It is now over twenty years since revisionis
form our understanding of early modern
between revisionists and their critics goes
sterile debate in which both sides are cor
conception of politics. Meanwhile scholars
opened new approaches to the political ⌐ ⌐⌐⌐ ⌐⌐ ⌐⌐⌐ English
Renaissance state, emphasizing the importance of representations
of authority and reading plays, poems and portraits as texts of
power.

Kevin Sharpe has been at the forefront of the dialogue between
historians and critics, and a leading exponent of interdisciplinary
approaches. In the essays collected here, and in an important new
remapping of the field, he revisits earlier debates from new perspectives and points to new texts for and approaches to the period.
Remapping Early Modern England urges a 'cultural turn' that will refigure our understanding of the history and politics of early modern
England and the materials and methods of our study.

KEVIN SHARPE is Professor of History, School of Research and
Graduate Studies, University of Southampton. His previous publications include *Criticism and Compliment* (1987), *Politics and Ideas in
Early Stuart England* (1989), *The Personal Rule of Charles I* (1992), *Culture
and Politics in Early Stuart England* (ed., 1994) *Politics of Discourse* (ed.,
1987) and *Refiguring Revolutions* (ed., 1998).

REMAPPING EARLY MODERN ENGLAND

REMAPPING EARLY MODERN ENGLAND

The culture of seventeenth-century politics

KEVIN SHARPE

CAMBRIDGE
UNIVERSITY PRESS

PUBLISHED BY THE PRESS SYNDICATE OF THE UNIVERSITY OF CAMBRIDGE
The Pitt Building, Trumpington Street, Cambridge, United Kingdom

CAMBRIDGE UNIVERSITY PRESS
The Edinburgh Building, Cambridge CB2 2RU, UK   www.cup.cam.ac.uk
40 West 20th Street, New York, NY 10011–4211, USA   www.cup.org
10 Stamford Road, Oakleigh, Melbourne 3166, Australia
Ruiz de Alarcón 13, 28014 Madrid, Spain

First published 2000

Printed in the United Kingdom at the University Press, Cambridge

Typeface: 11/12.5 Baskerville MT   *System:* QuarkXPress [SE]

A catalogue record for this book is available from the British Library

Library of Congress Cataloguing in Publication data

Sharpe, Kevin.
Remapping early modern England: the culture of seventeenth-century politics / Kevin Sharpe.
p.   cm.
Includes bibliographical references.
ISBN 0 521 66293 1 (hardbound)
1. Great Britain – Politics and government – 17th century. 2. Political culture – Great Britain –
History 17th century. I. Title.
JN339.S53   2000
942.06 – DC21   99–30158   CIP

ISBN 0 521 66293 1 hardback
ISBN 0 521 66409 8 paperback

Contents

Illustrations

Preface

There may be a number of explanations why historians gather their essays or articles into a collected volume. In most cases we can dismiss financial gain: only pieces that originated as journalism are likely to sell widely in book form. Perhaps for some scholars not suited to sustaining an argument at length, a volume of essays satisfies the desire or pressure to produce, and provides the wider audience that comes with, a book. But the most common motive is some form of vanity – or to put it less negatively, a belief that one has something to say and a desire to be read by as wide an audience as possible.

For the most part, when I read collections of historians' essays, I am not only convinced that they do have something to say, and that it should be read more widely; I am also struck by how reading discrete pieces together focuses and strengthens their argument, making the whole considerably more than the sum of the parts. In the best cases what I originally read as revisions to small parts of our history, I now see as refiguring a whole subject or period. And, at particular moments, the publication of such volumes serves to redirect the historiography and to change the questions and debate.

In 1989, I published my own first collection, *Politics and Ideas in Early Stuart England*, at a time when the controversies over revisionism were still raging. Looking back, I discern that I had a number of intentions in publishing the volume, not all of which were as clear to me then as they are now. Certainly I wanted to sustain and reinforce some of the important findings of revisionist scholarship, at a time when some scholars were hoping that they could simply return to the old Whig pieties. Secondly, I wanted to answer those critics who claimed that revisionist history was, and needed to be, history with the ideas left out, and to reassert my own claim to have always been a historian of ideas. But, most importantly, I wanted to look not backwards but ahead: to suggest a new agenda for early modern history and new approaches to its study. In particular, in a long opening essay, I urged a broadening of our concept of the political and address to a wider variety of texts as documents of politics in seventeenth-century England.

Since 1990, when I finished the first draft of my book on *The Personal Rule of Charles I*, I have attempted in essays, articles, edited volumes and forthcoming books, to follow my own prescription. As the quarrels over revisionism have faded or become sterile and bogged down, I have advocated a broader perspective and exploration of the English Renaissance state, and a different appreciation of how texts performed in Renaissance political culture. Most controversially, at least to political historians, I have in pursuing those ends proclaimed the value of interdisciplinary studies, and recently even critical theoretical approaches to the reading of texts and images.

My intention in this volume is polemic – or at least advocacy and exhortation: to a new history of early modern England and in part to a new rhetoric of history. In essays that return to earlier concerns, I have set out to eschew the artificial choices between models of conflict and consensus; in studies of political language and discourse, I have tried to extend the 'linguistic turn' to texts hitherto ignored by historians of ideas and politics; in a specialised essay and a more general overview I suggest the central importance of visual culture, representations and symbols to the politics of early modern England. More generally, I endeavour to draw attention to the perspectives of literary critics and art historians (whose work remains too little read) and to theories of the production and reception of texts; and in methodological essays to suggest how we might refigure political history. What unites them all is my firm conviction that it is time to leave behind the stale debates over revisionism which no longer advance our understanding and to embark on an exploration of the culture of early modern politics from the Reformation to the 1688 Revolution. Indeed the metaphor of my title and introductory essay makes my point: that as we leave a millennium it is time to take a new direction and to lay out differently the field and our exploration of it – time to remap early modern England.

Acknowledgements

Over the years that these pieces were written many historian friends and colleagues, old and new, have stimulated my thinking by encouragement, criticism and sometimes obvious expressions of disapproval at my readiness to enter into dialogue with other disciplines and critical approaches. Not only have they led me to try to justify interdisciplinary interests and methods; they have also helped me to eschew the obfuscatory language that has distanced historians from them. Literary scholars, cultural critics and art historians, meanwhile, have displayed unfailing hospitality towards a historian who ventured into their territory, generosity with their time and advice, and remarkable tolerance of my ignorance. If this volume persuades others to enter the conversations from which I have learned so much, both about the history of Renaissance England and our writing of that history, I feel sure that we will see over the next few years rich new expositions of early modern political culture and fruitful reflection on our approaches to it.

For their help, in different ways, I thank George Bernard, Mark Kishlansky, Peter Lake, John Morrill, Annabel Patterson, David Riggs, Mark Stoyle and Greg Walker. In particular I would like to thank Steve Zwicker whose work has stimulated so many of the most interesting questions and who has been the best of critics. Working with him has refigured my ideas about and approaches to the field. I wish also to record my thanks to the Press readers who enthusiastically endorsed this volume and to William Davies who encouraged me from the beginning and who saw the book smoothly through production. I am grateful too to my copyeditor Diane Ilott who carefully and helpfully edited the manuscript.

Once again I would like to express my thanks to all those institutions and individuals who have facilitated my researches with funding and the even more precious endowment of time. The British Academy and the University of Southampton have generously supported research; and I am grateful to Martin Ridge and Roy Ritchie at the Huntington Library and the Division of the Humanities at The California Institute of Technology for a productive year, in a stimulating region and environment. At Southampton, a former dean, Peter Ucko, believing that I had some important projects to pursue, generously (some might say foolishly) arranged a secondment to the School of Research, and to concentration on graduate studies; and I would like to thank him for the opportunity of time and an environment and teaching more conducive than a department to interdisciplinary work.

Essay 1, first given to John Morrill's seminar, appears in print here for the first time. Essay 2 formed the introduction to my *Politics and Ideas in Early Stuart England* (1989) and is now out of print; it belongs here, perhaps, more than in that collection. Essays 3, 4 and 5 explore discourse and power and appeared in K. Sharpe and P. Lake eds., *Culture and Politics in Early Stuart England* (Macmillan, 1994, pp. 117–38), J. Morrill, P. Slack and D. Woolf eds., *Public Duty and Private Conscience in Seventeenth Century England* (Oxford University Press, 1993, pp. 77–100) and in the *Historical Journal*, 40 (1997), pp. 643–65. I would like to thank the editors, Macmillan, Oxford University Press and the *Historical Journal* for permission to include them here. Essay 6, which attempts a general narrative of issues of style in political culture, was a chapter in J. Morrill ed., *The Oxford Illustrated History of Tudor and Stuart Britain* (1996, pp. 239–58) and is published with kind permission of the Oxford University Press. Essay 7 appeared in K. Sharpe and S. Zwicker eds., *Refiguring Revolutions: Aesthetics and Politics from the English Revolution to the Romantic Revolution* (1998, pp. 25–56) and is reprinted with permission of Steven Zwicker and the University of California Press. Essays 8 and 9 were published in R. Smith and J. Moore eds., *The House of Commons: 700 Years of British Tradition* (1996, pp. 83–100), a volume which emerged from a conference organized by the Manorial Society, and in C. Wright ed., *Sir Robert Cotton as Collector* (British Museum, 1996, pp. 1–39); I thank Robert Smith, Christopher Wright and the British Museum Board for urging me to write them and for allowing their republication in this volume. Essays 10 and 11 appeared in the *Huntington Library Quarterly*, 57 (1994), pp. 255–99 and the *Journal of Early Modern History*, 1 (1997), pp. 344–68 whose editors kindly granted permission to reprint. The final piece was written for this volume but appears too without illustrations in the *Historical Journal*.

Abbreviations

Add. MS	Additional Manuscript
Amer. Hist. Rev.	*American Historical Review*
Amer. Lit. Hist.	*American Literary History*
BL	British Library
Bull. Inst. Hist. Research	*Bulletin of the Institute of Historical Research*
Bull. John Rylands Lib.	*Bulletin of the John Rylands Library*
Cal. Stat. Pap. Dom.	*Calendar of State Papers, Domestic*
Cal. Stat. Pap. Venet.	*Calendar of State Papers, Venetian*
Cal. Treas. Books	*Calendar of Treasury Books*
Camb. Hist. Journ.	*Cambridge Historical Journal*
Camb. UL	Cambridge University Library
CJ	*Journals of the House of Commons*
DNB	*Dictionary of National Biography*
Eng. Hist. Rev.	*English Historical Review*
Eng. Lit. Hist.	*English Literary History*
Eng. Lit. Ren.	*English Literary Renaissance*
Hist. Journ.	*Historical Journal*
Hist. Mss. Comm.	*Historical Manuscripts Commission Report*
Hist. Polit. Thought	*History of Political Thought*
Huntington Lib.	Huntington Library
Hunt. Lib. Quart.	*Huntington Library Quarterly*
Journ. Brit. Studies	*Journal of British Studies*
Journ. Hist. Ideas	*Journal of the History of Ideas*
Journ. Interd. Hist.	*Journal of Interdisciplinary History*
Journ. Med. Hist.	*Journal of Medieval History*
Journ. Mod. Hist.	*Journal of Modern History*
Journ. Warburg & Courtauld Inst.	*Journal of Warburg & Courtauld Institutes*
Law Quart. Rev.	*Law Quarterly Review*
Midland Hist.	*Midland History*

New Left Rev.	*New Left Review*
Northern Hist.	*Northern History*
OED	*Oxford English Dictionary*
Parl. Hist.	*Parliamentary History*
Polit. Science Quart.	*Political Science Quarterly*
Polit. Theory	*Political Theory*
PRO	Public Record Office
Proc. Am. Philos. Soc.	*Proceedings of the American Philosophical Society*
Proc. Brit. Acad.	*Proceedings of the British Academy*
RO	Record Office (County)
Scottish Hist. Rev.	*Scottish Historical Review*
STC	A. W. Pollard and G. Redgrave, *A Short Title Catalogue* (1926)
Times Lit. Supp.	*Times Literary Supplement*
Trans. Am. Philos. Soc.	*Transactions of the American Philosophical Society*
Trans. Camb. Bib. Soc.	*Transactions of the Cambridge Bibliographical Society*
Trans. Royal Hist. Soc.	*Transactions of the Royal Historical Society*
VCH	*Victoria County History*

Frontispiece: satirical engraving entitled 'The world is ruled and governed by opinion'.
Blind opinion's tree is watered by a fool, a chameleon 'that can assume all cullors
saving white' perches on her wrist, and 'idle bookes and libells' fall from her branches.
Reproduced by permission of the British Library (BM Sat. 272).

PART ONE

Directions

CHAPTER ONE

Remapping early modern England: from revisionism to the culture of politics

The map we once conceived as a straightforward description of a terrain. What we have now learned, not least from recent criticism, is that the map projects the cartographer and his culture onto the land being charted, and even confirms and constructs the ideological contours and relief of his homeland as he perambulates other territory. Historians have not yet faced up to a similar postmodern reading of their own discipline: that 'the past', rather than a landscape simply elucidated by evidence, is a representation constructed by the historian from his own cultural vision as well as from the various representations that contemporaries created to discern meaning for themselves.[1] I offer here no theoretical or even working solution to this problem. What I wish to do is examine, and go some way to explain, the histories of early modern England that historians have constructed and – importantly – to urge us to pay attention to the representations that contemporaries presented of (and to) themselves: to urge a move from politics conceived (anachronistically) as the business of institutions, bureaucracies and officers to the broader politics of discourse and symbols, anxieties and aspirations, myths and memories.[2]

My essay is also unapologetically (as well as necessarily) personal.[3] Mid-career is a suitable time to review one's own earlier mappings, to examine where one has been the better to discern where one is going. In particular, now that its critical moment has passed, I want to explain and critique the movement known as 'revisionism' and to suggest a new

---

[1] Of all the humanities disciplines, history has remained for both better and worse, least influenced by theory. See however P. Joyce, 'History and Post Modernism I', *Past and Present*, 133 (1991), 204–9. Significantly a scholar often at the cutting edge sharply reacted, L. Stone, 'History and Post Modernism III', *Past and Present*, 135 (1992), 189–94.

[2] Peter Lake and I attempted such an agenda for early modern England in *Culture and Politics in Early Stuart England* (Houndmills and Stanford, 1994).

[3] This essay had its origins in an invitation from John Morrill to review my own scholarly career at a lively seminar in Cambridge, and was developed for a conference on Remapping British History at the Huntington Library.

agenda for the political history of early modern England, an agenda that involves not only a broader configuration of the political, but an openness to other critical perspectives on and interdisciplinary approaches to history – to the past and the exegesis of the past.

To understand approaches to seventeenth-century England we need to begin with the Whig view of history, not least because that phrase, though familiar, does more business than students usually appreciate. In the narrower sense, the Whig view of history was a necessary polemical response to the 1688 Revolution: the Whigs who forcefully removed James II to bring in William of Orange needed to make that violent fracture into a natural succession of government. They needed to marginalize the Jacobites and appropriate from them the languages of scripture, law and history through which all authority in seventeenth-century England was validated. Unlike their republican predecessors of the 1650s, the Whigs triumphed politically because they secured a cultural dominance.[4] By recruiting the most skilful pens and brushes, the Whigs assured a peaceful succession for William. And through a programme of editions, memoirs and histories, they created a pantheon of Whig heroes and a Whig interpretation of the past: an interpretation which emphasized parliaments and property, liberties and Protestantism in England from pre-Saxon times to 1688. Though they are obviously central, and though there are some signs that scholars have begun to address them, the processes by which the Whigs secured cultural hegemony and, to a large degree, control of the past await full investigation.[5]

In the larger and more familiar sense, of course, the Whig interpretation of history is a synonym for a teleological approach to the past: in general a quest to explain the present, in particular, in the wake of the Great Reform Bill, a self-congratulatory desire to trace the origins of reformed parliamentary government, the apogee, as the radicals saw it, of political development.[6] The figure who connects this larger vision to Whig politics is Thomas Babington Macaulay. Macaulay became a committed Whig and discerned even before 1830 that the course of parliamentary reform paved the way to a restoration of the Whigs to government. In parliament he was a leading spokesman for the Reform

---

[4] Cf. below, ch. 7; K. Sharpe and S. Zwicker eds., *Refiguring Revolutions: Aesthetics and Politics from the English Revolution to the Romantic Revolution* (Berkeley, Los Angeles and London 1998), introduction.

[5] See S. Zwicker, *Lines of Authority: Politics and English Literary Culture, 1649–1689* (Ithaca, 1993), ch. 6. There is no full study of the polemics of Augustan historical writing. For a less than satisfactory beginning see L. Okie, *Augustan Historical Writing: Histories of England in the English Enlightenment* (New York, 1992). [6] See H. Butterfield, *The Whig Interpretation of History* (1931).

Bill, the passing of which owed not a little to the power of his rhetoric.[7] In an early letter on the subject of reform, Macaulay invoked the name of Oliver Cromwell.[8] His vision of politics was, as he believed any vision of politics should be, informed by history. In his youth, Macaulay had penned essays on William III and Milton which, like his invocation of Cromwell, reveal how a reading of the seventeenth century shaped his approach to Whig politics in the nineteenth.[9] Indeed for Macaulay both those centuries, and history and politics generally, were inseparable. When the Whigs had enjoyed political dominance under William it was because a Whig view of history was also the prevailing orthodoxy. Accordingly the political resurgence of the Whigs in the 1830s required a history that would displace the popular *History of England* penned in the last years of Whig ascendancy by the Tory philosopher David Hume: it demanded a history that would attribute the very material progress of England to the political principles espoused by the Whig cause and party.[10] It was that history which Macaulay, after holding office in Lord Melbourne's government, turned to write: a history, as he described it, of 'all the transactions which took place between the 1688 Revolution which brought the crown into harmony with parliament and the 1832 Revolution which brought parliament into harmony with the nation'.[11] Macaulay's history displaced Hume's and imprinted its vision of the past on the imagination of the English. Though criticized in details, Macaulay's history, Whig history, became, in Trevor-Roper's words, 'part of the permanent acquisition of historical science'.[12] Macaulay's teleological framework was hard to escape. Even the great Samuel Rawson Gardiner, who was not uncritical of Macaulay and who followed Ranke in his efforts to engage with the past on its own terms, came to see the Victorian constitution as that historical terminus 'to which every step was constantly tending'.[13] And thanks to Gardiner, as Macaulay, historical narrative itself appeared to be – perhaps remains – Whig.

Though a history for its time, and as its author acknowledged, an insular history,[14] the influence of Macaulay's history extended beyond

[7] J. Clive, *Thomas Babington Macaulay: the Shaping of the Historian* (New York, 1973).

[8] Ibid., p. 152.

[9] Lord Macaulay, *The History of England*, ed. H. R. Trevor-Roper (Harmondsworth, 1979), 15–16.

[10] Ibid., 13, 20.   [11] Ibid., 20.   [12] Ibid., 33.

[13] Quoted in J. P. Kenyon, *The History Men: the Historical Profession in England since the Renaissance* (1983), 220.

[14] 'The book is quite insular in spirit. There is nothing cosmopolitan about it', quoted in Macaulay, *History*, ed. Trevor-Roper, 8.

the England of his lifetime. In the United States of America, sales of Macaulay's *History* were surpassed only by the Bible, as his message of progress and Whig politics struck a chord across the Atlantic. It was Macaulay's nephew, George Otto Trevelyan, whose *History of the American Revolution* 'supplied, in some sense, the originally intended conclusion to Macaulay's work'[15] and conjoined a view of seventeenth-century English history with the myth of the Manifest Destiny of the American people to extend benefits of freedom and progress across their continent – and beyond. A vision of seventeenth-century English history was (and remained) important to America because, in the words of the great American scholar of Stuart England, Wallace Notestein, it is 'the story of how human beings have learned to govern themselves . . . [the story of] the slow accumulation of parliamentary rights and privileges', hence a vital early chapter in what my own school textbook of American history called *The History of a Free People*.[16] Not least because such a national ideology retains power to this day, American historiography – especially on seventeenth-century England – has remained essentially Whig.

Moreover in Europe, the Whig view of the past drew impetus from another philosophical, historical and political movement – Marxism. At one level, Marxist may appear as distant from Whig historiography as Marx himself from Macaulay. Yet Marx's vision of history was, like the Whigs, teleological and, as for Macaulay, for Marx politics was a historical process just as history was 'that noble science of politics'.[17] More particularly, in both Whig and Marxist visions was a connection between material progress and the course of history, and a sense that in England's case the seventeenth century was pivotal. Where for the Whig the civil war witnessed the triumph of liberty and parliaments over despotism, to the Marxist the English revolution marks the overthrow of feudal monarchy and aristocracy by the rising gentry and merchant classes represented in parliament. Though their political ends were quite distinct, even antagonistic, Marx and Macaulay could find common ground in an interpretation of seventeenth-century England – an alliance that helped sustain as the dominant historical interpretation what had been polemically constructed to defeat the threats of Jacobitism.

[15] Macaulay, *History*, ed. Trevor-Roper, 25.
[16] W. Notestein, *The Winning of the Initiative by the House of Commons* (1924), 3. The textbook was used in 1967–8.
[17] Macaulay, *History*, ed. Trevor-Roper, 41. Cf. S. Collins, D. Winch and J. Burrow, *That Noble Science of Politics* (Cambridge, 1983), esp. ch. 6. And see the interesting study by A. Maclachlan, *The Rise and Fall of Revolutionary England* (Basingstoke, 1996).

Indeed a blend of Whig history, liberal Marxism and American intellectual and political culture formed the base ingredients for one of the
most influential textbooks of seventeenth-century history in our own
day: Lawrence Stone's *The Causes of the English Revolution*. This may
appear a controversial claim, for Stone rejects Whig and Marxist alike.[18]
Yet in passages about 'a strong desire for widespread change . . . towards
a "balanced constitution"', the thesis of the crisis of monarchy and the
'shift to new mercantile interests . . . organised to challenge the economic
monopoly and political control', the voices of Macaulay and Marx as
well as Tawney may be heard,[19] beneath the language of social theory
and models of revolution. And in its organization, Stone's history,
though never crudely so, is as inherently Whig as the politics of the historian with his 'belief in the limitless possibilities of improvement in the
human condition' – a belief, perhaps, by 1972 more widespread in
American than in English intellectual culture.[20]

Though then the product of a moment, or moments, the Whig view
of English history has sustained a dominance which calls for explanation. And the explanation is both ideological and historical. Perhaps
from the eighteenth century onwards, Whig history has been an important component of English and American nationalism and national
identity, of the moral foundations of colonial expansion and imperial
power. (Here it may be no accident that two leading critics of Whig
historiography – Sir Lewis Namier and Sir Geoffrey Elton – were
foreign.) Secondly and related, Whig history is also Protestant history
and in both England and America it underpinned an Anglo-Saxon
Protestant elite as the natural class of government.[21] Thirdly, Whiggery
has dominated historical interpretation because it infiltrated the records
we use to study the past and the methods by which we approach and represent it. Just as Milton and Ludlow were edited and re-presented as
protochampions of the Whig cause, so Thomas Rymer, the Whig
historiographer royal, and John Rushworth, former secretary to Oliver
Cromwell, compiled collections of documents which were intended as
'lectures of prudence, policy and morality' from which each could 'read

---

[18] L. Stone, *The Causes of the English Revolution, 1529–1642* (1972), 54, 38–9. Perhaps the term
'Marxisant' is better. See Maclachlan, *Rise and Fall*, 323, 419.

[19] Stone, *Causes of the English Revolution*, 30, 54; cf. 57 and Maclachlan, *Rise and Fall*, 164–8, 235,
320–3.

[20] Stone, *Causes of the English Revolution*, ix; cf. D. Cannadine, 'British History: Past, Present – and
Future?', *Past and Present*, 116 (1987), 69–91.

[21] Linda Colley stresses the importance of Protestantism in forging the nation in *Britons: Forging the
Nation 1707–1837* (1992), but the relationship of Protestantism to the Whig view of the past is not
explored.

to himself his own improvement'.[22] The polemic of these collections was
all the more effective in their restraint from direct partisanship or gloss.
As a consequence, the reading of history they promoted appeared inevitable. And Whig history, like Whig politics, performed the most subtle
of ideological moves in erasing the traces of its own polemic – to appear
the natural, national story, as it did again in Macaulay and has done until
recently.

At no point has the Whig view of history escaped challenge or criticism. The political opponents of Rushworth and later of Macaulay were
quick to demonstrate the partisan leanings of their judgements and use
of evidence.[23] There are, too, more fundamental objections to Whig
history. First, it is inherently an ahistorical approach to the past, concerned to explain a present rather than elucidate the autonomy and
differences of an earlier age. The Whig writes of Newton's mathematics and not his experiments in alchemy, of Ludlow's republicanism but
not his millenarianism. Whig history is also anachronistic in its address
to language: it invests seventeenth-century words such as liberty and
rights with later (different) meanings; and it ignores the vocabularies and
terms, like *ius* and grace, that were essential to early modern discourse
but later passed into insignificance.[24] It fails to explain why civil war
erupted in 1642 not, say, in 1637 or in 1629 when parliament was dissolved. In Whig histories, moments – moments when decisive actions
were taken or not taken – are reduced to points on a graph, or milestones
on a road that the men and women of the past were destined to follow.[25]

These were the objections that provoked the revisionist critique of
Whig history in the mid-1970s. What, however, has to be recognized is
that such criticisms were not entirely new; and what has still to be
explained is why in the mid-1970s the attack was escalated to the point
at which the Whig edifice toppled. In the 1960s, Geoffrey Elton and John
Kenyon had asked questions and offered new suggestions that wounded
the Whig interpretation of Stuart England.[26] But the mortal blow was

---

[22] See A. B. Worden ed., *Edmond Ludlow: a Voice from the Watch Tower, 1660–1662* (Camden Soc., 4th
ser., 21, 1978); S. Zwicker, 'Lines of Authority: Politics and Literary Culture in the Restoration',
in K. Sharpe and S. Zwicker eds., *Politics of Discourse: the Literature and History of Seventeenth-Century
England* (Berkeley, Los Angeles and London, 1987), 230–70, esp. 246–7; J. Rushworth, *Historical
Collections* (7 vols., 1659–1701), II, sig. A.

[23] See J. Nalson, *An Impartial Collection of the Great Affairs of State* (1682); Macaulay, *History*, ed. Trevor-
Roper, 31, 33–4.

[24] The 'linguistic turn' in historical studies, pioneered by John Pocock and Quentin Skinner, is
therefore fundamentally anti-Whig.

[25] The term 'milestones' is, notoriously, Stone's (*Causes of the English Revolution*, 94).

[26] See especially G. R. Elton, 'A High Road to Civil War?', in C. H. Carter ed., *From the Renaissance
to the Counter-Reformation* (1965), 325–47 (the metaphor anticipates and contests Stone's); J. P.
Kenyon ed., *The Stuart Constitution, 1603–1688* (Cambridge, 1966).

not struck for several more years – until on both sides of the Atlantic and within a short space of time, Conrad Russell, Mark Kishlansky and myself fired simultaneous salvos from different angles to the Whig citadel.[27] There have been few attempts to explain revisionism, and those few unsatisfactory. To Stone the narrow antiquarian empiricism of the generation trained through the Ph.D. saw a shift from the big picture to meaningless detail and pedantry.[28] Yet Russell has no Ph.D. and was an established scholar in mid-career as other revisionists were just graduating. The arguments of generational disenchantment with post-imperial Britain meet with similar difficulties.[29] As for politics and ideology, from what I know the leading revisionists came from quite different political sympathies, perspectives and experiences and shared few obvious ideological commitments or passions. Moreover, for all that they were lumped together, they had rather different historical points to make. Conrad Russell, in the seminal article of revisionism, argued for the impotence of parliaments both as legislators and controllers of the purse strings. Mark Kishlansky, through study of parliamentary procedure, posited that politics before the civil war was characterized by consensus not conflict. Having worked on the career of the antiquary Sir Robert Cotton, I was led to question the model of opposing sides of government and opposition and to suggest that political tensions and problems affected but were not caused by relations between crown and parliament. It is worth noting, since it may not be widely known, that, initially, the three of us worked independently and, as later publications have shown, were formulating rather different new approaches to early Stuart England. But what united the revisionists was a conviction that the old Whig history could no longer be modified or repaired. We questioned the model of escalating conflict between crown and parliament; calling for closer study of more evidence, we criticized the selective narrative constructed around high points of conflict; and we rejected teleological determinism as a historical philosophy. Whether the politics of that last move owed something to the decline of nationalism, whether a portrait of politics drawn in the chalks of interest and intrigue signalled a fading idealism (on both sides of the Atlantic) is not yet clear.

What is apparent is that to some of its critics revisionism meant more,

---

[27] C. Russell, 'Parliamentary History in Perspective, 1604–29', *History*, 61 (1976), 1–27; Russell, *Parliaments and English Politics 1621–1629* (Oxford, 1979); M. Kishlansky, 'The Emergence of Adversary Politics in the Long Parliament', *Journ. Mod. Hist.*, 49 (1977), 617–40; K. Sharpe ed., *Faction and Parliament: Essays on Early Stuart History* (Oxford, 1978), introduction and passim; Sharpe, *Sir Robert Cotton 1586–1631: History and Politics in Early Modern England* (Oxford, 1979).

[28] L. Stone, 'The Revival of Narrative: Reflections on a New Old History', *Past and Present*, 85 (1979), 3–24.   [29] Cannadine, 'British History'.

dangerously more, than a new interpretation of early seventeenth-century England. For Professor Hexter the removal of parliaments from the centre stage of Stuart history threatened to weaken the foundation of liberty in the modern world and he moved swiftly to try to counter the revisionist challenge and re-validate the traditional story.[30] Professors Rabb and Stone appeared more concerned about the consequences for historical study itself, fearing that the move from a big story to detail, and from an old certainty to question and confusion, robbed history of meaning and value.[31] Both were ideological critiques that subtly reveal the ways in which, as recent debates on multiculturalism have made noisily apparent, historical narrative underpinned Western liberalism. But whatever the sources of their discontent, the critics of revisionism, especially Derek Hirst, were right to object that some revisionists paid far too little attention to ideas and ideology in an era when men spoke passionately about values and beliefs.[32] To read some revisionist history is like watching a film without its noisy, dramatic soundtrack, to see politics reduced to a series of silent moves and manoeuvres.

In recent years therefore, in various essays, post-revisionist scholarship has returned – rightly – to the crucial issue of ideology. In some cases this has taken the form of undisguised political polemic or crudely simplistic history. Hexter's Center for the History of Freedom (financed by the conservative Heritage Foundation and Freedom Inc.) only thinly veils its twentieth-century ideological agenda.[33] Johann Sommerville's study of *Politics and Ideology 1603–40* too simply places political thinkers into predetermined and opposed boxes of 'absolutist' and 'constitutionalist' without engaging the complexities and contradictions that characterized them all.[34] But the best post-revisionist work, by Peter Lake, Ann Hughes and Richard Cust, has argued powerfully for ideological conflict in early Stuart England, without resorting to the old model of govern-

---

[30] See J. H. Hexter, 'Power Struggle, Parliament and Liberty in Early Stuart England', *Journ. Mod. Hist.*, 50 (1978), 1–50; Hexter, 'The Early Stuarts and Parliament: Old Hat and the Nouvelle Vague', *Parl. Hist.*, 1 (1982), 101–25.

[31] T. K. Rabb, 'The Role of the Commons', *Past and Present*, 92 (1981), 55–78; Stone, 'Revival of Narrative'; and in both cases conference addresses that I attended.

[32] D. Hirst, 'The Place of Principle', *Past and Present*, 92 (1981), 79–99.

[33] See, for example, J. H. Hexter ed., *Parliament and Liberty from the Reign of Elizabeth to the English Civil War* (Stanford, 1992) and Hexter, 'The Birth of Modern Freedom', *Times Lit. Supp.* (21 Jan. 1983), 51–4.

[34] J. P. Sommerville, *Politics and Ideology in England 1603–1640* (1986). For an effective critique, cf. G. Burgess, *The Politics of the Ancient Constitution: an Introduction to English Political Thought 1603–1642* (Basingstoke, 1992); Burgess, *Absolute Monarchy and the Stuart Constitution* (New Haven and London, 1996).

ment and opposition.[35] In the ideology of the 'country', they have suggested, may be discerned a set of values at odds with those of the court
and the beginnings of an erosion of trust in the government.[36] Only now
is a new generation of scholars beginning to take up their call for an
analysis of political rhetoric and the relationships of political discourse
to political tension and conflict.[37]

Some of the revisionists, responding to the charge that by removing
ideology they had made civil war inexplicable, pursued a different
agenda: the role of religion in engendering conflict.[38] With the rejection
of Whig history, the religious dimension for some time seemed lost. For
the old thesis of a revolutionary puritanism providing the ideology and
organization for resistance in England, as Calvinism had on the continent, had been questioned by Patrick Collinson and others.[39] However,
ecclesiastical historians identified a new source of instability in the reign
of Charles I in the rise of Arminianism which they claimed broke from
the Calvinist orthodoxy and shattered the consensus of the Jacobean
church, exciting fears of popery.[40] Conrad Russell included the seminal
essay in which that thesis was outlined in his early volume on the origins
of the civil war, and it evidently offered him some answer to the explanation of conflict which his own researches had rendered more
difficult.[41] Indeed for several revisionists religion appeared to solve the
central conundrum: of how a state which celebrated consensus and unity
fractured and divided into violent conflict. To John Morrill, it was religious commitments that would override the intrinsic localism and neutral-
ism of the English provinces and drive at least the leading protagonists
to take sides in what he came to describe as England's war of religion.[42]

---

[35] R. Cust, *The Forced Loan and English Politics 1626–28* (Oxford, 1987); R. Cust and A. Hughes eds.,
Conflict in Early Stuart England (1989); P. Lake, 'The Collection of Ship Money in Cheshire during
the 1630s: a Case Study of Relations between Central and Local Government', *Northern Hist.*, 17
(1981), 44–71.   [36] Cust and Hughes, *Conflict*, 19–21, 29–31.
[37] For example, Alastair Bellany (see his essay in Sharpe and Lake, *Culture and Politics*, 285–310) and
Glenn Burgess.
[38] This is notably the case with John Morrill, whose historiographical moves may now be traced
effectively through his collected essays, *The Nature of the English Revolution* (1993); see especially the
new autobiographical introductions to each section.
[39] The old thesis is well represented by M. Walzer, *The Revolution of the Saints* (Cambridge, Mass.,
1965) and C. Hill, *Puritanism and Revolution* (1958, 1962); cf. P. Collinson, *The Elizabethan Puritan
Movement* (1967) and *The Religion of Protestants* (Oxford, 1982).
[40] This thesis was outlined in the long unpublished dissertation by N. Tyacke, now published as
Anti-Calvinists: the Rise of English Arminianism c. 1590–1640 (Oxford, 1987).
[41] N. Tyacke, 'Puritanism, Arminianism and Counter-Revolution', in C. S. R. Russell ed., *The
Origins of the English Civil War* (1973), 199–234.
[42] J. S. Morrill, 'The Religious Context of the English Civil War', *Trans. Royal Hist. Soc.*, 5th ser., 34
(1984), 155–78.

Russell extended Tyacke's original argument beyond the Church of England. Pointing to the different religious settlements in the kingdoms of England, Scotland and Ireland over which the early Stuarts ruled, he pointed out how changes in the one church had profound and sometimes destabilizing consequences for the other. Religion was the most complex of the problems involved in ruling multiple kingdoms and when Charles I upset the delicate balance – not only in England – he started a British civil war which brought violence to England only last of his realms.[43]

The thesis of an orthodox Calvinism disrupted by the rise of revolutionary Arminianism, as I and others have argued elsewhere, seems fraught with too many problems to bear the interpretational edifice it is now asked to support.[44] Charges of Arminianism were heard little in early Stuart parliaments – and Ian Green's monumental new work suggests that, outside the universities and high ecclesiastical debate, Arminianism impinged little on life or worship in the parishes.[45] As for the 'British problem', it is not obvious that anyone other than the king saw the ecclesiastical issues in these terms, and, as John Morrill observes, it is far from clear that Charles I himself pursued a 'British' policy.[46] But perhaps the greatest objection to the religious explanations of the civil war is the attenuated notion of religion that informs them. Religion was not just about doctrine, liturgy or ecclesiastical government; it was a language, an aesthetic, a structuring of meaning, an identity, a politics.[47] As Peter Lake and others have argued, 'popery' conjured ideas of corruption, whoredom and anarchy, as well as doctrines of merit or the mass; and Protestantism became a polemical rhetoric and symbol as well as a faith.[48] We cannot fully understand the religious element of early Stuart conflict without an understanding of those broader significations – of the political culture itself.

And so for all the rich historical research, we were (and are) left with the problem of how the political culture failed to prevent civil war, indeed about the nature of, and changes in, the political culture of early

---

[43] See C. S. Russell, *The Causes of the English Civil War* (Oxford, 1990), ch. 5.

[44] See K. Sharpe, *The Personal Rule of Charles I* (New Haven and London, 1992), ch. 6; P. White, 'The Rise of Arminianism Reconsidered', *Past and Present*, 101 (1983), 34–54 and White, *Predestination, Policy and Polemic: Conflict and Consensus in the English Church from the Reformation to the Civil War* (Cambridge, 1992); J. Davies, *The Caroline Captivity of the Church* (Oxford, 1992). See now too I. Green, *The Christian's ABC* (Oxford, 1996), ch. 8, which undermines many of Tyacke's claims.

[45] Green, *The Christian's ABC*.

[46] J. Morrill, 'A British Patriarchy? Ecclesiastical Imperialism under the Early Stuarts', in A. Fletcher and P. Roberts eds., *Religion, Culture and Society in Early Modern Britain* (Cambridge, 1994), 209–37.   [47] Cf. below, ch. 10.

[48] P. Lake, 'Anti-Popery: the Structure of a Prejudice', in Cust and Hughes, *Conflict*, 72–106.

modern England. To be fair these were questions that some revisionists had always considered important. Such issues underline Kishlansky's arguments about the emergence of adversary politics. In my *Sir Robert Cotton*, I endeavoured to chart how perceptions of the medieval past revealed and intensified growing political anxieties, as in an essay on the Earl of Arundel I argued for the importance of ideas of aristocracy, counsel, stoicism, of attitudes to aesthetics and style in shaping political allegiances and positions.[49] Though such values and ideas did not to me sustain any thesis about government and opposition, they certainly evidenced ideological tensions and conflicts about values which required further exploration.

During the mid-1980s, again quite independently, two former revisionists extended their studies of politics into exegesis of broader political practices and texts. In his brilliant study of parliamentary s/elections, Kishlansky explained how a shift from the nomination and selection to the contested election of MPs signalled a broader social change: from a culture of honour and deference to one of division and choice – the process of politicization.[50] In a thesis that touched on transformations in social relations, values and discourse, Kishlansky interestingly opened with a reading of a literary text – Shakespeare's *Coriolanus* – and the 'clash of values' at which the playwright 'dimly hinted'.[51] At the same time, I had completed a study of drama, poetry and masques at the Caroline court as texts of politics. Whilst initially drawn to these in order to understand what was 'Cavalier' about pre-civil war court culture, I soon discovered that, far from simple paeans to monarchy, such texts themselves disclosed political debates within the court, and even anxieties about the exercise of authority and the style of monarchy. And I argued that, far from being confined to tract or speech, political ideas were articulated in the discourse of love in early modern England, and that that discourse could voice criticism as well as compliment.[52]

My own work (perhaps Kishlansky's opening pages too) was influenced at this time by the critical school of new historicism. After the publication in 1980 of Stephen Greenblatt's *Renaissance Self-Fashioning*, a group of critics turned to a new historicizing of Renaissance literary

---

[49] See Kishlansky, 'The Emergence of Adversary Politics'; K. Sharpe, 'The Earl of Arundel, His Circle and the Opposition to the Duke of Buckingham 1618–1628', in *Faction and Parliament*, 209–44; see also below, ch. 9.

[50] M. Kishlansky, *Parliamentary Selection: Social and Political Choice in Early Modern England* (Cambridge, 1986). [51] Ibid., 8.

[52] K. Sharpe, *Criticism and Compliment: the Politics of Literature in the England of Charles I* (Cambridge, 1987).

texts and an interrogation of literature, especially the drama, as debates
about power and authority.[53] Though the Foucaultian model underlying
much new historicism seemed reductive and its gestures to historicizing
often inadequate, it seemed to me that literature, again especially the
drama, presented the historian with uniquely rich evidence, the opportunity to hear contemporaries airing questions and anxieties that seldom
find expression in the traditional materials of political history.[54] A future
collaboration between critics and historians, it seemed, might promise a
richer exploration of both the politics of a variety of texts and the textuality of early modern politics. It was in order to advance such an
agenda that Steve Zwicker and I, after hours of fruitful dialogue at the
Institute for Advanced Study, embarked on a collection of essays that
was published in 1987 as *Politics of Discourse*.[55] As we submitted our
volume to press, Zwicker and I considered many other possibilities that
might be opened by interdisciplinary study: the royalist literature of exile
(philosophy, history and romance), the politics of Restoration comedy
and Rochester's pornographic verse, the power of Whig criticism that
marginalized cavalier lyric. But for me, *Criticism and Compliment* had
emerged from, but grown to interrupt, a different study. In 1980, at the
high point of revisionist historiography, I had commenced research for
what was expected to be a short book on the 1630s.[56] The project originated from questions central to the debate between revisionists and their
critics. How important were parliaments in early Stuart England? Why
did Charles I, who had called several, decide to rule without them? How
could or did government function without them? Did ideological lines
or religious divisions harden during that decade? What were Charles I's
aims and political values, and how did the 1630s contribute to the origins
of civil war? When I set out, I might have expected that these questions
could be answered from the normal sources of political history.
Research, however, confirmed the sense I had gleaned from the study of
Stuart historical writing, then drama and poetry, that the political

---

[53] S. Greenblatt, *Renaissance Self-Fashioning* (Chicago, 1980); J. Goldberg, *James I and the Politics of Literature* (Baltimore and London, 1983); S. Greenblatt ed., *Representing the Renaissance* (Berkeley, 1988). New historicism, as Maclachlan reminds us, was intrinsically anti-revisionist: *Rise and Fall*, 267.

[54] See H. Veeser ed., *The New Historicism* (1989); G. Harpham, 'Foucault and the New Historicism', *Amer. Lit. Hist.*, 3 (1991), 360–75.

[55] Sharpe and Zwicker, *Politics of Discourse*; cf. Sharpe, 'The Politics of Literature in Renaissance England', *History*, 71 (1986), 235–47, also in Sharpe, *Politics and Ideas in Early Stuart England* (1989), ch. 10.

[56] A preliminary report was written in K. Sharpe, 'The Personal Rule of Charles I', in H. Tomlinson ed., *Before the English Civil War* (1983), 53–78, 192–6; Sharpe, *Politics and Ideas*, ch. 3.

culture of Caroline England could not be understood from just the state paper or lieutenancy book, sermon or deposition. Charles I and his court represented themselves through a variety of media as well as pronounce-ments and the painting and architectural plan were as important to his vision of kingship as the proclamation. By the time I had written *The Personal Rule of Charles I*, whatever support it may have lent to revisionist arguments, it was not a book from which ideas, values, ideology were absent.[57] True, it rejected the thesis of court/country conflict, but it was not an argument that denied opposition nor its articulation in the poli-tics of ballad and symbol.[58]

During the 1980s, as I worked on *Criticism and Compliment* and *The Personal Rule*, I became increasingly dissatisfied with the historical methods and approaches of revisionism. As practised in particular by Conrad Russell, revisionist history privileged the manuscript (the more arcane the better) over the printed source and implicitly rejected literary, artistic or architectural documents. Such preferences emerge from and reinforce a view of history, and politics, as the story of the high intrigues of self-conscious political actors.[59] This view excluded from the picture the silent backbencher, and the wider public considerations of the leading political players. Such revisionism also rehearses a naïvely rigid distinction between reality and representation. It takes state papers as 'factual' documents that reveal, where pamphlets and plays, 'fiction', obscure or mislead. Yet this is both to ignore a rich vein of evidence for the perceptions of politics and to be deaf to the rhetoricity of all politi-cal locutions and performances. Remarkably, no historian of parliament studies the speeches as a rhetorical performance, as an act intended to persuade and constructed with (different) auditors and conventions of persuasion in mind.[60] Just as remarkably, Russell can write hundreds of pages about Charles I without ever referring to a picture.

To make these points is to remind ourselves how revisionist history, perhaps most political history, proceeded during the 1970s and '80s, largely oblivious to other critical and historical approaches that urged address to a broader political culture and different texts and methods for reading it. One, as we have seen, was new historicism. If new historicism

---

[57] *The Personal Rule* has been received mainly as a 'revisionist' book. *If* (and the if is important) it is revisionist in its conclusions, it departs widely from revisionism in its engagement with masque, play and portrait, and with genre and rhetoric, as the materials of politics.

[58] Ibid., see chs. 10–12.

[59] Here I am fundamentally at odds with Professor Russell: see Sharpe and Lake, *Culture and Politics*, introduction.

[60] There is no such analysis in Russell's major accounts of parliaments.

promised more than it delivered as a method, this was not least because few historians took up the challenge of situating and reading literary texts in their historical moment.[61] The best work, however, by Annabel Patterson, Michael Schoenfeldt and Steven Zwicker, has left us in no doubt of the wealth of insights to be gleaned from full exegesis of a text in its discursive and political moment.[62] Not only is it regrettable that so few historians have taken such scholarship on board, or extended enquiry into poems and songs written by princes.[63] It is unforgivable that they have failed to develop the critical skills of close reading, rhetorical analysis, sensitivity to genre and generic play, awareness of pronominal-ization and the authorial voice, and so on. Here the English historical establishment's (often healthy) contempt for theorizing has actually impoverished working methods – the capacity just to get on with it which is the empiricist's boast.

Two leading historians, of course, have pioneered a theoretical and critical address to such issues of language and rhetoric. Drawing on the work of linguistic philosophers and speech-act theorists, John Pocock and Quentin Skinner have revolutionized the history of political thought.[64] In a quest to recover the intentions of an author and the polit-ical performance of a text, Pocock and Skinner have redirected the history of political thought to the history of discourse and they have rewritten that history as a set of paradigmatic shifts of languages and idioms – Pocock arguing for a move from the validating discourses of grace and custom to those of rights and commerce.[65] More recently, both have moved from the author to the performance and reception of texts, drawing on the reception theorists such as Stanley Fish.[66] The bril-

---

[61] The exceptions were Blair Worden and myself. Worden published a wide range of essays which were noted for close historical situating and re-reading of Jonson, Marvell and Milton. See now his *The Sound of Virtue: Politics in Philip Sidney's Arcadia* (New Haven and London, 1996).

[62] See, for example, A. Patterson, *Fables of Power: Aesopian Writing and Political History* (Durham, N.C. and London, 1991); Patterson, *Reading Between the Lines* (1993); Patterson, *Reading Holinshed's Chronicles* (Chicago, 1994); M. Schoenfeldt, *Prayer and Power: George Herbert and Renaissance Courtship* (Chicago, 1991); Zwicker, *Lines of Authority.* See too below pp. 376–82.

[63] I am planning a study of royal writing from Henry VIII's love songs to James II's devotional writ-ings in exile. See below, pp. 23–4.

[64] See, for example, J. G. A. Pocock, *Politics Language and Time* (New York, 1971); Q. Skinner, 'Some Problems in the Analysis of Political Thought and Action', *Polit. Theory,* 23 (1974), 277–303; J. Tully ed., *Meaning and Context: Quentin Skinner and His Critics* (Cambridge, 1988).

[65] Q. Skinner, *The Foundations of Modern Political Thought* (2 vols., Cambridge, 1978); J. G. A. Pocock, *The Ancient Constitution and the Feudal Law* (Cambridge, 1957; 2nd edn 1987); Pocock, *The Machiavellian Moment: Florentine Political Thought and the Atlantic Republican Tradition* (Princeton, 1975); Pocock, *Virtue, Commerce and History* (Cambridge, 1985). Cf. Maclachlan, *Rise and Fall,* ch. 7.

[66] Pocock, *Virtue, Commerce and History,* 20; Pocock, 'Texts as Events: Reflections on the History of Political Thought', in Sharpe and Zwicker, *Politics of Discourse,* 21–34. Pocock cites approvingly S.

liance of their methodological reflections and their histories has rightly been credited with effecting a 'linguistic turn' in the history of political thought. But – curiously – little of this new perspective has informed the work of historians of politics. Though both Skinner and Pocock urged that it should not be, the history of political thought, even after the linguistic turn, remains dominated by the canonical text and no historians have traced the paradigmatic discursive or idiomatic shifts through genres such as the statute and proclamation, the parliamentary speech or assize sermon.[67] Early Stuart political history continues to be written innocent of the linguistic turn: in Conrad Russell's oeuvre there is no mention of Skinner.

Language is only one of the systems through which societies construct meaning. During the 1970s, Clifford Geertz in a brilliant study and collection of methodological essays reoriented the anthropological study of culture.[68] In *The Interpretation of Cultures*, Geertz argued that culture was always also politics, 'a set of control mechanisms . . . for the governing of behaviour', and that the representations a society constructs – in festival or play or display – embody and signify political codes and values.[69] Geertz's symbolic anthropology proved to be a major inspiration for the new historicists, especially Stephen Greenblatt who adapted and retitled the methodology a 'poetics of culture'.[70] Its influence on historians of culture and politics, however, has been less apparent. True, social historians of early modern England have recently paid fruitful attention to the charivari and shaming rituals through which village cultures constructed and reinforced a system of local order.[71] But again we note that in David Underdown's recent *Revel, Riot and Rebellion* there is no reference to Geertz or his critics.[72] A full reading of ritual and display, elite and popular, of games and pastimes as significations of social

Fish, *Is There a Text in This Class? The Authority of Interpretive Communities* (Cambridge, Mass., 1980). Skinner appears less enthusiastic about 'reader response' criticism, see Tully, *Meaning and Context*, 267–73.

[67] There are the glimmers of change. Under the supervision of John Guy, Stephen Alford has studied the rhetoric of draft legislation and legislation in Elizabethan England. See now, S. Alford, *The Early Elizabethan Polity* (Cambridge, 1997). I am grateful to Steve Alford for permission to see some of his work in advance of publication.

[68] C. Geertz, *The Interpretation of Cultures* (1975). [69] Ibid., 49.

[70] Greenblatt, *Renaissance Self-Fashioning*, 4–5; see too J. Bender, *Imagining the Penitentiary: Fiction and the Architecture of Mind in Eighteenth-Century England* (Chicago, 1987).

[71] See, for example, D. Underdown, 'The Taming of the Scold: the Enforcement of Patriarchal Authority in Early Modern England' and S. Amussen, 'Gender, Family and the Social Order 1560–1725', both in A. Fletcher and J. Stevenson eds., *Order and Disorder in Early Modern England* (Cambridge, 1985), 196–217. Neither refers to Geertz.

[72] D. Underdown, *Revel, Riot and Rebellion: Popular Politics and Culture in England 1603–1660* (Oxford, 1985).

relations and control mechanisms is needed. And, we might add, a full understanding of early modern politics and government requires consideration of Geertz's argument that power exists as 'really' in display and representation as in the institutions and mechanics of society.

It is, I think, a comment on the institutional arrangements and practices of English academic and humanistic culture that I was first led to engage with new historicism, the linguistic turn and Geertzian anthropology in the United States of America. In part this was the consequence of the happy accident of meeting Geertz at Princeton in 1981, and new historicist critics such as Jonathan Goldberg and others the same year. Yet, more than happenstance, it was my residence in an interdisciplinary institute, my release from the confines of a single academic department and an uncompromising English empiricism, that opened my thinking to these dialogues and perspectives.[73] The challenge of rethinking one's critical and working practices does not come easy and I resisted (regrettably still too much resist) the full implications of these schools in researching and writing history. All, however, have continued to influence my approach to evidence and choice of subject; and for some years I have thought about some fusion of these textual and ethnographical methods with the best trait of empirical and revisionist history: its close attention to the precise historical moment.

Indeed it was such reflections that led me to a first foray into what I see as a long-term future research agenda. In what remains for me the essay that I am most pleased to have written, I endeavoured to interrogate the questions of consensus and conflict in early Stuart England through a wide range of discourses, and, more broadly, demonstrated that politics embraced cultural practices such as horse-riding and beekeeping, music and games.[74] Work on the 'Commonwealth of Meanings' strengthened my sense that discourse analysis could fruitfully be extended to a broader corpus of texts – texts such as chess-playing manuals, in which our own culture would not expect to find such a politicized language.[75] Beyond that it also suggested that, as with equestrian portraits or horse-riding, discourse needed to be read alongside the ideology of performances and their traces in visual evidence. Increasingly it seemed to me that there was a myriad of other languages (besides the paradigmatic discourse traced by Pocock) in which systems

[73] The Institute for Advanced Study, Princeton was also where I first met Steven Zwicker who was, significantly, a visiting fellow working on Dryden in the School of Historical Studies.
[74] K. Sharpe, 'A Commonwealth of Meanings: Languages, Analogues, Ideas and Politics': below, ch. 2. This has been read too simply as another revisionist depiction of a consensual political culture: the plurals in the title are important.   [75] Or card-playing: cf. below, ch. 7.

of values and order were encoded – languages such as those of chivalry
and the pastoral. Thinking along these lines suggested a rather different
history – one that recognized that ideas of the 'country' were shaped by
paintings and poems, that attitudes to a favourite such as Buckingham
were formed by the codes of chivalry and reading classical histories, that
a fashion for Tacitus provided a language for articulating discontents
with corruption. I became certain that what we needed was a new
approach to early modern history that would ask both how a diversity of
languages and cultural texts provided ideological contexts (hence
meaning) to individual moments and occurrences; and (by corollary)
how specific episodes made immediate those texts and shaped the
reading of them by and for contemporaries.

My general sense of a need for a cultural turn in early modern studies
met its own particular moment when Macmillan invited me to edit a new
collection on the early Stuarts. Having still to finish *The Personal Rule*, and
questioning whether the time was right, I initially declined. However, I
soon came to see that this was an opportunity to move forward from the
sterile impasse of debates about revisionism and asked Peter Lake, a
post/anti-revisionist and friend with whom I had always enjoyed a stimulating dialogue, to join me in the enterprise. We determined that,
subject to the willingness of the best scholars in a variety of disciplines
to contribute, the volume would range over histories and translations,
poems and plays, paintings and architecture, popular pamphlets and
ballads.[76] Our joint purpose would be to reject the consensus v. conflict
model and to explore the performance of ideology in early modern
political culture, from a variety of perspectives and texts. What emerged,
as we argued in our introduction, was a set of common validating languages which contemporaries read, fused and glossed in quite different
ways (at times conflicting ways); and a struggle (unresolved) to claim
those languages and representations, to control meaning itself.

Whilst we would like to think that *Culture and Politics* marked an important move in early modern historiography, it raised more questions than
it answered. In particular it implicitly posed questions how, given
the multivalent and conflicting interpretations and constructions of
meaning performed by contemporaries, a culture of order and obedience held; and why in 1642 it fractured, turning interpretative conflict
into civil war. Beyond that, we might want to ask how after a violent revolution the political culture performed to reconstitute authority and

---

[76] Sharpe and Lake, *Culture and Politics*. The volume lacks essays on music and dance.

stability, how in 1688 the English nation avoided another civil war and how – to return to an earlier point – the Jacobite cause was culturally as well as politically subjected.[77]

In the second half of this essay, I want to sketch a map of this territory and of a number of approaches to it that I wish to explore. Before I do, however, it is worth recalling that half of the essays in *Culture and Politics* were written by scholars not in history departments, and that few historians have addressed the topics of literature, art and architecture they contributed. A recent survey of books on the seventeenth century led me to the conclusion that some of the most interesting explorations of early modern culture are not now being written by historians but by cultural critics interested in the politics of language and rhetoric, fable and romance, sexuality and gender.[78] Where literary scholarship has definitely taken a historical turn, historians, even young historians, have shown little interest in a more interdisciplinary praxis. Indeed some recent work indicates an intellectual retreat into the confines of the case study which, whatever its potential for broader illumination, has light thrown only on itself.[79] As Steven Zwicker and I argue elsewhere, the case study sits on a number of discursive and ideological trajectories and planes which it can help to examine and explore. To explore the intertextuality of meaning historians will need not only to transcend the barriers of their own subgenres (social history, gender history) but open their gates to a variety of critical practices and disciplines.[80]

II

One journey through the political culture of early modern England might see the terrain as follows. The Reformation marked the hitherto greatest ideological fissure in the English polity and society. The very divisions that were its consequence prompted, even necessitated, the construction and dissemination of an organic representation of the commonweal at a time when it faced the threat of fracture.[81] This was the tension at the centre of early modern political culture. Nervous governments went to some lengths to gloss those ambiguities and fis-

[77] Cf. Sharpe and Zwicker, *Refiguring Revolutions*, introduction.   [78] See below, ch. 10.
[79] For both interdisciplinary openness and case-study confinement see S. Amussen and M. Kishlansky eds., *Political Culture and Cultural Politics in Early Modern England* (Manchester and New York, 1995) and below, ch. 11.   [80] Sharpe and Zwicker, *Refiguring Revolutions*, introduction.
[81] The term 'commonweal' itself comes into currency at a time of the greatest threat of political fracture and social dissolution. See G. R. Elton, *Reform and Renewal* (Cambridge, 1973) and W. R. D. Jones, *The Tudor Commonwealth, 1529–1559* (1970).

sures. Homilies on obedience, Anglican apologia, the appropriation of religious rites in the art of majesty, the emergence of the court as a theatre of authority were all developed to underpin a culture of order and deference. To a large extent they succeeded: few voices articulated the language of resistance; condemned felons usually delivered a loyal speech of atonement on the scaffold; in the parishes and villages, social historians discover a popular culture of often rigid order and control that echoed the fears of anarchy and injunctions to obedience issuing from above.[82] The political reality of sixteenth-century England was quite other: the governing class and the realm were divided over religion, over loyalty to the faith and monarch, to self and state. If – and the if here is important – a fiction of unity veiled (the mixed metaphor is deliberately multi-media) that harsh reality, or permitted contemporaries not to confront it, that owed much to the brilliance of Tudor royal representation. Skilfully Henry VIII, most of all Elizabeth, appropriated the divisive rituals of religion for a unifying mystery of state.[83] An Erastian church and sacralized monarchy not only saved England from religious war; they elevated the Tudors to the height of divine-right rule. This fragile awe of majesty was punctured by the succession of James VI. The Reformation in Scotland had involved a more direct experience of, and open accommodation with, religious division and led to a demystification of state as well as church.[84] Less developed than in England, the Scottish court was far removed from the mystical rituals of Gloriana.[85] When he came thence to England, James revealed little interest in masques or sitting for portraits; his penchant for debate and participation in the political process rationalized the political culture, making debate about government, even monarchy, acceptable.[86] James may have been confident of his ability to win a war of words, but, as the newsbooks and political squibs of his reign make apparent, the harsh realities of debate knocked the monarchy from the pedestal of worship. Charles I endeavoured to remystify power. Eschewing political debate, he called on the arts of mannerism to re-elevate monarchy, to render its authority natural as well as divine.[87] Whether he would have succeeded remains

---

[82] K. Wrightson, *English Society, 1580–1680* (1982), esp. ch. 2; cf. K. Wrightson and D. Levine, *Poverty and Piety in an English Village* (1979); C. Herrup, *The Common Peace: Participation and the Criminal Law in Seventeenth-Century England* (Cambridge, 1987); Herrup, 'Law and Morality in Seventeenth-Century England', *Past and Present*, 106 (1985), 102–23.

[83] This is the persuasive recurrent theme of Roy Strong's works. See, for example, *Holbein and Henry VIII* (1967); *The Cult of Elizabeth* (1977). See too his *The Tudor and Stuart Monarchy* (3 vols., Woodbridge, 1995); below ch. 12.   [84] G. Donaldson, *The Scottish Reformation* (1960).

[85] See J. Wormald, 'James VI and I: Two Kings or One?', *History*, 68 (1983), 187–209.

[86] Cf. below, ch. 2, pp. 94–5.   [87] See below, ch. 3; Sharpe, *Personal Rule*, ch. 5.

open to question – more open to question than scholars have allowed when we consider the power of the royal image in the 1650s. It may be no accident that in Caroline Britain the first overt resistance to a re-iconized monarchy came from a Scotland where politics, rather than being etherealized, remained a harsh exchange of words.[88] One element of the British problem ignored by its proponents is that where in England authority was aestheticized, in Scotland it was the subject of discursive and rational scrutiny.

Ironically, in England it may have been the legacy of mystery that facilitated violent conflict when the fact of division could no longer be shrouded. Men fought for and about monarchy because they could not accommodate reasoned difference concerning it.[89] The civil war, however, produced a voluminous and powerful pamphlet literature in which all aspects of authority were opened to debate and interrogation – even by a wider public sphere outside the privileged discursive community of the elite. The civil war desacralized authority and fully politicized culture.[90] The body of the monarch, under Elizabeth the site of a culture that contained and denied difference, was itself cut in two – and on the stage of the most elaborate rituals of the theatre of state.

Regicide and civil war necessitated a new and altered political culture. Contest and division were inescapable realities of political life; if violence were not to be endemic they had to be controlled, not denied. The inherent weakness of the Commonwealth was that it constructed no new culture of authority, but depended for its survival on a monopoly of violence, on a standing army. Interestingly after the collapse of the Commonwealth, Cromwell, perhaps as iconophobic as any by instinct, became as Protector complicit in some remystification of rule – to make authority an object of desire.[91] Yet for all the stability he brought, royalist enemies and republican critics left him too dependent on an army and the nation on his death facing renewed civil conflict.

Gradually after 1660 a new political culture was constructed. True Charles II was greeted with triumphal arches and mythical tableaux celebrating Restoration,[92] but his character was very much down-to-earth and his exercise of monarchy anything but ethereal.[93] As political argu-

---

[88] On the Scottish pamphlets of the late 1630s, see Sharpe, *Personal Rule*, 813–24.

[89] See below, ch. 2, pp. 116–18.   [90] Cf. Sharpe and Zwicker, *Refiguring Revolutions*, introduction.

[91] See below, ch. 7, pp. 249–57.

[92] See J. Ogilby, *The Entertainment of His Most Excellent Majestie Charles II* (1662), ed. R. Knowles (Binghamton, N.Y., 1988); and G. Reedy, 'Mystical Politics: the Imagery of Charles II's Coronation', in P. Korshin ed., *Studies in Change and Revolution* (Menston, 1972), 19–42.

[93] See R. Hutton, *Charles II* (Oxford, 1989).

ments and differences were again articulated, the emergence of parties effected and announced important changes in the practices and culture of politics. Party not only institutionalized difference and contest, it acculturated division and disagreement, and so transmuted conflict from the battlefield to the political club and conversation. Religious toleration, the consequence of and vital step in that process of accommodating difference, began to neutralize a force for instability that had raised its head with the Reformation. By the end of the seventeenth century, a new political culture – of politeness – glossed the harsh fact of division and lent coherence, as once in quite different circumstances had the Virgin Queen, to the political nation.[94]

Of course there are numerous routes through this territory and approaches to its exploration. Many will question its very outlines. But it is a cultural history of politics, or a history of political culture that I wish to assay on the large scale, and in a number of complementary but separate projects.

Developing an earlier essay, I want further to examine the discourse of power through a study of royal writing and speech from Henry VIII to William III. Royal writings, I shall suggest, be they love poems, religious devotions or polemical treatises, were attempts to give authority cultural inscription, efforts to claim language and control meaning. From Henry VIII's songs, love letters and *Glass of Truth*, through Edward VI's diary and prayers, Elizabeth's translations and devotions, James I's Psalms and scriptural commentaries, Charles I's *Eikon Basilike*, to Charles II's narrative of his escape from the battle of Worcester and James II's memoirs penned in St Germain, monarchs struggled to write away challenges to their regality.[95] However, neither over discourse nor interpretation could sovereignty be exercised. And unwittingly by the acts of speech and writing, still more of publication, monarchs exposed themselves to answer and validated political debate. By the time of civil war royal words appeared on a page with counter-arguments and became commodified and democratized in the expanding market for pamphlet polemic. By the end of the seventeenth century, royal writing all but became a mere broadside of party discourse, as the royal word lost its

---

[94] See Sharpe and Zwicker, *Refiguring Revolutions*, introduction; P. Langford, *A Polite and Commercial People: England 1727–83* (Oxford, 1989); G. Barker Benfield, *The Culture of Sensibility* (Chicago, 1992).

[95] The fact that some of these works published in the monarch's name may not have been written by the ruler only adds a fascinating dimension to the complex relationship of authorship and authority and to the history of 'authorship' itself.

authority over the debate. A history of the changing relationship between royal authorship and royal authority promises to add to our understanding of the integrity of discourse to power, of the rhetorical nature of monarchy itself in early modern England.[96]

The other side of the coin – or rather page – is the *reading* of authority. If early modern historians have only just begun to investigate the ways through which meaning was produced in and disseminated by texts, they have ignored the study of hermeneutics, that is the habits of reading and strategies of interpretation according to which auditors and readers respond to texts. Historians of the book and of Renaissance humanist scholarship, such as Roger Chartier, Anthony Grafton and Lisa Jardine, have made a powerful case for the importance and possibility of understanding the culture of reading which, they demonstrate, is historically specific and ideologically freighted.[97] Yet as far as political history is still written, this important research might as well have never been conducted. The questions it raises however are essential for the historian of political culture. Could contemporaries choose how and where to read? What was the importance of the move to more private and solitary reading from the older habit of public and family reading aloud? Did personal reading foster a greater sense of self and an engagement of the individual with the text? Most importantly, to what extent was reading controlled by exposition, education, custom, and to what extent was the reader 'free' to perform his (or her) own interpretation, to refashion even the central texts of the culture (the Bible, or the law), to construct his own meaning? Such questions are not easily answered, but recent work has revealed the divergence and radicalism of readings of the classics, the politics of women's reading, and the significance of marks of reading as traces of ideological and political engagement.[98] For the work on mar-

---

[96] For some first thoughts see below, ch. 3.

[97] R. Chartier, *The Cultural Uses of Print in Early Modern France* (Princeton, 1989); Chartier, ed., *The Culture of Print: Power and the Uses of Print in Early Modern Europe* (Princeton, 1989); Chartier, *The Order of Books: Readers, Authors and Libraries in Europe Between the Fourteenth and Eighteenth Centuries* (Cambridge, 1994); L. Jardine and A. Grafton, ' "Studied for Action": How Gabriel Harvey read his Livy', *Past and Present*, 129 (1990), 30–78. For the eighteenth century cf. R. Darnton, 'Reading, Writing and Publishing in Eighteenth-Century France', *Daedalus*, 100 (1971), 214–56; Darnton, 'Readers Respond to Rousseau: the Fabrication of Romantic Sensitivity', in *The Great Cat Massacre and Other Episodes in French Cultural History* (1984), 215–56.

[98] D. Norbrook, 'Lucan, Thomas May and the Creation of a Republican Literary Culture', in Sharpe and Lake, *Culture and Politics*, 45–66; on women's reading I am grateful to Heidi Brayman for allowing me to read unpublished papers and her thesis 'Impressions from a Scribbling Age: Recovering the Reading Practices of Renaissance England' (Ph.D. thesis, Columbia University, 1995); on marginalia, I am grateful to Steve Zwicker for information and advanced copies of forthcoming work. See his 'Reading the Margins: Politics and the Habits of Appropriation', in Sharpe and Zwicker, *Refiguring Revolutions*, 101–15.

ginalia, or commonplace notes, on the material culture of the book and book market promises to add vital chapters to the history of the interpretations of, and responses to, authorized and authoritative texts. By study of the volumes of reading notes of a gentleman who also kept a parliamentary record and personal and public diary, I shall endeavour to argue that early Stuart Englishmen were able not only to read independently but, through reading, to construct private and public values quite at odds with the codes and norms of church and state.[99]

My third and major project will be a study of representations and images of power, of the culture of authority, from the Henrician Reformation to the 1688 Revolution. It starts from and explores the premise that in early modern England power rested in the representations as much as in the institutions of government and that, from Henry VIII onwards, monarchs exhibited an increased consciousness of their image as a vital source of their authority.[100] The study will venture the argument that the success of various regimes to a large extent depended upon these representations – in coronations and funerals, pictures and prints, coins and medals, escutcheons and seals, flags and buildings. The effectiveness of such representations, however, was not simply the skill of image-makers in imposing from above an image of kingship. The importance of these images lay as much in the desires of the subject as the intentions of the ruler. Successful representations, that is effective government, required the careful construction and maintenance of a cultural accord between monarch and political nation, and increasingly between government and the wider public.[101] In the Renaissance state, a measure of aesthetic affinity was essential to the maintenance of authority.

Through copies of paintings,[102] engravings and woodcuts, coins and display of royal arms, images of regality reached out into the country. In the provinces, as in London, rural and civic elites and humbler folk

---

[99] See my *Reading Revolutions: the Politics of Reading in Early Modern England* (forthcoming, New Haven and London, 2000), a study of the reading notes and parliamentary and political diaries of Sir William Drake.

[100] Strong sees Henry VIII as the monarch with the 'earliest deliberate propaganda programme . . . in English history', *Holbein and Henry VIII* (1967), 7.

[101] For a 'bottom up' argument along similar lines, see Herrup, *The Common Peace*, and now P. Griffiths, A. Fox and S. Hindle eds., *The Experience of Authority in Early Modern England* (Houndmills, 1996).

[102] There were many copies and 'afters' of Van Dycks, Lelys and Knellers etc. in aristocratic houses, and these images were therefore seen by local servants, retainers and visitors who did not have access to the elite galleries of Whitehall. Despite the connoisseurship of peers like Arundel, this was still an age that venerated the image as much as the artist (and the book, as much as the author).

read and responded to such images as they did to royal speeches and words. In the counties, corporations and villages, civic rituals, carnival and charivari, cartoons, squibs and acts of vandalism signalled responses to (both emulation of and dialogue with) the images of state. Just as with the language of scripture and law, certain symbols and images came to bequeath or validate authority and so had to be appropriated or claimed by any exercising authority. No government could allow others to take the scales or sword of justice; after Elizabeth's reign the phoenix rising from the ashes signified the best of rule. Together with the study of discourse, study of the representations and emblems of authority is central to an understanding of the exercise of and responses to power in early modern England.

Curiously and frustratingly, since the brilliant publications of Roy Strong, the art history of early modern England has tended to retreat from these historical questions into the narrower concerns of connoisseurship and formalist analysis.[103] Unlike the art history of the eighteenth century, we have few studies of the politics of placement, perspective, gesture, gendering, the accoutrements of office in the portraits of Hilliard or Van Dyck, Lely or Kneller.[104] Nor have art historians asked why or how a particular style came to dominate at a particular moment, creating as it were (in the case of Van Dyck) a representational community of courtiers whose values, religious beliefs and political allegiances were so strikingly different. Similarly no scholars have remarked the presence in Lely's canvases of blackamoors, tropical fruits and exotic birds as the badges of emerging empire, nor the association of such exotica with a more obviously sexualized portrayal of women (Figure 1). As Marcia Pointon and John Peacock have argued, portraits construct values and hierarchies and their material form and placement order communities and control our gaze, our perception of the representation of what/who is represented.[105] Thirty years ago, Strong lamented that 'the study of British art during this period has suffered because of isolation from the general currents of political, religious, cultural and social history' and urged that the image be relocated and read

---

[103] The excellent exception is David Howarth. See his *Images of Rule* (Basingstoke, 1996). I am grateful to David Howarth for his allowing me to read this invaluable book in advance of publication; below pp. 454–6.

[104] Though see J. D. Stewart, 'Sir Godfrey Kneller as Painter of Histories and Portrait Histories', in D. Howarth ed., *Art and Patronage in the Caroline Courts* (Cambridge, 1993), 243–63.

[105] M. Pointon, *Hanging the Head: Portraiture and Social Formation in Eighteenth-Century England* (1993); J. Peacock, 'The Politics of Portraiture', in Sharpe and Lake, *Culture and Politics*, 199–228.

Figure 1. Sir Peter Lely, 'Margaret Hughes, actress' (private collection)

in its broader 'ideological history'.[106] With one or two brilliant exceptions, Strong's case for such an art history of early modern England has
still not been answered. Art scholarship has not taken the historicist or
interdisciplinary turn that has characterized literary studies. Yet who can

[106] R. Strong, 'Proceedings of a Conference on British Art in the Sixteenth and Seventeenth
Centuries', 21 April 1965, on deposit at the Huntington Library and Mellon Centre in London.
It is remarkable how so many of the stimulating questions raised here remain untackled to this
day.

Figure 2. Sir Godfrey Kneller, 'William III on horseback'
(Royal Collection © Her Majesty Queen Elizabeth II)

doubt that the Dobson of William Strode gesturing to bountiful peace
while war looms behind must be read alongside the dramatist's own
engagement with art and allegiance? Who would not acknowledge the
power of the representation of William III on the white horse of the
apocalypse (Figure 2), or as the Protestant Hercules of the Fourth
Eclogue claiming scriptural and classical authority for his rule, and
return to scripture or editions of Virgil with a sharpened sense of their
valence for contemporary politics?[107] Is not the appropriation of a pow-

---

[107] Photograph in Huntington Art Library (Courtauld Witt B60/804 'Strode') of original at Knole;
O. Millar, *The Tudor, Stuart and Early Georgian Pictures in the Collection of Her Majesty the Queen* (1963),
plate 337; see J. D. Stewart, 'William III and Sir Godfrey Kneller', *Journ. Warburg & Courtauld
Inst.*, 33 (1970), 330–6.

erfully validating image evident in Van Somer's portrait of the faltering Prince Charles in the armour of his heroic elder brother (Figure 3), in Queen Anne's portrait in a dress worn by Elizabeth, or in Kneller's imitating Van Dyck in a portrait of George I that seems visually to naturalize his succession and erase his Hanoverian alterity?[108] Until we pursue an interdisciplinary address to such portraits, sensitive to the anxieties they disclose as well as the illusions they may seek to effect, we will not understand the political culture, and changes in the culture, of early modern England.

As with new historicism and the history of the book, such an address must involve a new approach to the politics of genre and consideration of the politics of material forms. Why did the miniature emerge as a fashionable genre at the court of Elizabeth, re-emerge as a token among royalists during the civil war, then fade after 1660? Why did the landscape, estate picture and battle scene become common only in the later seventeenth century? Was the sheer number of the coronation portraits of William III an endeavour visually to support his disputed succession? Do Kneller's Kit Kat Club portraits become more homogenized in style and form as party cohesion developed and collecting became conditioned by party affinity as well as aesthetic preference? The changing market for paintings, as a larger democratization of the aesthetic, is an important and neglected aspect of the study of representation and hence of politics itself.[109]

The most commodified (and increasingly democratized) of artistic genres were engravings and woodcuts. Until very recently historians of early modern England effectively ignored the woodcut as a text of popular culture. For Germany, Robert Scribner argued persuasively the importance for 'simple folk' of woodcut images which appropriated Catholic iconography and re-deployed it for Lutheran messages.[110] Now research on England – by Tessa Watt and Margaret Aston – has shown the fruits of such investigations for an understanding of English popular piety and Protestant polemic.[111] For, though England did not develop a significant woodcut industry in the sixteenth century, English publishers, like John Day, employed foreign craftsmen and the numbers of woodcut illustrations, though not large, increased. As Tessa Watt has

---

[108] National Gallery of Scotland, B4498; Kimbolton School (Courtauld Witt B79/928); Holyrood (Courtauld B76/2061 and A71/66).

[109] Cf. Sharpe and Zwicker, *Refiguring Revolutions*, introduction.

[110] R. W. Scribner, *For the Sake of Simple Folk: Popular Propaganda for the German Reformation* (Cambridge, 1981; 2nd edn Oxford, 1994).

[111] T. Watt, *Cheap Print and Popular Piety, 1550–1640* (Cambridge, 1991), M. Aston, *The King's Bedpost: Reformation and Iconography in a Tudor Group Portrait* (Cambridge, 1993).

Figure 3. Bernard Van Somer, 'Prince Charles in Prince Henry's armour'
(National Gallery of Scotland)

demonstrated, illustrations were a vital medium of popular religious books but were also displayed on walls in homes and alehouses, along with more secular representations illustrating ballads, tales, scandals or freaks of nature.[112] The image, as well as orality, shaped the consciousness of the illiterate, and helped to condition for the literate ways of reading, as well as seeing, ways of conceptualizing morality.[113] We are only just beginning to investigate the importance of such images for an understanding of popular politics. Watt quite reasonably excludes engravings from her study of cheap print on grounds of cost, but in doing so reminds us of how little we know about copperplate engraving and its market in sixteenth- and seventeenth-century England. And scholarly neglect here has led to serious misconceptions as well as ignorance. For even when they were quite expensive, engravings disseminated copies of portraits of monarchs and ministers, by the likes of Holbein and Van Dyck, far beyond the aristocratic elites who saw them at Whitehall or afforded a canvas for their country home. By the late sixteenth century, there was a growing market in England for engraved portraits of royalty, courtiers, bishops and men of learning, which may have reflected a broader participation in debate about politics (Figure 4).[114] During the early seventeenth century the range of subjects engraved grew so that, by the 1630s, numerous printsellers were in business, as the developed artistic tastes of Prince Henry and King Charles also spawned a small industry of copies by engravers such as Henry Holland and William Faithorne.[115] The man who dramatically responded to and revolutionized that market was Peter Stent. As the civil war further stimulated demand for some representations of actors newly emerged on the political stage or slain in battle, Stent turned from a high quality, small stock to a large list of cheaply executed engravings intended for 'the aspiring lower and middle classes', who could afford a few pence or a shilling.[116] As a consequence from the 1640s, thousands of Van Dycks of Charles I, images of Cavaliers and Parliamentarians, plates of Elizabethans and Jacobeans, maps and views, religious prints and satires hung framed or unmounted in merchants' homes across

[112] Watt, *Cheap Print*, passim.

[113] D. Freedberg, *The Power of Images: Studies in the History and Theory of Response* (1989); M. R. Miles, *Image as Insight: Visual Understanding in Western Christianity and Secular Culture* (Boston, 1985); Scribner, *For the Sake of Simple Folk* (1994 edn), new introduction.

[114] See A. M. Hind, *Engraving in England in the Sixteenth and Seventeenth Century* (3 vols., Cambridge, 1952–64); S. Colvin, *Early Engraving and Engravers in England* (1905).

[115] Hind, *Engraving in England*; L. Fagan, *A Descriptive Catalogue of the Engraved Works of William Faithorne* (1888); Colvin, *Early Engraving*.

[116] A. Globe, *Peter Stent, London Printseller c. 1642–1665* (Vancouver, 1985).

Figure 4. Broadsheet showing 'The royall line of kings, queenes, and princes, from the uniting of the two royall houses, Yorke, and Lancaster' (© Society of Antiquaries, London)

England. With the return from exile in the 1650s of Faithorne and Wenceslaus Hollar, the English engraving industry received further impetus and by the Restoration the collecting of engravings, as standardization of material form indicates, had become something of a fashion.

Because an art history dominated by questions of aesthetic originality and connoisseurship has neglected the engraving as ephemeral, we know too little about the changing forms, modes of production and distribution, price, purchasers or perceptions of engraved images. Yet the expanding inventory and commercial profits of the printseller suggest an important aspect of the relationship of aesthetic to political change that has never been explored. For as the purchasing subject desired to acquire and possess some representation of the figures of authority, in government, church and society, so those figures were placed, alongside other images and texts, in a domestic gallery ordered by the ordinary householder. As with expanding literacy, the wider market for engravings democratized a reading of what had once been icons, mysterious images hung only in quasi-sacred spaces, removed from vulgar eyes.[117] The marketplace also made the image a vital medium of polemic in an increasingly divided and contested political culture.

Increasingly from the late sixteenth century, engravings were used to make specific political arguments and affinities. The 1590 engraved map of Britain, with nobles, merchants and the head of Queen Elizabeth taking the place of Scotland, surely had a point to make shortly after the execution of Mary Queen of Scots (Figure 5).[118] The engraved image of Charles II in the 1650s, presented as a phoenix rising from the ashes, with his father's motto from the *Eikon Basilike* ('in verbo tuo spes mea') underlined the divine right of succession and the king's role as heir to the royal martyr and the Protestant Deborah.[119] Later Queen Anne's representation as a Stuart monarch, surrounded by ovals of her dynastic predecessors – James I, Charles I, Charles II and James II – gestures to recreate the family of the realm, after the divisive ruptures of William III's invasion and reign.[120] The engraving could also prove a powerful medium of opposition. During the civil war and republic, royalists brilliantly

---

[117] Cf. Scribner's remarks about print and sacred images in *For the Sake of Simple Folk* (1994 edn), new introduction. Interestingly, after the Restoration we see a significant increase in books on art and architecture which also explain these former 'mysteries' in everyday language.

[118] Huntington Library, Richard Bull Granger, vol. III, no. 9v.   [119] Ibid., vol. XII, nos. 7, 13.

[120] Ibid., vol. XXIII, no. 1. On Queen Anne, see also T. Bowers, *The Politics of Motherhood: British Literature and Culture* (Cambridge, 1996); I am grateful to Toni Bowers for allowing me to read chapters of this book in advance of publication.

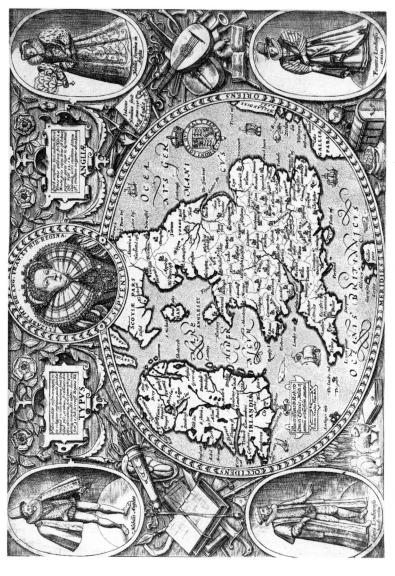

Figure 5. Map of Britain, with nobles, merchants and the head of Elizabeth I (reproduced by permission of the Huntington Library, San Marino, California)

exploited opportunities to caricature the Commonwealth as a dragon that shat taxes and consumed the realm – an effective charge of antipatriotism and a reassociation of the monarchy with the cult of St George.[121] Under James II, an engraving of bishops martyred a century before under Queen Mary skilfully played on fears of Catholic cruelties and despotism which had become part of English myth and memory.[122] Before we can begin to understand the effects of such images, their relationship to pamphlet polemic, ballad and a broader political consciousness, we must endeavour a full study of engravings – their production and appropriation, their changing aesthetic and political performance.

The valence of images in early modern political culture was not confined to 'aesthetic' objects – paintings and prints. In this heraldic culture, the blazon with the motto defined and publicized the lineage and values of the aristocratic or gentry family. The banner signified the business and virtues of the corporation, guild – or battalion. As the royal arms – on proclamations or in churches – signified the royal presence and power, so the seal authorized as well as authenticated letters of state and the correspondence of gentlemen. And coins of course made the monarch's image quite literally common currency. As soon as we recognize the ubiquity and ideological force of the image in early modern culture, we begin to pose a number of questions that have not been addressed. Was successful government in sixteenth- and seventeenth-century England as much a matter of a good image as of sound bureaucratic procedures and sensible policies? Was this why the Tudors succeeded and (some of) the Stuarts failed? Did, as I have suggested, the Commonwealth fail to establish a republican state because it never developed an iconographic or symbolic alternative to monarchy? If the right image was crucial to successful rule, what constituted the 'right image' and how did it change?

These lead to other obvious questions. Did the Tudors, as Roy Strong argued, inaugurate a new era in the deployment of image as political propaganda – or is such talk of a 'conscious revolution' 'misplaced'?[123] Who controlled the construction and dissemination of the royal image? Was it important that Elizabeth and Charles I exercised a measure of control over their visual representation, where other rulers (James I and

---

[121] Huntington Library, Richard Bull Granger, vol. x, no. 26. On the pre-war revival of the cult of St George, see Sharpe, *Personal Rule*, 219–22.

[122] Huntington Library, Richard Bull Granger, vol. ii, no. 159. See W. Maltby, *The Black Legend in England* (Durham, N.C., 1971).

[123] As Greg Walker argues in 'Henry VIII and the Politics of the Royal Image', in his *Persuasive Fictions: Faction, Faith and Political Culture in the Reign of Henry VIII* (Aldershot, 1996), 72–98.

II) did not? Did the Dutch dominance of the engraving industry lend powerful assistance to Protestant, and puritan, advocacy in sixteenth-century religious debate; and did the numerous Dutch engravings of James II surrounded by cardinals and the devil, fleeing England give a massive propaganda advantage to William III and the Whigs?[124]

Once we recognize the significance of the image, we are also led to the crucial historical question of change. How did representations of royal authority change from the early sixteenth to late seventeenth century? Did change in taste refashion the arts of political propaganda, or were they influenced by it? To what extent can we apply to the visual medium Pocock's model of paradigmatic shifts of symbolic motifs, and what may we read from them about altered political values and perceptions? Was the visual history of early modern England a narrative of mystification, desacralization and the construction after civil war of a new process of signification, as well as a new political order? How far did older images retain ideological force in changed aesthetic and political circumstances? Were the decline of the guild, the gradual end of the high age of chivalry, the fading interest in the emblem book, the conditions of a more rationalized and secularized culture and politics? Was the cartoon, as it emerged in Hanoverian England, a final marker (pace Jonathan Clark) of a demystified body – body both political and natural?

Such reflection leads us to recall that it is in the period from Henry VIII to William III that the most striking and memorable images of kings and queens were produced – images that few educated English people fail to recognize.[125] Was this, as some would argue, the accident of available artistic talent and a monarchy that did not need to account for its indulgences?[126] Or was it this fragile age of religious division and anxiety about civil conflict that was compelled to naturalize authority on canvas – as it did in the metaphors of the sun and the lion, the father and the body. By the very end of the seventeenth century, not only had many of the internal tensions been settled, England had emerged as a powerful nation, strong enough to defeat the forces of popery and to extend its rule over other cultures and terrains. When power appeared

---

[124] See, for example, Huntington Library, Richard Bull Granger, vol. XVIII, nos. II–IIV, 13, 24, 25, 29. On Elizabeth's censorship of depictions of herself, see E. W. Pomeroy, *Reading the Portraits of Queen Elizabeth* (Hamden, 1989), 17.

[125] I tried a recognition test on random groups of friends and students (some students of history, some not). Few failed to recognize most of the Tudors and Stuarts; very few could identify earlier or later monarchs (not even differentiating the Georges) – with obvious exceptions such as Queen Victoria.

[126] See the recent cautionary remarks of S. Anglo, *Images of Tudor Kingship* (1992).

intellectual and political history. Professor Pocock warned that narrow concentration on the practice of high politics reduces discourse to insignificance.[2] Professor Stone, as usual, is more polemical and more graphic: the revisionists, he writes, 'write detailed political narratives which implicitly deny that there is any deep-seated meaning to history except the accidental whim of fortune and personality . . . they are now busy trying to remove any sense of ideology or idealism from the two English revolutions of the seventeenth century'.[3] There is much substance in the criticism, but the passage quoted gives rise to a concern that was (and is) central to revisionists' historiography. For Stone equates ideology with a 'deep-seated meaning to history', with, I take that to mean, a belief that the past has been leading somewhere, indeed leading to the establishment of certain principles and values. This of course, though Stone might not like the term, is another manifestation of the Whig interpretation of history which the revisionist historians, especially those of the seventeenth century, set out to challenge.[4] From Macaulay to Gardiner those historians who studied the Stuart century as a crucial stage in the evolution of parliamentary government were as Whig in their history of ideas as in their history of politics; to question their political narrative as anachronistic is also to invalidate the history of seventeenth-century beliefs as they approached it – searching for those who heralded the future glories of the English constitution.[5] The revisionists rejected the teleological approach to the history of beliefs, as to the history of politics, but they were not intrinsically or necessarily hostile to the place of principle or ideology.[6] As yet, they have not written a revisionist history of ideas, but we have to consider how it might be written.

Over the last two decades, while the political history of the seventeenth century has been rewritten, a far more important revolution has taken place in the discipline of intellectual history. It is a revolution that can confidently be said to have been led by two scholars: John Pocock

---

[2] J. G. A. Pocock, *Virtue, Commerce and History* (Cambridge, 1985), 34.

[3] L. Stone, 'The Revival of Narrative: Reflections on a New Old History', *Past and Present*, 85 (1979), 3–24; quotation, 20.

[4] For evidence of the Whiggery cf. L. Stone, *The Causes of the English Revolution, 1592–1642* (1972), esp. 57, 117.

[5] Cf. J. C. D. Clark's comment on the early Hanoverian revisionists in *Revolution and Rebellion* (Cambridge, 1986), 65.

[6] Revealingly those who have castigated revisionists for taking the meaning and ideology out of history have also charged them with writing Jacobite or Tory history (see L. Stone, 'The Century of Revolution', *New York Review of Books*, 26 February 1987. The present writer was once introduced as a 'Tory historian'.) See also D. Cannadine, 'British History: Past, Present – and Future?', *Past and Present*, 116 (1987), 169–91.

and Quentin Skinner.[7] Greatly influenced by linguistic philosophers and semioticians, Pocock and Skinner have reoriented the methodology and practice of intellectual history to a study of languages in which, they argue, the beliefs and attitudes of an age are encoded. Such an approach has emancipated intellectual history from the limitations of the 'great texts' to study the vocabularies of the past revealed in all discourse – letters, sermons and plays, as well as pamphlets and political treatises. Quentin Skinner has argued that the great texts are in some respects the least representative of the thought of an age, rather the response to new problems – a response which in turn led to the reshaping of languages and ideas. For Pocock the great texts of political theory exemplify the most powerful minds of an era 'exploring the tension between established linguistic usages and the need to understand words in new ways'.[8] In order to comprehend those very texts, and more generally to understand the prevalent attitudes of the age, Pocock has proclaimed in methodological essays the need for the broadest study of vocabularies and languages, especially those languages that in any era become accredited to take part in public speech, or that were institutionalized.[9] The history of the changes in linguistic paradigms and accredited vocabularies, he has shown in practice, may then document the fundamental shifts in values – from a concern with grace to concern with custom and law, from a perception of virtue founded on civic humanism to one associated with the new world of rights, property and commerce.[10]

The history-of-languages approach to the history of thought has contributed far greater sophistication to the study of intellectual history and rightly problematized some simplistic (or even unpondered) notions.

---

[7] For a selection of methodological essays, see Skinner, 'Meaning and Understanding in the History of Ideas', *History and Theory*, 8 (1969), 3–53; Skinner, 'On Performing and Explaining Linguistic Actions', *Philosophical Quarterly*, 21 (1971), 1–21; Skinner 'Some Problems in the Analysis of Political Thought and Action', *Polit. Theory*, 2 (1974), 277–303; Pocock, 'The History of Political Thought: a Methodological Inquiry', in P. Laslett ed., *Philosophy, Politics and Society* (Oxford, 1956), 183–202; Pocock, *Politics, Language and Time* (New York, 1971); Pocock, 'Verbalizing a Political Act: Towards a Politics of Language', *Polit. Theory*, 1 (1973), 27–45; Pocock, 'Texts as Events: Reflections on the History of Political Thought', in K. Sharpe and S. Zwicker eds., *Politics of Discourse* (Berkeley, Los Angeles and London, 1987), 21–34; Pocock, 'Political Ideas as Historical Events', in M. Richter ed., *Political Philosophy and Political Education* (Princeton, 1980), 139–58. See also M. Foucault, *The Order of Things* (1970).

[8] I refer here to Skinner's methodological injunctions. In *The Foundation of Modern Political Thought* (2 vols., Cambridge, 1978) Skinner falls back on a study of great texts. Pocock, *Virtue, Commerce and History*, 13.   [9] Pocock, *Virtue, Commerce and History*, 8.

[10] Pocock, *The Machiavellian Moment: Florentine Political Thought and the Atlantic Republican Tradition* (Princeton, 1975).

The old idea of 'influence' has fallen to the new approach; problems of authorial 'intention' and the reception of texts have been complicated and clarified (if not resolved) by a developed understanding of the linguistic contexts of any discursive performance.[11] Perhaps most important of all, Professor Pocock's discussion and demonstration of a 'shared yet diverse linguistic context'[12] has furthered our understanding of the common beliefs and assumptions that still underlie the articulated tensions of an age, as in 1628 when crown lawyers no less than MPs argued in the language of custom and law.[13]

Yet for all these benefits, there are problems within Pocock's and Skinner's study of languages, and, more generally, limitations to and weaknesses within the linguistic methodology itself. Critics have drawn attention to fundamental philosophical problems of interpretation that have not been entirely satisfactorily resolved: the problems of the precise nature and definition of text and the related problems of the hermeneutic circle – that is the need to interpret texts from our broader knowledge of vocabularies which knowledge itself we derive from texts.[14] Despite his methodological injunctions, Skinner's own study of early modern political thought has still focused on the 'great' texts. And his exploration of the languages which provide the discursive context of those texts has been selective and even anachronistic: concentrating for example on natural law, but not theology or canon law. More generally, neither Skinner nor Pocock have pursued the relationships of languages to meanings or the perceptions of that relationship in the early modern period. Was language in the seventeenth century, as we might at times be led to deduce from a reading of the philological scholars or Ben Jonson's *Discoveries*, synonymous with the object ('Nomen et esse go together')?[15] Or did contemporaries perceive words, as did Bishop Arthur Lake's biographer, as a mode of representing meaning 'fitly

[11] Here the stimulus has come from literary critics: see especially H. Bloom, *The Anxiety of Influence* (1973); Bloom, *A Map of Misreading* (New York, 1975); S. Fish, *Self-consuming Artifacts* (Berkeley, 1972).

[12] Pocock, *Virtue, Commerce and History*, 3; Pocock, 'The Commons Debates of 1628', *Journ. Hist. Ideas*, 39 (1978), 329–34.

[13] I. Hampsher-Monk, 'Political Languages in Time: the Work of J. G. A. Pocock', *British Journ. Polit. Science*, 14 (1984), 89–116, esp. 107; Pocock, *Virtue, Commerce and History*, 4.

[14] Pocock, *Virtue, Commerce and History*, 4.

[15] W. Camden, 'The Antiquity and Office of the Earl Marshal of England', in T. Hearne ed., *A Collection of Curious Discourses* (2 vols., 1771), II, 90; K. Sharpe, *Sir Robert Cotton 1586–1631: History and Politics in Early Modern England* (Oxford, 1979), 21–4; B. Jonson, *Timber or Discoveries*, in C. H. Herford and P. Simpson eds., *Ben Jonson Works* (11 vols., Oxford, 1925–52), VIII, 621; A. Barton, *Ben Jonson Dramatist* (Cambridge, 1984), ch. 8.

compared by the ancients to a picture'?[16] What did contemporaries
understand by metaphor? How did they distinguish, as does Pocock,
between rhetorical and institutional languages? How conscious were
they of the linguistic turn as an ideological act?

Another unresolved difficulty is the old one – the precise relationship
within the linguistic methodology of ideas to events. Pocock attempts to
resolve the problem by (rightly) closing the difference between speech
and action – by seeing discourse as performances at moments in time.
But this approach does not itself explain *why* at any given moment languages undergo a shift, nor how changed events bring about linguistic
and ideological sea-changes.[17] Quentin Skinner, as Professor Tully
pointed out, acknowledges that ideologies are poor guides to action[18]
and ends up (curiously, given his methodological injunctions) in the
Foundations of Modern Political Thought with a blend of Whig history of
ideas and a resort to war as the motive force of political change – which
leaves the relationship of languages and events (the starting point of
Skinner's theorizing about intellectual history) far behind.[19] What both
these unresolved problems may suggest is that the relationship of ideas
to events, of intellectual and political history, cannot satisfactorily be
explored *only* through the history of verbal languages. Events not only
lead men to recast inherited terms, vocabularies and syntaxes. They
sometimes lead them to *act* and *experience* – I shall argue that the civil war
is one such case – in ways that their language does not, cannot, represent or accommodate, at least until some time after.[20]

This leads to an unfortunate (but not necessary) consequence of the
linguistic approach to the history of ideas: the neglect of other aesthetic
and cultural practices in which values and assumptions are encoded.
The tendency of all recent discussion has been to see verbal discourse as
the locus where all meaning is constituted.[21] Skinner defines an ideology
entirely in discursive terms as 'a language of politics defined by its con-

---

[16] A. Lake, *Sermons with Some Religious and Divine Meditations* (1629), 'A Short View of the Life and
   Virtues of the Author'. Cf. Puttenham's idea of language arising from consent, and Milton's
   description of language as an 'instrument', *OED* 'Language'.

[17] Hampsher-Monk, 'Political Languages in Time', 89–116, esp. 109.

[18] J. H. Tully, 'The Pen is a Mighty Sword: Quentin Skinner's Analysis of Politics', *British Journ.
   Polit. Science*, 13 (1983), 489–510, esp. 505.

[19] Skinner, *Foundations of Modern Political Thought*. Cf. the methodological articles cited above, n. 7,
   and see Tully, 'The Pen is a Mighty Sword'.

[20] Pocock's and Skinner's approach appears to be premised on the belief that experience and language are concurrent.

[21] J. E. Toews, 'Intellectual History After the Linguistic Turn: the Autonomy of Meaning and the
   Irreducibility of Experience', *Amer. Hist. Rev.*, 92 (1987), 879–907, esp. 898.

ventions and employed by its writers'.[22] This, however, is to ignore the picture and the building, the public procession and religious ritual, the games and pastimes in all of which the meaning a society identifies for itself is embodied and represented. In his discussion of 'the state of the art' of intellectual history, Pocock says nothing of the art of the state. In a period where a relationship of aesthetics to ideology is assumed, he therefore fails to explore important material for elucidating ideology and cultural values.[23] In their fruitful borrowings from semioticians, Pocock and Skinner have hitherto paid too little attention to the equally rich offerings of symbolic anthropology, for elucidating the ideologies of cultural practices.[24] At the beginning of the decade, reviewing the state of intellectual history William Bouwsma called for 'an expanded concern with the meanings expressed by every kind of human activity in the past'.[25] He saw the study of the history of music and dance as providing perhaps the most valuable future area of study. His agenda has not yet been followed, but in the extension of Pocock's and Skinner's approach into these territories may lie the most profitable future research.

Here the early modern period of English history offers especially rich possibilities, which may not have been fully appreciated. In the early modern period, as we have long known, men idealized a divinely ordained system which, never descriptive of the world, nevertheless presented a powerful normative depiction of it. In that representation, from the highest sphere of the planets, through the arrangements of societies, the composition of the individual and the hierarchy of beasts, a naturally appointed order was replicated.[26] Accordingly, the king of the commonweal corresponded to God in the heavens and the sun in the cosmos or to the father in the family and the lion, ruler of beasts, in the animal kingdom. Within man himself in his divine state the reason or soul was perceived to be the monarch; and by corollary the state was conceived as a human body, consisting of head and members, sinews and humours.

---

[22] Tully, 'The Pen is a Mighty Sword', 491.

[23] Pocock, *Virtue, Commerce and History*, introduction. Pocock does not explain the place of aesthetic or cultural practices in his approach to the history of political thought. This is not to say that Pocock's methodology cannot accommodate these non-verbal texts; only to observe that hitherto it has not extended to them.

[24] The inspiration here has come principally from C. Geertz; see esp. *The Interpretation of Cultures* (1975).

[25] W. J. Bouwsma, 'Intellectual History in the 1980s', *Journ. Interd. Hist.* 12 (1981), 279–91, quotation, 288.

[26] A. O. Lovejoy, *The Great Chain of Being* (Cambridge, Mass., 1936); E. M. W. Tillyard, *The Elizabethan World Picture* (1943); W. H. Greenleaf, *Order, Empiricism and Politics* (1964); R. Eccleshall, *Order and Reason in Politics* (Oxford, 1978).

These correspondences or analogues ran in both or several directions; that they were mutually adaptable was one of the ingrained habits of mind of early modern culture.

These analogues cannot be reduced to mere metaphor. Contemporaries were quite able to distinguish metaphor, which was a rhetorical device, from analogical thinking which 'discovered new truth by arguing from known to unknown'.[27] Pym, in reply to Strafford's long speech at his trial in which the earl had referred to the state by architectural, corporal and musical analogies, mentioned his 'metaphor of the intoxicating cup'; the analogues he took without comment as truths.[28] (Evidently Bacon did likewise when he described Aesop's fables as 'parabolic wisdom'.)[29] To be a father, in early modern England, *was* to be a king, and the reverse was also true. To observe the world of nature with its own hierarchies and laws was also a political experience; to master one's own unruly appetites and passions, to ride a horse and tame the unruliness of its nature, was to practise government and reconfirm the natural order of divine government.[30] It may take a considerable imaginative leap for us to comprehend that bee-keeping might be or become an ideological act. But when we turn from such practices to the discourse that in turn they generated, the need to make that imaginative leap is made both more compelling and easier. For we soon come to appreciate as we read seventeenth-century books and speeches how familiar and natural the transferences were: animal fables were popular moral texts not least because the animal kingdom corresponded to the human commonweal;[31] the *Game at Chess* was a powerful political polemic not least because the game was readily seen to replicate political action. The language of treatises on the body, on the family, on riding, on music, on the government of cattle, was highly political because each of these analogues (and others) corresponded in some way to the commonweal, as it related to them. Once we perceive this, we may see that not only the cultural practices but the texts they generated become invaluable documents of political ideas. Moreover, as we observe and read them from this perspective, we may discern that authors were not only aware of the political force of this seemingly apolitical matter, but capable of a

---

[27] S. L. Bethell, *The Cultural Revolution of the Seventeenth Century* (1952), 45.

[28] J. P. Kenyon ed., *The Stuart Constitution, 1603–1688* (2nd edn, Cambridge, 1986), 193–5.

[29] D. G. Hale, *The Body Politic: a Political Metaphor in Renaissance English Literature* (The Hague, 1971), 19.   [30] See below, pp. 99–100.

[31] The relationship of attitudes to animals and social and political ideas has been explored in K. Thomas, *Man and the Natural World, Changing Attitudes in England, 1500–1800* (1983) and H. Ritvo, *The Animal Estate: the English and other Creatures in the Victorian Age* (Cambridge, Mass., 1987).

sophisticated manipulation of the correspondence – bringing it into now closer, now more distant, focus.[32] So familiar were these correspondences that they often run quite casually across the various planes of the macrocosm, appearing to us like mixed metaphors. So, in *God Save the King*, Henry Valentine could speak of the king as the sun and 'The Sun is the beauty and bridegroom of nature.'[33] Similarly the preface to the *Commons Journal* on 19 March 1604 depicted the commonweal in a few lines in architectural, corporal and familial terms.[34] The analogies and correspondences came naturally to mind and were as naturally interrelated.

As well then as texts and languages, we shall need to study aesthetic documents, cultural practices, analogues, correspondences and the discourse that they in turn generated and which we have not been used to studying as political texts. An appreciation, however, of these ingrained habits of mind as political ideas requires the political historian as much as the historian of ideas, and it is here that the separation of the sub-disciplines has impoverished each. For in a general sense many actions in early Stuart England were political and political moments must be understood in the context of ingrained habits and cultural assumptions.[35] That is why Pocock sees political theory as emerging from ordinary political discourse in times of crisis, and why Professor Salmon found himself 'often unable to distinguish between political theory and political history'.[36] But more particularly, it is the political historian who may see the highly topical, immediate and (perhaps) radical comment in the articulation at a specific moment of the timeless trope or convention.[37] To discuss, in highly political terms, the reciprocal relations of love and duty between husband and wife, to urge that neither press it to a 'question of law' but for them to strive who should be most careful of each other's good, is one thing; in the year after Bate's case and the quarrel over the rights of kings and subjects it is sharply to specify a general analogy.[38] To rearticulate a conventional discourse of love

---

[32] Below, pp. 81–4. [33] H. Valentine, *God Save the King* (1639), 18.

[34] See *CJ*, I, 139 and the excerpt in Kenyon, *Stuart Constitution*, 10.

[35] Trial speeches offer another rich source for the specific assertion of norms; in so far as the approach suggested here is concerned, they have been neglected.

[36] Hampsher-Monk, 'Political Languages in Time', 105; J. H. Salmon, *The French Religious Wars in English Political Thought* (Oxford, 1959), preface.

[37] The phrase 'timeless trope', often used to designate the importance of an idea, is as unhelpful as it is problematic. Cf. below, p. 79. For a fine example of the historian's capacity to historicize the timeless trope see J. Fliegelman, *Prodigals and Pilgrims: American Revolution Against Patriarchal Authority* (Cambridge, 1982).

[38] B. Sk., *Counsel to the Husband* (1608), 53. Cf. below, pp. 108–9.

between monarchy and subjects at a time when that discourse was being redefined by the king was, as I recently argued in the case of Thomas Carew, to turn a gesture of praise into criticism.[39] Again contemporaries often exhibited a sophisticated capacity to manipulate the dialectic between the conventional trope and the moment – a sophistication which Jonson announced for example in declaring that his masques (which drew on Neoplatonic philosophy) were also to 'sound to present occasions'.[40] At times the 'occasion' that gives a conventional language or action its specificity may be beneath the surface of the broad familiar story: Davenant's poem *Madagascar*, I suggested, addresses the debate in Council in the winter of 1636–7 over aid to the Elector Palatine as well as a project to conquer the island.[41] Far then from revisionist historiography being intrinsically hostile to the history of ideas, a closer, detailed narration of political moments and manoeuvrings may enable us to historicize and particularize the timeless general trope and so to study the discursive performance or cultural act both as a political event and ideological gesture.

THE WORLD PICTURE

Traditionally studies of political ideas in the seventeenth century have moved quickly (and with an audible sigh of relief) to Hobbes, bemoaning the poverty of theory during the earlier decades of the century. Such studies equate political thought with political philosophy, with self-conscious theorizing of fundamental problems about the nature of the state. Others, the works of Christopher Hill chief among them, have attempted to explain the early deficiency of theory in comparison to a later ferment in political thought by reference to the operation of censorship before the 1640s.[42] Government censorship, however, not least because there were no adequate institutions or mechanisms through which to exercise it, was largely ineffective even when attempted and the evidence suggests it was attempted only in extreme cases. This myth of

---

[39] K. Sharpe, 'Cavalier Critic?: the Ethics and Politics of Thomas Carew's Poetry', in Sharpe and Zwicker, *Politics of Discourse*, 117–46.

[40] B. Jonson, *Hymenaei*, Line 17, *Works*, VII, 209, and see S. Pearl, 'Sounding to Present Occasions: Jonson's Masques of 1620–25', in D. Lindley ed., *The Court Masque* (Manchester, 1984), 60–77.

[41] K. Sharpe, *Criticism and Compliment: the Politics of Literature in the England of Charles I* (Cambridge, 1987), 95–6.

[42] C. Hill, *Intellectual Origins of the English Revolution* (Oxford, 1965), passim; Hill, 'Censorship and English Literature', in his *Collected Essays I: Writing and Revolution in 17th Century England* (Brighton, 1985), I, 32–71.

widespread censorship needs to be, and is currently being, dispelled.[43] More recently, however, scholars have questioned the absence of theory: an eminent medievalist has drawn attention to the fourteenth-century foundations of ideas voiced in the 1640s;[44] a literary scholar has demonstrated the familiarity of early Stuart England with the political treatises of George Buchanan;[45] most generally, a survey of political ideology has forcefully argued that the early Stuart English could draw from rich wells of indigenous intellectual traditions and continental theorists to justify their resistance to the monarch in 1642.[46]

While such scholars have greatly enriched our knowledge, their arguments, I believe, fail to convince. For though ideas of resistance, contract and popular sovereignty were available from the past and from the continent, they were not questions theorized or addressed by early Stuart Englishmen. To acknowledge that men did not articulate these ideas, that they did not see the relevance or the force of ideas that had emerged from political crises until they confronted their own crisis, may come close to saying (since all thinking is an act of selecting) that they did not think them. What is certain is that such theories were not in the foreground of their thinking about politics. And I would suggest that in general concentration on and search for such theorizing of political problems in early seventeenth-century England is anachronistic.[47] It is anachronistic because political theory approaches politics as both a sphere of its own and as a set of problems: it addresses the questions of political obligation, of why citizens should be subject or subject themselves to the authority of the state. It takes, that is, the state as an artifice which needs to be justified. This is a premise and approach essentially

---

[43] See, e.g., Sharpe, *Criticism and Compliment*, 36–9, 290–7; S. Lambert, 'The Printers and the Government, 1604–37', in R. Myers and M. Harris eds., *Aspects of Printing from 1600* (Oxford, 1987), 1–29 (I am grateful to Sheila Lambert for a copy of this important essay); B. Worden, 'Literature and Political Censorship in Early Modern England', in A. C. Duke and C. A. Tamse eds., *Too Mighty to be Free* (Zutphen, 1988), 45–62. I am grateful to Blair Worden for allowing me to read this important essay in advance of publication. Annabel Patterson in *Censorship and Interpretation* (Madison, Wis., 1984) writes, I now think, too much from an assumption that censorship was widely practised, but demonstrates how it was circumvented.

[44] B. Tierney, *Religion, Law and the Growth of Constitutional Thought 1150–1650* (Cambridge, 1982).

[45] D. Norbrook, '*Macbeth* and the Politics of Historiography', in Sharpe and Zwicker, *Politics of Discourse*, 78–116. Cf. J. H. Burns, 'The Political Ideas of George Buchanan', *Scottish Hist. Rev.*, 30 (1951), 60–8; H. R. Trevor-Roper, *George Buchanan and the Ancient Scottish Constitution (Eng. Hist. Rev.,* supplement 3, 1966).

[46] J. P. Sommerville, *Politics and Ideology in England 1603–1640* (1986); K. Sharpe, *Politics and Ideas in Early Stuart England* (1989), 283–8.

[47] Cf. J. Daly, 'Early Stuart England was not a congenial place for the production of the kind of mature theory which the latter part of the century has taught scholars to look for', 'Cosmic Harmony and Political Thinking in Early Stuart England', *Trans. Am. Philos. Soc.*, 69 (1979), 3.

alien to early Stuart thinking. It is one of the many marks of Hobbes's revolutionizing of political thought that he conceived his state as an artificial creation: 'for by art is created that great Leviathan called a Commonwealth . . . which is but an artificial man'.[48]

For before the events of civil war shattered the assumptions, the state was seldom conceived abstractly or as an 'other'. The commonweal, the term usually employed, was represented as a natural organism, like the family from which it grew. Man fulfilled himself as a man in so far as he was part of the commonweal, and had no social existence (Aristotle would have said no fulfilment of his humanity) outside it. Everything good in the created world, a preacher at the assizes in 1629 told his auditories, was ordered and under government: celestial bodies, beasts, men.[49] In a clock, he noted (revealing that even the observations of mechanisms could then complement rather than confront this worldview), the great wheels guided the small. And so the government of the commonweal reflected the divine plan and government of all nature.

We cannot but discern a justificatory tone to the preacher's assertions; he claimed authority for the government of the day – implicitly against its critics – by equating it with *an ideal*: of the divine government of nature. But that idealization itself manifests that in early modern England the question of order in the state was part of that of natural order – and of moral order in all human affairs, secular and spiritual. Political theory did not really exist as an independent study because politics was not a distinct and separate arena of thought or action.[50] That is not to say that there was no political thought, no debates or differences, no attitudes to politics. Rather the reverse: to reflect on the universe, the relationship of man to God or the hierarchy in the animal kingdom was also to reflect on the nature of the commonweal and of the order and degrees within it. As J. Robinson put it succinctly in his *Observations Divine and Morall*, 'It is a kind of impeachment of Authoritie to examine the Reasons of Things.'[51]

We tend in modern political discussion to think about various relationships: of individuals to each other, to institutions, of each to principles or ideals. In early modern England, commentators tended rather to represent the commonweal as an organism in which there was only one relationship: that of all to all, and of everything to one divine truth.

[48] T. Hobbes, *Leviathan*, ed. M. Oakeshott (Oxford, n.d.), 5.
[49] T. Taylor, *The Mappe of Moses, or A Guide for Governors* (1629), esp. 7–12.
[50] Daly, 'Cosmic Harmony', 26.
[51] J. Robinson, *Observations Divine and Morall, for the Furthering of Knowledge and Vertue* (1625), 65.

Because there was held to be one truth, there could no more be a contention over fundamental values in secular matters than in spiritual; the
two, the state and the church, promulgated and preached God's truth;
out of the bosom of the church, it was officially decreed, 'there is no
ordinary salvation'.[52] Again the organic conception was an ideal, but the
religious divisions and social dislocations that increasingly disrupted it
led not to the abandonment but the more forceful articulation of organic
unity. Hooker reasserted that those who questioned the Church of
England upset all order, as indeed their questioning reflected the disruption of their human order. Bishop Henry King denounced those 'giddy'
men who 'prefer their own fantasies' to public doctrines;[53] Gyles
Fleming wrote of the need to prefer 'the unity of God's church before
our own private phantasies and particular humours'.[54] Anglican apologists and antiquaries were so anxious to establish the historical origins of
the Church of England in the time of the apostles because it was essential to exonerate their church from the charge of schism.[55] For there
could be only one true religion; neither God nor his magistrates on earth
could really tolerate another faith. In a real sense recusants and nonconformists who rejected the church were also outside the commonweal;
their only hope was to come to see the light of truth.[56] This assertion of
the unity and oneness of truth was by no means just an official doctrine
of the church hierarchy. It was a normative ideology for long just powerful enough to contain the tensions that might have fractured it. Despite
the logic of the Calvinist doctrine of election – that is mass separation –
and the tensions to which (as we shall see) it gave rise,[57] surprisingly few
puritans were willing to separate from the church. Robert Bolton, a
Northamptonshire preacher, in *The Saints Sure and Perpetual Guide* revealed
his unease with the Laudian church, but counselled the godly not to separate.[58] The religious sceptics and rationalists too, for all they appear at
times to herald a future more liberal position, held to the idea of one
indivisible truth and religious community. Sir William Davenant, who
appears to have desired a more rationalist theology, upbraided the

---

[52] A. Fisher, *A Defence of the Liturgy of the Church of England or Booke of Common Prayer* (1630), 116. Sir
Robert Filmer preserved the manuscript of the treatise for publication (epistle dedicatory).
[53] H. King, *An Exposition upon the Lords Prayer* (1628), 18.
[54] G. Fleming, *Magnificence Exemplified and the Repair of St Paul's Exhorted Unto* (1634), 21. Fleming
defined 'gentem nostram, that is church and commonwealth' and urged that both be preferred
above individual considerations.
[55] F. J. Levy, *Tudor Historical Thought* (San Marino, 1967); J. Bruce and T. T. Perowne eds.,
Correspondence of Matthew Parker (Parker Soc., 1853).
[56] W. Struther, *A Looking Glasse for Princes and People* (1632), 84–6.
[57] Below, pp. 70–4.   [58] R. Bolton, *The Saints Sure and Perpetual Guide* (1634), 126–9.

puritans for separating themselves, like the Jews, as a sect.[59] The philosopher Lord Herbert, though impatient with dogma, in the words of his biographer, 'in spite of the appearance of some hard-hitting pragmatism responds to the idea of truth as to a mysteriosum fascinosum whose ultimate characteristic is the unification of all diversity'.[60] Herbert indeed responded to the sceptical Montaigne's contention that all was diversity by asserting (not arguing, for it was an axiom not to him in need of demonstration) that all was integrated by correspondences into one ordered universal structure.[61]

As idealized, then, the commonwealth was bound by one truth. It was also held, ideally, to express one good. The state, Aristotle had maintained, existed to make the virtuous life possible. It was a moral community and because it was both a moral and an integrated community there could theoretically (the practical tensions we will explore at length)[62] be no confrontation between the good of the individual and the good of the whole. The good of each person derived from and depended on the good of the community. What over a century later Rousseau went to elaborate lengths to argue (and failed), could be asserted in seventeenth-century England as a commonplace: 'That which tends to the common peace and safety must be practised by all.'[63] The imperative itself suggests a recognition that not all adhered to that commonplace. Indeed the most acute of the Tudor commonwealthsmen revealed a realistic awareness of the tensions that could exist between the individual and the community. But, for all that realization, they adhered to the traditional concept of society as an organism, 'depending for its health on the proper functioning of all its parts for the good of the whole body'.[64] After the religious disputes, economic crises and political tensions of the late sixteenth and early seventeenth centuries, John Pym could declaim in 1628 that:

The form of government is that which doth actuate and dispose every part and member of a state to the common good, and as these parts give strength and ornament to the whole, so they receive from it again strength and protection in their several stations and degrees. If this mutual relation and intercourse be broken, the whole frame will quickly be dissolved.[65]

---

[59] Sharpe, *Criticism and Compliment*, 71.
[60] R. D. Bedford, *The Defence of Truth: Herbert of Cherbury and the Seventeenth Century* (Manchester, 1979), 101. This is an important work which deserves to be better known.
[61] Ibid., 104–5. [62] Below, pp. 60–75.
[63] The phrase is from J. Davenport, *A Royal Edict for Military Exercises* (1629), 2. See also 6–7.
[64] A. B. Ferguson, *The Articulate Citizen and the English Renaissance* (Durham, N.C., 1965), 349. Ferguson documents the awareness among some writers of economic and private interest and yet the tenacity of traditional concepts and values. [65] Kenyon, *Stuart Constitution*, 15.

It may from hindsight seem ironic that Pym's speech was delivered at the impeachment of Mainwaring. Certainly that context powerfully reminds us that ideals are often asserted at the very moments when they are being undermined in practice; that a shared language about how things ought to be may mask damaging political conflicts about how to restore them to perfection. But it is equally important to note that when contemporaries recognized threats to common good and order posed by interests, personal acquisitiveness, selfish behaviour or circumstance, they responded – the Jacobean dramatists provide an excellent example – by a reassertion of community and integrity.[66]

Those who preferred a private course were, like the fanatics who followed the dictates of their own consciences, dismissed as irrational men. 'The order of reason', Nicholas Faret observed in *The Honest Man*, 'requires that the interests of private men should yield to the public.'[67] What we would delineate as 'private interest', distinct from and in confrontation with public roles and duties, was not accepted in early modern England.[68] Economic and social theorists such as Clement Armstrong, a philosopher like Thomas More, could discern it but never really accommodate or accept it.[69] Any society organized around service relationships may find it difficult to distinguish private and public realms and in early modern England there were few who did not either give or receive service; most did both. The politicization of the body expressed this world and these integrations.[70] Indeed what later ages would understand as private, the early seventeenth century viewed as 'privatus', deprived of the order and good of the commonweal, of, as the Solemn League and Covenant could still put it, 'the true public liberty, safety and peace of the kingdom, wherein everyone's private condition is included'.[71] What we would separate as private and public interest, the individual and the state, were harmonized in the concept of the commonweal.

Indeed the commonweal was represented generally as a condition of harmony. In this quality of course it corresponded in microcosm to the harmony of the celestial bodies and took as its model the harmony of

---

[66] E.g. L. S. Marcus, *The Politics of Mirth* (Chicago, 1986), esp. 33. Cf. J. Montagu, *The Workes of the Most High and Mighty Prince James* (1616), 212, James I saw the preference for private interest as a rejection of the 'mother, the Commonwealth'.

[67] N. Faret, *The Honest Man or The Art to Please in Court* (translated into English 1632), 125–6; George Wither went so far as to argue that injustice to an individual might be defensible in the name of the common good, *Britain's Remembrancer* (1628), 236.

[68] See *OED* 'Private', 'privacy' and J. Goldberg, *James I and the Politics of Literature* (Baltimore and London, 1983), passim.   [69] Ferguson, *Articulate Citizen*, passim.

[70] Below, pp. 111–13.   [71] Kenyon, *Stuart Constitution*, 240.

God's creation. It also macrocosmically corresponded to the harmony of humours in the well-ordered man. These are familiar statements but their implications have not perhaps sufficiently been pondered. For as God authored and maintained the harmony of the world so it was the role of the king to sustain the harmony of the commonweal.[72] Harmony is synonymous with balance and the balance is the symbol of justice. The business of kingship, then, is less the exercise of power than the distribution of justice to maintain, as an assize sermon put it, 'proportion'.[73] In the natural body of man, health depended on a harmony of the various humours, on a balanced constitution; and so, again, as the physician of the state, it was the duty of the king to preserve a balanced *constitution* (the word takes on its political sense in our period)[74] in the body politic.

These ideas of harmony are essential contexts for any understanding of attitudes to power in early modern England, and in particular help to make sense of what to us seem irreconcilable contradictions – such as Sir Thomas Smith's references to parliament as the highest power in the realm *and* to the king as absolute.[75] They also importantly suggest how disagreements and even disruptions could for long be accommodated to ideas of unity and wholeness: by treating political upheavals not (as we naturally do) as rival contests for power, but rather as temporary imbalances in the body politic.[76] The subject and the sovereign were not only analogues to the body and the soul, wrote Forset in his *Comparative Discourse*; they existed in the same balance.[77] What secured that balance, or harmony, was moderation – the avoidance of any extremes. In Aristotle's *Ethics*, moderation, the pursuit of the mean, was equated generally with virtue and specifically with justice.[78] Echoing Aristotle, Ralph Knevet writing in 1628 defined the most virtuous men, the aristocracy, as those who most harmonized or moderated their own parts.[79] In *The English Gentleman*, Richard Brathwaite wrote: 'Moderation is a subduer of our desires to the obedience of reason.'[80] The ruler then was a mod-

---

[72] J. de Santa Maria, *Christian Policie or the Christian Commonwealth* (1632), 105–9. Daly, 'Cosmic Harmony', 13.   [73] A. Fawkner, *Eiphnotonia or the Pedegree of Peace* (1630), epistle dedicatory.

[74] The *OED*'s first entry for 'constitution' in the political sense is 1610.

[75] M. A. Judson, *The Crisis of the Constitution* (New York, 1971 edn), 84. Cf. P. G. Burgess, 'Custom, Reason and the Common Law: English Jurisprudence 1600–1650' (Ph.D. thesis, Cambridge University, 1988), 192–7.

[76] Cf. the point of R. M. Smuts in *Court Culture and the Origins of a Royalist Tradition in Early Stuart England* (Philadelphia 1987), 260.

[77] E. Forset, *A Comparative Discourse of the Bodies Natural and Politique* (1606), 10.

[78] Aristotle, *Ethics*, bk II, ch. 6, ed. J. A. K. Thomson (Harmondsworth, 1955), 65.

[79] R. Knevet, *TPAT TIKON or A Discourse of Militarie Discipline* (1628), sig. F2.

[80] R. Brathwaite, *The English Gentleman* (1630), 306.

erator who, controlling his own appetite and balancing humours, sought to avoid all excess or extremes in the commonweal.[81] James I, who did not always succeed in the moderation of his personal pleasures, specifically proclaimed this as his axiom: 'I am for the medium in everything.'[82] Charles I's courtiers, I recently argued, reasserted the doctrine to a monarch who, they believed, had upset the balance both in his practice and theory of government.[83] The idea of cosmic harmony – of balance and moderation – far from a validation of unrestrained authority, was a normative ideology of self-restraint for rulers.

Power we most obviously think of as residing in individuals (or institutions), as the sway wielded by a superior over an inferior and as related to the exercise of the will. None of these associations gets to the heart of early seventeenth-century attitudes.[84] Early modern perceptions of power, it must be admitted, are beset by ambivalences and hard to pin down; but these, like the infrequent use of the term, may be revealing as well as frustrating for the historian. The power of the king, we know, was described as analogous to that of God. Yet, as James Daly pointed out, the position of God himself in the cosmic theory (like much of that theory) was itself ambiguous, since He was both the author of the chain of correspondences and also part of that chain.[85] Not surprisingly then, in itself the analogy of royal with divine power could support both relatively unrestrained action and action circumscribed by the need to act according to the principles – or laws – that maintained the cosmos in harmony. Most contemporaries, however, saw God as acting usually through the divine laws according to expectations discernible by reason, deploying only exceptionally His power of miracle which operated outside of natural law. That power was explicitly compared to the king's prerogative; in the words of John Donne: 'Nature is his Prerogative.'[86] Royal prerogative, the Earl of Strafford added in 1641, 'must be used as God doth his omnipotency', that is only on 'extraordinary occasions'.[87] The analogy of the king with God then limited as well as validated royal power. Moreover the king's inferiority to God and his derivation of power from God made the due exercise of that power an *obligation*.

---

[81] See below, p. 93.
[82] C. H. McIlwain ed., *The Political Works of James I* (Cambridge, Mass., 1918), 291.
[83] Sharpe, *Criticism and Compliment*, ch. 6.
[84] See R. Tuck, 'Power and Authority in Seventeenth Century England', *Hist. Journ.*, 17 (1974), 43–61.   [85] Daly, 'Cosmic Harmony', 10.
[86] J. Donne, *Essays in Divinity*, ed. E. M. Simpson (Oxford, 1951), 80–1; and F. Oakley, 'Jacobean Political Theology: the Absolute and Ordinary Powers of the King', *Journ. Hist. Ideas*, 19 (1968), 323–46, esp. 337–40.   [87] *Cal. Stat. Pap. Dom. 1640–1*, 542.

Early modern Englishmen were more used to thinking in terms of duties than of rights: Fulke Greville referred to the 'mutual duties to which man is born';[88] Francis Bacon wished to digest the duties of men to a science.[89] Notions of duty and obligation came more easily than the concept of power to a society organized around patron–client relationships. The more frequent assertions of the obligations and duties than power of the king (even their equation) therefore should not surprise us. The most obvious obligation was the need to account to God, in respect of whom, Owen Feltham put it in his *Resolves*, 'the greatest Monarch is more base than the basest vassal'.[90] P. Scot in his *Table-Booke for Princes* was more graphic: kings were never to forget their imminent need to account before the strictest of all judges – 'who knoweth but tomorrow they may be (where all kings before them are) the food of serpents and worms'.[91] Accountability to God, however, was not the only obligation. The king was obliged to subject his own will, not only to the regulation of his own reason, but to the common good, the custody of which defined his function.[92] In *A Looking Glasse for Princes and People*, a thanksgiving sermon for the birth of Prince Charles, the preacher William Struther reminded his congregation that the power of princes was 'not of themselves but lent of God and not for themselves but for him and his people'.[93] Charles I needed no reminding of this – even though he felt others did. 'Let me remember you', he told his Commons in 1628, 'that my duty most of all and everyone of yours according to his degree, is to seek the maintenance of this church and commonwealth.'[94] Charles I and his audience in 1628 evidently had a different sense of the good of the church and commonwealth. But what is important is that he, as they, believed that royal power was in no way synonymous with the king's will.[95] In *The Emperour of the East*, Massinger has a character go so far as to proclaim that 'absolute Princes/Have, *or should have* in policie less free will then such as are their vassals'.[96] His caveat strikes to the root of the

[88] F. Greville, *Poems of Monarchy*, in A. B. Grosart ed., *The Works of Fulke Greville* (4 vols., 1870), I, 92; cf. James I to his son, 'You are rather born to onus than honos', *Basilikon Doron*, in *Workes of James I* (1616), 138.

[89] F. Bacon, *The Advancement of Learning*, bk II, ch. 21, sections 7–10, ed. G. W. Kitchen (1965), 163–6.

[90] O. Feltham, *Resolves, Divine, Morall, Politicall* (1623), 30. It is worth emphasizing the accountability in divine-right theories of monarchy.

[91] P. Scot, *A Table-Booke for Princes* (1621), 10–11, 65.   [92] Ibid., 6.

[93] Struther, *A Looking Glasse for Princes and People*, 14. Struther, a preacher of Edinburgh, dedicated his thanksgiving sermon for the birth of Prince Charles to the king.

[94] R. C. Johnson et al. (eds.), *Commons Debates 1628*, (3 vols. New Haven, 1977), II, 3.

[95] P. Bethune, *The Counsellor of Estate* (1634), 77.

[96] P. Massinger, *The Emperour of the East* (1632), sig. E1; P. Edwards ed., *The Plays and Poems of Philip Massinger* (5 vols., Oxford, 1976), III, 432.

political problems left unresolved by theory: what was to be done if the monarch did not behave as he ought? To this problem the normative ideology had no answer other than a reassertion of the ideal. The exercise of royal power was, or ought to be, the exercise of self-restraint.[97] Sovereigns, Forset put it, governed by laws.[98] Power thus perceived and law were not at odds – which is why Knolles, in translating the *Six Livres de la République*, could combine praise of a Bodinian theory of sovereignty with celebration of the English common law.[99] Governing – exercising power – in early modern England was seen not as an individual act of will but as the expression of a cosmic and communal order by a monarch whose public body and will were inseparable from that order and community. Thomas Hobbes in his *Leviathan* came to see power in very different terms. But significantly before the civil war he defined power in communal terms – as having its foundation in the 'belief of the people'.[100]

The community participated in the exercise of power through the giving of counsel and presentation of petitions against things amiss. Juan de Santa Maria put the place of counsel boldly: 'Kings which do not hear by consequence do not understand. And not understanding they cannot govern.'[101] Here again the analogy with God reinforced the king's obligation to heed the voice of his subjects. Kings, John Bastwick argued (for once uncontroversially), are like gods 'in respect of invocation, only to be sought to and called upon of their subjects', as God was invoked by prayer.[102] We are familiar with the pervasiveness in early Stuart political discourse of the necessity for, and the king's obligation to heed, good counsel.[103] Indeed once again mounting anxieties about the course of government lay behind the persistent reiteration of the ideal. In good counsel, it was frequently argued, lay the very health of the body politic.[104] But we may be less familiar with how far the obligation could

---

[97] Scot, *Table-Booke*, 12.
[98] Forset, *Comparative Discourse*, 4; cf. Scot, *Table-Booke*, 4: 'scepters are not given unto kings (tyrant-like) to abuse their authority, but to be strict observers of the laws they impose upon others'.
[99] J. Bodin, *The Six Bookes of a Commonweale*, translated by R. Knolles, 1606, ed. K. D. Macrae (Cambridge, Mass., 1962); G. L. Mosse, 'The Influence of Bodin's Republique in English Political Thought', *Medievala & Humanistica*, 5 (1948), 73–83. Cf. Burgess, 'Custom, Reason and the Common Law', 194–7.
[100] T. Hobbes, *Eight Bookes of the Peloponnesian Warre written by Thucydides*, preface to the reader; I owe this reference to G. Oestreich, *Neostoicism and the Early Modern State* (Cambridge, 1982), 114.
[101] Santa Maria, *Christian Policie*, 164.   [102] See Sharpe, *Politics and Ideas*, p. 80 and n. 23.
[103] Cf. K. Sharpe ed., *Faction and Parliament* (Oxford, 1978; 2nd edn, London, 1985), 37–42.
[104] See, for example, *The Works of Joseph Hall* (1628), 231: 'As where no sovereignty so where no counsel is, the people fail; and contrarily where many counsellors are, there is health.'

be pressed. In the English translation of Juan de Santa Maria's *Christian Policie*, for example, the monarch who resolves business alone 'therein breaks the bounds of a Monarchie and enters into those of a tyrannie'.[105] Moreover, he is equally guilty if he acts 'against the opinion of his counsellors' – a point also made by George More in his *Principles for Young Princes*, a treatise which in general not only emphasized the obligations of princes but catalogued the horrible ends met by tyrants.[106] The obligation on the king to subordinate his own will to the concurrence of his councillors underlines how far the early seventeenth century was from seeing power as a distinct act of the individual will. And it is a further reminder why, despite the tensions in practice, it was not easy for them to theorize about the (potential) conflicts of prerogative and law.

On the continent, circumstances had forced England's neighbours to reflect on these and other fundamental political questions and problems. Such reflections had produced important and radical texts of political theory – especially in those countries where religious wars had led to violent antagonism between conscience and obedience, religious and secular obligations. Works such as the famous *Vindiciae Contra Tyrannos*, Buchanan's *De Iure Regni Apud Scotos* and several Dutch justifications of their revolt, were disseminated and well known in England.[107] Sympathy for the Dutch cause among the Sidney circle meant that even apologia for resistance could be received favourably, for all the queen's disapproval. The Sidney circle also had connections with French polemicists and with Buchanan, and questions concerning resistance and tyranny permeate Sidney's *Arcadia*.[108] After the 1550s, however, English Calvinists were not faced with the threat of suppression. Even in the ideological decades of the 1560s to 1580s, when the cause of international Protestantism perforce involved England in the European debates about the limitations to authority and obedience, there was in England no reinvestigation of the foundations of political theory.[109] Sir Thomas Smith's *De Republica Anglorum* was premised on the symbiosis, not conflict, of

---

[105] Santa Maria, *Christian Policie*, 7; cf. 60–1, 76, 164, 273.

[106] Ibid., 7; G. More, *Principles for Young Princes* (1611), e.g. 7, 29–30, 55–7, 59–61.

[107] The *Vindiciae* and the *De Iure* were available in Latin from 1579. The *De Iure* went to three editions by 1580. Thomas Wentworth collected in his youth aphorisms from works which included Duplessis-Mornay; J. W. Stoye, *English Travellers Abroad 1604–1667* (1952), 64. See also Salmon, *French Religious Wars*, and E. H. Kossman and A. F. Mellink eds., *Texts Concerning the Revolt of the Netherlands* (Cambridge, 1974).

[108] See J. E. Phillips, 'George Buchanan and the Sidney Circle', *Hunt. Lib. Quart.*, 12 (1948), 23–56; W. D. Briggs, 'Political Ideas in Sidney's Arcadia', *Studies in Philology*, 28 (1931), 137–61; D. Norbrook, *Poetry and Politics in the English Renaissance* (1984), 15, 96ff.

[109] Salmon, *French Religious Wars*, 12; Hale, *Body Politic*, 80.

authority and law.[110] After the threat to England receded in the 1590s, and after the peace with Spain of 1604, though travel to the continent was opened, England may have been in some respects more insulated from radical Protestant thought than before.[111] The Gunpowder Plot reinforced James I's desire for a polemical retort to the Jesuits and ultramontanes, but his reply was an ideological reinforcement of the commonweal (and Church of England).[112] James's Calvinism seemed to ease remaining tensions in radical Protestant political thought as in theology, and the king himself ruled Buchanan out of season.[113] As for the Catholics, despite their political proscription and marginalization, they proved, by the end of Elizabeth's reign, more anxious to demonstrate their loyalty than to flirt with resistance theories.[114]

The continental treatises of political thought that were translated into English in the early seventeenth century either emphasized the unitary nature of the commonweal and the need for monarchical authority, as did Bodin's *Six Books of a Commonweal*, or reiterated existing English conventions about monarchy and the state. Philip Bethune's *The Counsellor of Estate*, translated from the French in 1634, though it resonates with echoes of Commines, Machiavelli and Botero, defined the state as 'no other thing but an order' and stressed the necessity for religious unity, for good laws, mild government, counsel and sovereign monarchy.[115] Juan de Santa Maria's *Christian Policie*, published two years earlier, discussed the king analogically and conventionally as the reason, the father, the shepherd and the physician of the state, along with the traditional injunctions that the ruler must be just and virtuous. In places the language of such translations makes it clear that continental texts were being anglicized – not to censor their content but to make it comprehensible to English experience and convention.[116]

On occasions, however, even in the early seventeenth century, the very different nature of continental experience and ideas was made manifest.

---

[110] See Judson, *Crisis of the Constitution* (1971 edn), 83–4; E. O. Smith, 'Crown and Commonwealth: a Study in the Official Elizabethan Doctrine of the Prince', *Proc. Am. Philos. Soc.*, 66 (1976), 30–3.

[111] Stoye, *English Travellers Abroad* rightly illustrates the easier contacts between England and the Huguenots in the reign of James I, but the point here is that political circumstances in England, as in France itself, were less conducive to *radical* political thought.

[112] See McIlwain, *Political Works of James I*, introduction.

[113] Norbrook, '*Macbeth* and the Politics of Historiography', 82; Sharpe, *Sir Robert Cotton*, 89–90.

[114] P. Holmes, *Resistance and Compromise: the Political Thought of the Elizabethan Catholics* (Cambridge, 1982); I owe this reference to Keith Thomas.

[115] Bethune, *The Counsellor of Estate*, quotation, 2.

[116] There was, for example, little discussion of sovereignty in early Stuart England; and see Knolles, *Six Bookes* and Mosse 'Influence of Bodin'.

J. F. Le Petit's treatise *The Low Country Commonwealth* (translated in 1609) boldly concluded that the King of Spain had acted wrongly and the Dutch had 'been forced to oppose themselves and shake off his yoke'.[117] But there is almost no evidence that such knowledge or claims posed new questions about the commonweal in England. As Professor Salmon concluded: 'It was difficult for Englishmen to appreciate the relevance of ... ideas remote from their own legal traditions until an open breach between King and Parliament, an overt contest for the sovereign law-making power forced them to do so.'[118] In the 1630s and 1640s, circumstances led the Scots to draw anew on Buchanan;[119] in 1647 the declaration of the army referred to the rebellious Netherlanders and Portuguese 'proceeding from the same principles of right and freedom' as the soldiers claimed.[120] But before the divide, the fact and literature of resistance – on the continent or in the past – seem to have been of little relevance to early Stuart Englishmen. The exception to that generalization is the Cambridge lectures on Tacitus by Isaac Dorislaus in which, as well as defending the Dutch, the lecturer was believed to have hinted too at the application of his text to England. The episode caused a furore and the lecturer was silenced.[121] It is an episode that may demonstrate as much the paranoia of the king and government as any radical intents of the lecturer or his patron. In either case it suggests that the applicability of continental to English experience never required a long leap. Yet the fact remains that for most of the years before the civil war it was a step which was not taken.

    To apply the experiences and values of another country or culture to one's own world, to re-examine one's own organization and premises in the light of them, seems to us an obvious, indeed unavoidable gesture. It is, however, a gesture that depends upon a relativism largely absent from the world-view of early modern England.[122] Just as there could be no toleration of other faiths because God's truth was one, so other societies, or modes of government, were seen as imperfect or diseased organisms. French foppishness and tyranny, Dutch avarice and selfishness, Spanish unreliability and pride, Italian chicanery and amorality, were stereotypes not eroded by travel. It has been persuasively argued

---

[117] J. F. Le Petit, *The Low Country Commonwealth*, translated by E. Grimestone (1609), 303.
[118] Salmon, *French Religious Wars*, 12.
[119] See P. Donald, 'The King and the Scottish Troubles, 1637–1641' (Ph.D. thesis, Cambridge University, 1988).   [120] Kenyon, *Stuart Constitution*, 264.
[121] See Sharpe, *Politics and Ideas*, ch. 8.
[122] For an interesting discussion of the emergence of this relativism see B. Shapiro, *Probability and Certainty in Seventeenth Century England* (Princeton, 1983).

that in sixteenth-century Spain, the impact of the discovery of the Amerindian prompted a fundamental reappraisal of ideas about society, man and the state of nature.[123] There is little evidence that such rethinking percolated to England. Rather the travel literature of the early Stuart years displays either a curiosity with the bizarre (like that which led to the building of cabinets of curios) or a cultural imperialism discomforting to some modern readers. Sir Thomas Herbert's *A Relation of Some Yeares Travaile . . . into Afrique and the Greater Asia* offers some fascinating insights into the ceremonies and habits of the peoples but displays prurience and superiority more than a real desire to understand without judging.[124] Henry Lord's *Display of Two Foreign Sects in the East Indies* showed him only 'how Satan leadeth those that are out of the pale of the church around in the maze of error and gentilism'.[125] Travel in fact appears to have taught him, as it has so many Englishmen through the ages, the wisdom of staying at home. With regard to the experience of the other, 'I know not wherein it may be more profitable than to settle us in the solidness of our own faith.'[126] Heylyn's aptly titled *Microcosmus* did just what many English scholars since have: surveyed the globe from his study at Oxford and found it by English standards wanting.[127] Even those whose temperaments or circumstances made them sympathetic to other cultures appear incapable of evaluating them for themselves – as other, different. *A Relation of the Successfull Beginnings of the Lord Baltemore's Plantation in Maryland* went to great lengths to paint the Indians in good colours, as chaste, grave and friendly; but their greatest quality was their proximity to Christianity (only language hindered a complete conversion) and English civilization, their residence with a central fire being compared to the old baronial halls of England![128] The understanding of Indian culture was not likely to develop from comparisons of their idols with children's dolls in England, but the comparison does typify how other cultures, when experienced, were seen.[129] Societies were judged by one set of standards as churches by (theoretically) one gospel.

The greatest challenge to such a world-view was presented by the

[123] A. Pagden, *The Fall of Natural Man: the American Indian and the Origins of Comparative Ethnology* (Cambridge, 1982).
[124] Sir Thomas Herbert, *A Relation of Some Yeares Travaile Begun Anno 1626 into Afrique and the Greater Asia* (1634). Herbert unfavourably contrasted the behaviour of Madagascan women who revealed their pudenda for food with the modesty of the English (p. 15)!
[125] H. Lord, *A Display of Two Foreign Sects in the East Indies* (1630), 93.   [126] Ibid., 95.
[127] P. Heylyn, *Microcosmus: a Little Description of the Great World* (Oxford, 1629). See, for example, the nationalism on pp. 460–90.
[128] *A Relation of the Successfull Beginnings of the Lord Baltemore's Plantation in Maryland* (1634), 7, 8.
[129] Heylyn, *Microcosmus*, 771.

essays of Michel de Montaigne, translated into English by John Florio in 1603.[130] Montaigne found in nature no common uniform law discernible by man's reason: 'we see an infinite difference and variety in this world'.[131] As a consequence, systems of morality, law, order were also relative. The radical implications of Montaigne's assault on the metaphysical universe of the Renaissance did not pass unnoticed in England. Samuel Daniel, in a preface to the English translation, acknowledged the alternatives posed if Montaigne were right. Either men were unlearned, 'or els that truth hath other shapes then one'.[132] Lord Herbert of Cherbury engaged with Montaigne and reasserted man's capacity to discern the 'common notions' of one natural order.[133] Montaigne's relativism won no converts in England. Though he deserves, perhaps, an important place in Professor Shapiro's story of 'the gradual erosion of the distinction between knowledge and probability', it is a story with no really important chapters before the middle of the century.[134]

TENSIONS

A commonweal united as one, all its parts in harmony, all its citizens combined in the common interest, its ruler restraining his own will and governing for the public good, a realm untouched by the conflicts on the continent and the fundamental reappraisals of government which they had forced: it will already have been more than apparent that what I have sketched is an idealized picture, not an accurate representation of Tudor and Stuart society.[135] This idealization, however, is not that of the historian; it is a contemporary idealization, a representation that encodes the meaning that early modern Englishmen (especially those in authority) discerned in their universe and which they in turn represented to themselves and to each other. They were not of course ignorant that there were threats to their world, contradictions within it, indeed tensions which could become conflicts. Separatists challenged the very foundations of society, state and church, and, most seriously, rejected their integration. Theorists and pamphleteers wrote of economic self-

---

[130] M. de Montaigne, *The Essayes or Morall, Politike and Millitarie Discourses* (1603).
[131] Bedford, *Defence of Truth*, 43.
[132] J. Florio, *Essayes written in French by Michael Lord of Montaigne* (1613 edn), prefatory poem by Daniel, sig. A3.   [133] Bedford, *Defence of Truth*, 50.
[134] Shapiro *Probability and Certainty*, 17.
[135] Like other 'revisionists', I have been charged with idealizing the early Stuart age. From the Whig perspective of inevitable conflict, however, any depiction of the seventeenth century in its own terms is open to the charge of idealizing.

interest and the quest for power; dramatists staged naked ambition; magistrates and MPs daily encountered political differences; the populace at times rose in revolt. If then we are to maintain that before the civil war such realizations and experiences did not shatter their world-view, did not rewrite the vocabulary of political thought, we must examine these tensions, and how they were perceived and accommodated.

In the early seventeenth century, the tensions pervade the entire chain of being from the celestial plane to the little kingdom of man. The great speech on order from *Troilus*, cited by Tillyard as the summation of a world-view, is itself undermined by the character's position in the play. We have become all too familiar with Donne's lines from the *First Anniversary* about the impact of the new cosmology.[136] But it is worth quoting from the less-well-known Thomas Scot's *Philomythie* (1616) to see how closely the disharmony of the planets is associated with the subversion of all moral order:

> This earth we live on and do steadfast call
> Copernicus proves giddy brainde and all
> Those other bodies whose swift motions we
> So wonder at, he settled finds to be
> Till sanctified Ignatius and his brood
> Found out the lawfull way of shedding blood,
> And proved it plainly that a subject might
> Murther his Prince, we fondly usde t'indite
> Such persons of high treason: Now before them
> We kneele, we pray, we worship and adore them.[137]

At the other end of the chain, Thomas Browne was no less convinced of the macrocosmic significance of his own personal turmoil. In himself, rather than all being order, a mass of contrarieties contended for the mastery: 'the battle of Lepanto, passion against reason, reason against faith, faith against the Devil, and my conscience against all'.[138] In general the ordering of human sexual appetites was (and is) regarded as an important social problem: understandably so if the author of *The*

---

[136] J. Donne, 'An Anatomy of the World. The First Anniversary', in A. J. Smith ed., *John Donne, the Complete English Poems* (Harmondsworth, 1973), 270–83.

[137] T. Scot, *Philomythie or Philomythologie wherein Outlandish Birds, Beasts and Fishes are taught to speake true English* . . . (1616), sig. A2. The reference to Ignatius's brood is to the Jesuits who justified resistance to heretics and excommunicated monarchs. Cf. *Ignatius His Conclave, or his inthronizacon in a late eleccon in Hell*, entered in the Stationers company register in 1611 (III, 208).

[138] Cited in D. P. Norford, 'Microcosm and Macrocosm in Seventeenth Century Literature', *Journ. Hist. Ideas* 38 (1977), 409–28, 416. Cf. the battle of Romans and Carthaginians that raged at night around Ben Jonson's great toe, Barton, *Ben Jonson*, x.

Lawes Resolutions of Women's Rights was correct in arguing that without the protection of law no woman 'being above twelve years of age and under an hundred . . . should be able to escape ravishing'.[139] That sexual passion was often an analogue for man in the state of nature made this a problem of universal import. Social and political tensions were not comprehended only analogically (important though this is) from corresponding disorder in the macrocosm or microcosm; they were explicitly acknowledged in the commonweal. Jacobean city comedies and rogue literature speak to an obvious recognition of disharmony;[140] sermons and injunctions to hospitality, Herrick's poetry and Jonson's later drama address 'the breakdown of a system of communal obligations'.[141] James I acknowledged that though 'we are of all nations the people most loving and most reverently obedient to our Prince, yet we are . . . too easy to be seduced to make rebellion'.[142] George Wither's *Britain's Remembrancer* is permeated with a fear of imminent 'distraction', 'desperation' and specifically deplores those who have put their persons before the public weal.[143] The popularity of satire and criticism of the prince was freely recognized,[144] even though it sat uneasily with assertions concerning the love that existed between the king and his people.[145] Sir Thomas Wentworth even acknowledged that there were some who sought to divide the ruler from his people and sovereignty from subjection 'as if their ends were distinct, not the same, nay in opposition'.[146] A recurrent theme of tragedy was the tension between ideal and natural rulers. Juan de Santa Maria, for all his conservatism, almost took it for granted that no kings could be found without faults.[147] And so the catalogue could go on. But it is more important to ponder these acknowledgements of

---

[139] E. T., *The Lawes Resolutions of Women's Rights* (1632), 377.

[140] See M. Walzer, 'On the Role of Symbolism in Political Thought', *Polit. Science Quart.*, 82 (1967), 191–204, esp. 202; S. Greenblatt, 'Invisible Bullets: Renaissance Authority and its Subversion', *Glyph*, 8 (1981), 20–61.

[141] F. Heal, 'The Idea of Hospitality in Early Modern England', *Past and Present*, 102 (1984), 86–93; Marcus, *Politics of Mirth*, 143 and passim.   [142] *Workes of James I*, 211.

[143] Wither, *Britain's Remembrancer*, 221–4, 229. Though he recognizes these problems, Wither throughout sees their solution in the reassertion of traditional ideals. This is an important work which deserves a full discussion.

[144] See, for example, N. Carpenter, *Achitophel, or the Picture of a Wicked Politician* (1629), 10: 'He that goes about to persuade a multitude they are not so well governed as they ought to be shall sooner want argument than attention'; M. R., *Micrologia, Characters or Essays* (1629), 11: on the popularity of songs 'interlarded with anything against the state'.

[145] See below, pp. 109–11.

[146] Wentworth's speech as Lord President of the North, December 1628, Kenyon, *Stuart Constitution*, 16. Ironically this was one of the principal charges against Wentworth at his own trial for treason, article VII, F. Hargrave, *A Complete Collection of State Trials* (11 vols., 1776–81), I, 723.

[147] Santa Maria, *Christian Policie*, 21.

tension than it is to list more of them. What is immediately striking is how often they surface in works which may also be read as conventional treatises of cosmic harmony: Shakespeare's plays offer a vivid example, but Scot's treatise and Wentworth's speech of 1628 offer more prosaic instances.

In fact in most of the texts we examine, some recognition of division and dislocation is juxtaposed with the theory of unity and order.[148] There may be general reasons for that as well as particular ones: Clifford Geertz once observed (significantly while discussing Elizabethan England) that 'heresy is as much of a child of orthodoxy in politics as it is in religion'.[149] But their acknowledgement of disorder does not make our texts self-consuming artefacts. Rather in themselves subsuming those tensions within a theory of order, our writers may have textualized that exquisite poise that was normative for (though never simply descriptive of) social behaviour. Richard Hooker's *Laws of Ecclesiastical Polity*, often and rightly cited as a classic statement of harmony, is itself a document of tensions *and* of an attempted resolution of them – the reconciliation for example of consent and order.[150] In this context it is noteworthy that some of our best evidence of contemporary debate comes from early Stuart drama. Not only, one suspects, because the dramatic medium is one of debate, but because the stage offers a laboratory for the examination of a difficulty, displaced – but not too far – from reality. On the stage in Jacobean England therefore we find plays that lack closure, as dramatists dared to imagine their world without meaning. Ben Jonson, the author of one of the best of them, *Bartholomew Fair*, took the broken compass as his own mark.[151] The imaginary permits this licence because it enables reflection without practical consequences.[152] On the political stage such experiment was not possible: the tensions, though acknowledged, had to be resolved; the circle had to be complete; there had to be closure. The royal texts therefore, the

---

[148] Walzer, 'Symbolism', 202; Greenblatt, 'Invisible Bullets', passim.

[149] C. Geertz, 'Centers, Kings and Charisma: Reflections on the Symbolics of Power', in J. Ben-David and T. N. Clark eds., *Culture and its Creators* (1977), 168.

[150] Hale, *Body Politic*, 83; John Carey has related these tensions to Hooker's style, 'Sixteenth and Seventeenth Century Prose', in C. Ricks ed., *English Poetry and Prose 1540–1674* (1970), 379–90, esp. 384–7.

[151] See Barton, *Ben Jonson*, ch. 9; on the significance of the broken circle see the biography of Jonson by David Riggs: *Ben Jonson: a Life* (Cambridge, Mass., and London, 1989). I am grateful to Professor Riggs for showing me this important study in advance of publication and for stimulating discussions of Jonson at Stanford University. See also L. A. Beaurline, *Jonson and Elizabethan Comedy* (San Marino, 1978).

[152] I do not wish here to separate representation from reality, but rather to stress their interaction.

Basilikon Doron of James I and the *Eikon Basilike* of his son, had to find that balance which secured the harmony of the commonweal. Interestingly, a concern with exquisite poise, the resolution of tension, has recently been discerned in the paintings and architecture, as well as the literature, of Caroline England.[153] In each case the documents of kingship replicated and reinforced the picture of order not by ignoring its opposites but by controlling them. And this was the function of the king in practice: the act of recognizing threats, neutralizing them, reconciling contradictions – his own and others – and preserving balance through the destabilizing passage of time. Governing, Juan de Santa Maria acknowledged, was difficult;[154] had all been naturally harmonious, of course, it should not have been. The king's very position was ambivalent: he drew his authority from a world-view which at times only the due exercise of his authority could sustain.

Far then from a simple idealization removed from reality, the idea of correspondences, the metaphysical idea, was itself a way of resolving tensions, a way of holding the world together through coincidentia oppositorum.[155] The world was held together by an act of consciousness – though we would add a consciousness that was also translated into action. It is no accident that it was Francis Bacon who could clearly articulate what others only dimly suspected and even feared: human understanding, he wrote, 'easily supposes a greater degree of order and equality in things than it really finds; and although many things in nature be sui generis and most irregular, will yet invent parallels, conjugates and relatives where no such thing is'.[156] Along with the certainties and truths of the Elizabethan world-picture went the realization that all was not as it was represented, that authority could easily become over-rigorous, that kings could fail to take counsel, that the balance of humours was precarious, that order was on the edge of confusion. When these tensions were themselves systematized, encoded into a different representation of meaning or order, they posed the profoundest challenges to the prevailing ideology, perhaps challenges from which it never completely recovered. We must turn to examine three of these: the challenges of scepticism, Machiavellianism and Calvinism.

Scepticism and rationalism, we might think, posed the greatest threat to the Elizabethan world-picture and commonweal. To question the power or nature of God might analogically be thought to challenge his magistrate on earth. Certainly some of the activities of the sceptics

---

[153] Smuts, *Court Culture*, 193.   [154] Santa Maria, *Christian Policie*, 21.
[155] Norford, 'Microcosm and Macrocosm', 427.   [156] Hale, *Body Politic*, 110.

caused scandal. In tearing leaves out of a Bible in order to dry his tobacco the philosopher Thomas Allen quite literally deconstructed one of the prime texts of authority.[157] The sordid death of Christopher Marlowe pleasantly confirmed to many the swift arm of divine retribution against one who had danced with the devil. Yet the sceptics of the early Stuart age, I would suggest, were men of different, less radical stripes than their Elizabethan predecessors. It was not, perhaps, a small or insignificant group that took in Raleigh, Lord Herbert, Inigo Jones, the Earl of Arundel, the poet Sir John Suckling, the playwright Sir William Davenant, as well as the distinguished circle at Great Tew – especially Lord Falkland.[158] But listing them we see that these were very much men of the court and establishment. Their scepticism consisted in a rationalist, undogmatic approach to religion, in an emphasis on man's reason and capacity to discern the good, in a concern with ethical rather than narrowly doctrinal priorities. Accordingly in *Philomythie*, Thomas Scot allegorizes the sceptic as a chameleon; 'His Reason is his God.'[159] 'They make', William Pemble observed, 'the understanding the seat of all speculative habits.'[160] The ethics of the sceptics were derived as often from classical as Christian sources: they knew 'some Philosophy no Divinity', Scot charged.[161] In his popular treatise on *The English Gentleman* (1630) Richard Brathwaite asked: 'have we not read how divers naturally addicted to all licentious motions by reading moral precepts and conversing with Philosophers became absolute commanders of their own affections?'[162] In another widely disseminated *Guide of Honour* (1634), Anthony Stafford counselled his noble readers to love goodness in whatsoever religion they found it.[163] Both tenets confirm a sense that a more secular approach to ethics was a fashion among the upper classes and perhaps most of all the court milieu in the late 1620s and 1630s:[164] Sir Thomas Wentworth (to whom *The English Gentleman* was dedicated) and the Earl of Arundel were both Stoics;[165] Inigo Jones, like his patron

[157] M. C. Bradbrook, *The School of Night: a Study in the Literary Relationships of Sir Walter Raleigh* (Cambridge, 1936), 19.

[158] On Herbert, see Bedford, *Defence of Truth*; on Jones, J. Lees-Milne, *The Age of Inigo Jones* (1953), 52; on Arundel, K. Sharpe, 'The Earl of Arundel, His Circle and the Opposition to the Duke of Buckingham, 1618–1628', in *Politics and Ideas*, 201–6; on Suckling and Davenant, Sharpe, *Criticism and Compliment*, 71–2 and J. Suckling, *An Account of Religion by Reason* (1646); on Falkland, H. R. Trevor-Roper, 'The Great Tew Circle', in *Catholics, Anglicans and Puritans* (1987), 166–230.

[159] Scot, *Philomythie*, sig. E3; cf. J. Earle, *Microcosmographie* (1630), 53.

[160] W. Pemble, *A Plea for Grace* (1629), 133.   [161] *Philomythie*, sig. E3.

[162] Brathwaite, *The English Gentleman*, 97.   [163] A. Stafford, *The Guide of Honour* (1634), 16.

[164] See Smuts, *Court Culture*, 222–34.

[165] Thomas Wentworth to George Butler, November 1636, in W. Knowler ed., *The Earl of Strafford's Letters and Despatches* (2 vols., 1739), II, 39; D. Howarth, *Lord Arundel and His Circle* (1985), 85–6.

Arundel, paid more attention to the didactic qualities of classical art and architecture than to devout piety.

Some historians have gone further and posited a close connection between the sceptics and rationalists and the dominance of the Arminians at the court of Charles I.[166] There are some general reasons and particular passages to support this view.[167] Lord Herbert, for one, concluded that 'this principle of Evil cannot be derived from Adam, for all our sins and transgressions are our own meer voluntary acts'.[168] Meric Casaubon, dedicating to Laud the meditations of Marcus Aurelius Antoninus, announced it as, though the work of a heathen, one of the best guides to living virtuously.[169] Robert Harris, pastor of Hanwell, in 'A treatise of the New Covenant' seems to suggest theological connection: 'for whosoever is capable of Reason, the same is also capable of Grace (for what is Grace but reason perfected and elevated . . .)'.[170] Laud himself, however, would have none of it: he showed little sympathy for other courtiers' ease with the integration of the sacred and the profane. When his friend Wentworth sent him a treatise on the vanity of the world replete with references to poetry, art and the classics, Laud replied with unusual frostiness: 'If you will read the short book of Ecclesiastes you will see a better disposition of those things than in any anagrams of Dr Donnes or any designs of Van Dyck.'[171] The Laudian God, as Malcolm Smuts has put it, was a more 'tranquil deity'[172] than the interventionist God of the puritans; the Laudian Christopher Dow described as accidents events that Burton had catalogued as God's punishments of sabbath-breakers.[173] But neither Laud nor the Arminians walked with the rationalists and sceptics and significantly none of their enemies (who hurled every other accusation) charged them with doing so.

Yet though there was no obvious connection between Laudianism and the rationalists, the court of Charles I was especially conducive to a

---

[166] Smuts, *Court Culture*, 233.

[167] It is worthy of note that in N. O., *An Apology of English Arminianisme* (1634), Arminius speaks with more control and reason than 'Enthusiastus'.

[168] Cited by Bedford, *Defence of Truth*, 199.

[169] M. Casaubon, *Marcus Aurelius Antoninus His Meditations* (1634); the epistle dedicatory told Laud that in reading them he would read himself.

[170] R. Harris, *The Way to True Happinesse* (1632), 4–5.

[171] Knowler, *Strafford Letters*, II, 170; Bishop Hall wrote against the tendency to stoicism: 'Not Athens must teach . . . but Jerusalem', *The Works of Joseph Hall*, 73.

[172] Smuts, *Court Culture*, 233.

[173] C. Dow, *Innovations Unjustly Charged upon the Present Church and State* (1637), 10. Cf. Wither's concern in *Britain's Remembrancer* to prove that the plague did not, as others were claiming, arise from natural causes.

classical, pagan, as well as Christian world-view. Those like Alexander Grosse who counselled preachers to cite the Scriptures rather than secular authorities, or Richard James who urged that 'from Christ better than from the Stoic porch' morality may be learned, express the fear that a clear line between pagan and Christian culture was being eroded.[174] This may well have upset many – and not only the puritans. But it demonstrates that the rationalists and sceptics did not present a threat to the ideological foundations of the commonweal as perceived by the king and court. Rather, for all his piety, Charles I's own political values appear to synthesize classical and Christian influences.[175] The radical scepticism of Montaigne, we have seen, enjoyed little influence in England, and even the potential radicalism of the Elizabethan 'School of Night' faded into naught with the death of a generation. In the scepticism of Caroline figures such as Lord Herbert there was an intrinsic conservatism: the principle that since certainty was elusive, one should place one's trust in the laws and conventions of the realm.[176]

If Montaigne cast only a shadow across the moral horizon of the Elizabethan world, Machiavelli darkened its skies to near blackness. The impact of Machiavelli is all the more powerful when we recall that no English edition of *The Prince* was published until 1640, and no edition of the *Discourses* before 1636.[177] And yet Machiavelli was sufficiently popularly known to be represented on the stage as the devil himself,[178] the phrase 'old Nick' being his legacy to folklore. The man himself, or his reputation, became a text – debated, refuted, yet possessing power. Given that he was not widely read, except by the learned who could read him in Latin or Italian,[179] the fear that he aroused, the vehemence with which he was denounced, require explanation. At the simplest level, an explanation must be that Machiavelli not only challenged but subverted all the premises of the early modern English commonweal. He disrupted the notions of unity and wholeness by acknowledging and advocating the pursuit of interests; he substituted for ideas of divine harmony the capricious goddess Fortuna; he separated the exercise of power from virtuous action and detached authority from obligation; he broke the

---

[174] A. Grosse, *Two Sermons* (1632); R. James, *A Sermon Delivered in Oxford* (1630), sig. F2.

[175] Sharpe, *Criticism and Compliment*, 262, 300; Smuts, *Court Culture*, passim.

[176] Bedford, *Defence of Truth*, 40.

[177] E. D[acres], *Nicholas Machiavel's Prince* (1640), but even then 'with some animadversions noting and taxing his errors'; *Machiavels Discourses upon the First Decade of T. Livius* (1636).

[178] See F. Raab, *The English Face of Machiavelli* (1964).

[179] Machiavelli was widely read at Oxford; see M. Curtis, *Oxford and Cambridge in Transition 1558–1642* (Oxford, 1959), 119, 137.

correspondence between divine and regal behaviour by a defence of dissimulation. He opted for fear over love as the basis of government.[180]
More traumatically, he effected this bouleversement of conventions
through a discourse that employed the very vocabulary that had sustained them and so drew attention to the tensions which that language
had concealed.[181] He divested *reason* and *nature* of their divine, metaphysical, ethical, their normative value.[182] A more sophisticated explanation
for the fear that Machiavelli excited must be related to the ambivalence
of this conservative vocabulary and radicalism of meaning. Machiavelli,
to put it another way, was feared because he powerfully articulated existing tensions that the normative conventions and discourse had kept in
delicate control. And this ambivalence, I would suggest, revealingly sur-
faces in the treatises that denounce him as well as those that adapt, adopt
and attempt to neuter him. We need say little about the latter: the
'Machiavellianism' of men like Raleigh and Bacon has been extensively
argued;[183] politic historians such as John Speed anglicized and moral-
ized but nevertheless appropriated his goddess Fortuna (in English garb
she was reconciled, if not always synonymous, with Providence) as a
driving force of history.[184]

The denunciations are more interesting. Even diatribes such as
Machiavells Dogge (1617) take their agenda from him, setting back upright
each of the premises he was believed to have overturned.[185] One
wonders too whether in his conventional counsel to princes, George
More did not, in spite of scorning him, also see Machiavelli's relevance
to recent English experience: 'where Matchevils [*sic*] principle taketh
effect, there the subjects must be made poor by continual subsidies, exactions and impositions that the people may be always kept under as
slaves'.[186] In other works, the connection between Machiavelli and the
tensions within and the fragility of the conventions seems consciously to
be explored. In Scot's *Philomythie*, in which animals in turn deliver moral

[180] See for this last point, Q. Skinner, *Machiavelli* (Oxford, 1981), 46.
[181] Cf. Sharpe and Zwicker, *Politics of Discourse*, 19–20.
[182] J. H. Hexter, *The Vision of Politics on the Eve of the Reformation* (New York, 1973), 210–11 and chs. 3 and 4, passim.
[183] Raab, *English Face of Machiavelli*, 70–6; N. Orsini, *Bacono e Machiavelli* (Genoa, 1936); Pocock, *The Machiavellian Moment*, 355–7, 386, 388.
[184] Sharpe, *Sir Robert Cotton*, 233–4; Levy, *Tudor Historical Thought*, 196–9.
[185] *Machiavells Dogge* (1617). The classic denunciation of Machiavelli was Innocent Gentillet, *A Discourse Upon the Meanes of Wel Governing Against N. Machiavell* (1602). These extracted maxims, with Gentillet's rebuttals, were the only form in which Machiavelli was translated into English prior to 1640. I owe this point to David Riggs.
[186] More, *Principles for Young Princes*, 69.

tales, Aesop has to face the argument of Tortus (Cardinal Bellarmine's chaplain, who may stand for Machiavelli) that his morality may easily be inverted. Tortus charges that:

> In Kings he would no other vertue see
> Then what in lyons and in Eagles bee
> To prey on all, to make their will a law,
> To tyrannize, to rule by force and awe.[187]

Aesop's moral fables are subverted by Tortus just as Machiavelli overturns the normative paradigms of the age. The frontispiece depicts Aesop and Tortus, representing virtue and vice, contesting for the globe – we might say for the interpretative authority to determine values.[188] In *The Uncasing of Machivils Instructions to His Son* the very structure of the treatise addresses ambivalence. The first half *is* a Machiavellian treatise in which (ironically?) all are counselled to follow their own interest, wealth and power, to flatter and deceive, to use, not love their fellow men, to think of the present not the afterlife:

> Get all contentment that the world can give
> For after death, who knoweth how we live.[189]

The second half of the tract, however, offers 'The Answer to Machiavelli's Uncasing'. Here the coin is flipped and the reader is urged to ignore all that has preceded except 'by ill to know the good';[190] the anonymous author proceeds to conventional invocation to honesty, charity, honour, virtue, piety. Not only does this work acknowledge the force of Machiavelli's impact, it acknowledges too that the relationship of the ill and the good is as close (as well as opposite) as the two faces of a coin. The author shows Machiavelli's vain courses *and* how to avoid them. He counsels virtue but (unwittingly?) concedes that the interpretation of his janus text (the moral decision) rests with the reader: 'Machiavel's rules deny, yet use them as thy pleasure.'[191] Is the ambivalence of the last line unconscious? For we may deny Machiavelli's rules and yet live by them and thereby (rather than rejecting them) pursue *pleasure* (rather than virtue). The coin may be turned over again and again. It may be such a recognition that prompted the remarks of

---

[187] Scot, *Philomythie*, sig. A4. Mattaeus Tortus was Cardinal Bellarmine's almoner, under whose name Bellarmine had published his Response to James I's *Apology for the Oath of Allegiance*. At James's command, Bishop Andrewes replied to this work in his *Tortura Torti sive ad Matthei Torti Librum Responsio* (1609). Scot casts him as a Machiavellian figure, as Jesuits were often so branded by Protestant polemicists. [188] See jacket of Sharpe, *Politics and Ideas*.
[189] *The Uncasing of Machivils Instructions to His Son* (1613), 16. [190] Ibid., 29ff.
[191] Ibid., sig. G4 (the work is curiously paginated).

Edward Dacres in his preface to the translation of *The Prince*.
Machiavelli's maxims were condemned as pernicious by all, he confessed, but 'if thou consider well the actions of the world, thou shall find
him much practised by those that condemn him'.[192] Dacres could not
himself mask his grudging respect for the Italian even whilst penning a
critical commentary on his amoral tenets. Once again too he sees that
Machiavelli had demonstrated how this was the coin-edge that divided
the two heads. The ethical politics which Dacres's own day 'presup-
pose[d]', 'will never allow this rule, as that a man may make *this small
difference* between virtue and vice'.[193] But Machiavelli had made only a
small difference between them and it was only a *presupposition* (not quite
the same as a truth) that stood in his way. Old Nick raised demons that
could never be completely exorcized.

Machiavellianism and scepticism are ideologies which it is hard to
define rigidly. Puritanism, the last of our cases, appears from recent
historiography to be in danger of losing all meaning,[194] and the question
of its importance in relation to politics and the crisis of 1642 has dissolved into disagreement and confusion. Gardiner had no doubt that in
an important sense the English civil war was a puritan revolution; from
a different perspective, Christopher Hill concurred and Michael Walzer
in a stimulating study probed the revolutionary ideology and language
of the saints.[195] More recent historiography has questioned the radicalism of the puritans, has claimed that few theological differences distanced them from the established church, and even depicted them as the
vanguard defence of the status quo against the innovating Arminians,
on whose shoulders the blame for the crisis now rests.[196] Such revisions
have not (at least to this reader) proved convincing. For the moment let
us leave that controversy to make a different observation.

---

[192] *Nicholas Machiavel's Prince*, epistle to the reader.   [193] Ibid., 121, my italics.

[194] NB O. Feltham, *Resolves, Divine, Morall, Politicall* (1628 edn), 9–10: 'I find many that are called
Puritans; yet few or none that will own the name. Whereof the reason sure is this; that 'tis for
the most part held a name of infamy, and is so new that it hath scarcely yet obtained a definition; nor is it an appellation derived from one man's name, whose tenets we may find digested
into a volume: whereby we do much err in the application. It imports a kind of excellency above
another . . . As he is more generally in these times taken, I suppose we may call him a church
rebel, or one that would exclude order that his brain might rule.'

[195] M. Walzer, *The Revolution of the Saints* (1966).

[196] Notably N. R. N. Tyacke, 'Puritanism, Arminianism and Counter-Revolution', in C. R. S.
Russell ed., *The Origins of the English Civil War* (1973), 199–234; Tyacke, *Anti-Calvinists: the Rise of
English Arminianism c. 1590–1640* (Oxford, 1987). For an effective challenge see P. White, 'The Rise
of Arminianism Reconsidered', *Past and Present*, 101 (1983), 34–54; S. Lambert, 'Richard
Montagu, Arminianism and Censorship', *Past and Present*, 124 (1989), 36–68. I am grateful to
Sheila Lambert for an early view of this paper.

For that two quite contrary interpretations can be powerfully argued might lead us to suspect that both within puritanism and the Church of England there were ideological tensions to which circumstances could give a conservative or revolutionary face. Since much has been written of late about the former, it is probably appropriate here to re-emphasize the second, for strict Calvinist theology on several points squared uneasily with the theological and philosophical bases of the Elizabethan world-picture. First the logic of double predestination threatened the separation of grace (the gift only of God) from nature seen as irredeemably corrupt and fallen. This was potentially to question the divine, natural and normative condition of society which could now only be itself a product of the Fall. Richard Hooker, seeing the danger of their challenge, forcefully argued for God as the author of nature and man's reason as capable of acting according to the good.[197] The controversy about nature and grace was not resolved: Sidney's *Apology for Poetry* is a splendid document of the ambivalent perceptions of nature;[198] and the word continued throughout our period to be used in not only different but quite contrary senses – as the fallen and as the perfect state of man. It may be the rationalist classicism of the 1620s and 1630s, as well as the Arminians, that rearticulated and reintensified the differences. Both Burton and Prynne, of course, blamed the Arminians and went to great lengths to deny the ascription of grace to nature.[199] Classical humanism, however, was as difficult to reconcile with strict predestination as was Arminianism and the resulting tension, as Milton and the radical sects of the 1650s testify, was not just between theological enemies.[200]

With predestination came another emphasis that jarred with the conventional ideology: the emphasis on the power and will of a God who acted purely according to his volition and by no means necessarily in accordance with any rules or laws discernible to man.[201] In the Elizabethan world-picture the universe, as we have seen, was idealized as operating according to divine laws; God's exercise of his prerogative – miracle – was only an occasional intervention in a rational system: his will and his law were complementary not at odds. The Calvinist emphasis implied their separation and hence substituted a voluntarist for a legal perception of power in general; this by correspondence questioned the

---

[197] Bedford, *Defence of Truth*, 143.

[198] P. Sidney, *An Apology for Poetry*, ed. G. Shepherd (Manchester, 1973).

[199] H. Burton, *The Christian's Bulwarke Against Satan's Battery* (1632), 2; W. Prynne, *The Church of England's Old Antithesis to New Arminianism* (1629), sig. C2.

[200] H. R. Trevor-Roper, 'Milton in Politics', in *Catholics, Anglicans and Puritans*, ch. 5; C. Hill, *The World Turned Upside Down* (1972).   [201] Cf. Judson, *Crisis of the Constitution*, ch. 8, esp. 321–7.

harmony between prerogative and law in the commonweal as well as created world. James I, in a little-quoted passage of his famous speech on monarchy, recognized the importance of the parallel and reasserted the symbiosis of prerogative and law as well as of the divine and secular realms. Kings like God had power to create or destroy:

> But now in these our times we are to distinguish between the state of kings in their first original, and between the state of settled kings . . . for ever as God, during the time of the Old Testament, spake by oracle and wrought by miracles, yet how soon it pleased him to settle a church . . . then there was a cessation of both, he ever after governing his people and Church within the limits of his revealed will; so in the first original of kings . . . their wills at that time served for law, yet how soon kingdoms began to be settled in civility and policy then did kings set down their minds by laws.[202]

We perhaps need to look again at the perception of law in the sermons and speeches of puritans.[203] For though the logic of the voluntarist emphasis of Calvinism was not always pursued, there is a sense in which Hobbes's determinism drew on the puritans he hated.[204]

As well as emphasizing a wilful God operating outside a perceived system of law, Calvinism placed the personal conviction and personal relationship with God above the codes or community of the commonweal. The Calvinist community of the elect could not logically be synonymous with the community of the visible church. Whilst some ministers did not choose to press this to its conclusion, the puritans did distinguish themselves by their behaviour – by the zeal of their devotion to sermons, by the sobriety of their lives and by their distancing themselves from the pastimes of their neighbours whom they regarded as profane.[205] James I and others scorned the puritans as a 'sect rather than religion', a term that expresses the challenge they presented to the ideology of communalism.[206] There can be little doubt that the Books of Sports which licensed traditional pastimes were intended as responses to the puritan challenges to society as well as the church, and it may be that we need to study the pastoral idealizations of rural harmony that are a recurring motif of the literary and visual arts in Caroline England not

---

[202] James I's speech to parliament, 21 March 1610, Kenyon, *Stuart Constitution*, 12.

[203] For an earlier study, see D. Little, *Religion, Order and Law: a Study in Pre-Revolutionary England* (Oxford, 1970).

[204] L. Damrosch, 'Hobbes as Reformation Theologian: Implications of the Free-will Controversy', *Journ. Hist. Ideas*, II (1979), 339–52, esp. 350.

[205] P. Collinson, *The Religion of Protestants* (Oxford, 1983), ch. 5.

[206] McIlwain, *Political Works of James I*, 274; Sharpe, *Criticism and Compliment*, 70, 245–7. In the *Basilikon Doron*, James wrote of the puritans: 'before that any of their grounds be impugned, let King, people, law and all be trod under foot', *Workes of James I* (1616), 143.

as an innovation, but as a reassertion of conventional ideas of unity.[207] In their insistence on uniformity of ceremonies, Charles I and Laud appear, whatever the fear of their critics, to have been more concerned with the unity of the church and realm than with the theological and sacerdotal aspects of the liturgy.[208] The puritans, however, put conscience before uniformity, parish community, and indeed before family. This could not but have consequences for a society built on those very pillars, as contemporaries – not all fellow travellers with the high church party – were quick to recognize. In *The Looking-Glasse of Schisme*, Peter Studley, a minister at Shrewsbury, related the gory story of one of his parishioners, Enoch ap Evan, who had axed his brother and mother to death for kneeling in church.[209] To Studley the moral was clear: schism and zeal threatened the church and realm; it was natural to conclude in early Stuart England that fratricide was but one step from regicide. Owen Feltham found political language came naturally in describing those who 'in things but ceremonial' spurned at 'the grave authority of the church': 'I suppose we may call him a church *rebel*, or one that would exclude order that his brain might rule.'[210] Even the moderate Robert Sanderson who denounced the Arminians and went to some lengths to deny the 'effectual holiness' of ceremonies still condemned those who would fashion their own liturgy according to their taste: 'whereof what other could be the issue but infinite distraction and unorderly confusion'?[211] The stress on the individual conscience and the distinctness of the godly were, and were seen to be, political as well as religious and social gestures.

What then of the political conservatism of the puritans recently argued by historians?[212] This must I think be open to major qualification if not rejection. For in England as in Europe the loyalty of the puritans to princes was always conditional: in the case of Thomas Cartwright, as Scott Pearson put it, 'of such a conditional nature as to render it suspect'.[213] The author of *Christ's Confession* illustrates the point: whilst he maintained that Christ's kingdom was not prejudicial to Caesar's, he warned princes that if they were not obeyed by subjects it was because

[207] Cf. Marcus, *Politics of Mirth*.

[208] A point made by Sir Philip Warwick, *Memoires of the Reign of King Charles I* (1701), 74. I develop this argument in *The Personal Rule of Charles I* (New Haven and London, 1992). ch. 6.

[209] P. Studley, *The Looking-Glasse of Schisme* (1634).   [210] Feltham, *Resolves* (1628), 10–11.

[211] Robert Sanderson, *Twelve Sermons Preached* (1632), 26; cf. his reference to Arminius's corrupt doctrine, ibid., 35.   [212] E.g. W. Lamont, *Richard Baxter and the Millennium* (1979).

[213] A. F. Scott Pearson, *Church and State: Political Aspects of Sixteenth Century Puritanism* (Cambridge, 1928), 37.

they did not seek Christ's kingdom.[214] And those who were not with
Christ were against him. A godly man could serve his king when the
monarch walked the path of God: 'But if the prince they serve be an
idolator, an heretic or wicked, they can hardly hold their places.'[215]
Christ's Confession closes with a prayer that the king may see the light and
leaves the possible consequence of his not doing so undiscussed. The
implications, however, are those expressed more obviously in *The Fall of
Babylon*, a diatribe against the bishops published in Amsterdam in 1634:
kings are lords over men only in so far as they are subjects not as they
are Christ's disciples.[216] The unconventional division points to the
radical core of Calvinist political thought: the unnaturalness (in the normative sense) of the state and its subordination to the rule of the
saints.[217] For much of our period the radical, political implications of
Calvinism were quiescent. But they were not, as Johann Sommerville
would have it, of no importance.[218] For the Calvinists alone perhaps in
1642 had a set of beliefs that could turn the world upside down. 'At the
beginning of the English civil war, the work of ideological opposition to
the king was still done (largely) by the radical Calvinism of the sixteenth
century and its derivatives.'[219]

Our excursus into scepticism, Machiavellianism and puritanism may
seem to have led us far away from the commonweal of truth, harmony
and virtue which we earlier described. It is important therefore to recall
that we have not travelled to other realms, that sceptics, Machiavels and
puritans inhabited the commonweal even when others found it hard
ideologically to incorporate them. Not only were they part of the commonweal, they articulated clearly ambivalencies and tensions at its philosophical and theological centre. The perception of a rationally ordered
universe intelligible to human reason always contained the possibility of
a more secular world-view; in Protestant theology lay always the potential for a more individual relationship to a wilful God; and many in practice acted (and were seen to act) according to Machiavelli's principles.
The Elizabethan world-picture was not a flat, two-dimensional canvas.
The frame only just contained a swirl of action and contradiction, an
interplay of dark and light. Viewed from a different perspective all could
take on a different appearance. Or, to change the metaphor to a lan-

[214] J. P., *Christ's Confession and Complaint Concerning His Kingdom and Servants* (1629), 29–30.
[215] Ibid., 70; for a refutation of this argument see below, p. 106.
[216] *The Fall of Babylon* (Amsterdam, 1634), preface to the reader.
[217] Cf. Hale, *Body Politic*, 8.   [218] Sommerville, *Politics and Ideology*, 12.
[219] R. Tuck, *Natural Rights Theories* (Cambridge, 1979), 144.

guage that contemporaries frequently used, it was a drama which at first sight appears a simple morality play but on closer reading resonates with tensions and subversions only just held in artistic control. Until 1642, the early modern world was just that: held together by art, by the texts which mediated its ideological premises. As we turn to those authorizing texts, vocabularies, cultural practices and analogues, we must remain alert to the ambiguities and contradictions they reveal and endeavour to control.

TEXTS AND LANGUAGES

It is a mark of how approaches to the history of ideas have been revolutionized that where once we founded that history on key texts, the very existence or nature of a text is now called into question and doubt. It was called into question by literary critics who observed that what we call a text is no more than a speech act of agent (a) (whom we describe as an author) which is reinterpreted and hence rewritten by a set of subsequent agents (b to n) (whom we call readers, commentators, critics, etc.). These agents from their own linguistic and cultural paradigms reconstitute the meaning of the original verbal performance, themselves therefore become authors, and so by appropriating de-authorize, in both senses (displacing both the author and the authority of), the original performance. Many historians have ignored the radical challenge posed by Stanley Fish's question: *Is There a Text in This Class?*[220] John Pocock, however, has addressed it and reasserted 'the persistence of a literary artefact of a certain authority and *duree*".[221] The historian, Pocock argues, can, indeed does, accommodate the acts of reinterpretation and appropriation without abandoning the idea of text, viewed as 'a certain set of formulas or paradigms, which are to be applied each time the authority of the text is invoked'.[222] This goes a long way to answering the textual Pyrrhonists. One might here adduce to support Pocock's argument seventeenth-century instances in which a destruction of a text acknowledged an authority which could not easily be deconstructed. We have mentioned Thomas Allen's tearing up of his Bible; James I's ripping of the Protestation from the Commons Journal in 1621, and other concerns about entries in that Journal imply a recognition of its textual authority.[223] More generally the growing anxiety exhibited by the

---

[220] S. Fish, *Is There a Text in This Class? The Authority of Interpretive Communities* (Cambridge, Mass., 1980).   [221] Pocock, *Virtue, Commerce and History*, 21–2.   [222] Ibid., 22.

[223] See above, p. 65; James I tore out the Protestation at a Council meeting to which MPs were summoned with the journal, *Cal. Stat. Pap. Dom. 1619–23*, 326.

Privy Council over records and libraries – Sir Robert Cotton's was closed in 1629, Sir Edward Coke's papers were sequestered on his death – may reveal, if not the autonomous power of legal and historical documents, at least the greater authority of some readings than of others.[224] Indeed the need to reinterpret and appropriate certain texts itself bears witness to their authority.[225] It was essential to claim biblical endorsement for almost any action in early modern England, and the same was almost as true for Aristotle. Hugo Grotius, as Richard Tuck has pointed out, had to comb Aristotle in search of passages to support a very un-Aristotelian thesis.[226]

Yet this example reminds us too that textual authority and its subversion may be in a more complex relationship than Pocock allows. Texts, even as a set of linguistic formulas, may remain. But the authority of a *name* may become the veil for a subversion of the *meanings* originally connected to (we will not worry the problem of intended by) that name, leaving the survival of the text as original meaning act in doubt. A good case of this is offered by Charles Schmitt's rich study of Renaissance Aristotelianism.[227] Aristotle, Schmitt reminds us, was read from many different types of text – most of them printed with some form of commentary: 'like . . . Biblical knowledge, Aristotelian doctrine was available in many different forms, from the most learned annotated editions of the Greek text to the sketchiest of compendia in Latin or a number of different vernaculars'.[228] Centuries-old disputes over the editions and translations of the Bible, the difference between the Scriptures in the Vulgate and Geneva Bible forms, are enough to indicate how editions complicate speaking of the authority of the text. Not least because he was read in so many forms, and in so many different circumstances, in courts, in literary academies, in schools and universities, 'Aristotle could serve as a starting point for many investigations and result in varied approaches to understanding the world.'[229] At times the only unifier of such variety was

---

[224] Sharpe, *Sir Robert Cotton*, 80–2, 144–6; for Coke, *Cal. Stat. Pap. Dom. 1629–31*, 490; *Hist. Mss. Comm. Cowper*, II, 266. Cf. *Cal. Stat. Pap. Dom. 1631–3*, 567; PRO PC 2/42/419. I pursue this official concern with manuscripts further in *The Personal Rule of Charles I*, 655–8.

[225] Sharpe and Zwicker, *Politics of Discourse*, 12–13. Eccleshall has shown that after the Restoration, because Hooker's *Laws of Ecclesiastical Polity* had been used to justify opposition to Charles I, attempts were made to deny its authenticity. R. Eccleshall, 'Richard Hooker and the Peculiarities of the English: the Reception of the Ecclesiastical Polity in the Seventeenth and Eighteenth Centuries', *Hist. Polit. Thought*, 2 (1981), 63–117, 75.

[226] Tuck, *Natural Rights*, 63.

[227] C. B. Schmitt, *Aristotle and the Renaissance* (Cambridge, Mass., 1983); Schmitt, *John Case and Aristotelianism in Renaissance England* (Kingston, Ontario, 1983). I am grateful to the late Charles Schmitt for stimulating discussions on the reception of Aristotle in England.

[228] Schmitt, *Aristotle*, 61.   [229] Ibid., 36, 89.

Aristotle's name. Similarly the Platonism of the Renaissance has been recently defined as 'a kernel of Plato's doctrines along with Aristotle's reinterpretations admixed with Pythagorean mathematics, Stoic ethics, Plotinian and Christian mysticism, Hermeticism, Patristic theology, and cosmology, Florentine humanism and Neo-Platonism, a number of occult symbolisms, several types of logical theory and method, and a turbulent current of religious reformation'.[230] To what extent was there a Platonic text in this class? Clearly there was in the sense that Renaissance Platonists were so described and derived authority for their meaning from him. But as editions also lead us to recall, texts as well as conveying power are authorized by and dependent upon it. Their publication required licence; their teaching and discussion in schools and universities involved the support of teachers or a place in the curriculum. The authority of a text in other words always interacted with the institutions of power, political, social and intellectual. As Schmitt put it, 'The longevity of Aristotelian philosophy . . . certainly was tied . . . to the whims of those in political control, as well as to the structural continuity and acceptance of traditional practices.'[231]

Those texts which continued to have authority, then, may be those whose original meanings had least stability or rigidity; their formulas or paradigms, to dissent from Pocock, may not be so much reapplied as recast. They may have been authoritative because they have to a wide extent permitted and yet contained their own reinterpretations. Eclecticism, however, cannot ultimately be contained: as John Selden put it, 'Scrutamini Scripturas: These two words have undone the world.'[232] Nor are there *no* bounds to eclecticism. When the world in 1642 was undone, its authorizing texts were dethroned along with the king. The authority and subversion of the Bible, Aristotle and other texts is inseparable from the history of authority and subversion itself.

The close interplay of 'texts' and 'authority' is in particular demonstrable from a study of interpretations. Certain interpretations made by those in power became thereby authoritative in the broader sense of influencing other readings. Elizabeth I's identification of herself with Richard II[233] or James I's reading of the *Faerie Queen* as a commentary on his mother's (Mary Queen of Scots') trial shaped contemporary

---

[230] Bedford, *Defence of Truth*, 20.   [231] Schmitt, *Aristotle*, 113.
[232] Cited by Bedford, *Defence of Truth*, 148.
[233] L. B. Campbell, 'The Use of Historical Patterns in the Reign of Elizabeth', in L. B. Wright ed., *Collected Papers of Lily B. Campbell* (New York, 1928), 355; Campbell, *Shakespeare's Histories: Mirrors of Elizabethan Policy* (San Marino, 1947).

readings and responses.[234] But, as recent work has begun to demonstrate, the relationship between textual authority and organs of power may, especially in Renaissance England, be broader and closer still. Once we see a text as a set of paradigms that have acquired authority but which are also reinterpreted in time and circumstance, we may come to include as 'texts' other such performances, both discursive and enacted – especially by those in authority. Indeed James I's desire to have the story of his mother's reign rewritten[235] may become more explicable when we understand that royal authority itself in early modern England rested more on a set of presumptions and perceptions than on the instruments of power.[236] The power of a text, we might say, could then be crucial for the performance of power. And the monarchy itself we might study as a text – not least because the comparison came easily to contemporaries. Ben Jonson always regarded the king and poet as brothers in authority and shaped his own artistic performance in close parallel to royal speech and action: his *Works* appeared the same year as those of James I.[237] Shakespeare, David Bergeron has argued, fashioned his plays about families and politics from the model of the royal family, which became a text for him as much as the 'authorities' – North's *Plutarch*, Greene's *Pandosto* and others – on which he drew.[238] More importantly, the identification of monarch and artist came as naturally to the former as the latter: their roles as actors, icons and texts were acknowledged by Elizabeth, James and Charles and by their subjects.[239] The *Table-Booke for Princes* put it directly: kings are 'the subjects of all discourse; the objects of all men's eyes'.[240] The lives of princes, another wrote in 1634, 'should be set forth unto their people as specula, a supereminent watch tower whom their subjects everywhere might behold . . . and as speculum, a mirror wherein they might gaze on and strive to imitate their sovereign'.[241] In a mirror, however, one sees oneself. And these last lines from the preface to a life of Alfred indicate that the actions and lives of

---

[234] E. Edwards, *Libraries and Founders of Libraries* (1864), 164–5; another example is James I's interpretation of Revelation, *A Paraphrase upon the Revelation* (in *Workes of James I* (1616), 7–80).

[235] H. R. Trevor-Roper, *Queen Elizabeth's First Historian: William Camden and the Beginnings of English 'Civil History'* (1971).   [236] See Geertz, 'Centers, Kings and Charisma', 150–71.

[237] Marcus, *Politics of Mirth*, 11.

[238] D. M. Bergeron, *Shakespeare's Romances and the Royal Family* (Lawrence, Kans., 1985); see Sharpe, *Politics and Ideas*, 280–3.

[239] See, for example, *Basilikon Doron*, in McIlwain, *Political Works of James I*, 18; K. Sharpe, 'The Image of Virtue, the Court and Household of Charles I', in D. Starkey ed., *The English Court* (1987), 226–60, esp. 258; Sharpe, *Politics and Ideas*, ch. 5.   [240] Scot, *Table-Booke*, 9.

[241] R. Powell, *The Life of Alfred* (1634), 'To the Reader'; cf. Machiavelli's dedicatory epistle to Lorenzo Medici in *The Prince*.

monarchs, like other texts, were also reinterpreted; their original formulas or paradigms were rewritten.[242] By the 1610s and 1620s Elizabeth I's reign was employed as the hold-all for a set of values some of which she would have deplored.[243] *England's Elizabeth* was appropriated, albeit unconsciously, to authorize later attitudes.[244]

Texts then can be regarded as clusters of values which derive authority often from the name which holds them together; their histories may see the name and certain associations invoked, while the values are rewritten. In an important sense the text as object remains, as does the mirror, but historical subjects find in it representations of themselves. Though few historians would dissent from this formulation, many have not exploited the possibilities it presents. The phrases 'conventions' (often 'merely conventional') or 'familiar trope' are often employed by historians of ideas to denigrate the importance of a view or thinker:[245] the 'timeless' trope, by its label, has no history. But no conventions or tropes are without a history; and the changing selection, articulation and deployment of them requires, perhaps, closer attention than it has received. Consider the classicism of Ben Jonson and the Caroline poets and playwrights: literary scholars have for years been content to elucidate the 'imitations' or 'borrowings' from and 'influence' of Horace, Martial, Ovid and so on; and historians have fallen into the trap of dehistoricizing those who appeared to want to live outside of their own age. The classicism of English Renaissance poets, however, does not make them unoriginal.[246] We may say of them, as Professor Oestreich said of Justus Lipsius: though superficially he seems to be lost in the classical authorities he cites, 'yet it is his own pregnant formulations that stick in the mind'.[247] Indeed, the chronology of imitation and appropriation raises important questions. Why, we need to ask generally, was a pagan culture celebrated in decades of religious passion and division?[248] Why, we must ponder more specifically, does an interest in the classical motif of the happy country life come into vogue in the second quarter of the

---

[242] Powell's *Life of Alfred* is 'together with a Parallel of our Soveraign Lord K. Charles'.

[243] See A. Barton, 'Harking Back to Elizabeth: Ben Jonson and Caroline Nostalgia', *Eng. Lit. Hist.*, 48 (1981), 701–31; see, for example, D. Primrose, *A Chaine of Pearle: or a Memoriall of the Peerles Graces and Heroick Vertues of Queene Elizabeth* (1630).

[244] T. Heywood, *England's Elizabeth, Her Life and Troubles* (1632).

[245] Christopher Hill described the ideas of Thomas Carew as 'banal', evidently because they were conventional, *Times Lit. Supp.*, 1 January 1988, 17.

[246] See K. A. McEuen, *Classical Influence Upon the Tribe of Ben* (New York, 1968); T. M. Greene, *The Light in Troy: Imitation and Discovery in Renaissance Poetry* (New Haven, 1982); R. W. Peterson, *Imitation and Praise in the Poems of Ben Jonson* (New Haven, 1981).

[247] Oestreich, *Neostoicism*, 40.

[248] I am grateful to John Morrill for stimulating my thinking about this question.

seventeenth century?[249] Poets like Jonson, it has been suggested, treated their classical sources in the way that antiquaries drew on precedents:[250] they selected from a past what might convey qualities for living properly in the present; their texts and circumstances were in a dialogue.

Historians who can learn from eavesdropping on such conversations might pay more attention to the editions of and prefaces to classical texts, and still more perhaps to the genre of *observations* on authors who were popular in the early modern period. In these the re-readings and reconstitutions in the light of contemporary experience are obvious: in *The Honest Man or The Art to Please in Court* (translated into English in 1632), Nicholas Faret admitted that he had so mingled his own views with those of the ancients that he did not know how to unravel them.[251] Joshua Sylvester, in his prefatory remarks to C. Edmondes's *Observations upon Caesar's Commentaries*, wondered whether Caesar or Edmondes deserved the greater praise;[252] Samuel Daniel thought the *Observations* 'Makes Caesar more than Caesar to contain'. Ben Jonson revealingly described Edmondes as recreating Caesar.[253] A perusal of the work shows these comments to be more than mere praise. Edmondes draws for his commentary on other authors ancient and modern, on Livy and Guicciardini;[254] more importantly he invests Caesar's age with the cosmology of seventeenth-century England. Edmondes commends Caesar's address to his soldiers who had taken fright at the Germans, and his endeavour 'by the authority of his speech to restore reason to her former dignity, and by discourse . . . to put down a usurping passion, which had so troubled the government of the soul'.[255] In Edmondes's pages, recent historical figures such as the Admiral Coligny inhabit a world alongside Caesar and Tacitus. Similarly in *Augustus* (1632) Peter Heylyn drew on Guicciardini, moved easily to the reign of Richard III and never left behind his experience of the reign of Charles I.[256] These commentaries and observations are only one way in which classical conventions were rewritten and re-specified. Jonson's *Epigrams* and country house poems both imitate the ancients and address themselves specifically to the present; what is selected *and not selected* from each, the use of a trope to arouse an expectation which is then not pursued, such devices

[249] M. S. Rostvig, *The Happy Man: Studies in the Metamorphosis of a Classical Ideal* (New York, 1962 edn), 101.   [250] Smuts, *Court Culture*, 113.   [251] Faret, *The Honest Man* (1632), 404–5.

[252] C. Edmondes, *Observations upon Caesar's Commentaries* (1609), prefatory verse; in his own dedication to the prince, Edmondes reminded Henry that his father James I had recommended Caesar in his *Basilikon Doron*.   [253] Edmondes, *Observations*, prefatory verses.

[254] Ibid., sig. A5.   [255] Ibid., 40.

[256] P. Heylyn, *Augustus* (1632), 45, 50; NB also 126, 150, 186, 223–4.

and strategies give specificity to each act of classical imitation rather than dissolve them into timeless conventions.[257] In early modern England, the familiarity of anyone educated with the classical texts so adapted meant the specificity of such manoeuvres did not pass unnoticed.

This is true not only of the classics. Simon Birkbeck in *The Protestants Evidence* recruited Geoffrey Chaucer as a Protestant in his effort to prove the historicity of his faith;[258] the 1606 edition of *The Ploughman's Tale* announced that it showed 'by the doctrine and lives of the Romish clergie that the Pope is anti-Christ'.[259] Histories, ancient and modern, were frequently rewritten in the light of circumstances or as polemical gestures. By 1630, Elizabeth I's reign was being rewritten to demonstrate the queen's desire for further religious reform and her allegedly ever-harmonious relations with her parliaments.[260] More generally, as Annabel Patterson has cogently demonstrated, the fable tradition from its beginnings denies the distance between convention and specificity: the question of its author is itself one of historical interpretation; the fables are universal and political; they are both authoritative and open to endless different readings.[261] 'The story of the fable in England in the seventeenth century', Patterson concludes, 'is one that can teach us more than moral commonplaces. It helps to explain how ideology finds expression and how cultural formations appear and disappear in response to historical circumstances.'[262] We may take an illustration of our own from Scot's *Philomythie*, where he relates the tale of the sea horse and the crocodile contending to be kings of the Nile. The crocodile is lulled into a false sense of security by 'antique shews and masking merriments' and is warned:

> Beware of him that does extol you so
> And like a God adores ye as ye go[263]

The story is explicated as a moral about honour and baseness. As well as this moral commonplace, however, the author (Scot) recognizes historical circumstances: 'If any man enquire further after the tale, let him call to mind the late death of that renowned King of France.'[264] The

---

[257] See Peterson, *Imitation and Praise*. Structuralist and poststructuralist criticism has made us more sensitive to the politics of generic adaptation and manipulation. See Norbrook, *Poetry and Politics*; Sharpe, *Politics and Ideas*, 269–71.   [258] S. Birkbeck, *The Protestants Evidence* (1634), 64–5.

[259] G. Chaucer, *The Ploughman's Tale Shewing by the Doctrine and Lives of the Romish Clergie that the Pope is Antichrist* (1606).   [260] Primrose, *A Chaine of Pearle*; above, p. 78.

[261] A. Patterson, 'Fables of Power', in Sharpe and Zwicker, *Politics of Discourse*, 271–96.

[262] Ibid., 295–6.   [263] Scot, *Philomythie*, C2v–C3.   [264] Ibid.

invitation to historical readings is opened, seemingly to be closed by one. But 'if any man enquire [yet] further after the tale', one lulled by 'masking merriments' and flatterers in 1616 might well evoke more domestic and topical applications. Political and social circumstances, in other words, gave timeless fables constantly renewed specificity – as indeed they did other conventions and traditions.

This specificity itself has a longer and shorter historicity. In general the intellectual life of early modern London must be seen in relation to recent social developments: the residence in the fashionable West End of nobles and gentry for much of the year; the popularity of a gentry education at universities and the Inns; the emergence of the court as a cultural centre.[265] Professor Malcolm Smuts has made the interesting suggestion that the vogue for love poetry in the 1620s and 1630s reflected the return of powerful ladies to court, with the succession of Henrietta Maria.[266] The interdependency of ideas and circumstances can, also, have a much more detailed history. The publication and editions of texts emerge from present concerns: Professor Salmon observed that the *Vindiciae Contra Tyrannos* was translated into English at a time when England planned to intervene in the Low Countries.[267] Other historians have drawn attention to the vogue for Machiavellian works in 1650–1.[268] We might note the republication of Elizabethan and Jacobean writers about the same time, and the spate of Elizabethan material published around 1617–18, as further instances of circumstance as the motor for publication – a subject greatly in need of further study.[269]

Altered conditions and experiences in our period led to some famous and some less well-known rewritings and reinterpretations, across relatively short periods of time. Sir Edward Coke's view of the common law, we know, was coloured by his career and especially by his dismissal from office as Lord Chief Justice. Hobbes after 1642 abandoned his earlier equivocation to argue for the impossibility of renouncing man's right to self-defence and revised his account of the state of nature accordingly.[270] In the 1625 edition of his *Essays*, Francis Bacon recast his 'Of Ambition' to accommodate ambitious natures as he had not before, and in general exhibited less enthusiasm for a civil science that might explain human

---

[265] Smuts, *Court Culture*, ch. 3.   [266] Ibid., 189.

[267] Salmon, *French Religious Wars*, 17. This was an English edition of the fourth part.

[268] B. Worden, 'Marvell, Cromwell, and the Horatian Ode', in Sharpe and Zwicker, *Politics of Discourse*, 162–7.

[269] Sharpe, *Sir Robert Cotton*, 246. It is surprising how little use is made of the chronological cards of the STC for this purpose.   [270] Tuck, *Natural Rights*, 125.

behaviour by precepts and laws.[271] When, in 1535, Marsilio of Padua's *Defensor Pacis* was translated into English, his translator, William Marshal, omitted the chapter on the correction of secular magistrates as 'nothing appertaining to this realm of England'.[272] More careful analysis of these editions, translations and rewritings could provide valuable insights into important intellectual shifts.

Still more illuminating than such rewritings, however, is reflection about how seemingly unaltered conventions were *re-read* in different circumstances. At times such a study of reception and reader-response may be elusive. There can be little doubt about the suggestion that the ancient tales of murder and intrigue took on renewed vividness in the context of seventeenth-century phobias about Catholic plots, but it is difficult to pin down and document.[273] However, the publication of works around celebrated historical occasions clearly does suggest the likelihood of re-reading and specifying conventions. George More's reiteration of timeless counsel to justice, mercy and liberality in his *Principles for Young Princes* gained at least a renewed immediacy in the year after the creation of the first Prince of Wales since Henry VIII.[274] T. Pelletier's *Lamentable Discourse upon the Paricide . . . of Henry the Fourth* gave particular poignancy to the argument for sovereign authority in the year of the French monarch's assassination and that nation's drift into anarchy.[275] Two works (at least) published in 1628 clearly addressed the assassination of the Duke of Buckingham and the issues he had aroused as much as the lives of Aelius Sejanus and Edward II which were their avowed subjects.[276] Sejanus (with whom Buckingham had been identified in parliament) was depicted as ensuring Tiberius trusted no one else; Tiberius (with whom Charles I had identified himself) as regarding the attacks on his favourite as directed against him.[277] In *The Deplorable Life and Death of Edward II*,[278] Gaveston is portrayed as corrupting the king by masques,

---

[271] I. Box, 'Bacon's *Essays*: from Political Science to Political Prudence', *Hist. Polit. Thought*, 3 (1982), 31–50, esp. 37.   [272] E. W. Talbert, *The Problem of Order* (Chapel Hill, 1962), 7.

[273] Smuts, *Court Culture*, 26.

[274] More, *Principles for Young Princes*. See R. Strong, *Henry Prince of Wales and England's Lost Renaissance* (1986); Sharpe, *Politics and Ideas*, 288–91.

[275] T. Pelletier, *A Lamentable Discourse upon the Paricide . . . of Henry the Fourth* (1610). The interplay of general axioms and the specific moment characterizes this work.

[276] P. Matthieu, *The Powerfull Favorite or the Life of Aelius Sejanus* (Paris, 1628); Sir Francis Hubert, *The Deplorable Life and Death of Edward II* (1628).

[277] Cambridge Univ. Lib. MS Dd 12, 21, f. 99; F. Thompson, *Magna Carta, its Role in the Making of the English Constitution 1300–1629* (Minneapolis, 1948), 324.

[278] *The Deplorable Life* was first written in Elizabeth's reign, but was refused a licence. An incorrect edition appeared in 1628 and prompted Hubert to issue the correct text (see STC 13901). The circumstance of Buckingham's death clearly prompted the publication, *DNB*, Hubert.

by cutting him off from counsel, and by advising him that his will was
above the law.[279] Sometimes an action other than publication gives the
general a specific and political turn. It would be hard to deny this, for
example, in Henrietta Maria's escorting the visiting Elector Palatine to
the Blackfriars to see a revived Elizabethan play about the sufferings of
Germany under a medieval Spanish tyrant.[280] More generally we can
only imagine *how* a gesture, tone or aside made specific and topical a
history play, a sermon or a lecture.[281]

Fortunately we are in no doubt that audiences and readers were quick
to make such applications, and that writers responded to their enthusiasm to do so. In Massinger's *Roman Actor*, Paris protests, with less than
conviction, his innocence if some found themselves specifically touched
by what was only generally represented.[282] Thomas Scot's *Philomythie*, an
Aesopian collection of fables (the moral ambivalence of which we have
discussed), disclaims any particular application beyond the conventional
moral:

> If ought beside the moral you invent,
> Call it your owne, by me 'twas never ment.[283]

The disclaimer, however, turns out to be an invitation. As we begin to
read in the fables, the story of the bird of paradise's divorce from the
Phoenix to marry 'An unknowne foule, by th'ayre begot and bred'
appears to have in 1616, the year of the Overbury scandal, a more particular force than the injunction to chastity.[284] And as we progress further
we discern that the very structure of the work subverts the disclaimer in
order to assist closer parallels with Jacobean England. After the first part
of *Philomythie*, we meet a section entitled 'Certain Pieces of This Age
Parabolized'; as the generalities of the first part had specific resonance
so here the particulars of Jacobean experience are raised (if that is the
right word) to moral texts. In the second part the two come together as
ideals, moral tales and Jacobean experience are synthesized – in order
to praise, counsel and criticize the king and court in the light of the
moral qualities they mirror or neglect. 'O Princes', ends the debate
between the hart, the horse and the bull, 'banish faction from the
Court.'[285]

---

[279] *Deplorable Life*, 17–18, 23.   [280] M. Butler, *Theatre and Crisis, 1632–1642* (Cambridge, 1984), 33.
[281] For one example, see *Cal. Stat. Pap. Dom. 1639*, 140–1.
[282] P. Massinger, *The Roman Actor* (1629), sig. C2v. This is a frequent and frequently unconvincing
    disclaimer.   [283] Scot, *Philomythie*, sig. B2.
[284] Ibid., sigs. D2–D3; B. White, *A Cast of Ravens: the Strange Case of Thomas Overbury* (1965).
[285] Scot, *The Second Part of Philomythie*, sig. C2.

Circumstances could lead to the rewritings and re-readings of conventions to the point where they overturn rather than adjust the paradigms. One cannot but wonder how conscious John Pym was in 1640 when he refashioned the traditional identification of the king as the soul of the commonwealth and physician of the state to support his claims: 'A parliament is that to the Commonwealth which the soul is to the body, which is only able to apprehend and understand the symptoms of all such diseases which threaten the body politic. It behoves us therefore to keep the faculty of that soul from distempers.'[286]

The conceit was entirely traditional; its application radically novel. Some historians of ideas who prefer to find more autonomously intellectual influences behind changes in ideas might reflect that Thomas Hobbes, who had evidently become a Cartesian mechanist by 1630, did not develop his mechanist theory of the state until he experienced disruption and civil war.[287] A political crisis prompted a radical reappraisal, just as earlier, less traumatic, events had led to reinterpretations of existing texts and paradigms.

We have observed that the world-view of early modern Englishmen contained ambivalences and tensions. We have seen that social and political circumstances reinterpreted, some would have said subverted, the authoritative texts of that world-picture. As we turn from specific texts to the languages, cultural practices and analogues, through which early modern Englishmen mediated the meaning they identified in their society, we must keep in mind the dialectic of the ideal and actual, the stable and unstable which characterized the intellectual and political realms. Languages themselves operate simultaneously in many different and contrary ways. Speech acts are individual and yet, since the function of language is to communicate, are premised on what is shared; they not only convey ideas; they too evoke other responses – emotions, prejudices, past experiences, fantasies, in all of which, as well as in thought, meanings are constituted.[288] A common language runs throughout the commonweal of discourse, but performs quite differently in its various territories. It is not clear that Pocock's method allows sufficiently for this, especially where his accredited and institutionalized languages are

---

[286] Kenyon, *Stuart Constitution*, 184.
[287] R. Gray, 'Hobbes's System and His Early Philosophical Views', *Journ. Hist. Ideas*, 39 (1978), 199–215.
[288] We have not concentrated enough on the role of languages in communicating such sentiments and emotions.

concerned. Legal language, his first study, was undoubtedly an important idiom of political discussion in early modern England, but that shared language had different meanings and evoked different responses in law courts, in the Commons, and in common speech – as today economic terminology functions differently in business and everyday parlance.[289]

The shared language may be in general evidence of common values and ideals, but it is not synonymous with shared experiences or meanings. All – James I, Charles I, Pym, those outside the political arena – saw the king's prerogative and the common law as complementary, but experience showed them that they did not mean the same by that. In Hampden's case, for example, Fortescue was invoked by both sides.[290] Revealingly and importantly, however, the realization that a common, shared language could articulate different, even contrary positions did not lead to an abandonment of the legal idiom as a vocabulary for the discussion of political questions, but to a wish to codify the law as a means to resolving political problems.[291] (MPs as late as 1628 believed that once the law was *clear* their apprehensions would be settled;[292] and Charles I acted as though he believed the same thing in taking knighthood fines and ship money to the decision of the courts in the 1630s.)[293] James I, as so often, expressed the belief best. In the context of recent questions about the relationship of royal prerogative, civil and common law, James expressed his wish that the laws were in English, that contrary precedents and statutes be resolved and clarified ('all contrarieties should be scraped out of our books'), most of all that the law might have 'a settled text'.[294] A settled text might effectively end arbitrariness and dispute. Such a belief was echoed throughout the first four decades of the century – and even beyond in the interregnum interest in law reform.[295] The quest for that text demonstrates that, for all the tensions and disputes of the early Stuart decades, politics was still not conceived as a contested pursuit of power, but as a matrix of duties and rights held harmoniously in balance by law. It also suggests a belief that words

[289] On the different views of the common law that could be held by those who spoke the same language, see Burgess, 'Custom, Reason and the Common Law'.

[290] C. A. J. Skeel, 'The Influence of the Writings of Sir John Fortescue', *Trans. Royal Hist. Soc.*, 3rd ser., 10 (1916), 77–114, 97.   [291] Cf. below, pp. 115–16.

[292] Pocock, 'The Commons Debates of 1628'.

[293] W. J. Jones, *Politics and the Bench: the Judges and the Origins of the English Civil War* (1971).

[294] James I's speech to parliament 1610, Kenyon, *Stuart Constitution*, 82–3.

[295] S. E. Prall, *The Agitation for Law Reform During the Puritan Revolution 1640–1660* (1966); G. B. Nourse, 'Law Reform under the Commonwealth and Protectorate', *Law Quart. Rev.*, 75 (1959), 512–29; D. Veall, *The Popular Movement for Law Reform* (Oxford, 1970).

might themselves possess an authority which permitted no different interpretation – a belief that may open up an important aspect of the relationship between ideas and politics in early modern England.

The language of the ancient constitution is, of course, a historical as well as legal language. Among the gentry and educated of early modern England it was a common language, although the study of history had, until the 1620s, no formal place in the university curriculum. History was valued among the governing classes because, like the law, it was seen to offer rules for the conduct of affairs and especially statecraft. Historical thought and the languages and values bequeathed by the study of the past in the seventeenth century still await a comprehensive study.[296] What seems worthy of note, however, is that the philological studies of the Elizabethan period were not developed into a sophisticated sense of anachronism; rather in the early Stuart years the favoured histories were essentially didactic treatises peppered with axioms and often populated by figures who seem as shaped by present concerns as by evidence from the past.[297] History was not the study of the past as we would understand it but a glass in which man might observe universal truths: 'there', Bethune put it in *The Counsellor of Estate*, 'is seen the life of the world . . . the divers establishments of estates, the beginning, progress, middest and end, and the causes of the increase and ruin of empires'.[298] Hobbes in his preface to Thucydides' *Peloponnesian Wars* praised 'the actions of honour and dishonour' which were guides to the 'government of . . . life'.[299] The first history lecturer at Oxford, Degory Wheare, instructed his students to seek out from the particulars of their texts *universals . . .* by which we may be instructed to live well and happily'.[300] Gentlemen's commonplace books make it clear that the reading of historical works led often to collections of maxims and axioms evidently compiled as guides for the present.[301] The past and the present were not perceived as different; as there was theoretically one universal truth that united the divine system, so there had been one truth through all time. As the idea of one ordered universe prevented relativism, so it stayed the development of anachronism – even when the technical skills for its comprehension, philology and archaeology, for example, were emerging. The past like the present was studied not by the historical criteria of successful or

---

[296] The present writer plans a study of perceptions of the past and politics from Foxe to Burnet.
[297] Sharpe, *Sir Robert Cotton*, passim; J. Levine, *Humanism and History: Origins of Modern English Historiography* (Ithaca, 1987).   [298] Bethune, *The Counsellor of Estate*, 260.
[299] Hobbes, *Eight Bookes of the Peloponnesian Warre*, sigs. A1–A2.
[300] Sharpe, *Politics and Ideas*, ch. 8, 213.   [301] Stoye, *English Travellers Abroad*, 64–7.

unsuccessful but according to the moral absolutes of good and bad. Like
the Scriptures, history offered the way to the good life.

It did not escape contemporaries that from the past men justified their
wrongdoings and rebellions, as evil men claimed the Bible for their
authority. Such only demonstrated, however, that one needed to learn to
read the past and perhaps that, like the laws, histories needed codifica-
tion to distil the moral precepts which they yielded. Though in histories
men read of tyrants, as well as virtuous rulers, coups and rebellions, as
well as the calm of Augustan empire, none dissented from the view that
history was an ethical text, moral philosophy taught by examples, nor
from the position that good actions had the warrant of the past. It was
the civil war that severed the cord between past and present, between
history and morality.[302] The Levellers came to claim rights intrinsic to
man whether or not they had existed in the past; Hobbes claimed that
the civil war had been caused by the reading of histories.[303] Once again
it was a political crisis rather than the philological method itself that
changed thinking about the past. In the later seventeenth and early
eighteenth century, scholars began to develop the antiquarian scholarship of the Elizabethan age into what looks more recognizable as a
modern historicism. And simultaneously, but gradually, history began to
lose its status as the accredited language of politics. In early Stuart
England, history, for all the different meanings it might permit and
conceal, was a language both normative and shared.

History, in seventeenth-century England, was a branch of *literae
humaniores*, and the language it bequeathed was part of the discourse of
humanism and classicism. To the scholar, it is scarcely an exaggeration
to say that history was classical history; in England in the early seventeenth century, the antiquarian interest in the medieval past fell subject
to ancient history and histories penned according to classical models.[304]
An absorption in classical antiquity led to an absorption in classical
vocabularies and values, the significance of which we still have not
pursued.[305] Thomas Godwin's *Romanae Historiae Anthologia . . . An English
Exposition of the Roman Antiquities* drew very exact parallels between
England and Rome, and the ease with which seventeenth-century
Englishmen employed classical terms, such as senate, points to a wide-

[302] C. Hill, *Some Intellectual Consequences of the English Revolution* (1980), 59.
[303] C. Hill, 'The Norman Yoke', in *Puritanism and Revolution* (1958), 50–122; B. Worden, 'Classical
Republicanism and the Puritan Revolution', in H. Lloyd-Jones, V. Pearl and B. Worden eds.,
History and Imagination (1981), 182.   [304] Levine, *Humanism and History*.
[305] W. Notestein, *The English People on the Eve of Colonization* (1954), 53, 120.

spread identification.[306] In the ancients, some came to believe, was 'all that was requisit to be known'; classical values therefore might form the source of the good life.[307] In Ben Jonson we discern a clear belief that classical culture might be the powerful instrument of moral reform. Not least because Horace and Virgil located virtue in the rural estate, he revived and adapted their vision in the country house poem *To Penshurst*, as he restaged their world in Roman plays.[308] It was a vision widely shared. In *The Schoole of Pollicie* published in 1605, Henry Crosse discussed virtue in predominantly classical terms.[309] Anthony Stafford's *Guide of Honour* counselled a moderation of the passions and liberality which he called 'humanitas'.[310]

This secular classicism, as we observed, existed in tension with more spiritual priorities and texts; as Professor Kearney put it, there were 'two contrasting ideals of what a humanist education should be, the one drawing its inspiration from the values of the Italian courts, the other from the city states of Strasburg, Geneva, Basle and Zurich'.[311] One was lay, the other clerical. In discussing the common languages of early modern England, however, it is necessary to observe that even these tensions did not de-authorize classical idiom. The strict Calvinists shared an education with their less spiritual peers and the classics were as familiar to them.[312] Sir Simonds D'Ewes recalled immediately on learning of Henri IV's assassination Tacitus's account of the poisoning of Germanicus; Leighton and Prynne, puritans, addressed the House of Commons as 'senators'.[313] Professor Rostvig pointed long ago to similar praise of the classical value of the via contemplativa in the poetry of Catholics such as William Habington, of Anglicans like Drummond and Herrick, and of Milton.[314] Evidently Meric Casaubon and Thomas

[306] T. Godwin, *Romanae Historiae Anthologia Recognita et Aucta: an English Exposition of the Roman Antiquities* (1628); for examples of 'senate' and 'senators', see W. Prynne, *A Briefe Survey and Censure of Mr Cozens his Couzening Devotions* (1628), dedication to parliament; A. Leighton, *An Appeal to the Parliament* (1628), 1. Gustavus Adolphus was referred to as 'that Caesar and Alexander of our times' in *The Swedish Intelligencer* (1632), preface to the reader.
[307] P. Matthieu, *Unhappy Prosperitie, expressed in the histories of Aelius Sejanus and Philippa* (1632), 148.
[308] Peterson, *Imitation and Praise*; K. E. Maus, *Ben Jonson and the Roman Frame of Mind* (Princeton, 1984); P. J. Ayres, 'The Nature of Jonson's Roman History', *Eng. Lit. Ren.*, 16 (1986), 166–82.
[309] H. Crosse, *The Schoole of Pollicie* (1605), passim.
[310] Stafford, *The Guide of Honour*, 61, cf. 72–3, 129.
[311] H. F. Kearney, *Scholars and Gentlemen: Universities and Society in Pre-Industrial Britain 1500–1700* (1970), 43.
[312] See J. Morgan, *Godly Learning: Puritan Attitudes Towards Reason, Learning and Education 1500–1640* (Cambridge, 1986).
[313] J. O. Halliwell ed., *The Autobiography and Correspondence of Sir Simonds D'Ewes* (2 vols., 1845), I, 49; above n. 306.   [314] Rostvig, *Happy Man*, 122.

Wentworth found Marcus Aurelius's *Meditations* complementary to their Christian beliefs.[315] The classical idiom, in other words, was another shared language of values among the governing classes of England. It was an idiom that reinforced a vision of a moral universe and a harmony secured through moderated passions. Classical culture was a culture of discipline and self-regulation for governors and for subjects. In the 1650s, however, as Zera Fink has shown, the republican apologists found in the classics (especially in Cicero) authority for their radical cause.[316] In doing so they broke the link between the Elizabethan world-picture and the ancient world and put an end to the classical idiom as one of shared values. When the Augustans after years of upheaval rearticulated classical values they did so, it has been argued, more consciously and strategically, not naturally – in both its early modern senses. 'The superb formal imitations of Pope, Swift and Doctor Johnson' take us far from the classical world of Ben Jonson; they 'adjust the idiom of familiars who have lost their numinous ghostliness'.[317]

AESTHETICS AND CULTURAL PRACTICES

A belief that imitation of the classics might revivify the civilizing, moral force of the ancient world in early modern England was an ideology not confined to the literary arts. The adoption (and adaptation) of Roman styles in buildings, portraits, dress and manners expressed similar values and ideals. As Malcolm Smuts recently brilliantly explicated it, Inigo Jones's philosophy drew on Vitruvius's parallel between architecture and the human body.[318] The right proportion and harmony in stone might by correspondence promote a more rational ordering of the senses and the appetites in man; and in the body politic, by correspondence, the architect was partner to the statesman in moulding the raw materials of nature into a harmonic order. Inigo Jones thought that Stonehenge had been erected by the Romans in order to civilize the ancient Britons and his projected palace at Whitehall was to have served the same purpose. In default of its being completed the proscenium arches he designed for the masquing stage at Whitehall, most often in the Banqueting House which had been built as the first stage of the larger plan, announce the claim of architecture as a moral force and agency of government.[319]

---

[315] Above, p. 66.
[316] Z. Fink, *The Classical Republicans* (Evanston, Ill., 1945) and Worden, 'Classical Republicanism and the English Revolution'.   [317] Greene, *The Light in Troy*, 293.
[318] Smuts, *Court Culture*, ch. 6.   [319] Sharpe, *Criticism and Compliment*, 207–9.

Jones's claims appear to have baffled or disturbed Ben Jonson.[320] But they were not, I would suggest, unusual, except in the complexity of Jones's philosophical explications. The architectonic analogue came naturally to early modern England. Wentworth's famous speech about the arch of order seems to transcend a mere metaphor or simile for government: the authority of the king '*is* the keystone of the arch of order and government', he claimed.[321] In 1641 at his trial, he was to rearticulate the point. The 'pillars of this monarchy' had been fixed 'that each of them keeps due measure and proportion with [the] other'.[322] Sir Edward Coke depicted the common law in the same terms, as 'the main pillars and supporters of the fabric of the commonwealth'.[323] The analogue came naturally because the architect (like the poet) is a maker; like God (and his magistrate, the king) he creates that harmony which distils the order of perfect nature, and which holds the cosmos and commonweal together. The architect was a statesman in presenting models of harmony and proportion that might lead men to balance their own humours and so regulate the realm of their body, enabling subject and ruler in turn to love each other, as the father taught and loved his children.

In considering the relationship of aesthetics to politics, it is important to emphasize that the Elizabethan world-picture was just that: a picture, a representation of the ideology of the cosmos and commonweal. The word cosmos means both order and beauty.[324] The beautiful therefore was an ordering, a governing in itself. Beauty was, one writer put it in *An Apology for Women*, 'a kingdom without a general'.[325] It was 'called of Plato a prerogative of nature',[326] that is the effective power of a perfect nature holding all in harmony, or, in Owen Feltham's words, 'Beauty is the wit of Nature put into the frontispiece.'[327] Physical beauty was expected in Renaissance thought to express an inner perfection, a perfect harmony of humours in the microcosm of man or woman, or indeed beast. A horse was regarded as the noblest of creatures 'for the verdict of reason must pass according to the evidence of proportion'.[328]

---

[320] D. J. Gordon, 'Poet and Architect: the Intellectual Setting of the Quarrel between Ben Jonson and Inigo Jones', *Journ. Warburg & Courtauld Inst.*, 12 (1949), 152–78.

[321] Kenyon, *Stuart Constitution*, 16. My comment here is a convenient shorthand. The metaphors current in any age are among the most valuable documents of deep cultural values and deserve fuller explication as such.   [322] Ibid., 193.

[323] Quoted by J. W. Gough, *Fundamental Law in English Constitutional History* (Oxford, 1955), 41.

[324] Daly, 'Cosmic Harmony', 12.   [325] C. Newstead, *An Apology for Women* (1620), 37.

[326] Ibid., 36.   [327] Feltham, *Resolves* (1623 edn), 251.

[328] N. Morgan, *The Perfection of Horsemanship, drawne from Nature, Arte and Practise* (1609), sig. A2v.

Men's characters and qualities were read from their faces; outward beauty was praised only in so far as it reflected inner virtue.[329] If external beauty did not correspond to inner perfection the disjuncture had social and cosmic implications. For as beauty led men to the perfection of nature, artifice corrupted nature and the commonweal. False representation struck at an important foundation of the Elizabethan world-picture, the Neoplatonic philosophy of the relationship of perfect form to matter. It is such import that lies behind Ben Jonson's denunciation of fashion (and flattery) as the corruption of men and society.[330] Owen Feltham addressed the consequences in directly political language: 'Wickedness in beauty is a traitor of the bedchamber.'[331] When Laud spoke of the 'beauty of holiness' he voiced the same belief: that there must be a corresponding harmony, unity and order in the outward face of religion as there was in God, in his created world and in the soul wherein the beauty of created man, his natural power to order himself, resided. The liturgy, like Inigo Jones's buildings, indeed like St Paul's Cathedral to the refurbishing of which Laud devoted so much energy, might assist in bringing about an inner spiritual order. Church towers, Gyles Fleming reminded his congregation, expressed the triumph of the Christian over the pagan; and the act of ordered worship expressed a harmony between the worshipper and God.[332]

The corollary to the belief that the beautiful might bring about order and harmony is the belief that models of order should be visually represented. In histories and poems, characters of virtue and vice were verbally presented so that men might thence derive a moral sense. The visual representation of order had the same (some argued more) force.[333] 'Julius Caesar', one author claimed, 'but looking upon the image of Alexander the Great was thereby excited to the undertaking and performance of things truly great.'[334] The source of order in the commonweal was the monarch, who was, the phrase is often used, made in God's image. The

---

[329] Sharpe, *Criticism and Compliment*, 123–4.
[330] *Timber or Discoveries*, in Herford and Simpson, *Ben Jonson*, VIII, 581, 593; cf. ibid., IV, 33: 'To the Special Fountaine of Manners: the Court', dedication of *Cynthia's Revels*.
[331] Feltham, *Resolves* (1623 edn), 252.   [332] Fleming, *Magnificence Exemplified*, 42; cf. 40.
[333] Despite the famous quarrel between Jonson and Jones, the literary and the visual were usually regarded as complementary. In *Mythomystes . . . of the Nature and Value of True Poesy* [1632], H. Reynolds spoke of painting as 'a silent poesy' and poetry as 'a speaking painting' (dedication to Lord Maltravers); cf. Nicholas Faret, who described painting as 'a silent poem', *The Honest Man* (1632), 100. Peacham relates that Rubens had history or poetry read to him while he painted, *The Compleat Gentleman* (1634 edn), 110. See L. Gent, *Picture and Poetry, 1560–1620: Relations Between Literature and the Visual Arts in the English Renaissance* (Leamington Spa, 1981). I owe this reference to Keith Thomas.   [334] L. Anderton, *The Triple Cord* (1634), epistle dedicatory.

true king, as the Oxford play *The Royal Slave* reminds us, displayed his virtue, his regality, in his looks.[335] The king's image might therefore lead others to emulate his goodness. God stamped princes with majesty in their countenance, the preacher William Struther observed in *A Looking Glasse for Princes and People*. (The recurrent employment of the metaphor, in mirrors for magistrates, almost certainly relates to the belief that outward appearance revealed inner qualities.)[336] The countenance of the good monarch then could itself order and harmonize the raw materials of nature and society.[337] 'In the light of the King's countenance', Bishop Hall wrote, 'is life';[338] 'Every King . . .' Bishop Henry King concurred, 'is a rich medal cast in Christ's mould.'[339] It is no coincidence that the period of the English Renaissance in which the ordered picture of the cosmos was the predominant ideology was also the age in which monarchs took an interest in their own visual representation: in statues and pictures, on coins, medals and seals. This was neither vanity nor simple propaganda.[340] In an age when the king's touch cured scrofula and his word could be life and death, his image (which authorized coins as currency) conveyed power. Elizabeth I, we know, was converted by portraits into an iconic symbol, at times like the statue of a saint.[341] The queen loses her personality in a larger story of divine import, which both glorifies the queen *and* reminds us of that greater majesty to which she owes obeisance. Few if any portraits of English monarchs in the late sixteenth and seventeenth centuries appear to me as straightforward announcements of a king's power. Scholars have observed that in Van Dyck's portraits of Charles I, the king with the most sophisticated appreciation of the representation of kingship, one discerns rather a 'psychic balance', than swagger.[342] The calm of the king's demeanour, his subduing of a powerful horse, symbolize the passions ordered and thereby represent the king as the best ruler.[343] The monarch is depicted as an image of self-regulation. Interestingly in Massinger's *Emperour of the East*, Pulcheria,

---

[335] W. Cartwright, *The Royal Slave*, Act I, scene iv, in G. Blakemore Evans ed., *The Plays and Poems of William Cartwright* (Madison, Wis., 1951), 208; see Sharpe, *Politics and Ideas*, 133–4.

[336] Struther, *A Looking Glasse for Princes and People*, 12.

[337] It is worth noting here that it is the *sight* of the monarch that orders the wilderness of nature in the masques, for the king did not speak.   [338] *The Works of Joseph Hall*, II, 233.

[339] King, *An Exposition upon the Lords Prayer*, 105.

[340] The interest was avidly shared by subjects. Increasingly histories of kings were illustrated by pictures of the monarchs. See, for example, Henry Holland, *Braziliologia, a booke of Kings* (1618), a series of pictures of monarchs from William I. It was reissued in 1628 and in 1630 with copper engravings.

[341] Smuts, *Court Culture*, 143 and plate 6. R. Strong, *The Cult of Elizabeth* (1977); F. Yates, *Astraea* (1977).

[342] Smuts, *Court Culture*, 204.   [343] Below, pp. 99–100.

Beauty, makes the point explicitly: absolute princes have less free will than vassals.[344] Beauty, balance and order were seen as one in the cosmos, in society, and in the individual. The ideology of the visual and plastic arts still awaits careful explication. But in the canvases of Van Dyck we may see the contained tension between the majestic individual who through his own power might impose order on his environment and the monarch subsumed in a larger picture of order, subject to natural laws.

The history of these ideas cannot be limited to the study of texts, languages and visual artefacts. There is a politics of performances as well as a politics of discourse, and it may be that historians have not only largely ignored the former but erected over-rigid boundaries between the two. Ideology, in any culture, is encoded in symbolic systems, of which language is only one.[345] Like established texts and languages, certain cultural practices become accredited because they mediate shared values from which in turn they derive authority.[346] Such practices reveal the tensions within shared values and customs. As a consequence they offer the historian rich documents of perceptions of power and of the submerged differences beneath common practices. The artificiality of the distinction between discourse and other performances is most obvious in the case of the monarchy itself. Kings addressed their subjects in words – in speeches, proclamations – and through their actions – ceremonies, progresses, processions to chapel – and also through their manners, style, choice of advisers, organization of court and household, eating habits and so on.[347]

James I and Charles I had very different senses of their own performances. James chose to represent himself mostly through his words: few other monarchs published not only their political testament but their *Workes* as he did,[348] and contrarily showed so little concern for the consequences of his actions, his conduct. When he spoke of royal action, he soon came back to discourse: 'King's actions . . . are as the actions of those that are set upon the stage . . . and I hope never to speak that in private which I shall not avow in public'; 'One of the maynes for which God hath advanced me upon the lofty stage of the supreme throne is that my words . . . might with greater facility be conceived.'[349] In

---

[344] Massinger, *Emperour of the East*, sig. Er^v.
[345] Walzer, 'On the Role of Symbolism', 191–204, esp. 196.
[346] I am grateful to Professor Steve Mailloux of Syracuse University for discussions we had on this subject at the Stanford Humanities Center in 1986.
[347] The present writer is working on representations of royal authority in early modern England.
[348] See *Workes of James I* (1616), 'The Preface to the Reader'.
[349] Kenyon, *Stuart Constitution*, 81; *Workes of James I*, 382.

Jacobean England, the royal actor was an orator. Charles I, by contrast, seldom chose to represent himself through words. His affection, he wrote to Louis XIII, was to be found more in actions than words, 'me montant toute ma vie par mes actionnes'.[350] Unlike his father Charles regarded his daily conduct as a representation of his rule, and encouraged others in authority to do so. He was chaste, reserved, grave, moderate in his diet and dress, and ordered his court as a model of decorum, believing that 'every man should be a rule of order and abstinence in his own house'.[351] When – rarely – he spoke at any length, the words were still subordinate to other forms of representation. When he set down his declaration after the dissolution of parliament in 1629, the king explained that he had written 'that we may appear to the world in the truth and sincerity of our *actions*, and not in those colours in which we know some . . . would represent them to the public view'.[352] Discourse will not take us far into the nature of Charles I or his values, and it can never be more than one source for the study of monarchical ideology.

Historians have of course begun to study rituals of state. The coronation ceremony, we learn, 'acted out the reciprocal obligations owed the prince by the people, owed the people by the prince, and owed to God by the prince and people, within the frame of order and degree'.[353] Changes in the ceremony or in behaviour at the ceremony could subtly tilt its message. Yet we need to extend our study to more familiar practices and to the subtle but revealing shifts in such familiar customs and practices. The removal of the Garter ceremony from Windsor to London (by Elizabeth) or back again (by Charles) reflected very different emphases within the theory of order – perhaps from a civic to a more theological conception of monarchical ritual and authority.[354] The ending of jousts, the monarch's dancing (or not dancing), dining publicly (or not) all need explicating, as they have not been, as ideological performances. Performance, action, not mere 'external representation', Juan de Santa Maria wrote in *Christian Policie*, is the essence of kingship.[355] Every act was then also a real presentation of the monarchy and the system of order that it partook of.

---

[350] Charles I to Louis XIII (n.d.), Huntington Library MS HM 20365.
[351] Sharpe, 'Image of Virtue'; J. F. Larkin ed., *Stuart Royal Proclamations, Vol. II: Royal Proclamations of King Charles I, 1625–46* (Oxford, 1983), 80.
[352] Kenyon, *Stuart Constitution*, 71.   [353] E. O. Smith, 'Crown and Commonwealth', 8.
[354] R. Strong, 'Queen Elizabeth and the Order of the Garter', *Archaeological Journ.*, 119 (1962), 245–70; E. Ashmole, *The History of the Most Noble Order of the Garter* (1715).
[355] De Santa Maria, *Christian Policie*, 24.

Ceremonies, culturally accredited performances, especially by those in some position of authority, we are used to studying as symbols and enactments of values. This is not least, perhaps, because contemporaries often wrote about them and announced their political import. The allegorical pageants of Elizabeth's reign were recounted often in early Stuart England;[356] masques were published as texts (at times with high print-runs), as were some civic rituals. In 1629, the order of the mayor, aldermen and sheriffs of London 'for their meetings and wearing of their apparell throughout the whole year' was set down – presumably for a public wider than their eminences themselves.[357] Ceremonies were attended by a public which was evidently well schooled in reading their symbolic codes.[358] Recent work on the politics of popular ritual and festival has begun to open our understanding of the broader place of ceremonies throughout the symbolic commonweal.[359] Like royal coronations and progresses, village customs and rituals – May Day festivities, beating the bounds, rituals of inversion – were both expressions of and reinforcements of the ideology of wholeness, harmony and order. They represented its ideal form; they acknowledged and contained its tensions. Popular festivals served, Leah Marcus put it, 'to meld individuals into their *natural* surroundings and into a larger collective entity'.[360] That festivals were ideological and political performances is obvious from the political disputes to which they gave rise: magisterial complaints of disorder and subversion, arguments about the cohesion of the community and the importance of exercises to defence, the sharp divisions over the question of Sunday sports. Professor Underdown has argued, suggestively albeit not persuasively, that differing rural pastimes and festivals helped to *explain* political divisions in 1642.[361]

Historians of political ideas need to pay closer attention to the accredited rituals and ceremonies of social communities. And, in this context, religious practices would repay further study too. For again ecclesiasti-

---

[356] E.g. Heywood, *England's Elizabeth*, 181–2.

[357] *The Order of My Lord Mayor, the Alderman and the Sheriffes* . . . (1629).

[358] For a good example, see Bulstrode Whitelocke's account of the procession before the masque *The Triumph of Peace*, in S. Orgel and R. Strong eds., *Inigo Jones: the Theatre of the Stuart Court* (2 vols., Berkeley, 1973), II, 541–3.

[359] See P. Burke, *Popular Culture in Early Modern Europe* (1978). For a detailed study of a more modern festival, see D. Cannadine, 'Civic Ritual and the Colchester Oyster Feast', *Past and Present*, 94 (1982), 107–30.

[360] C. Geertz, 'Ritual and Social Change', in *Interpretation of Cultures*, 142–70; Marcus, *Politics of Mirth*, 149, my italics.

[361] D. Underdown, *Revel, Riot and Rebellion: Popular Politics and Culture in England 1603–1660* (Oxford, 1985); Sharpe, *Politics and Ideas*, 298–303.

cal historians have paid more attention to discourses – to sermons, theological works, polemical tracts and diatribes – than to religious performances, the art of preaching, pastoral care and acts of charity, the act of administering and receiving the sacraments and, importantly, the diversities in all such practices. The Northamptonshire preacher Robert Bolton was strong in his belief that the word read had not the force of the word preached; he prescribed elaborate preparation for the delivery of and listening to sermons, attaching, as did most puritans, importance to the *practice* of a sermon as well as the word.[362] *An Alarm to Awake Church Sleepers* literally offers such counsel, urging the congregation actively to participate by uttering short ejaculations during the sermon.[363] Others less precise in their religious inclinations also saw the importance of the performance of preaching. Owen Feltham thought that the stage had lured men away from the pulpit through the power of its performances: 'We complain of drowsiness at a sermon, when a play of doubled length leads us on still with alacrity. But the fault is not all in ourselves. If we saw divinity *acted* the gesture and variety would as much invigilate . . . The stage feeds both the ear and the eye and through this latter sense the soul drinks deeper draughts. Things *acted possess us more*.'[364] The word itself had to be performed to have most power. Yet the power of religion did not lie only in the word but in the sign, in the sacraments, in the gestures (kneeling, standing), in the place – cathedral, parish church, private chapel, or house. The sacraments Christopher Dow defended in 1637 as 'moral instruments to convey those graces unto the receivers which the outward signs visibly represent'.[365] To some churchmen they were in other words efficacious in instilling grace. The relative importance of the word and the sacraments was, of course, the subject of theological and indeed political controversy. But this was not a controversy between word and action, discourse and performance. Performance was at the heart of religious beliefs, puritan, Anglican and Catholic, and at the very centre of the ideology of order. When we consider religion as performance, it may lead us to see that many, some

---

[362] Bolton, *The Saints Sure and Perpetual Guide*, 212.

[363] *An Alarm to Awake Church Sleepers* (1640), 122ff., 141.

[364] O. Feltham, *Resolves or Excogitations with Resolves, Divine, Morall, Politicall* (1628 edn), 64–5, my italics; *An Alarm* also pointed out that, though men slept through sermons, they stayed awake for plays (p. 96).

[365] Dow, *Innovations Unjustly Charged Upon the Present Church and State*, 206. John Gerhard called the sacraments the visible word, *The Marrow of Divinitie* (1632), 239; Bishop Griffith Williams pointed out that 'we do often times adore and worship without any words', *The True Church* (1629), 163.

seemingly trivial, cultural practices also symbolically revealed and reaffirmed that ideology.

The symbolic significance of cultural practices in earlier ages has left its stamp on some familiar idioms. Perhaps no political metaphor has been more enduring and familiar than that of the ship of state. In the seventeenth century it came to speakers and writers naturally as a depiction of order and government. In *A Free Will Offering*, Samuel Hinde spoke of the church in these terms: 'In the ship of our English church sits the sovereign majesty of our Lord and King. His nobles, lords, judges, Councillors as representative pieces of his own Majesty sit in the steerage of estate and to them is committed the helm of government.'[366] The clergy, he added, were the pilots of that ship. The metaphor was open, of course, to various interpretations and left room for a radical deployment.[367] But what, I think, we need to consider here is the practice that produces the metaphor: the act of sailing, navigating, provisioning a large ship, of commanding its crew, of steering through rocks and storm-tossed seas. Did not such an experience *actually* replicate the art of ordering the self, the family, the commonweal in a world beset by tempests internal and external? In the case of the puritan emigrés, as David Cressy has recently shown, the experience of crossing the ocean was a spiritual as well as physical journey.[368] I would suggest that we need to reflect more generally and imaginatively on the meaning of such experiences, on, in other words, correspondences between such an action and an ideology in early modern England. Not least because contemporaries give us warrant to do so. For example, the ubiquity of the theatrical metaphor, the frequent depiction of social and political life as a play, may lead us to understand that experiencing a play in early Stuart England was itself an extension of political as well as social life.[369] The popularity of the satirical *Game at Chess* might indicate too that it was not only plays and politics that shared a discourse and meaning; the chess-board seemed naturally to replicate the political world. Arthur Searle's manual *The Famous Game of Chesse Play* announced the game as 'an exercise . . . fit for princes' and its language is politicized at every turn.[370] Searle observed the limitations to the king's freedom of movement for all his

[366] S. Hinde, *A Free Will Offering* (1634), 83.   [367] Sharpe, *Criticism and Compliment*, 92.

[368] D. Cressy, *Coming Over: Migration and Communication between England and New England in the Seventeenth Century* (Cambridge, 1987), ch. 6.

[369] Interestingly, Joseph Hall pursued generic classification so far as to say that on the world stage the good acted out a comedy and the wicked a tragedy, *Works*, II, 27.

[370] A. S., *The Famous Game of Chesse Play* (1614). Searle points out that it originated from martial discipline.

importance; the power of a queen; the capacity of a mere pawn to threaten the king; the relative strength of dukes (rooks) and knights in comparison to bishops; most of all the need for co-operation among all the orders for security and success.[371] Other players clearly left the board with political reflections to the fore: 'there is much difference between the king and the pawn', Owen Feltham noted in his popular *Resolves*; 'that once ended they are both stuffed into the bag together . . . and who can say whether was most happy, save only the king had many checks, while the little pawn was free and secure'.[372] The force of Middleton's play seems more compelling in this context. No less, a full appreciation of the country house poem requires a similar imaginative grasp of the Stuart perception that gardening, ordering the raw material of nature, was an ideological and political pursuit.[373] We find these connections across a broad range of cultural practices. In *The Art of Archerie*, for instance, Gervase Markham linked the sport to the inculcation of virtue, reminding his readers that Aristotle had defined virtue as the mean and that the archer practised so as not to go 'wide of the mark'[374] (a phrase which has retained its familiarity whilst losing its ideological force).

Perhaps the best illustration of the ideological significance of cultural practices comes from horse-riding – not least because it generated extensive contemporary discussion. In his *Observations Divine and Morall, for the furthering of Knowledge and Vertue* (1625), J. Robinson depicted the vicious, brutish man, 'swayed and led by the affections as a foolish wagoner by his horses'.[375] Owen Feltham echoed the sentiment: 'man's will without discretion . . . is like a blind horse without a bridle'.[376] The taming of the passions was represented as analogous to the art of riding. That this, again, was not mere simile becomes clear when we examine treatises such as Nicholas Morgan's *The Perfection of Horsemanship, drawne from Nature, Arte and Practise* (1609). Since the fall, Morgan begins, the obedience of creatures to man could no longer be assumed; it had to be secured by art. Nature, however, desired restitution to her primary perfection, and all creatures desired a return to their original nature. The art that might restore it was reason – 'all Art worketh by true reason'.[377]

[371]   'And coming at the last in place,
          Where knights and lords did dwell,
          Their king shall give to them like grace,
          Because they served him well.' (Ibid., 'To the Reader'.)
[372] Feltham, *Resolves* (1623 edn), 31.
[373] As is evident from the masques, Sharpe, *Criticism and Compliment*, ch. 6; cf. R. Strong, *The Renaissance Garden in England* (1979).   [374] G. Markham, *The Art of Archerie* (1634), 6.
[375] Robinson, *Observations Divine and Morall*, 274.   [376] Feltham, *Resolves* (1623 edn), 108.
[377] Morgan, *Horsemanship*, 6.

Even after the fall, man's reason could be efficacious: 'our natural reason is obscured by the disobedience of our first parents, and yet nature may not be said to be unperfect or faultie, for it hath put into all things possibility and aptness, and also act and perfection'.[378] It is significant that Ben Jonson had uttered the same belief.[379] Just as he believed poetry might assist in man's moral regeneration, so Morgan argued that the art of horse-riding might restore the original order of nature and man's nature. Taming a great beast was a taming of nature's wildness and so, like the Caroline masques and paintings in which disordered nature is calmed, represented an act of government. In a marginal comment to his translation of Machiavelli's *Prince*, Dacres, moralizing his text, observed that Plutarch maintained 'a Prince excells in learning to ride the great horse, rather than in any other exercise: because his horse being no flatterer, will show him he makes no difference between him and another man, and unless he keep his feet well will lay him on the ground'.[380] The prince who learnt to keep his feet well, by corollary, learnt how to govern. The emperor on horseback depicts the man fitted to rule because he has tamed his own nature and learnt to order the wildness of nature herself. His mastery of the great horse expressed his virtue. And this was true not only of the prince. Dukes, marquises and knights, Morgan noted, all took their titles from the names of horsemen.[381] The aristocracy, the most virtuous men, were the most skilful riders; when they rode they re-enacted the moral paradigms which underpinned hierarchy and government.

Whilst many other such particular practices require consideration in this way, we need to re-emphasize generally here that *being* a nobleman or gentleman was itself a cultural practice of ideological significance. The vogue for courtesy books and manuals for gentlemen in early modern England reflects not only the fluidity of social status, the development of the court and the civilization of society; it speaks to a new awareness of the responsibility of the gentry and nobility in society. Gentlemen were to serve the state, not only in the narrow sense of counselling the prince, sitting in parliament, or attending the Quarter Sessions. The JP's role 'to mediate, attone and determine all such differences as arise between party and party' was the gentleman's role.[382] Gentlemen were to be patterns, Richard Brathwaite instructed them, of temperance and moderation: 'a true and generous moderation of his

[378] Ibid., 58.   [379] Herford and Simpson, *Jonson*, VIII, 567, 607, 619.
[380] E. D[acres], *Nicholas Machiavel's Prince*, 197.   [381] Morgan, *Horsemanship*, 10.
[382] Brathwaite, *The English Gentleman*, 147.

affections . . . hath begot in him an absolute command of himself'.[383] When a man was ennobled, he had thoughts he never had before. 'A gentleman *will do* like a gentleman.'[384] To be a gentleman was a performance; to do like a gentleman was to enact a political ideal. Like kings, noblemen had the power to mould society. 'Blame none but yourselves', Nicholas Caussin admonished them, 'if you create not a world, that you banish not vice from the earth and make a golden age return again.'[385]

ANALOGUES, PRACTICES AND NEW SOURCES

Acting and being, everyday behaviour and existence: the historian of modern political ideas is not used to taking these as his documents. *Political ideas* are ideas articulated by those involved in the discourse or performance of politics. We have seen, however, that in a system of correspondences all related to all. Order was observed and sought in all experienced, believed (and perhaps imagined), and the constitution of order is of course the matter of politics. As we turn then to treatises on gardening, music, on marriage, the family, on the body, we shall not be surprised to find their language politicized at every turn.[386] And we shall gain a brief glimpse of how the discourse of these analogical practices and experiences offers a rich fund of texts for the history of political ideas.

In the case of the works dealing with the natural world, the multivalence of the very word nature in seventeenth-century usage is enough to alert us. The term could describe a state of perfection, an Eden, God's creation, man's innocent condition, that which was normative; or anarchic wilderness, the condition of fallen man. The natural world therefore was a glass in which the tensions between order and disorder, the ideal and the actual, the spiritual and the secular were reflected; a glass into which contemporaries looked to see the world. Animals, because they knew no artifice, might teach man lessons from a less corrupted nature. To a conservative Catholic like Matthew Kellison, nature itself demonstrated the argument for hierarchy over Calvin's 'anarchy': all creatures turned to monarchy; 'Nature and natural reason seem to plead for a

---

[383] Ibid., 457.
[384] Ibid., 266. Cf. the simultaneous acknowledgement and satire of this perception in *The Winter's Tale*, Act V, scene ii, lines 124ff.   [385] N. Caussin, *The Holy Court* (1634 edn), 41.
[386] As I first read through the STC I was struck by the politicization of language over a broad range of works. And even when this is not obviously the case the prefaces appear to invite a politicization of the treatise which follows.

monarchy.'[387] To other observers, nature presented a more complex text, but one no less readily politically read. The inspiration for such readings came no doubt in part from Virgil's *Eclogues*, but again the adoption and adaptation addressed topical concerns.[388] The seventeenth-century writers who shared, for example, his fascination with the kingdom of bees, had their own reasons for taking an interest in the subject. For as the title of Charles Butler's detailed examination brings starkly home, the bees were subject to *The Feminine Monarchy*.[389] That potentially discomforting fact aside (perhaps the recent memory of Elizabeth I made it less disturbing of the traditional politics of gender), the bees seemed to offer a model of nature's virtue: 'In their labour and order at home and abroad they are so admirable that they may be a pattern unto men both of the one and of the other.'[390] The bees had the ideal commonwealth, 'since all that they do is in common without any private respect'.[391] Temperate and averse to idleness, they laboured together for the common good. Bees abhorred polyarchy and anarchy, loving a monarch 'of whom above all things they have a principal care and respect'.[392] They protected their estate, trained to use of their 'poisoned spear' in defence of their perfect kingdom. They were so naturally inclined to piety that when a woman placed a sacramental wafer in their hive to make them produce honey, they constructed a little chapel around it![393] The keeping of bees therefore was a pastime that was a lesson in statecraft and also one in personal conduct. For loathing impurity, being chaste and clean, bees were inclined to sting vicious keepers. If you do not want to be stung, Butler advised the prospective beekeeper, 'thou must be chaste, cleanly, sweet, sober and familiar'.[394] What the author himself learnt from his observation comes as a startling conclusion to his study: a condemnation of all who withheld tithes from the church and a diatribe against the 'new fangled Brownist' who separated.[395] The 1619 translator of Vigil's *Eclogues* pursued more secular observations – whilst noting that in the beehive some were designated to toil 'by a covenant made' amongst themselves.[396] One can only guess what other meanings those who read such tracts, more importantly those who kept bees, derived from the observation of their commonwealth.

---

[387] M. Kellison, *A Treatise of the Hierarchie* (Douai, 1629), 49.

[388] See the fine study of P. Alpers, *The Singer of the Eclogues: a Study of Virgilian Pastoral* (Berkeley, 1979).

[389] C. Butler, *The Feminine Monarchy: or a Treatise Concerning Bees and the Due Ordering of Them* (1609).

[390] Ibid., sig. A1.   [391] Ibid., sig. A1–A1^v.   [392] Ibid., sigs. A2–A3.

[393] Ibid., sig. B3.   [394] Ibid., sig. A5^v.   [395] Ibid., 'The conclusion to the Reader'.

[396] J. Brinsley, *Virgil's Eclogue* (1619), 121. The language is significant; Brinsley was a puritan divine of note, see *DNB*.

The same is even more true of other everyday habits and pastimes. Not least because few historians have as yet followed Bouwsma's agenda, we know considerably less than we would like about the politics of music and other such recreation.[397] The term *recreation* itself suggests that quest to reorder fallen nature, which we have seen to inform poetry and the visual arts. In the case of music the analogic significance becomes clear as soon as we recall that the celestial bodies were believed to move to music, according to musical harmonies of divine composition. Music was a gift of heaven, Peacham taught the complete gentlemen, bestowed on men so that they might praise their creator.[398] Hymns were sung, prayers were chanted or intoned, because music was a means of coming closer to God – a belief, for all the different forms it took, that held as good for the puritans as the high church party. The author of *Mottects or Grave Chamber Musique* (1630), dedicating his work to the new Lord Brooke, reminded his patron that Brooke's predecessor had loved harmony and music 'the being whereof is beyond mortalitie and regulates the whole frame of nature in her being and motions'.[399] Music's haters, Sir John Davies of Hereford put it, 'have no forme nor soule'.[400] In the individual, the right music might harmonize the humours and set the soul free, as Campion claimed, from the passions.[401] The musician knew how to regulate himself. The brother composers Henry and William Lawes were, the poet Aurelian Townshend praised them, 'lawes of themselves, needing no more direction'.[402] Music that led to self-government assisted too with the government of others: indeed the two were one in their dependence upon harmony. The Earl of Strafford perhaps revealed one of his own recreations as well as much else when he observed in his defence speech of 1641: 'as on the lute if anything be too high or too low wound up you have lost the harmony, so here the excess of a prerogative is oppression, of a pretended liberty in the subject disorder and anarchy'.[403] Thomas Ravenscroft in his *Brief Discourse of the True . . . Use of Charact'ring the Degrees . . . in Music* compared what he saw as the disordered state of music with that of a commonweal. Music lamented 'my laws violated, my precepts neglected'.[404] Arts

---

[397] Bouwsma, 'Intellectual History in the 1980s', 288–91.

[398] Peacham, *Compleat Gentleman*, 96.

[399] M. Peerson, *Mottects or Grave Chamber Musique* (1630), dedication to Lord Brooke.

[400] Prefatory verse to T. Ravenscroft, *A Brief Discourse of the True . . . Use of Charact'ring the Degrees . . . in Music* (1614).   [401] Ibid., prefatory address by Campion.

[402] C. Brown ed., *The Poems and Masques of Aurelian Townshend* (Reading, 1983), 122.

[403] Kenyon, *Stuart Constitution*, 193.

[404] Ravenscroft, *Brief Discourse*, 'Apologie'; cf. Thomas Carew's identification of problems on the stage and in the state, R. Dunlap ed., *The Poems of Thomas Carew* (Oxford, 1949), 96.

were 'much altered from their Pristine State/Humors and fancies so praedominate'.[405] But, as a prefatory verse put it, in frank acknowledgement of the tensions we earlier identified, such problems were not new:

> Concord and Discord still having been at ods,
> Since the first hour the heathens made them Gods

the flats and sharps contending along with them.[406] Ravenscroft, however, in ordering music into degrees contributed to a larger order:

> But heere is One, whose Dove – like Pen of Peace
> Strives to out flie such strife and make it cease;
> And Discord brings with Concord to agree
> That from their strife he raises Harmonie.[407]

Ravenscroft himself described the power of music in language that evokes the court masques: 'we see the sovereignty of Music in this Affection, by the cure and remedy it affords the dispassionate . . . thereby to assuage the turmoils and quell the tempests that were raised in them'.[408] We would like to know more about the score for masques, how the antimasque cacophony of knackers and bells gave way to harmony,[409] as we would like to know more about the choreographical transformation from antic to measured paces in the dance. For like the playhouse, music and dance in early Stuart England appear to have presented a cosmological, social and personal drama of reason and passion, order and disorder. The injunction that the family be like a well-strung instrument, 'every thing in his place keeping his note and height',[410] leads us onto how contemporaries saw that political play enacted also on the domestic stage.

The description of the king as the father of his people was a familiar idiom of political discourse from Aristotle's *Politics* to the Victorian age.[411] In those centuries when kingship was lordship and the king's household not different in kind from those of his noble retainers, the language was literally as well as metaphorically appropriate. The network

[405] Prefatory verse of M. Pierson to Ravenscroft's *Brief Discourse*.
[406] Prefatory verse of William Austin.
[407] Ibid., cf. Shakespeare *Henry V*, Act 1, scene ii, lines 178–83.
[408] Ravenscroft, *Brief Discourse*, sig. A3. See S. K. Heninger, *Touches of Sweet Harmony* (San Marino, 1974); J. Hollander, *The Untuning of the Sky: Ideas of Music in English Poets 1500–1700* (Princeton, 1961).
[409] See M. Chan, *Music in the Theatre of Ben Jonson* (Oxford, 1980); M. Lefkowitz, *William Lawes* (1960); M. McGowan, *L'Art du ballet de cour en France 1581–1643* (Paris, 1963); B. Pattison, *Music and Poetry of the English Renaissance* (1970).   [410] B. Sk., *Counsel to the Husband*, 38.
[411] Significantly one of the powerful Victorian images here came from the seventeenth century. See R. Strong, *And When Did You Last See Your Father? The Victorian Painter and British History* (1978).

of clientage relationships that bound the monarch to his nobility and through them to all his subjects was not unlike an extended kinship network. Monarchical government was personal, to some extent household government until at least the later seventeenth century. There were important changes that become apparent by the end of the sixteenth century: the monarch was perceived as not just an overlord but as the ruler of a nation; and the court developed spectacularly to become a centre of the realm, as well as the household of the king.[412] The system of personal relationships had to accommodate these subtle shifts of perception and a growing political nation. The royal 'family' became the realm – as indeed during the crises of the mid-Tudor years the safety and survival of the realm depended upon the royal family. The power of this political analogue is demonstrated in its persistence through the reigns of a boy, two women and a virgin queen. Indeed Elizabeth I, always so skilled in the personal appropriation of the ideologies that sustained monarchy, took advantage of her childless condition to emphasize her place in the politic family: 'Though after my death', she told her subjects in 1563, 'you may have many stepdames, yet shall you never have a more natural mother than I mean to be unto you all.'[413] The succession to the throne after Elizabeth of two fathers underlined the associations of the king's personal and politic families.[414] James I frequently played on the association in his speeches; Charles I in the paintings of his family. Both penned their political testaments as personal advice to their sons. The force of the representation was acknowledged by the king's enemies in the civil war: those who drafted the Army Remonstrance of November 1648 pointed out to parliament that for all his (as they saw it) chicanery and evil, the king 'comes in the only true Father of his People, you being proved the cruel foster-fathers'.[415] Milton perhaps recognized the power of the paterfamilias icon as part of the force of the *Eikon Basilike* when he dismissed the politic father as a conceit best left to the Muses.[416] During the early modern period, however, it was not confined to poetic territory, but was an accredited analogue of all political discourse.

Though historians have frequently pointed to the analogue and studied the images of father and family in political speeches and treatises, they have paid little attention to the tracts on the family and

---

[412] Cf. D. Starkey, 'Court History in Perspective', in *The English Court*, 1–24.
[413] J. Neale, *Elizabeth I and Her Parliaments* (2 vols., 1953), I, 109.
[414] Bergeron, *Shakespeare's Romances*; Sharpe, *Politics and Ideas*, 282.
[415] Kenyon, *Stuart Constitution*, 286.
[416] Walzer, 'On the Role of Symbolism', 195. Milton grudgingly recognized its power for an 'image doting rabble', cited by Trevor-Roper, *Catholics, Anglicans and Puritans*, 268.

household, and the political reflections which they venture or imply.[417] Yet as soon as we examine such works, we immediately discern an address to public as well as domestic issues. Pierre Ayrault's *A Discourse of Parents Honour*, translated into English in 1614, was written by a French civil lawyer in the 1580s, during the wars of religion.[418] The English dedication, to Tobie Matthew, prefaced it as a tract for an age inclined to disobedience. The nature of authority and obedience are its subjects from the opening pages. 'A commonwealth is nothing else but a body incorporate of so many private families and so founded and begun by parents.'[419] Good government in the commonwealth began with good order in the home. The father Ayrault interestingly compares to a rider with his bit, spur and switch; it was for his children, as his horse, to obey his direction.[420] Some, Ayrault notes, had raised the question whether obedience were owed to unjust fathers. 'The determination of such questions' he saw as 'exceedingly dangerous' – because of their political repercussions. 'Whether the Bishop of Rome be above or under a General Council, whether the Emperor be above the people . . . whether in religion contrarietie of sects may be tolerated, at first sight [such questions] be set forth with a marvellous fair show, but if you mark them well there is poison served in . . . for upon these and such like other disputes, every day ensue schisms, seditions, civil wars & *this question now in handling* [of obedience to fathers] *is much after the same sort.*'[421] Ayrault concluded that the obligations of parents and children were mutual and that natural bonds could not be broken. 'To take away filial obedience, and duty to parents, is to grab up nature by the root.'[422] He who renounced that obedience 'having begun with his father is like enough to finish it with insurrection against his Prince'; 'farewell all government when parents cannot be obeyed'.[423] In particular, Ayrault denied that differences of religion could break the bonds between father and son. This was not a surprising concern in the France of Henri III, but there was relevance there for England too.

In his *Observations Divine and Morall*, Robinson repeated the denial – in the cases both of families and commonwealths. 'No difference or alteration in Religion how great soever, either dissolves any natural or civil

---

[417] Susan Amussen announced her intention of pursuing them in 'Gender, Family and the Social Order', in A. Fletcher and J. Stevenson eds., *Order and Disorder in Early Modern England* (Cambridge, 1985), 196–217. See now S. Amussen, *An Ordered Society: Gender and Class in Early Modern England* (Oxford and New York, 1988).
[418] P. Ayrault, *A Discourse of Parents Honour* (1614), dedication to Tobie Matthew.
[419] Ibid., 39.   [420] Ibid., 18.   [421] Ibid., 43, 45, my italics; above, p. 73.
[422] Ibid., 156.   [423] Ibid., 45, 157.

bond of society . . . A king, husband, father . . . though a heathen, idolator, atheist or excommunicate, is as well and as much a king, husband or father.'[424] To break the bond with parents was an irreligious act that no sectarian preference could justify. As Ayrault put it, 'do but once prove disobedient to parents, and presently you fall down headlong into atheism'.[425] The threat of religious difference to the politic and domestic family is dispelled by a reassertion of the obedience due naturally to fathers.

As well as parent–child relations, the family is the microcosmic stage of that enduring drama: the relations of the sexes. Once we might have read the many assertions of male authority in early modern England as straightforward descriptions of their world. More recent work, however, has pointed to tensions and strains in gender relations which surfaced in a variety of cultural practices and community actions: skimmingtons, shaming rituals, accusations of witchcraft, carnival inversions.[426] In default of any study, one is tempted to wonder what impact the (acknowledged) success of Queen Elizabeth's reign had on the traditional taboo of female government. What we can say is that questions were being aired and books being published about the position of women in the family and society and that such discussions have significance for the historian of political ideas. C. Newstead's *An Apology for Women* (1620) offers an interesting example, largely because it is far less apologetic than its title suggests. For Newstead argued the natural superiority of women. Their beauty itself, he noted, was a 'prerogative of nature' and displayed their virtues.[427] The temperature of their bodies made them wittier, we might say more intelligent, than men; they were more prudent in the management of household matters, and 'our politic prudence sprung first from oecumenical'.[428] As no element predominated in their bodies so no passions usurped their souls. In consequence they were more faithful and chaster than men because less slave to their appetites. 'It is the greatest conquest, when the body is the chariot, that carries the mind triumphing over its affections.'[429] Women ruled the family, nourishing and educating their offspring. Far from the male standing independent and commanding, 'there is nothing more repugnant to man's nature than solitude'; 'a man is never perfect until he is married'.[430]

---

[424] Robinson, *Observations Divine and Morall*, 48.   [425] Ayrault, *Discourse of Parents Honour*, 157.
[426] Amussen, 'Gender, Family and the Social Order' and D. Underdown, 'The Taming of the Scold: the Enforcement of Patriarchal Authority in Early Modern England', in Fletcher and Stevenson, *Order and Disorder*, 116–36.   [427] Newstead, *An Apology for Women*, 36.
[428] Ibid., 33.   [429] Ibid., 17.   [430] Ibid., 42, 47. I detect no obvious irony in this treatise.

Few went so far in their claims for the natural superiority of women. But even in the more conservative treatises we detect a debate about gender relations which both drew from and in turn contributed to political discourse. The author of *Counsel to the Husband* (1608) declared the broadest political significance in familial relationships: 'there belongeth more to a family than governors, servants, household stuff, and provision: there must be laws and discipline, order and instruction, a watchman and overseers'.[431] Families had been subverted by wives disobeying and husbands ruling badly; disagreement between the husband and wife resulted in confusion. The *Counsel* therefore endeavoured to prescribe the model, natural relationship. Here the husband's predominance is taken for granted and he should not 'give over his sovereignty unto his wife', any more than he would don her apparel.[432] Her place was to take light from him ('as the moon is said from the sun') and to labour for his wealth and credit, in whom her own were subsumed.[433] The woman's subject status, because natural, was no condition of debasement. 'If . . . in a kingdom, or family, there must of necessity be those degrees and that we see men so subject to princes, that they constantly delight therein, and neither count it slavishness . . . should not the wife look unto the hand of God, which made her the wife, and not the husband . . . to govern otherwise, is not to rule but to usurp.'[434] But while the husband was possessed of natural authority he was expected 'to command yet with love'.[435] What then when the reality fell short of this ideal harmony, when the woman withheld obedience or the man ruled not lovingly but 'tyrannously'?[436] In the year after Bate's case when the question of love and obedience between the king and his people had exercised the judges, the *Counsel* expressed a 'wish that it might never grow to question of law between man and wife whose is the duty . . . but for them to strive who should be most careful of each other's good'.[437] If the conduct of family affairs continued to be mishandled, if prayers were not said, the wife might counsel and ask 'for the reformation of those amiss'. Her only course was to persuade 'by warmth and fair means'.[438] 'As there is no striving with a prince because of his power; so there is (*or should be*) no contending with the husband . . . because of that absolute sovereignty which is in his hand.'[439] The greatest reproach to a wife (as James I might

---

[431] B. Sk., *Counsel to the Husband*, 11.
[432] Ibid., 42. Given the frequency and at times ritual accreditation of cross-dressing in early modern England, the fragility of the assertion is clear.   [433] Ibid., 49.
[434] Ibid., 50.   [435] Ibid., 49.   [436] Ibid., 55.   [437] Ibid., 53.
[438] Ibid., 62, 69. The language echoes that of a parliamentary petition.
[439] Ibid., 63. My italics: the parenthetic aside of the original both speaks to a recognition of tensions and a desire to pretend that they do not exist.

have said to a parliament?) was to be 'Solomon's contentious woman'.[440] The virtuous obedient wife, however, 'is a crown to her husband'. Fulfilling her obligations, she obliged her husband to honour his: to 'not disdain to be counselled by his wife'; to love and understand her, 'so to govern that he give not occasion by foolishness to be despised nor by overmuch severity to be hated or feared'.[441] In its recognition of strains and exhortation to mutual love and duty, *Counsel to the Husband* at every point politicizes the relations between husband and wife. That it also so often seems to echo with the language, issues and tensions of Jacobean politics is not least because marriage and love were, like the role of the father, analogues of political life.

Love we like to think of as the most private and personal of matters – perhaps despite evidence to the contrary in our own age. In the seventeenth century love did not describe only personal but also cosmic, spiritual and political relationships.[442] God's act in creating the world was perceived as an act of love. In his *Heavenly Academie*, Francis Rous wrote that 'love itself is a likeness to him who is love'.[443] God, Robinson put it simply in his *Observations Divine and Morall*, 'is love'.[444] Love bound the whole cosmos chain in a network of relationships within and between the corresponding spheres. Lovers who could not join together were indeed 'star-crossed'. In his philosophical enquiry *De Veritate*, Lord Herbert of Cherbury wrote of love as that which mediated between the world of spirit and the material world.[445] It brought man closer to God; love, his poem 'The Idea' shows, might lead to knowledge, liberty, unity and harmony.[446] Recently I have shown how in the Caroline court masques love was the force that led men to virtue, to a perfected nature, to self-government. Herbert's poem, significantly 'Made at Alnwick in his Expedition to Scotland with the Army 1639', was no less political. Love was the unifying element in the cosmos, in families and in kingdoms. As a consequence of the fall, however, love also had become corrupted by appetite and required regulation. Christianity prescribed marriage as the institution through which man's sexual appetite might, instead of casting him down into the bottomless pit of sin, procreate virtue and assist in his regeneration.[447] The marginalia to the Genevan

---

[440] Ibid., 76.   [441] Ibid., 77, 85, 88.

[442] See A. J. Smith, *The Metaphysics of Love* (Cambridge, 1985); Sharpe, *Criticism and Compliment*, ch. 6. See Sharpe, *Politics and Ideas*, ch. 9 and 262–4.

[443] F. Rous, *The Heavenly Academie* (1638), 115.

[444] Robinson, *Observations Divine and Morall*, 204.   [445] Bedford, *Defence of Truth*, 121.

[446] Ibid., 6.

[447] Cf. Herbert, 'the feeling which relates to the perpetuation of the species, so long as it is not infected with unlawful lust or concupiscence, is humane and may spring from the faculty which seeks the general good', Bedford, *Defence of Truth*, 121.

Bible pointed up the Pauline analogy of the married couple to Christ and the church; the Book of Common Prayer described marriage as a condition of paradise and remedy against sin.[448] Marriage was a polity; it regulated lust by its laws. Love and marriage were normative analogues and vocabularies in early modern England and so came naturally in political discourse to men for whom the ideal of government was the replication of God's divine order founded on love. Love expressed harmony and balance; in loving relationships authority and subjection were as one, not in contention; love unified the community. In his *Resolves* Owen Feltham praised the Church of England because it 'constitutes so firm a love among men'.[449] John Doughty, a fellow of Merton College Oxford, exhorted controversialists in the church in 1628 to 'love and unanimity', as the notes of Christians.[450] In a Christian commonwealth, the relation between the monarch and his people had to be founded on love. James I in a speech of 1624, in this as in other respects, saw it as his duty to model himself on God:

it is a very fit similitude for a king and his people to be like a husband and wife, for even as Christ, in whose throne I sit . . . is husband to the Church and the Church is his spouse, so I likewise desire to be your husband and ye should be my spouse; and therefore, as it is the husband's part to cherish his wife, to entreat her kindly, and reconcile himself towards her, and procure her love by all means, so it is my part to do the like to my people.[451]

The king so wed to his people also believed that 'there was such a marriage and union between the prerogative and the law as they cannot possibly be severed'.[452] It is important to appreciate that the political tensions and quarrels of the early Sutart decades did not invalidate this discourse. Sir Thomas Wentworth and John Pym once again spoke a shared language, referring to the 'mutual intelligence of love' between king and people and the 'lust' that depraved the realm if the bonds of law were not upheld.[453] Illustrations of this discourse could be multiplied. It is more important to flip the coin and see that as politicians naturally employed the vocabulary of love and marriage, so the representations of love and marriage offer documents of political ideas.

[448] R. Greaves, *Society and Religion in Elizabethan England* (Minneapolis, 1981), 118; J. E. Booty ed., *The Book of Common Prayer 1559* (Washington DC, 1976), 290–1.
[449] Feltham, *Resolves* (1628 edn), 49.
[450] I. Doughty, *A Discourse Concerning the Abstruseness of Divine Mysteries* (1628), 20.
[451] Kenyon, *Stuart Constitution*, 43. Professor Kenyon did not draw attention to the frequency and importance of this language.
[452] Speech of the Earl of Salisbury reporting James I, 8 March 1610, ibid., 11.
[453] Ibid., 16, 196.

Recently I attempted to explicate the politics of love from the poetry and drama of three Caroline writers. The subject needs broader exploration: not only in Elizabethan and Jacobean plays and poems, but in paintings, sonnets, courtly airs, dance, the etiquette of courtship, wedding ceremonies, divorce cases and so on. Jacobean drama, we know, illustrates political tensions and ideals in plays about love and marriage. In the Lord Mayor's show in London, the mayor was portrayed as the bridegroom of the city.[454] At the level of court, civic and county elites as well as the village community a *political* history of love and marriage would offer invaluable insight into the history of political thought.[455]

The public condition, the politics of the family, of marriage and of love leads us to what we might think of as the last sanctuary of private space: the self, the body. The phrase 'body politic', however, though now emasculated of its analogic force, remains to inform us of an age when the body was not only politicized, but stood as the most familiar of all analogues for the commonweal. The analogue, like that of the family, goes back to pagan, classical times, and to the time of the apostles.[456] But it is in the Renaissance period that the natural, not merely the rhetorical or idealized body, was explicitly analogized to the state, and in that age that the analogy was developed and worked out in detail. As has been well argued, Menenius's comparison of the state and body in *Coriolanus* 'is more than a device of rhetoric; it is a statement of truth'.[457] This analogue of the natural body may tell us much about changing attitudes towards the self and the community: the image realized the multiple forces in man and contained the disparateness of society. It also brought the individual and the polity together. The image was a means of overcoming a metaphysical problem of distance between subject and object.[458] The many treatises entitled 'An Anatomy of . . .' indicate the desire to relate and reduce the universe to human experience. In the political realm the image (like the whole world-view) not only unified a fragile state; it elevated and incorporated the person of the king into that larger body of the commonweal at a time when the monarch as personal overlord was becoming a monarch as ruler of the nation.

The general use of the image in political discourse in Renaissance

---

[454] Daly, 'Cosmic Harmony', 14.

[455] In Burton's *Anatomy of Melancholy*, love is the unifier of families and kingdoms. Significantly Scot (*Philomythie*, sig. C2ᵛ) saw 'The bond of marriage betwixt man and woman; the bond of loyal obedience between subjects and sovereigns' as the knots which the pope sought to cut asunder.

[456] See I Corinthians 12, verses 8–31.   [457] Hale, *Body Politic*, 12.

[458] Cf. Norford, 'Microcosm and Macrocosm'.

England, because it is familiar, need not detain us long.[459] John Pym in 1640 took it for a truism that 'A king and his people make one body: the inferior parts confer nourishment and strength, the superior sense and motion.'[460] Significantly the most detailed working out of the analogy is found in one of the few self-pronouncedly political treatises of the early Stuart years. In his *Comparative Discourse of the Bodies Natural and Politique*, Edward Forset anatomized the king's councillors as the understanding; his favourites as the fantasies; disordered manners as diseases; 'nimble headed pragmatics' as amateur doctors.[461] What it is more important to observe – and a subject still not investigated – is how the image of the body was subject to varying interpretations and adapted according to circumstances.[462] The emphasis on the king as the head and the people as the body was traditional and conservative. But as James Daly pointed out, it left the political counterpart of the soul in a 'dangerously ambiguous position'.[463] Archbishop Laud in a 1628 sermon spoke of the church as the soul which unified the bodies politic and natural and so potentially forged a division between the ecclesiastical and secular power which, had its implications been pursued, would have damaged the Elizabethan world-picture.[464] Pym, as we have seen, more radically claimed that parliament was the soul of the commonwealth.[465]

The metaphor of the king as the head was by no means a justification of absolute authority. The king could no more change the laws of the body politic, George More pointed out in his *Principles for Young Princes*, than the head could alter the sinews on which it depended.[466] In order to rule the body too, the head itself needed to be free of corruption. Again Pym was to claim that it was for parliaments to ensure that 'the intellectual part . . . be kept from distemper', and he was not the first to draw such conclusions from the metaphor of head and body.[467] Buchanan had described the laws as a check on the passions of the king, reminding us that in the head itself reason and appetite contended for government.[468] Ponet and Parsons even foresaw that 'decapitation is a

---

[459] Two full studies are Hale, *Body Politic* and L. Barkan, *Nature's Work of Art: the Human Body as Image of the World* (New Haven, 1975).   [460] Kenyon, *Stuart Constitution*, 192.

[461] Forset, *Comparative Discourse*, 85; Hale, *Body Politic*, 91.

[462] Barkan shows how the analogue was attractive to those who watched the disintegrating polis of the fifth century, *Nature's Work of Art*, 65.

[463] Daly, 'Cosmic Harmony', 16. Forset identified the soul with the sovereign, *Comparative Discourse*, 3.

[464] W. Scott and J. Bliss eds., *The Works of . . . William Laud* (7 vols. in 5, Oxford, 1847–60), I, 151–82, esp. 162–3.   [465] Above, p. 85.   [466] More, *Principles for Young Princes*, 1.

[467] Kenyon, *Stuart Constitution*, 184.   [468] Burns, 'Political Ideas of George Buchanan', 63.

reasonable remedy for a diseased body politic'.[469] Few drew such conclusions in early seventeenth-century England, but the emphasis on the
natural body of which the politic was seen to be the analogue, drew
attention to the frailties as well as authority of the head/king. 'To prescribe a man', Nicholas Coeffeteau wrote, 'that is not moved with any
passion were to deprive him of all humanity.'[470] The king was human
and *ergo* subject to the passions of humanity, for all that as the head he
represented the source of reason. Monarchs then needed to order their
affections and appetites. More's *Principles for Young Princes* shows concern
for the actual body of the ruler in injunctions to the prince to moderate
his diet because 'the body being full of meat corrupteth the judgement
as maketh a man neither fit to . . . govern in a commonwealth'.[471] The
prince should learn to know himself 'and his imperfections'.[472] More
did not explore the consequences if the ruler failed in either that self-
knowledge or self-government which qualified him to rule. But the
acknowledged 'passions', 'imperfections' and possible distempers in the
person of the king sit uncomfortably with the dictum that the king could
do no wrong and open the way for others to question the unreasonable-
ness of royal command. Such tensions are a common subject of
Elizabethan and early Stuart plays – *The Winter's Tale* and *Lear* are two
obvious examples – in which royal passions rob monarchs of the basis of
their authority while leaving them the externals of power.[473] Such plays
still await the full political readings that they invite.

More generally, however, we need to see the political import of any
discussions of the relation of passion and appetite to reason, and so
the politics of attitudes to learning, madness, emotion and zeal.[474]
Contemporary writers readily politicized their mental conditions. Owen
Feltham described his own 'passions and affections' as 'the chief distur-
bers of my civil state: what peace can I expect within me while these
rebels rest unovercome?'[475] Bishop Joseph Hall frankly applied the rules
of civil policy to the mind because, he believed:

Every man hath a kingdom within himself. Reason, as the princess dwells in the
highest and inwardest room; the senses are the Guards and attendants on the
court . . . The supreme faculties (as will, memory etc.) are the Peers; the outward

[469] Hale, *Body Politic*, 81.   [470] N. Coeffeteau, *A Table of Humane Passions* (1621), 67.
[471] More, *Principles for Young Princes*, 44–5.
[472] Ibid., 42; cf. Marcus on Ben Jonson and James I, *Politics of Mirth*, 11, 102, 122–3.
[473] See also Sharpe, *Criticism and Compliment*, 39–44, ch. 2.
[474] Michael McDonald argues that the wife's desire to leave her husband was seen as a psycholog-
    ical disturbance, *Mystical Bedlam: Madness, Anxiety and Healing in Seventeenth Century England*
    (Cambridge, 1981), 98–105, 101.   [475] Feltham, *Resolves* (1623 edn), 48.

parts, and inward affections, are the Commons. Violent passions are as rebels.[476]

The royal condition was also human; the human psychology also political. Once we see this, we may come to see the political significance of changing attitudes to human psychology. In the *Table of Humane Passions*, translated into English in 1621, Nicholas Coeffeteau attempted an analysis of human psychology. Man he saw as motivated by pleasure and pain. Passions he defined as 'a motion of the sensitive appetite caused by the apprehension of good or evil, the which is followed with a change or alteration in the body'. This he regarded as 'contrary to the laws of nature'.[477] Writing two decades later, however, when the laws of nature were less easily equatable with order and reason, Thomas Hobbes was to turn the theory of motion not only into a new mechanistic psychology but into a radically novel political philosophy.

IDEAS, POLITICS AND THE ENGLISH CIVIL WAR

We have viewed the world-picture of early modern England as one might study a court masque. We have examined the philosophy that informed it, the ideals it expressed, the perfect harmony and government it represented. We have, too, detected the antimasque figures and tempests that threatened its ideal images: Machiavels and sectaries, foreign furies and disordered passions at home. At times, it seemed, the tensions might not be contained. But they were. They were fused into and artistically subsumed by the final scenes of calm landscapes, civilized cities, measured dances and royal power in which the cosmic order was framed and represented at Whitehall.

Whitehall, I think, may be the key to intellectual as to political history. Historians rightly viewing the English civil war as an intellectual revolution have – perhaps naturally – searched for its intellectual origins.[478] The search never produced results that quite convinced. They detect those of radical political views like Buchanan or even Fulke Greville; they find ardent Calvinists and presbyterians like Cartwright, providentialists like Raleigh. They point to the emergence of a common law tradition led by Sir Edward Coke, to the novel epistemology heralded by the new science of Francis Bacon. But they never satisfactorily explain

[476] Hall, *Works*, I, 14.
[477] Coeffeteau, *Table of Humane Passions*, 5, 31; hope and despair are differentiated 'by reason of the divers motions they excite', 49.
[478] Most notably, Hill, *Intellectual Origins of the English Revolution*.

how these men and movements for long accommodated – in many cases within the court itself – came in 1642 to turn the world upside down. For all the puritan unease, Sir Edward Coke's quarrel with James I, or Baconian empiricism, the languages and analogues of political debate remained the same: the languages of scripture, of the law, of history and the classics; a discourse of politics in terms (often derived from Aristotle) of the family, of love and marriage, of the body. What we from hindsight see as revolutionary intellectual discoveries did not produce a revolution. Thomas Hobbes evidently became acquainted with the new mechanism in Paris as early as 1630. There is no evidence that it then led him to a new politics.[479]

There is little sign then that in the early seventeenth century new theories or ideas affected the course of politics. The course of politics, however, subjected prevailing ideals and axioms to the greatest strain. Bate's case and the debates over impositions raised uncomfortable doubts about the harmonious relationship between monarchical authority and the law.[480] The demands of war in the 1620s, the courses pursued by king and Council in order to raise, equip, feed and transport troops, revealed and fostered tensions between, on the one hand, individuals and their private property and, on the other, the state and commonweal. The debates in parliament leading to the Petition of Right began to make it clear that the shared language of law and common good could express different meanings and perceptions in practice.[481] And, like the debates over religion, they also demonstrated that there were very different views on how to right what was amiss. A shared sense of what ought to be did not prevent conflict about how to restore an earlier (idealized) harmony and unity. The articulation of such differences, certainly of different emphases, undoubtedly damaged the model of order. What weakened it most was the erosion of the cement that held the world-view together: trust. By 1629 there were some, by 1640 many, who were no longer sure that Charles I could be trusted to rule for the common good. Moreover, events suggested that the traditional antidotes to such a distemper were no longer effective. The decisions in the Five Knights Case

---

[479] Above, p. 85 and cf. p. 48.
[480] See the speeches of Nicholas Fuller, Thomas Hedley, James Whitelocke and William Hakewill, in E. R. Forster ed., *Proceedings in Parliament 1610* (2 vols., New Haven, 1966), II, 152–65; I, 70–97, 221–4; S. R. Gardiner ed., *Parliamentary Debates in 1610* (Camden Soc., 1st ser., 81, 1861), 79–83; F. Hargrave, *A Complete Collection of State Trials* (11 vols., 1776–81), II, 407.
[481] See C. Russell, *Parliaments and English Politics* (Oxford, 1979), ch. 6; J. A. Guy, 'The Origins of the Petition of Right Reconsidered', *Hist. Journ.*, 25 (1982), 289–312; R. Cust, 'The Forced Loan and English Politics' (Ph.D. thesis, London University, 1984).

and the Ship Money Case led many to fear that the law was no longer a safeguard of balance and harmony. Charles's choice of advisers, personal prominence in government, and wilful rule left – as some saw it – the cry for good counsel unanswered. Doubtless in some gentry houses and vestries the question was pondered: what could be done when the king did not do as he ought?

Yet when all this is said, what remains noteworthy is that such realizations and disputes did not before 1642 rewrite the *language* of politics. The debates on the Petition of Right still confirm that heated words, different emphases and attitudes, did not develop into a contest of rival ideologies, of two opposed theories of the commonweal.[482] Speakers still talked of differences between the king and Commons as a marital tiff which could be made up through love, a temporary imbalance which the reason of the law (shared by all) would resettle.[483] They held onto the ideal of one truth, one commonweal; there could be no alternative ideology because there was no moral order, no political life outside it. The solutions to the problems remained traditional. Those who disagreed with the king sought not to remove him but to persuade him, because they could think of no government that was not his. The language and the ideals it expressed survived the confrontations of the 1620s. Even after the personal rule of the 1630s, there were no proponents in 1640 of an alternative parliamentary government. There were those who in practice were prepared to try to compel the king to heed good counsel, but it was good monarchical government, not any opposed model, that they sought. Their values and discourse were traditional. For all the gulf that separated them, it is, as we have seen, remarkable how close is the *language* spoken by Pym and Strafford at the latter's trial for treason in the winter of 1640. There was little sign even in a political crisis of Englishmen drawing on the radical pamphlets of the wars of religion.

Events, however, had brought those foreign experiences much closer to home. For in 1637 a British kingdom had rebelled against the divine order of monarchy. Still more the Scots had justified rising in defence of their religion and liberties and against the institution of episcopacy. Though protesting their loyalty to the king, they drew on Buchanan to justify, in the words of one newswriter, 'what tenets they hold and what

---

[482] Pocock, 'The Commons Debates of 1628'; Judson, *Crisis of the Constitution*, passim. J. Sommerville has argued otherwise (*Politics and Ideology*). See my comments in *Politics and Ideas* 283–8.

[483] C. Russell, 'The Nature of a Parliament in Early Stuart England', in H. Tomlinson ed., *Before the English Civil War* (1983), 123–50, 132.

invasion they would make upon the civil and temporal parts of the king's office'.[484] This is not the place to consider in detail the difficult question of the impact of the Scots' rising on English attitudes.[485] On the one hand, Charles I and several of his courtiers described, at least initially, the Scots trouble in conventional language: of 'factious spirits', of 'disease', of 'a burning fever', in Wentworth's words, 'a war of liberty for their own unbridled inordinate lusts and ambitions'.[486] Others, however, saw a greater ideological challenge in the Scottish rebellion. The French ambassador viewed the pamphlets distributed in England as 'fort dangereux pour cette monarchie'.[487] 'I should believe', an English newsletter concurred, 'the question . . . a king or no king.'[488] The Scottish rebellion, in other words, had shaken the very trunk of the tree of order and some had begun to wonder whether it would stand. A letter allegedly written from the camp at Berwick in the spring of 1639 reported: 'the contempt of religion brings discord and confusion, treadeth virtue under foot, giveth authority unto vice, and soweth quarrels and dissentions amongst men . . . and *in the end open and civil wars*'.[489] The language of the opening phrases is conventional, but the recognition, the fear in the last words, takes us into a new world: a world in which the axe would be laid to the root of the tree.

Drawing upon the radical Calvinist pamphlets of the sixteenth century in order to justify their actions, the Scots were perhaps as important to the intellectual as to the political upheavals of the 1640s. Yet in 1642, in England, king and parliament drifted into civil war, confused at events, not controlling them by the blueprint of an ideological agenda. Each side claimed the authority of the Scriptures and the law; each claimed to defend the unity and harmony of the Christian commonweal against heretics, schismatics and factions. They did not go to war because they articulated fundamentally opposed political ideologies. They went to war because they could not trust each other to maintain what they still believed to be common values and ideals. On both sides the civil war was waged between men who believed passionately that their enemies sought to undermine order and truth, and the law and church that sustained them. Both sides waged a war for defence of the commonweal against schismatics. One might say they fought because

---

[484] John Castle to the Earl of Bridgewater, Huntington Library, Ellesmere MS 7824.
[485] The subject is thoroughly treated in Peter Donald's Cambridge thesis, above n. 119.
[486] Huntington Lib., Hastings MS 1349; Ellesmere MS 7828, *Hist. Mss. Comm. Cowper*, II, 227.
[487] PRO 31/3/71, f. 23, dispatch of 3 March 1639.
[488] Bodl. MS Tanner 67, f. 53.   [489] Bodl. MS Rawlinson B210, f. 16, my italics.

they could not accommodate difference to their world-view.[490] The shared languages and absolutes they continued to express had for long held their world together; now they obstructed a political settlement that might have saved it. For a settlement in 1642 would have required the *recognition* of difference and contest and a politics that could incorporate them. And, in the words of Brian Tierney, 'none of the conceptual apparatus available – neither the language of mixed constitution, nor of corporation law (nor indeed of classical republicanism) provided a solution for the problem of conflict'.[491] Events outran ideas; new political crises could not be contained within the frame of order, but the old picture was still the only pattern men could make of the world. Even after the fact of war, they tried for some time to restore it, to touch it up here and there, but leave it intact.

The civil war, however, fractured the Elizabethan world-picture – and irreparably. In itself the war, especially when it proved to be more than a temporary outburst of passion, shattered the ideas of wholeness and harmony. The commonweal as one community was no more.[492] The Commonwealth that emerged in the 1640s bore no relation to the old ideal – beyond perhaps the desire to appropriate a value-laden term. It was a body now without a head, the government too of a (minority) party. After the Restoration, the term 'Commonwealthsman' described a hardline republican Whig, and was often employed as a term of abuse.[493] The very word that had summed up a whole world and shared ideology had become the label of a faction and of, by 1660, discredited tenets.

With the demise of the commonweal, a world of interlocking values fell too. As armies marched through the countryside, billeted on homes, evicted MPs from the Commons and seized, then executed, the king, it was impossible to sustain an ideal of harmony and increasingly hard to think of government and obedience as reciprocally founded on duty and obligation. Naked power backed by the force of arms became visibly divorced from authority, from its divine, metaphysical and moral base. Men began to speak less of duties than of rights, less of the common

---

[490] Malcolm Smuts makes the point that the perception of politics as a world of contending passions waging a struggle against public interest 'led individuals on both sides of any serious issue to place the worst possible construction on the motives and designs of their opponents', *Court Culture*, 275.   [491] Tierney, *Religion, Law and the Growth of Constitutional Thought*, 98.

[492] D. W. Hanson, *From Kingdom to Commonwealth: the Development of Civic Consciousness in English Political Thought* (Cambridge, Mass., 1970), ch. 10.

[493] See Sharpe and Zwicker, *Politics of Discourse*, 5.

good than the preservation and advancement of their own interest.[494] Laws were seen now to be at the mercy of the sword. Writers like Henry Parker saw the inadequacy of the common law language and traditions to deal with these circumstances. Hobbes claimed that the political situation led him to abandon other projects to write *De Cive*. When he sat down later to write *Leviathan*, Hobbes had to confront what was now a clear and novel problem: the need to reconcile power and interest, the need to find a means of overriding the conflicting interests of citizens who might not believe in God or any natural order or authority.[495]

Hobbes's state was a *Leviathan*, a monster, an 'artificial' creature. The civil war robbed the state of its foundation in nature. As the chain that linked the heavens, the commonweal and the natural world was broken, the state, civil society, had to be justified; it could not longer be assumed. Hence arose the fundamental questions concerning why men should subject themselves to government, what rights they had and could or should surrender, what limits there were to authority. Because he was forced to answer questions that would have been, quite literally, unnatural to his predecessors, Hobbes wrote the first work of political philosophy in England;[496] thereafter it was difficult to write about political life in any other way. With the state now detached from its natural origins, politics had to find its own moral codes – or accept that it had none.

The conflict not only shattered the unity of the commonweal, it cast its shared languages into the arena of contest. The Bible, the language of the Scriptures, was anarchically appropriated by every sect or individual who claimed divine inspiration. The readers made their own texts of scripture now to overturn the authority it had once supported – and not only the authority of the government and church. Women priests, advocates of free love, fanatics, Quakers and fifth monarchists overturned the order of gender, morality, temporality and rationality as they had been known.[497] As for the texts and languages of histories and the classics, the religious radicals rejected them for revelation; the Levellers claimed history itself had been a yoke, making bondsmen of men who

---

[494] Tuck, 'Power and Authority'; Hanson, *From Kingdom to Commonwealth*; J. W. A. Gunn, *Politics and the Public Interest in the Seventeenth Century* (1969).

[495] D. Wootton ed., *Divine Right and Democracy* (Harmondsworth, 1986), 61.

[496] Hampsher-Monk writes of Pocock's belief that 'Political theorizing emerges from ordinary political discourse in times of crisis' ('Political Languages in Time', 105). But it is not clear from his discussion *how* this occurs, and it seems more likely that Hobbes was driven by experience to depart from rather than develop the paradigms of ordinary political discourse. Cf. D. Johnston, *The Rhetoric of Leviathan: Thomas Hobbes and the Politics of Cultural Transformation* (Princeton, 1986).   [497] Hill, *The World Turned Upside Down*.

had rights not by precedent but naturally by being men.[498] Intellectual radicals dethroned Aristotle and planned new curricula for universities and colleges.[499] The authorizing texts and languages of early modern England were appropriated, deconstructed or simply destroyed.

With the destruction of the idea of cosmic order and the languages through which it had been articulated, the whole nature of discourse was revolutionized. The metaphysical conceit which spoke across the correspondences gave way to the plain prose that spoke to only one discursive territory.[500] The need to address a broader audience in the 1640s and 1650s, the people, led the most poetic of imaginations to prose, and the more prosaic to plain simplicity. The visual symbols of a world-view – in churches, paintings, statues, masques – fell prey to iconoclastic fury.[501] The king's art collection was dispersed, and the Commonwealth and Protectorate regimes displayed some discomfort with any visual mode of representation.[502]

The final destruction of the world-view took place, of course, in 1649, on the scaffold at Whitehall. On 30 January 1649, it was not only Charles Stuart who met his end: the father of the politic family was executed; the keystone of the arch collapsed; the head of the body was decapitated; the light of the Sun of the commonweal was extinguished. At the sight of the severed head, the watching crowd was said to have uttered a deep groan. Pregnant women, on hearing the news, miscarried.[503] Analogically this was the end of the family, of civil society, of nature, of the cosmos itself. And yet, for all the confusion, for all the world turned upside down, the heavens did not fall, the beasts did not overcome man. By the 1650s there was even some order in the realm. England was governed without a king – and even humiliated her ancient rivals the Dutch.

---

[498] Hill, 'Norman Yoke'; cf. Overton's claim: 'whatever our forefathers were or whatever they did or suffered, . . . we are the men of the present age and ought to be absolutely free from all kinds of exorbitancies, molestations or arbitrary powers'. *A Remonstrance of Many Thousand Citizens*, in W. Haller ed., *Tracts on Liberty in the Puritan Revolution* (3 vols., New York, 1934), III, 354–5.

[499] See H. R. Trevor-Roper, 'Three Foreigners: the Philosophers of the Puritan Revolution', in *Religion, the Reformation and Social Change* (1967), 237–93.

[500] See Carey, 'Sixteenth and Seventeenth Century Prose'. In his preface to *Troilus* Dryden said of Shakespeare that many of his 'words, and more of his phrases are scarce intelligible . . . and his whole style is so pestered with figurative expressions, that it is as affected as it is obscure' (cited in W. Griswold, *Renaissance Revivals* (Chicago, 1986), 116). The comment aptly summarizes the revolution in style.   [501] See A. L. Rowse, *Reflections on the Puritan Revolution* (1986).

[502] An important observation here is made by Professor Underdown: 'The republic's reliance on verbal means of establishing its legitimacy . . . reflects the characteristic puritan preference for rational discourse over pictorial modes of communication.' *Revel, Riot and Rebellion*, 257. This is a subject that awaits a full discussion. See below ch. 7.

[503] Hill, *Intellectual Origins of the English Revolution*, 5.

The pieces remained and even co-existed, even when everything which (as it had been believed) held them together had collapsed. If 1642 showed their coherence was not certain or natural, the 1650s suggested, radically, that it was not necessary.

After 1660, most of the old political and social order was brought back. At first sight we might be tempted to think that the old intellectual order came with it, that the old world-picture was dusted off and restored. Some believed that, or at least acted as if, it was. Charles II referred to his crown as 'that right which *God* and *Nature* hath made our *due*' (my italics);[504] Clarendon referred to the restored House of Lords as the 'Great Council' of the realm.[505] The languages of law, custom, history and scripture became again Pocock's accredited and institutionalized vocabularies. Yet though the idiom persisted, the contest for and partisan deployment of these normative languages had made inroads into the community of belief from which they had drawn their authority. The changes were profound. Even in the Declaration of Breda, Charles II himself had offered religious toleration to presbyterians. There was to be no one religious truth. Those who denied them toleration did so not in the name of unity, but from the interests of a section – what would soon be called a party.[506] The Declaration even offered a pardon to rebels – as though their treason against a king could be separated from their sin which only God could forgive. The office of monarch was restored by a political (and military) act; the monarch was granted an annual revenue for peacetime government; by the 1670s some spoke of transferring the office to another not the successor to the throne; in 1688 they did so. The army's 1648 claim that authority resided in the office 'and but ministerially in the person'[507] was aired in the rhetoric of Exclusion, and again in 1688. The pursuit of interest overshadowed the old bonds of obligation and loyalty; even the king and the court felt the need to build an interest through a direct exchange of pension and place for service and co-operation in the Commons. Though it was to be some time before the language of contract widely permeated the discourse of politics, relations had indeed become contractual (the abolition of feudal tenures is significant)[508] – even

[504] Kenyon, *Stuart Constitution*, 331.   [505] Ibid., 421.

[506] Bedford points out that where nonconformists had before been prosecuted in the name of truth, by Locke's day the concern was with good order, *Defence of Truth*, 231. For remarks on the intellectual importance of the accommodation of party see Sharpe and Zwicker, *Politics of Discourse*, 7.   [507] Kenyon, *Stuart Constitution*, 264.

[508] This has been underestimated. The end of feudal tenures marks a crucial shift from personal monarchy to the king as a public figure, governing a nation.

between ruler and ruled. Society and government recoalesced not around the normative foundations of an organic community and divine order, but around the coincident interests of individuals who elected to enter into relationships with each other, but who yet retained an identity outside of the community. John Locke offers us the best verbal exposition of these changes which had taken place, but they are evident too in a myriad of cultural practices and mores: the emergence of politics as a self-conscious pursuit, the rise of party, the separation of morality from sin, the developed idea of privacy, perhaps the acknowledgement, with all its profound consequences, of the autonomous self.[509]

These profound changes were not sudden, or obvious. The survival of old vocabularies makes them difficult to date.[510] Men were still loath to credit parties with more dignity than the name of factions; the old terminology of 'court' and 'country' co-existed with the new party labels.[511] But at times now one senses an archaism, a strategic conservatism in their usage and deployment. The old languages and texts were no longer universally normative but appropriated to serve a particular cause. By the end of the century, Charles Schmitt observed, reference to the authority of Aristotle was *reactionary*: 'scholastic philosophy had an ideological rather than an intellectual role to play'.[512] Scriptural politics having been shown to open the door to all confusion, the language of the Bible less often informed political discourse. The classics lost their force as the texts of moral philosophy to be consciously imitated by the 'Augustans' who aped the style of a civilization which they saw to be quite different from their own.[513] Slowly the study of history induced a sense of anachronism and relativism, little developed in England since its faint beginnings in the philological enquiries of the Elizabethan antiquaries.[514] Along with the ideology of order, its authoritative texts and languages, the analogues and correspondences fade too.[515] There are

[509] See M. McKeon, 'Politics of Discourses and the Rise of the Aesthetic in Seventeenth-Century England', in Sharpe and Zwicker, *Politics of Discourse*, 35–51; McKeon, *The Origins of the English Novel, 1600–1740* (1987) and J. Bender, *Imagining the Penitentiary: Fiction and the Architecture of Mind in Eighteenth-Century England* (Chicago, 1987). I am grateful to John Bender for stimulating discussions at Stanford in 1986.
[510] S. L. Bethell argued that 1660 is still 'the best date to choose as a dividing line' (*Cultural Revolution*, 12). I would suggest that 1649 marks the crucial divide.
[511] D. Hayton, 'The Country Interest and the Party System 1689–c. 1720', in C. Jones ed., *Party and Management in Parliament 1660–1784* (Leicester, 1984), 37–79.
[512] Schmitt, *Aristotle*, 107.   [513] Cf. the remark of T. Greene, above, p. 90.
[514] Just as it took the Reformation for the medieval church to be seen in historical perspective, so the civil war induced a sense of anachronism and change in secular as well as religious affairs.
[515] Cf. Walzer, 'Once those images and analogues had been called into question, it was not impossible, but it was increasingly difficult to think the old thoughts', 'On the Role of Symbolism', 193–4.

fewer references to the king as father of his people; and in society the family becomes more private.[516] The world of nature was no longer an analogue for virtue and government: Bernard de Mandeville's *Fable of the Bees* posited a society built on natural vice, prosperity and self-interest.[517] As for the body politic, the phrase lived on as a metaphor shorn of its literalism as ideas of interest and contract invalidated it.[518] With the collapse of such analogues and correspondences, literary styles and reputations were overturned. Pope and the Augustans appear not to have greatly valued metaphysical poetry, perhaps because the metaphysical conceit, the encapsulating of a world, a cosmos, in a microcosm, had passed;[519] some have even suggested that what we delineate as reason and feeling had become separated.[520] In its place there was a new literary genre which arose from the gradual acknowledgement of the autonomous self, as well as from a world in which the aesthetic had found its own space – the novel.[521]

One cannot place a year-date on ideological and cultural changes such as these. It 'took a long time for the interconnections and cross-references to disappear from the corpus of human learning'.[522] But if we accept that, for all that, we are by the end of the seventeenth century in a new intellectual world, the best date to pick in order to understand that profound shift is 1649. And 1649 must lead us to conclude that whilst the new political history will be the poorer if ideas are left out, the intellectual history of early modern England must – still more than it has been – be also a political history.

---

[516] Amussen, 'Gender, Family and the Social Order'.
[517] B. Mandeville, *The Fable of the Bees* (1714).   [518] Hale, *Body Politic*, 8.
[519] I am grateful to A. J. Smith for discussions on this subject; cf. above, n. 442 and Sharpe, *Politics and Ideas*, 264.
[520] Bethell, *Cultural Revolution*, 115. Cf. T. S. Eliot, 'The Metaphysical Poets', in *Selected Essays* (1969), 281–301. This argument now appears too simplistic, but the suggestion pays careful consideration. See also Sharpe, *Politics and Ideas*, 263–4.
[521] See the works by Michael McKeon cited in n. 509.
[522] Bethell, *Cultural Revolution*, 12.

PART TWO

Texts and power

CHAPTER THREE

The king's writ: royal authors and royal authority in early modern England

In recent years literary and cultural critics have made us more aware of the inextricable interrelationship of discourse and power. Speaking, writing, discursive performances, they have shown, not only reflect social arrangements and structures of authority; they are themselves acts of authority. It is no coincidence that some of the most stimulating research in this field has been in the literature and politics of the Renaissance state.[1] For in Tudor England, the power of the crown and state depended largely upon its representation of authority. The monarch had no standing army or independent bureaucracy to enforce his will; both the co-operation of the political nation and the obedience of the lower orders rested more on a culture and ideology of order than on physical coercion. Images of royal power, palaces and pictures, coins and seals, festival and procession shaped that culture of authority and obedience which sustained the state. Most of all in the first century of printing, the royal word, through letters, proclamations and speeches, conveyed the king's power to the corners of the realm. During the sixteenth century in England, both the revival of interest in the classics and the growth of Protestantism emphasized the importance of the word – both as rhetoric and as signification. Words and names, Plato and Aristotle had argued, expressed the essential nature of animals and objects; language, theologians maintained, was the key to divine truths; to Protestant reformers such as John Bale, the word offered unmediated access to divinity.[2]

During the Tudor century, as we know, monarchs increasingly

---

[1] M. Foucault, *Power/Knowledge*, ed. C. Gordon (New York, 1980); D. Macdonnell, *Theories of Discourse* (Oxford, 1986); G. Kress and R. Hodge, *Language as Ideology* (1979), esp. ch. 4; J. G. A. Pocock, *Politics, Language and Time* (New York, 1971); S. Greenblatt ed., *The Forms of Power and the Power of Forms in the Renaissance* (Norman, Okla., 1982).

[2] On the increasing importance of the word, E. Eisenstein, *The Printing Press as an Agent of Change* (Cambridge, 1980); cf. D. Katz, 'The Language of Adam in Seventeenth Century England', in H. Lloyd-Jones, V. Pearl and B. Worden eds., *History and Imagination* (1981), 132–46.

claimed that they ruled as God's lieutenants on earth, that is they represented his divine justice, reason and will in the commonweal. Like God, the monarch through his word bestowed grace or anger and decreed life and death. In Shakespeare's *Richard II*, Bolingbroke, commenting on his sentence of banishment, compares the power of royal with divine discourse:

> How long a time lies in one little word!
> Four lagging winters and four wanton springs
> End in a word: such is the breath of kings.[3]

As Richard II himself makes poignantly clear, the king's very power lay in the authority of his word.[4] And in the Tudor state as on the Tudor stage the monarch claimed authority over other voices and discourses: publication depended on royal licence; parliamentary debate was bounded by royal definition of 'free speech'; condemned traitors had, as their last act, to read what was almost an official script damning themselves and praising royal rule. The king spoke; good subjects, like good wives and children in early modern England's patriarchal society, listened but were not heard.[5]

Ironically, however, the very developments that led to the predominance of the word in the exercise of political authority also sowed the seeds of challenge to a monopoly or control of discourse, hence to power. First, rhetoric, ideally a device for the communication of truths, could become a mode of deception. Machiavelli counselled the prince to deploy language as a tool of self-interest, ambition and power untrammelled by moral norms; and others, as Shakespeare's Richard III reminds us, were to follow his advice.[6] Secondly the rise of Protestantism and religious division led to different interpretations of the Bible. Because the Holy Scripture was also a treatise for government such different interpretations fractured a common discourse of state into rival languages of power. By the end of the sixteenth century, radically in the Netherlands, France and Scotland, more quietly but no less significantly in England, the Calvinists turned God's word into a subversive political discourse.[7]

Faced with these threats to shared ideological vocabularies, monarchs

---

[3] *Richard II*, Act I, scene iii, lines 213–15.

[4] Ibid., Act IV, scene i. Cf. *Henry V*, Act I, scene i, lines 36ff. for a comparison of Henry's discourse with his authority.

[5] S. W. Hull, *Chaste, Silent and Obedient: English Books for Women 1475–1640* (San Marino, 1982); A. Fraser, *Weaker Vessel: Woman's Lot in Seventeenth Century England* (1984).

[6] Machiavelli, *The Prince*, ed. Q. Skinner (Cambridge, 1988), 61–3; *Richard III*, Act III, scene vii, lines 141–74. [7] Cf. M. Walzer, *The Revolution of the Saints* (Cambridge, Mass., 1965).

endeavoured in the new circumstances they confronted to re-establish their authority by a reassertion of their interpretative power over rival voices. James I's patronage of a new authorized version of the Bible – the King James Bible – was as much an act of power as of piety: an official translation proscribed the Geneva Bible and sought to define the parameters of hermeneutic freedom opened by the translation of the Scriptures.[8] But monarchs did more: by the force of their own words they attempted to reclaim, appropriate and re-authorize the discourses and metaphors that had validated royal authority. Royal speeches and writings – exegeses of scripture, translations of classics, epic poems – endeavouring to contest and contain challenges to order and sovereignty, were acts of government and power. Royal authorings, we might say, had become central to the sustenance of royal authority.

As a woman Elizabeth's allotted role was one of silence. Yet as a queen she is famous for her skilful oratory and familiar speech. Not least through her skill with words, Elizabeth turned the disadvantages of her sex into a powerful claim to sovereignty. Little attention, however, has been paid to the queen's writings – as self-presentation and as representation of monarchy. Yet from youth to old age Elizabeth wrote, translated and published a variety of works which invite analysis as texts of power. Elizabeth's volumes of devotions and prayers may be read as private and personal meditations, but their language and address is also directed to public and political concerns. Elizabeth's language is strongly gendered and erotic. The soul's deliverance from sin she compares to that of the birth of a child from the womb; she prays 'o most meek father . . . thou untie and loose me'. Such language places Elizabeth's prayers within the conventions of medieval Catholic female piety and, at a time when it was desirable to carve a path between religious extremes, there may be significance in that. More generally, the queen's metaphors and her language are often directly political. Having taken God as her husband, she will 'keep but one household with Him'; God's 'sovereignty sounds as a major note throughout the devotions'.[9] Elizabeth politicizes the Christian struggle for faith. Sin she describes in her prayers as an internal insurrection needing to be quelled if she were to rule her own

---

[8] The epistle dedicatory is politically explicit, speaking of the need to tread between 'popish persons and self-conceited brethren who run their own ways'.

[9] Elizabeth I, *A Godly Medytary on the Christian Soule* (1548), ff. 15–17, 19–19ᵛ, 21ᵛ, 22ᵛ, 24, 25ᵛ, 26ᵛ–27, and passim; Elizabeth I, *The Mirror of the Sinful Soul*, ed. P. W. Ames (1897), 12, 15, 23–5, 31, 43, 63; *Christian Prayers and Meditations* (1569), sigs. cii, ki; BL MS facs. 218; W. P. Haugaard, 'Elizabeth Tudor's *Book of Devotions*: a Neglected Clue to the Queen's Life and Character', *The Sixteenth Century Journal*, 12 (1981), 79–105, 83.

person: 'I would subdue all evil affections but they daily rebel and rise against me and will not be subject unto my spirit.'[10] Only when subject to God did she feel free, 'the prerogative of a free mind always minding heavenly things'.[11] Elizabeth's prayers echo with the language used of kings: God was a 'perfect physician', as the prince was to the common-weal; she prayed he would incline to her 'petitions', the medium of sub-jects' address to monarchs; she hoped her people might become 'heavenly citizens'.[12] As her subjects looked to her as queen, so she told God in her Latin prayers of 1563, 'Tu es ipse Rex meus.'[13] Elizabeth's prayers were undoubtedly her personal plea for God's grace and counsel. But published in 1563, 1569 and 1571, as well as circulated in manuscript, they were also public texts.[14] Indeed the texts of the queen's personal subjection to God became a validation of her public claim (contentious in the eyes of Catholics) to be His chosen ruler. Her per-sonal prayers enabled Elizabeth to appropriate the ideal of the good prince, one who made 'thy people my crown, . . . thy service my govern-ment, . . . thy gospel my kingdom'.[15] Moreover the prayers, more than self-guidance, became admonitions to all governors: 'This the Lord commandeth', she prayed, 'keep equity and righteousness, deliver the oppressed from the power of the violent . . . and shed no innocent blood in this place.'[16] Significantly Elizabeth's books of devotions reveal no narrow denominational preferences: they are Christian rather than obviously Protestant. Writing in Latin, French, Italian and Spanish as well as English, the queen established her own universality, her learning and her capacity to discern God's will.[17] God's words, she once wrote, 'are oftentimes mystical/And are not rightly understood by all'.[18] In her prayers Elizabeth interpreted and mediated God's word for her subjects. In the contentious decades of the 1560s, when many were vying to deter-

---

[10] *The Queenes Prayers* (1571), sig. D3v; cf. sig. C4ᵛ.   [11] Ibid., sig. B.

[12] *Christian Prayers and Meditations* (1569), sigs. Fiii, Kiii, Niv, piiᵛ–iii. This compilation, known as 'Queen Elizabeth's prayerbook' (see sigs. Kiiii, piiᵛ), is published with the queen's arms at the front and back and a frontispiece woodcut of Elizabeth at prayer. It underlines the ambiguity of 'authoring' and 'authorizing' in sixteenth-century usage. I shall explore this in a fuller study of royal texts.   [13] *Precationes Private Regiae* (1563).

[14] Haugaard makes too little of this, 'Elizabeth Tudor's *Book of Devotions*', 80–1.

[15] BL MS facs. 218 f. 34v. The 1569 *Christian Prayers* contains a section of 'Certain Sentences taken out of Promises, Admonitions and Counsels to good kings . . .'.

[16] *Christian Prayers*, sig. Ee iiᵛ.

[17] Haugaard, 'Elizabeth Tudor's *Book of Devotions*', 92; *Christian Prayers*, sigs. Gg i–ii; Elizabeth uses the familiar 'tu' when discoursing with God.

[18] *The Argument Against Transubstantiation with Queen Elizabeth's Opinion Concerning the Erroneous Doctrine* (1735), 30. Haugaard refers to the queen's 'priestly function', p. 103.

mine the nature of worship, the queen's interpretations were very much acts of authority too.[19]

As well as scripture, the classics were validating texts in a Tudor society that looked to Greece and Rome as the pinnacle of civilization. Interestingly, during the 1590s, Elizabeth took time from the business and cares of government to translate Boethius's *Consolation of Philosophy*, Plutarch's essay *On Curiosity* and Horace's *On the Art of Poetry* – both in prose and in verse. The translations were done quickly, are by no means exact and may not have been completed.[20] Though they were not printed in the queen's lifetime it is not clear whether they were intended for publication: a copy is found in State Papers.[21] Nor is the motive for writing obvious: translation was a common pedagogic exercise in which Elizabeth had been well schooled, but her age dispels any such explanation and the dictation of the works to a clerk of the signet suggests more public import. If, as has been argued, Elizabeth 'chose to translate those things which were most central to her own thoughts', we need to ponder which contemporary concerns her 1590s translations addressed.[22]

Boethius's *Consolation* was a moral dialogue arguing the victory of philosophy over fate. Boethius, banished and awaiting death, laments his condition, having ruled wisely, protected the poor and followed his conscience. He fears all is governed by chance. Philosophy (a female figure) reassures him that the world is 'ruled by divine reason' and urges him to adhere to 'conscience truth'.[23] It is difficult not to read Elizabeth's choice of subject and translation as a form of confession and search for reassurance. The 1590s were a difficult decade for the queen in which literally and politically the glamour faded from her regime. Through a reabsorption of Boethius in her own words perhaps Elizabeth (who in youth took 'Semper Eadem' as her motto) reassured herself of the continuance of reason and order in a volatile world. But the translation was more than just a personal document. The presentation of a female figure who triumphed over 'outward and mean matters' might itself have reinforced Elizabeth's authority.[24] More generally the *Consolation* proclaims the

---

[19] The prayers begin the process of constructing Elizabeth and her people as God's chosen. *Christian Prayers*, sigs. Kiiii, Kkiv, Ggi. See *Queen Elizabeth's Opinion Concerning Transubstantiation* (1688).

[20] C. Pemberton ed., *Queen Elizabeth's Englishings* (1899), introduction, esp. viii–xiii, 140, 149. *De Curiositate* is in Elizabeth's own hand.

[21] PRO SP Elizabeth 289; Pemberton, *Queen Elizabeth's Englishings*, 101, 141, 149.

[22] Pemberton finds it hard to explain how a busy queen found time for these translations (p. xii). See A. Somerset, *Elizabeth I* (1991), 12.   [23] Pemberton, *Queen Elizabeth's Englishings*, 18, 53.

[24] Ibid., 32.

divine origin of all order and its necessity for human existence. All, Philosophy tells Boethius, partake of a unity framed by the creator; but it was a fragile unity: 'everything shall last while it is one, but when it leaves that order it perisheth'.[25] Men, she continues, consist of lust and appetite but also enjoy reason. The virtuous, those in whom reason rules, work for 'the common end of all things'. Breaking God's order was not freedom; rather those that upset order 'are vexed with slaying affections which increasing . . . they heap that bondage to themselves . . . and are . . . captivated by their own liberty'.[26] The thrust of the *Consolation*, we can see, was a reinforcement of the organic concept of the state. 'Let persuasion of sweet rhetoric', Philosophy urged Boethius, 'assist thee' to reaffirm faith in divine reason.[27] Against rival discourses, Elizabeth too reasserted the ideology of order.

Perhaps we may also discern in the translation a more particular address. One of the mounting threats to the idea of the commonweal as a replication of divine order came from the puritans whose theology of predestination and an invisible church of the elect fractured the community of church and state.[28] Certainly Boethius is at odds with puritan and Calvinist tenets at several points. The argument that 'nature hath ingraft in men's mind desire of truest good' suggests a rejection of Calvinist emphasis on the condition of fallen man.[29] Predestination is specifically countered: 'there is no liberty in man's counsels nor acts which God's mind . . . constrains to one end'; 'there remains a sure liberty of will to mortal folkes' – a liberty to come to knowledge of God's reason.[30] If these sound rather like ideas that Hooker was to develop into a philosophy of church and state, therein may be the point. Boethius's *Consolation* offered a counter to the Calvinists' radical separation of grace and nature, as to other challenges to order. 'What place can there be left for rash men', Philosophy asks, 'where God in all order keepeth.'[31]

During the 1590s, Elizabeth also translated in her own hand Plutarch's *De Curiositate*, one of the essays in which he explored types of virtue and vice and the nature of a moral being. *De Curiositate* denounces those who seek to criticize the deficiencies of others, collect gossip and pry – even into courts. Such are directed to self-examination, self-regulation and real learning rather than idle tattle. Curiosity is categorized as one of the senses that dethrone reason in man. Elizabeth renders Plutarch's admonition that 'no man ought permit his sence abrode to range':

[25] Ibid., 66.   [26] Ibid., 79, 104.   [27] Ibid., 20.   [28] See above, pp. 70–4.
[29] Pemberton, *Queen Elizabeth's Englishings*, 44; cf. 96.   [30] Ibid., 107, 120.
[31] Ibid., 102.

> And than againe in thy selfe with reasone make abodd
> and ther abide not strayinge out of office charg.[32]

That use of 'office' seems to politicize the moral counsel into advice for citizenship. Again, though it has been said that Elizabeth translated the piece for her private exercise, the tone suggests address to others as much as self address. During the 1590s, growing disenchantment with the regime was expressed in satires, newsletters and topical 'opposition' plays.[33] Plutarch's essay, not least in its specific injunction to shun the theatre, offers a reply.[34] More generally Plutarch, whose essays were held as a model for the 'heroically moral man', associated virtue with self-regulation, the ruler with reason. He also expounded the argument 'that the philosopher should converse especially with princes'.[35] In her translation, Elizabeth, demonstrating her own learning and acquaintance with philosophy, reclaimed natural authority. And she reaffirmed what was increasingly becoming a polemical position whilst seeming to remain above the polemical exchange. A royal translation that could rebut the assault of Tacitean satire and 'classical republicanism' was an act of power indeed.

Elizabeth self-consciously took up the interrelationship of discourse and government in the last of her translations, her englishing of Horace's *De Arte Poetica*, which she wrote in 1598. In one of the most important works of classical and Renaissance critical theory, Horace, following Aristotle, expounded the relationship of good writing to wisdom and virtue. The purpose of poetry, he maintained, was moral: 'the giving of pleasure with some useful precepts for life'.[36] Because the poet possessed a didactic power to direct men, so his deployment of language was a social responsibility that he must never forget:

> Nor eloquence shal he want nor ordar cleare
> For Grace and Vertu shall he place, or forbeare.[37]

Horace went so far as to associate the power of words with that of armies, in determining victory or defeat:

> If speakars wordz unfit their fate,
> The army all with skorne will them deride.[38]

---

[32] Ibid., 136, 140–1. Elizabeth read Cicero's *De Officiis* in prison at Woodstock: Haugaard, 'Elizabeth Tudor's *Book of Devotions*', 88.   [33] See A. Kernan, *The Cankered Muse* (New Haven, 1959).

[34] Pemberton, *Queen Elizabeth's Englishings*, 137.

[35] *Encyclopaedia Britannica* (1973), XVIII, 70.

[36] Horace, *On the Art of Poetry*, in T. S. Dorsch, *Classical Literary Criticism* (Harmondsworth, 1965), 90–1.   [37] Pemberton, *Queen Elizabeth's Englishings*, 143.   [38] Ibid., 146.

The right order of words could represent the natural order – 'let all things be as sorteth best their place' – and, by representing, reinforce it. It may be that at the time of factional strife, economic hardship and disaffection, Elizabeth hoped that the *De Arte Poetica* could revitalize a belief in natural order, that, as she translated him, Horace could 'with new shewe the hiden yore expound'.[39]

Certainly the queen had an acute sense of the importance of her own word in the exercise of her rule. In a letter to James VI, she once reminded him of Isocrates' counsel to his emperor that royal words were the 'ensigns' of royal authority – badges or banners around which a ruler might gather force to counter rival or antagonistic ideologies and discourses.[40] Similarly in a speech to Cambridge University in 1564 the queen recalled an axiom of Demosthenes which she paraphrased: 'the words of superiors have the weight of books with inferiors; and the sayings of princes retain the authority of laws with their subjects'.[41] Elizabeth's neglected writings, her devotional works and translations, no less than her famous speeches, were themselves acts of command and organs of government.

II

Elizabeth's successor, James VI and I, was probably the most literate and learned king to have occupied the English throne: a monarch who not only read all the classical texts of statecraft, but one who believed the schoolmaster's life closest to that of kingship. Moreover, James possessed 'an indomitable faith in the significance of the printed word'.[42] He commissioned a new history of his mother's reign in Scotland because he knew the ideological power of such representations; he dictated 'every word' of proclamations because he believed that control of their language was vital to their authority.[43] So great was his trust in words that, James himself jested, his chancellor had had to remind him that 'my house could not be kept upon epigrams; long discourses and fair tales will never repair my estate'.[44] James's verbosity was more than a vain desire to parade his learning, more too than an understanding of the

---

[39] Ibid., 144–5.
[40] J. Nichols, *The Progresses and Public Processions of Queen Elizabeth* (3 vols., 1823), II, 627.
[41] Ibid., I, 177.   [42] T. A. Birrell, *English Monarchs and Their Books* (1986), 30.
[43] H. R. Trevor-Roper, *Queen Elizabeth's First Historian: William Camden and the Beginnings of English 'Civil History'* (1971); W. Notestein, F. H. Relf and H. Simpson eds., *Commons Debates 1621* (7 vols., New Haven, 1935), IV, 71.
[44] J. O. Halliwell ed., *Letters of the Kings of England* (2 vols., 1848), II, 146–7.

force of rhetoric. 'One of the maynes for which God hath advanced me upon the lofty stage of the supreme throne', he wrote, 'is that my words uttered from so eminent a place . . . might with greater facility be conceived.'[45] If the King of Scotland spoke and wrote much it was because by doing so he fulfilled the first duty of a ruler: serving God.

Historians are familiar with what their editor C. H. McIlwain collected as James's *Political Works*: his speeches and addresses, *Apology for the Oath of Allegiance*, most of all his *Trew Law of Free Monarchies* and *Basilikon Doron*, his advice book to his son. The last, written originally in Middle Scots, was an attempt to counter the contractual theories of government advocated by Buchanan and John Knox, theories which had justified the deposition of his mother in 1567. But there is more to these works than polemical exchanges. In the *Trew Law*, James glossed the familiar metaphor of the king as head and the subjects as members to argue: 'As the *discourse and direction* flows from the head and the execution thereunto belongs to the rest of the members . . . so it is betwixt a wise prince and his people.'[46] It was because discourse and direction were so interdependent to him that James advised his son of the importance of his words which 'will remain as true pictures of your mind'.[47] The *Basilikon Doron*, written when James believed himself to be on his deathbed, was the king's own last 'testament' and his (as the title means) 'royal gift' of word to his son.

While there is much to be said about the *Trew Law* and *Basilikon Doron*, it is more important to appreciate that all James's writings were penned as acts of government, not only in the sense of a polemical response to challenges, but in the broader didactic sense: as attempts to lead men to God's reason and goodness through royal representation of His divine truths. The preface to James's published *Workes* of 1616 makes the point clear. Bishop Montagu, James's editor, acknowledged that some might think it fitter for kings to wield a pike than a pen. But God, the King of Kings, became the word and his chosen Moses, David, and Solomon wrote to lead men to understanding. Similarly, he claimed, 'we have seen with our own eyes the operation of his Majesty's works in the consciences of . . . men so far as . . . there have been [those] that have been converted by them'.[48] In the frontispiece to the volume James stands beside a table on which is placed a book bearing the title *Verbum Dei*;

---

[45] C. H. McIlwain ed., *The Political Works of James I* (Cambridge, Mass., 1918), 169.
[46] Ibid., 65 (emphasis mine).
[47] J. Craigie ed., *The Basilikon Doron of King James VI* (2 vols., Scottish Text Soc., Edinburgh, 1944–50), I, 184. [48] *The Workes of the Most High and Mighty Prince James* (1616), preface.

beneath the picture a caption announces: 'Knowledge makes the king most like his Maker.' 'God hath given us a Solomon', Montagu explained, and beneath the king's picture the Lord spoke as he did to Solomon: 'Ecce do tibi animum sapientem et intelligentem.' It was God's divine understanding that James was offering through his *Workes*.

The first of James's writings in the volume is his *Paraphrase Upon the Book of Revelation*. In what is essentially a commentary, James melds his own reading with the biblical text itself to turn exegesis into his own interpretation and world-view. As he decodes the figurations he points out how 'the popedom is meant by the pale horse in the fourth seal', how Rome is the false monarchy.[49] There is admonition perhaps to puritans as well as Catholics in the passage the king rendered 'I have reserved the secret power of election and reprobation only to myself.'[50] In his closing remarks, James warned others against imposing their own opinion upon scripture. For himself he presented not an interpretation of Revelation but a mediation of God's word; and so he joins his own words with St John's: 'and [God] said unto me write and leave in record what thou hast seen'.[51] Montagu drew attention to Revelation, the book of the last things, in his preface: 'Kings', he pointed out, 'have a kind of interest in that book beyond any other'; and James, he added, possessed an understanding beyond the measure of men. When we consider how Revelation had been (and was soon again to be) a primary text of revolution, we begin to grasp how great was that royal 'interest' and how important was an authorized royal reading of its ambiguities and opacities.

In his Meditation upon chapters of the first book of 'the Chronicles of the Kings' James was explicit about the politics of his reading. He desired that 'these meditations of mine may after my death remain to . . . posterity as a certain testament of my upright and honest meaning'.[52] The king reflected on King David's first act after victory, his moving the ark of the Covenant to his house, 'whereof', he observed and advertised, 'we may learn first that the chief virtue which should be in a Christian prince . . . is a fervency and constant zeal to promote the glory of God'.[53] James invites the reader into his private meditation on scripture to witness that the realm was blessed with a godly ruler. More particularly he again explores the text to see 'how pertinently this . . . doth appertain to us and our present estate'.[54] James compares the biblical elders to the burgesses of parliament and notes in a description that is also prescrip-

---

[49] Ibid., 19.   [50] Ibid., 11.   [51] Ibid., 65.   [52] Ibid., 81.   [53] Ibid., 82.   [54] Ibid., 87.

tion: 'that a godly king finds as his heart wisheth, godly estates concurring with him'.[55] In passing he is even able to find a passage describing the dancing of David to show his puritan subjects that 'dancing, playing and such like actions . . . are of themselves indifferent'.[56] Exegesis of scripture once again becomes royal command. Indeed James's *Meditation Upon the . . . XXVII Chapter of St Matthew* became a treatise on the office of kingship dedicated to Prince Charles. Interpreting the mock coronation of Christ with thorns, he reaffirms his sense of duty to God and his people, but also reminds his people as well as the prince that kings received their crowns from God only and were 'mixtae personae', partaking of His divinity as well as humanity. A passing jibe at 'foolish superstitious puritans' who refused to kneel connects nonconformity to broader challenges to authority, in a work which transforms private meditation into a powerful revalidation of divine monarchy.[57]

James's *Meditation Upon the Lords Prayer* was written in 1619, the title page announces, 'for the benefit of all his subjects especially of such as follow the court'. The Lord's Prayer, of course, was a fundamental text for all Christians. James skilfully appropriates it to validate his vision of the Church of England and to exclude those, especially the puritans, who did not accept his vision. 'Trust not', he urges, 'to that private spirit or Holy Ghost which our Puritans glory in for then a little fiery zeal will make thee turn separatist.'[58] Against the threat of separatism, James reasserts the Hookerian axiom: 'everyone of us is a member of a body of a church that is compacted of many members'. As for puritans who rejected the visible church – 'to the woods and caves they must go like outlaws and rebels, to their sermons and divine exercises".[59] The passage 'and lead us not into temptation' leads James to a theological ruling in what was becoming an increasingly contentious issue. Arminians, he observed, would not like the passage because it stressed God's will. But, he added, 'we are also to eschew the other extremity of some puritans who by consequent make God author of sin'. For, 'He doth force none to fall from Him.'[60] James turns the Lord's Prayer into a diatribe against the puritans and a defence of the true visible church as it then was, he claimed, in his kingdom.

That James's exegeses of biblical texts found no place in McIlwain's edition of his political works may be revealing. For though they are

[55] Ibid., 83.   [56] Ibid., 86.
[57] James I, *A Meditation Upon the . . . XXVII Chapter of St Matthew* (1620), 12, 35–6, and passim. Cf. below, ch. 4.   [58] James I, *A Meditation Upon the Lords Prayer* (1619), 18.
[59] Ibid., 14, 22.   [60] Ibid., 116–19.

deeply politicized and partisan texts they claim a space above polemical exchange; they announce themselves as meditations on, rather than interpretations of, scripture. James states it to be his duty 'to defend all those who profess the same faith'.[61] But it was also a necessary support to his rule, which is why he was led to intervene in the theological debate in the Netherlands sparked by the writings of Conrad Vorstius. Vorstius disputed 'the sacred and ineffable essence of God' and so, in the words of James's tract included in his English *Workes*, was a 'sworn enemy not only to divinity but even to all philosophy both human and natural denying God to be actus purus but having some kind of diversity or multiplicity in himself, yea even the beginnings of a mutability'. Diversity, multiplicity and mutability were in early modern Europe political as well as theological heresies. When James against Vorstius reasserted that 'God is unity and verity is one', he revalidated the premise on which all order and government was founded. Not surprisingly he also went to pains to denounce as an Anabaptist heresy Vorstius's argument that none could exercise authority over others in spiritual matters. For against his domestic 'precisians' who 'out of self will and fancy refuse to conform themselves to the orders of our church', no less than Vorstius, he declaimed it 'unlawful' to speak of the mysteries of God other than as the church prescribed.[62] The power and mystery of his lieutenant on earth depended upon it.

James VI and I's poetry has received no historical and little critical evaluation. Evidence of revision, however, suggests that the king may have intended a complementary volume of poetical works after his prose works of 1616. Certainly he returned actively to writing poetry which he had been famous for in Scotland, especially during the 1580s. Like his religious writings, James's poems, though often personal and meditative in tone, are permeated with the language and experience of power, difference and contest. Like them, too, they seek through discourse to shape the reader's moral vision to accord with the king's observation and will. One of James's earliest poetic enterprises was his verse translation of the Psalms. As with his other prose exegeses, James mediates scripture through royal discourse and melds the king's words with those of King David and the King of Kings to whom he sang. The Psalms read as counsel to the self as well as other rulers, as James writes how 'cruel and bloodthirsty tyrants' are 'cursed' and how good kings are just, open to petition and 'serve the lord with fear'. But translating, as the title puts it,

---

[61] *Workes of Prince James*, 361.   [62] Ibid., 365, 368, 371–2.

the 'Psalmes of His Majesty', James also presents himself as that good king who heeds God's counsel and speaks with Him:

> nou knou I godd preserves his oinctid king
> & from his holy Heavinns doth heare him well.[63]

The king 'does firmly put his trust in Jehovah' and becomes one with him. It is probably no coincidence that James began his Psalms during the 1580s when he sought to restore the prestige of Scottish kingship against the challenges of the presbyterians and contract theorists who forged, not least from scripture, an ideology for rebellion.

Such circumstances also underlay James's major poetic enterprise of the decade, his verse translation of *The Furies*, which he rushed into print in 1591, describing its author – the 'divine' Du Bartas – as a mirror for the age.[64] *The Furies* tells the story of the fall of man and the collapse of natural order. When Adam sinned he not only cast the harmony of God's created universe into chaos and contest, he surrendered command over his own world.

> Man, in rebelling thus against
> The soveraigne great, I say,
> Doth feele his subjects all enarm'd
> Against him everie way.[65]

Even the animals formed 'rebellious bands' against man. Wolves, leopards and bears

> Most jealous of the right divine
> Against their head conspire.[66]

War ensued. And within the microcosm of man the Fall dethroned reason, leaving 'the king of beasts . . . of himselfe . . . not the maister now'. As passions rose against reason, so good government gave way to 'false contracts', 'unlawful measures' and 'oppressors'.[67] As with Elizabeth's *Boethius*, in his translation of *The Furies* (a text, he claimed, 'quite transformed by me'), James associates royal authority with divine order and the subject's constitutional health.[68] In a fallen world the only hope lay with those who were 'Dame Nature's counsellors and the Almighty's agents ay'.[69] Godly kings were the Almighty's lieutenants and divine poets like Du Bartas were Nature's counsellors. Uniquely the poet/king might help reverse the Fall; meanwhile he associated with that first damnable rebellion of man all who contested with authority.

[63] J. Craigie (ed.), *The Poems of James VI of Scotland* (2 vols., Scottish Text Soc., Edinburgh, 1955–8), II, 11, 34. [64] *The Furies*, ibid., I, 98. [65] Ibid., I, 126. [66] Ibid., I, 134.
[67] Ibid., I, 184, 190. [68] Ibid., I, 194. [69] Ibid., I, 176.

The subject of James's own original epic poem of the 1580s seems at first a surprising one. His *Lepanto* celebrates the famous Spanish victory over the Turk in 1571; and James himself acknowledged that some (especially the hotter sort of Protestants) might think it inappropriate for him to praise a 'foreign popish bastard'.[70] Throughout, however, in its references to election and the certainty of salvation, the poem is Protestantized. But more interestingly in its representation of 'Christians' (James carefully avoids denominational tags) united against a common enemy, the poem gestures to an ecumenical hope for a reunified *respublica Christiana* which James cherished throughout his life. Not only perhaps a plea for ecumenism, the epic is also a cry for community. In passages reminiscent of Virgil (whom he invokes in his preface), in which the king vividly compares the preparations for the crusade with the labour of bees in the hive, there is a powerful, classical and Christian, evocation of and injunction to community. And in lines that are both polemical and admonitory, the devil's attempts to sow discord in the ranks are associated with all disobedience, indeed with individualism. At Lepanto such disaster was averted by strong and able leaders who formed 'voluntaires of conscience' – the pun is surely significant – into one co-operative force:

> Yet did the wisdomes of the Chiefes
> And of the generall most
> Compound all quarrels and debates
> That were into that Host
> Preferring wisely as they ought
> The honor of the Lord,
> Unto their owne, the publicke cause
> To private mens discord.[71]

James's *Lepanto* did not only celebrate a battle; it portrayed an ideal Christian commonwealth, in which virtuous rulers led all to subordinate their private conscience to the good of the community.

When James resumed writing poetry – in England after 1616 – his verse was more overtly partisan and polemical. When, in 1618, a comet raised fear of some impending doom, not least the possible success of the unpopular marriage negotiations with Spain, James sharply condemned the dangerous conjectures of gossips and puritans. 'To guess at God Almighty's mind', he snapped, was not the prerogative of subjects; the king might discern 'treason in him whose fancy overrules his

---

[70] *The Lepanto of James the Sixth*, ibid., I, 198.   [71] Ibid., I, 218.

Reason'.[72] In 1622, fascinatingly, James penned a mocking poem commanding nobles to leave London, in the hope that verse might disperse them whom 'scarce a Proclamation can expel'.[73] Most extraordinarily James replied in mock doggerel to the 'raylinge rhymes and vaunting verse' which lampooned the Spanish match. In their own language he reminds his critics:

> God above men kings inspires
> Hold you the publique beaten way
> Wonder at kings and them obey.[74]

The obvious question to which these outbursts give rise is why James responded to attacks in verse. While they reiterate the themes of the need for reason and order in the human and political constitution, these poems can scarcely claim to stand over the polemical fray like his earlier Scottish epics. Yet evidently James believed in the power of poetry to make his case – at the popular level as in more learned lines. In the case of his most famous political testament, the *Basilikon Doron*, the 'argument of the book' is distilled in a prefatory poem. With Sir Philip Sidney, James believed that poetry might 'lift up the mind' of fallen man to an understanding of God's natural order.[75] 'A breath divine', he wrote, 'in Poets brests does blowe':

> Wherethrough all things inferiour in degrie
> As vassals unto them doe hommage showe.[76]

The political language associates poetry with government. Like kings, poets were God's lieutenants, trusted with raising men to virtue through representation of perfect nature. Poets were 'Nature's trunchmen, heavens interprets trewe'.[77] In other words verse, like James's exegeses of scripture, mediated God's divine order and reason. And so in turn, the king became also a poet, in Ben Jonson's carefully chosen words of flattery, the 'best of Poets' as the 'best of kings'.[78] James himself conjoined royal and poetic authority in his *Urania*, through the familiar metaphor of the seal which authorized letters and documents:

---

[72] Ibid., II, 172.   [73] Ibid., II, 179–82.

[74] 'King James His Verses Made Upon a Libell . . .', ibid., II, 182–91.

[75] P. Sidney, *An Apology for Poetry*, ed. G. Shepherd (Manchester, 1973), 104; James wrote an epitaph on Sidney, *Poems of James VI*, II, 104. The Scottish tradition of the 'flyting' may help explain James's decision to contest in verse. I would like to thank Greg Walker for this point.

[76] Craigie, *Poems of James VI*, II, 68.

[77] James VI, *The Essayes of a Prentise in the Divine Art of Poesie*, ed. E. Arber (1869), 29.

[78] I. Donaldson ed., *Ben Jonson Poems* (Oxford, 1985), 223.

For as into the wax the seals imprent
Is lyke a seal, right so the Poet gent
Doeth grave so vive in us his passions strange,
As makes the reader halfe in author change
For verses force is sic that softly slydes
Throw secret poris and in our sences bydes
As makes them have both good and eville imprented
Which by the learned works is represented.[79]

But if poetry were to fulfil its responsibility, like government it required
– as Horace had appreciated – manuals, rules and law, so James therefore wrote, along with his political advice books, a *Short Treatise Containing
some Reulis and Cauteles to be Observed and Eschewed in Scottis Poetrie*. 'If Nature
be chief', he explained their purpose, 'reulis will be an help and staff to
Nature.' Poets' words, he urged, should literally 'vividly represent', their
epithets describe 'the natural of every thing'.[80]

In the *Basilikon Doron*, James had counselled his son to make his own
example an exemplary text: 'let your own life be a law book'.[81] In his writings he hoped that text would wield authority. Like Elizabeth's, James's
writings, through representation and self-presentation, attempt to
reaffirm and re-authorize paradigms that sustained his divine right; and
to control the arena of interpretation and discourse. Just as the Authorized
King James Bible and his exegeses of scripture claimed contested texts for
the crown, so royal poetry, with its echoes of Virgil and Horace, Cicero
and Sidney, appropriated an ambiguous classical tradition, which some
deployed to defend republics, for the monarchy. There was more than flattery in the epistle dedicatory to James's *Essayes of a Prentise in the Divine Art
of Poesie*: 'Caesar's workes shall justly Caesar crowne.'[82]

III

After the death of Prince Henry in 1612, James bequeathed to Prince
Charles his royal words: the *Basilikon Doron*, the 1616 *Workes* and the meditation on St Matthew's Gospel. In a painting of the late Jacobean
period, Charles is depicted as the 'inheritor of the royal word'.[83] Charles,
however, unlike his father, presented himself as a man of silence. It did
not, the new king told his first parliament in 1625, 'stand with my nature

---

[79] James VI, *Essayes of a Prentise*, 31.   [80] Ibid., 54–6, 63–4.
[81] Craigie, *Basilikon Doron*, I, 104.   [82] James VI, *Essayes of a Prentise*, p. 9.
[83] *Workes of Prince James*, dedication to Prince Charles; James I, *Meditation Upon St Matthew*, dedication. J. Goldberg, *James I and the Politics of Literature* (Baltimore and London, 1983), 94.

to spend much time in words'; he was often to repeat the statement.[84] Charles's silence is traditionally attributed to a speech defect that caused him to stutter. But there is plentiful evidence that he was capable of eloquence; moreover such an impediment does not explain his disinclination to *write*. Clearly, as I have argued elsewhere, Charles was aesthetically more inclined to visual culture, but visual and verbal were not necessarily antagonistic media and the Caroline court continued to be a rich ambience for poetry and drama.[85] Charles in fact was neither uninterested in words nor as silent as is sometimes believed. As prince and king he read widely – in Tasso and Spenser and Donne, in Sandys, Bacon, Erasmus, Dallington, Beaumont and Fletcher and Harington. Interestingly he read and carefully annotated Aristotle's *On Rhetoric*, Bacon's *Advancement of Learning* and Shakespeare's *Works*.[86] And he often painstakingly corrected and amended drafts of letters that went out in his name, spending hours alone with papers in his study.[87] Indeed Charles began to edit his father's poetry and penned occasional verse of his own, composed volumes of prayers, gathered all his papers for the two-volume edition of his works which appeared in 1662, and most probably substantially wrote the famous *Eikon Basilike*.[88] But if Charles's reputation for taciturnity is in part a misconception, it is one the king himself fostered. And the fact remains that the bulk of his writing comes from later in his reign, especially the period after 1640. What we need to understand is that in Charles's case the chronology of both silence and speech/writing is significant in his discourse of power.

During the early part of his reign, Charles spoke and published regularly whilst claiming his aversion to both. The business of war, he told his parliament, 'needeth no narrative'. 'Three of the best rhetoricians', he added, 'Honour, Opportunity and Safety plead for expedition.' In 1628 he desperately urged, 'the times are now for action, action I say not words'.[89] To Charles the obligation of his people to support the monarch in war was not an argument that needed to be made, but a truism that ought to be self-evident. To accept the need to persuade men to do their duty would be to acknowledge that there was no commonweal. The reluctance and brevity of the royal word were themselves an ideological articulation: the reaffirmation of an ideal that was not sustained by his

---

[84] *The Workes of Charles I* (2 vols., 1662), I, 357, 377; K. Sharpe, *The Personal Rule of Charles I* (New Haven and London, 1992), 179–80. [85] Above, pp. 94–5.
[86] M. Pickel, *Charles I as Patron of Poetry and Drama* (1936), 20–2. I have seen the Aristotle and Shakespeare in the Royal Library. [87] Sharpe, *Personal Rule*, 198–205.
[88] Pickel, *Charles I*, 14, 177–8; BL Add. MS 24195. [89] *Workes of Charles I*, I, 357, 361, 365.

political experience. We can sense Charles's uncomfortable negotiation with this problem in the declarations he issued after the dissolutions of unsuccessful parliaments. The king, Charles explained introducing the first of these in 1626, owed no account to any but God. Yet he felt the need to justify himself to the world and reply to criticism. Ideally, he continued, kings could remain silent, their virtue and sense of duty being their best rhetoricians, but some had doubted the monarch. Charles could not, however, accept, and certainly not articulate, that this signalled fundamental divisions in the body politic. Sincerely therefore he concluded that his parliament no less than himself had been 'abused by the violent and ill-advised passions of a few members', that 'the common incendiaries of Christendom have subtly . . . caused these divisions'.[90] The explanation reinforced the ideal of an organic Christian society challenged only by Satan, and so marginalized dissent as disease or evil. The conceit was continued and developed in 1628 and 1629. Protesting again his freedom from the need to give an account to his subjects, Charles presented himself 'in the truth and sincerity of our actions', that having 'laid down the truth and clearness of our proceedings', all 'wise and discreet men' could know their duty.[91] In these declarations, Charles literally endeavoured to write away a political world of interest, difference and contest and rescript a validating ideology of order. When his last parliament in 1629 failed to act their part, the king silenced their discordant discourse. In a lengthy declaration explaining the dissolution, Charles presented a selective and personal narrative – of all that had been plotted since his succession by 'envenomed spirits which troubled . . . the blessed harmony between us and our subjects'.[92] It was literally the last word on the matter, for the accompanying proclamation banned even discussion of future parliaments.[93] But it was, as we shall see, by no means the last time that Charles deployed the partisan narrative as a genre that claimed a space above political polemic.

It is the period of Charles's personal rule in which the king most deserves his reputation for silence. The parliament doors were closed; there were fewer proclamations; reforms of the court, church and administration were enacted without long declarations or justifications; the decade was characterized more by the visual representation of the king on Van Dyck's canvases than by verbal exchange. Charles did write and publish volumes of prayers in which he presented himself as the

---

[90] *Bibliotheca Regia* (1659), part II, 355ff.   [91] Ibid., 385.   [92] Ibid., 394–417.
[93] J. F. Larkin ed., *Stuart Royal Proclamations II: Royal Proclamations of King Charles I 1625–46* (Oxford, 1983), 226–8.

conscience of the nation, praying that each of his subjects 'would be a magistrate unto himself and his whole family'.[94] But in the court masques to which he devoted so much attention, the king remained silent. The debates of antimasque were eclipsed by his very appearance as the embodiment of reason, love, harmony and order. Masques, like Van Dyck's paintings, depicted royal authority as 'natural', needing no gloss or spokesman. Yet it is consummate artifice of technique and stage machinery that secures that 'naturalism', and seeks to re-present it to the observer. The king's animated silence is central to the ideology of that representation: a belief that a natural ruler 'need not speak but simply be'.[95]

It is significant that Charles's most virulent critics, the radical puritans, charged his government with censorship. For while there was no effective control of literary production, there was a larger truth to their claims: the king had triumphed over *debate*. And it is revealing that when the king encountered opposition from his Scottish subjects from 1637, the conflict that ensued was as much a propaganda war as a military campaign. From the beginning the Covenanters published and disseminated thousands of pamphlets denigrating the government. Charles was forced to break his silence. And in his proclamation denouncing their 'seditious practices', he listed the 'multitude of their printed pamphlets' as the first of the Scots' 'traitorous' acts. A breach of his control of discourse, he went on to explain, was a decisive challenge to his authority:

they have now assumed to themselves Regal power; for whereas the Print is the kings in all kingdoms these seditious men have taken upon them to print what they please though we forbid it, and to prohibit what they dislike, though we command it; and with the greater affront have forbid and dismissed the Printer whom we established.[96]

Proclamations ordered English subjects to read no pamphlets sent from Scotland. But Charles could no longer rely on silence, and he announced a 'large Declaration coming forth containing all the particular passages which have occurred in this business'. The *Large Declaration*, published in 1639, broke the royal silence in a truly massive way. In its pages, Charles took up the narrative on the grand scale as a device of polemical control.[97] The Prayer Book rebellion ended the authority of silence in

---

[94] Charles I, *A Form of Common Prayer* (1625, 1636).
[95] P. Thomas, 'Charles I. The Tragedy of Absolutism', in A. G. Dickens ed., *The Courts of Europe 1400–1800* (1977), 195. [96] Larkin, *Proclamations*, 662–7, 664.
[97] [W. Balcanquall], *A Large Declaration Concerning the Late Tumults in Scotland* (Edinburgh, 1639).

Caroline England and instigated a new politics of discourse in which power depended upon the articulation of the royal voice.

For some time Charles sought to deny the new circumstances and retreat from verbal engagement. In his Declaration to his loving subjects published in 1641, he expressed himself 'sorry . . . there should be such a necessity of publishing so many particulars'.[98] Even in his answer to parliament's message concerning control of the militia, he held to the belief that 'it is below the high and royal dignity (wherein God hath placed us) . . . to trouble ourself with answering those many scandalous seditious pamphlets and printed papers'. Now, however, circumstances necessitated he 'take more pains this way by our own pen than ever king hath done'.[99] In his declaration of 12 August 1642, Charles graphically linked the drift to arms with contested discourse. To sustain the truth and expose the pretences of his enemies, he was, he wrote, now 'enforced to use a dialect rougher and different from what we have used to treat in'.[100]

During the 1640s, with others now claiming divine support or natural right, Charles perforce became a rhetorician, a writer, in some ways a politician. He spoke frequently and issued a large number of declarations skilfully directed to their audience. His published volumes of prayers now cohered in communal worship a party rather than a nation. 'Deliver me', the king paraphrased the Psalms of David, 'from the hand of mine enemies.' Like Absalom and the conspirators of Korah, the Roundheads 'smite down thy people oh Lord'. After Edgehill Charles published a prayer of thanksgiving for the 'God of Hosts who goest forth with our armies'. Royal victories taught the enemies of the Lord 'that to take up arms against thy vice gerent is to fight against heaven'.[101]

Charles needed to appropriate the texts of scripture and the law because even during civil war these remained validating vocabularies for any legitimate rule. But in the king's case his authority depended on their being not partisan but unifying ideologies, the 'common inheritance', as he put it to the freeholders of York, of king *and* people.[102] Charles therefore continued in his speeches and declarations to use the language of unity and community. The monarch was, he said, the father of the realm, the head of the body politic. Although there was 'a great misunderstanding betwixt the head and the body', 'these ruptures may yet

---

[98] *Workes of Charles I*, II, 73.
[99] *His Majesty's Answer to a Declaration of Both Houses, 5 May 1642* (E148/13), 1–2.
[100] *Workes of Charles I*, II, 134.
[101] *A Form of Common Prayer Appointed by His Majesty* (Oxford, 1643), 3, 13–14; *A Collection of Prayers . . . used in His Majesty's Chapel and His Armies* (1643), 3–4 and passim.
[102] *His Majesty's Declaration to Ministers and Freeholders of the County of York, 3 June 1643* (E149/27).

in good time be made up'.[103] Once again the king attributed the troubles to 'an unquiet spirit' that infected the realm.[104] Charles used such language because he could not be seen to head only a party. But he used it also because (like many) he continued to believe in unitary principles and truths that were above politics and narrow interest – even his own. And he considered himself bound by conscience to uphold those principles whatever the short-term disadvantages. On occasions during the 1640s, most famously in sacrificing Strafford, the king was persuaded to put expediency first. Increasingly however, he came to believe that 'the obligation of mine oath' was a principal 'point of conscience' and that a monarch could not, for any immediate political benefit, recede from promises even when they had 'been obtained by force'.[105] During the last years of his life, Charles carefully translated into English and revised Bishop Sanderson's *De Juramento*, in which promises were described as a 'bond' not only to men but 'of divine natural law'.[106] If he were to reauthorize the divine laws that were the foundation of the commonweal, the king's words had to stand, uncompromised, above polemic and politics.

Accordingly after 1646 Charles again abandoned the war of words and began to construct himself as a martyr to higher truths, fulfilling the offices of a Christian and a king. At his trial, he would not debate, speaking only of his trust from God. On the scaffold, Christ-like, asking forgiveness for his enemies, he claimed to eschew partisan rhetoric: 'I have delivered my conscience.'[107]

On 30 January 1649 Charles returned to silence. But from the silence of the grave he bequeathed his most famous discourse and most powerful act of authority: the *Eikon Basilike*, the '*portraiture* of his Majesty', which went through thirty-five editions within a year of the king's death. Surprisingly it has received little critical analysis.[108] What I wish to argue is the genius of the text in fulfilling what Charles had struggled to attain throughout the 1640s and even before: answering every charge or challenge whilst positioning the royal author above the polemical fray. That success lay as much in its literary as its political strategy, in the authority of its writing as much as its discourse on authority.

---

[103] *His Majesty's Last Speech to . . . Privy Council* (1642) (E83/44), 4, 7; *A Joyful Message* (1642) (E109/1), 3.
[104] *His Majesty's Speech to the Gentlemen of Yorkshire, 4 August 1642* (E109/26), 1–2.
[105] C. Petrie ed., *The Letters, Speeches and Proclamations of King Charles I* (1935), 166; *Workes of Charles I*, I, 246.
[106] R. Sanderson, *De Juramento . . . Revised and approved under his Majesty's hand* (1655).
[107] *Workes of Charles I*, I, 430–5, 455.
[108] For bibliographical analysis see F. F. Madan, *A New Bibliography of the Eikon Basilike* (Oxford, 1950).

The *Eikon* opens with a narrative commencing with the calling of the Long Parliament and continues through chapters on Strafford's death, the Triennial Act, the king's departure from Westminster and the raising of armies. It then goes back to the Covenant and Irish rebellion. Like Charles's earlier accounts of his 1620s parliaments, this was a narrative very much under the king's control and written from his perspective. Throughout the narrative is inscribed not with the third person 'his Majesty' but the authorial I, its repetition underlining the personal control of events and their representation. The *Eikon* presents the king, as Charles always had, traditionally, as the head of an organic body politic. Where his enemies acted from 'the partialities of private wills and passions', he stood for 'Reason and public concernments', a reason which mediated 'the divinest power'.[109] And that reason, for the good of all, curbed the passions which threatened the constitution both of a Christian commonweal and of man. 'Condemn us not', the king prayed for all his people, 'to our passions which are destructive both of *ourselves* and others.'[110] Far from being the interest of a party, royal authority was presented as the interest of each and all. Central to its organic conception was the reiterated argument for one church and law. Differences in religion, the *Eikon* argues, could not remove 'the community of relations, either to parents or princes'. Without mention of them by name, the saints' call for an invisible church of the godly is silenced. Threats to the law, Charles claimed, came not from him (in 'preserving laws . . . my interest lies more than any man's') but those who 'look more to present advantages than their consciences'.[111]

Such claims were made by many in the pamphlets of the 1640s. The power of the *Eikon Basilike* comes from its self-presentation as a text of conscience and its condemnation of rhetoric and politics. Where politicians 'wrap up their designs' in pretences, the king prayed, 'o never suffer me for any reason of state to go against my reason of conscience'. When others hid behind verbal artistry, 'I am content . . . my heart . . . should be discovered to the world without any of those dresses or popular captations which some men use in their speeches.'[112] In the pages of the *Eikon*, the king becomes what Elizabeth in her devotions and James in his exegeses of scripture had claimed to be: not the rhetorician but the direct mediator of God's word and will.

Indeed, like James's paraphrases of Revelation or St Matthew's Gospel, the *Eikon Basilike* is a meditation on scripture in which skilfully

---

[109] *Eikon Basilike* (1876 edn), 32, 114.   [110] Ibid., 141.   [111] Ibid., 23, 106, 187.
[112] Ibid., 10, 88, 157.

the king's own words meld with holy writ, and his conscience blends with God's will. At the end of each section, the king turns, as if in one of his earlier books of devotions, from his earthly reader to prayer to his God, as though through the king's words, like a priest's mediation, the subject came closer to the Lord. When we review the structure of the text we begin to read the narrative passages, framed by the prayers, as sermons in a text for a service conducted by a king who in the *Eikon* expressed his belief that 'both offices regal and sacerdotal might well become the same person'.[113] The frontispiece, almost like the proscenium arch to the masque, frames the reading: looking to a heavenly crown, Charles kneels with a crown of thorns in his hand before an altar on which an open book bears the text 'in verbo tuo spes mea' (see Figure 10, p. 215). In the king's words too, it would claim, lay the hope and salvation of all men.

The responses to the *Eikon Basilike* offer eloquent testimony to its political/rhetorical power. The questioning of Charles's authorship (which began as soon as the *Eikon* was published) and royalist counterarguments for its 'authenticity' underline the mutual associations of text and authority. Milton took up his pen immediately, sensing the *Eikon*'s polemical capacity to 'catch the worthless approbation of an inconstant, irrational and image-doting rabble'.[114] Writing at far greater length than the *Eikon Basilike*, Milton painstakingly contests all its claims, replacing them into the arena of verbal contest above which its author had succeeded in elevating them. Most interestingly he also recognized that to challenge the arguments or assertions of the text was not enough; in *Eikonoklastes*, Milton was forced to critique the *Eikon Basilike* as text: as a work of literature and authorial performance. 'I began', he wrote in his preface, 'to think that the whole book might be intended [as] a peece of poetry' and it was the aesthetic power of the text, its aestheticization of the king's (to him) contentious claims, that Milton felt most need to undermine. Accordingly he derided its verbosity and metaphor, mocked its form and genre, and questioned the originality of its composition – pointing to prayers stolen from Sir Philip Sidney and Shakespeare.[115] Making the aesthetic into an accusation led Milton, as Steven Zwicker has recently argued, into some uncomfortable positions.[116] Yet he had no choice. The

---

[113] Ibid., 174.
[114] J. Milton, *Eikonoklastes*, ed. W. H. Haller in *The Works of John Milton* v (New York, 1932), 309. See too *Eikon Basilike*, ed. P. A. Knachel (Ithaca, N.Y., 1966), introduction.
[115] Ibid., 84–9, 125; cf. 162.
[116] S. Zwicker, *Lines of Authority: Politics and English Literary Culture, 1649–1689* (Ithaca, 1993). I am grateful to Steve Zwicker for a chance to read this brilliant book in typescript.

power of the *Eikon Basilike* lay in its literary properties as much as its politics: the two were one. To challenge its authority Milton had to undermine it as authorship – both as the king's words and as a piece of mere poetry. For all his skill he failed. With more editions over the next decade, the *Eikon* ensured that the king's writ ran current throughout the realm. It was Charles I's most authoritative performance.

About the time of the publication of the *Eikon Basilike*, in exile in Paris, Thomas Hobbes was attempting to devise a philosophical justification for the state and defence of sovereign power in circumstances in which the naturalness of the commonwealth and authority could no longer be assumed. Language Hobbes saw as central to his problem and purpose. For in the state of war each man called 'good' or 'bad' what attracted him or served his interest. Society, however, required a shared public language: 'The power of Hobbes's sovereign was thus above all an *epistemic* power, to determine the meanings of words', to impose a common language.[117] Before civil war had thrown them irrecoverably into contest, Elizabeth, James and Charles had spoken and written to reinforce, authorize and control the common languages on which their power was founded. Their authorings were as vital to their exercise of authority as the authority of Hobbes's sovereign was necessary for a common discourse of state.

[117] Hobbes, *Leviathan*, ed. R. Tuck (Cambridge, 1991), xvii, 39.

CHAPTER FOUR

Private conscience and public duty in the writings of James VI and I

Conscience: 'a man cannot steal, but it acuseth him; a man cannot swear but it checks him; a man cannot lie with his neighbour's wife but it detects him. 'Tis a blushing shame fac'd spirit that mutinies in a man's bosom . . .'

2nd Murderer, Richard III, I. iv. 133–9

> Let not our babbling dreams afright our souls;
> Conscience is but a word that cowards use,
> Devis'd at first to keep the strong in awe.
> Our strong arms be our conscience, swords
>   our law.

Richard III, v. iii. 308–11.

'Private conscience' and 'public duty' are in our usage terms that usually imply opposites. Though numerous events and controversies – politicians' sexual indiscretions, the publication of offensive books, the responsibility for riot and disorder – belie a simple distinction between them, we adhere to a belief in the separateness of private and public spaces. Indeed, commitment to that separateness and the idea of the ownership of the self are fundamental to both modern psychology and the modern state. Almost from the time that the word became respectable, the business of politics has been that of a negotiation between the individual and the state, private interests and public interests. Indeed, the acceptance and validation of a world of politics – of contest and party, lobby and propaganda – marked a recognition of the artificiality of the social state, and of a public morality that might differ from the ethical values that governed personal behaviour. Brave would be the historian who endeavoured confidently to assign an exact date to, or list of causes for, what were truly revolutionary developments. But we know that by the end of the seventeenth century, despite lingering pejorative associations, parties had become enshrined in the social and political life of the nation; that the Toleration Act signalled a degree of separation of

church and state; and that the language of 'interest' had gained respectability.[1] Such developments, it has been suggested, were inextricably
linked with a new attitude to the autonomous individual and a sphere of
self-determination.[2] By the end of the seventeenth century the conscience was defined as part of that sphere: as, in Locke's words, 'nothing
else but our own opinion or judgement of the moral rectitude or pravity
of our own Actions'.[3]

Before the civil war, however, such distinctions were not so readily
made and ideas of conscience were correspondingly different and less
individualistic. The normative texts of politics were the works of
Aristotle and the Bible. Following Aristotle, it was held that the state was
an ethical community and there was no contradiction between the good
person, the good citizen and the good ruler. The concept of the commonweal precluded clear delineation of the public and the private. The
human body and 'self' were as much a part of the public as the 'body
politic' was anthropomorphized. Because it was natural, the commonweal united all in one interest. Because all were members of a Christian
commonweal that shaped its laws and codes according to God's decrees,
there should no more have been contention over the 'right course' in
public action than in private.[4] There was one God, one scripture, and
therefore – in theory – one conscience for the commonwealth.
Conscience was the inner law-giver, the 'deity within us', that element of
knowledge of God that remained even in fallen man. Those who
claimed God or scripture spoke to them differently from the prescriptions of the commonweal were, it was held, betrayed by a false conscience or pretended to conscience, *as they themselves knew*, out of evil
intent. Nor, in this model, was conscience at odds with duty. Both
implied a moral obligation, that is an obligation to a shared morality.
The Geneva Bible's translation of Ecclesiastes 12:13 enjoined: 'Feare
God and keep his commandments: for this is the duty of man.'[5] Among
God's commandments was obedience to divinely instituted authority. As
the conscience was God's lieutenant in the soul, so the king was God's
lieutenant in the commonweal, responsible for guiding the *respublica
Christiana* according to the divine decrees. Loyalty to the king was an act
of conscience as well as a duty and an interest. Resistance to the ruler

---

[1] See S. Zwicker, 'Lines of Authority: Politics and Literary Culture in the Restoration', in K.
Sharpe and S. Zwicker eds., *Politics of Discourse: the Literature and History of Seventeenth-Century England*
(Berkeley, Los Angeles and London, 1987), 230–70; also 5–7.
[2] M. McKeon, *The Origins of the English Novel, 1600–1740* (1987).
[3] J. Locke, *An Essay Concerning Human Understanding* (1824 edn), 25.
[4] Cf. above, pp. 48–51.   [5] *OED*, s.v. 'Conscience'.

was rebellion not only against God but against the self, the rise of ignorance and passion against the knowledge and reason which distinguished men from beasts.

Such ideal prescriptions had perhaps always been compromised by observed human experience: theological controversy, popular and baronial revolt, conflicting loyalty to family and ruler. But the rent of Christendom massively exacerbated the tensions and bequeathed to the era between the Reformation and the age of toleration fundamental practical and theoretical problems which could not be resolved nor even fully conceptualized within the prevailing paradigms. Many of those problems and questions – the nature of 'true religion', the extent of obedience to the prince, the relation of man to God and his fellows, the ends and organization of society and the state – were intimately bound up with and revolved around issues of 'conscience'. As old vocabularies and value systems lived on in radically new circumstances, the very word conscience, once a symbol of unity, was deployed to defend violence, rebellion and division. As a consequence a few thinkers, most notably Niccolò Machiavelli, advocated the radical course of freeing public life and government from religion and morality. But, to an age which still hoped for an ecumenical solution to the division of Christendom, Machiavelli's secular politics were anathema.[6] Faced, then, with the enduring ideals of Christian humanism and the experience of religious division and contest, rulers and citizens had to define – and redefine – their own conscience. It is hardly surprising that in doing so they faced contradiction – not only from others, but also within themselves.

Often in early modern England the theatre staged (and attempted to contain) those contradictions. As our opening quotations remind us, Shakespeare glaringly presents a world in which conscience both preserves some of its unifying moral authority and yet lies at the mercy of 'Machiavels' – illegitimate princes – who would subject it to personal ambition and force. It is no coincidence that, in the works of Shakespeare and other Elizabethan and Jacobean dramatists, we encounter debates about conscience in plays self announcedly about kings.[7] For many of the tensions and contradictions in early modern English society were examined through a notion which had an 'important heuristic function in the period of transition from medieval to

---

[6] Above, pp. 67–70; F. Raab, *The English Face of Machiavelli* (1964).

[7] As well as *Richard III, Richard II, Henry V, Lear, Hamlet* and *The Winter's Tale* are obvious texts in which the king's conscience both faces dilemmas and is yet central to the integrity of the realm.

modern political thought': the concept of the king's two bodies.[8] On the one hand, in his mystical body, the king was the head, the reason, the conscience of the commonweal, exemplifying the oneness of private and public, duty and interest. On the other, in his natural body, the king was 'but a man as I am', as Henry V puts it, having but 'human conditions' and being subject to human frailties.[9] The virtuous king was he who harmonized his natural to his mystical body, who subjected his passions to his reason, and so through his own example of wholeness applied holistic medicine to the body politic. Yet, even in the case of Shakespeare's good king, questions and tensions remained. The virtuous quality of sincerity required that the king display his 'crystal heart' to his subjects, but diplomacy and discretion, in Henry V's case even intercourse with his subjects, necessitated disguise and deceit. Though the king was responsible for his subjects, yet 'he is not bound to answer the particular endings'.[10] Similarly the king might keep the conscience and command the duty of the realm, 'but every subject's soul is his own' and it was for every subject to 'wash every mote out of his conscience'.[11] As Professor Goldberg reminds us, even this most heroic monarch and mirror for princes appears to different observers – within and outside the play – differently; 'whether he is most Machiavellian or most pious has divided critical response to him'.[12]

Historians have similarly been as divided over their characterization of Tudor and Stuart monarchs. Was Henry VIII a ruthless manipulator of circumstance, or a man who sincerely governed himself as well as the polity according to his conscience? Was Charles I genuine in his claim to rule only for the weal of his people, or did he act – in *both* senses – only to establish his power as absolute? The historiographical differences of interpretation of 'actual rulers', like the critical disagreements about Henry V and other kings represented on the stage, owe much to the self-contradictions of the age and so especially of its rulers, particularly over questions of conscience and duty.[13] In one case, we are fortunate to have a monarch who not only reigned during the period of the richest dramatic representations of these tensions, but also, in (what we would

---

[8] See E. H. Kantorovicz, *The King's Two Bodies: a Study in Mediaeval Political Theology* (Princeton, N.J., 1957), passim and p. 447.

[9] E. Forset, *A Comparative Discourse of the Bodies Natural and Politique* (1606); D. G. Hale, *The Body Politic: a Political Metaphor in Renaissance English Literature* (The Hague, 1971); Shakespeare, *Henry V*, Act IV, scene i.   [10] *Henry V*, Act IV, scene i.   [11] Ibid.

[12] J. Goldberg, *James I and the Politics of Literature* (Baltimore and London, 1983), 161. I am grateful to Jonathan Goldberg for his brilliant insights both in this work and in discussion.

[13] The historiographical disagreements are especially heated for early modern British history, not least because the period set itself contrary criteria of judgement.

delineate as) both public and more private genres of writing, contributed to the debate of these issues. Indeed it was in 1599, the year of the first performance of *Henry V*, that James VI penned his own reflections on kingship, the *Basilikon Doron* or 'His Majesty's Instructions to his dearest son, Prince Henry'.

James VI and I's most public pronouncements on kingship, as well as the *Basilikon Doron*, *The Trew Law of Free Monarchies*, the *Apology for the Oath of Allegiance*, the *Remonstrance for the Right of Kings*, and the speeches to parliament, have been easily available in C. H. McIlwain's *The Political Works of James I* since 1918. It is surprising that they have attracted little critical study as political theory or discourse.[14] Perhaps even more regrettably, no study has been made of James's letters, devotional tracts, commentaries on scripture and, especially, his poetry as self-examinations and as self-explications of the king's person and concept of office. Central to any such investigation must be an understanding of James's perceptions of conscience and duty – his own, and his subjects' in a Christian commonweal – and of the contradictions within them.

In his most public and avowedly political works, James outlined what conscience and duty meant to him. No more for his subjects than for himself could they be divided. It was the duty of the people to obey their sovereign 'in all things except directly against God', and subjects were 'bound to obey their princes for conscience sake'.[15] 'The bond of conscience', James once wrote to James Hamilton in Scotland, was 'the only sure bond for tying of men's affections to them whom to they owe a natural duty'.[16] Herein, of course, lay the central problem of the early modern state: if conscience were the foundation of the duty of obedience to princes, yet conscience informed some subjects that the ruler acted 'directly against God', how could monarchy and the commonweal survive? James himself conceded that it was the duty of the clergy to encourage disobedience of commands contrary to God's – 'it is always better to obey God than man' – yet continued to maintain that there was no conflict, rather a harmony, between faith and allegiance.[17] In part this seeming contradiction was resolved in theory by another: the notion of

[14] They find no place in Quentin Skinner's survey, *The Foundations of Modern Political Thought* (2 vols., Cambridge, 1978). See, however, L. Avack, *La ragione dei re. Il pensiero politico di Giacomo I* (Milan, 1974).

[15] *The Trew Law of Free Monarchies*, in C. H. McIlwain ed., *The Political Works of James I* (Cambridge, Mass., 1918), 61; *Apology for the Oath of Allegiance*, ibid., 72; *Hist. Mss. Comm.*, Salisbury, XV, 300, James I to Thomas Parry, Nov. 1603.

[16] G. P. V. Akrigg, ed., *The Letters of King James VI and I* (1984), 166–7.

[17] *A Remonstrance for the Right of Kings*, in McIlwain, *Political Works of James I*, 213.

civil obedience. In the case of his Catholic subjects, the king separated
their civil obedience from their conscience. Never believing that 'the
blood of any man shall be shed for diversity of opinions in religion',
James left them to their 'opinion', requiring only subscription to an oath
of allegiance.[18] That oath he regarded as the solution to the pull between
conscience and the duty of obedience: 'I never conceived the difference
between real obedience and promise by subscription to obey.'[19]
However, the promise involved in an oath itself rested on one's obligation and accountability to God – in other words on conscience.[20] In
order to reconcile the conscience and duty of his Catholic subjects,
James was forced to separate what he intrinsically believed should be
inviolable – the civic and the religious.

For, whilst his defence of the Oath of Allegiance seemed to imply it,
elsewhere James denied that the sphere of conscience could be separated as a personal realm outside the public. In *A Premonition to All Most
Mighty Monarchs* he went so far as to refute the sacred secrecy of the confessional when the public interest was at stake.[21] Most of all he was at
pains to deny the puritan claim to personal conscience, that is to a personal interpretation of what God ordained. Parity of conscience, he
realized, would soon lead to equality (and hence anarchy) in the commonwealth.[22] Conscience was not identical with mere opinion: sinners
confused the dictates of conscience with those of appetite, and many did
'prattle of' a conscience they did not feel.[23] True conscience was not
opinion but knowledge, 'the light of knowledge that God hath planted
in man'.[24] 'Conscience not grounded on knowledge', James once put it,
'is either an ignorant fantasy or an arrogant vanity.'[25] Knowledge of
God came to man through scripture, the principal tutor to the conscience. Therefore, 'in making the Scripture to be ruled by their conscience and not their conscience by the Scripture', the puritans
subverted conscience no less than they did authority.[26]

In matters of dispute, of course, the interpretation of scripture rested
with the church. So, though on occasions he appears to regard con-

---

[18] *Letters*, 204; *Apology for the Oath of Allegiance*, in McIlwain, *Political Works of James I*, 72 and passim.
[19] *Letters*, 223.
[20] See R. Sanderson, *De Juramento: Seven Lectures Concerning the Obligation of Promissory Oaths* (1655), a
work revised by Charles I.   [21] McIlwain, *Political Works of James I*, 167.
[22] James I, *A Meditation Upon the Lords Prayer* (1619), 18: 'trust not to that private spirit or Holy Ghost
which our Puritans glory in, for then a little fiery zeal will make thee turn separatist'.
[23] J. Craigie ed., *The Basilikon Doron of King James VI* (2 vols., Scottish Text Soc., Edinburgh,
1944–50), I, 40, 124.   [24] Ibid., I, 40.
[25] James I, *Flores Regii, or Proverbes and Aphorismes . . . Spoken By His Majesty* (1627), 104–5.
[26] *Basilikon Doron*, I, 16.

science as an individual's personal negotiation with God, for the most part James believed in a 'common quality conscience' in which all (himself included) shared, rather than 'distinct individual consciences'.[27] Perhaps, he saw that acceptance of the idea of individual conscience ultimately threatened not only diversity of religious sects but moral and religious relativism. What most upset James about the teachings of Conrad Vorstius was his contention that God had 'some kind of diversity or multiplicity in himself yea even a beginning of a certain mutability'.[28] Against Vorstius no less than Montaigne, James reasserted a theoretical axiom of the early modern polity: 'God is unity itself and verity is one.'[29] But, though necessary, the belief in a common conscience of the commonweal was fraught with difficulties and inconsistencies. For in certain passages the king discerns the light of conscience in all men. God, he concludes in the second book of the *Basilikon Doron*, has 'imprinted in men's minds by the very light of Nature the love of all moral virtues' and an awareness of wrongdoing.[30] Even malefactors retained, like Richard III's murderer, a sense of their own evil, a residual conscience which, as James described it in his *Daemonologie*, 'haunted' them, until 'the purging of themselves by amendment of life from such sins as have procured that extraordinary plague'.[31] But, if such were the case, why could not a man's conscience be autonomous? How was it that puritans professed a conscience that was false or pretended, if God planted the light of his knowledge in all? Or, to put the question simply and fundamentally, why did all not agree about the right course for a Christian commonweal?

At times James wants to claim that they did. 'You know in your conscience', he told Members of the House of Commons in 1624, 'that of all the kings that ever were . . . never was king better beloved of his people than I am.'[32] But there is a silent *ought to* implicit before that 'know', a silent phrase that alone can bridge the gap between the theory of common conscience and James's experience, not least with his parliaments, of fundamental disagreement. Whatever should be, conscience was not common to all. Their conscience led the puritans to become a 'sect', as James described them, whose members 'refuse to obey the law

[27] *OED*, s.v. 'Conscience', history of usage.
[28] *A Declaration Concerning the Proceedings with the States General of the United Provinces . . . in the Cause of D. Conradus Vorstius*, in *The Workes of the Most High and Mighty Prince James* (1616), 365.
[29] Ibid., 372.   [30] *Basilikon Doron*, I, 160.
[31] James I, *Daemonologie*, in *Workes of Prince James*, 125.
[32] *Cobbett's Parliamentary History of England* (36 vols., 1806–20), I, 1376.

and will not cease to stir up a rebellion'.[33] Theirs led the Powder Plotters into 'denying the king to be [their] lawful sovereign or the anointed of God'.[34] God had his own ways of expressing the dictates of true conscience. When Catesby and others were wounded when the powder for their plot exploded on them, James thought they were 'wonderfully stroken with amazement in their guilty consciences, calling to memory how God had justly punished them with that same instrument which they should have used for the effectuating of so great a sin'.[35] Yet it was the role of the state to lend some assistance even to 'the wonderful power of God's justice upon guilty consciences'. Accordingly, Guy Fawkes was imprisoned (and, not mentioned, tortured) to help him to 'advise upon his conscience'.[36] Conscience may have been to James the foundation of his authority, but, paradoxically, his authority was an essential prop of a true conscience. To answer the cynic, then, who would dismiss the whole notion as a disingenuous disguise for power, we must look at how James interpreted conscience and duty when he turned to examine his own.

Too much that has been written about the king's theory of divine right has failed to grasp that James saw his position as God's lieutenant not as a power but as a duty – and an awesome duty, in the sense of religious observance as well as feudal obligation, at that. 'Being born to be a king,' he instructed Prince Henry, 'ye are rather born to ONUS than HONOS: not excelling all your people so far in rank and honour as in daily care and hazardous pains in the dutiful administration of that great office that God hath laid upon your shoulders.'[37] A king owned himself even less than private men. For the commonweal, James wrote in 1593, 'I am born more than for myself'.[38] Even as a parent, a king did not own his son. Henry was 'not ours only as the child of a natural father, but as an heir apparent to our body public in whom our state and kingdom are essentially interested'.[39] If the king's body and flesh were not his own, no more was his conscience. As in his mystical form he was head of the body politic, so the king's conscience was not only personal but the conscience of the realm. James was explicit about how his conscience was bound to the codes of the polity that it was his duty to rule – to law, justice, and equity. 'Certainly,' as he put it in *The Trew Law of Free Monarchies*, 'a king that governs not by his law can neither be countable to God for his administration.'[40] 'A King that will rule and govern justly', he told his

---

[33] *Basilikon Doron*, I, 26.
[34] *A Discourse of the . . . Discoverie of the Powder Treason*, in *Workes of Prince James*, 231.
[35] Ibid., 245.   [36] Ibid., 241.   [37] *Basilikon Doron*, I, 6–7.   [38] *Letters*, 25.
[39] *Hist. Mss. Comm., Salisbury*, XV. 302.   [40] McIlwain, *Political Works of James I*, 63.

parliamentary audience in March 1610, 'must have regard to conscience'.[41]

Now, our cynic (or Dr Sommerville) might point out that justice was the king's justice and that the laws too were – James himself used the possessive – 'his'. The conscience of the king's mystical self was then one and the same with his personal conscience and so autonomous and untrammelled. James, however, had sworn a coronation oath to see law, justice, mercy and truth maintained, and felt himself as bound to execute that promise as were the Catholics by the Oath of Allegiance.[42] It had been, he recalled in a speech of 1616, his principal care to keep his conscience clear in all points of his coronation oath.[43] For an oath was to God as well as to the other party and so, as Bishop Sanderson was to put it, 'not to be taken with a relucting and unsatisfied conscience'.[44] That conscience was inextricably part of the honour of the king, 'without which', James proclaimed in 1607, 'I have no being'.[45] Indeed, so much was the king's conscience the realm's as much as the king's own that at times, it would appear, he came close to subordinating his 'private conscience' for the sake of the commonweal. Where his policy towards the papists was concerned, for example, 'I must', James acknowledged in a speech in the Lords, 'put a difference betwixt mine own private profession of mine own salvation and my politic government of the realm for the weal and quietness thereof.'[46] He did so because, 'as I would be loather to dispence in the least point mine own conscience for any worldly respect than the foolishest precisian of them all; so would I be as sorry to straight the politique government of the bodies and minds of all my subjects to my private opinions'.[47] In theory, of course, in the ideal commonweal there should have been no such disjuncture. The king's personal and public consciences should have accorded with each other and those of his subjects. The reality was otherwise. The reality of politics threatened the separation of the king's two bodies at a time when their conjunction was essential for – indeed was a device for – the cohesion of the body politic.[48] It was not least because he fully grasped that necessity that James struggled to reconcile and to harmonize all those consciences: to be (as we shall argue) the crystal mirror in and through which his subjects could come to a shared knowledge of God.

[41] Ibid., 318.
[42] See *The Ceremonies, Form of Prayer and Services Used in Westminster Abbey at the Coronation of King James 1st* (1685).   [43] McIlwain, *Political Works of James I*, 329.
[44] Sanderson, *De Juramento*, 144, 197–8, 236, 269.
[45] McIlwain, *Political Works of James I*, 298.   [46] Ibid., 274.   [47] Ibid.
[48] Cf. above, pp. 111–13, 120–1.

In the first place, James went to some lengths to remove and deny any barrier between his private and public selves. Kings, he advised Prince Henry, should have no secret thoughts that they were afraid publicly to avouch. A prince ought to keep 'agreeance and conformity . . . betwixt his outward behaviour and the virtuous qualities of his mind'.[49] 'By the outward using of your office . . . testify the inward uprightness of your heart.'[50] 'I never with God's grace', he once wrote to Cecil, taking his own counsel, 'shall do anything in private which I may not without shame proclaim upon the tops of houses.'[51] Because discourse was 'the true image' of the king's mind (a 'testament' as he called the *Basilikon Doron*), it was important that monarchs spoke and wrote what they meant.[52] Accordingly James vowed to his parliament that he would promise nothing which he intended not to deliver.[53] His 'tongue should ever be the true messenger of his heart'.[54] Today we would be inclined to interpret this as a *claim* to sincerity – something we tend to doubt in public figures, dismissing such talk as itself political rhetoric or strategy. And this is the point. James was intending more than to secure belief in his word. He was specifically opposing those Machiavels who sought to justify deceit and disguise as stratagems of power in an amoral political universe.[55] And his counter-argument not only opposed Machiavellian premises; it deployed to opposite purpose Machiavelli's own language. As a king James spoke 'without artifice'; 'as a prince', he wrote to Elizabeth, perhaps choosing his self-description carefully, 'it becomes me not to feign'.[56] In 1621, subverting the metaphors of *The Prince*, he condemned orators who 'fox-like . . . seem to speak one thing and intend another'.[57] The king's own discourse was itself a denial of the new 'politics' and a reassertion of the Aristotelian premise that the good ruler and the good man were one. Because the political reality was otherwise, and James was a shrewd observer, that realization crept into his speech even as he sought to deny it. He knew and evidently articulated that 'in civil actions he is the greater and deeper politic that can make other men the instruments of his will and ends and yet never acquaint them with

---

[49] *Basilikon Doron*, I, 15.   [50] Ibid., I, 200.   [51] *Letters*, 192.   [52] *Basilikon Doron*, I, 21–2.
[53] McIlwain, *Political Works of James I*, 305.   [54] Ibid., 280.
[55] Though Machiavelli was not available in English until 1640, *The Prince* was translated into Scots by W. Fowler, a court poet, who contributed a celebratory verse to James's own collection of poems. See *His Maiesties Poetical Exercises at Vacant Houres* (Edinburgh, 1591), sig. A4; *The Essayes of a Prentise in the Divine Art of Poesie* (Edinburgh, 1585), sig. 3v; T. Craigie ed., *The Poems of James VI of Scotland* (2 vols., Scottish Text Soc., Edinburgh, 1955–8), I, xxii.
[56] W. Notestein, F. H. Relf and H. Simpson eds., *Commons Debates 1621* (7 vols., New Haven, 1935), V, 85; *Letters*, 162.   [57] *Commons Debates 1621*, II, 12.

his purpose'.[58] But knowing was not accepting, and certainly not author-izing: James's use of 'politic' here appears pejorative. Elsewhere he is forcefully condemnatory of deceptions. It was a '*tyrant*', he told Cecil in 1604, who gave 'fair words till he had gotten his turn done, and then but have kept his promise as he had thought convenient'.[59] A 'just king' opened his mind 'freelier'. Whatever the politic might do, James would swear: 'never shall I for compulsion either speak, promise or write other-wise than I think and that which is honest'.[60] And his subjects could then place trust in his meaning as 'ever one and alike in all his royal resolu-tions'.[61]

James's denial of the rhetoric of artifice and dissimulation had a purpose beyond a negation of Machiavellian politics – a more construc-tive, or perhaps we should say *re*constructive, purpose. In his written tracts and in speech after speech James went to great lengths to display to his subjects, and to assure them that he was displaying, 'the true image of my very mind'.[62] He expressed his wish to parliament 'that there were a crystal window in my breast wherein all my people might see the secretest thoughts of my heart'.[63] In 1610 he offered a 'rare present', 'a fair and crystal mirror . . . such a mirror or crystal as through the trans-parentness thereof you may see the heart of your king'.[64] In 1621 he delivered yet again 'a true mirror of my mind'.[65] The recurrence and doubleness of the metaphor is important. The word *crystal* had a dual meaning in early modern England: the crystal was, as we understand it, transparent; it was also another term for a mirror, which, of course, reflects. James, I would suggest, intended both. In 1618, in *The Peace-Maker or Great Britain's Blessing*, he described honour as a rumour of vir-tuous action which redounded from the soul, to the world and, by reflection, onto ourselves.[66] Conscience, we have seen, was often coupled by James with his honour. Because the king was God's lieutenant, when the subject looked into the king's heart he looked as through a crystal at God's laws and decrees, the codes of his own conscience. When he looked at the mirror of the king's mind, he saw how his own conscience fell short of God's decrees as they were reauthorized (that is rewritten and revalidated) by the king. That is why James believed it 'necessary that a king should deliver his thoughts to his people'.[67] Mediating God's

---

[58] *Flores Regii*, 125; cf. *Commons Debates 1621*, IV, 72.   [59] *Letters*, 240.   [60] Ibid., 68.
[61] *Hist. Mss. Comm., Salisbury*, XVI, 395.   [62] *Basilikon Doron*, I, 22.
[63] McIlwain, *Political Works of James I*, 285.   [64] Ibid., 306.   [65] *Commons Debates 1621*, II, 2.
[66] *The Peace-Maker or Great Britain's Blessing* (1618), sig. D4.
[67] E. R. Foster ed., *Proceedings in Parliament 1610* (2 vols., New Haven, 1966), I, 45.

will and decrees as his lieutenant, the virtuous king might become an image of God and a pattern for men, acting like God, in 'wakening up their zeal' for the good.[68] This was the duty of authority, 'persuasion and example of life being more proper means to reclaim men's consciences than compulsion'.[69]

Kings most fulfilled their duty, then, when they not only acted according to, but enacted and transmitted, the will of God. As James put it in a speech in Star Chamber on 20 June 1616, 'no king can discharge his accompt to God unless he make conscience . . . to declare and establish the will of God'.[70] The king, in other words, was not only God's lieutenant; he was – both in actions and discourse – his exegete. We are familiar with the concept that the king as head was the reason of the body politic. But we do not always accord it the deep theological meaning that reason carried: the idea of acting divinely, according to the 'light of knowledge that God hath planted in man', before the Fall, a light that still flickered in all and shone in the godly.[71] By acting as a representation of Christ, the king might kindle that light in his subjects. Prince Henry, therefore, was advised by his father in words that Christ had spoken: 'let it not be said that you command others to keep the contrary course to that which in your own person you practise'.[72] Following that counsel himself, James vowed to follow that 'alike Christian as politic rule to measure as I would be measured unto'.[73] 'Peace be with you', James took as the fit 'motto of a king' because 'the blessing of a God'.[74]

James's tracts, speeches and letters contain constant applications of scripture to issues and problems of state. Scripture was for him a text of state because the Christian and political realms were one and shared a discourse. 'Let our souls be bound for our bodies,' he urged in 1618, 'our bodies for our souls, and let each come in at the General Sessions to save his bail, where he shall find a merciful judge.'[75] No less than his actions, the king's words, his *Workes*, were mediations of God's will, as revealed in scripture. Their function, as Bishop Montagu saw it when he introduced them to their readers in 1616, was to operate on men's consciences so that they might be 'converted by them'.[76] James described his own *Basilikon Doron* as a 'discharge of our conscience'.[77] *Basilikon Doron* means the royal gift. James so described others of his works, dedicated to Prince Charles or the Duke of Buckingham. In a larger sense, they were, when

[68] *Daemonologie*, in *Workes of Prince James*, 126.   [69] *Commons Debates 1621*, V, 426.
[70] McIlwain, *Political Works of James I*, 327.   [71] See above, n. 24.
[72] *Basilikon Doron*, I, 102.   [73] *Letters*, 181.   [74] *The Peace-Maker*, sig. A4.   [75] Ibid., sig. E4v.
[76] *Workes of Prince James*, epistle to the Reader.   [77] *Basilikon Doron*, I, 22.

published, gifts to all his subjects. For, by bringing readers closer to God, leading them to know him, James might indeed convert men by bringing them to the knowledge of God, which, when shared, united all in a Christian commonweal. The author (writer/authorizer) of the tag to the frontispiece to James's works was the earthly no less than the heavenly king: 'Ecce do tibi animum sapientem et intelligentem.'[78]

A king who saw it as his duty to be an apostle as well as a prince, to mediate God's word and will, faced an awesome responsibility to ensure the uprightness of his own conscience. And, in the main, he faced it alone. It may be the duty of MPs 'upon *your* consciences plainly to determine' for 'the weal both of your king and your country'.[79] And the king had his counsellors, bishops and chaplains close to his bosom. But these were men chosen 'out of my own judgement and conscience' who owed loyalty and service to their master.[80] The acclaim of others could not be relied upon as a mark of the king's virtuous courses. Reputation, James once wrote, was but other men's 'opinion' – and for that a prince should not risk his soul.[81] Ultimately the keeper of the nation's conscience was alone – with his own, before God. In his epistle to the Reader of 'His Majesty's Instructions to his . . . son', James explained his resolution 'ever to walk as in the eyes of the Almighty, examining ever so the secretest of my drifts, before I gave them course, as how they might some day bide the touchstone of a public trial'.[82] Kings had, he put it in the *Trew Law*, 'the count of their administration' to give to God.[83] Not only was that an account more strict than that any other servant owed his master; it was a count of each and every word and deed. Justice demanded of kings that, 'as we reign by [God's] grace . . . we should turn all our energies and thoughts to His glory'.[84] This was not rhetoric. Every day, James commanded his son, he should take the reckoning with himself, his conscience, and his God:

remember ever once in the four and twenty hours, either in the night or when ye are at greatest quiet, to call yourself to account of all your last days actions, either wherein ye have committed things ye should not, or omitted the things ye should do, either in your Christian or kingly calling: in that account let not yourself be smoothed over with the flattering $\Phi\iota\lambda\alpha\mu\tau\iota\alpha$ . . . but censure yourself as sharply as if ye were your own enemy.[85]

---

[78] *Serenissimi Potentissimi Principis Jacobi . . . Opera* (1619), motto at foot of frontispiece depicting the figures of Religion and Peace.   [79] McIlwain, *Political Works of James I*, 288.

[80] *Letters*, 261.   [81] *The Peace-Maker*, sig. D4.   [82] *Basilikon Doron*, I, 12.

[83] McIlwain, *Political Works of James I*, 54.

[84] J. O. Halliwell ed., *Letters of the Kings of England* (2 vols., 1848), II, 68.

[85] *Basilikon Doron*, I, 44.

Never, he concluded, 'ever wilfully or willingly . . . contrare your conscience'. The king more than any must fear as well as serve God.[86] 'Let
hell afright thee', he advised his fellow rulers, 'and let thy conscience
describe it to thee.'[87] When alone taking the count of his obedience and
service to God, the king needed only to turn to scripture – 'the statutes
of your heavenly king' – to determine whether he had acted (as good
kings should) as a true subject of *his* sovereign.[88] 'Would ye then know
your sin by the law? read the books of Moses . . . Would ye know . . .
Christ? looke the Evangelists.'[89] With scripture, especially the books of
Kings and Chronicles, James told his son, he should be familiarly
acquainted: 'for there will ye see yourself (as in a mirror) either among
the catalogues of the good or evil kings'.[90] Self-knowledge, conscience,
the same as the knowledge of God, came from meditation upon *His*
word, as in turn the king's *Workes* written and enacted were the mirror
in which subjects saw their God and themselves.

It is in this context that we must glance specifically (if briefly) at the
more neglected of James I's writings: the king's own exegeses of and
commentaries on scriptural texts. James called them 'paraphrases' and
'meditations'. And they stand, indeed, as evidence of his personalizing
the Scriptures, meditating upon their message to himself and communicating their meaning to his subjects. The king's *Paraphrase upon the
Revelation* is an exegesis, a decoding of that most complex of biblical
books and a specific application of its symbolic figurations to his own
and his contemporaries' world. James deconstructs, as we would now
say, the visions of chapter 10, explaining how Christ was the Angel fore-
told and how the rainbow signified His covenant with his elect. Similarly
the woman of chapter 12 represents the church, he explains, and the
twelve stars stand for the prophets and the patriarchs.[91] Throughout
James puts his own words as if they were spoken by St John and so joins,
as if in a dialogue, the text of Revelation and his reflections upon it. As
a consequence it is no less the king's than the apostle's words we read
when he writes 'and [God] said unto me, Write and leave in record what
thou hast seen'.[92] James saw much that was for the edification of himself.
He read again, as scripture in many places showed him, that 'the hearts
of the greatest kings as well as of the smallest subjects are in the hands
of the Lord'. The book of the last things forcefully urged him: 'Be watch-

---

[86] Ibid., 5, 'The Argument'.　　[87] *The Peace-Maker*, sig. C2.　　[88] *Basilikon Doron*, I, 5.
[89] Ibid., I, 34.　　[90] Ibid.
[91] *Paraphrase upon the Revelation*, in *Workes of Prince James*, esp. 13–14, 19–21, 36–9, 63–4, 78.
[92] Ibid., 65.

ful then and sleep no longer in negligence and careless security . . . revive your zeal and fervency.'[93] His discursive dialogue with scripture sharpened his conscience. As he turned to meditate on some verses of the fifteenth chapter of the first book of Chronicles (which he had, we recall, recommended to Prince Henry), he was reminded clearly of the first duty of kings.[94] David after his victory over his enemies immediately translated the ark of the Covenant to his house, 'whereof *we* [*sic*] may learn first that the chief virtue which should be in a Christian prince . . . is a fervency and constant zeal to promote the glory of God'.[95] James applied his text closely to his place, comparing the elders of the Chronicles to the barons and burgesses of his kingdom and underlining his own responsibility for 'choosing good under-rulers'.[96] At all points the 'opening up of the text' was the basis for examining 'how pertinently the place doth appertain to us and our present estate', guiding the king, for example, on the lawfulness of Sunday sports.[97]

James's meditations on scripture were a form of self-counsel, a didactic engagement with the commands in scripture as a means of tutoring conscience. And not only his own. The meditation on the twentieth chapter of Revelation reads also like a sermon. Introducing his meditation upon the first book of Chronicles, James expressed his desire that 'these meditations of mine may after my death remain to the posterity as a certain testimony of my upright and honest meaning'.[98] Like the overtly *Political Works* (as McIlwain defined them) from which they have been artificially separated, James's paraphrases and explications of scripture were a discharge of his conscience, an image of the king, at once a crystal and a mirror for all men as well as for magistrates.

Perhaps we see their public and, as well as personal, heuristic function most clearly in two little-studied works, the *Meditation Upon the Lords Prayer* of 1619 and the *Meditation Upon the . . . XXVII Chapter of St Matthew* of 1620. The first, though dedicated as a New Year's gift to the Duke of Buckingham, was 'written by the King's Majesty for the benefit of *all* his subjects, especially of such as follow the court'.[99] The meditation was a plea for Christian unity at a time of mounting tension and division; as in *The Peace-Maker* of 1618 James had called on the 'monarchical bodies of many kingdoms' to 'be one mutual Christendom',[100] so he now urged

---

[93] Ibid., 11, 56.
[94] *A Meditation Upon the XXV, XXVI, XXVII, XXVIII, XXIX Verses of the XVth Chapter of the First Book of the Chronicles of the Kings*, in *Workes of Prince James*, 81–90; see p. 164.
[95] Ibid., 82.   [96] Ibid., 83.   [97] Ibid., 86–7.   [98] Ibid., 81.
[99] *Meditation Upon the Lords Prayer*. The full title includes this address.
[100] *The Peace-Maker*, sig. B1.

all his subjects to join in the fellowship of the sacraments and prayer. The Arminians, he wrote, sought to rob God of his secret will; at the 'other extremity', 'some puritans . . . make God author of sin'.[101] Exposition of the prayer taught by Christ warned all to 'trust not to that private spirit which our Puritans glory in' but to remember, through the words 'Our Father', that 'every one of us is a member of a body of a church that is compacted of many members'.[102] James commends confession to churchmen for the clearing of the conscience and, through reflection on the Lord's Prayer, finds the 'true visible church . . . now in this kingdom' the best hope for salvation.[103]

The *Meditation Upon . . . St Matthew* began, James informed his son Charles, as a private reading 'to myself the passion of Christ'.[104] But, as he thought on the crown of thorns, James contemplated 'the thorny cares which a king . . . must be subject unto as (God knowes) I daily and nightly feel in mine own person'.[105] As he meditated further, 'I apprehended that it would be a good pattern to put inheritors to kingdoms in mind of their calling by the form of their inauguration' and 'whom can a pattern for a king's inauguration so well fit as a king's son and heir being written by the king his father and the pattern taken from the king of all kings'. And so the work became for Charles what the *Basilikon Doron* had been for Henry, James's gift of knowledge of God to his son. Indeed, James informed the reader of his meditation that, if God gave him days and leisure, he intended to expand it to cover 'the whole principal points belonging to the office of a king'.[106] Meantime, the *Meditation Upon . . . St Matthew* was a forewarning of the heavy burden of kingship: 'make it therefore', he instructed the prince, 'your vade mecum'. As he laid out for his son the verses describing Christ's crowning with plaited thorns and mock coronation with sceptre of reed and the soldiers' laughing 'obeisance', James detailed the cares and duties of the prince who was to take his 'pattern' from Christ. The thorns, he explained, made a king remember 'that he wears not that crown for himself but for others'; the reed sceptre instructed a ruler to correct gently and govern 'boldly yet temperately'. In general, Christ's crowning passion reminded kings that they were 'mixtae personae . . . bound to make a reckoning to God for their subjects' souls as well as their bodies'.[107] 'In a word', James con-

---

[101] *Meditation Upon the Lords Prayer*, 42, 116–17.   [102] Ibid., 18, 22.   [103] Ibid., 62, 66, 15.
[104] *Two Meditations of the King's Maiestie* (1620), epistle dedicatory.
[105] *A Meditation Upon the . . . XXVII Chapter of St Matthew or A Pattern for a King's Inauguration* (1620), epistle dedicatory.   [106] Ibid., advertisement to the Reader.
[107] Ibid., 25, 50, 124 and passim.

cludes, 'a Christian king should never be without that continual and ever wake-riffe care of the account he is one day to give to God of the good government of his people and their prosperous estate both in souls and bodies, which is a part of the health of his own soul.'[108] As often with James, it was counsel to himself as well as to his son. Just as Pilate proclaimed Christ King of the Jews in Hebrew, Greek and Latin, so 'upon St George's day and other high festival times the chief Herald Garter . . . proclaims my titles in . . . Latin, French and English'.[109] We can almost hear James meditating with himself as he tells Prince Charles that the purple robe of office was to remind him 'to take great heed of his conscience, that his judgements may be without blemish or stain'.[110]

Our final texts of the king's conscience have all but rested unexamined by historians – doubtless, not least, because they are poetry. James, however, was a major influence on the Renaissance poetry of Scotland, and both his poems and treatise on poetry are rich in evidence of his values and ideals. Like his paraphrase of Revelation, James's verse translations of the Psalms of David were a form of meditation on scripture, by means of absorbing its meaning into his own words – a placing 'before thy holy throne this speech of mine'.[111] Translation, James decreed, did not license reinterpretation of scripture; those who adulterated holy writ with their own opinions were accursed.[112] The translator was a glass through which scripture could be read, and poetry might be the instrument by which it was read most clearly.[113] So the King of Scotland, through David, the King of Israel, addresses, as in prayer, his heavenly King, a 'king that last for ever shall quaire all the nationis perish & decayes'.[114] Through David, James learnt (as he taught) that the Lord was a lord of justice, that he abominated the 'creuell and bloodthristie tyran' and those false princes who 'speake with pleasant lippes and dowble myndis'.[115] He read that the Lord preserved his anointed king and bestowed his grace on the virtuous, 'thaim of conscience iust & pure'.[116] James therefore prayed for protection from his enemies without and from temptations of wickedness within; he asked 'lett all my judgement ay proceid from thy most holy face'.[117] Urging, as he was to do in the *Basilikon Doron*, 'all princes sonnes yield to the lorde', he vowed to place his trust 'in Iehova's might'.[118] Trust here meant not only his

---

[108] Ibid., 125–6.   [109] Ibid., 78–80.   [110] Ibid., 120.
[111] BL Royal MS 18 B xvi, f. 9; *Poems of James VI*, II, 11. James's father-in-law, the King of Denmark, had written too a manual of selected psalms which 'was his continual vade mecum' (*Meditation Upon the Lords Prayer*, 96).   [112] *Paraphrase upon the Revelation*, 72.
[113] Bodl. MS 165 f. 20.   [114] *Psalmes of His Maiestie*, in *Poems of James VI*, II, 20.
[115] Ibid., II, 11, 23.   [116] Ibid., II, 42.   [117] Ibid., II, 21, 26, 27.   [118] Ibid., II, 9, 36.

confidence but his responsibility, his kingdom. In the exercise of his office James, with David, knew the Lord would guide and 'counsaile me', as in turn he would give account to God how he had heeded His counsel:

> the lorde doth iustice give unto the nationis sure
> then judge me lorde according to my iustice great & pure[119]

James's Psalms, *The Psalmes of His Maiestie* as they were titled, were not his only poetical exercises that we should consider as meditations on God and self-examination of the royal conscience. Only when we recall James's admonition to his son to reflect upon God and take his reckoning with himself at quiet moments free from worldly business may we understand the significant epithet in *His Maiesties Poeticall Exercises at Vacant Houres*. In his translation of 'divine' Du Bartas's *The Furies*, a poem about the Fall, James advised that the reader (and reader/writer) might 'see clearly, as in a glass, the miseries of this wavering world: to wit, the cursed nature of mankinde and the heavie plagues of God. And especialle heere maye thou learne not to flatter thyselfe, in cloaking thy odious vices with the delectable coulour of vertue.'[120] In *The Furies*, we read how authority had once been natural and kings could rule, like Adam over beasts, not by force but with a wink or a nod. But disobedience to God had as its consequence the collapse of all natural hegemony, as well as the disintegration of order and harmony into chaos. The animals now formed 'rebellious bands' against Man:

> Man in rebelling thus against
> The soveraigne great, I say,
> Doth feele his subjects all enarm'd
> Against him everie way . . .[121]

Wolves, leopards and bears now challenged the lion, king of beasts:

> Most jealous of the right divine
> Against their head conspire.[122]

Even kings themselves were stained by the Fall:

> The King of beasts . . . of himselfe
> Is not the maister now.[123]

Yet poetry, Sir Philip Sidney had claimed, could bring fallen man closer again to God. As James himself summarized him: 'a breath divine in

---

[119] Ibid., II, 14, 26.   [120] *Poems of James VI*, I, 98; *Workes of Prince James*, 328.
[121] *The Furies*, lines 224–7, in *Poems of James VI*, I, 126.
[122] Ibid., lines 381–2 (I, 134).   [123] Ibid., lines 1359–60 (I, 184).

Poets breasts doth blow'.[124] Through *The Furies*, therefore, James learnt and taught the emptiness of man's 'outward show', the illegitimacy of princes who advanced themselves 'by false contracts and by unlawfull measures', and the wisdom of those who had 'the feare of God / Imprinted deepely' and who obeyed his will.[125] Similarly, from his verse account of the battle of Lepanto we know James learnt and taught the duty of kings: to be God's generals against the devil, to prefer the 'honour of the Lord' before all else, and to be 'volunteers of conscience' in the Lord's ranks.[126]

In and through his poetry, which awaits a critical/political reading, James, as the poet Gabriel Harvey put it, 'read a . . . lecture to himself'.[127] He did more than tutor his own conscience, however. The 'heavenly furious fire' of poetry, he believed, might re-ignite the embers of conscience and knowledge of God in all men.[128] Poets are 'Dame Natures trunchmen, heavens interprets trewe'.[129] So James offered instruction in the art of poetry as he penned advice on the art of kingship. And, in his *Essayes of a Prentise in the Divine Art of Poesie*, he prayed that he, as poet and king, might have the power to represent the wind, the seas and the seasons, nature – the created works of a living God whom men through verse may come to know and follow:

> For as into the wax the seals imprent
> Is lyke a seale, right so the Poet gent
> Doeth grave so vive in us his passions strange,
> As makes the reader, halfe in author change
> For verses force is sic that softly slydes
> Throw secret poris and in our sences bydes
> As makes them have both good and eville imprented
> Which by the learned works is represented.[130]

David, Job and Solomon had been poets as well as kings. The poet like the good king prayed to his God 'That I thy instrument may be', so that, as *The Furies* concludes, 'this worke which man did write' also 'by the Lord is pend'.[131] Poetry for James VI and I, like his devotional works, was a meditation with himself and God and a representation to his subjects of himself and God – his purest crystal. In purifying his own conscience,

---

[124] *Poems of James VI*, II, 68.   [125] *The Furies*, lines 1167–8, 1451–2, 1461–2 (I, 175, 190).
[126] 'The Lepanto of James the Sixth', lines 283, 317–18, in *Poems of James VI*, I, 216–18, and passim.
[127] *Poems of James VI*, I, 274. Cf. Goldberg, *James I*, 17–28. I am preparing an essay on 'The Politics of James VI and I's Poetry'.   [128] *Poems of James VI*, II, 70.
[129] James VI, *The Essayes of a Prentise in the Divine Art of Poesie*, ed. E. Arber (1869), 29.
[130] Ibid., 29.   [131] *The Furies*, lines 29, 1515–16 (I, 114, 192).

he equipped himself to teach; by teaching, he learnt. So the wise poet of *Uranie* was told:

> In singing kepe this order showen you heir,
> Then ye your self, in feeding men shall leir
> The rule of living well . . .[132]

And, thus, the king published rules for poetry as well as for government, that 'reading thir rules ye may find in yourself such a beginning of Nature'. In the words of the sonnet to the reader, 'Sic docens discens'.[133]

In early modern Europe, as circumstances challenged traditional beliefs, all rulers faced difficult choices. Either they accepted the realities and were forced to compromise long-held beliefs and codes, or they fought to reassert the paradigms and to reconstruct a shattered world. Even though faced with the obvious fact of religious wars in Europe and theological wrangles at home, James VI and I pursued hopes of, and policies towards, an ecumenical resolution to the divisions of Christendom. He endeavoured to make the Church of England a platform for the reunification of a truly Catholic church, a *unum corpus* of which all Christians could be members. In his own countries he sought to minimize dispute over theology and ceremony. And we now see that, as an essential part of his ambitious designs, he sought to lead his subjects to a knowledge of God's dictates, so that all might partake of a common conscience, as well as be members of one church and commonweal. He faced, inevitably, inconsistencies in his own exposition of his ideal, because the means to obtain his goal (a coincidence of private and public belief) were the goal itself. His only answer to the new challenges was the reassertion of the old ideals. James, however, went beyond reassertion; his *Workes* were a strategy of re-enactment. By his own example, he attempted to demonstrate that conscience was neither mere opinion, nor, as the 'politics' would have it, a disguise, nor yet the inevitable victim of force. And he tried to heal the divisions in the commonwealth, by resolving the disjunctures in himself – between his natural and mystical body, his person and office – ruling his own conscience and his kingdom, as he claimed, according to scripture.

In the public sphere it is clear that he failed: religious differences and even moral positions continued to polarize. The king perforce took

---

[132] *Essayes of a Prentise*, 37.
[133] James VI, *An Schort Treatise Containing Some Reulis . . . to be Observed . . . in Scottis Poesie*, ed. E. Arber (1869), preface to the reader, p. 55, sonnet of the author, p. 56.

political decisions which accorded uneasily with his conscience. Furthermore, even in his own person James exemplified not only the ideals but also the failings he discussed, to the point that he became a microcosm of the human frailties that always threatened a Christian society. In his quest for the English crown after Elizabeth's death, the young James acquiesced in his mother's execution, for all his formal protest, and so failed in the filial devotion he believed was owed to parents.[134] Similarly, for all his injunctions to honesty, it would appear that he was prepared to mislead about his willingness to convert to Rome.[135] More tragically still, the king who thundered against the vices of intemperance, drunkenness and especially sodomy (a crime he exempted from pardon and which, he told Henry, 'ye are bound in conscience never to forgive') was a drunkard and homosexual.[136] How, then, could James counsel his son not to commend what he did not practise or boast, as in 1616, that 'both our theorique and practique agree well together'?[137] The simple answer would be that James was a straightforward hypocrite, but it would be too simple an answer. For James's denunciations of what were also his own sins were part of his meditations, and may have been a form of the confession that he recommended to others, for 'amendment of life'. We cannot know how, in his private moments, James faced his God and himself. But knowing, as he told his son, that Christ did not come for the perfect, he found 'in the religion we profess . . . so much comfort and peace of conscience'.[138]

---

[134] See *Letters*, 81–2; J. Bruce ed., *Letters of Queen Elizabeth and King James VI of Scotland* (Camden Soc., 1849), 46; Goldberg, *James I*, 14–17.   [135] Akrigg, *Letters*, 308.

[136] Ibid., 315; *Basilikon Doron*, I, 64, 102, 122, 136, 168.

[137] James I, *Workes of Prince James*, 379.   [138] *Hist. Mss. Comm.*, *Salisbury*, XV. 302.

CHAPTER FIVE

Private conscience and public duty in the writings of Charles I

Perhaps no monarch in English history succeeded to the throne better briefed in the responsibilities of office than Charles I. Though James had penned it for his elder son and, primarily, for a Scottish context, his *Basilikon Doron* passed, as if by inheritance, to Prince Charles on Henry's death. As James himself put it in 1619, Henry having died, 'it now belongs to my only son Charles who succeeds to it by right as well as to all the rest of his brother's goods'.[1] The *Basilikon Doron* was not the only book of 'instructions' James bequeathed to his son. In 1618 and 1619 James wrote meditations on chapters of the books of St Matthew and Chronicles, works which began as personal meditations but which he published and dedicated to Charles because 'I apprehended that it would be a good pattern to put inheritors to kingdoms in mind of their calling.'[2] And if paternal injunction itself was not enough, the editor of James I's *Workes*, Bishop James Montagu, dedicated the volume to Charles, presenting it as 'a portion of your inheritance'. 'Let these workes therefore most gracious Prince', Montagu enjoined from the pulpit of his preface, 'lie before you as a Patterne; you cannot have a better. Neither doth the Honour of a good sonne consist in anything more than in imitating the good Presidents of a good father.'[3] These, Montagu explained to his royal reader, and all readers, were works that carried 'in them so much divine truth and light' which might 'operate' on the 'conscience' of men, to lead them to that truth and light. 'God hath given us a Solomon.' It was for Solomon's only surviving son to be an 'alter idem, a second self'.[4]

In his *Remonstrance for the Right of Kings*, James had, quite conventionally, asserted that the duty of a son to obey his father was enshrined in

---

[1] *The Workes of the Most High and Mighty Prince James* (1616), dedication to Prince Charles; James I, *A Meditation Upon the Lords Prayer* (1619, STC 14384), sig. A4; J. Craigie, ed., *The Basilikon Doron of King James VI* (2 vols., Scottish Text Soc., Edinburgh, 1944–50).

[2] James I, *A Meditation Upon the . . . XXVII Chapter of St Matthew* (1620, STC 14382), epistle dedicatory to Charles; *Meditation Upon the Lords Prayer*.   [3] *Workes of Prince James*, dedication.

[4] Ibid., preface to the reader.

the law of nature; that it was an obligation to God the Father as well as
the natural parent.[5] From such a premise James, again conventionally,
developed the idea and articulated the language of the king being father
to his subjects. The latter, by the law of nature, owed the king obedience
as he was similarly bound to love, protect them and govern for their
good.[6] In reality, in the most personal and particular cases, James's relationships with his sons fell somewhat short of the ideal. Henry clashed
with his father over matters of policies and style and, it has been argued,
established a court that became a centre of opposition to James.[7] As for
Charles, from quite an early age, there was evidently a chilly distance
between father and son. James seems to have devoted more of his paternal affection to his favourites, especially Buckingham, his 'child', who
reciprocated by addressing himself to his 'dear Dad'. Charles was left to
seek Buckingham's mediation with his father when James 'ill interpreted'
his son.[8] Moreover, the differences of style were profound. James, as
Jenny Wormald has demonstrated, was very much the product of his
Scottish environment and upbringing. He was informal, familiar and
jocular; he could be bawdy, coarse and crude. Despite his strictures to
the contrary, he overindulged in the drink – and perhaps other vices –
he anathematized.[9] Charles by contrast was chaste, prudish and moderate in his appetite. His court, unlike James's, was a model of decorum;
if Bishop Burnet is to be believed, he was alienated by his father's 'light
and familiar ways'.[10] And yet, Charles never spoke of his father but with
reverence, nor referred to his policies (as in Scotland for example) but as
a pattern. It may be that, as king as well as prince, Charles displayed a
'*dutiful* respect and love' for his father rather than personal warmth.[11] But
it is worth remembering that, for all his protestations of consistency
between his 'theory' and 'practice', what James wrote was quite other
than how he behaved.[12] It was therefore quite possible for his son genuinely to embrace his father's 'instructions', even follow the 'pattern' of
his *Workes*, whilst rejecting James's personal example.[13]

There is much to suggest that Charles quite literally took his father's

---

[5] James I, *A Remonstrance for the Right of Kings*, in C. H. McIlwain ed., *The Political Works of James I* (Cambridge, Mass., 1918), 224ff.   [6] E.g. McIlwain, *Political Works of James I*, 307.

[7] See R. Strong, *Henry Prince of Wales and England's Lost Renaissance* (1986), esp. ch. 2.

[8] J. O. Halliwell ed., *Letters of the Kings of England* (2 vols., 1848), II, 122, 149, 158–9; G. P. V. Akrigg ed., *The Letters of King James VI and I* (1984), 373–4, 376, 386–7.

[9] J. Wormald, 'King James VI and I: Two Kings or One?', *History*, 68 (1983), 187–209.

[10] Quoted in M. Lee, *The Road to Revolution* (Urbana, 1985), 6.

[11] Halliwell, *Letters of Kings of England*, II, 122.

[12] *Workes of Prince James*, 279; see also above, pp. 170–1.

[13] *The Workes of the Most High and Mighty Prince James* (1620) (Bodleian Lib. Vet A2 C17), dedication to Prince Charles.

words to heart. He annotated and corrected a volume of his father's poetry.[14] In proclamations and speeches he echoes phrases and passages from those which (as James himself tells us) his father penned himself.[15] Adages and advice that James wrote or uttered, Charles repeated or paraphrased into his own words. Various collections of axioms of the two monarchs ascribe to both the same adages and there is no reason to attribute the dual ascription to confusion.[16] Even the frontispiece of the *Eikon Basilike*, depicting Charles holding a crown of thorns (see Figure 10 on p. 215), may have owed much to the *Meditation* on verses of St Matthew that James had dedicated to his son, telling him 'the crown of thorns went never out of my mind remembering the thorny cares which a King . . . must be subject unto'.[17] Charles, we know, took particular comfort from the coincidence that the twenty-seventh chapter of St Matthew was the reading for the day he ascended the scaffold. Perhaps he did so not least because his father in his *Meditation* on the same passage had urged his son to 'prepare yourself for the worst'.[18] It would appear that Charles literally followed Montagu's injunction to take his father's *Workes* as a pattern. Not for nothing in one of the few Jacobean royal family portraits does Charles stand next to the Bible and James's *Workes*, as the inheritor of the divine word of both a heavenly and natural father.[19] Even after his death, James was represented as enthroned, with his son, the new king, standing as his word become flesh.[20]

James left the *Basilikon Doron* as 'my testament' and 'your counsellor', urging his son to keep it by him as had Alexander the *Iliad* of Homer.[21] Charles's sense of duty and conscience were – to a degree greater than we have appreciated – formed and shaped by it. The first book details 'a King's Christian Duty Towards God'. James instructs his successor to frame his affections according to the rules set down in scripture, to take the Bible as a mirror for self-examination, to fear as well as love God. He enjoins the prince to be 'a loving nourish father to the Church', to be a benefactor to the ministry, and to punish the enemies of the church – the puritans – 'in case they refuse to obey the law'.[22] Accordingly, the

---

[14] BL Add. MS 24195.

[15] W. Notestein, F. H. Relf and H. Simpson eds., *Commons Debates 1621* (7 vols., New Haven, 1935), IV, 71.

[16] Cf. *The Princely Pelican* (1649) and *Effata Regalia: Aphorismes Divine, Moral, Politick . . . of Charles I* (1661), with *Flores Regii* (1627); B. A., *King James his Apothegmes or Table Talk* (1643) and *Regales Aphorismi; or a Royal Chain of Golden Sentences* (1650). See too *Witty Apothegmes Delivered . . . by King James, King Charles* (1658). [17] James I, *Meditation Upon St Matthew*, epistle dedicatory.

[18] Ibid.; F. Hargrave, *A Complete Collection of State Trials* (11 vols., 1776–81), I, 1042.

[19] See J. Goldberg, *James I and the Politics of Literature* (Baltimore and London, 1983), plate p. 92.

[20] Ibid., plate p. 93. [21] *Basilikon Doron*, I, 8. [22] Ibid., 16, 24–52, 78, 80.

Prince Charles who was taunted by his elder brother as fitter to be an archbishop than a monarch became the most unerastian of kings, praised by Bishop Wren as a protector of the church.[23] Charles never doubted, as he passed on the words to his own son, that 'the chiefest duty of a king is to maintain the true religion'.[24] He endeavoured to increase the wealth and power of the clergy, protect the church from its enemies, and preserve the authority of the episcopate. In the end he also knew 'my obligation to be' never 'to abandon God's cause'.[25]

The second book of the *Basilikon Doron* concerned a 'King's Duty in his Office'. It urged the prince always to retain an awful sense of his responsibility for the protection and welfare of the commonwealth for whose good rather than his own he was born. What differentiated, James wrote, a legitimate king from a tyrant, was that 'the one acknowledgeth himself ordained for his people, having received from God a burden of government whereof he must be countable . . . the other thinketh his people ordained for him'.[26] The good king subjected his own desires 'ever thinking the common interest his chiefest particular'.[27] No less than his father, Charles felt 'daily and nightly' the cares and burden of his office.[28] It is, he told his parliament in 1628, 'my duty most of all' as well as 'everyone of yours according to his degree . . . to seek the maintenance of this church and commonwealth'.[29] Perhaps because the strains of political problems bore on him more than on his father, Charles more stridently stressed the need for 'affection to the public' to triumph over private interests.[30] More, perhaps, than his father he thought of a 'state' to which, no less than his subjects, he owed his service.[31] 'I have a trust', he put it at his trial, 'committed to me by God . . . I will not betray it.' For Charles, as for James, 'power' was not the agency of the royal will but the means, granted by God – 'lent unto us', as Charles put it – to execute that trust.[32] If the monarch extended his power, James had advised in 1620, it would only be 'where necessity shall require it' to fulfil his responsibility.[33] So Charles argued in 1642 against those who sought to divest him of the militia: 'that he cannot consent to divest himself of the just power which God and the laws . . . have placed in him for the defence of his people'.[34] 'Nature and duty' bound the king to have 'most

---

[23] See C. Carlton, *Charles I, the Personal Monarch* (1983), p. 10 and note.
[24] Halliwell, *Letters of Kings of England*, II, 417.   [25] Ibid., II, 384.   [26] *Basilikon Doron*, I, 54.
[27] Ibid.   [28] James I, *Meditation Upon St Matthew*, epistle dedicatory.
[29] W. Cobbett ed., *The Parliamentary History of England* (36 vols., 1806–20), II, 218.
[30] Ibid.; K. Sharpe, *The Personal Rule of Charles I* (New Haven and London, 1992), 194–5.
[31] *The Workes of Charles I* (2 vols., 1662), I, 430.   [32] *Cobbett's Parliamentary History*, II, 352.
[33] James I, *Meditation Upon St Matthew*, 124.   [34] *Cobbett's Parliamentary History*, II, 1107.

care of your preservations', he had announced in the 1620s.[35] Even in more adverse circumstances, he maintained that 'without the power which is now asked from us, we shall not be able to discharge that trust'.[36] When Charles spoke of the obligations to 'the general good of my kingdom . . . which I am bound to preserve' before 'my own interests', we can almost hear him echo his father's own words and injunction to make the discharge of his responsibility 'the principal butt ye shoot at'.[37]

As he detailed the policies and principles of good kingship, James penned a script for the reign of his second son. Behind Charles's injunctions against enclosures and depopulators we read his father's instructions to check proud oppressors and proffer justice to poor and rich alike.[38] From James's defence of 'plays and lawful games in May', 'good cheer at Yule' and innocent recreation on Sundays, Charles, like his father, drew his *Book of Sports*.[39] The court of Charles I, the 'most regular and splendid in Christendom', seems almost to have been fashioned according to the blueprint of the *Basilikon Doron*, where James counselled the temperance, virtue and godliness from which his own court fell so sadly short.[40] Only from James's advice to 'hold no Parliaments but for necessity of new laws' did Charles obviously dissent, assembling those of 1626 and 1629, for example, more to resolve a problem than to pursue a legislative programme.[41] For all the differences of their style and between their practice, Charles most often followed his father's advice to the letter.

Indeed, even in his most personal habits and demeanour, Charles regarded it as his duty to obey his father's decree, having no more the freedom of his own passions or body, than James had of a son who was 'heir apparent to our body politic' as well as his natural child.[42] James laid down the curriculum for a prince's education: in history and mathematics as well as holy writ, and in active, physical exercise as well as contemplative study.[43] A connoisseur, expert horseman, musician, student of history, inventor and lover of antiquities, Charles became the embodiment of his father's belief that 'all arts and sciences are linked every one with other', as he took 'the counsel of all crafts'.[44] In his mod-

---

[35] Ibid., II, 218.   [36] *Workes of Charles I*, II, 98.
[37] *Eikon Basilike* (1876), 31; *Basilikon Doron*, I, 206.   [38] *Basilikon Doron*, I, 68ff.
[39] Ibid., I, 94–5; S. R. Gardiner, *Constitutional Documents of the Puritan Revolution, 1625–1660* (Oxford, 1899), 99–103.
[40] Sir Philip Warwick, *Memoires of the Reign of King Charles I* (1701), 113; *Basilikon Doron*, I, 136.
[41] *Basilikon Doron*, I, 60.   [42] *Hist. Mss. Comm., Salisbury*, XV, 302.
[43] *Basilikon Doron*, I, 34, 142–52; *Meditation Upon St Matthew*, dedication.
[44] *Basilikon Doron*, I, 142, 144.

eration in food, drink and dress, and in remaining 'pure' until marriage and faithful afterwards, Charles lived according to his father's dictates. Even his wife he endeavoured to govern by James's precepts, not permitting her (for most of his reign) 'to meddle with the politic government of the commonwealth'.[45] Most of all, tutored by his father as well as by experience that 'people are naturally inclined to counterfeit . . . their Princes' manners', Charles followed 'a virtuous life in his own person', so that his 'good example' might aid the 'alluring of his subjects to the love of virtue'.[46] In his own words, Charles sought to stand as a 'rule of order', or, as James put it, the 'vive image' of God, the 'author of all virtue'.[47]

That last injunction reminds us that, though the tensions of a perceived reality occasionally fractured it, James adhered still to the ideal that the good ruler was the good Christian, that government was an ethical activity. 'As you are a good christian', he opened his book on the duties of the regal office, '*so* you may be a good king.'[48] Indeed, the repetition of an ideal and prescription that had been theoretically challenged by Machiavelli surpassed naïveté and nostalgia. James appears to have believed that the monarch, by resolving the contradictions within his own person – between the public and private interest, order and anarchy, the moral and the expedient – might ease the tension that threatened the commonwealth.[49] Accordingly, James stressed to his son the importance of an 'agreeance and conformity . . . betwixt his outward behaviour . . . and the virtuous quality of his mind', and the need to present an image of self-regulation as a didactic microcosmic model for society. 'He cannot be thought worthy to rule and command others', he urged, 'that cannot rule . . . his own proper affections and unreasonable appetites.'[50] A king, by contrast, who mastered his own passions made his 'own life . . . a law book and a mirror to your people, that therein they may read the practice of their own laws'.[51] In the end, then, good kingship came down to self-regulation, the willingness to order oneself according to God's divine decree, the knowledge of which he had planted in all created man, and especially his lieutenant on earth. It was, in fact, a matter of conscience. 'Above all then (my son)', James counselled first Henry, then Charles, 'labour to keep sound this conscience';

---

[45] Ibid., I, 134; Sharpe, *Personal Rule*, 172–3.   [46] *Basilikon Doron*, I, 102–4.
[47] Ibid., I, 160; J. F. Larkin ed., *Stuart Royal Proclamations, Vol. II: Royal Proclamations of King Charles I, 1625–1646* (Oxford, 1983), 80; PRO LC5/180, p. 1.   [48] *Basilikon Doron*, I, 52.
[49] Above, pp. 160–3.
[50] *Basilikon Doron*, I, 15, 24. Charles paraphrased this adage in a margin note to his copy of Bacon's *Advancement of Learning* (1640).   [51] *Basilikon Doron*, I, 104.

'Remember . . . in all your actions of the great account you are one day to make.'[52] Because, even more than his father, Charles daily laboured and never forgot, he encountered greater difficulties in the exercise of his office.

Certainly Charles held firmly to the idea that public actions no less than private should be conducted by the same ethical codes. 'As for princely policy', he once put it, 'I hold none better than sincere piety':[53] the good king was the good Christian. Where James, however, had been in practice prepared to act 'politically', Charles for most of his life took the injunction literally as a working rule of government. Circumstances and experience made it ever more obvious that not all princes shunned Machiavelli's contrary precepts and some at home counselled courses that separated strategy from morality. Charles's own frequent references to 'policy' even echo their language. He recognized that some spoke, and might even believe *he* spoke and wrote, 'out of design or policy'.[54] He was ready to acknowledge that in treating one did not offer concessions all at once, reserving some 'to be drawn on by degrees upon debates'.[55] But for the most part, Charles's perception of this disjuncture between moral and politic courses led not to an acceptance of realpolitik, rather to a determination to do what he thought right, even if it was quite evidently *not* good strategy. One of the things, Charles said, that he most disliked the puritans for was their belief that their ends justified their means; for 'what good man had not rather want anything . . . than obtain it by unlawful and irreligious means'.[56]

This is I suppose what Conrad Russell and John Reeve mean when they describe Charles I as a poor politician, unfit for rule.[57] This is a judgement both accurate and anachronistic, for while we are ready to accept a 'political sphere' of action at times divorced from morality and even admire it, the early modern age, whatever some practised, in theory did not. Charles thought his first responsibility was to do according to God's dictates, as his reason and conscience discerned them, rather than act 'politically'. 'A king', he explained, 'having so many strict ties of conscience upon him hath *least liberty of prudence*.'[58] And (he maintained), as if in posthumous answer to Conrad Russell, 'if the straitness of my conscience will not give me leave to swallow down such camels as others do

---

[52] Ibid., I, 42–4.   [53] *The Princely Pelican*, 5.   [54] *Workes of Charles I*, II, 326.
[55] W. Bray ed., *Memoirs Illustrative of the Life and Writings of John Evelyn Esq.* (1818), 84–5.
[56] *Eikon Basilike*, 41.
[57] L. J. Reeve, *Charles I and the Road to Personal Rule* (Cambridge, 1989), 3–4 and passim; C. Russell, *The Causes of the English Civil War* (Oxford, 1990), ch. 8 and passim.
[58] *Effata Regalia*, 86, my italics.

of sacrilege and injustice . . . they have no more cause to quarrel with me than . . . that my throat is not so wide as theirs'; 'although I may seem a less politician to men yet I need no secret distinctions or evasions before God'.[59] During the 1640s, as we shall see, circumstances fractured Charles's moral universe to present a stark choice between political compromise and moral principles. Charles continued to claim their harmony: 'the best rule of policy', he argued, 'is to prefer . . . the peace of conscience before the preservation of kingdoms'.[60] Though under pressure he dabbled with them, and in doing so gained a reputation for duplicity, only after he suspended experiments at compromise to resume a rigid stand was 'His Majesty . . . very much as ease with himself, for having fulfilled the offices both of a Christian and of a King'.[61] Ironically, it was ultimately through death that he reconciled them.

The king's tongue, James had written in the *Basilikon Doron*, should be 'the messenger of the mind'; what he said and promised should be what he meant, and meant to perform.[62] Again, as I have argued, James was occasionally willing in practice to encourage expectations that he did not propose to fulfil or hint at intentions that he did not hold.[63] And once again Charles appears to have more rigidly followed his father's theory than his example. Evidently he believed strongly in the sanctity of oaths and promises – be they to his ministers, foreign princes, his wife, or the commonwealth as a whole. So when he was about to recommend the Bishop of Ross for the see of Elphin in Ireland, Charles, remembering that he had promised the nomination to Wentworth, informed his Lord Deputy, that 'if you hold me strictly to my engagement, I cannot go from it'.[64] No less the promise Charles made to respect Henrietta Maria's religion he kept despite personal as well as political problems and though, as he told her frankly, 'the oath I took not to seek to convert thee hath been of great prejudice to me'.[65] Even in matters of diplomacy, Charles, though willing to take refuge in unspecific phrases, was not ready blatantly to deceive. In 1627 he ordered Buckingham to be careful in laying out his manifesto to the Huguenots lest circumstances forced him to renege on a declaration, 'which I should be loath should fall out'.[66] Even in August 1641 when it was not to his best advantage to fulfil his promise, he believed himself 'so far now engaged to the Spanish

[59] *Eikon Basilike*, 25, 70.   [60] *Effata Regalia*, 3.   [61] *Workes of Charles I*, 263.
[62] *Basilikon Doron*, I, 178–82.   [63] Above, pp. 170–1.
[64] Halliwell, *Letters of Kings of England*, II, 321.
[65] J. Bruce ed., *Charles I in 1646: Letters of King Charles I to Queen Henrietta Maria* (Camden Soc. 63, 1856), 22.   [66] C. Petrie ed., *The Letters, Speeches and Proclamations of King Charles I* (1935), 51.

ambassador . . . that I cannot now go back'.[67] At home Charles frequently assured his parliaments that he would perform what he promised. And for all the disputes about what had been agreed in 1628, he sincerely felt in 1640 that 'I never said anything in way of favour to my people but that, by grace of God, I will really and punctually perform it.'[68]

His own obligation to honour his coronation oath and promises, Charles believed, imposed on his subjects a reciprocal bond to trust in 'the word of a king'.[69] The failure of that trust more than anything else was incomprehensible to him. Still in 1642, he snapped at the Earl of Holland, saying 'it was a high thing to tax a king with breach of promises'.[70] And even in treating with rebels, he could not entirely condone a breach of his word. Following James's own counsel that in dealing with rebels, though 'direct promises' should still not be made, it was legitimate to gain time by 'fair general speeches', he instructed the Marquis of Hamilton, his commissioner to the rebel Covenanters in 1638, 'in a word gain time by all the *honest means* you can'.[71] 'Flatter them with hopes', he continued, so long as 'you engage not me against my grounds'.[72] The sanctity of oaths, Charles continued to maintain throughout the 1640s, overrode political expediency and hard circumstance. He evidently approved of the rather Hobbesian view that even an oath made to a thief was made voluntarily and was binding – not least because an oath was to God as well as man.[73] Accordingly he ordered the future Charles II that, though his restoration might be on hard conditions, 'whatever you promise, keep'.[74] Despite his own hard conditions, Charles told Alexander Henderson during the debate on the church at Newcastle, it was not least his coronation oaths that bound him to sustain the bishops.[75] The sanctity of oaths was essential to the very existence of a Christian commonwealth.

Beyond the obligation to fulfil his promises, James, in happier times, had instructed a future king to eschew any public rhetoric that did not voice his innermost thoughts, urging 'his tongue should ever be the true

---

[67] Bray, *Memoirs of Evelyn*, 5.   [68] *Workes of Charles I*, I, 376.
[69] *Cobbett's Parliamentary History*, III, 293; cf. James I's insistence that when he spoke the word of a king 'you are bound to believe me', McIlwain, *Political Works of James I*, 317.
[70] *Workes of Charles I*, I, 397.
[71] *Basilikon Doron*, I, 182; Petrie, *Letters, Speeches and Proclamations of Charles I*, 7, my italics.
[72] Petrie, *Letters, Speeches and Proclamations of Charles I*, 106.
[73] R. Sanderson, *De Juramento: Seven Lectures Concerning the Obligation of Promissory Oaths*, 'revised and approved under his Majesty's own hand' (1655), 138–9.
[74] Petrie, *Letters, Speeches and Proclamations of Charles I*, 240.   [75] *Workes of Charles I*, I, 325.

messenger of his heart'.[76] The denial of a distinction between the 'public' and 'private' voices of a ruler was, I have argued, itself a rejection of the Machiavellian notion of a distinct sphere of 'politics' and the reaffirmation of the harmony of virtue and government.[77] If Charles learned this from his father, he also read that scripture condemned feigning and enjoyed a singleness of heart. It was, he believed, the Jesuits' and puritans' mental reservations to their oaths and promises, the gap between language and intention, that more than anything made them a threat to a commonwealth of discourse into which 'a sense mixed of verbal and mental parts is no wise to be admitted'.[78] For a mental reservation implied an individual conscience separate from and at odds with the values and truths which, it was still believed, were shared across the commonwealth. Like his father, therefore, Charles often expressed his desire 'that the clearness and candour of his royal heart may appear to all his subjects'.[79] This was more than a mere claim to sincerity or a plea for trust; it was an invocation to his subjects to be instructed in what was right by looking into the king's conscience. 'We will not be drawn to pretend', he explained to the Commons during the debate on the Petition of Right, when 'our judgement and conscience are not satisfied'. The king's conscience was not the servant of any private interest; it was the custodian of 'the public good and safety of us and our people', a conscience for the commonwealth.[80] Because he would 'not affirm that to men what in my conscience I denied to God',[81] the king, as his father had counselled, would act as a crystal through which his subjects would see and come to join with him in knowledge of God and of his decrees for a Christian society.

Charles adhered to the concept of a shared national conscience, even as the realm fragmented and divided into civil war. Like the law, conscience was a shared code for conduct across the commonwealth. The judges, the custodians of the common laws, he explained, he had left 'wholly to their consciences and whensoever they offended against that they wronged his Majesty no less than his people'.[82] And yet, he also accepted, necessarily, the fact of individual beliefs, arguing – in significant language – that 'every private believer is a king and a priest'.[83] Like James in his treatment of his Catholic subjects, Charles endeavoured to maintain that 'different professions in point of religion cannot . . . take

---

[76] *Basilikon Doron*, I, 182, 280; McIlwain, *Political Works of James I*, 280, 307.
[77] Above, ch. 4.   [78] Sanderson, *De Juramento*, 198, 202.
[79] *Cobbett's Parliamentary History*, II, 573.   [80] Ibid., II, 352.   [81] *Eikon Basilike*, 21–2.
[82] *Workes of Charles I*, II, 334.   [83] *Eikon Basilike*, 175.

away the community of relations either to parents or to princes'.[84] However if God was 'the only king of men's consciences', those who did not share the king's religion would not, in the end, follow his conscience – or continue their allegiance.[85] In the end, in the absence of an ecumenical reunion of Christendom or a readiness to tolerate difference of belief and to separate conscience and politics, Charles was left denouncing those who challenged the codes of the commonwealth as misled by false conscience, or by none. The malignant, he replied to the parliamentary petition of 1641, threatened the common peace under '*pretence of religion and conscience*'.[86] The lecturers appointed by puritan patrons, he told '*all* his loving subjects' in August 1642, were men of '*no conscience*'; the private interests and vices of 'ambition, malice and sedition' had 'been hid under the visors of conscience and religion', for 'under the colours of piety ambitious policies march'.[87] As true religion sustained the co-operation and hierarchy of the commonwealth, self-interest and rebellion could only be 'the pretensions of religion in which politicians wrap up their designs'.[88] Moreover, Charles appears to have held to the conviction that, so powerful was the force of God's code, the pretenders knew in their hearts the nature of their deception – of themselves as well as others. Those, he proclaimed in his declaration from York in June 1642, who accused others 'themselves in their consciences know that the greatest and indeed only danger . . . is in their own desperate and seditious designs'.[89] 'Few men's consciences', he once opined, 'are so stupid as not to inflict upon them some secret impressions of that shame and dishonour which attends all unworthy actions'; 'even dishonest men are so far touched with some conscience'.[90] The king's role was to expose the pretenders, to develop the residual sense of right and wrong in all, and to protect and defend the common conscience of the realm until the misguided came to see the light or were defeated and saw God's own displeasure.

Charles had hopes of all three. From the publication of his majesty's *Large Declaration* in 1639, Charles set out to expose the pretence of conscience claimed as justification for their actions by enemies to episcopacy.[91] He was optimistic, he recalled by way of answer to the Nineteen Propositions, that even during the Long Parliament those who had combined to alter this government 'would . . . have been converted in their

---

[84] Ibid., 106.   [85] Ibid., 109.   [86] *Workes of Charles I*, II, 77, my italics.
[87] Ibid., II, 149, 159, my italics.   [88] *Eikon Basilike*, 88.   [89] *Workes of Charles I*, II, 107.
[90] *De Juramento*, 205; *Effata Regalia*, 88.
[91] See [W. Balcanquall], *A Large Declaration Concerning the Late Tumults in Scotland* (Edinburgh, 1639).

consciences by the clearness and justice of our actions'.[92] And at the very end, he believed that those who voted to block all further treating with him, knew in their consciences that he had 'satisfied your desires in every particular since this treaty'.[93] Sinners, however, resisted the injunctions of conscience (even when it dimly still spoke to them) to do their duty. The king could never be deaf to its call. 'If you', he had warned his MPs as early as 1628, '. . . should not do your duties . . . I must in discharge of my conscience, use those other means which God hath put into my hands to save that which the follies of some particular men may otherwise hazard to lose.'[94] The king, in other words, to provide what 'the state . . . needs', had to reinforce God's voice of conscience in his subjects – by example and persuasion, and ultimately, if need be, by authority and force.

It was a familiar political analogue in early modern England to characterize the king as the reason of the body politic. As the court masques evidence, Charles represented his authority as the rule of reason over passions and appetites. When, however, at Holdenby, he referred to 'the Reason which God hath given him to judge by for the good of him and his people', we can see that what Charles means by that reason was a special judgement and capacity to discern God's will, in other words a right 'conscience'.[95] If it was the king's duty, as he believed, to put 'the salvation of men's souls above the preservation of their bodies and states', so God had equipped him to perform it.[96] The conscience, Charles told Alexander Henderson, was God's 'vicegerent'; and as God's vicegerent on earth, the king's duty was to be the conscience of his people.[97] So in 1625, in a public prayer of Charles's own devising, the people of England were taught to pray: 'rule the heart of thy chosen servant Charles, our king and governor, that he knowing whose minister he is may above all things seek thy honour and glory and that we his subjects duly considering whose authority he hath may faithfully serve, honour and humbly obey him, in thee and for thee'.[98] The king's conscience then was never in theory at odds with his practice of government; it was the essence of his kingship. 'To look to my own conscience', Charles put it, was 'the faithful discharge of my trust as a king'.[99] Those who advised Charles to compromise his conscience on certain matters so as to preserve his throne sought to separate what he saw as inviolably married: his conscience and his regality. The king who had condemned

[92] *Workes of Charles I*, II, 136.   [93] Ibid., I, 293.   [94] *Cobbett's Parliamentary History*, II, 218.
[95] *Workes of Charles I*, II, 616.   [96] *Eikon Basilike*, 86.   [97] *Workes of Charles I*, I, 174.
[98] *A Form of Common Prayer together with an Order of Fasting* (1625), sig. I2.   [99] *Eikon Basilike*, 78.

the Jesuits' and puritans' mental reservations would not conceal his own knowledge of God's wishes: 'I have never', he told the Speaker of the House of Commons in 1647, 'dissembled nor hid my conscience'.[100] To dissemble it was to be unkinged:

> A quiet conscience in the breast
> Has only peace, only rest
> The wisest and worst of kings
> Are out of tune unless she sings.[101]

The compromise of the royal conscience, Charles believed, signalled the surrender to appetite and the breakdown of all social relations. 'If I should forsake my conscience', he writes in anguish to his beloved wife, 'I cannot be true to . . . thee.'[102] In compromising his conscience, the king surrendered along with his regality, his trust, his honour, his very humanity. Matters of conscience could not be negotiated or treated, because the conscience was 'more dear' than life. As a consequence, Charles Stuart concluded it was 'better for me to die enjoying this empire of my soul, which subjects me only to God, so far as by reason or religion He directs me, than live with the title of a king, if it should carry such a vassalage with it as not to suffer me to use my reason and conscience . . . as a king'.[103]

'The dictates of conscience', Bishop Sanderson wrote in a work that Charles I himself revised, '*whether right or erroneous* ever bindeth at the least not to act against it.'[104] The trust placed in kings, however, necessitated that their consciences should not err. James therefore had advised his son to take the reckoning with his conscience daily: 'remember every once in four and twenty hours, in the night or when you are at greatest quiet to call yourself to account of all your last days actions . . . censure yourself as sharply as if you were your own enemy'.[105] Charles therefore resolved that, as vital to 'the conscientious execution of that regal office whereto He hath called me . . .', 'with a strict and impartial scrutiny will I examine my heart'.[106] It was for the king, he told the Commons, to take their counsel but to weigh it with 'the reason, which have prevailed with our own conscience', that is after conversing along with 'that mighty Counsellor who can both suggest what is best and incline his heart steadfastly to follow it'.[107] James, we have seen, commended confession to his

---

[100] *Workes of Charles I*, I, 243.
[101] M. Pickel, *Charles I as Patron of Poetry and Drama* (1936), 177–8, a poem ascribed to Charles I.
[102] Bruce, *Charles I in 1646*, 71.   [103] *Eikon Basilike*, 29.   [104] *De Juramento*, 84, my italics.
[105] *Basilikon Doron*, I, 44.   [106] *The Princely Pelican*, 9.
[107] *Effata Regalia*, 38; Petrie, *Letters, Speeches and Proclamations of Charles I*, 120.

son and meditated on scripture always as the best tutor to and mirror of a king's conscience. Charles regularly confessed his sins, indeed retained a confessor, and in addition evidently took his most difficult cases of conscience to his trusted clergy – to Archbishop Laud and to Bishop Juxon.[108] Moreover, like his father, he meditated alone on passages of scripture, finding special comfort in the Psalms, which his father had translated and which he 'would usually upon occasion repeat . . . by heart' after meditation.[109] 'God's sovereignty', he knew, was 'the . . . King of men's consciences', and of none more especially than the king's own. 'When a King retires to God', he once uttered, 'he most enjoys himself', his own being, as monarch and man.[110] There can be no denying Charles's performance of that 'strict . . . scrutiny' of self he proclaimed nor doubting what Richard Watson was to call his 'self-clearing and sometimes . . . self-condemning disposition of conscience'.[111]

When James VI described his *Basilikon Doron* as a 'discharge of our conscience', he meant it in (at least) two senses. The work was a dialogue with God, a mirror for himself and an instruction to his son(s) – and beyond to all other readers. Similarly, I have suggested, his meditations on the books of Revelation and Chronicles and St Matthew's Gospel were private conversations with God that he published because they were mediations of God, so fulfilling a king's duty to bring his subjects to knowledge and fear of the Lord.[112] Charles did not follow his father's course in writing on books of scripture. Though learned in the Scriptures and Fathers, he was less of a theologian than James; his character, perhaps too his faith, were less logocentric than his father's. But in his own ways, Charles was as concerned to communicate to his subjects his conscience and knowledge of God – through icons and texts, finally through his death making himself both icon and text, apostle and martyr of Christ.

Few scholars have paid any attention to the prayers Charles composed or published under his name. Prayer, Charles was to define as the 'soul's . . . immediate converse with the divine majesty', 'thoughts devoted and dedicated to God . . . when the mind is most at quiet'.[113] As we read them, we cannot doubt that for Charles prayers were what his father's biblical exegeses had been for James: a meditation on, a personalizing of scripture – and a baring of the conscience before God. Where James grappled in his study with the hermeneutics of holy writ to discern God's

---

[108] Sharpe, *Personal Rule*, 281.   [109] *The Princely Pelican*, 10.
[110] *Eikon Basilike*, 109; *Effata Regalia*, 92.   [111] *Effata Regalia*, epistle dedicatory.
[112] Above, pp. 164–7.   [113] *Eikon Basilike*, 113; *The Princely Pelican*, 19.

will, Charles's less intellectual piety led him to kneel in prayers of emotional self-subjugation. The prayers have a confessional tone: 'look down at me', he prayed, 'thy unworthy servant who has prostrated myself at the footstool of thy throne of Grace'.[114] Acknowledging his failure to do all the duties of a Christian, the king yet fulfilled 'our burden and necessary duty to confess our sins freely unto thee'.[115] These intensely personal devotions, however, were not private. From the very beginning of his reign to his death, Charles also sought to lead his people through prayer to a knowledge of and subjection to the divine will. The plague that afflicted the land in the very year of his succession starkly underlined the need for prayers of atonement and the monarch's duty to take, as it were, the confession of the nation. Charles therefore, with the assistance of his bishops, composed a prayer and service, which, a proclamation of 3 July enjoined, should be

generally observed and solemnized . . . that when both prince and people together through the whole land shall join in one common and solemn devotion, of sending up their faithful and repentant prayers to Almighty God at one instant of time, the same shall be more available to obtain that mercy, help and comforting from God.[116]

The service reminded subjects that, as a mark of God's wrath, plague signalled the need for national repentance and fasting – ends 'to a more deep consideration of their consciences'.[117] His people felled by pestilence, the biblical King David had asked God to spare them, 'and rather to turn his ire himward'; the like had Josaphat and Ezechias. So Charles subjected himself – 'I am poor and in misery' – and by his example taught the humiliation his people, 'miserable and wretched sinners as we are', owed to God.[118] The 1625 prayers and service he devised were a form of national confession and purgation. 'Our conscience' (we note the singular noun), all prayed, 'doth accuse us and our sins do reprove us': 'if we should excuse ourselves our own consciences would accuse us before thee'. Prayer united the realm: all prayed for the king to serve God and for themselves and all subjects to 'humbly obey him in thee and for thee'. All confessed the nation's vices: drink and gluttony, fornication and swearing, false weights and measures, polluting the Lord's day, criticizing authority – the last underlining how a virtuous king not only implored God's mercy for the realm but spoke as the voice of its collective conscience.

<hr/>

[114] *Workes of Charles I*, I, section D IV.   [115] Ibid., I, 196.
[116] Larkin, *Proclamations*, II, no. 19, pp. 46–8.   [117] *A Form of Prayer* (1625), preface.
[118] Ibid., sig. C3v and passim.

The second outbreak of plague in 1636 saw another service together with another proclamation for a weekly fast, both intended 'by serious humiliation to implore the grace and favour of that Supreme offended majesty who hath smitten the land'.[119] This time, with the plague severe and (to be) enduring, it was acknowledged dangerous to detain assemblies in infected places for long services. The prescribed public service was shorter, and 'all other duties of prayer and humiliation requisite' were left to 'be observed by every person in their private families, at home'.[120] However, though circumstance limited the practice, the principle of communal uniform public worship was reaffirmed. In places not infected, 'His majesty requireth that the said fast be publicly solemnized, not only by reading the said [new] book, but by the use of sermons, or homilies . . . and for the more orderly solemnizing thereof, without confusion, his majesty . . . hath directed that the book of Prayers formerly set forth . . . shall be reprinted.' This the king 'commands to be used in all churches and places at these public meetings . . . as they tender the favour of Almighty God'.[121] Charles was directly connecting his authority to his own prayers, his kingship with a role as priest, overriding the false conscience of hypocrites (as he put it in thinly veiled denunciation of the puritans), to lead a national humiliation and worship.

In these volumes of prayers, the king's conscience virtually stands for the very being – or ideal – of the Christian commonwealth. Indeed, like James's paraphrases of scripture, Charles's effort to cohere and articulate a national conscience can be read as an attempt to resist the challenges to that ideal and to revalidate both the organic concept of the state and the authority of God's lieutenant to speak to him for it. After the outbreak of civil war, however, a war fought in part over religious differences and fears, the fiction of a common conscience was harder to sustain. Initially Charles endeavoured through prayers to uphold it, almost classifying civil war as another plague from outside. So his 1643 devotions led all in prayer 'for the averting of God's judgement now upon us; for the ceasing of this present rebellion; and restoring a happy peace in this kingdom'. Because all had too much followed their own hearts, and rebelled against the Lord, they prayed for obedience to him, the devotions closing with the homily against disobedience to all magistrates taken from the book published in Queen Elizabeth's reign.[122] But as division hardened, the king had to acknowledge that his conscience

[119] Larkin, *Proclamations*, II, no. 229, pp. 538–40; *A Form of Common Prayer together with an Order for Fasting* (1636).   [120] Larkin, *Proclamations*, II, no. 229, p. 539.   [121] Ibid., 540.
[122] *A Form of Common Prayer to be used upon the Solemn Fast appointed by His Majesty's Proclamation* (1643).

and prayers articulated those of a party rather than the whole commonwealth. Prayers were now of thanks for victory to a 'God of Hosts who
goest forth with our Armies' and 'against them that strive with Him'.
Though the king prayed the Lord to 'strike the minds of the perverse
with a true touch of that conscience which they go about to stifle and a
true sense of that duty to thine anointed', the coupling (of conscience
and obedience) was more artificial and the definition of conscience more
partisan. Charles himself acknowledged it; he was banished from his
garden of Eden, in which all men knew and obeyed God and king.
Though he prayed for peace and concurrence, he knew that some 'do
pursue their own private ends' and followed their *own* consciences.[123]

During the 1640s, amid the war of pamphlets and propaganda that
was no less important than the conflict of arms, we hear Charles struggling with this dilemma. The king retained a strong belief in, and saw
clearly the need for, a common conscience if the commonwealth were
to be repaired. Yet others now claimed conscience to justify violence and
sectarianism; and circumstances and even the king's friends urged the
need for expedient courses to secure his victory over his enemies. As
early as 1641 the Earl of Strafford argued that by going to the scaffold
he might act as a scapegoat and purge the nation's ills. Knowing the earl
to be innocent, however, Charles could not 'satisfy myself in honour or
conscience' without assuring him that he would not suffer.[124] 'I must tell
you', the king informed the Lords, 'that in my conscience I cannot
condemn him of high treason':

> My lords I hope you know what a tender thing conscience is; and I must declare
> unto you that to satisfy the people I would do great matters: but in this of con-
> science neither fear nor any other respect whatsoever shall make me go against
> it.[125]

After attainder and sentence, Charles could hardly bring himself to sign
the earl's death warrant, for 'conscience draweth itself by its own
light'.[126] The king's privy council, however, pressed on him the necessity
that absolved him from guilt. Four prelates were sent to Charles to 'pro-
pound how the tenderness of his conscience might safely wade through
this insuperable difficulty'. They argued that because high 'judges' had
found Strafford guilty the king 'may suffer that judgement to stand

---

[123] *A Collection of Prayers and Thanksgivings used in His Majesty's Chapel and his Armies* (1643); *A Form of Common Prayer for Blessing on the Treaty now Begun* (1644).
[124] Halliwell, *Letters of Kings of England*, II, 327.   [125] *Workes of Charles I*, I, 387–8.
[126] J. Hacket, *Scrinia Reserata: a Memorial Offer'd to the Great Deservings of John Williams* (1693), 160.

though in his private mind he was not satisfied'.[127] It was an argument that, in separating public from private belief, the conscience of the commonwealth from that of the king, undermined all Charles held dear as man and monarch.

Charles repented his concurrence in Strafford's death right up to his own last day. And not merely because he had let down a friend. Of the courses open to him in 1641, he had chosen 'rather what was safe than what seemed just, preferring the outward peace of my kingdoms with men before that inward exactness of conscience before God'. 'O never', the king prays in the *Eikon Basilike*, 'suffer me for reason of state to go against my reason of conscience.'[128]

Strafford's death, however, was by no means the only occasion on which the king faced a dilemma of conscience. Throughout the 1640s, negotiations for peace centred on religious issues and especially the episcopal government of the church. In 1641, the year in which he suspended many of his beliefs in the name of settlement, Charles conceded the taking away of bishops' votes in parliament, in the hope of abating the hostility to the episcopate itself. As the assault on them escalated, he came to repent an expedient act for which 'I have been most justly punished.'[129] But the issue would not fade away, and Charles's belief in the divinity of episcopal government had to be weighed in the scales with his duty to mend the rent in the commonwealth. In 1646 the prospect of peace hung on the bishops and Charles consulted Bishop Juxon, knowing his worth 'in resolving cases of conscience'. Some, Charles told Juxon, persuaded him to presbyterianism which was 'against my conscience', but he could not ignore his obligation to effect a peace. Could he, therefore, he asked, offer a temporary compliance, conceding presbyterian government for three years?[130] Though Juxon evidently answered in the affirmative, the concession was still too much for Charles's comfort. In February 1646 he had expressed his belief that a temporary concession 'may palliate not excuse my sin'.[131] We hear him endeavouring to convince himself that he had not 'thereby any whit abandoned . . . the great and not to be foresaken argument of my conscience'. 'It is', he tried to persuade himself, 'but a temporary permission to continue such an unlawful possession which for the present I cannot help, so as to lay a hopeful ground for a perfect recovery of that which to abandon were directly against my conscience.'[132]

---

[127] Ibid., 160–1.   [128] *Eikon Basilike*, 6, 10.   [129] *Workes of Charles I*, I, 196.
[130] Halliwell, *Letters of Kings of England*, II, 422.   [131] Bruce, *Charles I in 1646*, 19.
[132] Halliwell, *Letters of Kings of England*, II, 430, 434.

During 1646 and 1647 Charles not only negotiated with Scots and with English presbyterians and independents, he negotiated between his desire for peace, which required compromise, and his conscience, which held him to rigid principles. Though he could justify deceiving the commissioners of an illegal parliament (as he saw it), he tried to stop short of outright deception by forms of words. Though he gave parliament 'leave to hope for more than he intended', he comforted himself that he had promised only to 'endeavour' their satisfaction.[133] Such linguistic sleights, however, appeared to many as duplicitous. The capture of royal letters after the battle of Naseby had revealed the gap between Charles's public protestations and secret thoughts and intentions; and, not least because of his stand on his honesty, greatly damaged his cause.[134] Though a sizeable peace party in the House of Commons remained willing to trust the king, evidence of his deceit and evasiveness undoubtedly fed a party – in parliament and more dangerously in the army – that came to regard his oath as a lie and his person as an obstacle to peaceful settlement, a man of blood.[135] Throughout all the negotiations, Charles was probably trying to pursue constant goals through changing means dictated by altered circumstances. But if he lost more than he gained by such politicking, it would also appear that the king was himself discomfited by it and in his heart knew that it was best to adhere to principle 'howsoever it shall please God to dispose of me'.[136]

Certainly when it became clear that a stark choice had to be made about the nature of the church, he took a stand even against his own beloved wife. Henrietta Maria had no doubt that her husband should ditch the bishops. Their quarrel over the matter, conducted through correspondence, was the most painful disjuncture between private affection and public duty in Charles's life, and the most powerful document of his conscience. Charles tried to explain to his wife why he rejected her counsel; he pleaded for her respect in this, one of their few clashes: 'albeit we differ in matters of religion, yet thou must esteem me for having care of my conscience'.[137] Finally, in a moving sentence, he asked her to 'consider that if I should quit my conscience how unworthy I make myself of thy love'.[138] After periods of hesitation Charles came to assert what he had always known, that his conscience was his very being

---

[133] Bruce, *Charles I in 1646*, xxvii.
[134] Carlton, *Charles I*, 289; D. Underdown, *Pride's Purge: Politics in the Puritan Revolution* (Oxford, 1971), 60.
[135] Underdown, *Pride's Purge*, 6off. and passim; P. Crawford, 'Charles Stuart, that Man of Blood', *Journ. Brit. Studies*, 16 (1973), 41–61.   [136] Bruce, *Charles I in 1646*, xvii.
[137] Ibid., 24; cf. 7.   [138] Ibid., 21.

as a Christian; that to compromise it was to show 'more fear of man than of God'.[139]

Indeed by 1646 Charles had already come to believe in the necessity of a stand on conscience, even if it cost him his life. That is, he attempted to appropriate to himself and his cause the validation of conscience, to marginalize his enemies by denying their claim to it, and most of all to reunite the realm by publicly renouncing personal interest so as to speak once again as the conscience of the commonwealth. Some of Charles's thinking on the issue is undoubtedly reflected in Bishop Robert Sanderson's lectures on the obligation of promissory oaths, the work 'revised and approved under his Majesty's own hand'. Scripture, the lectures affirm, enjoined singleness of heart: the obligation to mean what one says. Promises were made always to God as well as men and so 'no injury done to us by men can give us just cause to injure God'. Because 'the obligation of an oath is of divine natural law', 'the dictates of conscience . . . ever bindeth at the least not to act against it'. The Christian, Sanderson's treatise concludes, should not prefer external peace to the quiet of his conscience.[140]

Increasingly, as military was followed by political defeat, this was the stance of Charles's public pronouncements. In his reply in May 1647 from imprisonment at Holdenby to proposals from parliament, the king coupled his divine right, authority and conscience: 'without disclaiming that Reason which God hath given him to judge by for the good of Him and His people, and without putting the greatest violence upon his own conscience', Charles argued, he could not 'give his consent to all of them'.[141] In September he similarly wrote from Hampton Court that he could not consent to new terms 'without violation of his conscience'.[142] The next year, in his stand for episcopacy, Charles hinted that he would die to preserve his conscience and to enshrine the principles of conscience as the basis of action in a Christian commonwealth:

if his own Houses shall not think fit to recede from the strictness of their demands in these particulars, his Majesty can with more comfort cast himself upon his Saviour's goodness to support him and defend him from all affliction, how great soever that may befall him, than for any public consideration . . . deprive himself of . . . inward tranquillity.[143]

Finally at his trial, Charles eschewed political engagement and refused to answer charges but 'delivered my conscience', a conscience

[139] *Eikon Basilike*, 6.   [140] Sanderson, *De Juramento*, 41–2, 84, 197, 234, 236 and passim.
[141] *Workes of Charles I*, II, 616.   [142] Ibid., II, 629.   [143] Ibid., I, 349.

which 'I call dearer to me than my life'.[144] During the last weeks of his life, far from concurring with John Reeve and Conrad Russell that he should have been more politically astute, Charles was anxious to erase from the public memory the occasions on which he had played the politician; indeed to confess his own lapse from fidelity to conscience as the cause of his troubles. In a prayer he was alleged to have composed in his 'life of sufferings', the king asked God's (and his people's) forgiveness for having made concessions – to the Scots and over the rights of bishops: 'with shame and grief I confess that I therein followed the persuasion of worldly wisdom forsaking the dictates of a right informed conscience'.[145] Charles prayed: 'keep me from the great offence of enacting anything against my conscience'.[146] By his final stand and confession of his recent 'errors' – errors of negotiating, politicking, conceding – Charles cast all recent events as plagues brought on the nation, like those of the 1620s and 1630s, by its *and his* sins. And his personal confession and reaffirmation of faith was an invitation to his people to follow him, to go with their conscience.[147] For, as an editor of the king's works glossed the royal message, 'a good conscience . . . draweth away all sadness . . . And it is that which I wish unto all who fear God and honour the King.'[148] By mediating God's will to his people, the king's conscience might lead his subjects back to God – and so in the future to his lieutenant on earth.

In order to do so, either Charles or his intimates constructed a powerful text of the royal conscience that might live after him, and invalidate the rival claims to interpret God's will made by the godly. The *Eikon Basilike* more than anything else denied the victory to Charles's enemies by elevating the sphere of conscience above that of state.[149] The text opens with a repeated royal confession of his sin in sending Strafford to the block:

I have often with sorrow confessed both to God and men as an act of so sinful frailty that it discovered more fear of men than of God. I see it a bad exchange to wound a man's own conscience thereby to salve state sores.[150]

---

[144] Ibid., I, 442, 455.

[145] *His Majesty's Prayers which he used in his Time of his Sufferings* (1649, E1317/2), sig. A4v.

[146] E. R., *The Divine Meditations and Vows of His Sacred Majesty in his Solitude at Holmby House* (1649, E560/27), p. 7.

[147] E.g. Halliwell, *Letters of Kings of England*, II, 361, 430, 432; *Workes of Charles I*, I, 196; Hargrave, *A Complete Collection of State Trials*, 1043; *Eikon Basilike*, 6–10, 225–6.

[148] E. R., *Divine Meditations of His Majesty*, preface to the reader.

[149] See *Eikon Basilike*, 144, where Charles says of his enemies: 'They have often indeed had the better against my side in the field, but never, I believe, at the bar of God's tribunal, or their own consciences.'   [150] Ibid., 6.

Having learned his error, however, Charles announced how he thereafter determined to live by his conscience and 'although I may seem a less politician to men yet I need no several distinctions or evasions before God'.[151] And what he hid not from God he concealed not from men either. Where his enemies hid their real intent behind 'disguises', 'pretensions' and in 'deceitful dalliances', the king acted only from conscience assured, now he was true to him, of God's favour and protection.[152]

Acting on his conscience was also more than a personal satisfaction; it was, the *Eikon* puts it, 'the faithful discharge of my trust as a king'. For it was the duty of a king to consider 'the salvation of men's souls above the preservation of their bodies and estates' and so to make their sins appear to their consciences as the king's had to him.[153] God was the 'king of men's consciences' and it was the duty of his lieutenant to teach it. But, in learning subjection to God, subjects came to an understanding of their bond of obedience to the godly king, 'bonds which thy word . . . have laid on their conscience'. For those who sinned against the king's conscience sinned also 'against thee'.[154] It was those who rejected conscience who elevated power above the law, hid sedition under the cloak of religion and ultimately surrendered their own natural freedom, the 'empire' of their own souls. For God saw through their disguises and worked to 'accuse them in their own thoughts'. Their 'black veils' could not hide the king's 'shining face while God gave me a heart . . . to converse with him'.[155]

It is as a text of royal conscience that the *Eikon Basilike* turned the tables on the king's enemies. Obviously the king's stance as *the* interpreter of God's will undercut the whole godly justification of their actions in the name of conscience. But the potential force of this text goes well beyond that. Just as he had in his prayers of the 1620s, Charles in the pages of the *Eikon* conducts a national service of worship and atonement. Once we read it, we, willy-nilly, participate in that service and acknowledge the king's sacerdotal role. Or we cast ourselves outside, as one excommunicated from the church. Indeed, Charles's appropriation of the language and role of Christ made rejection of the earthly simultaneously a turning away from the heavenly king. The king's conscience in other words had become the text of God's will, rendering all other claims to conscience not only rebellious or flawed, but ungodly.

Milton discerned both the power of this stance and the urgent need

---

[151] Ibid., 25.   [152] Ibid., 26, 88.   [153] Ibid., 78, 86.   [154] Ibid., 98.
[155] Ibid., 111, 144.

for the puritans to contest it. The *Eikon*, he confessed, read as though 'the very manuscript of God's judgement had been delivered to [Charles's] custody and exposition'.[156] In order to undermine it, therefore, he both denied the authenticity of the king's own conscience and refuted any claim for monarchical conscience to dictate to others. Strafford's trial, Milton argued, demonstrated the errors of Charles's conscience in its opposition to a 'solemn piece of Justice' and the 'welfare, the safety, and . . . the unanimous demand of three populous Nations'.[157] If the king claimed conscientious scruples about Wentworth's execution, he continued, it was only 'because he knew himself a Principal in what the *Earl* was but his accessory'.[158] Charles's vacillations over Strafford's condemnation – his insistent refusal to find him guilty, his subsequent acquiescence and then passionate regret – Milton used as evidence of the king's 'subtle dissimulation', of his worldly political manoeuvres masked by a rhetoric of conscience which was (the very charge Charles had levelled at his enemies) a 'specious plea'.[159] Even had the royal conscience not been corrupted, Milton denies its authority over others. In answer to Charles's poignant laments about the assault on his conscience, Milton replies that the grant to the king of his own conscience should not be a 'permitting him to bereave us of ours'.[160] Charles I, Milton implies, not altogether inaccurately, deployed the authority of his conscience as a prop to the exercise of absolute government. 'It was not the inward use of his reason and of his conscience that would content him, but to use them both as a law over all his subjects.'[161] Against Charles's claim to have 'his conscience . . . a universal conscience, the whole Kingdom's conscience',[162] Milton asserted the rights of subjects in their own, and indeed the role of parliaments in protecting those rights of conscience, as they did the property of subjects, from incursion. 'The parliament . . . hath had it always in their power to limit and confine the exorbitancy of kings, whether they call it their will, their reason, or their conscience.'[163] For no monarch, Milton concluded, could 'counterfeit the hand of God': 'he who . . . takes upon him perpetually to unfold the secret and unsearchable Mysteries of high Providence is likely . . . to mistake and slander them'.[164] The claim to die for conscience, *Eikonoklastes* asserts against the very core of the *Eikon Basilike*, does not make Charles I a martyr, if it is the unconstitutional claim to power of an erroneous or specious conscience.

[156] J. Milton, *Eikonoklastes*, ed. W. H. Haller, *The Works of John Milton* V (New York, 1932), 272.
[157] Ibid., 91.   [158] Ibid., 93.   [159] Ibid., 138.   [160] Ibid., 132.   [161] Ibid., 132.
[162] Ibid., 176–7.   [163] Ibid., 181.   [164] Ibid., 272.

The vast pamphlet war sparked off by the *Eikon Basilike* essentially revolved around this issue: the claims made for and the integrity of the royal conscience.[165] *The Princely Pelican*, a work of observations extracted from his majesty's divine meditations, reports the king saying: 'As for princely policy, I hold none better than sincere piety.'[166] Accordingly he promises that 'with a strict and impartial scrutiny will I examine my heart'.[167] *The Princely Pelican* represents the lone godly prince in the wilderness of sin, finding comfort in the psalms. Against the charge that the royal meditations were deceit or hypocrisy, the author retorts that 'his princely pen hated nothing more than to play the subtle sophist with their soul'.[168] The contest, charge and countercharge went on. A 1661 edition of the *Aphorisms Divine Moral [and] Politick of Charles I* announced their primary value as texts of the king's 'self-clearing and sometimes . . . self-condemning disposition of conscience'.[169]

But the king's opponents did not simply negate the claims of the *Eikon Basilike* and its defenders. Milton's reference to providence reminds us that, albeit in different language, others besides Charles I made claim to discern God's ways and will in the world. For the puritan, the ability to discern God's providence was a mark of election, a prerogative of the saints. Though such a belief was common throughout the early modern period, Blair Worden is surely right to observe that it was the time of the Great Rebellion or civil war in England 'when Puritan providentialism enjoys its most widespread influence'.[170] During the civil wars, events – revolutionary events – required a justification that the discourse of law and politics did not readily provide. The doctrine of providence offered the most powerful counter to the pretensions to divine right by an unelect king (as he was seen) and appropriated God's will and intervention to override arguments from law, custom and tradition. Monarchy might be limited by arguments from custom and law, but it was the discourse of providence that gave a script to regicides. Moreover, providence not only made sense of these apparently confused and turbulent years; it was a concept and language which, far from dictating rigid courses and principles, permitted major shifts of policy and action, as God revealed his mysterious will at each turn of events. Oliver Cromwell, of course, not only illustrates these observations; he

---

[165] For a brilliant discussion of *Eikonoklastes* see S. Zwicker, *Lines of Authority: Politics and English Literary Culture, 1649–89* (Ithaca, 1993), ch. 2.
[166] *The Princely Pelican's Royal Resolves presented in Sundry Choice Observations* . . . (1649), 5.
[167] Ibid., 9.   [168] Ibid., 10, 23.   [169] *Effata Regalia*, epistle dedicatory.
[170] B. Worden, 'Providence and Politics in Cromwellian England', *Past and Present*, 109 (1985), 55–99, 59.

exemplifies, one is tempted to say epitomizes, them. Whatever his early
uncertainties and doubts about the trial and execution of the king, God's
providence overcame them. And if he on all matters often changed his
mind, it was but because he came to know God's will the better.[171] The
providence that contended with Charles I's claim to conscience was
claimed ironically by the Lord Protector as *his* validation – for military
decision, for political manoeuvre, for the acquisition of power, for the
defence of his authority.

Whether or not Cromwell was always entirely sincere in his invocation of providence is a question we neither can, nor perhaps need to,
answer. What is important is that – like Charles I's claim to conscience
– it was contested. It is worth remembering, since it is an obvious point
too often passed over, that, even in military defeat, the royalists themselves remained committed to the idea of providence and denied that
their enemies enjoyed its aid or validation.[172] God may have chastened
sinful cavaliers with defeat in battle, but it was only to raise them again
in the future. The Cromwell who claimed providence they lampooned
as an evil Machiavel who sought only to conceal his ambition and expediency.[173] Such charges were only to be expected from royalist sympa-
thizers, but increasingly they also came to be levelled at the Protector
from fellow puritans and comrades-in-arms for the Good Old Cause. As
one of his querulous and uncooperative parliaments told Cromwell, 'the
providences of God are like a two edged sword which may be used both
ways' – or, more accurately, several ways.[174] The Ludlow, Vane and
indeed Milton who had followed Cromwell's sense of the providential
call to arms came to very different interpretations of God's script for a
holy commonwealth.

It is not surprising then that the doctrine of providence, as Blair
Worden put it, 'lost its edge' during the 1650s nor, as I would add, that
the parallel claim to be the conscience of the realm was blunted along
with it.[175] Observation of others' shifts and manoeuvres encouraged
cynicism about, and the charge of duplicity against, those who claimed
to interpret God's will. And in the midst of civil war, changes of regime
and successions of loyalty oaths 'even those who avoided open changes
of allegiance were frequently forced to equivocate, to dissemble, and

---

[171] Ibid., passim.   [172] Ibid., 87–8.
[173] There is a vast contemporary pamphlet literature painting Cromwell as Machiavelli. See F.
Raab, *The English Face of Machiavelli* (1964), ch. 5.   [174] Worden, 'Providence', 85.
[175] Ibid., 98.

sometimes to swallow their principles'.[176] In such a world, it began to seem, in James Howell's graphic phrase, that conscience was all too 'apt to follow the conqueror' – to be at the mercy of whosoever wielded power.[177] Against what he observed to be happening, Howell denied the autonomy of particular consciences and reasserted the need for conscience to take guidance from legitimate authority. From a rather different perspective Thomas Hobbes concurred. Listing the claim to individual conscience, along with the 'pretence of inspiration' (his sense of providence), as a doctrine 'repugnant to Civil Society', Hobbes both pressed the need for a 'public conscience' and located it in the secular text of the law rather than scripture.[178] The anarchy of the sects led others to distrust both scriptural politics and the appeal to individual conscience as forces of social instability.

Perhaps nothing more obstructed settlement during the 1650s than divisions over the authority of church and state, and the freedom of individual conscience. The gentry, some of whom had at least for a time been prepared to believe otherwise, articulated their fear that freedom for individual conscience signalled the dissolution of all society and government and pressed for a national church to act as the conscience of the realm. In 1660, it even appeared that they invited Charles II back to be what his father had claimed to be in the *Eikon*: the conscience of his people.

But, though long before it became obvious, it was not to be. For one, the new monarch's private faith was, almost certainly, not that of the church over which he presided as head. Moreover, Charles II seems genuinely not to have shared the belief of his propertied subjects that toleration of tender consciences was anathema to political stability. But more importantly, the world after 1660 had changed – for all the attempts to paper over the fact. The civil war had schooled the realm in an art that since Machiavelli had first published most Englishmen had attempted to deny: the art of politics. And politics, though it took some time to acknowledge it, is a sphere of activity distinct from the realm of conscience.[179] The politics of Restoration England, it has been argued, was characterized by dissimulation and disguise, that very distance between

---

[176] D. Woolf, 'Conscience, Constancy and Ambition in the Career and Writings of James Howell', in J. Morrill, P. Slack and D. Woolf eds., *Public Duty and Private Conscience in Seventeenth Century England* (Oxford, 1993), 243–78, quotation p. 243.   [177] Ibid., 268.

[178] T. Hobbes, *Leviathan*, ed. R. Tuck (Cambridge, 1991), 223 and ch. 29 passim.

[179] Cf. M. McKeon, 'Politics of Discourses and the Rise of the Aesthetic in Seventeenth-Century England', in K. Sharpe and S. Zwicker eds., *Politics of Discourse: the Literature and History of Seventeenth-Century England* (Berkeley, Los Angeles and London, 1987), 35–51.

the heart and the tongue that James I and Charles I had denounced.[180] Even for monarchs, speaking to God and addressing their people involved different, at times contrary, discourses. The emergence of party vitiated a politics governed by the notion of a public conscience. The logic of such developments led, of course, to the Toleration Act. But it led too to a new attitude to conscience, not as a shared common code, but as an individual and autonomous entity from which men derived moral principles – that site or space which came to be called 'character'.[181] As John Locke put it, in his *Essay Concerning Human Understanding* (1690), 'conscience is nothing else but our own opinion or judgement of the moral rectitude or gravity of our own actions'.[182]

It was a definition and concept far removed from that for the defence of which Charles I had given his life. By the end of the seventeenth century the king's claim to be the conscience of the commonweal had lost its force. Yet then, in changed circumstances, the consequence was not the dissolution of authority and society that Charles I and many of his contemporaries had feared. For though political authority had lost the validation that came from acting as the public conscience, toleration and what we might call the privatization of conscience[183] ended the threat of revolutionary providentialism. Both for rulers and rebels conscience was no longer the central discourse of the public sphere.

[180] S. Zwicker, *Politics and Language in Dryden's Poetry: the Arts of Disguise* (Princeton, 1984).
[181] For a brilliant discussion, see K. Thomas, 'Cases of Conscience in Seventeenth-Century England', in Morrill, Slack and Woolf, *Public Duty and Private Conscience*, 29–56. Keith Thomas's essay appeared after this essay was drafted but offers an excellent broader context for the shift I am arguing.   [182] *OED*, 'Conscience'.
[183] Cf. T. Corns, *Uncloistered Virtue: English Political Literature, 1640–1660* (Oxford, 1992), 34.

PART THREE

Visions of politics

CHAPTER SIX

Stuart monarchy and political culture

INTRODUCTION

The sixteenth century bequeathed an ambivalent legacy to the Stuart dynasty. The development of the Privy Council and more frequent meetings of parliaments made England a 'mixed polity'. Yet the king remained the hub of a network of clientage and patronage which was the system of government. And the Reformation made the ruler spiritual as well as secular head of the realm. Long before James VI succeeded to the English throne, Tudor propaganda had schooled his subjects in the divine right of kings. James I inherited a system of government in which the person of the ruler was central and a political culture in which the monarchy had been exalted to its greatest height (Figures 6 and 7).

At the heart of the governmental system and the political culture was the court. The court was traditionally, and to some extent remained, less a fixed place than a body of men and women in attendance on the monarch. It is best to define the personnel of the court loosely rather than over-precisely – as the entourage surrounding the king, from consorts and children, mistresses and ministers, attending aristocrats and foreign dignitaries, down to barbers and pastry chefs, guards and gardeners. But there can be little doubt that by the beginning of the seventeenth century, the court had changed fundamentally from the courts of medieval monarchs. In the first place, though still peripatetic when the monarch went on progress, the court was increasingly centred in the royal palaces – St James's and Hampton Court, most of all Whitehall, since Henry VIII's reign the monarch's principal London residence. More and more during the sixteenth and seventeenth centuries, as monarchs travelled less, attendance at court meant coming to London. The building of aristocratic houses in the Strand, the development of Covent Garden and the West End, the fashionable squares and the theatres, the

Figure 6. Robert Peake, 'Henry, Prince of Wales (1594–1612) in the hunting field'
(Royal Collection © Her Majesty Queen Elizabeth II)

emergence of the London season, are all evidence of the mounting importance of the court in the nation. Secondly, the court grew considerably in size from the few hundred who attended Henry VII to the thousands who waited on Charles II and James II. This growth stemmed not only from the increased numbers of nobles and gentry who visited Whitehall, but, as the evidence of portraiture and engravings shows clearly, from a broadening of the membership of the court. Playwrights and painters, like Jonson, Davenant and Lely, scene designers and engravers (such as Inigo Jones and Robert White), mathematicians and virtuosi (Newton and Aubrey, for example), astrologers and philosophers, like Boyle and Hobbes, joined the ranks of noblemen, ministers,

Figure 7. Studio of De Critz, the 'Sutherland' portrait of James VI and I
(© Sotheby's Picture Library)

judges and personal servants to constitute a court that became the intellectual and cultural as well as the political headquarters of the nation.
Not surprisingly both the functioning of the court and perceptions of
the court were central issues in the political debates and discourses of
seventeenth-century England.

The court's most important political function was as a centre of patronage and access to the monarch. The decline in the royal progress
made the court, increasingly Whitehall, the forum to press a suit or plead
for a pension, place or favour. Not all, however, could easily travel to
London; and with the monarch increasingly distanced by changes in
palace architecture and the elaboration of formal ceremony, still fewer
could gain direct access to the ruler. Leading courtiers with personal
access to the sovereign, therefore, emerged as brokers to advance the
suits (and sometimes views and grievances) of others. Courtiers, from the
well-established nobility, like the Howards or Herberts, to bedchamber
servants such as Endymion Porter, became patronage managers. The
role of patronage was to bind the most important governors of the localities to the king at the centre and ensure that lines of communication
remained open so that none, despairing of a hearing, pursued the politics of violence rather than petition. The authority of each monarch
depended, as we shall see, on the extent to which his court successfully
fulfilled that function.

As well as the headquarters of patronage, the court was the show-case
of personal monarchy. Throughout early modern English society, from
the aristocratic household to the hamlet, status and authority depended
on degrees of magnificence and display. The Tudor monarchs showed
the most sophisticated appreciation of the need for the royal household
and court to outshine any rival in abundance, conspicuous consumption
and magnificent display. For elaborate dress and precious jewellery, huge
feasts of thirty dishes and Hollywood-budget spectacles not only
announced (as they still do today) to foreign rulers and English subjects
alike the wealth and power of the sovereign; they also, through the awe
they inspired, fostered the culture of obedience and deference on which
the authority of early modern government rested. Those who came to
court in early modern England attended a 'theatre of monarchy' whose
images and special effects represented power as a divine mystery. No less
than the modern cinema, they moulded the perceptions of the age. Nor
was the impact of the court, as some argue, confined to those who
attended at Whitehall. As the monarchs increasingly employed a host of
impresarios – painters and engravers, pamphleteers and numismatists –

the image of the ruler was disseminated more broadly to the country. Civic rituals and festivals echoed courtly spectacles; engravings of royal and courtly portraits adorned provincial town halls and homes; woodcuts and ballads relayed images and tales of the court to the country.

Indeed as some monarchs had always hoped, the court became a model as well as focus for the rest of the nation. Nobles and gentry began to redefine their own role less as warriors, more in terms of service at court, and to emulate the fashions of the court, in architecture, dress and deportment, in their houses in the country. English advice books for young gentlemen, like Henry Peacham's bestseller *The Compleat Gentleman*, are known as '*courtesy* literature' (Figure 8). Words for the practice of amorous pursuits – 'court' for example – suggest that the influence of the royal court on many aspects of life spread to circles beyond the propertied elites. Perhaps not surprisingly the court and courtiers often failed to live up to the ideal image of themselves that they projected. The ideals of devotion to the interests of the commonweal, service to the monarch, chivalric conduct and gallantry were compromised at times, especially in James I's or Charles II's reign, by factional war, personal vendetta, sexual scandals (like the Overbury affair) and unseemly, even vulgar, behaviour – not least by the king himself. From the last decade of the sixteenth century, we discern a growing disenchantment with the court in the country. There emerged – not least from within the circles of the court itself – a body of acerbic critics and satirists who lambasted the corruption and debauchery of the court and courtiers. Such critics began to contrast the failings of the court in reality, with the ideal courts of romantic and chivalric literature; and as a counter to its failings they constructed an alternative idyll, the ideology of the country as a locus of traditional values – honesty and integrity, innocence and purity, fellowship and community. Such a rural idyll bore no more relation to the reality of local rural life than the actual court to its ideal archetype. But the language of 'court' and 'country' was an important aspect of contemporary discourse and perception, and it bears witness to the extent to which political questions and debates in early modern England centred on the ideal and experience of courtly life.

ROYAL COURTS AND STYLES

It is tempting to discuss the Stuart court as if it were an unchanging entity. Indeed the institutions, offices and rituals of court life were to a

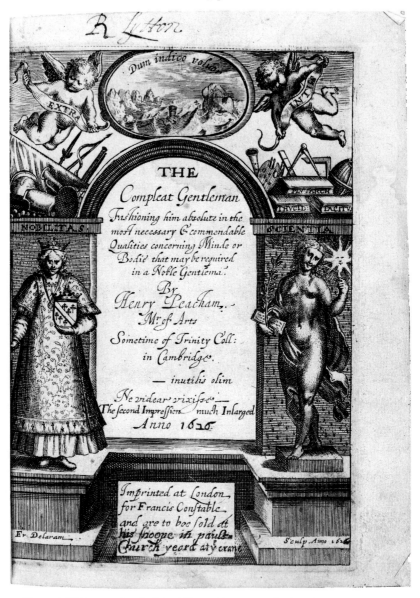

Figure 8. Title page dated 1626 of Henry Peacham, *The Compleat Gentleman*, 1627
(© the Trustees of the British Library)

large extent continuous – surprisingly even during the Protectorate and across the gulf of regicide and republic, to the years of Restoration and beyond. Yet, in many respects, the court changed in structure and, as importantly, in style with each reign, sometimes with changing political circumstances within the span of a single reign. Most obviously, the marital status and sex of the ruler determined the most basic arrangements, with significant political consequences. Elizabeth I, having no consort or children, had a single court. Here she was attended, in the most intimate quarters of her bedchamber, by women who could not easily, in the patriarchal structures of the age, convert their proximity to the queen into major political influence. All of her Stuart successors were married and had children. As a consequence there was always more than one court at Whitehall (and other royal palaces) around which servants and aspirants gathered. The disharmonies in any family make it easy for us to appreciate that the courts of the king, queen and royal children did not always act in concord; in James I's reign, the courts of Anne of Denmark, Prince Henry and Prince Charles each became rival centres for the disaffected who wished to pursue policies quite different from the king's. By the early eighteenth century, indeed, the 'reversionary interest', consideration of the likely policy and patronage preferences of the heir to the throne, became an acknowledged aspect of political calculation.

Such consideration reminds us that the age and experience of the ruler were no less important for the court – or courts we should probably say – than the monarch's marital status. James I was well into middle age when he ascended the throne, James II in his fifties when he succeeded his brother. Both Charleses were under thirty. The political consequences of such generational differences have been little studied and require research, but, at the most obvious level, age influenced the choice of personnel, the manner and style of the court, the attitude of the monarch, and the political influence wielded, and political calculations made, by magnates, courtiers and factions. The Duke of Buckingham for one might have been less inclined to link his fortunes to Prince Charles had James been younger and in better health. James II's age might have kept him on the throne had not the birth of his son threatened the continuation of his unpopular Catholic policies. Nationality, of course, was another factor: not only the nationality of the ruler, but of the consort and the entourage. The politics of Queen Elizabeth's reign had been dominated by considerations of the nationality, and hence religion, of any prospective consort. The prevalence and influence of his Scottish compatriots in the English court undoubtedly soured James I's relations with his parliaments. And the foreign Catholic wives of Charles I, Charles II and James II fuelled the anti-popery which in all three reigns lit the fire of political crisis. In 1688 William of Orange was welcomed or accepted as king, as a counter to a detested French influence as well as to Catholicism.

Most of all, it was the personality of the ruler which shaped the arrangements and fashioned the style of the court. The monarch's attitudes to the dispensation of patronage, to festivals and entertainments, to rituals and customs such as touching to cure the king's evil, profoundly affected the functioning of and attitudes to the court and monarchy. Similarly, royal preference for formality or familiarity, sexual mores and recreations determined the degree of access to the monarch, the style of counsel and debate, and the fortunes of magnates and factions – that is to say, the nature of all political life. If then we are to understand the political culture of the Stuarts and their courts, we need to have some sense of how each royal (not just monarchical) personality reconstituted the court and the politics of patronage, of place and of the representation of authority.

THE SCOTTISH SUCCESSION: JAMES VI AND I

The arrival of the Scottish king James VI to be the new head, as James I, of the English court presented a shock both to the monarch and his subjects. Queen Elizabeth, whose long reign had spanned a whole generation, had founded her authority on the exploitation of her femininity and the cultivation of a mystique behind which, especially in her later years, she retreated, remote from direct engagement with her courtiers. Her court was large and complex, its rituals were sophisticated and elaborate, the royal show was carefully stage-managed and packaged. James came from a poor country whose court was small and simple, and its style more open and direct. Where English political thought had developed the idea of the divinity of kings, in Scotland the Presbyterian Kirk had stressed the contractual nature of kingship and the limitations to royal powers. Scottish politics were still in part clan politics and successful royal rule depended more on agility at the cut and thrust of personal exchange with the lairds than skilful acting on the stage of majesty. The contrast between the two courts, as contemporaries were very quick to notice, was marked. It was compounded by the personal style of the king. For all his considerable intelligence and intellectualism (Figure 9),

Figure 9. Title page of James VI and I's *Workes*, 1616
(by courtesy of Cambridge University Library)

James was a practical, down-to-earth character, with little sympathy for rituals and florid formalities, let alone entertainments presenting the monarch as a god of love and nature. The Scottish king could be insensitively blunt and grossly indecorous. Though his detractors exaggerated his personal failings and contributed to his bad press, James himself showed little concern with public relations. He presided over evenings of drunken debauchery and was personally slovenly and unkempt. Such lack of decorum, compounded by James's own homosexual relations and the sexual scandals of his reign, both sharpened the criticisms of the court and diminished the authority of majesty which depended as much on style and image – ways of doing things – as on the talents and policies of the ruler. The king and court that became the target of scatological broadsheets and pornographic ballads squandered the Tudor legacy of royal mystique and divinity.

James's personal style in some ways reorientated the court for the better. During the last years of her reign the isolation of and difficulty of access to Elizabeth had dangerous repercussions – most obviously manifest in the rebellion of the Earl of Essex, who despaired of securing her favour. Arguably too the prevaricative style of the queen, her reluctance to engage, had glossed over problems that needed to be confronted. James, in complete contrast, was willing to acknowledge and ready to tackle problems; and he remained open to a wide variety of influence – from Catholics and Protestants, those counselling peace and war, or men urging a variety of domestic reforms. No figure or faction during the early years of the reign needed to despair of persuading the king to advance their persons or policies; the court functioned, as it was meant to, as the centre of all political positions and groups.

The royal family contributed to this openness, and more. Though she has been accorded insufficient attention by historians, James's queen, Anne of Denmark, was politically astute and active. Though sexually estranged from her husband, she evidently continued to wield influence upon him, and from her own courts at Denmark House and Greenwich she manœuvred behind the scenes in conjunction with courtiers to supplant favourites and advance her own candidates – most infamously George Villiers. The king's eldest son, Prince Henry, not only provided at St James's a home and patronage for many alienated from his father's favours and by his policies, he established a court so radically different in style from that at Whitehall that some even viewed it as a centre of opposition to the king. Unlike his father, Henry was chaste, decorous, devoted to the tilt, and a champion of belligerent intervention in Europe. The entertainments at his court announced as well as reflected his martial values. After his early death in 1612, the court of his younger brother Prince Charles also functioned as a centre for those frustrated by the king's foreign policy and, by 1624, as a campaign headquarters for the war party. Moreover, the influence of Anne, Henry and Charles effected another shift in the court. The patronage of continental artists, architects and gardeners and the fashion for the elaborate twice-yearly entertainments of music and dance called masques (which owed most to Anne and her sons) brought the politics of the Renaissance court portrait and spectacle to an England still largely isolated from European fashions.

While James's personality made for healthy openness and his family offered alternative centres of patronage, the king's capriciousness and sexual infatuations with attractive young men were forces for instability. James's predilection for the young Scot Robert Carr, and his promotion of this relatively obscure figure from page to viscount, then earl, alienated the ancient aristocracy and upset the scales of influence the king had so shrewdly balanced during the first decade of his reign. Still worse, his obsession with George Villiers, elevated to be Duke of Buckingham, led James to allow one figure to acquire a virtual monopoly of patronage, which dangerously narrowed the court's connections to the powerful political elites of the localities. Buckingham's dominance of the court and king and James's public demonstrations of their sexual relationship not only offended sensibilities; sodomy was in this period a felony for which the penalty was execution. The rise of an ambitious personal favourite to political dominance drove courtiers and natural allies of the crown into disaffection and opposition, exacerbated difficulties between the king and his parliaments, and effectively destroyed his foreign policy. As the nexus of patronage and public-relations headquarters of monarchy, the Jacobean court, for all the king's personal qualities, was an all too conspicuous failure.

ORDER AND FORMALITY: CHARLES I

The immediate revolution in court life effected by Charles I might well have been a deliberate reaction to the style of his father. Charles had left Scotland as a boy of four and not returned before he succeeded as king in 1625. Unlike his father he was naturally withdrawn and inclined to formality, and these traits, developed by his admiration for the splendidly regulated Spanish court which he visited in 1623, dictated the organization and tone of his royal household. In contrast to the easy approachability of James, Charles tightly regulated access to his person, strictly delineating and limiting the courtiers who had entrée to his privy quarters, and secured his privacy by changing locks in the privy lodgings. Under Charles the daily life of the court was, as it had been under Elizabeth, organized around a set of elaborate rituals and ceremonies from the king's waking, dining and going abroad to his retreat at night. In his court, as in his church, Charles attached great importance to such rituals because he believed them to be the essential expressions of reverence for sovereignty. The rules he devised for the governance of his household and court are marked by their emphasis on the awe of majesty. No one was permitted to come too close to the king's person, his chair or canopy, and articles in contact with his person were treated as sacred objects to be cherished. The court entertainments make explicit the ideas informing these practices. Where James seems to have favoured rollicking good entertainment and took pleasure most in the dancing, the Caroline court masques enacted a philosophy and ideology known as Neoplatonism. In these entertainments, the king appeared as the force who by his very being transformed darkness to light, wilderness to harmony, vice and chaos to virtue and order. Such an ideology of kingship was promulgated no less in the paintings of himself and the royal family which Charles commissioned from Van Dyck: the virtuous king, having mastered his own passions, stands as the force who might civilize all men and lead them to self-regulation by example. Though silent in masques and on canvas, Charles articulated through the culture of his court a philosophy of rule which he desired and expected others to emulate.

The changes in organization and style at court are central to understanding the politics of the reign. More distant, less easily influenced than his father, and, unlike James, personally very happy in his marriage, Charles did not govern through favourites. After the death of his friend Buckingham, the king himself very much led from the front, leaving his ministers to their respective responsibilities. As in James's early years, a wide variety of factions and views were again represented at court. Moreover, the court of Charles's queen, Henrietta Maria, provided patronage and a centre for not only her Catholic entourage but some magnates who, critical of the king's foreign policy, sought a French alliance and war against Spain. For much of the 1630s, Charles's court functioned politically as it should: to accommodate differences and contain conflicts.

Both within and outside the court, however, were the seeds of future troubles, some sown by the king himself. Charles was sparing with his favours and affections and did not easily gain the love, trust and loyalty he expected. While open to advice, his rigidity once he had made up his mind fostered the politics of inflexibility and principle rather than negotiation and compromise. When civil war came, nearly half the king's Privy Councillors and courtiers failed to support his cause. And though he won respect for the moral reforms he effected, Charles's court became tainted by a fatal suspicion: that the court – and perhaps the king himself – were governed by papists. Such fears, which echoed through the country, were fostered by the enhanced emphasis on religious ceremony, still more by the public worship of English Catholics at the queen's chapel and the conversions to Rome of some prominent courtiers. The fears were misplaced; Charles was devoted to the Church of England. But in religion as in politics, he too often failed to feel the need to explain his position until it was too late. In consequence the court which Charles constructed as his model for the whole nation was perceived by many as the headquarters of the popish Antichrist, to be destroyed, if need be by violent revolution.

COMMONWEALTH AND COURT

At first we might be led to think that the revolution which decapitated the king, abolished the monarchy and established a republic also destroyed the court, root and branch. Certainly the court as it was under Charles I was dismantled for all time: England's first true Renaissance court was also its last. The personnel of the court were divided and dispersed; some fought for parliament; some made their peace with the new regime; some fled to exile. Royal palaces were sold off to raise money, as was much of the spectacular artwork the connoisseur king had collected as a beacon of his majesty. The puritan tendency to iconophobia – to suspicion of sensuous imagery in state and church rituals – was accompanied by the republicans' preference for a plainer style – in speech, dress and display. Nevertheless, in important senses, the remnants of a court, still more the image of kingship, remained even during the earliest years of the republic, from 1649 to 1653. First, the Council of State, the successor to the Privy Council, continued to meet at Whitehall Palace, where ambassadors were received. Though we know little about the nature of the Council's entertainments, a Master of Ceremonies continued in office; and royal furniture, tapestry, some paintings and plate – often engraved with the royal arms – were retained for the government's use. Whilst there were fewer courtiers of the old type in evidence, the Commonwealth's civil service, the larger court, expanded and its costs surpassed those of the king's. Whatever the reality, the regime attracted the charges of corruption, incompetence and extravagant waste that had fuelled country critiques of the royal courts of the Stuarts.

The Council of State was even less successful than the royal court in binding the powerful men of the localities to the centre – not least because it was less representative of the political nation. And even more than the courts of the Stuarts, the Commonwealth failed to present an image that sustained its authority. Not that it failed to try. A new great seal, commemorative medals struck after victories in battle, a new vocabulary of legitimation cast in the language of providence rather than divine right, indeed official organs of propaganda, were instituted to replace the image of the court and king with the symbols of a new regime. They failed. The *Eikon Basilike* (Figure 10), supposedly Charles I's own account of his kingship, the person of his son, the literature of royalist nostalgia, popular memory and custom, the very palaces and artefacts deployed by the Commonwealth, sustained the memory of the king and belief in the need for government with something of the monarchical in it. And Charles II's attempts to regain his throne kept him constantly in the minds and hearts of the people of England.

When the Commonwealth government was dissolved in 1653, the first steps back to a king and court were taken when Oliver Cromwell was appointed Lord Protector – of 'England, Scotland, Ireland etcetera'. From the beginning the change in style was more marked than historians have noticed. Cromwell was installed in 1653 with a ceremony monarchical in character; an inauguration medal was struck; his great seal featured an equestrian portrait of the Protector evocative of the famous portrait of Charles I by Van Dyck; the Protector's arms were topped with an imperial crown nearly exactly resembling the one used by Charles I (Figure 11). Not surprisingly from 1654 there was debate as to whether Cromwell should take the title as well as trappings of kingship. While many in the army, and perhaps Oliver himself, were resistant, it rapidly became clear that a quasi-king and a court were, as the lawyers and parliamentary gentry urged, necessary institutions for the government of England.

So, even though he declined the actual title, Cromwell restored the monarchy and court in all but name when he became hereditary

Figure 10. Frontispiece to *Eikon Basilike*, 1649 (reproduced by permission of the
Huntington Library, San Marino, California)

Protector in 1657. The reinvestiture ceremony, with coronation oath and
enthronement, followed a royal coronation in all its stages but for anointing and crowning. Not only did Cromwell move into Whitehall Palace,
other former royal palaces, such as Hampton Court, were repurchased
as retreats for 'His Highness'. Though smaller than that of Charles I, a
royal household and entourage was re-established. Cromwell had a
guard of halberdiers resembling the Yeomen of the Guard and his servants and watermen were clothed in the Protector's livery. His court –
and contemporaries began now customarily to refer to it as such –
became more hierarchical and more marked by ritual and ceremony.
Cromwell, a good country gentleman himself, may have seen its political value as a bridge to secure support for his regime from the local
gentry who increasingly returned to govern the shires. He created peer-
ages and restored an Upper House. He received visitors and revived

Figure 11. Cromwell's seal as Lord Protector
(© the Trustees of the British Museum)

something of the old court life, entertainments and display. More of the late king's goods were brought in to enrich his surroundings; paintings and miniatures of the Protector were distributed; the Banqueting House was used for receptions; a form of masque was even revived – by William Davenant, the deviser of Charles I's last entertainment. Soon, in pane-gyric, Cromwell was lauded in the traditional language of royal paeans, as the father of this people, the Sun of the cosmos, God's lieutenant on earth. His magnificent funeral was a more stately and majestic occasion than that of James I. After standing under a canopy of state flanked by

500 candles, Cromwell's effigy was led in an elaborate cortège formed by his household servants from the Strand to Westminster. The court, albeit of a deceased substitute prince, was again visible to the crowd who thronged the way.

Both in its failure and its success, Cromwell's Protectorate and court advanced the restoration of monarchy and royal court. Because of his dependence on the army, whatever his own preferences, Cromwell could not dispense all his patronage to the gentry, who were determined to end military rule. As a consequence his court, though it restored a welcome sense of normality, never functioned politically to win the nation to an indefinite Protectoral rule. For the conservative gentry, Cromwell did not go far enough, either in substance or style, to restoring the old ways. By contrast, to the stricter republicans in the army and the country, he went, by a long way, too far: his court symbolized his betrayal of the Good Old Cause for which they had fought in 1642. Indeed Cromwell's failure is exemplified in his court which simultaneously announced him as a traitor to republicans and a usurper to royalists. Yet in that he had succeeded during his lifetime in providing some stability, not least by a partial appropriation of old customs – and symbols – Cromwell and his court accelerated the political flow that led to the Restoration.

RESTORATION OR RECONSTITUTION?

Every effort was made in 1660 to present the Restoration as a straightforward return to the old order. The rhetoric of healing in panegyrical discourse announced the body politic restored to health after eleven years of sickness. Charles II, who had of course dated his realm from the day of his father's execution, was, like Charles I, celebrated as the Father, the Solomon, the Moses, the King David of his people. The coronation ceremony, on the king's birthday and St George's Day, was regarded as the most magnificent ever. The City of London erected a series of triumphal arches and allegorical tableaux, celebrating peaceful Restoration and the defeat of rebellion, to entertain the king and his entourage and to awe the spectators with the power of majesty reinstated. In Westminster Abbey the coronation was enacted with sacred solemnity, all the nobles touching the crown as a token of their allegiance. Charles II played his part in the pageant well. En route to England from exile, he offered to many the magical royal 'touch' for cure of the 'king's evil' (scrofula); at his coronation he pronounced a pardon of unprecedented extent; he conducted himself with solemnity and dignity before his public (Figure 12). Knights of the Bath joined Knights of the Garter to enrich the ceremony and underline the restoration of a culture of kingship and courtliness as well as of the monarchy itself.

The reality was different from the spectacle. For in reality the royal regalia, Arthur's chair, Edward the Confessor's crown, orbs and sceptres were not simply restored to Charles Stuart; melted down during the Commonwealth, they had to be remade. In important senses the same was true of the monarchy and political culture of the age. Cromwell's embalmed body was exhumed and burnt, his head was publicly displayed on a stake, and Charles I's statue restored, but the memory of regicide and republic could not be so easily erased. During the 1650s the nation had been well governed and in foreign affairs and commerce had enjoyed glory and gain under republican rule. Whatever the official cult of royalism, even some panegyrists were reluctant to condemn totally the republican regimes and even willing to draw some lessons from them.

Not least the lessons of the 1650s were also etched on the king himself. During years of exile and hardship, sheltering with and receiving help from ordinary folk, Charles had undergone the unusual royal experience of close engagement with his people, which influenced his personal style of monarchy. Though he could exhibit a strong sense of the reverence due to majesty, he was – quite unlike his father – a down-to-earth figure, witty and affable, familiar and often vulgar. Though he continued to 'touch', Charles II never revived the masques or rituals through which his father had represented the mystique of monarchy. As the reign progressed, the court descended into public debauchery that even shocked the French and the king's vulgarity tended to base crudery. Charles's series of young mistresses – the first since Henry VIII's reign – were paraded scandalously in public and even represented on the coin of the realm or engraved sacrilegiously as madonnas. The vices of drink, whoring and pox were soon seen to be symptomatic of the political ills of corruption, arbitrary government and popery. The mystique of kingship was greatly dimmed when 'the angel clothed in flesh' began to appear altogether more fleshly than angelic.

If the Commonwealth irrevocably demystified monarchy, it left a still more important legacy: the fact of permanent divisions in the body politic. In 1660 the language may have been that of union, harmony and public interest, one king and one church, but between the lines echoed the fear of division, intrigue and insurrection. For all the popularity of the Restoration, politically it was the victory of a party not the nation.

Figure 12. Dirk Stoop, 'Charles II's cavalcade through the city of London, 22 April 1661' (by courtesy of the Museum of London)

Remarkably soon political debates and disagreements made it clear how far issues and divisions remained – over the prerogative and religion. An astute politician, Charles II was able not only to adapt to this new political world but even to turn it to his advantage. He recognized the need for compromise; he acknowledged the need at times to feign and disguise. With parliaments now a regular institution, he learned the first lessons in the art of political management to win support; he played on fears of instability to strengthen his hand. Arguably though the mystique of monarchy had been damaged, in practice he was stronger than any of his predecessors. But as divisions hardened into parties, the illusion of Restoration gave way to a new political order in which the monarch had to play skilfully a careful political game.

The truth of this was made painfully clear by the refusal of Charles II's successor to play that game. The open Catholicism of James, Duke of York, had been the principal force for instability during the later years of Charles's reign. When his brother skilfully defeated attempts to exclude him from the succession, James wrongly interpreted it as a victory for himself and his cause, rather than as a triumph of political management. As a monarch he displayed pride, rigidity and a reluctance to heed counsel, failing in the essential political arts of realism and manœuvre. The new king had much going for him in 1685. Charles had discredited the Whigs and won over the Tories. James had a reputation as a fearless soldier and fine admiral (Figure 13). After the profligacy of his brother's reign he presented a welcome contrast of style. He was careful with money; he reduced waste and extravagance at court. And whilst he never entirely resisted the temptations of mistresses, James was relatively discreet and in public set a moral tone for his court. He banished drunkards and blasphemers; he insisted on marital fidelity; he had little time for balls and plays and worked hard with a devotion to duty.

Unfortunately his court and kingship were to contemporaries more obvious for their Catholic than moral tone. Unlike his brother, James was not prepared to disguise his faith; like his father he was committed more to fixed principles than to politicking. James's central objective as king was to secure toleration for Catholics and to advance their faith and cause. Contrary to Whig legend, he attempted no Catholic monopoly, nor arbitrary rule. But, uninterested in the politics of explanation or representation, James failed to dispel the fears that he aspired to popish absolutism. Rather, the complexion of his court confirmed them. Charles II had learned to stick by his friends the Tories for fear that otherwise they would not support him. James by contrast removed the

Figure 13. Sir Godfrey Kneller, 'James II'
(by courtesy of the National Portrait Gallery, London)

Protestant nobility, surrounded himself with committed Catholics and so made his court a narrow party enclave rather than the nexus of all politics. In 1688, when he fell to an invading force led by William of Nassau, James failed to secure the aid of the Tories as well as Whigs. Rather than earthing him to the most powerful currents of the political nation, James's court and patronage had left him isolated at Whitehall, then cast him into exile.

The debates about the rights of James II's deposition and William and Mary's claim to the throne – debates centred on elective kingship, the contracts between rulers and subjects, the quarrels between and within parties – again suggest that, for all the attempts to put the clock back, the civil war and Commonwealth had changed the nature of politics, and so changed the political culture and the royal court. The king's person, personal style, household and entourage were still the centre of government and politics, but now more obviously part of, than *above*, the political fray. The administrative changes, long wars and absences of William III during the next reign were to throw the court and monarchy into the maelstrom of the bitterly contested and sharply divided politics of party. Stormed by parties and factions which limited the king's room for manœuvre, the court more reflected and promoted the new politics of division and contest than the harmonious residence of God's lieutenant on earth.

CHAPTER SEVEN

'An image doting rabble': the failure of republican culture in seventeenth-century England

Only a short time ago almost all historians agreed with E. M. W. Tillyard that Tudor ideas of order and harmony presented monarchy as the natural, divine mode of government and rendered alternative polities literally unimaginable.[1] More recently, however, scholars have detected in repeated homilies on obedience anxieties about dissenting views. In particular, it has been argued, a republic in early modern England was not only thinkable but was thought.[2] Radical Calvinists facing persecution on the continent read in the Bible of resistance to ungodly tyrants and were in turn read in English puritan circles.[3] And all educated Englishmen learned from the Greek and Roman past the achievements and virtues of the classical republics and studied their contemporary and later humanist historians and apologists. Towards the end of Elizabeth's reign, some suggest, as criticism of the regime intensified, republican ideas became fashionable in the intellectual circles of Sidney and Essex and bequeathed a language and a vision of politics that remained to critique and contest the official discourse of monarchy and state.[4]

Such suggestions and revisions prompt questions that have yet to be pondered. If the languages of tyrannicide and republic ran current in early modern England, was civil war and regicide the violent and incom-

[1] E. M. W. Tillyard, *The Elizabethan World Picture* (1943); cf. A. O. Lovejoy, *The Great Chain of Being* (Cambridge, Mass., 1936).
[2] P. Collinson, 'The Monarchical Republic of Queen Elizabeth I', *Bull. John Rylands Lib.*, 69 (1987), 394–424.
[3] J. H. Salmon, *The French Religious Wars in English Political Thought* (Oxford, 1959); J. E. Phillips, 'George Buchanan and the Sidney Circle', *Hunt. Lib. Quart.*, 12 (1948), 23–56.
[4] M. Smuts, 'Court-Centred Politics and the Uses of Roman Historians, c. 1590–1630', in K. Sharpe and P. Lake eds., *Culture and Politics in Early Stuart England* (Houndmills and Stanford, 1994), 21–44; D. Norbrook, 'Lucan, Thomas May, and the Creation of a Republican Literary Culture', in ibid., 45–66; B. Worden, 'Classical Republicanism and the Puritan Revolution', in H. Lloyd-Jones, V. Pearl and B. Worden eds., *History and Imagination* (1981), 182–200; Worden, 'The Commonwealth Kidney of Algernon Sidney', *Journ. Brit. Studies*, 24 (1985), 1–40.

prehensible shock to Englishmen that we have traditionally presented it as being? Was a commonwealth erected in 1649 not because of unforeseen and unintended events but because the idea was already established in the political and cultural imagination? Or, alternatively, have recent revisions exaggerated the power and importance of republican languages and beliefs? In pursuing these questions, I shall argue that, not least because they have largely ignored the visual, the symbolic and the emblematic, historians of republican discourse have underestimated the pervasiveness of monarchy in the culture of early modern England. In early modern England government was not just a matter of institutions or rational arguments but a nexus of customs and cultural practices. The forms through which authority had traditionally expressed itself became the forms through which any authority must express itself. Since these were forms shaped by kings, then something essential of the royal remained, whatever the constitution, policies or personnel. And I shall suggest that it was because the culture was so inscribed and coloured with monarchism that a commonwealth was never established as the government of seventeenth-century Englishmen. The failure of republican politics was a failure to forge a republican culture that erased or suppressed the images of kingship, images that sustained a monarchical polity, even in the absence of the king.

THE COMMONWEALTH ESTABLISHED?

The Commonwealth was not established when the axe separated Charles I's head from his body on the scaffold at Whitehall. A king had been executed but the institution of monarchy had not been abolished. Not until March did the Rump pass an act 'for abolishing the kingly office' as 'burdensome and dangerous to the liberty, safety and public interest of the people' and even then somewhat ambiguously decreed that 'the office of a king in this nation shall not henceforth reside in . . . any one single person'.[5] The faltering tone expressed the fundamental questions of 1649: What was the nature and authority of the new government? What were the people to expect from parliament and what, as Isaac Pennington put it, from 'their supreme governor or governors'?[6] Novelty and uncertainty, it was recognized, threatened the new regime.

---

[5] *An Act for Abolishing the Kingly Office in England, Ireland, and the Dominions thereunto Belonging* (1649), BL, Thomason Tracts, 669 f14/2.
[6] I. Pennington, *The Fundamental Right, Safety, and Liberty of the People* . . . (1651), BL, Thomason Tracts, E629/2.

As John Goodwin put it in his *Defence of the Honourable Sentence Passed upon the Late King*, 'the first apparition of things new and strange, especially when the reasons and causes of them are unknown . . . are usually disturbing and offensive to their apprehensions'.[7] The new commonwealth had to construct its own authority in 1649. This, in part of course, was a question of time. Apologists for the regime, arguing that all could not be 'perfected with one swap', believed that 'a year or two will habituate the present government'.[8] In *The Case of the Commonwealth of England Stated*, Marchamont Nedham predicted confidently: 'Let the Commonwealth have leave to take breath a little in the possession of a firm peace, then they would soon find the rivulets of a free state much more pleasing than the troubled oceans of kingly tyranny.'[9] Time undoubtedly could dull the sense of shock and gradually dispel the feeling that the new government was a temporary aberration. But time in itself was not enough. To establish the authority of the new regime, the language and image of a republic had to be instilled in and the language and image of monarchy erased from the political culture of early modern England. The kingdom of England had to be 'turned into a commonwealth'.[10]

Much Commonwealth propaganda was necessarily defensive, a justification of the shocking events that had brought it into being. *A Declaration of the Parliament* rejected the right of a son to succeed to a father who had forfeited the crown, condemned the prodigality of kings and courts, and asserted the right of the people to determine the fate of kings as they had originally instituted them.[11] *The Obstructors of Justice* denied any obligations to kings who did not discharge their trust.[12] Many writers cited necessity as the reason for the rejection of monarchy.[13] More originally, *The Case of the Commonwealth*, pointing to European neighbours who had cast off the yoke of kingship, suggested that the cycle of history itself had turned against monarchy.[14] Most famously, in *The Tenure of Kings and Magistrates* (and in *Eikonoklastes*), Milton attacked 'lawless kings', justified the trial and regicide, and defended the Commonwealth.

---

[7] J. Goodwin, *The Obstructors of Justice, or A Defence of the Honourable Sentence Passed upon the Late King* (1649), E557/2, dedication.   [8] A. Warren, *The Royalist Reform'd* (1649), E582/4, pp. 20, 43.
[9] [M. Nedham], *The Case of the Commonwealth of England Stated* (1650), E600/7, p. 93.
[10] *Panegyric to Cromwell* in F. Peck, *Memoirs of the Life and Actions of Oliver Cromwell* (1740), 70.
[11] *A Declaration of the Parliament of England Expressing the Grounds of Their Late Proceedings* (1649), E548/12.   [12] Goodwin, *Obstructors of Justice*, 46, 59.
[13] See, for example, *The Bounds and Bonds of Publique Obedience* (1649), E571/26, p. 7. *Reasons Why the Supreme Authority of the Three Nations . . . Is Not in the Parliament* (1653), E697/19, p. 3, where it is claimed that 'most of the Parliamentarian writers' make 'Necessity . . . the main reason for turning the monarchy of this land into a state'.
[14] [Nedham], *Case of the Commonwealth*, 4.

Milton's texts, however, exemplify the problem of such propaganda: the *Tenure*, still more *Eikonoklastes*, 'operate within terms of reference' defined by Charles I, his trial and his own book.[15] As such they, as much as royalist polemic, vividly sustained the memory of the king and too narrowly discussed the new commonwealth in relation to (corrupted) monarchy.

Some, quick to see that the negative arguments against kingship did not establish the authority of the new regime, shifted to more pragmatic justification. Urging all to submit to those who now possessed power, *The Bounds and Bonds of Publique Obedience* argued that 'so soon as one supreme power is expelled by another, law, life and estate fall into the hands of the succeeding power'.[16] Authority, others concurred, came from power. When scripture, some argued, enjoined obedience to authority, it meant any who possessed power.[17] Yet more boldly *The Case of the Commonwealth* asserted that 'the sword creates a title'; as a result of the defeat of the king 'the old allegiance is cancelled and we are bound to admit a new'.[18] Though the de facto arguments moved the debate away from the monarchy, they also threatened to take it outside the discourse of history, law and divinity in which all politics had been conducted. As such they were vulnerable to the counterarguments of royalists and other enemies who could more easily deploy the power of those legitimating vocabularies and familiar tropes.

More positive polemics, therefore, rather than ignoring traditional history and language, endeavoured to rewrite them. From 1649 pamphlets like *King Charles' Trial Justified* argued that the historical origins of power lay in the people.[19] The 1650 tract *The Government of the People of England Precedent and Present the Same* not only pursued the historical argument of its title but proclaimed as its slogan: 'All government is in the people, from the people and for the people.'[20] The author of *The True Portraiture of the Kings of England*, tracing the power of the people to determine government from the time of the Saxons, claimed that now parliament had returned affairs 'to their first natural and right principle'.[21] The force of these arguments, however, was undercut not only by the persistence of arguments against or about monarchy in their pages and titles.[22] As the agitation in the army and Leveller pamphleteering had

---

[15] See T. Corns, *Uncloistered Virtue: English Political Literature, 1640–1660* (Oxford, 1992), 208 and ch. 6.   [16] *Bounds and Bonds of Publique Obedience*, 20–1.

[17] *The Lawfulness of Obeying the Present Government* (1649), E551/22, pp. 6–8 and passim.

[18] [Nedham], *Case of the Commonwealth*, 23, 31.

[19] R. Bennet, *King Charles' Trial Justified* (1649), E554/21, p. 4.

[20] *The Government of the People of England Precedent and Present the Same* (1650), E594/19, p. 7.

[21] *The True Portraiture of the Kings of England* (1650), E609/2, p. 15.   [22] Below, pp. 230, 233–4.

graphically demonstrated, the language of popular sovereignty could undermine as well as underpin the government of the Rump and sustain a radical politics that alienated elites, parliamentarian as much as old royalist.[23] Significantly this was an argument that was used with caution in official circles and one that faded as the regime survived the anxious first months of existence.

There is perhaps one surprising silence in the Commonwealth propaganda of 1649 and 1650. Although Nedham drew on the classical past to argue that Rome's greatness stemmed from the overthrow of kings and to expound the virtues of republican democracy, classical arguments for republican government are hard to find in the pamphlets collected by George Thomason.[24] A Short Discourse between Monarchical and Aristocratical Government of October 1649 cited Tacitus as evidence of the fundamental incompatibility between liberty and monarchy, but in defence of the middle way the author appealed to the Netherlands and Venice rather than to Rome.[25] While the language used to describe Roman heroes and emperors was early applied to Cromwell, classical antiquity scarcely featured in arguments for the new republic.[26] If anything, classical republican language developed in reaction to Cromwell's (as some saw it) imperialism in an English context in which the republic had died in all but name.[27]

It was in scripture rather than the classics that Commonwealth propagandists found justification for their existence. The revealingly titled Logical Demonstration directly stated that both king and parliament had appealed to God and that he had passed his sentence.[28] Scripture, claimed the author of Monarchy No Creature of God's Making, showed that the people should be governed by parliaments and that Providence so directed events to re-establish godly government.[29] The mutations of commonwealths, the case went, followed God's will and, fearful Englishmen were consoled, 'a bright star of Providence leads us'.[30]

[23] A Short Discourse between Monarchical and Aristocratical Government (1649), E575/31, pp. 19–20, denounces Leveller arguments on these lines.
[24] [Nedham], Case of the Commonwealth; on Nedham see J. G. A. Pocock, The Machiavellian Moment: Florentine Political Thought and the Atlantic Republican Tradition (Princeton, 1975), 379–84; J. Scott, Algernon Sidney and the English Republic 1623–1677 (Cambridge, 1988), 110–12; and now B. Worden, 'Marchamont Nedham and the Beginnings of English Republicanism, 1649–1656', in D. Wootton ed., Republicanism, Liberty, and Commercial Society, 1649–1776 (Stanford, 1994), 45–81.
[25] A Short Discourse, 12, 15.
[26] For example, Veni, Vidi, Vici: the Triumphs of the Most Excellent . . . Oliver Cromwell (1652), E1298/1; The Establishment (1653), E720/1.   [27] Below, pp. 260–2.
[28] A Logical Demonstration of the Lawfulness of Subscribing the New Engagement (1650), E590/11, pp. 5–6.
[29] Monarchy No Creature of God's Making (1652), E1238/1, dedication, p. 116 and passim. Cf. G. W., The Modern Statesmen (1653), E1542/2, p. 56.   [30] A Short Discourse, 18.

Cromwell, of course, was from the beginning the most famous spokesman of the providentialist arguments for regicide and republic.[31] These
victories, he wrote to parliament after successful campaigns in Ireland,
'are seals of God's approbation of your great change of government'.[32]
But the argument from Providence was a dangerously malleable rhetoric and an instrument that could, as circumstances changed, be wielded
by enemies as well as friends. Just as Oliver used this argument to support
his Protectorate, his critics asserted that the Lord's will ordained a free
commonwealth for his people.[33] And it is important to note that after
Charles II's 'miraculous' escape from the battle of Worcester, royalists
appropriated the language of Providence to contest republic and to
claim God's protection of the king.

One of the weaknesses of republican polemics was – understandably
– an uncertainty about the strategies for argument and justification. Was
the government after 1649, as some had it, a continuation of the true
constitution after the pruning of a corrupt excrescence from the body
politic? Or was the Commonwealth the outcome of a revolution effected
by Providence? Were the arguments for obedience pragmatic – the need
for some authority – or religious: the obligation to follow God's decree?
Such dilemmas and uncertainties expressed a still greater problem that
faced the regime and its apologists: the problem of language itself.

Language is inextricably interwoven with the structures of power and
the culture of authority. Words derive their force from the institutions,
personalities, customs they describe, but in addition words as validating
terms can endow with power and construct and create authority. A successful new regime in 1649 had not only to undermine the lan-
guage/power of its enemies but speak and write a new discourse that
would utter and inscribe its own authority.[34] There is some indication –
and if there is anything in the suggestion it would repay further investigation – that this was a situation that Cromwell sought to address. For in
his letters to parliament in 1650 we can hear him endeavouring to write
a new community, a new commonwealth into existence.[35] Avoiding the
authorial *I*, Cromwell wrote as the voice of the army ('We thought fit to
take the field'),[36] as the servant of the public ('your instruments', 'you

[31] B. Worden, 'Providence and Politics in Cromwellian England', *Past and Present*, 109 (1985), 55–99.
[32] *A Letter from the Right Hon. the Lord Lieutenant of Ireland to . . . William Lenthall* (London, 1649), 2.
[33] Worden, 'Providence', passim.
[34] E. Skerpan, *The Rhetoric of Politics in the English Revolution* (Columbia, Miss., 1992), 84, speaks of
'the *opportunity* to create a new political community out of language' (my italics). It was also a
need.   [35] I am grateful to Ross Parry for discussions on this subject.
[36] *A Letter from the Lord Lieutenant of Ireland . . . 25 February 1649/[50]*, p. 3.

whom we serve'),[37] and as God's soldier against his 'enemy' 'for England and his people'.[38] And, perhaps acknowledging the importance of these letters as language, the Rump ordered them printed and read from the pulpits as a new litany of state. But even as he struggled for a new discourse, Cromwell's speeches and letters at times resonate – 'We beg of you not to own us but God alone' – with the rhetoric of warrior kings like Shakespeare's Henry V.[39] And because Cromwell always addressed his letters to Speaker William Lenthall, the wider issues of the nomenclature appropriate to the new government were left unaddressed. Petitions to 'the present visible Supreme Power Assembled at Westminster' indicate that at the most fundamental level – its own name – language was a problem for the Commonwealth government.[40] And the problem permeated language and metaphor used to it, of it and by it. In 1650 *The Government of the People of England* slipped naturally into metaphors with royal valence in discussing the vigilant physicians of the Commonwealth, as the author of *The Fundamental Right . . . of the People* (1651) perhaps not innocently wrote of 'the head and the members' that existed in every body politic.[41] Such usages were not trivial. Did the very metaphors and language of politics which kept the memory of monarchy alive imply that language itself was royal(ist)?[42] The issue is graphically illustrated in an account of the reception of the new republic's ambassadors in the United Provinces. Relieved that the Dutch government was willing to recognize the regime, the apologist for the Commonwealth in *Joyful News from Holland* celebrated the validation of its ambassadors and its authority in the '*Royal* entertainment given by the States'.[43] While such language ran current (in both republics), monarchy was never erased from the perceptions of power. Throughout the republic's brief life the problem of language undermined its authority. With another change and challenge in 1653, one pamphleteer, uneasy about how to describe the regime, attempted to brush aside the problem:

[37] *A Letter from the Lord Lieutenant of Ireland, 30 October 1649,* p. 8; *A Letter from the Lord General . . . 21 July 1650,* p. 5.

[38] *Letter 21 July 1650,* p. 6; *A Letter from the Lord General Cromwell from Dunbar, 3 September 1650,* in *Original Memoirs during the Great Civil War, Being the Life of Sir Henry Slingsby* (Edinburgh, 1806), 302.

[39] *Original Memoirs,* 303.   [40] BL, Thomason tracts, 669 f13/77 (1649).

[41] *The Government of the People of England,* 13; Pennington, *The Fundamental Right, Safety, and Liberty of the People,* 17.

[42] During the 1640s Parliamentarians had endeavoured to undermine the Royalists' monopoly of this language with some measure of success. But it remained a language of monarchy, for all the differences about the nature of kingship. I am grateful to Joad Raymond for a discussion of this issue.

[43] *Joyful News from Holland Showing the Royal Entertainment Given by the States of the United Provinces to the Lords Ambassadors of the Commonwealth of England* (1651), E626/18, my italics.

'What is the matter of words,' he asked, 'or how the Supreme Authority be called, provided the country be well-governed?'[44] But as more astute polemicists discerned, it did matter. In his *History of Britain* Milton recognized both the absence of an indigenous language to describe the new commonwealth and the need for such a language to create it. 'Many civil virtues', he maintained, must 'be imported into our minds from foreign writings and examples of best ages, we shall else miscarry'.[45] Nedham made some effort to translate those foreign examples into English idioms before he turned 'Protectorian'. And in Milton's case, as Blair Worden has argued, 'his reading . . . freed him from the conceptual limitations of contemporary political debate'.[46] Most, however, remained citizens of an English discursive commonweal ignorant of foreign writings and the civil virtues they advanced.[47] Milton's hopes were dashed not only by his elitism. In his disdain for an 'image doting rabble', he not only showed contempt for the uneducated; he exhibited his blindness to a need perhaps greater than that of language itself: the need for a new government, in an intensely visual and emblematic culture, to supplant the image of monarchy and construct effective representations of its authority.[48]

It was a need that the Rump government failed to meet. For all the power of satiric cartoons lampooning the court in the 1620s and 1630s and the importance attached to standards and banners during the war, few visual representations of Commonwealth government were produced, whether we survey paintings, engravings (which were reaching a wide audience by mid-century), or engraved or woodcut illustrations in books or on broadsides.[49] At a time when a powerful and evocative image of the king was, as we shall see, polemically coloured and widely disseminated, the near absence of a contesting representation of the Commonwealth is striking. In part the explanation lies in puritan iconophobia: certainly the word was to be the foundation of the new commonwealth's representation as it was of its justification. But, as

---

[44] *Reasons Why the Supreme Authority . . . Is Not in the Parliament*, 11.

[45] J. Milton, *History of Britain*, quoted in J. Scott, 'The English Republican Imagination', in J. Morrill ed., *Revolution and Restoration* (1992), 36.

[46] Blair Worden, 'Milton's Republicanism and the Tyranny of Heaven', in G. Bock, Q. Skinner and M. Viroli eds. *Machiavelli and Republicanism* (Cambridge, 1990), 231.

[47] It is interesting that there was little translated from or written about Dutch or Venetian political debate.

[48] Milton, *Eikonoklastes*, ed. W. H. Haller, *The Works of John Milton* V, (New York, 1932), 309. See below, pp. 261–2.

[49] Such portraits and engravings as there are depict members of the Council in sober, black dress, conveying a godly but not republican representation.

important, was the absence of any model for a visual representation of republic suitable for the English polity. There is evidence of the odd gesture towards its construction. In 1650 the *Government of the People of England* carried on its title page an engraving of two hands clasping a bound bundle of arrows (with individual broken arrows on the ground) to symbolize the strength that lay in the unity of the people. But neither the Thomason tracts nor a major collection of engravings yields many such positive images of republican government.[50] Artists painted and engraved godly figures or military heroes of campaigns in Ireland and Scotland – Fairfax, Essex, most of all Cromwell – but in many such cases the image was more regal than republican. In 1651 *A Perfect List of All the Victories Obtained by Oliver Cromwell* was dominated by an engraving of Oliver (Figure 14) with his left hand on his sword and his right holding a baton of command. The page who ties a sash around his waist adds to the courtly air – a regal impression reinforced by his standing between the act of parliament constituting him Captain General and the propositions sent by Charles II to the pope.[51] Such an image, in the traditional iconography of royalty, evoked the absent king and court. In visual representation the image of the Commonwealth never broke free of the cult of personality and dynasty, nor of the genres and forms of courtly iconography.

With seals and coins the regime took more trouble to mark the change of government. The new great seal of the Commonwealth, removing the representation of a single person who had given documents their authority, had the arms of England and Ireland (not yet conquered) on one side and a representation of the House of Commons in session on the other, with a motto that endeavoured to rewrite history: as the 1651 seal has it, 'in the third year of freedom by God's Blessing Restored'.[52] New coins were minted depicting the St George Cross, the harp of Erin, the palm of victory and peace, and bearing mottoes in the vernacular such as 'God with Us' or simply 'The Commonwealth of England'.[53] Such images skilfully associated parliament with the nation and promoted the idea of an English state, forged in victory and protected by

[50] I spent several months with the large collection of engraved British portraits in the Huntington Library's Richard Bull copy of James Granger's *Biographical History of England* (1769). All illustrations to this essay are reproduced with the kind permission of the Huntington Library. See M. Pointon, *Hanging the Head: Portraiture and Social Formation in Eighteenth-Century England* (1993), ch. 2.

[51] BL, Thomason tracts, 669 f16/23. The engraving is based on a Robert Walker portrait, of which there are several variants and copies.

[52] Huntington Library, Bull/Granger, vol. 10, no. 34.

[53] Huntington Library, Bull/Granger, vol. 12, no. 34

Figure 14. Engraving of Oliver Cromwell, 1651 (reproduced by permission of the
Huntington Library, San Marino, California)

God.[54] Though these representations were important, several factors limited their effectiveness in erasing the royal image. Not least because it had many other pressing matters to handle, the Rump took some time to issue the new seal and coins.[55] Moreover, the regime never had enough bullion to replace royal coins so 'at no point . . . did the output of new style coinage threaten to swamp the circulation of coin issued by the Royal mints'; because few coins of small denomination were minted, little of the new money circulated among the ordinary people.[56] Most of all the life of the new images was short. Cromwell as Protector swiftly reverted to a regal style on seals and coins – a decision that may tell us as much about the hold of a royal image (and the failure of republican forms to replace it in the imagination of the nation) as about the ambitions or preferences of Cromwell himself.[57]

THE ROYAL PRESENCE

In many ways the early years of the Commonwealth evoke the old royal Presence Chamber: the accoutrements of monarchy were there; the king was symbolically present even in his absence. Through all the discussion of his person, deeds and trial, negative as well as positive, Charles I dominated the political discourse for some time after his death. And the issue of monarchy remained the central subject of political debate throughout the 1650s. 'The King's person in England never dies says the law', the *Second Part of the Religious Demurrer* reminded readers.[58]

There can be little doubt that his manner of dying was the most popular thing Charles I ever did. The king's bravery in battle, his deportment at his trial and his accomplished performance on the scaffold did much to erase earlier failings, and criticisms, from the national memory. As one writer claimed, even Charles's critics and enemies admired his fortitude of spirit and stand on conscience.[59] As for the people, Arise Evans believed they 'knew not the sweetness of King Charles his Nature and Love to them until he declared it upon the scaffold'.[60] Royalist

---

[54] See M. Seymour, 'Pro-Government Propaganda in Interregnum England, 1649–1660' (Ph.D. thesis, Cambridge University, 1987), 125: 'The badge of a nation replaced the head of a king; the language of the people replaced the language of the law; the title of Commonwealth . . . replaced that of personal dominion; and the palm and laurel spoke of the peace brought by victory.' [55] Most of the coins I have seen are from 1651 or later.

[56] Seymour, 'Pro-Government Propaganda', 120–4, quotation 120.

[57] See below, pp. 253–4. [58] *A Second Part of the Religious Demurrer* (1649), E530/31, p. 7.

[59] *Comparatio inter Claudium Tiberium Principem et Olivarium Cromwellium Protectorem* (1657) (Huntington Library, not in Wing), p. 16. See above, ch. 5.

[60] A. Evans, *The Euroclydon Winde Commanded to Cease* (1653), E1491/2, p. 6.

panegyrics in 1649 proclaimed that the king would never be forgotten. The sheer quantity of royalist hagiography ensured that the king was remembered. But the most eloquent testimony to the power of the royal memory comes from those who opposed it. *The Life and Reign of King Charles, or The Pseudo Martyr Discovered*, for example, exhibits an unease that even denunciations contributed to the 'frequent occasions to rake over his ashes'.[61] An apologist for the Commonwealth, acknowledging the force of the axiom that the king can do no wrong, rued 'how hard it hath been to make the people think the king could offend or was liable to any guilt'.[62] It is revealing that the Commonwealth government did not attempt to make 30 January a commemoration day on the ritual calendar. Though literature critical of the king began to be more effective from 1652 or 1653, the memory of Charles as a virtuous martyr survived his detractors. Throughout the years of the Commonwealth, the king, as a monument of 1649 had put it, did 'live in each true subject's heart'.[63] That he did was largely a result of the power of the king's image in the culture and imagination of the nation.

Only recently has close attention been paid to the extraordinary rhetorical power of the *Eikon Basilike*, 'the image of the king'.[64] The *Eikon* towered over the literature of 1649 and the continuing debate over the authorship not only kept Charles I at the centre of political discussion, it pointed up the need to deprive the king of a language that carried such authority. The king's book, however, succeeded in (re)claiming a number of validating vocabularies for the royalist cause: as one elegist put it with astute use of possessive pronouns: 'Thy book is our best language.'[65] Not least on account of its own appropriations of biblical language, the *Eikon* was held by many to be 'next to hallowed writ and sacred page'.[66] Testament to its authority, the *Eikon* spawned an industry of extracts, copies and imitations. And it continued, seemingly unabated. As late as 1657 the *Psalterium Carolinum*, which rendered in verse and music 'the devotions of His Majesty in his solitude and sufferings', was sold at The

---

[61] *The Life and Reign of King Charles, or The Pseudo Martyr Discovered* (1652), E1338/2, preface. Cf. *The Non Such Charles His Character* (1651), E1345, where after a damning condemnation of the monarchy the author acknowledges 'the smile of a king can send comfort unto the very heart of men' (p. 182).   [62] *A Short Discourse*, E575/31, p. 12.

[63] *The Monument of Charles I* (1649), 669 f14/36.

[64] See Skerpan, *Rhetoric of Politics*, ch. 5; Corns, *Uncloistered Virtue*, 80–91; above, ch. 3, pp. 147–50; most of all the brilliant analysis in S. Zwicker, *Lines of Authority: Politics and English Literary Culture, 1649–1689* (Ithaca, 1993), ch. 2.

[65] *An Elegie upon the Death of Our Dread Sovereign Lord King Charles* (1649), 669 f14/42.

[66] *An Elegie on the Meekest of Men* (1649), 14.

Bell in Paul's Yard.[67] The *Eikon Basilike* did what Charles had foreseen his martyrdom would do: it raised the king above the polemical fray, enshrined his memory, and so denied the fruits of victory to his conquerors. As *Virtus Redeviva* was to put it, 'by Thy Book thou gainst the greatest victory'.[68] Milton was not the only one to appreciate the need to contest its power and royal authorship.[69] The *Eikon Alethine*, anxious about the damage the *Eikon* inflicted on the new regime, systematically analysed the book to prove that it was neither the king's work nor even a fair reflection of his views or style, then closed with the caution that if this had not persuaded the readers, they should realize that it is 'not writing but acting well that adorns a king'.[70]

What most dismayed the critics of the *Eikon Basilike*, however, was what has received least scholarly attention: its visual evocation and the power of its emblematic frontispiece (see Figure 10 on p. 215). The author of *The Portraiture of Truths Most Sacred Majestie*, recognizing that 'multitudes biased by affection to the late king would readily and very credulously take for current anything stamped with his effigies', asked his readers why the book so prevailed with them: 'Will you be frighted by his image whose person could neither frown nor flatter you from fidelity to your country?'[71] The answer, as he suspected, lay in the question. Or, as *The Pseudo Martyr Discovered* put it, the royalists had won the victory 'by presenting this book with his picture praying on the frontispiece purposefully to catch . . . the people . . . canonizing him for a saint, and idolizing his memory for an innocent martyr'.[72] The principal artifice of the impostor who compiled the *Eikon*, he continues, was that he 'garnished the approaches to his collections with the king's picture in some places standing, in others kneeling, and as it were ejaculating his prayers to God and those dressed with sundry devices and mottos and all this to invite the eye if not the understanding of the silly beholder to a belief that he died an innocent martyr'.[73] The pamphleteer accepted the power of the appeal to 'the eye', as he acknowledged in suitably military language that it had 'so much taken in the opinion of the vulgar belief and [was] esteemed to be such an impregnable rampier encircling his innocency that it hath been thought not accountable', that is, above reproach.[74] The visual power of the *Eikon*, ignored by logocentric historians, was

---

[67] *Psalterium Carolinum: the Devotions of his Sacred Majestie* (1657), E1076, an important and neglected work.   [68] *Virtus Redeviva: a Panegyrick on Our Late King Charles I* (1660), E1806, p. 26.
[69] See the appendix to *Monarchy or No Monarchy in England* (1651), E638/17, especially pp. 81ff.
[70] *Eikon Alethine: the Portraiture of Truths Most Sacred Majestie* (1649), E569/16, pp. 2–6, p. 6.
[71] Ibid., sig. [A1]: epistle to reader.   [72] *The Life of King Charles* (1652), preface.
[73] Ibid., 148–9.   [74] Ibid., 178.

clearly obvious to contemporaries, whether they were enemies or allies. And royalists ensured that the image, like the text, continued to circulate in a number of different forms. For one, there were many copies and variants of the famous frontispiece, sold as engravings and reproduced in books and polemical tracts. Some engravings carried verse explaining the symbolism or biblical passages glossing its meaning.[75] Artists entered the disputes over authorship by depicting the king seated, writing.[76] Badges of emblems from the *Eikon* were circulated, one depicting a skull inscribed 'CR' and a celestial crown of glory.[77] There was almost no visual response to these images. Though the *Eikon Alethine* reinforced its argument that the king's book was a prelatical forgery by an illustration of a curtain drawn aside to reveal a priest writing, the opportunity to mock or desecrate the image – by caricature or cartoon, for example – was not taken.[78] If Milton's contempt for images expressed a broader reluctance to engage on these terms, it was a polemical disaster. The image of the king dominated the visual culture of the Commonwealth; given the force of symbols and emblems the absent king, as we shall argue, remained a presence and power in the political culture too.

We must also recall that the *Eikon Basilike* addressed in general the nation, in particular a figure who, more than any emblem, bore the king's image: his son. The *Eikon Basilike* closed with an address to the prince; by the time of publication he was the new king. Charles II and his supporters were quick to imitate the discursive and visual polemics of the king's book in speeches, declarations and engravings that proclaimed the succession. At Scone in 1651 a ceremony marked Charles's coronation as King of Scotland (in contrast to the uncelebrated change of government in England in 1649) and thereafter raised not only the royal profile but the threat of invasion to restore the Stuarts to the throne of England.[79]

The continuous presence, symbolic and physical, of the two kings also ensured that traditional political and religious ideas remained alive in the national consciousness and the nation's conscience. Albeit debated and contested, theories of divine right, the duty of obedience and the

[75] Huntington Library, Bull/Granger, vol. 6, nos. 23, 24.

[76] *Eikon e Piste, or The Faithful Portraiture of a Loyal Subject* (1649), E573/11, an engraving of Charles writing, with accompanying verse.

[77] H. Farquar, 'Portraits of the Stuarts on the Royalist Badges', *British Numismatic Journal*, 2 (1906), 23–30.

[78] *Eikon Alethine*: see the verse 'Presumptious priest to slip into the throne / And make his King his bastard issue owne', frontispiece.

[79] *The True Manner of the Crowning of Charles of the Second, King of Scotland* (1651), E669 f15/82; R. Douglas, *The Form and Order of the Coronation* (Aberdeen, 1650), Wing 2030B.

sanctity of oaths survived the battles of civil war; indeed the *Eikon Basilike* and royalist propaganda successfully reclaimed the divine for Charles I and his son. Immediately after the execution, *A Serious and Faithful Representation of Ministers of the Gospel* was presented to the General Council and published to the nation. 'You cannot but know', the London ministers asserted as though it was indisputable, 'how fully and frequently God's word commandeth and enforceth obedience and submission to magistrates.'[80] 'No necessity', they continued, anticipating Commonwealth counterarguments, 'can . . . dispense with lawful oaths'; to oppose princes, they concluded, was the doctrine of Jesuits, not Protestant Englishmen.[81] In a similar vein *The Rebels Looking Glass, or The Traitors Doom*, echoing James I's words that 'Kings are God's vicegerents', accused MPs of breaking their oath not only to the king but to God and recalled God's punishments on Corah, Absalom, Achitophel, Shimei and Shiba for the sin of rebellion.[82] Several pamphlets took up the themes of the divine nature of monarchy, the binding religious obligation of oaths, the sin perpetrated by the regicides and the divine judgement that awaited them. The point here is not that such arguments and beliefs were new or original: they were traditional and commonplace. What is important is that having been questioned and contested they were reinforced and reappropriated by the *Eikon Basilike* and by skilful royalist polemics and sustained throughout the short life of the Commonwealth. And they planted in the consciences of many the fear that to fall in with the new government was to sin.

Monarchy in England was not only sanctioned by scripture, it was at the heart of the nation's law and of its history – of its identity. 'I have late heard much of a Commonwealth,' Robert Sprye wrote in *The Rules of Civil Government*, 'but know not what it meaneth.'[83] History had determined what government was. *A Brief Chronology of Great Britain* made a powerful ideological point in its one-page history from biblical times to Charles I, as did royalists who depicted the Stuarts as the thread that connected England to 600 years of history.[84] Commonwealth writers could respond to the historical case in two ways. One was to press a different reading of history.[85] Accordingly, *The True Portraiture of the Kings*

---

[80] R. W. K. Hinton ed., *A Serious and Faithful Representation of Ministers of the Gospel* (Reading, 1949), 11. [81] Ibid., 12, 17. [82] *The Rebels Looking Glass* (1649), E554/23.

[83] R. Sprye, *The Rules of Civil Government Drawn from the Best Examples of Foreign Nations* (1653), E1484/3, sig. A3.

[84] *A Brief Chronology of Great Britain* (1656), 669 f20/35; *Three Propositions* (1659), E985/17.

[85] Nedham, we recall, took up a cyclical rather than linear view of history in *The Case of the Commonwealth*, 4.

of England exposed the myth of seamless continuity to show that the succession in England had often been interrupted since Saxon times, leaving but a 'broken and usurped title'.[86] *The Number and Names of All the Kings of England and Scotland* began a catalogue of the monarchs from Brutus, with brief entries starkly listing all those 'killed', 'beheaded', or 'murdered'.[87] More positively, *The Continuation of an Historical Discourse* argued that the nation had been in ancient Saxon times a commonwealth and 'as I found this nation a commonwealth, so I leave it'.[88] The alternative strategy was to reject history altogether. So *The Royalist Reform'd* sought to sweep aside tradition by asserting simply that 'the chief books about governments were written in old dark times when tyrants were the only kings'.[89] History in itself was not what mattered, the author of *A Short Discourse* agreed: 'Antiquity is an argument for nothing but truth and goodness.'[90] History, however, could not be so easily dismissed in a seventeenth-century England where gentlemen's education, titles, houses and lands as well as the nation's institutions were defined by it, where custom was the very basis of the common law. Because Commonwealth apologists could never overcome a feeling that history (destiny) was against them, the weapon of history remained in the hands of the royalists, who used it to effect: 'Our realm is a Monarchy', the author of *The Immortality of the King* proclaimed, 'successive by inherent birthright'; '*were* there an interregnum there would be a time, like the present with us, in which the statutes and common law should neither be of force or use'.[91]

Neither the law nor scripture, of course, were royalist property. Yet though the Commonwealth justified itself from readings of the Bible, the constitution and the English past, it was royalist propaganda that was most effective when it evoked these normative languages. 'The God of order', *A Dissection of All Governments* put it, 'intended . . . monarchical government' and kings had linearly descended since the Conquest in fulfilment of God's will.[92] In a similar blend of legal and divine discourse, another announced: 'England in her best and loudest language the law hath largely declared the sacred sovereignty of her kings.'[93] Christian time, history, they were claiming, was the time of kings: 'Monarchy was

---

[86] *The True Portraiture of the Kings of England*, 11–15, quotation 15.
[87] J. T., *The Number and Names of All the Kings of England and Scotland* (1650), E1246/3.
[88] N. Bacon, *The Continuation of an Historical Discourse of the Government of England* (1650), E624/1, p. 357.   [89] Warren, *The Royalist Reform'd*, 10.   [90] *A Short Discourse*, 18.
[91] *Majestas Intemerata, or the Immortality of the King* (1649), E1347/1, pp. 118–19. We await a good study of the rhetoric and polemic of histories written and published during the civil war and interregnum.   [92] W. J., *A Dissection of All Governments* (1649), E545/23, pp. 5, 12 and passim.
[93] W. Juxon, *The Subjects Sorrow . . .* (1649), E546/16, p. 26.

created with and will end with the world.'[94] Such rhetoric, not least the appropriation of the apocalyptic, undercut pragmatic defences of the new regime and made it appear an 'interruption' to history itself – illegitimate and ungodly.[95] Other vocabularies and metaphors, seemingly effortlessly but often artfully employed, served to connect God, king and nation. When the elegist of *Jeremias Redevivus* spoke of a regicide that had 'widowed our whole nation', he evoked not only the political marriage of king and realm but the mystical union of Christ and his church.[96] References to 'nursing fathers' and to biblical kings bound monarchy, scripture and church.[97] And such representations of monarchs as divine, natural rulers, the protectors of church and law, are not only a commonplace of royalist texts; they were the recurring motif of the skilfully polemical paintings and engravings that may have reached an even wider audience.

We have glanced at the frontispiece to the *Eikon Basilike* and its importance for that text. More generally, we need to examine the images of Charles I and Charles II which both kept them in the public eye and continued the argument for restoration by different means. First, we should note the very large number of portraits of the royal family in aristocratic and country houses. For every known great master (many were sold and dispersed widely in the 1650s), there were scores of copies, 'afters', and imitations in a society that still venerated the image more than the artist. There was scarcely a country house in which some image of the king or court did not hang, daily observed by family, visitors, retainers and servants.[98] More important, because neglected, many formed the templates of hundreds more engravings and woodcuts, a surprising number of which have survived – perhaps because they became treasured possessions. Such portraits of king and courtiers evoked memories, doubtless sustained royalist communities, and retained mystical, iconic power with plain folk.[99] (Not for nothing did radical soldiers shoot at the paintings

---

[94] *The Royal Legacies* (1649), E557/1, p. 49.

[95] *An Exercitation concerning Usurped Powers* (1649), E585/2, p. 64: 'We therefore swear to obey Princes . . . whilst it pleaseth God to continue them to us; and this tie a present interruption of government . . . cannot dissolve.'　　[96] *Jeremias Redevivus* (1649), E556/33, p. 2.

[97] See, for example, *Observations upon Aristotle's Politics*, sig. A5; *God and the King* (1649), E550/2; *The Royal Legacies*, 78 and passim.

[98] The photoarchives at the Huntington Library and Courtauld Institute reveal dozens of copies of the famous Van Dycks which are too often discussed as images seen only at court.

[99] Quite literally in the case of the engraving of Charles I surrounded by loyal supporters, sold by Sam Speed at the Rainbow in Fleet St. (Huntington Library, Bull/Granger, vol. 6, no. 26). Engravings were also made of statues that were removed during the Commonwealth: e.g., a Le Sueur statue preserved by a brazier in Holborn (ibid., vol. 6, no. 16).

of kings.)[100] Appearing in a wide range of contemporary books, these portraits sustained the connection of royalty with a number of cultural practices. Engravings, moreover, were often directly polemical and partisan. Sometimes the argument resided in a simple juxtaposition of image and words: the *Pious Instructions* (Figure 15) found hanging in Charles I's closet consisted of an engraving of the king above injunctions concerning daily life, diet and apparel, thoughts ('heavenly'), prayer ('faithful', 'frequent') and remembrance ('judgement');[101] Simon's engraving of the king's trial was captioned 'the picture of the royal martyr . . . in the pretended High Court of Justice'.[102] Often the image provided its own symbolic meaning. The frontispiece to *The Subjects Sorrow*, to take a case, depicted Charles on his deathbed above which angels held a crown, while in the distance a cross stood on a hill, associating the king's sacrifice with Christ's.[103] Other engravings represented Charles coming to the defence of the tree of religion against ruffians who lopped at its branches (Figure 16) or reaching out to raise a fainting figure of Ecclesia, crowned and bearing the sceptre in one hand, Magna Carta in the other.[104] In some cases the image encapsulated the symbolic presence of the king even in his absence. The engraving of Judge Jenkins, who opposed the regicide, holding Magna Carta or the map of London churches with a prominent St Paul's bearing the device 'O Theater of Royal Love', visually conjoined king, church and law.[105] The toppled oak, with water from heaven pouring down on its stump, promised restoration.[106] And the promise was made real in the portrayals of Charles II. A simple engraving of Charles I giving thanks for the birth of his son underpinned the succession, as less subtly did that of Charles II with the sword of faith in his hand, a book with 'In Verbo Tuo Spes Mea' (the words of Charles I in the *Eikon*), looking heavenward to a crown inscribed 'Carolus ad Carolum'.[107] As many Englishmen contemplated their sin, a complex engraving showed the Scots presenting a pistol to an armoured Charles II behind whom a monster trampled Charles I. On top of the Banqueting House the figure of justice with uneven scales and broken sword associates regicide with the destruction of law, as the whole calls on the English to join the fight for the newly

[100] *Mercurius Rusticus* (1647), E1099/1, pp. 203, 212–13.
[101] Huntington Library, Bull/Granger, vol. 6, no. 20.   [102] Ibid., vol. 6, no. 22.
[103] Juxon, *The Subjects Sorrow*.   [104] Huntington Library, Bull/Granger, vol. 6, no. 25.
[105] Huntington Library, Bull/Granger, vol. 7, no. 122; vol. 11, no. 38.
[106] Ibid., vol. 10, no. 26, dated 30 January 1649, with verses from Job 14:7–9. This is also British Museum, engraved portrait, no. 737.
[107] Huntington Library, Bull/Granger, vol. 6, no. 30; vol. 12, no. 7.

PIOUS INSTRUCTIONS,

Which were found   hanging up in a

Black Ebony Frame,   written in Gold, in

King Charles I's   C L O S E T,

foon after his Death,   *Ann. Dom.* 1648.

CHARLES,I,KING OF ENGLAND,&c.
*His Sufferings & his Death with truth proclaim :
For He got Glory, but the Nation Shame .*

1 Thoughts	{ Heavenly, Timerous, Religious.	6 Diet	{ Moderate, Meet, Frugal.
2 Will	{ Firm, Obedient, Mature.	7 Apparel	{ Comely, Clean, Decent.
3 Words	{ Few, Honeft, Unfeigned.	8 Sport	{ Honeft, Short, Seldom.
4 Works	{ Profitable, Godly, Pure.	9 Prayer	{ Brief, Faithful, Frequent.
5 Behaviour	{ Difcreet, Courteous, Chearful.	10 Sleep	{ Temperate, Quiet, In due Time.
	{ Remembrance of	{ Death, Judgment, Punifhment.	{

In the Chariot of Wifdom, the firft Step is, to know thy felf.	*A fpecial Refpect of thy Ways, is to be had ; Cuftom will make it pleafant.*

Figure 15. *Pious Instructions* (reproduced by permission of the Huntington Library, San Marino, California)

Figure 16. 'The shepherds oracles': Charles I defends the 'tree of religion' (reproduced
by permission of the Huntington Library, San Marino, California)

proclaimed king.[108] Engravings of the coronation in Scotland in them-selves gave visual reinforcement to Charles II's legitimate succession;[109] Hollar's Jupiter and Minerva crowning Charles as he triumphed over the dragon of rebellion announced a new St George, a king blessed by wisdom and the gods themselves.[110]

Royalist visual propaganda, as well as authorizing the royalist cause, lampooned the Commonwealth in graphic cartoons. In one (Figure 17) the Commonwealth is depicted ruling with a standing army represented as a large dragon whose tail is a chain and which shits out excise and taxes.[111] Caricatures of ministers like Hugh Peter show him as avaricious and lascivious, while tub preachers in general fanned fear of parity in state as well as church.[112] Where the Commonwealth failed to draw on the tradition of the scatological cartoon, in defeat the royalists employed this as other visual genres to polemical effect. By 1653 the visual had almost become identified with the royal – perhaps a point made in the portrait of Charles I in armour that illustrated William Sanderson's *Graphice . . . or The Most Excellent Art of Painting*.[113] Certainly as the Cromwellian Protectorate began to take more pains over its image, its style too became more regal.

Visuals held such sway in early modern culture because symbols were held to represent truths. It is important therefore to understand that even after the execution of the king, the universe of symbols – coins, heraldic escutcheons, processions, card games and a myriad of social practices – were inscribed with and by monarchy. In a woodcut of 1649, *The King's Last Farewell*, the royal coffin is flanked by two standard-bearers whose banners are blank, without escutcheons.[114] Can, the image leads us to ask, there be a universe of signs, meaning, without a king? And, as if by answer, *The Royal Charter* reminded readers that the throne, the crown and the sceptre stood for justice, honour and strength and that there was need for 'the signs *and* the things signified'.[115] To be fair, the Rumpers, not least because they were part of this culture, recognized the author-ity of signs. As well as a new seal, they ordered a new parliamentary mace, new civic maces, with more republican motifs, new arms for courts, naval yards and ships, and new liveries for coachmen and water-

---

[108] BL, Thomason tracts, 669 f12/88.

[109] Huntington Library, Bull/Granger, vol. 10, nos. 3, 3ᵛ, vol. 12, no. 6.

[110] Ibid., vol. 12, no. 31ᵛ.   [111] Ibid., vol. 10, no. 26.

[112] For example, ibid., vol. 10, no. 72v.

[113] W. Sanderson, *Graphice: the Use of the Pen and Pencil, or The Most Excellent Art of Painting* (1658), E1077/2.   [114] *The King's Last Farewell to the World* (1649), 669 f1/79.

[115] *The Royal Charter* (1649), E1356/1, p. 18.

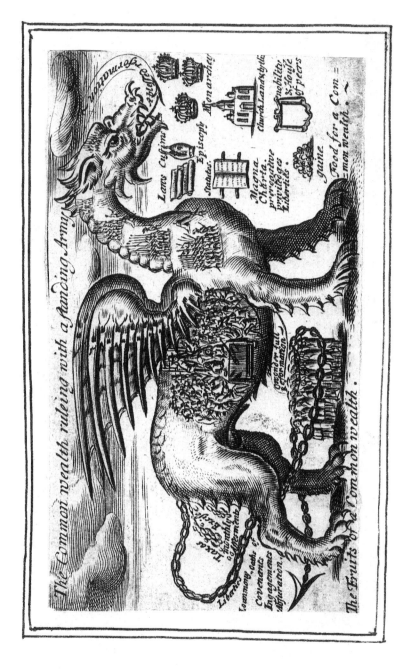

Figure 17. 'The Common wealth ruleing with a standing army' (reproduced by permission of the Huntington Library, San Marino, California)

men.[116] But the endeavour to create a new symbolic system was faltering and problematic. When the Rump planned a medal to commemorate the victory at Dunbar, Cromwell advised a picture of parliament on the one side, the army on the other, but parliament insisted on Cromwell's bust after his portrait by Walker.[117] As well as flattery of the Lord General, their decision also points up the difficulty of symbols detached from persons in a heraldic culture. Significantly, when Oliver became Lord Protector the arms of the Commonwealth, detached from any dynasty or family, were replaced by a new device incorporating his own escutcheon.[118]

If new symbols were hard to create, it was even more difficult to remove the old. When the Commonwealth witnessed citizens 'going a whoring after the [king's] image set up in the old Exchange' they took it down and placed there the words 'Exit Tyrannus Regum ultimus Anno Libertatis Angliae Restituto primo AD 1648 Jan 30.'[119] Words, however, did not replace such icons; statues removed were preserved and engraved. Moreover, the site remained in the national memory as the *Royal* Exchange.[120] In the capital and in the provinces daily life involved daily encounter with the symbols of royalty. Many had purchased royal goods, from great paintings to close stools; more fingered the king's coin.[121] Aristocrats and gentlemen bore arms crossed with royal emblems, more humble folk drank or shopped in 'The King's Head in the The Old Bailey' and such like.[122] There, no doubt, they continued to drink the king's health, since drinking the Rump's was neither ordered nor mentioned.[123] Some played the 'Royal Game at Pickett'; any who played cards could share the lament that 'I lost the game for lack of a king.'[124] At every game chess players were reminded that their whole purpose as a player was to protect the king.

The historian does not have to imagine the connections contemporaries made between such play and politics.[125] The *Game at Chess* used the

---

[116] F. Peck, *Historical Pieces* (1740), 56; for information about the mace, I am grateful to Sean Kelsey.

[117] H. W. Henfrey, *Numismata Cromwelliana: Coins, Medals, and Seals of Oliver Cromwell* (1877), 3–4.

[118] See below, pp. 253–4.   [119] *Monarchy or No Monarchy* (1651), E638/7, pp. 118–19.

[120] N. G. Brett-James, *The Growth of Stuart London* (1935), 18, 43, 323.

[121] O. Millar, *The Inventories and Valuations of the King's Goods* (Walpole Soc., no. 43, 1972); A. MacGregor ed., *The Late King's Goods* (London and Oxford, 1989). Little attention has been paid to the purchasers of Charles I's goods (who include leading members of the Council of State) or to the significance of items with royal arms being distributed and displayed throughout the life of the republic.

[122] *The Government of the People of England* (1650) was printed and sold at the King's Head!

[123] See *Enthusiasm Displayed* (1743), 21; *The Right Picture of King Oliver* (1650), E858/7, p. 8.

[124] *The Royal Game at Pickett* (1656), E886/4.

[125] See above, ch. 2, pp. 98–101. It is interesting that the Convention in France tried to change such symbols.

board as a political allegory in 1623; thirty years later the author of *The Royal Game at Pickett* satirized Cromwell and his generals by means of an imagined card game. Images of monarchy continued to pervade the visual and symbolic universe. The material culture, which is also the political culture, remained a royal culture, and the royal icon continued to shape the forms and genres of social and political life.

'It is easy', the author of *A Short Discourse* wrote in 1649, 'to frame the idea of a new government . . . but not so easy to alter an old one.'[126] This was true not just of the institutions but of the customary practices and forms that had themselves become inextricably associated, indeed endowed, with authority. Let us consider acts and proclamations. These partook of a set visual form, with decorated initial letters and Gothic script, a standard form of address and a language peculiar to the genre. So identified did the act become with its generic markers that the new regimes found it necessary to continue the old forms. Though, as royalists protested, the Rump altered 'the ancient, regal and legal style of writs' to remove oaths of allegiance, they retained the regalia of form.[127] An Act for bestowing the powers of the Lord Warden and Lord Admiral on the Council of State deployed Gothic script, a large ornamental B on 'Be it enacted', angels and cornucopia, even a crowned (Tudor) rose.[128] When the Protector was invested, he was proclaimed at the familiar London landmarks – the Strand, Temple Bar, the Exchange.[129] Cromwell's own proclamations adopted a distinctly regal style and in letters patent he resumed the royal address 'Right trusty and well beloved Counsellor'.[130] Proclamations for fast days and commemorations (of Dunbar, for example) connect the familiar form to a continued familiar practice; the commemoration of Guy Fawkes's Day in particular could not but evoke a king, a Stuart saved by the hand of God.[131]

Whatever the Commonwealth's desire to silence the bells of some festivals and birthdays, such rituals were (and are) integral to government. Indeed, so was the culture of the aristocracy and the court. *Honor Redivivus* was consciously royalist in stating that the king was 'the true fountain from whence all these rivulets and swelling streams of honour spring'; but even a bare list of the dukes, earls and barons in 1652 could

[126] *A Short Discourse*, 19.   [127] *The English Tyrants* (1649), E569/10, p. 12.
[128] *An Act Establishing the Powers of Lord Admiral . . . as Lord Warden of the Cinque Ports upon the Council of State* (1651), 669 f15/80. In 1660 satires mocked Commonwealth proclamations; see, for example, *St George and the Dragon* (1660), 669 f23/66.
[129] *The Commonwealth Mercury*, 2–9 September 1658.   [130] Peck, *Historical Pieces*, 60–1.
[131] See D. Cressy, *Bonfires and Bells: National Memory and the Protestant Calendar in Elizabethan and Stuart England* (1989), ch. 9.

hardly avoid mentioning the 'especial grace and favour of the several kings' who had 'admitted [them] into the honour of their ancestors'.[132] The House of Lords may have been abolished, but the aristocracy remained – in London and on their estates – the heads of local society and patronage. Any permanent political settlement needed to embrace them and, as part of his quest for settlement, Cromwell felt it increasingly necessary to re-establish a court as a centre of display and a point of contact between Whitehall and the shires.[133]

With an aristocracy and a court went aristocratic pastimes and courtly culture. Cromwell, as John Adamson put it, may have preferred to read of the zeal of Phineas to chivalric romances and the like, but most aristocrats did not share his preference.[134] In 1653 *The Card of Courtship, or The Language of Love* published a guide to writing amorous letters and to forms of compliment that, for all puritan objections, reminds us of the continuing symbiosis of love and politics.[135] By 1658 *The Accomplished Courtier* was advising on all modes of behaviour at court, asking 'Qui enim non vivit in Aula?'[136] *The Mysteries of Love and Eloquence* meanwhile addressed terms used at horse-races and balls, how to woo fair ladies, 'the choice of a gentleman usher', and included love poems, cavalier carpe diem songs, and (often vulgar) jests.[137] By 1658 the open revival of such practices was seen by contemporaries to presage a return to monarchy. But they had never gone away. Throughout the 1650s courtly literature was read and courtly practices pursued, all pointing to the absence at the centre: the absence of the king.

The same is true of plays. It is often wrongly believed that because the public theatres were closed all experience of drama ended during the republic. Certainly the republic's opposition to theatre was political as well as religious. As the prologue to the first play revived at the Cockpit in 1660 put it: 'They that would have no king would have no play' for fear that the ghosts of Harries and Edwards would 'still on the stage a march of glory tread' and 'teach the people to despise their reign'.[138] Yet,

[132] *Honor Redevivus* (1655), E1458/2, p. 61; cf. pp. 48, 62 and passim; *A New Catalogue of the Dukes, Marquesses, Earls, Viscounts, Barons . . .* (1652), E1238/2.

[133] See R. Sherwood, *The Court of Oliver Cromwell* (1977).

[134] J. S. A. Adamson, 'Chivalry and Political Culture in Caroline England', in Sharpe and Lake, *Culture and Politics*, 194.

[135] *The Card of Courtship* (1653), E1308/2; cf. K. Sharpe, *Criticism and Compliment: the Politics of Literature in the England of Charles I* (Cambridge, 1987), ch. 7.

[136] *The Accomplished Courtier* (1658), E1824/1, title page.

[137] *The Mysteries of Love and Eloquence* (1658), E1735, pp. 104, 155ff., 176 and passim; cf. Corns, *Uncloistered Virtue*, 244–68, and D. Hirst, 'The Politics of Literature in the English Republic', *The Seventeenth Century*, 5 (1991), 135–55.

[138] *Prologue to His Majesty at the First Play Presented at the Cockpit in Whitehall* (1660), 669 f26/26.

for all that, across the decade old plays were still read, new ones published, some performed with official sanction and, doubtless in aristocratic houses, many more without. In 1653, for example, five new plays
by Richard Brome were published, including *The Court Beggar*.[139] Two
years later *Hymen's Praeludia*, the third part of the romance *Cleopatra*, was
translated and published – with a preface rich in political language.[140]
William Davenant staged a number of entertainments for Cromwell,
while in 1653 James Shirley, author of the famous *Triumph of Peace*,
devised the masque *Cupid and Death* for the entertainment of the
Portuguese ambassador.[141] Davenant, we now know, was advancing
schemes for a new reformed drama that might inculcate civic virtues
through 'heroic representations', but he and Shirley were playwrights to
the former king and, as the 1660 prologue stated, plays were about courts
and kings.[142] In one case a play drew dramatic attention to a living king
and dynasty: *The Nuptials of Peleus and Thetis* (1654), published in English,
to be sold at the Anchor in the lower walk of the New Exchange, a
masque performed at Paris by the king, the Duke of Anjou, Henrietta
Maria and the Duke of York. It closed with the lines: 'By this we find
adversity to be / The surest road to true felicity.'[143]

Like play, procession was integral to the political culture of early
modern England but because of its associations with royal festival presented a difficulty to the Commonwealth government. The new regime
had to express itself ceremonially but was never certain how. The years
1649–53 were not devoid of procession and celebration. There were
several receptions for Cromwell after returns from victories in Ireland,
in Scotland and at Worcester. There were state funerals for Isaac
Dorislaus, Henry Ireton and others. But stripped of the allegories,
myths, pageants and tableaux vivants scorned by puritan iconoclasts,
such occasions became little more than military parades.[144] Still too
focused on personality for staunch republicans, denuded of the mysteries and spectacles that awed the mob, the Rump celebrations failed to

---

[139] R. Brome, *Five New Playes* (1653), E1423.   [140] *Hymen's Praeludia* (1655), E1459/2.
[141] S. J. Wiseman, 'History Digested: Opera and Colonialism in the 1650s', in T. Healy and J.
    Sawday eds., *Literature and the English Civil War* (Cambridge, 1990), 189–204; J. Shirley, *Cupid and
    Death: a Masque* (1653), E690/4.
[142] See J. Jacob and T. Raylor, 'Opera and Obedience: Thomas Hobbes and *A Proposition for
    Advancement of Moralitie* by Sir William Davenant', *The Seventeenth Century*, 6 (1991), 205–50. Cf. N.
    Smith, 'Popular Republicanism in the 1650s: John Streater's "Heroick Mechanicks"', in Q.
    Skinner and D. Armitage eds., *Milton and Republicanism* (Cambridge, 1995), 137–55. I am grate-
    ful to Nigel Smith for his having allowed me to read this interesting essay in advance of publi-
    cation.   [143] *The Nuptials of Peleus and Thetis* (1654), E228/3.
[144] See Seymour, 'Pro-Government Propaganda', ch. 6.

find 'a suitable vehicle for spectacular presentation of itself'.[145] Significantly, there were no Lord Mayor's shows from 1643 to 1655.[146] Joyful, grand celebration and pageant therefore remained in the public mind as regal occasions, and those who rued their end could not but be led to regret too the demise of their raison d'être. When in 1656 *London's Triumph* described and defended the mayoral pageant that did 'dazzle and amaze the common eye . . . to make them know there is something more excellent in magistracy than they understand', its author linked 'those ancient customs of joy and entertainment' to princes who delighted to behold them.[147]

Across a broad spectrum of genres, surviving cultural forms kept kingship at the centre of political and social life and undermined the Commonwealth's establishment not just in the institutions but in the material culture of England. Time might have made the difference, but one of the reasons that the Rump government did not enjoy more time was because it failed to establish itself as the government of the nation. There was no great public outcry when Cromwell dissolved parliament in April 1653. There is, however, something revealingly poignant about his trifling with the mace, his dismissing as a 'bauble', 'a jester's staff', one of the symbols of its authority to which the Commonwealth had devoted attention.[148] After 1653 the style of government as well as the constitution was to change profoundly. The Oliver Cromwell who as Lord General in the early 1650s had endeavoured to write a new script for a republic became – from the start, then progressively more so – a monarchical figure. Whether he aped the king out of ambition or came to a sense that there was no real alternative image for government we do not need to judge. The question that matters is whether his appropriation of royal words and idioms erased the memory and power of monarchy itself or whether it turned men to thinking that the thing signified was as necessary as the signs.

THE PROTECTORATE

When Cromwell dissolved the Rump he knew that it had failed to establish a republic or erode the hold of kingship on the nation. As he

---

[145] Ibid., 224; cf. 229: 'There was perhaps no convenient way to advertise the merits of a political collectivity.'   [146] Ibid., 196–9.

[147] *London's Triumph, or The Solemn and Magnificent Reception of . . . Robert Tichborn, Lord Maior* (1656), E892/7, p. 9.

[148] See W. C. Abbott, *Writings and Speeches of Oliver Cromwell* (4 vols., Cambridge, Mass., 1937–47), II, 642–3.

explained in his *Declaration . . . Showing the Grounds and Reasons for the Dissolution of the Late Parliament*, the supreme authority had been entrusted to 'men fearing God and of approved integrity' 'hoping thereby the people might forget monarchy'.[149] The experiment was an even greater failure. As one panegyrist wrote, when the Barebones assembly dissolved itself, they were saying, 'Cromwell we are deserted. You only remain: the finishing of all our affairs is returned to you: on you it relies.'[150] The battery of second person singular pronouns makes the point: from 1653 government by a single person was effectively re-established in England. The year 1653 marked a major shift in the form and style of government, bringing the monarchical, albeit not the monarchy, back to centre stage. By no means did all contemporaries see things this way or intend that they should be. Going through the constitution line by line, Nedham presented the Protectorate as the mean between extremes, the best of all governments. Nedham, however, throughout felt the need to make a case against the Stuarts and to press the distinctions between a monarch and a Protector.[151] That he felt such a need from the very beginning is not surprising when we read *A Declaration concerning the Government of the Three Nations* (1653).[152] For this account of Cromwell's investiture as Protector sketched a ceremony that, as we shall see, appeared familiarly regal, with oaths, a chair of state, the surrender of the seal and sword, a procession to the Banqueting House, and a grand feast.[153] Contemporaries of all political shades saw significance in the occasion. Supporters believed revealingly that the ceremony at last validated the government: '*Now* this commonwealth is become the wonder and emulation of Europe.'[154] But others, the same writer admitted, 'begin to breathe forth a disowning and dislike of this great and unparalleled change'.[155]

The sense on all parts that a major change had taken place is manifested – what else would we expect – in the issue of nomenclature and language. Some thought the title General, as honourable to the Romans as Imperator to the Germans, the best for the Protector; others thought of him as the head of a Sanhedrin or noted that the title Protector was

[149] *A Declaration of the Lord General and His Council . . .* (1653), E692/6, p. 4.
[150] Peck, *Memoirs of Cromwell*, 122.
[151] *A True State of the Case of The Commonwealth* (1654), E728/5, pp. 3, 28, 32ff., 51 and passim.
[152] *A Declaration concerning the Government of the Three Nations* (1653), E725/2.
[153] Ibid.; E. J. Porter, '"Imperious Dictators and Masters of Words": the Discourse of Legitimacy in Cromwell's England, 1653–1655' (Ph.D. thesis, La Trobe University, 1992), 162–8.
[154] *Declaration concerning the Government*, 6, my italics.   [155] Ibid., 6.

given to governors of Israel, like Joshua and Moses.[156] Some accepted the title was known 'but little' but knew what a Protector should be.[157] Others, however, had no doubt that it was a form of kingship. The royalist *Character of a Protector* mocked the title and office as a debased monarchy:

> What's Protector, tis a stately thing
> That Apes it in the non-age of a King.

A Protector was counterfeit and insubstantial: 'a brasse farthing stamped with a Crowne', the 'fantastick shaddow of the Royal head'.[158] But it was not only royalists who feared Cromwell had appropriated the kingship. Critics were quick to charge that 'the pomp and vanity in court is now up again' and to jeer at the title.[159] Almost all who defended the Protectorate felt the need to reply to accusations that it was but an ersatz monarchy. Cromwell himself in his speeches to parliament, drawing attention to his dislike of the hereditary principle, defended the protectoral constitution as the mean between kingship and democracy, effected by God's providence.[160] Whatever their interests or bias, however, contemporaries were right to suspect that, notwithstanding the constitution, the culture of monarchy was returning and the few tender shoots of a new republican style withering before they were even established.

From its inception the Protectorate involved the restoration of a court and courtly life. The republican *Picture of a New Courtier* sneered at the 'gentlemen ushers and gentlemen waiters, the grooms of the stool, gentlemen sewers besides the fiddlers and others . . . which shine in their gold and silver'.[161] As the author rightly observed, Cromwell occupied old royal palaces and enhanced them with 'new rivers and ponds', enclosed parks for sport outside and employed 'trumpet, harp, lute and organ' for recreation within.[162] Sweetmeats and delicious wines were served and the pomp, it was claimed, outstripped that of the king. Nor was pomp and ceremony confined within the precincts of the Protector's

---

[156] *Reasons Why*, (1653) E697/19, pp. 7, 18; J. Cornubiensis, *The Grand Catastrophe* (1654), E726/12, pp. 7–8; J. Moore, *Protection Proclaimed* (1655), E860/5, To the Reader; S. Richardson, *Plain Dealing* (1656), E865/3, p. 10.
[157] G. Wither, *The Protector: a Poem* (1655), E1565/2, 'to the readers', pp. 17ff.
[158] *The Character of a Protector* (1654), E743/2.
[159] S. Richardson, *An Apology for the Present Government* (1654), E812/18, p. 10; *Declaration of a Freeborn People* (1655), 669 f19/70.
[160] See *A Declaration of His Highness . . . 22 January 1654* (1655), E826/13, and Abbott, *Writings and Speeches of Cromwell*, III, 451–60.
[161] *The Picture of a New Courtier* (1656), E875/6, p. 11. Smith suggests it may be by Streater ('Popular Republicanism', p. 139 n. 4).   [162] *Picture of a New Courtier*, 13.

palaces. Days after his investiture, the City invited Cromwell to a grand feast at Grocers' Hall, to which he set forth in 'great . . . pomp and magnificence'.[163] When, soon after, he called his first parliament, Cromwell rode to Westminster in a full procession, with his gentlemen 'very richly clad', followed by the Captain of the Guard, Commissioners of the Seal and members of the Council, and he entered the abbey with four maces and the sword and purse of state borne before him.[164] To celebrate the peace with the Dutch in April 1654, an elaborate entertainment was prepared by Oliver Fleming, Master of Ceremonies. The Dutch envoys having passed through the city in the Protector's coach, attended by fifty other coaches of the nobility, were greeted by trumpets in Palace Yard. The next day they were brought in similar style to the Banqueting House, 'which was hung with extraordinarily rich hangings', where, after formal audience, an elaborate dinner was served which greatly impressed the visitors.[165]

On such occasions the style adopted to and by Cromwell was regal and it therefore comes as no surprise to hear contemporaries soon using royal language to discuss the Protectorate and the Protector. From the beginning Cromwell was celebrated by panegyrics that revived the traditional genres, language, and metaphors of paeans to kings. The Protector was called 'Sovereign', 'Prince', in Latin 'Maxime Princeps'. He was described as 'Sun', 'husband', 'father of your country', 'nursing father', 'pilot', 'universal medicine', 'the body politic's doctor'.[166] In one panegyric, metaphor extends to fully developed royal simile: 'As the world looks gay with rays everywhere diffused over it by the Sun, so all England was exhilarated by the news of your welfare.'[167] The author of *The Unparalleled Monarch* took such language and praise to its heights, applying all the standard symbols of monarchy to Cromwell: the pilot, the oak, the physician.[168] But this tract praises Cromwell in a language and style that borrows directly from royal panegyric and that makes an important departure from any language employed since 1649. Cromwell is described as a natural ruler who bore regality in his looks, a heroic prince whose very actions seemed the stuff of fable and romance.

[163] S. Carrington, *The History of the Life and Death of . . . Oliver Late Lord Protector* (1659), E1787/1, p. 167; *The Perfect Politician* (1660), E1869/1, pp. 253–4.   [164] *The Perfect Politician*, pp. 265ff.

[165] *The Whole Manner of The Treaty . . . between His Highness the Lord Protector and the Lords Ambassadors of the United Provinces* (1654), E731/14, pp. 5–7; Sherwood, *Court of Oliver Cromwell*, 140–1.

[166] For example, *The Unparalleled Monarch or The Portraiture of a Matchless Prince*, 'epistle to the reader' sig. [A6v], pp. 11, 51; P. Fisher, *Piscatoris Poemata Vel Panegyricum Carmen* (1656), Wing F 1034; J. Field, *Museum Cantabrigiensium Luctus . . .* (1658), p. IV; sig. H1, H4; G. Lawrence, *Peplum Olivarii* (1658), 12, 33.   [167] Panegyric in Peck, *Memoirs of Cromwell*, 109.

[168] *Unparalleled Monarch*, 'to the Reader'.

Beyond, mere mortal celebration, 'Methinks', the author wrote, 'I see a kind of dawning of celestial beauty in his courts as if some rays and little glories of heaven were descending on earth.'[169] Cromwell's glory, he continued, 'cannot be fully illustrated unless I could use the sunbeams for my pencils and blend the virtues and graces with the angelical beauties', for such a man appeared to have 'the general applause and acclamations of angels'.[170] Such extravagant vocabulary extends far beyond the discourse of Providence to present Cromwell as a prince who carried some kind of divinity in his person – as the 'anointed of God', a 'saint'.[171] Against the spirit of regicide and Commonwealth it mystifies (his) power, as an authority possessed of supernatural, even magical, qualities: 'his sovereignty is mysterious'.[172] And significantly *The Unparalleled Monarch* deploys the language of masque: an intensely symbolic, visual language and a form in which the very presence of the prince has transformative and transcendent power.

This tendency to more regal forms is seen clearly in the visual representations of Oliver Cromwell as Protector. At the simplest level this renewed vision is manifest in the larger number of paintings, miniatures and engravings that date from the Protectorate. But it is manifest also in the style of such portraits and the use to which they were put. Interestingly and significantly, in May 1653, shortly after Cromwell had dissolved the Rump and during a period when it might have seemed logical for him to assume power, a portrait of the Lord General was put up at the Royal Exchange, with verses beneath enjoining him 'Ascend these thrones . . .'[173] The visual, in other words, was associated with the regal. And for all the gestures to a different, more Roman image portraying Oliver, toga'd as a Roman military hero, for all the resistance to idealizing implied in Cromwell's famous preference for 'warts and all', the images of the Protector were predominantly royal images. Indeed the Faithorne engraving of 'Olivarius Britannicus Heros' depicted Cromwell mounted as St George in a manner that appropriated for the Protector not only a traditional English royal icon but one that had been reinvested with symbolic power by Charles I himself.[174] In a still more striking and audacious appropriation of the royal, the engraver Peter Lombart reworked the plates of Van Dyck's *Charles I on Horseback with Mr St Antoine* and substituted Cromwell's head for that of the king.[175] Such

---

[169] Ibid., 42.   [170] Ibid., sig. [A10].   [171] Ibid., 61.   [172] Ibid., 66.

[173] Peck, *Historical Pieces*, 56.

[174] Huntington Library, Bull/Granger, vol. 10, no. 12. On the Garter, see K. Sharpe, *The Personal Rule of Charles I* (New Haven and London, 1992), 219–21.

[175] Huntington Library, Bull/Granger, vol. 10, no. 22v.

images not only reflected but endeavoured to effect a change in the government and culture – the birth of a new kingship of, as one engraving by Faithorne was titled, 'Olivarius Primus'.[176] Evidently the change was approved if not directed by Cromwell himself, for in devising his seal as Protector Oliver fundamentally rejected the Commonwealth model and directly copied royal antecedents. On one side the great seal bore Oliver bare-headed and mounted, his right hand on the baton of command; behind lay the Thames and London and around the edge was written once more in Latin 'Olivarius Dei Gra Reip Angliae Scotiae et Hiberniae &c Protector'. On the obverse the shield topped with the imperial crown and quartered for St George's cross, St Andrew's cross and the harp of Erin also carried Cromwell's family arms, the white lion and his motto 'Pax Quaeritur bello' (see Figure 11 on p. 216).[177] Here, in the new great seal, which became the model for others, the joining of Cromwell's with the nation's arms symbolized the return to personal, even dynastic rule. Cromwell indeed changed his crest as Protector from a demi-lion holding a halbert to the demi-lion with a diamond ring in his paw 'to signify his political marriage to the imperial crown of the three kingdoms'.[178] Not for nothing did Thomas Simon, chief engraver at the Mint, submit his account for work on seals executed 'in imitation of Charles Stuart'.[179] Coins similarly abandoned the republican style and adopted the royal. The representation of parliament – the central image of the old commonweal – disappeared to be replaced by an imperial bust of Cromwell, the fifty-shilling piece bearing a large imperial crown 'nearly exactly resembling the one used by Charles I'.[180] Cromwell's medals and coins, like his sign manual with its large signature and flourish, appeared to herald the return of monarchy.

Not surprisingly contemporaries began to regard Cromwell as a king – and by descent as well as desert. In 1656 the writer of *The Unparalleled Monarch* argued that Cromwell was 'the offspring of some worthy ancient descended of great and mighty kings'.[181] 'He is a king,' he added, 'and will not put on a crown.'[182] Since 1653, however, Cromwell had symbolically put on a crown. And from 1653 the discourse was no more of the nature of a republic. More than historians have recognized, the political debate and political culture were dominated by the question of kingship.

---

[176] Ibid., vol. 10, no. 17.

[177] Ibid., vol. 10, no. 35; Henfrey, *Numismata Cromwelliana*, plate 8. See also K. Pearson and G. M. Morant, *The Portraiture of Oliver Cromwell* (Cambridge, 1935).

[178] Peck, *Memoirs of Cromwell*, 130.   [179] Henfrey, *Numismata Cromwelliana*, 219.

[180] Ibid., 103.   [181] *Unparalleled Monarch*, 8.   [182] Ibid., 13.

Historians such as Charles Firth and Roy Sherwood have seen the issue of kingship as one that came to the fore after 1656.[183] Yet we know that Cromwell and Bulstrode Whitelocke debated the importance of the title as early as 1652, and recent scholarship has shown that the question remained vital thereafter and throughout the life of the Protectorate.[184] Those who in 1653 erected the picture of Cromwell at the Royal Exchange, urging him to be king, were not alone.[185] The same year the author of *The Only Right Rule for Regulating the Laws and Liberties of the People of England* felt it necessary to counter the prevailing view that the only way to re-establish the law and government was to restore monarchy.[186] In *A True State of the Case of the Commonwealth*, Nedham, while he concentrated on defending the new regime against the charge that it reintroduced monarchy, appeared also to want to keep his options open, simultaneously reminding readers that they had fought Charles I not because he was king but because he was a tyrant. Rather than a desire for monarchy it was 'hankering after that family' he was most eager to dispel.[187] Did his ambivalence express an uncertainty in official circles, even a wavering in Cromwell's own mind as early as 1654? While the evidence does not permit a clear answer to that question, it does yield many other examples of uncertainties, anxieties and hedged bets. The pseudonymous Cornubiensis, for example, in *The Grand Catastrophe* set out to persuade readers that 'it is a gross mistake' to regard the Protectorate as 'monarchical or kingly government'.[188] It was not a single person but the distribution of power, he contended, that made a monarchy, and there was no reason to suspect the Protector of a desire for more power. Yet between the lines, as well as in its very title, *The Grand Catastrophe, or The Change of Government* revealed its anxieties that kingship was returning. Some, the author had heard, had drawn up a pedigree to prove Cromwell's descent from Cadwallader as part of a design to make him king. 'There are those', he told Oliver, 'who suspect you'll king it' – and he may well have deep down been among them as he prayed: 'Let him be the shame of men . . . if he make his Protectorship a step to kingship.'[189] Similarly George Wither, though he called on all to obey the new government, could not disguise his doubts about the title and its

---

[183] C. Firth, 'Cromwell and the Crown', *Eng. Hist. Rev.* 17 (1902), 429–42; 18 (1903), 52–80; Sherwood, *Court of Oliver Cromwell*, appendix A.

[184] Abbott, *Writings and Speeches of Cromwell*, II, 589; Porter, '"Imperious Dictators"', ch. 7.

[185] Above, p. 253.

[186] *The Only Right Rule for Regulating the Laws and Liberties of the People of England*, E684/33, p. 3.

[187] M. Nedham, *A True State of the Case of the Commonwealth* (1654), E728/5, pp. 3–4, 47.

[188] Cornubiensis, *Grand Catastrophe*, 11. [189] Ibid., 12–13, 15.

holder, nor his fears that all might return again to the monarchy against which he had 'put on arms'.[190] During 1654 and 1655, as the failure of parliaments signalled the broader failure to settle, royalists and others called for a return to monarchy and urged Cromwell to be the instrument for the restoration of the Stuarts.[191] During the winter of 1654 there was even a rumour circulating that Cromwell's daughter Frances might marry Charles II and so unite their families in royal rule.[192] Time – and the developing regal style of the Protector's court – strengthened the calls from several quarters for Cromwell to accept the crown. *A Copy of a Letter Written to an Officer of the Army*, purportedly by 'a true commonwealthman and no courtier' who supported the Protectorate, was frank in its admission that most desired the old government back and were happier with hereditary rule.[193] John Hall in *The True Cavalier* had no doubt that 'the present government . . . is monarchy' and assured Cromwell that old royalists would find no difficulty in obeying him as a king.[194] The author of *The Unparalleled Monarch*, as the title indicated, thought Cromwell a 'matchless prince' already, lacking only the 'crowning' that the envy of a few had denied him.[195]

Only in the context of these debates and positions can we fully understand parliament's offer of the crown to Cromwell in 1657. Whether Oliver himself desired it has been the subject of a contentious historical debate in his own day and ever since, one that goes to the core of Cromwell's complex personality and one we cannot hope to resolve here. But the remark in one later vindication of the Protector that Cromwell 'well [knew] that the power of a king was universally understood and reverenced by the people of this nation' is helpfully suggestive.[196] Oliver had once said that he would not contest over forms of government.[197] But as his own changing rhetoric and representation hints, he may have come to see that the forms were an essential adjunct of any authority, that to continue to enact his ideals and programmes he needed to adopt and adapt the familiar forms of the old (royal) government. So, leaving aside his personal ambition, Cromwell may easily have been led to the view that only a royal style enabled the settlement he so desperately sought. And though he rejected the crown, he did all to mit-

---

[190] Wither, *The Protector*, 'to the readers', and pp. 4, 17, 28, 31 and passim.
[191] *For the Lord Protector* (1655), 669 f19/66.   [192] Porter, '"Imperious Dictators"', 285.
[193] *A Copy of a Letter* (1656), E870/5, pp. 14, 20, 36–7.
[194] J. Hall, *The True Cavalier* (1656), E885/10, preface, pp. 101–2.
[195] *Unparalleled Monarch*, 50.   [196] *A Modest Vindication of Oliver Cromwell* (1698), 60.
[197] Abbott, *Writings and Speeches of Cromwell*, I, 527–8.

igate his refusal and further symbolically to portray himself as the monarch in all but name. This was dramatically apparent in the ceremony that marked Cromwell's second investiture as Lord Protector, with the power (one he had earlier denounced) now descending in his family. Into Westminster Abbey, with MPs and aldermen seated around 'like a theatrum', marched the great officers of the household and heralds before His Highness, 'richly dressed, habited with a costly mantle of estate, lined with ermines and girt with a sword of great value'. With 'loud acclamation' the Protector was 'enthroned' and, with his son and successor standing behind, was presented with the Bible, sword and sceptre, the symbolism of each explained as they were bestowed on him. The Speaker then administered the oath, after which the trumpets sounded and the shout of the spectators proclaimed him: 'Long live his Highness.'[198] As Roy Sherwood long ago argued, 'The only significant ingredients of a true coronation that were missing at the reinvestiture . . . were the anointing and the crowning';[199] in all other respects Cromwell was invested as a king and the objections against the office were subtly circumvented. The language of contemporaries reveals that many saw the occasion as in essence a coronation.[200] Fittingly then an anagram of 1658, greeting him as a new monarch and St George, turned Cromwell's name into 'Rule welcome Roy.'[201]

Most of all, the signs that the Protector had become a king were manifested at every point in the state funeral that followed Cromwell's death in September 1658. *The Commonwealth Mercury* for 18 November describes how the actual body of his late Highness was privately removed from Whitehall to Somerset House, but there an effigy was displayed to public view. After passing through the Presence Chamber, the Privy Chamber and the Withdrawing Chamber, all hung with black and with a chair and cloth of estate symbolizing the king's presence even in death, the mourners came to the room where lay the effigy 'apparelled in a rich suit of uncut velvet, being robed first in a kirtle robe of purple velvet, laced with a rich gold lace and furred with ermine'.[202] On 23 November the effigy, looking for all like the icon of a medieval king, was placed on a hearse and 'vested with royal robes, a sceptre in one hand, a globe in

---

[198] *Mercurius Politicus*, 25 June–2 July 1657; J. Prestwich, *Prestwich's Respublica; or a Display of the Honors, Ceremonies and Ensigns of the Commonwealth* (1787), 3–20.

[199] Sherwood, *Court of Oliver Cromwell*, 163; see also 160–5.

[200] See too *The Life and Death of Oliver Cromwell* (1659), E1787/1, pp. 202–3.

[201] *The Tenth Worthy or Several Anagrams . . . upon the Name . . . Oliver* (1658), 669 f21/9.

[202] *The Commonwealth Mercury*, 18–25 November 1658, p. 2; cf. *The True Manner of the Conveyance of His Highness's Effigies* (1658), E1866/2.

the other and *a crown on the head*'.[203] Covered with a canopy of state 'very rich', the carriage, adorned with plumes and escutcheons, conveyed the effigy 'all along the way from the Strand to Westminster', attended by the household, the Council, public officers and private servants, the mayor and aldermen, judges, ambassadors, 'a great part of those of the nobler sort' and heralds. As thousands watched, the procession made its slow way to Westminster Abbey, where the effigy was placed with elaborate ceremony 'in a most magnificent structure built to the same form as one before had been . . . for King James, but much more stately'.[204] There in the abbey too Cromwell's body was laid in the chapel of Henry VII, the resting place of kings. This was the most magnificent state funeral of the century, with thousands spent on building, painting, gilding and the hundreds of escutcheons, shields, banners, badges and crests that decorated lying-in rooms, coaches and streets.[205] Careful attention to detail, to the politics of places, the conjunction of escutcheons, the situation of objects (most of all the crown) and the pose and appearance of the effigy lying and standing in state, ensured that, however he had lived, Cromwell died a king. As one astute observer put it, 'The senate hath deservedly adorned him dead with a crown and other regal ensigns which living he refused.'[206] After 1657 few panegyrists denied him the title that the funeral rituals had at last bestowed on him. In his *Plea for the Lords*, newly revised in 1658, William Prynne did not hesitate to write of the 'new king' established recently.[207] A poem of 1658 foresaw deified amid a heavenly throng 'so rare a monarch'; the next year a panegyrist after hymning his virtues wrote simply: 'Such was our prince.'[208]

Understandably, amid the pomp and the panegyrics, from 1657 some began to hope and others to fear that the Humble Petition and Advice had increased the possibility that the Stuarts might be restored. It was said that Charles II himself believed that Cromwell had laid the foundations for restored monarchy – by which, of course, he meant Stuart monarchy.[209] As a 1659 pamphlet reminded readers, Oliver Cromwell

[203] *Commonwealth Mercury*, 18–25 November 1658, p. 5, my italics. See Pearson and Morant, *Portraiture of Cromwell*, plate 8, for the effigy 'standing in state'.
[204] *Commonwealth Mercury*, 18–25 November 1658, 5–6; Carrington, *The Life and Death of Cromwell*, 233–40; *The Perfect Politician*, 346.
[205] See *Prestwich's Respublica*, 182–203, for the banners, escutcheons and shields.
[206] Lawrence, *Peplum Olivarii*, 31.
[207] W. Prynne, *A Plea for the Lords* (1658), E944/1, 'to the ingenuous reader'.
[208] Field, *Museum Cantab. Luctus*, sig. G4v; E. Waller, *Three Poems upon the Death of His Late Highness* (1659), Wing W526, p. 8.
[209] *Eikon Basilike, or The True Portraiture of His Sacred Majesty Charles II* (1660), E1922/2, book III, p. 4.

himself had once argued against the hereditary principle and government by one, and the author added that 'if first they bring in a single person and grant that, the next dispute will be whether the one family or the other has most right'.[210] Despite the uncertainties, however, Richard Cromwell succeeded his father without trouble. On 3 September 1658, not only the day of Dunbar and Worcester but the same day as the accession of Richard I, Richard Cromwell was installed in a ceremony in London.[211] Much augured well for the perpetuation of the hereditary Protectorship, which some still praised as the best 'midway between a monarchical and democratical', which others would readily see become a crown.[212] In the country the peaceful succession appears to have been a cause of joy. Richard was proclaimed with trumpets, feasts, running claret, bonfires and bells, salutes and cheers throughout the provincial towns of England. From many came addresses of condolence and congratulation that they had a 'rightful successor', new 'prince and ruler' to whom they happily rendered homage and obedience.[213] In the autumn of 1658 it might have seemed that Cromwell had at last succeeded in erasing monarchy from the canvas of politics and establishing protectoral government. But the regime was unstable and indeed destabilized, albeit from two quite contrary positions, by the question of monarchy. Because he was not quite a king, Richard could not rely on those who wished for a monarchy. Because he was too much one, he soon attracted the suspicion and opposition of sections of the army for whom his succession seemed to signal another step towards monarchy. 'Have you not given way to the monarchical foundation of government', the apologists for Richard were asked, with vehement disapproval.[214] And the revival of hagiographical lives of Charles I and panegyrical characters of Charles II in 1659 appeared to answer the question in the affirmative.[215] But the demise of Richard Cromwell did not, as we know, lead smoothly to the Restoration of Charles Stuart. That it did not owed much to the powerful articulation of arguments and voices that for long had been silent or but faintly

[210] *A Brief Relation Containing on Abbreviation of the Arguments Urged by the Late Protector against the Government . . . by a King* (1659), E965/4, p. 7.

[211] Carrington, *The Life and Death of Cromwell*, 232.

[212] Ibid., 164–5; *A Character of . . . King Charles II* (1659), E1836/3.

[213] *A True Catalogue, or An Account of the Several Places and Most Eminent Persons . . . Where and by Whom Richard Cromwell was Proclaimed Lord Protector* (1660), E999/812.   [214] *A True Catalogue*, 66.

[215] Examples of lives of Charles I and Charles II: *The Faithful Yet Imperfect Character of a Glorious King* (1659), E1799/1; *A Dialogue between the Ghosts of Charles I . . . and Oliver* (1659), E985/24; *Bibliotheca Regia* (1659), E1718/1; *A Character of His Most Sacred Majesty King Charles II* (1659) E1836/2; L. Wood, *The Life and Reign of King Charles* (1659), E1760/2.

heard: the voices of the commonwealthmen and republicans, of the champions of the Good Old Cause.

THE GOOD OLD CAUSE AND THE SURVIVAL OF REPUBLICAN DISCOURSE

The Good Old Cause has, as its name implies, a long history. Even if we do not accept a story that goes back to Saxon times, the cause was one for which many had fought in 1649. But what I wish to argue is that it was the *reaction* to the monarchism of the Protectorate that cohered and strengthened a party and position that had failed to establish itself in the early years after regicide. From his appearance as a military leader and commanding personality, Cromwell attracted the charge that he was an ambitious schemer who grasped at the crown. Royalist propaganda depicted all the regicides, and Cromwell in particular, as greedy for power.[216] But unease about Cromwell's designs was not confined to royalists. A new regime that was endeavouring to revise the government of a single person was concerned (as, ironically, was Cromwell himself) to play down the cult of personality. Cromwell felt the need to defend himself against accusations that he pursued his own ambition rather than the Good Old Cause. Yet from the time of his brutal suppression of the Levellers, there were those in the army and the nation who feared Cromwell would betray their trust; and the dissolution of the Rump in 1653 dramatically confirmed those fears. His taking the title Protector in a government in which much executive power returned to a single person threatened to surrender all the victories for which so much blood had been spilled. As an apologist for the Protectorate admitted in 1653, Cromwell drew from some quarters 'a dislike of this great and unparalleled change'.[217] With the investiture of 'His Highness' the Lord Protector, the author of *An Honest Discourse* lamented the betrayal of all their protestations and declarations against the king: 'Now proud monarchy seems to step up again as high if not higher than before.'[218] Moreover the talk was of 'the Protector's secret aim and drift to make himself and family great'.[219]

After the dismissal of the first Protectorate parliament, such attacks on Cromwell intensified. The developing court and regal style of the

---

[216] See, for example, *Monarchia Transformata in Respublicam Deformatam* (1649), 669 f14/75; cf. W. Prynne, *The Machiavellian Cromwellist* (1648), Wing P4007A; and see *Hypocrisie Discovered* (1655), Wing 3887.   [217] *Declaration Concerning the Government*, 6.
[218] *An Honest Discourse* (1655), E840/10, p. 3.   [219] Ibid., 13.

Protectorate gave further ammunition to its opponents' fire. *The Picture of a New Courtier* deployed the old 'country' dialogue between 'Mr Time Server' and 'Mr Plain Heart' to deride the pride, pomp and extravagance of a Protector who violated the laws and cozened the people.[220] In 1656 *An Appeal from the Court to the Country*, by an MP excluded from the Commons, called for forceful resistance, claiming it would have been 'much better . . . for us patiently to have borne the yoke of kingly government' than Cromwell's.[221] By 1656, of course, the revival of kingly government was very much in the air. And as it looked as though King Oliver I might soon be enthroned, the champions of the old commonwealth waged a powerful – and successful – campaign against it.[222] Effectively returning to the evidence of scripture, *English Liberty and Property Asserted* demonstrated 'that God did never institute or approve the office of a king' and that 'this new modelled kingship' was directly opposed to the will of Christ.[223] A direct petition *To the Parliament of the Commonwealth of England* asked, 'What is in your minds that ye are now about to set up a king over us again?' and it warned against re-entangling the nation in a tyrannical bondage.[224] *A Narrative of the Late Parliament* railed against the ambitions of an upstart Protector and his courtiers and condemned 'the hot attempts to build again the cursed ruins of kingship'.[225] Cromwell's death checked what some still feared, even after his refusal of the crown: an inexorable drift towards monarchy. George Wither believed that the Lord 'took hence our Protector' because Cromwell had planned to take the crown the day he died. And in *Salt upon Salt* he penned an attack on a Cromwell who had re-erected the idols of monarchy he had pulled down and on 'the costly puppet play' of a funeral at which his 'Image' had literally been 'crowned in his place'.[226]

Rather than the events of 1649, it was the Protectorate, still more the threat of the kingship, that galvanized the republican cause and case. James Harrington's *Oceana*, published in the autumn of 1656, and Henry Vane's *Healing Question* of the same year are only the most famous

---

[220] *The Picture of a New Courtier* (1656), E875/6. The author condemns the Protector's pomp and pride as worse than kings'.   [221] *An Appeal from the Court to the Country*, E891/3, p. 6.

[222] The campaign against the revival of royal government, however, was not a united campaign. See J. H. Hughes, 'The Commonwealthmen Divided: Edmund Ludlow, Sir Henry Vane, and the Good Old Cause, 1653–1659', *The Seventeenth Century*, 5 (1990), 55–70.

[223] *English Liberty and Property Asserted* (1653), E905/2, pp. 6–7.

[224] *To the Parliament . . .* (1657), E905/3, p. 1.

[225] *A Narrative of the Late Parliament* (1658), E935/5, p. 28.

[226] G. Wither, *Salt upon Salt* (1658), E1827/2, pp. 18, 31, 33–5 and passim.

manifestos of a republicanism now more forcefully argued and articulated.[227] From then until the very eve of restoration – and beyond –
pamphleteers not only mustered a powerful argument against kingship
but the case for a perpetual Commonwealth. Yet the author who argued
that all who desired a monarchy should be sent to Bedlam also epitomizes the tone of desperation that sounds in many republican treatises
of the late 1650s – desperation born of a fear that, far from being erased
from popular memory, consciousness and culture, monarchy would be
the choice of the people of England.[228] It is a desperation everywhere
audible in that last great call to erect a republic. Milton's *Readie and Easie
Way to Establish a Free Commonweal* was published in February 1660 and
revised by the first week of April during elections to parliament.[229]
Following Harrington and Vane, Milton laid out a constitution for
government by an elite, an aristocracy of virtue and a Sanhedrin of the
godly. As for the multitude who, he knew, were now 'so mad upon' a king,
he despised an abject people's 'perpetual bowings and cringings' to a
monarchy, their 'deifying and adoring him' as a 'demigod'.[230] Ten years
earlier, in *Eikonoklastes*, he had similarly derided the 'image doting rabble'
as he had struggled against the power of the royal image.[231] The repetition of bitter invective evidences not only Milton's frustration on the eve
of the Restoration but perhaps also his own awareness that the failure of
republican politics lay, as much as anything, in the failure of the republican culture.

CONCLUSION

The events of January 1649 removed the head from a king and monarchy from the constitution. But the languages, still more the symbols and
images of kingship remained and were not replaced by republican discourse and representations that imprinted themselves on the imagination or the culture of Englishmen. Indeed from the early 1650s a cult of
personality began to develop around Cromwell and contemporaries
began to apply to him the language familiarly used of a royal head of
state. From 1653, when his emergent authority was officially recognized
in the title 'His Highness the Lord Protector', Cromwell increasingly
adopted the rhetoric and style of a king. And in turn that style prompted

[227] See Pocock, *The Machiavellian Moment*, 384; Hughes, 'Commonwealthmen Divided'.
[228] *A Secret Word to the Wise* (1659), E986/8.
[229] See H. Erskine Hill and G. Storey, *Revolutionary Prose of the English Civil War* (Cambridge, 1983),
      203–29.   [230] Ibid., 211, 220.   [231] Above, pp. 230–1.

the offer of the crown – a gesture that reflected a cultural change more
than created it. Language and image were central to the exercise of
power and the short-lived Commonwealth never succeeded in rewriting
and redrawing them as republican vocabularies and signs. The
Cromwell who sent his portrait to Queen Christina of Sweden acted not
just out of ambition but from a pragmatic grasp of the power of such
signs and the semiotics of power.[232]

On the eve of the offer of the kingship to Oliver, one apologist for a
republic put forward an acute analysis of what had gone wrong.
Despondent again at the 'high and ranting discourse of personal prerogative and unbounded monarchy', the author of *The Excellency of a Free
State* set out to answer why the people had not learned what true freedom
was.[233] He recalled, in a passage of wonderful insight, that Gracchus had
advised the Romans about 'the negligence of their ancestors who when
they drove out kings forgot to drive out the mysteries and inconveniences
of kingly power'.[234] And, he continued, 'Not only the name of King but
the thing King (whether in the hands of one or many) was plucked up
root and branch, before ever the Romans could attain to a full establishment in their rights and freedoms.'[235] Those who ousted Tarquin took
care therefore 'to imprint such principles in men's minds as might
actuate them with an irreconcilable enmity to the former power, in so
much that the very name of king became odious to the Roman
people'.[236] They brought up their youth to dislike royal government and
Brutus 'brake all the images and statues of the Tarquins and he levelled
their houses with the ground that they might not remain as temptations
to any ambitious spirits'.[237] Cromwell instead lived in those houses
(Whitehall and Hampton Court) and was surrounded by those royal
images – the paintings, tapestries and silver of kings.[238] Because the
'thing king' was never 'plucked up root and branch' from the culture of
England, the principles of a free commonwealth were never fully established.

If the Commonwealth failed, however, and the discourse of a republic was never dominant, that is not to argue that they were of no importance. That England had been stably governed at home and won

---

[232] Pearson and Morant, *Portraiture of Cromwell*, plate 40.
[233] *The Excellency of a Free State, or The Right Constitution of a Commonwealth* (1656), E1676/1, 'to the
reader'.   [234] Ibid., 6.   [235] Ibid., 10.   [236] Ibid., 14.
[237] Ibid., 163. The criticism of Oliver Cromwell who had recently moved into royal palaces is
obvious.
[238] See MacGregor, *The Late Kings Goods*, ch. 1; see the list of goods reserved for Cromwell's use in
Millar, *Inventories and Valuations of the King's Goods*, via index.

spectacular victories abroad without a king was an ineradicable fact of history. And for all the failure of a republican image, a republican language had been created for and spoken in an indigenous English context. As a sermon delivered at Lyme Regis in 1660 was to put it, for some years the name of a commonwealth had been 'beaten into us'.[239] It would no longer be sufficient for a new king to stand as 'silent rhetoric' for kingship: the case would have to be argued.[240] And behind all the scenes of pageant and celebration, between the lines of panegyric lauding the monarchy as historic, natural, divine, the king as Sun, head and father, one discerns an anxiety: that more than ever the case for monarchy needs to be repeated because it cannot be assumed.[241] If the Protector had felt the need to appropriate royal rhetoric and metaphor, the royalists in 1660 thought it prudent to boast that it was 'kingly government' that 'incorporated the perfections of a free Commonwealth'.[242] And if the royal regalia, melted in the civil war, had to be remade, that was true, to a degree, of the monarchy itself.

The memories of civil war and regicide were not erased at the Restoration. None would ever forget that the title itself could not save the king's head.[243] The trials and speeches of the regicides – of Harrison, Peters and Scott, of Jones and Carew – were forceful reassertions of the principles of the Good Old Cause of which, they claimed, 'their blood will make many more hundreds persuaded'.[244] Though their enemies tried 'to suppress and destroy those that did not think the king's person sacred', the republican cause, Carew prophesied, would live on.[245] The inscription 'Exit Tyrannus' that had been placed where Charles I's picture stood had now been erased, 'yet', Charles II was warned, 'it was written with the pen of a diamond on the hearts of many thousands'.[246] A republican cause and a Commonwealth party were born from 1649 and, though they failed to establish a dominant culture and government,

---

[239] A. Short, *God Save the King, or A Sermon Preached at Lyme Regis May 18, 1660* (1660), E1919/2, 'to the unprejudiced reader'.   [240] On the politics of silence, see above, ch. 3, pp. 142–4.

[241] I intend to explore this subject. For some evidence of such anxieties in the drama, see N. Maguire, *Regicide and Restoration: English Tragicomedy, 1660–1671* (Cambridge, 1992).

[242] *No King but the Old King's Son* (1660), 669 f24/30.

[243] See *A Sudden Flash* (1657), E1584/3, p. 18.

[244] *The Speeches and Prayers of Maj. Gen. Harrison . . . Mr John Carew . . . Mr Justice Cooke, etc.* (1660), E1053/1, p. 13. The accounts of the executions and speeches skilfully blend the old Foxeian martyrology as deployed by Prynne, Burton and Bastwick with motifs appropriated from Charles I's own trial.   [245] Ibid., 13.

[246] F. Phillips, *Veritas Inconcussa* (1661), E1925/2, 'to Charles II'. The quotation continues: 'There are too many amongst those many that made acclamations and seemed to rejoice in your Majesty's return . . . who have not changed their spots.'

they remained to destabilize the English royal regimes of 1660 to 1688 and, both chronologically and geographically, some beyond.

More than forging a minority party, those who did not think the king's person sacred won a bigger victory still. For all the prevailing 'mysteries' of kingship that dogged the republican cause, something had impercept-ibly but fundamentally changed in the 1650s. As a consequence, gradu-ally but undoubtedly, authority – not just monarchy – became demystified, and all governments had to argue their case. The process of demystification and (provided we are wary of anachronism) rationaliza-tion is part of a bigger story and a broader change in the political culture of late Stuart England. That story – of the decline of chivalry and emblems, the demise of masque and metaphysical poetry, the changes in portraiture and prose – has yet to be told and cannot be told here. But it begins in the 1650s and continues even through the euphoria of the Restoration. Charles II touched for the king's evil, and his coronation pageant was rich in the symbols and mysteries of monarchy.[247] Yet his personal style was – consciously? – down to earth, physical and coarse. By the end of his reign he was described – even by allies – as debauched and poxed. If the king's body was slowly demystified, so too his power was plunged into the maelstrom of debate and contest, the subject of pamphlet polemic and party politics. Perhaps because he adapted so well to a new world, even shaped his rhetoric and representation to it, Charles II died peacefully in his bed and left a strong monarchy at his death. But it was never quite the old monarchy. If the English revolution never fully forged a republican culture and government, the republic nevertheless effected a radical transformation of royal culture and power.

---

[247] See J. Ogilby, *The Entertainment of His Most Excellent Majestie Charles II* (1662), ed. R. Knowles (Binghamton, N.Y., 1988). I shall be discussing Restoration festival in the study *Images of Power in England, 1500–1700*.

PART FOUR

Re-writings

CHAPTER EIGHT

Re-writing the history of parliament in seventeenth-century England

When we look at an object what we see is conditioned by a number of factors: the distance at which we stand (or crouch), the angle from which we view, the nature of our eyesight in the biological sense; what we might call our 'cultural vision' (what we have been trained to see). And we might add to such a list a wide variety of possible technical aids, from the simple telescope, to 3D, X-ray, and the infra-red lens. In the cultural and technological senses, what we see is a product of history and change, and in turn what we see reshapes history. To take a seventeenth-century case, the first audiences at Inigo Jones's new perspective stage in Jacobean Whitehall, untrained in its mathematical principles, were confused about what was going on. Before long, however, the perspective stage was the normal arena of theatrical production. Moreover, by placing the king and courtly spectators according to the lines of perspective, the new way of seeing reinforced the position of the monarch and the lines of authority among the audience as well as actors, so connecting a privileged vision to a vision of privilege and status.[1] Similarly, the invention of X-ray, infra-red and ultra violet have affected our sense of reality as well as vision, providing the possibility and stimulating the language of looking *through* as well as *at*. Computer graphics take us still further into the possibilities of constructions and simulations in three dimensions of what is 'observed' only on two planes, apparently enabling the observer to view an object from a number of positions simultaneously.

All of this is obvious enough to a contemporary photographer or a historian of the image. But it has been curiously lacking in much recent work of the historians of seventeenth-century parliaments who nevertheless have written, revealingly, of placing parliaments in 'perspective'

[1] S. Orgel, 'The Royal Theatre and the Role of the King', in G. F. Lytle and S. Orgel eds., *Patronage in the Renaissance* (Princeton, 1981), 261–73.

rather than in *a* perspective.[2] The significant omission of the indefinite article, I would like to suggest, has led to the generation of more heat than light and ultimately left the subject still in the dark.[3]

In the last twenty years, the most heated debates among English historians of any period have been about seventeenth-century parliaments: their 'nature', their power and importance, their role in the origins of the English civil war, their place in the larger story of English history and, beyond, their contribution to the history of freedom in the West. In part, those discussions have been prompted, as new historical interpretations and debates often are, by the discovery or availability of new evidence: the papers of individual MPs and elections in local archives, the use of manuscript versions of the Commons and Lords Journals rather than the hotch-potch compilations of eighteenth-century editors; most of all the listing and printing of numerous private diaries for almost all the early Stuart sessions, published by the Yale Center for Parliamentary History. Rather than settling disagreements, as some might expect, the profusion of new evidence has sharpened scholarly disputes. This is not only because all the evidence can be viewed from a number of angles, but also because the search for evidence, certainly the type of evidence given greatest weight, has also been determined by historians' angle of vision.[4] Enamoured of the 'big story' of English liberties, J. H. Hexter and T. K. Rabb have little patience with the sources dominated by daily minutiae or localist preoccupations; viewing parliament as an organ of business rather than debate, Sir Geoffrey Elton is more concerned with the clerks' notes than the diarists' self-promoting rhetoric; suspicious of printed matter on principle and of *post hoc* perspectives in general, Conrad Russell spurns the contemporary broadsheets and the later narratives which polemically constructed and distributed the perceptions, fears and hopes of a number of early Stuart actors and their heirs.[5]

---

[2] See the seminal article by C. Russell, 'Parliamentary History in Perspective, 1604–29', *History*, 61 (1976), 1–27; also K. Sharpe, 'Parliamentary History, 1603–29: In or Out of Perspective?', in K. Sharpe ed., *Faction and Parliament: Essays on Early Stuart History* (Oxford, 1978; repr. London, 1985), 1–42. But compare J. S. Roskell, 'Perspectives in English Parliamentary History', in E. B. Fryde and E. Miller eds., *Historical Studies of the English Parliament* (2 vols., Cambridge, 1970), II, 296–323.

[3] On the revealing nature of this slip, compare Russell's observation that the title of his book is often misquoted: C. Russell, 'The Nature of a Parliament in Early Stuart England', in H. Tomlinson ed., *Before the English Civil War* (1983), 125.

[4] R. Cust and A. Hughes eds., *Conflict in Early Stuart England* (1989), 12–13; K. Sharpe and P. Lake eds., *Culture and Politics in Early Stuart England* (Houndmills and Stanford, 1994), 1–20, esp. 4–5. The footnotes in Cust and Hughes, *Conflict*, offer a bibliographical entry to the debate over seventeenth-century parliaments.

[5] J. H. Hexter, 'Power Struggle, Parliament and Liberty in Early Stuart England', *Journ. Mod. Hist.*, 50 (1978), 1–50; T. K. Rabb, 'The Role of the Commons', *Past and Present*, 92 (1981), 55–78; G. R. Elton, *The Parliament of England, 1559–1581* (Cambridge, 1986).

Observing (as any historian must) from a particular standpoint and preferring some types of evidence over others, each scholar has studied seventeenth-century parliaments from and in *a* perspective. It may be time
to see whether, rather than simply selecting one photograph and
renouncing the rest, we cannot examine the shots taken by different
lenses from different angles: to see whether some composite picture
might be constructed which draws upon them all. Though any such
arrangement, collage or computer model must itself be a personal
design, it at least compels an incorporation of 'perspectives' and dispels
the illusion of any authoritative *one* perspective.

Let us start with the photograph taken with the wide-angle lens, more
usually referred to as the Whig interpretation of the seventeenth century.
This is a picture of the past taken with the viewfinder framing the seventeenth-century and Victorian House of Commons. Its most famous
photographer was Thomas Babington Macaulay, an historian, MP and
Secretary for War in Lord Melbourne's government.[6] It offers a panorama of English history intended to explain the origins of the Victorian
constitution to which, in the words of Samuel Rawson Gardiner, 'every
step was constantly tending'.[7] The author of the massive and learned
ten-volume history of England from the accession of James I to the outbreak of the civil war, Gardiner's name should be a sufficient reminder
that, pace some revisionists, the Whig view of the past need not eschew
detail. Indeed, within the parameters of this subject, Gardiner worked
chronologically, so that his account was written as he proceeded from
strictly contemporary rather than later documentation – rather as revisionists have attempted to do. But for all his fine, often unsurpassed,
miniatures, Gardiner's vision of history, like Macaulay's, was focused on
a large picture that was determined by the stance of his own age and
intended to explain to him its constitutional triumphs.[8] The wide-angle
lens was deployed not only by the Whigs. From the nineteenth century,
Marxist historians offered an alternative panorama of the past, with the
viewfinder not primarily focused on the constitution, but ranging over
the landscape from feudal institutions to the triumph of the proletariat.
In the case of English history, where too many objects failed to fit, the

---

[6] T. B. Macaulay, *The History of England* (Harmondsworth, 1979), introduction by H. R. Trevor-
Roper.
[7] J. P. Kenyon, *The History Men: the Historical Profession in England since the Renaissance* (1983), 214–22;
quotation at 220.
[8] On Gardiner, see Kenyon, *The History Men*; R. Usher, *A Critical Study of the Historical Method of
Samuel Rawson Gardiner* (St Louis, 1915); R. C. Richardson, *The Debates on the English Revolution
Revisited* (1988), 82–6; J. S. Adamson, 'Eminent Victorians: S. R. Gardiner and the Liberal as
Hero', *Hist. Journ.*, 33 (1990), 641–57; S. R. Gardiner, *History of England from the Accession of James
I to the Outbreak of the Civil War* (10 vols., 1883–4).

photograph required some elaborate touch ups in the studio, which successions of Marxists have continued to refine.[9] While the Victorian constitution is undoubtedly identifiable, whatever significance we may give
to it, the triumph of the proletariat has had to be 'painted in' on the negative of English history and the studio has never succeeded in masking
the artifice of its production or selling it as a natural image of the past.
Finally, more familiar with the wide open spaces, several American historians have fitted a wider angle lens still. To Professor Wallace
Notestein, the big picture of English history opened onto a larger picture
still. If the English past showed how human beings had learned to
govern themselves, the panorama of history embraced the spread of
that lesson to America whose historical Manifest Destiny it had been and
was to preserve and disseminate that lesson in self-government.[10] It has
taken only refinements of Notestein's technology to enable Professor J.
H. Hexter to get into his frame this history of freedom and its establishment and advancement throughout the Anglophone world.[11]

In some of these photographs, as critics have complained, the wide
angle has reduced the seventeenth-century House of Commons to an
indistinct blur. But in each case, though indistinct in detail, early Stuart
parliaments are central to the large composition, and derive importance
from it. To the Whigs, the Stuart Commons was the arena in which
English subjects fought to preserve their liberties and properties against
absolutist monarchs, and the civil war and 1688 Revolution the occasions of their decisive victories in that struggle. For the Marxist historian
of England, the English revolution represents the overthrow of a feudal
monarchy and aristocracy by a rising bourgeois class of trade and
capital, and the emergence of radical Levellers and Diggers, the brief
dawn of a truly proletarian revolution that was (inconveniently for the
Marxist model) aborted. The early seventeenth century, too, witnessed
for Notestein, Hexter and others the emigration from old to new
England which exported the institutions and values of parliamentary

[9] R. Samuel, 'British Marxist Historians, 1880–1980', *New Left Rev.*, 120 (1980), 21–95; C. Hill, *The English Revolution, 1640* (1940; 2nd edn, 1949); B. Manning, *The English People and the English Revolution* (1976).

[10] W. Notestein, 'The Stuart Period: Unsolved Problems', *Annual Report of the American Historical Association . . . for the year 1916* (Washington, 1919), 389–99; Notestein, *The Winning of the Initiative by the House of Commons* (1924).

[11] J. H. Hexter, 'Introduction', in *Parliament and Liberty from the Reign of Elizabeth to the English Civil War* (Stanford, 1992), 1–20. This is one volume of a projected series on *The Making of Modern Freedom*, centred on English history and directed by Hexter. See now too R. W. Davis, *The Origins of Modern Freedom in the West* (Stanford, 1995) and D. Wootton ed., *Republicanism, Liberty and Commercial Society, 1649–1776* (Stanford, 1994).

government and liberties to the wider world. In each case, younger generations have criticized the technique, composition and vision of these historical pictures. Against the Whig picture it is argued that early Stuart MPs were not seeking parliamentary government, nor did they secure it: no parliament was in session in 1688 when a Whig coup brought William III to the throne. The Marxist picture is rejected on the grounds that the civil war was not a bourgeois revolution, but an aristocratic rebellion whose outcome saw no permanent social revolution. After 1660, the English state remained an *ancien régime* run by an aristocratic oligarchy of land and birth.[12] As for the Americans' Manifest Destiny and the history of freedom, the English revisionists have been quick to deride pictures which seem obviously drawn by contemporary ideological perspectives, and focus little on the meaning of 'liberties' and indeed 'parliaments' to those who spoke of them in the seventeenth-century House of Commons. At the core of all the criticisms are charges of anachronism, teleology or, to return to our metaphor, distortion in the Whig/Marxist, wide-angle pictures which reveal so little of the details of seventeenth-century parliaments that we are unable to see what they were, or how they worked.[13] While this is undoubtedly true, such criticisms may amount to disliking a mural done in broad strokes because it is not a miniature of filigree delicacy. The panoramic photo of the Grand Canyon may lose the detail of rock-formation shown by the close-up, but it remains *a* picture which represents what we see when we look up and around. If some historians in the nineteenth and early twentieth centuries could see the seventeenth century in a clear sweep of the camera that panned to their own time, there is importance and validity enough in that. If by the late seventeenth century we find men, some of whose experiences and memories went back decades, already sketching that picture, already seeing themselves in that perspective, we must keep it on our table, as a perspective we cannot lose sight of.[14]

For the moment, however, we turn to its opposite: the close-up photograph. It was Sir Geoffrey Elton who first asked historians to focus on seventeenth-century parliaments rather than sweep across or over them,

[12] For a review of criticism and some sharp critical observations, see J. C. D. Clark, *Revolution and Rebellion* (Cambridge, 1986).

[13] G. Burgess, 'On Revisionism: an Analysis of Early Stuart Historiography in the 1970s and 1980s', *Hist. Journ.*, 33 (1990), 609–27.

[14] We await a good study of the ideological constructions of history written in the later seventeenth and early eighteenth centuries. See, however, R. Macgillivray, *Restoration Historians and the English Civil War* (The Hague, 1974); A. B. Worden ed., *Edmund Ludlow: a Voyce from the Watch Tower, 1660–1662* (Camden Soc., 4th ser., 21, 1978); J. Sawday, 'Re-writing a Revolution: History, Symbol and Text in the Restoration', *The Seventeenth Century*, 7 (1992), 171–99.

and John Kenyon who began to show how differently they would appear viewed through a lens that spanned only their own century – or half century before 1642.[15] During the 1970s, a new generation of scholars set out with their cameras and a kit bag, from which the wide angle was banned, to take a number of new shots of the early Stuart parliamentary scene. All were engaged in close-up work. One focused on one MP, another on an election, yet another on the passage of a bill, or some weeks of a parliamentary session. With more ambition and experience, Conrad Russell set out to re-photograph each of the parliaments of the 1620s and, in consequence, to reorientate our vision of them all.[16] With reels of film devoted to the details of what had been a point on a larger panorama, the historical picture of parliaments was radically transformed – often beyond recognition. Indeed, the detailed close-up at times revealed the opposite of the hazier wide angle. Where the Whigs saw the Commons forging their way to power at the expense of the crown, Russell found MPs uninterested in taking the reins of government and reluctant to oppose the monarch, or to use their control of subsidies to get their way. Where the Whigs panned their camcorder to present a continuous narrative of parliaments growing from childhood to confident maturity, Russell presented intermittent snapshots of a faltering adolescent body which had little continuity of institutional life, which jumped from issue to issue and which declined in significance during the decades before the civil war. Far from the Commons being the centrepiece of the picture and the champions of constitutional rights, Russell showed an assembly which failed to discharge its functions and one whose members' frustrations reflected political problems beyond their resolution and even in some cases their comprehension.[17]

Some of those dissatisfied with Professor Russell's pictures were just too set in their angle of vision to see things another way. But there were legitimate worries about the new pictures, worries that have grown as the excitement of their first publication has passed. In the first place, even on Russell's videotape, for all the quality of the picture, the sound is missing. There was noise and passion in early Stuart parliaments and much heated discussion of them which finds only intermittent voice

[15] G. R. Elton, 'Studying the History of Parliament', in his *Studies in Tudor and Stuart Politics and Government* (Cambridge, 1974), II, 9; J. P. Kenyon ed., *The Stuart Constitution, 1603–1688* (Cambridge, 1966; 2nd edn, 1986).
[16] For examples, see Sharpe, *Faction and Parliament*, and C. Russell, *Parliaments and English Politics 1621–1629* (Oxford, 1979).
[17] Russell, *Parliaments and English Politics*; Russell, 'Parliamentary History in Perspective'; and see now C. Russell, *Unrevolutionary England, 1603–1642* (1990), introduction.

here, leaving in places an eery quiet where an animated soundtrack should be.[18] For all its use of the newly published parliamentary diaries, Russell's book is more confident in analysing political moves and manoeuvres than in examining the rhetoric of parliamentary speeches. Secondly, Russell is inclined to view the Commons from the perspective of the 'county community' and a historiography, now criticized, that depicted MPs as preoccupied with local questions and interests, rather than as men participating in the government of the nation or the public sphere of discourse about it.[19] Most seriously, the narrow focus on the 1620s restricted the historical vision and exacerbated the problems of historical explanation. If the Commons was so insignificant and declining in importance why was it called in the 1620s so frequently?[20] How did the issues and mood of the House in the 1620s compare with Elizabethan assemblies? How, if parliaments were a series of events, did some MPs attain a sense of institutional identity and pride? How did the experience of parliaments and memory of past parliaments shape individuals' political consciousness – to the point that MPs, like Pym in 1641, were to appeal to it with such telling effect?[21] Professor Russell, rightly critical of the fuzzy lines of the big Whig picture, was nevertheless wrong to claim that he had placed seventeenth-century parliaments in perspective. He had, very ably, shot them from a different perspective, which highlighted important features and details lost in the big sweep, but which also fragmented and cut off aspects – some would say the core – of its subject. We must endeavour to put the pieces together again.

The microscope enables us to probe beneath the surface of objects to see how they function and what parts they consist of. In the first case, the old Whig view was concerned more with the function of the House of Commons in the long historical story, than how contemporaries viewed it in early seventeenth-century England. If any consideration was given to the latter, it was assumed that early Stuart MPs saw themselves as fighting a historic struggle for parliamentary government, whose preservation and advancement was their primary function. This, of course, too easily ignored the fact that it was the king who summoned parliaments,

---

[18] My metaphor, but the point is well made by D. Hirst, 'The Place of Principle', *Past and Present*, 92 (1981), 79–99.

[19] C. Holmes, 'The County Community in Stuart Historiography', *Journ. Brit. Studies*, 19 (1980), 53–73; A. Hughes, 'Warwickshire on the Eve of the Civil War: A County Community?', *Midland Hist.*, 7 (1982), 42–72.

[20] Compare D. Hirst, *Authority and Conflict in England, 1603–1658* (1985), 39.

[21] In the Grand Remonstrance, printed in S. R. Gardiner ed., *Constitutional Documents of the Puritan Revolution, 1625–1660* (Oxford, 1899), 202–32.

presumably for some other reason than their advancement at his own expense. The view of the crown was that parliaments were called to vote taxes in extraordinary circumstances, to pass legislation, to offer advice and – too seldom mentioned – air grievances and criticism. As they looked closely at the workings of parliaments, the revisionist historians discovered paradoxically that the crown's view of their functions was shared by most MPs, but that they were functions the Commons was failing to perform.

In the case of taxation, the theory governing royal and parliamentary attitudes – that the king should live of his own revenues in peacetime – had long been unrealistic. Perhaps by the thirteenth century, the royal demesne was insufficient to bear the costs of government. Though the century of war with France brought almost permanent taxation, it hid the reality that even in peacetime the crown did not have the resources to sustain its obligations to defend and protect its subjects. A real opportunity to restore the monarchy to fiscal strength and independence was presented to Henry VIII when he inherited the Yorkist, Lancastrian and Tudor estates and added to them the lands of the dissolved monasteries. However, as a true Renaissance prince, Henry preferred the glories of war against France to pacifism and fiscal rectitude. By the end of his reign, most of his substantial resources had been dissipated, and the beginnings of the greatest inflation ever known quickly eroded the rest.[22] This was also the century when changes in weapons and tactics, sometimes called the military revolution, escalated defence costs even faster than the runaway inflation that rocked a realm used to stable prices.[23] Even withdrawal from continental warfare would not alone solve the problems: after the break from Rome, England was always the likely target of a Catholic crusade, and the realm needed to be kept in a state of preparedness for defence and war.[24]

The gap between the needs of the crown and its resources grew to a chasm. This is the gap that, Whig historians argued, Elizabethan and early Stuart MPs took advantage of, to force the crown to concede more

---

[22] G. L. Harriss, *King, Parliament and Public Finance in Medieval England to 1369* (Oxford, 1975); Harriss, 'War and the Emergence of the English Parliament 1297–1360', *Journ. Med. Hist.*, 2 (1976), 35–56; Harriss, 'Medieval Doctrines in the Debates on Supply', in Sharpe, *Faction and Parliament*, 73–103.

[23] G. Parker, *The Military Revolution: Military Innovation and the Rise of the West* (Cambridge, 1988).

[24] As Queen Elizabeth put it to her Commons in 1593, 'it is needful for a prince to have so much always lying in her coffers for your defence in time of need, and not to be driven to get it when she should use it'. (W. Cobbett ed., *The Parliamentary History of England* (36 vols., 1806–20), I, 893.) Compare James I's witty remark to the 1610 parliament 'that provision for war after its outbreak was like mustard after dinner' (E. R. Foster ed., *Proceedings in Parliament 1610* (2 vols., New Haven, 1966), II, 106).

power in return for votes of subsidies. Conrad Russell argued, from close examination, that if anything the Commons was weakened by these developments. Though he showed that from Elizabeth's reign onwards the Commons voted increasingly frequent and large grants of taxation, even in peacetime, the value of such levies declined, as assessments for the subsidy failed to keep pace with inflation.[25] In 1628, after parliament had granted five subsidies, the Privy Council was frantically endeavouring to get a yield per subsidy that matched that of 1572: they failed; subsidies declined in value from £130,000 to £50,000.[26] The only light at the end of the tunnel of fiscal gloom was the rising value of customs duties with expanding trade, and the value of extraordinary measures such as the grants of monopolies. In so far as the Commons questioned royal fiscal expedients as grievances, they threatened to cost as much as they contributed. As a source of revenue therefore, Russell argued, the Commons had all but lost its function. This is a provocative conclusion, hard to square with the frequency with which parliaments were called, especially in the 1620s. Though the crown necessarily resorted to fiscal expedients, as much to reward its servants as to gain revenue, what is still remarkable about early Stuart England is the crown's limited exploration of extraparliamentary revenue. In early Stuart England, there was no large-scale sale of hereditary offices like the *paulette* in France.[27] The monarchy and the Commons were both caught up in a set of traditional customs which were strained at the edges but not broken, leaving the crown unable to govern and the Commons, rather like modern critics of the health service, irritated at deficiencies and grumbling at the costs. Had it wished to loom large in government, the Commons perhaps could have done so through the voting of an annual revenue even in peacetime, but it showed little enthusiasm, in 1610 for example, to do so. It took the fact of civil war and parliamentary government to change the fiscal system. Before 1642, the Commons may have failed to meet the crown's fiscal needs in practice, but it did not veer much from customs and traditions in which king and parliament were both trapped.

[25] Russell, 'Parliamentary History in Perspective'.
[26] Hampshire Record Office, Herriard MS 021; F. C. Dietz, *English Public Finance, 1558–1641* (London and New York, 1932; repr., 2 vols., London, 1964), II, 391–3; M. J. Braddick, 'Parliamentary Lay Taxation, *circa* 1590–1670: Local Problems of Enforcement and Collection with Special Reference to Norfolk' (Ph.D. thesis, Cambridge University, 1987), esp. chs. 1–3.
[27] Most proposals for improving royal revenue were conservative in nature. Significantly, the few radical proposals – for an excise, for example – were not adopted. See Sir Robert Cotton, 'The Manner and Means how the Kings of England have from time to time Supported and Repaired their Estates', in J. Howell ed., *Cottoni Posthuma* (1651), 163–200; cf. BL Cotton MS Titus F. V; BL Add. MS 34234, f.169; K. Sharpe, *The Personal Rule of Charles I* (New Haven and London, 1992), 13.

The second important function of a parliament was legislation. Strangely, the Whig wide angle paid little attention to parliamentary bills and acts, concentrating on moments of constitutional dispute – the Apology or Protestation – which impeded the progress of legislation. Yet legislation was arguably what gave English parliaments their power and importance. By the sixteenth century, statute law was held to be supreme and royal proclamations were used only to enforce or gloss rather than to change the law. For all his claims to Caesaro-papism, Henry VIII enacted his Reformation through statute and the Elizabethan religious settlement was made in parliament. Scholars have long observed that from the reign of James I the number of official acts declined, and Conrad Russell has developed the point to argue that, after the failure of his project for full union with Scotland, James had no legislative programme and parliament's role as a legislator declined. The statistics show a decline in the number of acts from Elizabeth's reign.[28] But it is worth remembering that in terms of royal legislation, the sixteenth century with the need for religious settlement and new treason laws, was exceptional rather than typical.[29] During the early seventeenth century, the number of royal proclamations remained stable, and reached their lowest during the 1630s when no parliament assembled.[30] The absence of official bills then did not signal a monarchy looking to enact its will outside parliament, but a return to stability after the heady changes consequent on the Reformation.

What is more interesting is the paucity of public bills initiated by the Commons in this period – even on matters about which they expressed concern.[31] In part, this was due to incompetence and bureaucracy. For all Notestein's talk of procedural developments, the Commons often appears disorganized, unfocused and badly led.[32] Many bills of no obvious contention disappeared into committees from which they never emerged, perhaps because more educated MPs (rather like academics on committees) talked much but resolved little. Jennifer Loach, however, has interestingly suggested that the Elizabethan House of Commons was reluctant to legislate against the burden of monopolies because they

---

[28] R. W. K. Hinton, 'The Decline of Parliamentary Government under Elizabeth I and the Early Stuarts', *Camb. Hist. Journ.*, 13 (1957), 116–32, esp. 116.

[29] M. A. R. Graves, *The Tudor Parliaments* (1985), 77–9.

[30] J. F. Larkin ed., *Stuart Royal Proclamations, Vol. II: Royal Proclamations of King Charles I, 1625–46* (Oxford, 1983), xi. The average, 1603–29, was twelve a year, the same as in Mary's reign. Hinton does not discuss proclamations in his comments on extra-parliamentary government.

[31] A large proportion of the bills that became statutes in Jacobean parliaments were concerned with claims to title and estates, restorations, naturalizations and marriage settlements.

[32] See my introduction to *Faction and Parliament*, 25–8.

trusted the crown to reform the abuse.[33] If this were the case, the succession of James, who announced his enthusiasm to listen and reform, may have added extra goodwill to the traditional honeymoon for a new monarch and led to fewer bills and more petitions to the king. The range and number of petitions to the king is striking, and his response no less so.[34] It may be James's willingness to suspend patents by proclamation, for example, that took the heat out of the issue; for it was not until 1624 that a statute against monopolies was passed, and then with the active encouragement of the Prince of Wales. Though James's openness to reform and petition did not fulfil the hopes for reform of abuses, it did mean that those hopes, like the hopes of the religious reformers, were never dashed.[35] The obstacle to reform and to legislation, as the debates about purveyance or the Great Contract reveal, was a conservative resistance to fundamental change – among MPs as much as, if not more than, by the crown. After 1618, the focus shifted from domestic to foreign affairs with the eviction of James I's daughter and son-in-law from their lands in the Palatinate and the outbreak of the Thirty Years War. Politics and pressure (from outside as well as within the Commons) took over from legislation, the session of 1621 producing no legislation but the subsidy act. While the succession of the more rigid Charles I ultimately changed the atmosphere of openness to petition and reform, the new king began with a fund of goodwill, not least owing to memories of his championship of reforms in 1621 and 1624.[36] War and high politics dominated the parliaments of 1625–8, but for all their frustrations at burdens, policies and ministers, the Commons still preferred to reform through petition to the king rather than legislation – even in 1628 when the procedure by bill was dropped for a Petition of Right. After 1610 and before 1640, therefore, the crown had a minimal legislative programme and the Commons preferred petition to statute. Curiously, even when the Long Parliament met after eleven years of non-parliamentary government, it took more than six months before a series of reforming bills became law. Though the removal of what were perceived as excrescences on and abuses of customary government was sought by the backbenches, the manoeuvres for a resolution of the main political crisis were going on elsewhere. Legislation in early seventeenth-century England failed

[33] R. Smith and J. Moore eds., *The House of Commons: 700 Years of British Tradition* (1996), ch. 3.

[34] R. C. Munden, 'James I and the "Growth of Mutual Distrust": King, Commons and Reform, 1603–1604', in Sharpe *Faction and Parliament*, 46–9.

[35] R. E. Ruigh, *The Parliament of 1624* (Cambridge, Mass., 1971), 151, for James recommending remedial legislation against monopolies and other abuses; Russell, *Parliaments and English Politics*, 191.

[36] Sharpe, *Personal Rule*, 1, 7–9.

because (with the exception of the union) neither the monarchy nor the Commons considered pursuing the radical reforms of the system that necessitated statute. It was not an index of the redundancy of parliaments, but of the stranglehold of conservatism on all government.

The third function of parliaments, and especially of the Commons, no less in the eyes of the crown than of the MPs themselves, was advice. The whole theory of personal monarchy as it developed in England was based on the centrality of counsel – from ministers, magnates and Privy Councillors and from the representatives of the political nation in the shires. Before the development of party institutionalized the connections, good counsellors were the vital link between the crown and the political nation, the essential component of that trust on which the workings of the system depended. MPs came to Westminster with a unique knowledge of the problems and views of the counties and boroughs they represented and, even when the advice they gave the king was unwelcome or unpalatable, it was important and valued.[37] Or nearly always. James's openness to petition and counsel appears to have been dented by the Commons' response to his scheme for a union of Great Britain, a response which he believed (not unreasonably) to be dictated by nationalism, avarice and fear of rivalry for trade and places rather than considerations of the public weal. During the 1620s, the Commons' advice on foreign affairs he viewed – again not unreasonably – as ill-informed, if not ignorant, few MPs having any idea of the intricacies of European diplomacy or the costs of war. In Charles I's eyes, fighting a war as soon as he ascended the throne, the Commons' counsel was not only misguided, but inconsistent with its earlier exhortations; and members were downright irresponsible in denouncing the measures that the war they had urged necessitated. The crown's growing disenchantment not with the theory of counsel but with the Commons' unhelpful advice was matched by MPs' growing dissatisfaction that their counsel was either not heard or went unheeded. In some respects, the Duke of Buckingham, who, a recent biographer suggests, was greatly misunderstood and undervalued, became the scapegoat for a breakdown of parliament's role as an adviser: a breakdown as important as the fiscal problems of the regime.[38] For kings traditionally called parliaments for

---

[37] G. R. Elton, 'Tudor Government: the Points of Contact: I. Parliament', *Trans. Royal Hist. Soc.*, 5th ser., 24 (1974), 183–200. On James's attitude to parliamentary advice, see W. Notestein, F. H. Relf, and H. Simpson eds., *Commons Debates, 1621* (7 vols., New Haven, 1935), II, 4.

[38] R. Lockyer, *Buckingham: the Life and Political Career of George Villiers, First Duke of Buckingham, 1592–1628* (1981).

advice, even when they did not seek supply; the crisis of counsel, as MPs themselves discerned, threatened the survival of parliaments.[39] By 1629, it was because Charles I had resolved that their counsel was more a hindrance than aid to his government that he embarked upon a period of rule without them. For all his action was understandable, however, it underlined the importance of parliament's counsel. Superficially, the eleven years of non-parliamentary government appear to support arguments for their declining function and significance. Government continued and worked reasonably well. But the government lost a vital opportunity to communicate and explain its programmes and a sounding board to test the mood of the nation. As Charles I found in the late 1630s and Oliver Cromwell in the 1650s, the absence of regular parliaments detached the central government from the political nation, placing strains on the patronage chains of command.

For all then that, as Professor Russell argued, parliament appeared to be losing its usefulness – as a supplier, as a legislator, as a source of counsel – it never lost importance. The kings, and indeed the Protector, continued to view parliaments as the only organ for granting supply (all else were expedients), the only way to change the law, and a vital source of counsel. Still more they recognized its importance as a symbol of the traditional courses. Neither Charles I's nor Cromwell's speeches about the importance of parliaments should be dismissed as insincere rhetoric. They believed in parliaments and were as confused at the Commons' failure to act in harmony with them as MPs were devoted to monarchy and unable to understand why it failed to heed them. Interestingly, for all Conrad Russell's observations, the decline (and perceived decline) in parliament's functions did not lead to any reduction of the importance contemporaries (councillors and commoners) attached to them. If anything, as we shall suggest, the reverse was the case.

While we are observing through the microscope, we need to examine the structure and form of parliaments. Superficially, we do not need to look very closely to see that they consisted of king, Lords and Commons – though, having recognized that, much of the historiography has in practice ignored the first two. What we do need to appreciate and study is that the relationship of the constituents – of the Lords to the Commons, of the king to each House, of the full House to its committees – changes over time, as does the membership, the procedure and the practice. Such changes in parliaments were a consequence of broader

---

[39] Sharpe, *Faction and Parliament*, 37–42.

social and political shifts, and in turn tended to shape those broader developments. The Whigs, knowing already what they wanted to see, pronounced confidently after the briefest of looks, on what important changes the seventeenth century saw in the structure and constitution of parliaments. A new dynasty of kings, Scottish, ignorant of English law and traditions, bent on absolute rule, faced a new class of MPs, men newly educated in the universities and Inns of Court, whose humanist and legal studies equipped them to be champions of the resistance and fight for freedom and democracy. The Marxists, too, quickly discern a shift that fits into their wide-angle picture. During the sixteenth and seventeenth centuries, they detect the decline of a feudal aristocracy and the rise of a gentry and bourgeois class, often of men who had risen through trade, who came from the counties and especially the boroughs determined to dismantle the vestiges of feudal authority and to remake the constitution in their own interests. While they have returned to the laboratory and made minor modifications to the theory, whole generations of students have followed their Marxist professors, from Christopher Hill through Lawrence Stone to Derek Hirst, and most recently (albeit old experiments only recently published) Robert Brenner.[40] Recent research, however, has convincingly demonstrated that in their enthusiasm for their own model, these scholars were blind to some very important data. In the brilliant *Parliamentary Selection*, Professor Mark Kishlansky showed that, far from being revolutionized by social change, the processes of selecting members for parliament were characterized by norms of deference and consensus, and dictated by traditions of aristocratic patronage and honour. As a consequence, MPs sent to Westminster until at least the eve of civil war came from the same social class, and often the same families, as their forebears.[41]

As for the House of Lords (curiously ignored by the Whigs), as other scholars have shown, the peers refused to act as the declining class that the Marxists believed they saw. As a class, the peerage still expected and were accorded deference; and as a House, the Lords was prominent in the parliaments of the seventeenth century. In 1621, for example, the impeachments of the patentee, Sir Giles Mompesson, and the King's

---

[40] Hill, *English Revolution*; Hill; *Puritanism and Revolution* (London, 1958); Hill, *Collected Essays* (3 vols., Brighton, 1985–6); L. Stone, *The Causes of the English Revolution, 1529–1642* (1972); D. Hirst, *The Representative of the People?* (Cambridge, 1975); R. Brenner, *Merchants and Revolution: Commercial Change, Political Conflict and London's Overseas Traders, 1550–1653* (Cambridge, 1993). Despite its publication date, the last is very much old wine in new bottles.

[41] M. Kishlansky, *Parliamentary Selection: Social and Political Choice in Early Modern England* (Cambridge, 1986).

Lord Chancellor, Francis Bacon, depended upon the House of Lords, the revival of whose judicial powers enhanced their political importance for the rest of the decade. In 1628, in seeking redress of their grievances by a petition of right, the Commons were – necessarily – anxious at all points to have the support of the Lords. Without it they could do little. The support the Lords gave the lower House in 1628 directs us, far from the Marxist focus, to a problem still in need of exploration: why, by the late 1620s, had the Lords ceased to be the reliable supporters of the crown?[42] Detailed studies have shown how leading magnates such as the Earls of Arundel and Bristol became disaffected by the rise of a favourite in the 1620s, and conspired with their clients in the Commons to bring the Duke of Buckingham down.[43] Close analysis of the politics of the winter of 1640–1 has shown the centrality of the magnates in the machinations to resolve political crisis by changes in the King's Council.[44] A young scholar, researching the activities especially of the Earl of Essex and Lord Saye and Sele, has argued suggestively that, far from a revolution of a new rising bourgeoisie, the English civil war originated in the revolt of a baronage steeped in the history and values of their Lancastrian predecessors.[45] Though it is not here our central object of focus, it is clear that, in order better to understand the House of Commons, we need to know a great deal more about a House of Lords whose membership rose from 55 in 1603 to 126 in 1628. How far did the great expansion and, in some cases, change in the membership affect the politics of the House of Lords?[46] Did divisions within the Lords undermine its value to the king? Were the difficulties James I and Charles I faced with the Lords occasioned by more than the rise of a parvenu favourite? How did 'opposition' peers come to control the House in 1641 so as to secure the execution of the king's chief minister? Such questions dictate the need for a full study of the politics of the Lords from the failure of the Jacobean union to the civil war – and beyond. Evidently, Oliver Cromwell came to regard the absence of an upper chamber in

---

[42] J. Miller, 'The English Kill their Kings – from Divine Right to Parliamentary Monarchy: the Stuarts, 1603–1714', in J. S. Moore and R. Smith eds., *The House of Lords: a Thousand Years of British Tradition* (1994), 66–86.

[43] V. F. Snow, 'The Arundel Case', *The Historian*, 26 (1964), 324–50; K. Sharpe, 'The Earl of Arundel, His Circle and the Opposition to the Duke of Buckingham 1618–1628', in *Faction and Parliament*, 209–44.

[44] C. Roberts, 'The Earl of Bedford and the Coming of the English Revolution', *Journ. Mod. Hist.*, 49 (1977), 600–16; Sharpe, *Personal Rule*, 946–9.

[45] J. S. Adamson, 'The Baronial Context of the English Civil War', *Trans. Royal Hist. Soc.*, 5th ser., 40 (1990), 93–120; Adamson, 'Politics and the Nobility in Civil War England', *Hist. Journ.*, 34 (1991), 231–55. [46] Miller, 'The English Kill their Kings'.

the 1650s as an impediment to constitutional settlement, and to consider the conferring of titles an essential element in social and political stability.[47] After 1660, the House of Lords and the peerage were central to the politics of the restored kingdom, and the improved relations between crown and peerage provide a key to the political stability of the years after 1688.[48] Given what we have begun to learn about the links between the Houses at particular moments in the 1620s, a better understanding of the Lords promises to place the Commons in a very different perspective.

That, however, should not detract from the extensive research that still needs to be done on the House of Commons and its members. While Kishlansky is right to counter the claim that MPs came from a new class, it cannot be denied that the speeches reveal members better educated – in the classics, the law and scripture. Whether this better equipped the House to articulate its grievances against royal policies or bogged its proceedings in self-promoting speeches of hours' duration is a moot point.[49] The speeches themselves, their purpose, their rhetoric, the responses they received, inside and outside the House, have been curiously neglected. In some recent scholarship, too little consideration is given to the relationship of the speakers and rhetoricians to the 'silent' backbenchers whom the orators were presumably trying to persuade.[50] Were the silent those more concerned with the business of the House, where the orators sought to capture attention outside it? Were MPs ambitious for office and place pursuing quite different courses from those whose social and political ambitions were centred on representing their county? How were local and national perspectives weighed by men of strong local attachment, but education in and experience of national affairs? While scholars have debated some of these questions in general, we still have few case studies of MPs, either as individuals or representatives of a county; and those we do have are of members such as Eliot, Wentworth or Pym who (in different ways) were quite untypical.[51] The microscopic analysis of seventeenth-century parliaments has scarcely begun.

---

[47] M. Seymour, 'Pro-Government Propaganda in Interregnum England, 1649–1660' (Ph.D. thesis, Cambridge University, 1987), ch. 5.

[48] Clark, *Revolution and Rebellion*, 33, 75–7; Clark, *English Society, 1688–1832* (Cambridge, 1985), ch. 2.

[49] One about which contemporaries too were in doubt (Sharpe, *Faction and Parliament*, 7–8).

[50] E.g. C. Russell, *The Fall of the British Monarchies* (Oxford, 1991).

[51] J. N. Ball, 'The Parliamentary Career of Sir John Eliot, 1624–29' (Ph.D. thesis, Cambridge University, 1953); C. V. Wedgwood, *Thomas Wentworth, Earl of Strafford, a Revaluation, 1593–1641* (1961); S. P. Salt, 'Sir Thomas Wentworth and the Parliamentary Representation of Yorkshire, 1614–28', *Northern Hist.*, 16 (1980), 130–68; C. Russell, 'The Parliamentary Career of John Pym', in *Unrevolutionary England*, 205–30.

Such microscopic study, however, must not preclude study of the surrounding tissue. Ironically, the Whig wide angle and the Russell close-up on parliaments have failed fully to study them in relation to the other organs of government, as participants in the government, still more in the broader political culture and public sphere. Traditionally, the relationship of the House of Commons to the Privy Council and the court was described as one of contest or opposition. But as soon as we acknowledge that seventeenth-century politics was characterized more by personal relations than institutional parameters, we see how inappropriate it is to study parliaments discreetly. Nearly all Privy Councillors were Members of Parliament, and many MPs too were a part of the court – either narrowly defined (as the royal household and entourage) or more broadly conceived (as all who held office of the crown, including keepers of royal manors, forts and castles, or escheators of crown lands like Pym). Moreover, during the seventeenth century, several MPs, most famously Wentworth, Noy and Digges, became Councillors and courtiers – and it was perfectly natural rather than exceptional for them to do so.[52] If MPs sometimes took the route to office, it was no less true that Councillors and courtiers at times championed parliamentary grievances; and in turn used their allies in the Commons to win a dispute within the King's Council, even to put pressure on the monarch himself or, since the case is very well demonstrated for Elizabeth, herself.[53] Historians have demonstrated this for particular episodes and in the specific context of faction.[54] But the interrelations of parliament, Council and court went beyond the narrow politics of faction and we await a study of the Commons in the context of these broader, complex and fluid arrangements – in the context of patronage.[55]

Similarly, the relationship of various MPs to their localities needs to be reconfigured in the light of recent scholarship. During the 1960s and 1970s, the historians of the county communities presented a picture of the typical county MP sent to Westminster with provincial political perspectives and ends, keener to press for the repair of Dungeness

---

[52] P. Zagorin, 'Did Strafford Change Sides?', *Eng. Hist. Rev.*, 101 (1986), 149–63; *DNB* (1899), LX, 268–83; F. K. Sharpe, *Sir Robert Cotton 1586–1631: History and Politics in Early Modern England* (Oxford, 1979).

[53] P. Collinson, 'Puritans, Men of Business and Elizabethan Parliaments', *Parl. Hist.*, 7 (1988), 187–211.

[54] The history of faction added an important dimension to the study of Tudor and Stuart politics, but historians of faction have been too prone to over-schematize faction and to see political relations too narrowly in factional terms.

[55] A sketch for a possible study is outlined in K. Sharpe, 'Crown, Parliament and Locality: Government and Communication in Early Stuart England', *Eng. Hist. Rev.*, 99 (1986), 321–50.

lighthouse or the bridge over the river Nene, than to be involved in
national issues. As Clive Holmes, Ann Hughes and others have argued,
this is only a half truth.[56] Most MPs were lifted beyond their county hori-
zons by university, often a period at one of the Inns of Court and by business, kinship and marriage. Moreover, when sitting at Westminster, they
shared the experiences of other members and became part of an active
London culture which was the metropolis of news as well as (often political) entertainment. How did individual MPs negotiate their duties of
serving their locality, serving the crown, and advancing the public weal?
Such questions of choice and conscience always were, and still are, part
of being an MP. But if, as has been persuasively argued, the tensions
between centre and locality were increasing, it was natural that they were
reflected in parliament. If the Commons was only the barometer indi-
cating stormy political weather, we cannot hope to explain the storm
only by staring at the barometer. We need to examine the broader political structures, political culture and, as important, contemporaries' perceptions of them.

     Once, historians of ideas confidently described early modern political
culture as characterized by order, harmony and obedience, not least
because contemporary writers rehearsed such terms almost as a litany of
state.[57] What we now appreciate is that the repetition of such axioms
announced insecurities about their cohesion and fears about their subve-
sion. As on the continent, the English Reformation threw up awkward
questions about personal faith and conscience in relation to duty and obedience to the magistrate: questions that went to the heart of the nature of
power, authority and obedience. Subjects began to read the Bible, the
classics, the law in very different ways and came to different conclusions
about the priorities of government. Such real tensions and fissures were
often masked by a language of consensus and by rituals of community
which served to shelve and exacerbate the problems: problems not only of
religion, but of the role and authority of the state (at a time of military
escalation and endemic warfare) in relation to the rights and properties of
subjects.[58] Themselves a microcosm of a larger cultural incapacity to
acknowledge differences, the rituals and rhetoric of parliaments emphasized unanimity and concordance. To MPs whose (or whose constituents')
experience was rather one of discord and division, this led to confusion

---

[56] See above, n. 19.
[57] The *locus classicus* of this view is E. M. W. Tillyard, *The Elizabethan World Picture* (1943); A. O.
     Lovejoy, *The Great Chain of Being* (Cambridge, Mass., 1936; repr. 1953; New York, 1960).
[58] Sharpe and Lake, *Culture and Politics*, 18–20 and passim; above, ch. 2.

and frustration, and a need to place the blame somewhere 'outside'. Like the European witch craze, English hysteria about popery undoubtedly signals a larger psychological phenomenon: a need to explain ills that could apparently be ascribed to no natural causes. But if these were problems for parliaments, they were not problems caused by them. They were the problems of a culture which could not easily voice opposition and acknowledge conflict, the first steps in the resolution of problems.[59] Each MP's experiences of the Council, the court and his county, his own readings of the supposedly shared texts and codes of the political culture, are the essential contexts for an understanding of parliaments.

Nearly all historical analysts of Stuart parliaments have taken it as given that they were an unusual specimen, exhibiting abnormalities that revealed ills in the body politic. If, however, we are to conclude that, and explain how, seventeenth-century parliaments were abnormally contentious, we need a comparative sample of others of supposedly greater normality and harmony. Yet historians of medieval parliaments have been less inclined to see the seventeenth century as special or very different from the mix of harmonious and stormy scenes that characterized the twelfth to fifteenth centuries, or from the crises of Richard II's, Edward II's or Henry VI's reigns which led to the deposition and murder of anointed kings.[60] To come closer to the early Stuart decades, recent researches on Elizabeth's reign have not only shown that beneath the rhetoric of love and harmony were sharp clashes over the queen's marriage, the succession, religious and foreign policy, but also that, as in the 1620s, Privy Councillors were often behind the pressure voiced noisily in the Commons.[61] After the civil war, the hero of the parliamentarian cause, Oliver Cromwell, found it no easier to work with parliaments than his royal predecessors, and was dogged by the same issues (unparliamentary taxes, religious disputes) that had plagued them.[62] Noise, division and conflict, in other words, were the practical norms of parliaments, for all the rhetoric of harmony; and it is not absolutely obvious that the early Stuart parliaments were any worse than most. Indeed, even during the 1620s, there were occasions of co-operation and accord (as in 1624) rather than a smooth graph of escalating contention. Such observations

[59] This argument is pursued further in K. Sharpe and S. Zwicker eds., *Refiguring Revolutions: Aesthetics and Politics from the English Revolution to the Romantic Revolution* (Berkeley, Los Angeles and London 1998), introduction.
[60] Smith and Moore, *The House of Commons*, 1–2. Elizabeth and James I often referred to these earlier periods of crisis, e.g. C. H. McIlwain ed., *The Political Works of James I* (Cambridge, Mass., 1918), 246. [61] C. Haigh, *Elizabeth I* (1988), ch. 6; J. Loach, *Parliament under the Tudors* (Oxford, 1991).
[62] B. Coward, *Oliver Cromwell* (1991), chs. 6–7.

pose a conundrum. If tension and contention were normal to the history of parliaments, why did seventeenth-century conflicts lead to violent civil war where others – if not all – were resolved by more peaceful means? Here it is worth remembering that throughout the 1620s and even in 1641, the measures pursued to restore harmony were steeped in precedent and tradition. What was different about the so-called Bedford plan, to place trusted magnates in the King's Council, was the context rather than content of the proposals: the presence of a Scottish army and demobilized English troops. What this constituted, far more serious than a 'British problem', was a condition of violence in which, as often, political solutions were nigh impossible to negotiate. Thereafter, thanks to the Irish rebellion of 1641, there was never a window of demilitarized opportunity for peaceful settlement. After 1660, significantly, for all that the issues returned to parliamentary politics, as sharp and divisive as ever, their resolution always stopped short of battle. The memory of civil war and, related, the determination to exclude any standing armies in England, again provided a context for the resolution of normal political conflict by the normal processes of negotiation and compromise. Later, the party system institutionalized those processes and also reduced the likelihood of clashes between crown and parliament by requiring royal ministers to have a base of trust in the Commons. Even the perceived hysteria about popery did not again erupt into internecine violence. If sharp conflicts between crown and parliament were not themselves a sufficient cause for civil war, the history of early seventeenth-century parliaments may have been written to explain what they did not cause.

Our laboratory analysis may also benefit from continental as well as chronological comparisons. Certainly, such a comparison is implicit in the traditional Whig history. English parliaments, the assumption goes (like the English race, then spreading its beneficence to the colonies), were more robust than and morally superior to those of other nations.[63] Where the English Commons 'won the initiative' (against the odds?), the French Estates General meekly accepted its own demise in 1614 and succumbed to the growth of Bourbon absolutism; and the Paris parlement proved pusillanimous and compliant. In Spain, English ambassadors were struck by the willingness and generosity of the Cortes in granting taxation.[64] Where the English Commons held to the principle of no

[63] Russell points out that Sir John Fortescue began the myth 'that there was something especially English about parliaments' (Cust and Hughes, *Conflict*, 14).
[64] E.g. letter of Sir Arthur Hopton to Windebank, 7 February 1640: 'the Cortes do every year give more and it is strange to see how patiently the people bears being laid on by the insensible way of sisa' (Bodleian Library, Oxford, Clarendon MS 18, no. 1349). Cf. William Drake's observa-

extraparliamentary levies, the French and Spanish crowns taxed without consultation. Such observed differences were not just in the imagination of staunch Victorian patriots. Seventeenth-century Englishmen and MPs drew attention to the eclipse of representative institutions overseas and some feared their own would follow.[65] While the differences between English and continental assemblies were undoubtedly important, I wish to suggest that their importance has been misunderstood. Rather than weakening the monarchy, the English parliaments were a source of strength to the crown, and one which continental monarchs lacked. At first it appears odd that the Venetian ambassador to England should in 1607 describe James I as having 'reached such a pitch of formidable power that he can do what he likes'.[66] But if this was to go too far, it was pardonable exaggeration. During the sixteenth century, uniquely, the English monarchy had been able to carry through a break from Rome, a Protestant reformation, a return to Rome, and the resumption of reform without religious civil war. Henry VIII's (sincere) rhetoric that he never stood so high as when in parliament was proved by events.[67] In England, the negotiations between the crown and the political nation, the cynosure of *all* early modern governments, were worked out in parliaments rather than through aristocratic risings and revolts. The most important, and least pondered, difference between English and continental parliaments further enhanced social stability and the power of the crown. In England, taxes were paid as well as voted by the nobility and gentry who, in France, were largely exempt from payment. The burdens were not simply transferred to the poorest, and early modern England was largely free of the peasant uprisings which were endemic on the continent. There was surprisingly little class warfare in England; even the civil war saw no agrarian revolution, and its relative social cohesion strengthened the English state.[68] Secondly, the fact that the propertied in England were the taxpaying class presented a phenomenal potential for raising revenue, not at the disposal of foreign monarchs.

tion that the French monarchy was 'the most absolute, for the king doth what he pleaseth both for making laws or laying impositions' (University College London, Ogden MS 7/7 f.105).

[65] As Sir Robert Phelips put it in 1625, 'we are the last monarchy in Christendom that yet retain our original rights and constitutions' (S. R. Gardiner ed., *Debates in the House of Commons in 1625.* (Camden Soc., NS, 6, 1873), 109–10).   [66] *Cal. Stat. Pap. Venet., 1603–7*, 509–10.

[67] G. R. Elton ed., *The Tudor Constitution* (Cambridge, 1960, 2nd edn, 1982), 270; compare James I's speech to the parliament of 1605 that parliament was 'that most honourable and fittest place for a King to be in for doing the turns most proper to his office' (McIlwain, *Political Works of James I,* 284).

[68] J. Morrill and J. Walter, 'Order and Disorder in the English Revolution', in A. Fletcher and J. Stevenson eds., *Order and Disorder in Early Modern England* (Cambridge, 1985), 137–65.

While, as we have seen, for much of the period medieval attitudes to finance trapped the king and Members of Parliament, taxation bought Oliver Cromwell military and naval victories over powerful neighbours.[69] In the 1690s, with king and Commons in partnership, William III, supported by the new National Debt, crushed a Louis XIV who struggled to raise money for long campaigns from private creditors.[70] As Henry VIII had believed and predicted, the king in parliament could be the mightiest monarch of all and, as the country MPs might have said during the 1690s, with a parliament managed by patronage and place, the most absolute at home. There were no intrinsic peculiarities in the English parliament that secured its strength at the expense of the crown.

As we lay out our photographs of parliaments, some old and faded, some new, wide-angle, close-up, microscopic, some of the Commons alone, some with other subjects in the frame, we are struck by the fact that they appear to be images of quite different objects, but in reality are visions of the same one. That recognition prevents us simply discarding any photograph and suggests that we should endeavour to make some composite of them all.

Was the seventeenth century after all a period of unique constitutional conflict between crown and parliament, and was it a quest for power by the Commons that led to civil war? As soon as we return to these basic questions, we are immediately struck by a number of paradoxes. Although on the one hand, many MPs expressed anxiety about the survival of parliament, we have seen that parliament did less and less; moreover, there were few demands that it should meet more frequently, and absenteeism remained from Elizabeth's reign onwards a problem.[71] Even in 1641, when momentous matters were being discussed, the Commons ceased to be quorate. Secondly, if the Commons wished to participate more in government during the early Stuart decades, it is remarkable how slowly and reluctantly they took up the reins of power in the 1640s, and how willing they were to surrender them to a Protector, a new royal dynasty in the house of Cromwell, and in 1660 to the Stuart heir – with no extra guarantees of their position or restraints on the crown. Evidently, what the Commons wanted, as they often said, was traditional government by a king in parliament, ruling in the interests of the gentry. This is what a succession of monarchs also claimed to desire,

[69] This awaits a full investigation, but see W. Kennedy, *English Taxation, 1640–1799* (1913).
[70] P. G. M. Dickson, *The Financial Revolution in England, 1689–1756* (1967; repr. Aldershot, 1993); J. Brewer, *The Sinews of Power: War, Money and the English State* (1989).
[71] Haigh, *Elizabeth I*, 107–8; D. H. Willson ed., *The Parliamentary Diary of Robert Bowyer* (Minneapolis, 1931), 96; *Cal. Stat. Pap. Dom., 1623–5*, 209.

so we need to understand why it did not happen. Professors David Willson and Hugh Trevor-Roper once suggested that the explanation lay in a failure of royal management: that where Elizabeth and Burleigh managed the Commons, James I did not ensure adequate numbers of privy councillors in the House; and Cromwell failed to rig the elections to secure a compliant following.[72] Stability returned only with the brilliant skills of a Danby, or a Walpole, who forged a sense of common interest between king and Commons.[73] While there may be some truth in this, it is one more complicated than personalities. The English state was stronger in Walpole's time, the patronage at the crown's disposal greater; but just as importantly the king and political nation had been shaken out of an unworkable set of values and arrangements by the experience of civil war and later developments.

The early modern period, in England as on the continent, had seen new problems and tensions which placed peculiar strains on a still essentially medieval polity. The alleged 'absolutism' of the Stuarts was not a cause, but sign of these strains. James I and Charles I were not more 'absolutist' than Henry VIII, Elizabeth or the first two Georges.[74] But they reigned during a time when the expanding business of government and the dangers to national security occasioned by religious division, necessitated some extension of the executive. To carry out their traditional duties of protecting the realm, the monarchs had to pursue some untraditional courses. MPs and others who feared that the old customs and balances were being upset were right. But their proposed solution, from outside the circles of government, was adherence to the very traditions that could not serve the new circumstances. King, Lords, Councillors and Commons were all trapped by (sincere) devotion to custom – a dilemma nicely illustrated by ministers like Sir John Coke who as MP abhorred the novelty of the measures he took as Secretary of State in wartime.[75] The experience of government during the 1640s broke the stranglehold of custom. It was a parliamentary government that instituted peacetime taxation, excise and monthly assessments, set

[72] D. H. Willson, *The Privy Councillors in the House of Commons, 1603–1629* (Minneapolis, 1940; repr. New York, 1971); H. R. Trevor-Roper, 'Oliver Cromwell and his Parliaments', in his *Religion, the Reformation and Social Change* (1967; 2nd edn, 1972), ch. 7.

[73] J. H. Plumb, *The Growth of Political Stability in England, 1675–1725* (1967).

[74] Despite the claims of J. P. Sommerville, *Politics and Ideology in England 1603–1640* (1986). See K. Sharpe, *Politics and Ideas in Early Stuart England* (1989), 283–9; C. Russell, 'Divine Rights in the Early Seventeenth Century', in J. Morrill, P. Slack and D. Woolf eds., *Public Duty and Private Conscience in Seventeenth-Century England* (Oxford, 1993), 101–20.

[75] R. C. Johnson, M. Keeler and M. Cole eds., *Commons Debates, 1628* (4 vols., New Haven, 1977), III, 189; see also R. Cust, *The Forced Loan and English Politics 1626–28* (Oxford, 1987), 44, 69–71.

up a salaried Protector and established not only a powerful naval defence, but military basis for successful war and colonial expansion. Participation in government led the Commons to a greater understanding of the problems of rule and to a renewed basis of partnership between the ruler and the political nation. That partnership also depended on the gradual diminution of the heat of religious conflict. The break from Rome and spread of protestantism bequeathed fundamental problems which a Hookerian rhetoric of harmony and an official policy of *via media* served more to conceal than cure. Recently, some historians have argued that the English civil war was a 'war of religion' that resulted from divisions and fears that eroded trust between the crown and significant parts of the political nation.[76] Again, a shared rhetoric of concern for the Church of England masked long-standing differences about what the church was and should be, different visions for which a few were willing to fight. For all the talk of the success of Elizabethan moderation, it was perhaps only after the experience of radical extremes during the 1640s and 1650s (Catholic uprising and revolutionary sectarianism) that the political nation was bonded by a common support for one church and faith, whatever men's private beliefs and preferences.[77] A civil settlement of the religious problem was one of the important consequences of civil war – albeit it took until 1689 before the passing of a Toleration Act neutralized the threat of denominational division to political concord.

By the late seventeenth century, then, such changes in state and church helped to resolve the issues that had strained the relations between the crown and the political nation. They were not issues created or caused by parliaments, but problems that parliaments (that is king, Lords and Commons) had to tackle, but were ill-equipped to solve. Custom, the mantra of early modern political discourse, was the obstacle to settlement, to the re-establishment of the mixed polity in new circumstances, and so the destroyer of the Commons as well as the crown. The civil war led not to the triumph of Commons over the crown, but to a polity in which both increased in effectiveness and strength.

At the centre of the problems before 1642 lay the disjuncture, on all parts, between reality (the reality of change) and perception (the percep-

---

[76] J. S. Morrill, 'The Religious Context of the English Civil War', *Trans. Royal Hist. Soc.*, 5th ser., 34 (1984), 155–78.

[77] I. M. Green, *The Re-Establishment of the Church of England, 1660–1663* (Oxford, 1978), ch. 9; J. Spurr, *The Restoration Church of England, 1646–1689* (New Haven, 1991), ch. 3 and passim.

tion that things should be as they were). In that disjuncture too lies some of the explanation for the great differences between historians of Stuart parliaments. Professor Russell points revealingly to the political realities of declining subsidies, administrative weaknesses and the diminishing functions of parliaments. But, as Cust and Hughes argue, he pays inadequate attention to the devotion to parliaments and customary ways loudly articulated in speeches and pamphlets attacking the crown. If this appears contradictory, our own experience reminds us that our sense of the importance of institutions is often most vocalized when they appear not to be working – to the frustration of all concerned. The expressions of passionate commitment to parliaments were not confined to members of the Commons. They should be read not as the creed of a party seeking more power, but as a shared hope and anxiety of men living in a period of instability and change which they could not conceptualize or verbalize in the paradigms of custom that dominated their values.[78] Ironically, it was revolution that enabled the re-establishment of the traditional polity they desired – a renewed traditional partnership only made possible by an altered political culture.

[78] Cf. above, ch. 2, pp. 117–20.

CHAPTER NINE

Re-writing Sir Robert Cotton: politics and history in early Stuart England

I

When I first encountered him over twenty years ago, Sir Robert Cotton proved as useful to me as he had to many of his contemporaries. I was interested in exploring the interrelationship of scholarship and politics in early modern England, and in particular in investigating how study of the past and political experience shaped each other in an age that venerated custom and antiquity. For the twentieth-century historian, as for the Jacobean and Caroline antiquary and politician, all roads led to Sir Robert Cotton's library, the unique repository of precedents used by scholars, English and continental, and, as much, by men of affairs. Cotton and his library became for me the focus of a study which was intended to illuminate what were then (and in some sense remain) dark corners of the history of early Stuart England: historical scholarship and its relationship to continental humanism, circles of patronage, court and parliamentary politics, attitudes and ideological tensions and differences.[1]

Some reviewers, quite justifiably, commented that as a consequence Cotton himself remained in the shadows and criticized my study for neglecting key aspects of Sir Robert's life or for eschewing a more straightforward biographical approach.[2] Some (curiously in one or two cases the same reviewers) doubted whether Cotton was of any particular importance as a historian, political figure or thinker and wondered whether my claims for him to be taken more seriously did not surpass the evidence to sustain them.[3] Certainly there is a tendency natural among scholars (and especially enthusiastic young scholars) to exaggerate the importance of their subject. In this case, however, I would rather plead guilty to failing to do Cotton justice than concur with the view that

---

[1] K. Sharpe, *Sir Robert Cotton 1586–1631: History and Politics in Early Modern England* (Oxford, 1979).
[2] B. Worden, 'Unmatched Antiquary', *London Review of Books* (21 Feb. 1980), 22; J. P. Kenyon, 'Antiquarian at Court', *Times Lit. Supp.* (16 May 1980), 563; F. Levy, *Amer. Hist. Rev.*, 86 (1981), 127.
[3] Kenyon, 'Antiquarian at Court'; C. Holmes, *Hist. Journl.*, 24 (1981), 1026; see below, p. 333.

he did not, or does not, merit study. For Cotton proved to be of the first importance to early modern history and historiography. In my own case (and perhaps others') he led to the fundamental questioning of prevailing orthodoxies about, and towards a reconfiguration of, early seventeenth-century politics – a development that came to be known as 'revisionism'.[4] And, beyond, he and his circle pointed me to other investigations of the politics of scholarship and the broader culture of politics, which I am continuing, and to a more nuanced understanding of the political valence of all literary and historical texts in Renaissance England.[5]

Indeed since 1979 the whole landscape of the political and intellectual (I would now prefer the term cultural) history of early modern England has been redrawn – both by theory and by empirical research. The revisionists' emphasis on court faction and consensus over crown-parliament conflict and ideological fissure has itself been revised;[6] new historicism has elucidated the interrelationship of all writing and structures of authority and power;[7] and reader-response criticism and the history of the book have helpfully complicated, historicized and so politicized the very acts of reading and writing which we used to take as 'natural' activities unchanging through the centuries.[8] But, if our understanding of the broader contexts of early Stuart scholarship and politics has been revolutionized, Cotton, who was a central figure in those worlds, has largely been left behind. Though Professor Fritz Levy quite appropriately commented in 1980 that the 'absence of a full biography [of Cotton] is astonishing', no scholar has come forward to attempt it, or even to take up the many loose threads left dangling from my own study.[9]

---

[4] See K. Sharpe ed., *Faction and Parliament: Essays on Early Stuart History* (Oxford, 1978) and 'Revisionism Revisited' (preface to 2nd edn, 1985); also see C. Russell, *Parliaments and English Politics 1621–1629* (Oxford, 1979), 8, n. 1.

[5] K. Sharpe, *Politics and Ideas in Early Stuart England* (1989); K. Sharpe and S. Zwicker eds., *Politics of Discourse: the Literature and History of Seventeenth-Century England* (Berkeley, Los Angeles and London, 1987); K. Sharpe and P. Lake eds., *Culture and Politics in Early Stuart England* (Houndmills and Stanford, 1994).

[6] See most importantly R. Cust and A. Hughes eds., *Conflict in Early Stuart England* (1989), and D. Hirst, 'The Place of Principle', *Past and Present*, 92 (1981), 79–99.

[7] The most obvious examples are Stephen Greenblatt, *Renaissance Self-Fashioning* (Chicago, 1980); Greenblatt ed., *The Forms of Power and Power of Forms in the Renaissance* (Norman, Okla., 1982); L. Montrose, 'A Poetics of Renaissance Culture', *Criticism*, 23 (1981), 349–59; J. Goldberg, *James I and the Politics of Literature* (Baltimore and London, 1983).

[8] See E. Freund, *The Return of the Reader: Reader-Response Criticism* (New York, 1987); R. Darnton, 'What is the History of Books?', *Daedalus*, 111 (1982), 65–83; R. Chartier, *The Cultural Uses of Print in Early Modern France* (Princeton, 1989); L. Jardine and A. Grafton, '"Studied for Action": How Gabriel Harvey read his Livy', *Past and Present*, 129 (1990), 30–78.

[9] *Amer. Hist. Rev.*, 86 (1981), 127.

Of course, the notable, and excellent, exception is Dr Colin Tite, who was embarking on a thorough re-examination of the Cotton manuscripts even as my *Sir Robert* went to press.[10] In a series of important articles and now in his Panizzi Lectures he has added immensely to our knowledge of the collection, its creation, development and history.[11] And his work has not only served as the basis of a major exhibition of Cotton manuscripts in the British Library; it has stimulated a whole series of studies on Cotton's collections, and (to a lesser extent) writings and life.[12] The publication of such new research prompts us again to take stock of Sir Robert Cotton and his library and to re-evaluate their importance in the (newly reconfigured) context of early modern scholarship and politics.

II

One of the most important scholarly advances has been the beginnings of a historical reconstitution of the Cottonian collection. For all too long, though its deficiencies were glaringly obvious to librarians and manuscript scholars, the catalogue of the Cotton manuscripts has been treated as though it were a reasonably reliable guide to the manuscripts collected by Sir Robert Cotton. Further research has demonstrated in a number of ways just how far that is from the truth. Colin Tite has calculated that as a result of Cotton's generous lending and careless recording of loans, as many as one-tenth of his manuscripts strayed in his lifetime. He has found manuscripts with marks of Cotton's ownership in the Bodleian, the Royal Library (now the Royal MSS in the British Library) and Archbishop Ussher's manuscripts in Dublin.[13] Several Harleian Manuscripts (105, 513, 525, 547) have Cotton's name on the first folio; a catalogue of charters in Add. MS 5161 bears his hand and other manuscripts written by him and now in other repositories (his notes on Chancery, for example) were likely to have once resided, in some copy, in his own collection.[14]

---

[10] C. G. C. Tite, 'The Early Catalogues of the Cottonian Library', *British Library Journal*, 6 (1980), 144–57.

[11] See C. G. C. Tite, '"Lost or Stolen or Strayed": a Survey of Manuscripts Formerly in the Cotton Library', *British Library Journal*, 18 (1992), 107–47, reprinted in C. Wright ed., *Sir Robert Cotton as Collector* (British Museum, 1996), 226–306, and *The Manuscript Library of Sir Robert Cotton*, 9th Panizzi Lectures, 1993 (1994). I am grateful to Colin Tite for his generosity in allowing me to read these important lectures in advance of publication and for other advice.

[12] *British Library Journal*, 18 (1992), passim.

[13] Tite, '"Lost or Stolen or Strayed"', 268–70; and *The Manuscript Library of Sir Robert Cotton*, 1–39, esp. 15.   [14] BL Add. MSS 5161, ff. 1–8; 36106; Harl. MS 6018, f. 150.

Yet, if the current Cottonian collection is missing large numbers of manuscripts once owned by Sir Robert, it undoubtedly includes many which came into the library after his death. Sir William Dugdale contributed books to the collection while he was its custodian during the civil war and Commonwealth period.[15] Cotton's and Sir Simonds D'Ewes's charters were confused when the two libraries shared a home in the early eighteenth century; some manuscripts from the Royal Library strayed into the Cotton collection when both were housed in Ashburnham House; forty-four volumes of Thomas Rymer's manuscripts were placed in the Cottonian library in 1715.[16] Other manuscripts appear to have entered the library after the end of the seventeenth century from unknown sources: Caligula A. XVII, XVIII and E. XIII, for example, do not appear in Thomas Smith's catalogue of 1696, nor do Claudius C. XII, Nero E. VIII, Galba A. XX–XXI, E. XIII, Otho E. XIV, Vespasian A. XXIV, Vespasian D. XXIII–XXVIII, Titus F. XIV or Faustina A. X.[17] Examination of these manuscripts shows they bear no marks of Cotton's ownership; others listed in Smith's catalogue which bear no traces of Cotton's ownership (Otho C. XV, D. X, Vitellius F. XVII, Titus C. XI, for instance), but do have Thomas Cotton's inscription (Julius D. IX, Tiberius C. XII, D. XXII) suggest at least that they may have been acquired later.

Fortunately, we do not have to depend solely upon the printed catalogues of Cotton's library. Scholars have drawn valuable attention to the manuscript listings drawn up in, and shortly after, Cotton's lifetime, which add much to our knowledge of the development of the collection and which deserve to be edited and better known. Unfortunately, the exact status of these listings, even after Colin Tite's thorough examination, remains unclear.[18] In the case of the only list drawn up in Cotton's lifetime, the so-called catalogue of 1621 (Harleian MS 6018), there are many reasons for thinking that it was never completed, and may not even have been intended as a full inventory of the collection. Harleian 6018 lists only 413 manuscripts, well less than half the 958 manuscripts in the Cottonian collection in 1731, at the time of the fire at Ashburnham House; even allowing for Sir Robert's later acquisitions and gifts to or strays from the library after his death, we are left with the strong suspicion that Harleian 6018 was far from complete. It is confirmed by Cotton's own promise to Bishop Ussher in 1622 that he would send him

---

[15] Tite, '"Lost or Stolen or Strayed"', 276.   [16] Ibid., 283; *Cal. Treas. Books*, XIX (1957), 642.

[17] I would like to thank Godfrey Davis for sharing with me his research on Cotton manuscripts.

[18] Tite, 'Early Catalogues'; Sharpe, *Sir Robert Cotton*, 68–73.

a catalogue of his manuscripts when it was drawn up.[19] This was not ready by 1626 when Dr Bainbridge told Ussher that Cotton's books were 'not yet ordered in a catalogue' and evidently remained unfinished at his death when the Privy Council required a catalogue.[20]

Just as important as the deficiencies in any contemporary lists, there is more than the 'possibility' (as it is considered by Colin Tite) that 'there were manuscripts in the library that were not incorporated into it'.[21] Faustina C. I, for example, has notes in Sir Robert's hand but does not appear in the lists of 1621, 1635, 1654 nor any catalogue before 1696; Nero C. VIII, a wardrobe book collated by Cotton, does not appear in a list until 1696; Titus F. IV, which I suggested may have been Cotton's own parliamentary diary, is listed neither in 1621 nor 1635 but appears on Cotton's loan list in the same manuscript as the 1621 catalogue.[22] In general it would appear that Cotton's estate and financial papers were not incorporated into his library, and may even have remained in his house at Conington.[23] And in London, it may well be that loose papers in the process of arrangement and binding may not have been fully incorporated into the library, or given any classification or call mark.

In 1638 Sir William Dugdale informed his friend Nathaniel Johnstone: 'Sir Thomas [Cotton] told me he had two large bales of ancient papers of state and other things . . . which had never been opened since they were so packed by his father.'[24] These may have been included among the volumes of manuscripts on England's relations with Rome (Vitellius B.), with Spain (Vespasian C. I–XII), with Flanders (Galba B.) and the Netherlands (Galba C–E) which Dugdale compiled from Cotton papers, which did not appear in the lists of 1621 or 1635. According to W. Hamper, his biographer, Dugdale sorted papers of Wolsey, Cromwell, Burleigh and Walsingham, letters of Mary Queen of Scots and the Duke of Norfolk 'methodically both as to time and other-wise and caused them to be bound up with clasps and Sir Thomas Cotton's arms'.[25] Though almost certainly in Sir Robert Cotton's pos-session before his death, these more than eighty volumes may have entered the library proper only after a process of compilation and editing by another. If there are other such instances, we not only begin to see how the library apparently 'grew' between Cotton's death and

---

[19] R. Parr, *The Life of James Ussher . . . with a Collection of 300 Letters* (1686), 79.
[20] Ibid., 230; PRO PC 2/41, p. 91.   [21] Tite, '"Lost or Stolen or Strayed"', 281.
[22] Sharpe, *Sir Robert Cotton*, appendix, 251–2; BL Harl. MS 6018, ff. 159, 164v.
[23] Some are now in Huntingdonshire RO, Conington Papers, 2B Steeple Gidding Papers, Conington Papers Rental Estate books, Charters Box 14, Conington Lincoln diocese papers. See below, pp. 326–7.   [24] *Hist. MSS. Comm., 6th Report App.*, 453.
[25] W. Hamper, *The Life, Diary and Correspondence of Sir William Dugdale* (1827), 9.

Smith's catalogue; we also begin to appreciate how complex is the question of what constituted the Cottonian collection during Cotton's lifetime.

The later history of the library only compounds the problem. We know very little of what happened to the collection during the 1640s and 1650s, though there is evidence of gifts enhancing it: Titus C. XVI and XVII, for example, were given by Sir Edward Walker after 1645. In 1650 the library was evacuated to Stratton, Bedfordshire, but it is not clear when it returned to Cotton House. John Selden, a parliamentarian friend of the Cottons, protected the collection from plunder and he, Dugdale, Dodsworth and other scholars continued to work there. Figures of importance in the affairs of the Commonwealth, the Earl of Manchester and Bulstrode Whitelocke, borrowed from the collection, but there are no very substantial loan lists for this period, nor do we know the circumstances that led to the compilation of two more catalogues of the manuscripts in the 1650s.[26] Because we lack this information and because there has been no systematic comparison between the lists of 1621, *circa* 1635 and 1656/7, we have little sense of what manuscripts were lost or lent and not returned during these crucial decades or where to look for them among the collections of borrowers.[27]

If the library was less used during the troubled years of civil war, the Restoration and the revival of a political culture in which disputes were solved by precedent rather than violence placed the Cottonian library again at the centre of the overlapping circles of scholarship and politics. Elizabeth Teviotdale's inventory of the large numbers and arrangement of catalogues of Cotton's manuscripts in private hands, and in the hands of men like Samuel Pepys, Thomas Gale, High Master of St Paul's, William Petyt, Edward Stillingfleet, Bishop of Worcester, and William Sancroft, underlines the need for a thorough investigation of the use made of the Cottonian manuscripts in the scholarly and political polemics of the Augustan age.[28] Not least such an investigation, starting with the collections of those who had catalogues of the Cottonian library, might well unearth items that went missing between the 1650s and

---

[26] BL Harl. MS 6018, ff. 178, 182, 190; Cotton MS App. XLV, art. 13.

[27] To add examples, Claudius C. VII is found in no catalogue before 1654, Otho B. VI appears in the 1621 list but not 1654, Otho A. XVIII is on a 1635 list but has disappeared by 1654; Vitellius B. I disappears from view in the 1656 catalogue.

[28] That it remained a controversial collection is evident from the remark of Cotton's grandson in 1687, that the time was not appropriate for a catalogue because the Library contained much 'very cross to the Romish interest': Tite, *The Manuscript Library of Sir Robert Cotton*, 71; E. Teviotdale, 'Some Classified Catalogues of the Cottonian Library' in Wright, *Sir Robert Cotton as Collector*, 194–207.

Smith's catalogue of 1696 (such as Nero E. VIII, Tiberius B. VII and Vitellius B. I which were recorded in 1654, but had disappeared by 1656/7).

If the fate of the Cotton manuscripts during the period from Sir Robert's death to the issue of the first published catalogue remains vague and uncertain, we might be tempted to think their subsequent history has been a straightforward, albeit a tragic, one. We know that in 1700 Cotton's grandson bequeathed the collection to the nation and that in 1731 a fire at Ashburnham House consumed a large number of the treasures of the Cotton (and Royal) collection. But, as we now see, the events and their consequences are far from straightforward and add yet a further set of complications to our attempts at a reconstitution of the Cottonian manuscripts. From the very beginning there was significant disagreement about the nature and extent of the damage. A report was prepared for the parliamentary committee investigating the fire by Rev. William Whiston, Clerk of the Records in the Chapter House, Westminster, and by David Casley, deputy librarian of the Cotton library. According to a schedule dated 29 January 1732 in the Antrobus Papers, of the 958 manuscripts in the library 120 were deemed to have been entirely burnt, and 114 were listed as defective.[29] Whiston, however, gave the figures slightly more optimistically – as 114 and 98 respectively; by 1777 those lost had been reduced to 114 in a catalogue of that year.[30]

Andrew Prescott's essay now makes startlingly clear what lay behind these seemingly trivial discrepancies. For, as he shows, where manuscripts were concerned, 'destruction' is a matter of judgement and of history and technology. Emergency conservation and subsequent restoration work have ultimately reduced the list of manuscripts destroyed to only thirteen; but the history of these processes also revolutionized the nature and organization of Sir Robert Cotton's library.

Working under the constraints of time – not least to prevent mould further damaging manuscripts soaked in the water used to douse the fire – Whiston broke up many manuscripts and had them rebound. As Prescott warns us, it has become almost routine to assume that, where the leaves of a particular manuscript are out of sequence, this is due to interference by Sir Robert Cotton. In fact, it is just as likely that disordered collations of this sort are the result of the efforts of Whiston and

[29] Cambridgeshire RO, Antrobus MSS.
[30] A. Prescott, '"Their Present Miserable State of Cremation": the Restoration of the Cotton Library', in Wright, *Sir Robert Cotton as Collector*, 392; *A Catalogue of the Manuscripts in the Cottonian Library* (1777).

his colleagues to preserve what they could of Cotton's collection.[31] Whiston and his assistants placed 'a very great gulf between the modern user of the Cotton library and the library as it existed before the fire'.[32] Later efforts only widened this gulf. The survival of loose sheets, the movement of items for restoration work and new experiments led to future confusions – reordering, reconstruction – and indeed to losses as well as gains. Whilst scholars are greatly indebted to Sir Frederic Madden for his indefatigable labours in identifying, flattening and binding thousands of loose leaves, there is no doubt that in some cases his interpretations and reconstructions bore no relation to the original Cottonian compilation.[33] Albeit in the name of scholarship, the rear-rangements of Sir Robert's manuscripts have been on a scale greater than his own separations and compilations of the medieval documents that came into his hands.

What all these complications point to is the urgent need now for a full and thorough re-examination of the Cottonian library: an edition and careful comparison of the various 'catalogues' or lists of the collection from 1621 to 1696; a search of the archives (where they still exist) of those listed as borrowing from the collection for manuscripts with marks of Cotton ownership; a reinvestigation of volumes we know to have been restored either by Whiston or Madden, using ultra-violet light and other techniques not available to them; a search for transcripts of burnt Cotton manuscripts made by Cotton's contemporaries (such as Ralph Starkey who copied many) and later users of the library (like Selden and Dugdale) as was recommended after the fire at Ashburnham House;[34] in fine, a study of each individual manuscript (in conjunction with loan lists and catalogues) for evidence of provenance, ownership marks, fire damage and compilation. The results would not only lead to the cata-logue raisonné, the need for which was identified in 1732, and so provide a proper entrée to the collection for scholars;[35] they would also add inval-uable chapters to the history of scholarship and politics in Cotton's day and beyond.

---

[31] Prescott, '"Their Present Miserable State of Cremation"', 393–5. [32] Ibid., 395.
[33] Ibid., 429.
[34] Cambs. RO, Antrobus MSS, Memo on Cotton Library. For Starkey, see C. E. Wright, *Fontes Harleiani* (1972), q.v. See too H. Love, *Scribal Publication in Seventeenth-Century England* (Oxford, 1993), 86–7. Harold Love's study has much to contribute to an understanding of Cotton's library and the importance of Cotton's writings. Colin Tite is planning an edition of the loans lists.
[35] Antrobus MSS, Memo.

III

The Cottonian collection, as we have always known, was never the manuscripts alone.[36] But it is only recent work that is enabling us to evaluate
the importance of Cotton's books, and more particularly his stones and
monuments, coins and medals and seals in the collection, for the historical scholarship of his contemporaries and of our own age. In 1979, after
some investigation, I was forced to conclude that Cotton's printed books
remained a mystery.[37] Colin Tite now offers the fascinating hypothesis
that the list of 575 titles in Add. MS 35213 may be a list of an earlier collector's books acquired by Cotton; and whilst the case is by no means
concluded, it certainly provides a list of items to be searched for evidence
of Cotton's ownership when they are found in the collections of his
known contemporaries.[38]

Most welcome is the attention now being paid to the stones, medals and
coins. Cotton probably attributed almost as much importance to physical
artefacts as to manuscripts. Though Camden made famous the fruits of
his and Cotton's tour of Hadrian's Wall and the stones and objects found
and excavated, it is not often enough noted that Cotton continued to seek
out such artefacts throughout his lifetime: in 1622 he was still actually
tracking down stones;[39] in 1629 John Barkham was endeavouring to obtain
statues on his behalf.[40] Other agents sent Cotton medals from Paris and
Roman coins from Dublin;[41] he evidently gathered the coins of all the
Roman emperors from Pompey to Mauritius, the coins of all kings of
England from the Saxons to Charles I, and the seals of monarchs from
Edward the Confessor to Richard II as well as 'divers medals' of the
Asians and Egyptians.[42] Like the manuscripts, these were intended for *use*.
Cotton drew diagrams of artefacts as well as copying inscriptions.[43] As
well as Camden and Speed, Cotton and his co-author of the
'Topographical Description of England' referred to the stones and coins
for elucidation of the history of the realm.[44] When in *Nero Cæsar*, Cotton's
friend and fellow antiquary Edmund Bolton pleaded for greater study and
use of coins in recalling the great deeds of the past, it is most likely that
his sense of their value derived from Cotton's finds and collection.[45]

---

[36] Cf. Sharpe, *Sir Robert Cotton*, 56–7, 66–8.   [37] Ibid., 57.

[38] C. G. C. Tite, 'A Catalogue of Sir Robert Cotton's Printed Books?', *British Library Journal*, 17
(1991), 1–11, reprinted in Wright, *Sir Robert Cotton as Collector*, 183–93.

[39] BL Cotton MS Julius F. VI, f. 314: Roger Dodsworth to Cotton.

[40] BL Cotton MS Julius C. III, ff. 15, 16.   [41] Ibid., f. 26 (William Bold); f. 388 (James Ware).

[42] BL Add. MS 35213, f. 42.   [43] See BL Cotton MS Julius C. IX, f. 101.

[44] BL Sloane MS 241, ff. 27ᵛ, 68ᵛ; W. Camden, *Britannia* (1610), 88; J. Speed, *History of Great Britaine*
(1614), 322, 593; Sharpe, *Sir Robert Cotton*, 38.

[45] E. Bolton, *Nero Cæsar, or Monarchie Depraued* (1627), 14–15. See too Bodl. MS Ashmole 1149, f. 113.

Glenys Davies, David McKitterick and Gay van der Meer have greatly helped us to see how important the stones and coins were. Davies's descriptive catalogue of Cotton's stones vividly underlines the unique contribution they made to an appreciation of British antiquity and may suggest a vital link, even if one not pursued by the antiquaries themselves, between such scholarship and the beginning of an aesthetic interest in collecting Roman statuary.[46] We are left to ponder whether the location of Cotton's stones – at his Huntingdonshire seat in Conington, rather than London – did not limit their effecting a historical and aesthetic revolution. McKitterick has no doubt that the results of Cotton's finds, especially along Hadrian's Wall, 'were as dramatic as any in the history of British archaeology' and fascinatingly suggests how Cotton's stones may even have come to inform Ben Jonson and Inigo Jones's court masques.[47] Van der Meer's discovery of an inventory by Nicolas Claude Fabri de Peiresc of Cotton's Anglo-Saxon coins not only gives a sense of what has gone missing from the collections in material artefacts as well as manuscripts (how many coins Cotton had that were unknown to Speed), but opens the exciting prospect of further research enabling a reconstitution of the original collection – not least through identifying lists in Cotton's manuscripts as catalogues of his own holdings.[48] As more becomes known about Cotton's cabinet, his rarities (we should not forget his excitement about the excavation of a fossilized fish)[49] and his monuments, we may understand better how the various elements of the Cottonian collection complemented – and even were acquired to complement – each other, to provide a new range of material for the study of the British past.

IV

The contents of the collection, however, are only one part of the story. The other is Cotton's treatment of, we might even more generally say his relationship to, his collection. And here, I would argue, work on the Cottonian collection has yet to ask the most interesting questions raised by library scholars and historians of the book. Though some work has

---

[46] Arundel provides an obvious link; see below, pp. 322–3.

[47] D. McKitterick, 'From Camden to Cambridge: Sir Robert Cotton's Roman Inscriptions, and their Subsequent History', in Wright, *Sir Robert Cotton as Collector*, 105–28.

[48] G. van der Meer, 'An Early Seventeenth-Century Inventory of Cotton's Anglo-Saxon Coins', in Wright, *Sir Robert Cotton as Collector*, 168–82.

[49] G. Keynes ed., *The Letters of Sir Thomas Browne* (1941), 337; Sir W. Dugdale, *The History of Imbanking and Drayning* (1772), 172–3.

been done on listing the various catalogues of Cotton's manuscripts, there has been no satisfactory analysis of them: of what they show about how Cotton described (or remembered) his books, why he first listed them in numerical sequence, then adopted the famous imperial press-marks, and how the latter related to the former.[50] Similarly, although the loan lists have been cited as evidence of who consulted the collection (and to a limited extent how they used the manuscripts they borrowed), scholars have not seen their importance for Sir Robert Cotton himself. How he described and remembered books he loaned (perhaps especially when he could not recall the name of the borrower) may tell us much about how he viewed the importance of particular manuscripts – and items within bound volumes – as well as how he acquired them. 'The book of St Albans having the history in pictures' not only reminds us that we each have individual mental devices for recalling items, it may indicate Cotton's sense of the importance of the illustrations.[51] His large thick book of precedents in ecclesiastical courts, Cotton remembered particularly as 'of good use'.[52] Though he did not remember the name of the borrower of a volume on the history of religious orders, he did recall that 'it had at the end of it the prophecy of John of Bridlington and somebody borrowed it off me for this prophecy, I remember'.[53] Some books Cotton identified in terms of their source rather than subject – a book he had of 'Mr Whitt the scrivener', a volume that 'was the Earl of Salisbury's book'; a book given by Mr Griffith, parson of Hinckley.[54] Interestingly Cotton described several of his books in terms of their bindings. Evidently he himself deployed a variety of different materials and colours – and it would be worth pursuing how the choice of cloth, leather, vellum or velvet might speak to his valuation of a manuscript, or whether the colour related in any way to manuscripts that he arranged or intended to consult together.[55] If there is any consistency to the loan lists, we may also deduce that Cotton bound only some of his manuscripts with clasps and/or with his arms; and regarded some loose papers as obviously fit for binding in a collection at the time of lending

[50] Though Tite's suggestion that the imperial pressmarks followed Charles I's purchase of Titian's Caesars is an interesting one: *The Manuscript Library of Sir Robert Cotton*, 86.
[51] BL Harl. MS 6018, f. 154.   [52] Ibid., f. 159.
[53] Ibid., f. 174; cf. f. 160, 'Books lent, I know not to who'.
[54] Ibid., ff. 148ᵛ, 158ᵛ; cf. ff. 154, 156, 162, 174, 176. On Griffith, see now R. Ovenden, 'Jaspar Gryffyth and his Books', *British Library Journal*, 20 (1994), 107–39, which appeared after my essay was written.
[55] See, for example, Harl. MS 6018, ff. 157, 170, 174. When he lists a book as 'new bound', Cotton seldom mentions its colour.

them.[56] Examination of a number of the manuscripts in the light of Cotton's brief descriptions of content, condition and binding might well open further avenues into his priorities and values as a collector. One obvious area for fruitful study is the little-known engravings that form the title-pages of some volumes: Nero B. II and Galba B. IV (by William Hole), Cleopatra E. I–III (by Richard Elstrack), Cleopatra F. I–II (by K. Sichen), Vespasian C. II, Julius C. V, Tiberius B. I (anonymous). (There is also an anonymous drawing in Vespasian C. XII.)[57] Why did Cotton privilege these manuscripts with the charge of engraved title plates? Did he intend to publish them? What may we learn from Colin Tite's obser-vation that in binding Cotton made no effort to preserve recently written marginalia?[58] Twentieth-century scholars have fortunately abandoned the anachronistic judgements of earlier bibliographers who condemned Cotton (and his contemporaries) for their treatment of manuscripts: dividing originals, disrespecting provenance, rebinding separates, writing on documents. But as yet they have made little study of how we might use such physical practices as evidence of attitudes to the manu-scripts – and indeed to affairs outside the world of books. For in some cases it seems obvious that a volume Sir Robert compiled can be traced to a particular moment, patron or need. The collection on heralds and arms (Titus C. I), for example, may well be related to Cotton's advising the Earl of Northampton when the latter was appointed a commissioner for the office of Earl Marshal;[59] Cotton's sense that his papers on England's relations with Spain might make 'a great book' may well have been prompted by his own role in the negotiations for a Spanish mar-riage.[60] More research might fruitfully tie other Cotton collections, their organization, condition and his description of them, to particular moments.

Most surprisingly, there has been no systematic investigation of Cotton's marks of ownership (permanent or temporary) or reading in the manuscripts in his library, or those once owned by him but now else-where. We are just beginning to realize how serious is this neglect. Historians of the book have not only drawn our attention to the need to situate historically the activity of 'reading' – aloud or silent, in public or

---

[56] Harl. MS 6018, ff. 152ᵛ, 174ᵛ; ff. 148, 150, 153, 154v, 159, 161, 162 (arms), 148, 163, 176 (clasps).

[57] I owe my knowledge of these engravings to Godfrey Davis.

[58] Tite, *The Manuscript Library of Sir Robert Cotton*, 48.

[59] BL Cotton MS Titus C. I, f. 140 and passim; Sharpe, *Sir Robert Cotton*, 26; BL Add. MS 25247, f. 46.

[60] Harl. MS 6018, f. 174ᵛ; Cotton loaned these to Secretary Sir Ralph Winwood who held the office from 1614 to 1617. For Cotton's role in negotiations with Spain, see Sharpe, *Sir Robert Cotton*, 131–3.

private, as 'reader' or listener; they are also beginning to study marks such as marginalia, interlinings, even casual scribblings and ephemera of a domestic or personal nature in books as evidence of engagement with the text: by agreement, dispute, emphasis, degree of interest.[61] In cases where the documentation is rich, as with Gabriel Harvey's copy of Livy, brilliant exegesis has enabled historians to show us how 'Livy's early Rome change[d] contours, shadows and colours as Harvey inspected [it] . . . on successive occasions', and how readings were determined by the needs of patrons and moments.[62] The Cottonian collection offers a rich opportunity for the application of these approaches to early modern manuscripts as well as printed books. Careful study of hand, ink and annotations in the context of what we know about the manuscript, Cotton's acquisition and/or compilation, his description (or lending) of the item, and of his scholarly and political activities might offer invaluable insights into Cotton's readings and possibly re-readings and their relationship in his activities and values. Like divisions, compilations and bindings, marks are evidence that the acquisition, ownership and reading of books or manuscripts expressed values; that they were, it is not too much to say, ideological practices.

So was lending itself. Cotton's generosity in lending his books of manuscripts is of course well known. Yet it has largely been studied in the context of losses from the library rather than in terms of Cotton's and his contemporaries' attitudes to manuscripts – or ideas. It is not too simple a question to ask why Sir Robert was willing to lend the manuscripts that he had so painstakingly, and expensively, garnered – especially to men whom, as in some cases, he did not know.[63] After a time it must have been apparent to him that, as a consequence of his openness, losses were incurred but the loan lists indicate no diminution in the ranks of those permitted to borrow.[64] Even some of Cotton's contemporaries appeared to be surprised at the freedom with which he lent, surprised – as Bolton puts it – at his not exploiting the monopoly that he had.[65] Did

---

[61] Prof. Steven Zwicker is currently writing a book on reading practices in early modern England. I am enormously grateful to him for stimulating discussions on this subject as I am also to Heidi Brayman, who is completing an important and impressive Ph.D. thesis on Renaissance reading, and Bill Sherman who is soon publishing his case study of John Dee's marginalia. (See now H. Brayman Hackel, 'Impressions from a Scribbling Age: Recovering the Reading Practices of Renaissance England' (Ph.D. thesis, Columbia University, 1995) and W. H. Sherman, *John Dee: the Politics of Reading and Writing in the English Renaissance* (Amherst, Mass., 1995).)

[62] Jardine and Grafton, '"Studied for Action"', 66.

[63] E.g., BL Cotton MS Julius C. III, ff. 3 (Simon Archer), 5 (Edmond Ashfield), 171 (John Everard).

[64] Ibid., f. 30.

[65] And the number of signed receipts for books borrowed does not increase over time.

Cotton see himself as providing a service, supplying privately a resource nowhere else available when his and others' petition for a public library came to naught.[66] Was the collection compiled as his own research base – not for the 'pure' pursuit of scholarship but to equip him to rise to the ranks of adviser to magnate and MP, minister and monarch – and as a stock he could also lend, the interest being his advancement?

The answer to such questions, and to the larger issue of the importance of Cotton's library to his age, awaits the large study, never even attempted in miniature, of how borrowers *used* the manuscripts for their own purposes: scholarly, personal and political. Why, for example, did John Selden borrow, as well as medieval and legal manuscripts, the *Sententiae* of Guicciardini and how did his reading of that inform his own writings?[67] What might Arundel have read in the book on the Earl Marshal's office while he was in the Tower?[68] How did Dudley's book of accounts of Henry VII's reign affect Treasurer Cranfield's practices or reforms?[69] For what entertainments did Inigo Jones use the books of triumphs he borrowed?[70] A re-examination of the works, both written and performed, of Cotton's contemporaries (and successors) in the light of what they borrowed from him, and when, and how they deployed it, would not only add in general invaluable chapters to the history of Renaissance reading practices. It would enable us to see how Cotton's manuscripts performed and were deployed differently in a myriad of contexts, how scholarly research and politics interacted in a number of careers and moments.[71]

For this moment, it is time for us to reconsider how they interacted in Sir Robert Cotton himself.

v

In 1979, I made a number of claims for Cotton's importance in the historical scholarship of his day, some of which have proved to be contentious. One was the argument that Sir Robert Cotton arrived at an understanding of the nature of the knight's fee and of the feudal system before Sir Henry Spelman 'discovered' feudalism and published his findings in his *Archaeologus* of 1626. The argument had broader implications: if Cotton and his fellow antiquaries arrived at an understanding of

---

[66] Sharpe, *Sir Robert Cotton*, 27–8.   [67] Harl. MS 6018, f. 147, '2 February 1622'.
[68] Ibid., ff. 149–149v.   [69] Ibid., f. 150.   [70] Ibid., f. 179v.
[71] For instance, the King's goldsmith, Mr Williams, borrowed volumes on Welsh law and the life of St Dunstan; the parson of Conington, Mr Williamson, had Sir Henry Cobham's letters (ibid., ff. 158ᵛ, 160).

feudal tenures and the changes effected by the Norman Conquest, then we must question J. G. A. Pocock's thesis that early Stuart historical and legal thought was restricted by ignorance of such historical developments, and characterized by an insular belief in the unbroken continuity of immemorial English customs, as asserted by Sir Edward Coke.[72] If Cotton and others were aware of what English legal developments owed to the French, then Coke becomes less the paradigm of a universally held view, rather the forceful spokesman for a selective view of the past, a polemical argument that owed more to contemporary Stuart political debate than historical knowledge of the medieval past.[73]

Not least because the implications of these suggestions were wide reaching, the debate about the antiquaries' understanding of feudalism has continued. In 1979, quite independently in a study of natural rights theories, Richard Tuck questioned *The Ancient Constitution* and, observing that practising lawyers and members of the Society of Antiquaries were quite able to contemplate historical change in English law, argued that 'the real puzzle is why men like Sir Edward Coke did not'.[74] Others, notably Hans Pawlisch, published studies that raised doubts about the Pocock thesis.[75]

In 1987, Professor Pocock himself returned to the theme, to what he regarded as the efforts of his critics 'to transform a mentalité [of the ancient constitution] into a series of "moves"'.[76] Pocock acknowledged that early Stuart scholars knew of law outside their realm, including Roman civil law, and accepted too that in the light of Hans Pawlisch's findings he had exaggerated the insularity of Sir John Davies, Attorney General for Ireland. What he continued to doubt was the willingness of the English to apply this knowledge comparatively, to place indigenous customs and law in a broader historical and legal context: 'as a key to their past, the English knew of one law alone'.[77] And Pocock took the newly printed debates on the Petition of Right to sustain his point that Englishmen in 1628 still debated using the insular language of custom

---

[72] J. G. A. Pocock, *The Ancient Constitution and the Feudal Law: English Historical Thought in the Seventeenth Century* (Cambridge, 1957); cf. D. Kelley, 'History, English Law and the Renaissance', *Past and Present*, 65 (1974), 24–59.

[73] Sharpe, *Sir Robert Cotton*, 22–5; C. Brooks and K. Sharpe, 'History, English Law and the Renaissance', *Past and Present*, 72 (1976), 133–42; Kelley's reply, ibid., 143–6.

[74] R. Tuck, *Natural Rights Theories* (Cambridge, 1979), 83.

[75] H. S. Pawlisch, 'Sir John Davies, the Ancient Constitution and Civil Law', *Hist. Journ.*, 23 (1980), 689–702; Pawlisch, *Sir John Davies and the Conquest of Ireland* (Cambridge, 1985).

[76] J. G. A. Pocock, *The Ancient Constitution and the Feudal Law: a Reissue with a Retrospect* (Cambridge, 1987), 262. [77] Ibid., 282, 30.

and common law.[78] 'Defenders of the view that royal authority operated according to a plurality of leges terrae had no counter history to offer';[79] 'the common law still furnished the only historic past which could be visualized by those engaged in English government'.[80]

This, however, – possibly a recurring weakness of Pocock's methodology – is to take language at face value and out of context.[81] In 1628 all participants in debate were anxious to find a form of agreement. Charles I, no less than the proponents of the Petition of Right, believed in custom and common law. But he did not necessarily mean the same as all of them by it. He appears to have believed that prerogative actions outside the law had come to be part of the common law, obviating any need for a counter history or discourse to support his position. His father had clearly enunciated such a view. In the context, as he acknowledged, of fears that he intended to elevate civil law and alter the nature of government, James reasserted the divine origin of royal authority, comparing the king's prerogative to God's power of miracle. As God seldom intervened directly, preferring to govern through natural law, so in a settled state kings governed in accordance with the established forms and laws. Those who did not rule according to law, in such settled circumstances, were to be deemed tyrants. But, like God's power of miracle, the prerogative was a divinely given power that remained to kings for them to discharge their 'accompt to God'. As such James regarded it as a power that did not contest with common law but completed and fulfilled it; nevertheless his view had the potential to clash with the Cokeian doctrine of immemorial custom.[82]

The complexities of these positions have recently been clarified by Glenn Burgess's re-examination of the ancient constitution.[83] Burgess enables us to understand how, whilst James's speech expressed a tension or ambiguity in contemporary thought, it did not conflict with most ideas of English law, except as they were enunciated by Coke.[84] (And he suggests too that even in 1628 it was not Charles I's theory, but his articulation of it in an inappropriate time and context, that was chiefly at issue.)[85] For the most part, the languages of common law and civil law

---

[78] Ibid., 299–301; R. C. Johnson, M. Keeler and M. Cole eds., *Commons Debates, 1628* (4 vols., New Haven, 1977).   [79] Pocock, *Ancient Constitution*, 303.   [80] Ibid., 304.

[81] Cf. Sharpe, *Politics and Ideas*, 32–4.

[82] See James I's speech in J. P. Kenyon ed., *The Stuart Constitution* (Cambridge, 1966), 12; cf. F. Oakley, 'Jacobean Political Theology: the Absolute and Ordinary Powers of the King', *Journ. Hist. Ideas*, 19 (1968), 323–46.

[83] G. Burgess, *The Politics of the Ancient Constitution: an Introduction to English Political Thought 1603–1642* (Basingtoke, 1992).   [84] Ibid., 155, 158, 168.   [85] Ibid., 201.

were held together in the 'Jacobean consensus', which only later circumstances fractured.[86] Such a nuanced analysis may provide a helpful context for studying the developing ideas and politics of a number of early Stuart lawyers and antiquaries – including Cotton. What it is important to note here is that, revising Pocock, Burgess posits Coke as the exceptional figure of his age and identifies several lawyers – notably John Dodderidge – who saw the law as mutable, and a product of history as well as reason.[87] Dodderidge was a member of the Society of Antiquaries and with Cotton one of the joint petitioners to Queen Elizabeth for the erection of a public library.[88] His scholarly development, like Spelman's, may have owed much to the Society's discussions and debates. For, as Burgess reminds us, the Society of Antiquaries had come to an understanding of the historical fact of conquest in English society, and 'indeed it can be said that it was the growth of antiquarianism that led to the writing of recognizable histories of the law'.[89] In the intellectual world of those antiquarian debates and the facilities in Cotton's library, the insularity of Coke was not only exceptional; it was, rather than a *mentalité*, a choice – or 'carefully developed principle'.[90] Like the Brutus legend, the myth of the ancient constitution was articulated out of polemical strategy rather than scholarly ignorance.

Cotton's and other antiquaries' understanding of the Conquest and the *feudum* derived from their familiarity with the etymological scholarship of the continental humanists. In *Sir Robert Cotton*, I suggested that Cotton continued to be an important link between continental and English scholars, perhaps even after Camden's retirement from London to Chislehurst, and death in 1623. At least one reviewer countered that this was to overestimate Sir Robert who was only introduced to European circles by Camden and who always remained in the shadow of the older man.[91] This is not an unreasonable criticism. Cotton never published, like Camden, works that secured him an international audience. But here, as in English scholarship (and politics), his role as a facilitator should not be negated. Clearly Cotton's library was essential to European scholars such as Peiresc, De Thou, Fronto du Duc, André Duchesne, Pierre Dupuy, Lucas Holstenius, Janus Gruter, Franciscus Sweertius and others. Not least because the library was the hub where so many European and English scholarly roads intersected, Cotton may well have effected intro-

---

[86] Ibid., 199.   [87] Ibid., 40–2, 51 and ch. 2 passim.
[88] BL Cotton MS Faustina E. V, ff. 89–90.   [89] Burgess, *Politics of the Ancient Constitution*, 83, 59.
[90] Ibid., 81.
[91] F. Levy, *Amer. Hist. Rev.*, 86 (1981), 127. See the caveats in Sharpe, *Sir Robert Cotton*, 102.

ductions that bequeathed continental connections to the younger generation of scholars. Here much new research is needed in continental
archives, but there are already hints that when it is done Cotton's stature
is more likely to increase than diminish. Van der Meer's discovery in The
Hague of Peiresc's inventory of Cotton's Saxon coins indicates at least
that Cotton's collections may have been known in detail on the continent,
and other than just by scholarly hearsay.[92] If Colin Tite's identification is
correct, we also begin to obtain a sense of the high profile of continental scholarship in Cotton's library of printed books as early as 1595.
Under almost all the headed sheets on which book titles were pasted, we
find books published in Antwerp, Cologne, Frankfurt, Paris and Venice.[93]
In addition, we know that Peiresc and other continental scholars sent
Cotton books, including the *Historiae Normanorum Scriptores Antiqui*.[94] The
list of printed books Cotton lent to Selden in 1622 includes works in
French, Dutch, Italian and Portuguese, as well as Latin works published
on the continent.[95] Further research may well reveal Cotton's collection
to be of importance for printed continental works as well as for manuscripts. If, as Daniel Woolf maintains, in early Stuart England 'many less
well known historians were indebted to earlier and contemporary continental authors', it was also to the scholarship of the Society of
Antiquaries and Cotton's library that they were indebted.[96]

Cotton may have contributed more than the loan of manuscripts to
his continental contemporaries. There is the odd reference to his being
asked to write for a project, and it may be that pages by him or based on
his notes are contained within the works of Duchesne or Peiresc, as they
are in Speed or Ussher.[97] In one particular case, against the long-estab-
lished tradition, I argued that Cotton rather than Camden wrote the
history of Mary, Queen of Scots's reign which was forwarded to De
Thou for incorporation in his *Historia Sui Temporis*. It is rather surprising
that no one either challenged or developed the suggestion. I would now
add Thomas Leke's letter to Northampton, informing him that James
was anxious that Cotton progress with the history to be sent to De Thou,
which adds a point of confirmation.[98] Recently, however, Daniel Woolf

---

[92] See van der Meer, 'An Early Seventeenth-Century Inventory'; Peiresc advised Dupuy to secure
   a list of Cotton's manuscripts, J. P. Tamizey de Laroque ed., *Lettres de Peiresc* (7 vols., Paris,
   1888–98), I, 57.   [93] Tite, 'A Catalogue of Sir Robert Cotton's Printed Books?'
[94] Sharpe, *Sir Robert Cotton*, 58, 103. Duplicates were sent from France to Camden and Cotton: for
   those sent to Camden, see Bodl. MS Smith 89, f. 1.   [95] BL Harl. MS 6018, f. 147.
[96] D. Woolf, *The Idea of History in Early Stuart England* (Toronto and London, 1990), xii.
[97] See, e.g., Sharpe, *Sir Robert Cotton*, 97.
[98] BL Cotton MS Titus C. VI, f. 189; cf. Julius C. III, f. 59.

has filled out the story, using Peiresc's and De Thou's correspondence from the Bibliothèque Nationale. Whilst he confirms my story in outline, he is able to add the valuable information that Francis Bacon believed Cotton to be the author not only of the material sent to De Thou but also of the *Annales*, and that James ordered Cotton to correct the second part for publication, after Camden's death in 1625.[99] David McKitterick cites the royal warrant to publish the first part in 1615 issued to both 'our wellbeloved servants Sir Robert Cotton Knight and Baronett and William Camden Clarenceux one of our Kings of Arms'.[100] And Nigel Ramsay's discovery of Cotton's list of services to the crown, among which he includes compiling memoirs to be sent to De Thou, clinches the case.[101] So if what I thought a strong suggestion has become a certainty, we must not only wonder how much of what scholars persist in calling Camden's *Annales* was in fact written, drafted or corrected by Cotton, but also re-read the text with that possibility in mind.

The memoirs he sent to De Thou *may* have been Cotton's greatest written contribution to European scholarship. That they emerged from a royal need and directive sharply reminds us of a truism that still discomforts many scholars: that in early modern England at all points historical scholarship inhabited a world of authority, power and politics.[102]

VI

'The personal ownership of the past', writes Sir John Plumb, 'has always been a vital strand in the ideology of all ruling classes.'[103] It was especially so in early modern England when precedents were looked to both to reinforce views and resolve novel problems. Men studied history primarily for its use and application for contemporary affairs rather than, as we still often wish, to advance historical understanding. When Cotton and Dodderidge petitioned Queen Elizabeth to establish a library, they stressed the utility of history – and not merely as a rhetorical point. Edward I, they reminded the queen, had made use of historical records in establishing his claim to rule Scotland, as had Henry VIII in freeing the realm from the usurped authority of the Roman pontiff.[104] Later

---

[99] Woolf, *Idea of History*, 117–23.
[100] D. McKitterick, 'Sir Robert Cotton's Roman Inscriptions', in Wright, *Sir Robert Cotton as Collector*, 115.
[101] N. Ramsay, 'Sir Robert Cotton's Services to the Crown', in Wright, *Sir Robert Cotton as Collector*, 71–2.
[102] Here a new historicist approach to literary texts would pay dividends in the historicizing of works of history.   [103] J. H. Plumb, *The Death of the Past* (Harmondsworth, 1973), 26.
[104] BL Cotton MS Faustina E. V, ff. 89–90.

Cotton himself was to readvise Prince Charles about the rights of English kings to France not, as he boasted, 'by way of pleasing discourse as in these days is in use but by sound ground and substantial arguments' from history.[105]

Historians of the arts, drama and court festivals of the Renaissance write naturally of the driving force of patronage and politics on artistic production.[106] In a system of personal monarchy, monarchs did much to shape an intellectual culture, even when they did not directly commission works. The shift in cultural style from the reign of Elizabeth to that of James, or from James to his son, is manifest in changes in portraiture and architecture, poetry and plays, masques and music. We still need to see historical writing in this context: to study the changes in genre from chronicle to antiquarian treatise to 'politic history' as an expression of, as well as influence on, these broader changes, as a political as well as intellectual history.[107] Daniel Woolf has incisively observed that the type of narrative history that flourished under Elizabeth and James entered the doldrums under Charles I; and, significantly, the same has been argued about the drama.[108] Histories in verse too appear to have had their heyday in the late years of Elizabeth's reign and James's reign when, for all Sidney's distinctions, historians and poets (among them King James himself) often wrote to the same ends. The issues of early modern politics informed historical, as all other, scholarship, even when historians were not directly employed by the state. Camden's *Britannia* cannot be separated from the threats to England in the 1580s; John Speed's *Theatre of the Empire of Great Britain*, with its engraved frontispiece of a Roman, Saxon, Dane and Norman, flanked by an ancient Briton, clearly speaks to James I's self-styling as King of Great Britain and royal plans for union. It may even be that Cotton's and Camden's excavation of Hadrian's Wall in 1600 was stimulated by their perceived expectation that the two old hostile kingdoms might soon share one sovereign.[109] Ben Jonson for one used one of the stones they found for his court masque celebrating union.[110]

[105] BL Lansdowne MS 223, f. 7.
[106] See, for example, G. F. Lytle and S. Orgel eds., *Patronage in the Renaissance* (Princeton, 1981).
[107] See Sharpe and Lake, *Culture and Politics*, passim.
[108] Woolf, *Idea of History*, 243; A. Harbage, *Cavalier Drama* (New York, 1964).
[109] Cf. Sharpe, *Sir Robert Cotton*, pp. 199–202.
[110] McKitterick, 'Sir Robert Cotton's Roman Inscriptions', 116–17. On the masque *Hymenaei* celebrating political union, as well as the marriage of Essex and Frances Howard, see D. J. Gordon, '*Hymenaei*: Ben Jonson's Masque of Union', in his *The Renaissance Imagination*, ed. S. Orgel (Berkeley and London, 1975), 157–84.

History, like the law, the Bible, the classics, was a validating text. Yet like all those other texts, as well as sustaining authority, it could be deployed, appropriated and interpreted by others. James VI had seen clear evidence of this as King of Scotland, when the presbyterians' reading of the Scottish past formed the basis of their contractual theory of politics. In the *Basilikon Doron*, he advised his son Prince Henry to read histories, but not those of John Knox or George Buchanan.[111] In Jacobean England, the Earl of Arundel was to accuse Sir Edward Coke and his precedents of stirring up subjects against their sovereign.[112] Woolf is right to maintain that before the civil war there were no fundamental historical controversies expressing rival and antagonistic views of the past, but he goes too far in writing of a 'monochromatic image' of the national past.[113] Like the law, history was still a shared language; but men – often to their consternation – did read it differently, or at least with different emphases. Historical scholarship, therefore, was not only in general shaped by political conditions and questions, it was coloured by political tensions and differences.[114]

As the past became a disputed text, the custody of records became a political question too. Given her famous sensitivity to unflattering historical parallels, it is surprising that Queen Elizabeth did not accept Cotton's offer to pool his books with the royal collection to form a national library. As yet, the attitude to public records remained somewhat cavalier: state papers were allowed to drift; Burleigh gave to Camden official correspondence which was never returned; Secretaries of State kept their papers as private possessions.[115] Behind Cotton's petition may have been a political sense that there was a need to safeguard the records of state. Later, in urging that commissions to ambassadors be enrolled in Chancery and delivered into the Exchequer, he recalled that in Elizabeth's time the King of Denmark had insisted on a clause in a past negotiation and the English could not discover whether they were bound to it or not![116] Papers were in private hands, Cotton advised,

---

[111] J. Craigie ed., *The Basilikon Doron of King James VI* (2 vols., Scottish Text Soc., Edinburgh, 1944–50), I, 149; for the context, see J. Wormald, 'James VI and I, *Basilikon Doron* and *The Trew Law of Free Monarchies*: the Scottish Context and the English Translation', in L. Peck ed., *The Mental World of the Jacobean Court* (Cambridge, 1991), 36–54.

[112] BL Harl. MS 389, f. 133.   [113] Woolf, *Idea of History*, xiii.

[114] Above, pp. 87–8. We await a study of the politics of historical writing and of the readings of history in early modern England.

[115] Woolf, *Idea of History*, 120; R. B. Wernham, 'The Public Records in the Sixteenth and Seventeenth Centuries', in L. Fox ed., *English Historical Scholarship in the Sixteenth and Seventeenth Centuries* (Dugdale Soc., Oxford, 1956). See too *Hist. Mss. Comm., Cowper*, II, 234.

[116] BL Cotton MS Titus B. V, f. 3.

that ought to be kept safe in the public records. Given what we know of how many he 'acquired', Cotton's advice may sound like blatant hypocrisy. It may be, however, that he regarded his own library, open to all, as a safe repository, a supplement to the official records in the Tower. Others, however, who began to share his concern about the public records, did not concur that he was the right custodian. Thomas Wilson, Keeper of the Records in the Tower, issued warnings about Cotton's acquisitions of state papers and even advised that papers bequeathed to Cotton should be retained by the crown.[117] Clearly attitudes were changing and the factional rivalries and political tensions of the 1620s focused attention on the custody of the records of precedents that all looked to for support and ammunition. In 1621, Francis Bacon was evidently prevented from access to official records and to Cotton's library, at the time of judicial proceedings against him.[118] In 1626, when he himself was facing impeachment, the Duke of Buckingham recommended that Cotton's library be closed.[119]

The debates on the Petition of Right, centred on precedent in general and on Magna Carta (of which Cotton had copies) in particular, exacerbated the concern about ownership of the records of state. In 1629, Attorney General Heath, who, we now know, was not averse to altering official documents to sustain a claim,[120] observed: 'There are found in Sir Robert Cotton's study not copies or transcripts but the very originals of records . . . which indeed are not fit for a subject to keep.'[121] Interestingly, however, one of the leading protagonists of the Petition of Right in the Lords had come to quite a different view. The Earl of Bedford had supported the search for precedents to bolster the liberty of the subject: 'The records as he thought were the subjects . . . he judged it no offence if out of them he desired to know the utmost both of his right and duty.'[122] Never one to share his father's love of debate, and dismayed at some of the arguments promulgated in 1628, Charles I moved quickly to establish control over archives of state: he impounded Sir Edward Coke's papers, and ordered his Attorney to purge his reports of dangerous matter; he perused Attorney William Noy's and Secretary Dorchester's papers on their deaths, removing 'such as the state may have any use of'. Charles required his Keeper of the Records to recover

---

[117] *Cal. Stat. Pap. Dom. 1611–18*, 305; *Cal. Stat. Pap. Dom. 1623–5*, 548.
[118] Tite, *The Manuscript Library of Sir Robert Cotton*, 21.
[119] T. Birch, *The Court and Times of Charles I*, ed. R. F. Williams (2 vols., London, 1848), I, 98.
[120] See J. A. Guy, 'The Origins of the Petition of Right Reconsidered', *Hist. Journ.*, 25 (1982), 289–312.   [121] Bodl. MS Rawlinson C 839, f. 7v.
[122] Bodl. MS Rawlinson D 1104, f. 17.

documents that had been (as he now saw it) 'embezzled'. He forbad prisoners access to Tower records.[123]

And, most importantly for us, he closed Sir Robert Cotton's library. The king's concern to restrict and control access to records expressed not only his authoritarian personality and desire for order. Historical records and historical scholarship were becoming increasingly not just political, but politically contentious, objects and pursuits. Historians and antiquaries were embroiled in political disputes. Rubens may have regretted his friend Selden's involvement in a political controversy that led to his confinement and wished that he had restricted himself to scholarship, but – as the Ambassador Rubens of all people knew – it was something of a false distinction. Even Sir Henry Spelman, who appeared to remain most aloof from the political fray, was reading Oliver St John's treatise against benevolences in 1625.[124] For his part, Cotton was in the thick of it. To better understand his importance for early modern scholarship we have further to examine his political activities and attitudes.

VII

Just as we can only truly elucidate Cotton's collecting and scholarship in the broader context of the politics of culture, so his political career needs to be studied in the culture of politics in early modern England. Since I began work on Sir Robert Cotton in 1971 that broader landscape has been transformed. In 1975, my study of Cotton's career graphically demonstrated what was wrong with the prevailing Whig interpretation. At a time when, it was argued, conflict between crown and parliament, court and country was inevitable and escalating, Cotton resisted categorization or placement on either 'side'. A Huntingdonshire gentleman and baronet with (as we shall see) pride in his ancestry and locality, he was also connected to powerful magnates and monarchs; he advised princes as well as MPs; his criticisms of royal policies and favourites never transmuted into 'opposition' to the king or royal government; rather he offered counsel to reinvigorate royal government. Like others, Cotton remained devoted to the idea of the commonweal and exemplified the shared values and languages that, I then argued, characterized the political culture.

---

[123] PRO C 115/M36/8432; K. Sharpe, *The Personal Rule of Charles I* (New Haven and London, 1992), 655–8.
[124] M. F. S. Hervey, *The Life, Correspondence and Collections of Thomas Howard, Earl of Arundel* (Cambridge, 1921), 284; Sharpe, *Sir Robert Cotton*, 110; BL Add. MS. 34599 f. 93.

Since then, further research and debate have refined and developed our canvas, with implications for Cotton's place in it. For one, Dr David Starkey has directed historical attention away from the major officeholders of state and towards lesser figures, bedchamber men and the like, who enjoyed intimacy with the king and could act as channels of communication for others.[125] Though Starkey did not have figures like Cotton in mind, it is helpful to reconsider him in this light, as a figure who served and had direct contact with favourites, princes and monarchs and who was seen by others as able to advance suits and suggestions to the government. More importantly, critics have questioned or rejected some of the revisions that Conrad Russell and I offered towards a remapping of the Stuart terrain. The 'post-revisionists' argue that we exaggerated the importance of court faction, underplayed ideological commitments and differences and underestimated the importance of parliaments and of conflict between king and parliament.[126] Re-reading Sir Robert Cotton (as Harvey re-read his Livy) we can see how he can certainly lend support to some of those criticisms. Though undoubtedly attached to Howard patrons, Cotton, on the evidence we have, questions an undue emphasis upon faction. He served Somerset, but may have deserted him; he worked for Arundel but advised Arundel's enemy the Duke of Buckingham – even when the Earl Marshal was confined.

In other respects, however, re-reading Cotton suggests that post-revisionist premises themselves require re-examination. Even as I attempt it again, I find it difficult to place Cotton on any 'side'. Clearly – and I would now wish to emphasize it – Sir Robert exhibited real concern about the course of politics in the 1620s, and even fears for the liberty of the subject. But, as we now know, his concerns were shared by Privy Councillors as well as MPs. Indeed, the commissioning of Cotton to advise on the state of the realm before the calling of the 1628 parliament to me seriously questions Richard Cust's argument that by 1626 lines were hardening and the king's hostility to such counsels was manifest.[127] Cotton too gives the lie to all those scholars who persist in perpetuating the myth of widespread censorship in early Stuart England.[128] Amidst much heat, light has been shed by scholars like Blair Worden and Sheila Lambert who have demonstrated that censorship of literature

---

[125] See D. Starkey ed., *The English Court from the Wars of the Roses to the Civil War* (1987); Starkey, 'Representation through Intimacy', in I. Lewis ed., *Symbols and Sentiments* (1977).

[126] Some of these criticisms are gathered in Cust and Hughes, *Conflict*.

[127] R. Cust, *The Forced Loan and English Politics 1626–28* (Oxford, 1987), passim.

[128] Notably C. Hill, 'Censorship and English Literature', in his *Collected Essays I: Writing and Revolution in 17th Century England* (Brighton, 1985), 32–71.

was seldom effective and rarely attempted.[129] Middleton, Massinger and Jonson were punished and jailed, but continued to perform regularly at court. Similarly Cotton was twice confined, yet also appointed to a number of offices and commissions and considered as a candidate for Secretary of State. Even in 1630, when his library was closed, he was appointed as one of the 'persons of trust and quality' who made up the royal commission on fees.[130]

What Cotton's career undoubtedly underpins is the post-revisionists' injunction to give more emphasis to ideology. With that I would never have disagreed: in 1979 I wrote that it would be essential for the historian of politics 'to investigate intellectual interests and values'.[131] Here the leading revisionist, Conrad Russell, has signally failed. The way forward is not to be found, however, in a retreat to the old model of ideological conflict, but in a more richly complicated reconfiguration of the meaning and performance of ideology in the political culture generally and in individuals like Cotton in particular.[132] Already new questions pose themselves. Did Cotton's interests in stones and coins commend him to an Arundel whose own collecting of marbles and medals expressed wider values and beliefs?[133] Did Franciscus Junius, author of *The Painting of the Ancients*, come to work in Arundel House through his link with Janus Gruter, one of Cotton's continental correspondents?[134] What did Henry Peacham learn as a Huntingdonshire schoolmaster from his antiquarian neighbour that led him to dedicate his *Art of Drawing* to Cotton in 1606?[135] Did he owe his place as tutor to Arundel's son to his link with Cotton? Were, as Blair Worden has powerfully argued, Ben Jonson's values formed amidst the circles of historians in which he moved: notably Selden, Camden, his schoolmaster, and Cotton, a fellow student, who incidentally hung Jonson's picture in his library?[136] Did shared concerns about the course of politics underlie the writings of dramatists, poets and historians who dedicated works to each other and many of whom borrowed from Cotton's library? Were those values and ideas more shaped by reading or political experience – or is

[129] B. Worden, 'Literature and Political Censorship in Early Modern England', in A. C. Duke and C. A. Tamse eds., *Too Mighty to be Free* (Zutphen, 1988), 45–62; S. Lambert, 'The Printers and the Government, 1604–37', in R. Myers and M. Harris eds., *Aspects of Printing from 1600* (Oxford, 1987), 1–29. [130] Sharpe, *Sir Robert Cotton*, 145. [131] Ibid., 220.
[132] Cf. my critique of J. P. Sommerville's *Politics and Ideology in England 1603–1640* (1986) in *Politics and Ideas*, 283–8; and see Sharpe and Lake, *Culture and Politics*, introduction.
[133] Hervey, *Life of Arundel*, 267. [134] Sharpe, *Sir Robert Cotton*, 100.
[135] Cf. McKitterick, 'Sir Robert Cotton's Roman Inscriptions', 118.
[136] B. Worden, 'Ben Jonson among the Historians', in Sharpe and Lake, *Culture and Politics*, 67–90, 336–41.

the distinction itself unhelpful when both activities involved processes of interpretation and application? Did James I as scholar and poet, as well as king, himself encourage a culture in which history and poetry were favoured discourses of political participation and counsel?[137] And did his more taciturn son's succession effect a change in this broader political culture, with consequences we have yet to explore? A full biography of Cotton (or of Camden, Selden or Jonson[138] for that matter) would have to consider such large questions and would undoubtedly contribute towards answering them. In the space that remains we can only return to a few episodes that may take on a renewed importance in the light of recent research.

Since *Sir Robert Cotton* was published in 1979, historians have focused much more attention on a subject to which Cotton made an early contribution: the succession of James VI and the union of England and Scotland. Bruce Galloway and Brian Levack have studied the vast pamphlet literature that the debates on union produced, and the obstacles to James's scheme.[139] Questions about the extent of union (full incorporation, federal union or mere dynastic union), about the union of law, about the uniformity of religion and church government, about trading rights and commercial union, and about the adoption of the name of Great Britain preoccupied lawyers, poets, historians and antiquaries such as Sir John Dodderidge, John Hayward, Sir Henry Spelman and Sir Francis Bacon. James himself, under all heads, favoured complete union, which did not secure widespread support. Cotton, however, was wholeheartedly behind the scheme. In the tract he penned within two days of Elizabeth's death, Cotton wrote of 'both kingdoms being of one descent in blood, of one language . . . the religion all the same . . . their municipal laws near alike', their estates of 'self name and nature'.[140] Reading in the *Basilikon Doron* of James's intent to 'reduce these two potent kingdoms to that earlier state wherein it stood of old', Cotton recommended 'Britain' as the name most fit: 'for the first these kingdoms of England and Scotland were received under that name about 2000 years ago . . . for a second as a title sovereign it is the

---

[137] See Sharpe, 'The King's Writ: Royal Authors and Royal Authority in Early Modern England', above ch. 3.

[138] There are helpful suggestions in D. Riggs, *Ben Jonson: a Life* (Cambridge, Mass., and London, 1989).

[139] B. Galloway, *The Union of England and Scotland* (Edinburgh, 1986); B. Galloway and B. Levack, *The Jacobean Union: Six Tracts of 1604* (Scottish Hist. Soc., Edinburgh, 1985); B. Levack, *The Formation of the British State* (Oxford, 1987).

[140] PRO SP 14/1/3: 'A Discourse of the descent of the King's majesty from the Saxons'.

far oldest and so most honourable . . . After Caesar his invasion that name this kingdom held and our kings that title.'[141] The antiquary rapidly surveyed the history of the name, citing ancient and medieval authorities before concluding: 'Sithence then so many regards of peace and safety, the affinity of language, law and religion, the former domestic precedents, foreign examples and modern intentions do bring such a confluence of convenience to rebuild entire up this glorious empire it may pass happily with all acclamation by the name of Great Britain.'[142]

It was a powerful support for union before James had even arrived in London. With his patron Henry Howard, Earl of Northampton, Cotton continued to back the scheme in parliament where most MPs expressed fears of constitutional change or of Scottish competition for trade and patronage. Sir Robert (was his title a reward for his service?) continued to argue for the antiquity of the name where others objected that 'we should lose the ancient name of England' or feared 'the precedency of England in danger';[143] he tried to resolve the dispute and arguments about naturalization;[144] he laboured to promote the bill to abolish hostile laws;[145] he supported free trade, arguing that it enhanced wealth and shipping; he insisted that the Scots were not aliens but 'the offspring of an English root'.[146] Few went so far in their support of James's plans for full union, for 'one kingdom entirely governed, one uniformity in laws'.[147] Recent historiography has suggested how perceptive he may have been. Conrad Russell has argued that the problems of ruling multiple kingdoms, bequeathed by the failure of full union, were a force for political instability that contributed significantly to civil war. In particular, he contends, religious differences between the kingdoms created a problem of 'explosive force', which detonated in 1637.[148] Historians and antiquaries who defended the union concurred in this diagnosis. 'Where there is no unity of religion', John Dodderidge wrote in his *Brief Consideration of the Union*, 'there can be no hearty love'; the two realms, he thought, should embrace the episcopal form of government to strengthen church and state.[149] Cotton clearly felt religious uniformity should be restored, recalling that Scottish bishops 'from their first erec-

[141] Ibid.   [142] Ibid.   [143] *CJ*, I, 176, 19 Apr. 1604.
[144] Ibid., I, 339; BL Harl. MS 293, f. 179.
[145] PRO SP 14/27/44; L. Peck, *Northampton: Patronage and Policy at the Court of James I* (1982), 191–2.
[146] BL Lansdowne MS 486, f. 86ᵛ; Peck, *Northampton*, 190–1; Levack, *British State*, ch. 5.
[147] Levack, *British State*, 72; Galloway, *Union of England and Scotland*, 97, 99.
[148] C. Russell, *The Causes of the English Civil War* (Oxford, 1990), ch. 2 and passim, quotation on p. 214. Russell makes too much of an interesting perspective.
[149] Dodderidge, 'Brief Consideration', in Galloway and Levack, *Jacobean Union*, 9; Levack, *British State*, 150.

tion a long time were under the see of York in all spiritual causes, thence all receiving their consecrations'.[150] One is left wondering whether, had more in parliament shared these views, James I might have effected a full conformity of church government and so left a far more stable legacy to his son.

Cotton's service to the Earl of Northampton and advocacy of administrative reform may also now profitably be placed in a broader context. After the publication of *Sir Robert Cotton*, Professor Linda Peck developed my and her earlier arguments for Henry Howard to be re-evaluated as a leading proponent of reform in Jacobean government.[151] In an important chapter of *Northampton* she shows how the earl fought for reform of household expenditures, purveyance, the ecclesiastical courts, the navy, the Earl Marshal's office and of the practice of duelling. In every part of his campaign it would appear that Cotton was his leading adviser, not merely lending manuscripts or compiling lists of precedents, but drafting speeches, position papers and reports. Sir Robert presented evidence of the punishments suffered by duellers in the past; he drew up notes on purveyance; he prepared a volume of papers in connection with Northampton's endeavour as a commissioner to reform the College of Arms; most importantly he was Northampton's full partner in the investigation into abuses in the navy; in 'The Manner and Means how the Kings of England Have from time to time Supported and Repaired their Estates', he counselled the end of waste in the royal household and economy, to 'reduce' it again 'to the best, first and most magnificent order'.[152] More than Northampton's amanuensis, Cotton and his patron shared the same values and spoke the same language to the point where it is impossible (and inappropriate) to determine who most influenced whom. Northampton wrote passionately to Somerset about the need for reform: 'without some care to pull up those suckers that draw the very moisture radical from the root it is no more possible for this exhausted monarchy to subsist'.[153] Cotton, deploying the same metaphor, recommended immediate action against corruption because 'these privy stealths are the petites fleaux . . . that by silent progressions and augmentations eat daily into the very marrow and consume the radical moisture of this state'.[154]

[150] PRO SP 14/1/3.
[151] Peck, *Northampton*; Peck, 'Problems in Jacobean Administration: Was Henry Howard, Earl of Northampton, a Reformer?', *Hist. Journ.*, 19 (1976), 831–58.
[152] Sharpe, *Sir Robert Cotton*, ch. 4 passim; Peck, *Northampton*, ch. 8; James Howell ed., *Cottoni Posthuma* (1651), 168–9.   [153] BL Cotton MS Titus C. VI, f. 123.
[154] BL Egerton MS 2974, f. 83ᵛ.

Sir Robert endeavoured to promote the campaign for reform after his Howard patron's death in 1614. He advised Somerset on the reformation of the Heralds' office; he sat on the commission to enquire into fees charged in courts. The war years halted reforming initiatives, but in 1628 Cotton urged the Duke of Buckingham to champion the cause; and he counselled reduction of expenses and waste and the eradication of corruption. It was not long before another minister took up Northampton's and Cotton's programme, advocating a thorough reformation of the administration and state. We know little of Cotton's relationship with Thomas Wentworth who came to prominence towards the end of the antiquary's life. But it may be, as we shall suggest, that Cotton provided an important bridge between the Jacobean and Caroline movements for reform.

The broader historical context in which we must study Cotton's political activities in the 1620s has been radically rewritten since 1979. Conrad Russell has constructed a famous new narrative countering the thesis that the decade was one of crisis in relations between king and parliament, and arguing that war was the principal cause of political tension.[155] Roger Lockyer has published a revisionist biography of Buckingham, offering a more positive evaluation of the Duke's abilities, aims and policies.[156] Tom Cogswell has restudied the parliament of 1624 and the onset of war with Spain, Richard Cust the forced loan which was an expedient of war finance, and John Reeve the origin of Charles I's decision to rule without parliament that initiated the eleven years' Personal Rule.[157] Though they by no means concur, and this is not the place to review their respective contributions, all these publications do cast valuable light on the shadows and inconsistencies in Cotton's career.

In the first place, Russell's analysis not only exonerates us from an obligation to place Cotton in the court or parliamentary camp, it enables us to make sense of Cotton's aiding the government with wartime fiscal expedients, whilst expressing concern at the perceived threat to liberties of unusual exactions and courses and his desire for a parliament. As Richard Cust demonstrates the concern over the illegality of the loan was shared by some Privy Councillors as well as MPs; a figure like Sir John

---

[155] Russell, *Parliaments and English Politics*.
[156] R. Lockyer, *Buckingham: the Life and Political Career of George Villiers, First Duke of Buckingham, 1592–1628* (1981).
[157] T. Cogswell, *The Blessed Revolution: English Politics and the Coming of War, 1621–1624* (Cambridge, 1989); Cust, *Forced Loan*; J. Reeve, *Charles I and the Road to Personal Rule* (Cambridge, 1989).

Coke could deplore and yet appreciate the necessity that had dictated new courses.[158] Lockyer's *Buckingham* makes it easier to understand Cotton's initial support for the Duke and his reluctance until the end to give up on his being rewon for the public service. For, more than any, Buckingham sponsored reform of the navy, a new commission for which was issued in 1626.[159] Cotton may also in 1624 have been one of those (elucidated by Professor Cogswell) who ardently advocated a war with Spain after the chicanery and assaults to national honour over a decade of marriage negotiations, in which Cotton had himself played a role, and so supported the Duke as a new-found champion of the cause; certainly his relation of the Spanish 'disguises' was well publicized. If the war was a cause dear to him, we can also better understand how Cotton, like other frustrated 'patriots', came to be despondent at the disastrous military outcome and to despair of Buckingham in whom so much hope had been placed. Sir Robert's seeming volte-face from serving to attacking the Duke needs no factional explanation: Buckingham had failed the nation.[160]

Because he wished to continue the war – he opposed those who counselled peace[161] – Cotton was willing to continue to help with means, even dubious means, of raising money.[162] But he feared that ineptitude and waste made the country less inclined to pay and doubted the effectiveness of extraparliamentary courses.[163] Whatever his reservations about the Duke, Cotton did not advocate his impeachment. He urged a thorough ongoing reform as a prelude to another parliament, which he hoped would restore normal courses and see the more successful prosecution of the war. Somewhat surprisingly Cotton was not prominent in the 1628 parliament: he clearly understood the fears of MPs about arbitrary courses; he and his patron Arundel had been on the receiving end of Buckingham's vindictiveness; yet Cotton could also understand the plight of the government and saw nothing fundamentally wrong that vigorous good counsel would not put right. Recent scholarship enables us to re-read Cotton as a more explicable, less inconsistent figure, who, like so many, experienced heightened political tensions in the period 1626–8, but as yet felt no harsh alternative between serving king and country.

---

[158] Cust, *Forced Loan*, ch. 3.   [159] PRO SP 16/42/17; Lockyer, *Buckingham*, 341–4.

[160] Cogswell, *Blessed Revolution*, ch. 5 and passim; Sharpe, *Sir Robert Cotton*, 131–4, 171–5.

[161] D'Ewes to Mede, 10 Dec. 1628; BL Harl. MS 383, f. 76.

[162] BL Cotton MS Julius C. III, ff. 192, 236, 269–70; Lansdowne MS 209, ff. 176–234; Harl. MS 383, f. 92; Birch, *Court and Times of Charles I*, I, 327.

[163] Birch, *Court and Times of Charles I*, I, 155–7; Cotton, 'The Danger Wherein the Kingdom now Standeth and the Remedy', *Cottoni Posthuma*, 316ff.

Nigel Ramsay's important discovery of Cotton's own list of his services to the crown also refines and develops our understanding of the antiquary's position during the 1620s.[164] Most important here, the dating of some Cotton tracts places them and their author in a different light and perspective. First, that Sir Robert was asked for advice on ways of raising money and men 'in the distress of the Pallatinat' suggests that as early as 1620 or 1621, the antiquary was consulted about a war, even though his patron, Arundel, was against belligerent courses.[165] It may be this service that brought Cotton to Prince Charles's attention and so helps explain the role he played in 1624. Secondly, we must, in the light of Ramsay's document, redate Cotton's tract arguing 'That the Sovereign's Person is Required in Great Councils'. Where I ascribed this to 1621 and the judicial proceedings against Bacon, it now appears that the treatise relates to the impeachment of Buckingham in 1626. This not only indicates that Charles I was considering permitting the judicial proceedings to continue, but with himself present; importantly it also suggests that Cotton was not yet regarded as an implacable enemy of the Duke, even after the 1625 parliament.[166] If this is the case, it would add to my argument that by 1626 the lines were not yet drawn and Charles was not yet bent on unparliamentary courses.

How then are we to explain Cotton's last years and the events that led to his confinement and the closure of his library? Was Cotton punished, on a spurious pretext, by clients of Buckingham for his support of the liberties of the subject in 1628? Or was Sir Robert prosecuted for the alleged dissemination of Dudley's tract which advocated non-parliamentary government and, if need be, the use of force? If the tract were the central issue, was Cotton behind it and, if so, did it express views he had come to hold in 1629, or tendencies he perceived and felt compelled to publicize and possibly answer? Even after the recent work on 1629 by Reeve and David Berkowitz, it is not easy to give a straightforward answer to these questions.[167] Factional politics is clearly not a sufficient explanation: those named as informants against Cotton and others in 1629 include Wentworth who was no friend to Buckingham, Arundel who had long been at odds with the Duke and a patron of Cotton, and Manchester, Cotton's kinsman who had sought his advice and who in 1630 was to plead for his pardon and restoration to favour.[168]

[164] Ramsay, 'Sir Robert Cotton's Services', 68–80.   [165] Ibid., 74.
[166] Sharpe, *Sir Robert Cotton*, 177–82.
[167] Reeve, *Charles I*, 158–64; D. Berkowitz, *John Selden's Formative Years* (Washington D.C., 1988), 268–76.   [168] Reeve, *Charles I*, 158 and n. 184.

Similarly the names of Wentworth, the leading proponent of the Petition of Right, and Arundel, a supporter in the Lords, question whether divisions over the issues of 1628 are central to the story. Reeve is right to argue in general that 'there is a wider political and ideological significance to the Cotton case'; and he reminds us that contemporaries associated it with the trial of Sir John Eliot and others after the parliamentary session of 1629; but he remains uncertain as to what use Cotton intended to make of the pamphlet – whether to discredit the government or prompt a debate about recent political developments.[169] The evidence suggests that the whole episode may have been based on a series of misunderstandings. When the tract came into his hands, Cotton, possibly suspecting that it represented extreme and unpalatable advice to Charles I, apparently set out to *answer* the treatise. When a search of his study revealed 'drafts for an answer to [the] proposition' the Council exonerated Cotton from the charge of authorizing the pamphlet.[170] Further investigation revealed it as an old document, sent from Florence by Sir Robert Dudley in 1614 to the Earl of Somerset, from whose papers it had entered Cotton's library. Sir Robert was still not entirely free of the suspicion that he might have deliberately published it in 1629 to foster fears of innovation in government, but the government began to relax as it became apparent that there had been no conspiracy; and the prisoners were first released and then discharged when the birth of the prince offered an occasion to show mercy. Sure enough, both Cotton and his co-defendants and the government had exhibited distrust and edginess: Sir Robert may have genuinely feared the courses the Dudley pamphlet outlined, the Privy Council a conspiracy to paint the government in the colours of tyranny. But the distrust was not irreparable in 1630, not least because Charles I – as Wentworth's elevation manifests – was himself still capable of distinguishing between criticism and sedition. Despite his criticism of some courses Sir Robert evidently believed it still possible, by recounting his past services, to reassure the king of his 'uprightness and loyalty'.[171] Cotton's library remained closed, pending the completion of a catalogue. But where Sir John Eliot and other MPs festered in the Tower, Cotton was free; he reappeared in court circles and again sat on the commission on fees. In November 1630 the Councillors examining Cotton's library praised his readiness to serve the king and newsletters reported the reopening of the

---

[169] Ibid., 159–61.
[170] *Acts of Privy Council May 1629–1630*, p. 176; Berkowitz, *John Selden*, 272; Ramsay, 'Sir Robert Cotton's Services', 78–9. [171] Ramsay, 'Sir Robert Cotton's Services', 78.

library and his restoration to royal favour. Had he lived longer, Cotton
may have embarked on a whole new political career as an adviser, like
William Noy, during the Personal Rule.[172]

VIII

During the proceedings against Cotton, the Earl of Manchester
informed Sir Edward Montagu that the business 'makes a great noise in
the country'.[173] We are beginning to learn more about Cotton's own
country, his relationship to his seat in Huntingdonshire and their importance for understanding his intellectual and political activities. First, it
seems that Conington Castle may have been a second major repository
for the Cottonian collection. We know that Sir Robert kept his stones
there and built a special summerhouse for them, though it is not clear
whether this was for practical reasons – ease of transport, space – or to
make a local impression, or indeed what it suggests about how the antiquary regarded his collection as a whole.[174] Camden refers to Cotton's
'cabinet' at Huntingdon, a term which implies rarities other than
stones.[175] He evidently kept estate papers and documents at Conington,
and may have had books there: Sidney Montagu promised to return borrowed books to Conington and a loan list in Cambridgeshire may have
drifted from Cotton family papers.[176] Scholars too visited Conington as
well as Cotton's London residence; many who saw his stones, for
instance, must have viewed them there.[177] Huntingdonshire also featured more than has been noted in Cotton's scholarly activities: he
searched for books there; he excavated and found there a fossilized fish;
and he collected material for a history of the county.[178]

It is also becoming clearer that Cotton's scholarly activities were as
much related to local as they were to national politics. David Howarth
poses the crucial question why Cotton erected cenotaphs to Scottish
princes in the middle of the Fens and is surely right to answer that
Cotton was keen to vaunt his ancestry and relationship to Robert the

---

[172] Sharpe, *Sir Robert Cotton*, 145–6.   [173] *Hist. Mss. Comm. Buccleuch–Whitehall*, I, 269.
[174] D. Howarth, 'Sir Robert Cotton and the Commemoration of Famous Men', in Wright, *Sir Robert Cotton as Collector*, 42–4. It is worth remembering that Cotton had a substantial garden in Westminster.   [175] McKitterick, 'Sir Robert Cotton's Roman Inscriptions', 114–15.
[176] BL Harl. MS 7002, f. 65; Cambs. RO, Antrobus MSS; Hunts. RO, Estate papers.
[177] Antrobus MSS, Cotton's Commonplace Book; Camden's and Jonson's residence at Conington during the plague is well known.
[178] Parr, *Life of Ussher*, 338; above, p. 303; Cambs. RO, Antrobus MSS: Commonplace Book; note-book on history of Huntingdonshire and Cambridgeshire; Hunts. RO dd M 20/A/10, Cotton's notebook on the parishes of Huntingdonshire; BL Cotton MS Julius F. VI, f. 395.

Bruce, not least against his rival Sir Simeon Steward.[179] Scholarship was also put to more practical, some might say sinister, uses. Professor Manning shows how when the copyholders of the manor of Glatton filed in Chancery a complaint against Cotton, his uncle John and son Thomas, Sir Robert responded with a carefully supported cross bill which 'illustrates the application by Sir Robert Cotton of antiquarian research to the task of estate administration'.[180] Cotton was indeed embroiled in local politics – in boundary disputes, also with the tenants of Glatton, and in quarrels about drainage schemes;[181] he was threatened with proceedings for failing to repair a highway in Conington.[182] And, though he spent little time in his house and county, both remained important to him, as to other county gentlemen whose careers took them to London or to court.[183] He continued to oversee his rental accounts; he was involved in purchases of more land and of advowsons; he continued to build and improve Conington Castle up to his death.[184] Sir Robert also held local office – as sheriff, as one of the commissioners to raise an aid for the marriage of James I's daughter Elizabeth, as a surveyor of a royal manor, and as a member of the commission for sewers.[185] It is worth remembering that Cotton wished to be buried not in London, but in the south chapel of the parish church in his native Conington, the name of which often featured as part of his inscription in books and manuscripts.[186] Though he became a JP for Westminster in the 1620s, Cotton remained a country squire: we may need to think further about the importance of that for Cotton's attitude to his collection and still more for his perception of politics.

Further research on Huntingdonshire may throw light on the facets of Cotton not illuminated by the glare of London and court politics. Yet there are shadowy corners of the personality which will pose a challenge to the biographer who sets out to paint Cotton – not only in the flesh but

[179] Howarth, 'Cotton and Commemoration', 45–6.
[180] R. B. Manning, 'Sir Robert Cotton, Antiquarianism and Estate Administration: a Chancery Decree of 1627', in Wright, *Sir Robert Cotton as Collector*, 96; see also Manning, 'Antiquarianism and the Seigneurial Reaction: Sir Robert and Sir Thomas Cotton and their Tenants', *Historical Research*, 63 (1990), 277–88.
[181] Hunts. RO, Heathcote collection 12/1596, Inspeximus: Queen Elizabeth to Cotton et al., 1596; *VCH, Huntingdonshire* (3 vols., 1926–36), III, 268.
[182] BL Cotton MS Julius C. III, f. 20.
[183] Thomas Cotton said his father spent not four years residing there in forty. Howarth, 'Cotton and Commemoration', 44.
[184] Hunts. RO, Heathcote collection, dd Con II/C1–110; Conington Papers 2A, 2B; Charters box 14; Steeple Gidding boxes; bundles 5/1–5; *VCH, Hunts.*, III, 144.
[185] BL Cotton MS Julius C. III, ff. 408, 321–2, 119, 131; Harl. MS 298, f. 14; Add. MS 33466, ff. 56, 174ff., 201. [186] PRO, Prob. II 1 St John 159/68 (67).

warts and all. Historians of the early modern period tend to write the biographies of political and administrative figures, perhaps too of scholars, as though they had no life outside the office or study. It greatly changes our view of him, even as Secretary of State, to read of Sir John Coke in his seventies discussing the latest fashions with his tailor.[187] Certainly it would seem Cotton had a colourful side. He gathered and may have written verse; he enjoyed the company of poets and was obviously the host to lively gatherings of a social and scholarly nature.[188] Passion was certainly not unknown to him. The young man who bemoaned to his commonplace book the shortage of faithful and trustworthy women proved to be a philanderer and adulterer.[189] At some early point, probably by 1603, Cotton left his wife and lived at Lady Hunsdon's residence, possibly as her lover. And while D'Ewes tells us Cotton was reconciled to his wife after the fall of Somerset, the evidence suggests other instances of infidelity.[190] It was said that Sir Robert employed as an assistant *one* of his bastard sons;[191] and the conspiracy to set up the antiquary in a compromising position with a woman so as to blackmail him makes far more sense if Cotton had a reputation for extramarital affairs.[192] Cotton took aphrodisiacs in his fifties.[193] Such a side to an otherwise serious character may help to explain how Cotton befriended men like Ben Jonson, who was also given to overindulgence, and the other wits who met at the Mermaid, as well as more sober figures. Unless, however, we are able to find out more, we can only imagine how the several passions in his life, sexual and scholarly, integrated in the man. Cotton is still 'in danger of being lost amidst the many volumes of manuscripts which he collected'.[194] But if we cannot find him, we should at least remember that he is there.

IX

A full evaluation of Cotton's writings demands a greater knowledge of the circumstances that produced each piece, and of the personality of the man himself – knowledge that we may never have. But Graham

---

[187] Sharpe, *Personal Rule*, 154.
[188] W. H. Kelliher, 'British Post-Mediaeval Verse in the Cotton Collection', in Wright, *Sir Robert Cotton as Collector*, 307–90; Sharpe, *Sir Robert Cotton*, 202–3, 226–7; BL Add. MS 4712.
[189] Antrobus MSS, Commonplace Book: 'Ah me poor wretch that never yet could find / Ne faith ne trust in fruitless woman kind'.
[190] J. O. Halliwell ed., *The Autobiography and Correspondence of Sir Simonds D'Ewes* (2 vols., 1845), I, 80.
[191] BL Harl. MS 7002, f. 218.   [192] Halliwell, *Autobiography of Sir Simonds D'Ewes*, II, 42.
[193] BL Add. MS 14049: 'An Abstract and all the proofs of the conspiracy of Stevenson and others against Sir Robert Cotton'.   [194] Sharpe, *Sir Robert Cotton*, ix.

Parry makes an invaluable contribution to directing our attention back to the pieces collected in *Cottoni Posthuma* and Cotton's 'counsels'.[195] *Cottoni Posthuma* by no means contains all Cotton wrote. We have already remarked on sections by Sir Robert folded in the work of others: in Camden's *Annales*, in *Britannia*, in Speed's *History*; in addition he helped Ben Jonson pen a history of Henry V which burned in the fire at Jonson's house; he started with John Hayward a history of the House of Norfolk; and he wrote on arms and seals.[196] On the more obviously political side, Cotton considered the question of jurisdiction in ecclesiastical affairs; he drew, according to D'Ewes, a full declaration outlining the breach with Spain in 1624 (that was never published); fragments and allusions in correspondence suggest other works undertaken and either unfinished or lost.[197] Moreover, as with other antiquarian and historical works, Cotton may have been the ghost writer behind official speeches and declarations: like 'reading', 'authoring', as we are beginning to appreciate, is not a straightforward matter.[198] The volume *Cottoni Posthuma* itself wrongly attributes a treatise to Cotton and includes under its title two essays which are acknowledged as written by others. But *Cottoni Posthuma*, if only a selection of Cotton's œuvre (chosen as we shall see for its editor's purposes in 1651), offers an opportunity to analyse some of the texts for which, albeit they were not all then published, Cotton was known in his day.

What strikes the reader immediately is how few of the pieces are works of history as we understand them. Though several draw on knowledge of precedent, others offer straightforward political analysis, and all feel written at some distance from the rich manuscript holdings and massive erudition of Cotton's library. Even the most obviously historical piece, *The Life and Reign of Henry the Third*, reads, according to Parry, 'like the precis of an Elizabethan play of the 1590s in which the action is historic but the relevance contemporary'.[199] Parry's acute observation alerts us to the artificial barrier scholars have erected (and still police) between literature and history; and makes apparent what still discomforts us: that Cotton's purposes as a historian were political. Another commentator shows how little regard Cotton had in fulfilling

---

[195] G. Parry, 'Cotton's Counsels: the Contexts of *Cottoni Posthuma*', in Wright, *Sir Robert Cotton as Collector*, 81–95; it is interesting that a literary scholar has turned to a historicized reading of this text. See also Love, *Scribal Publication*, 49, 83–9, for the wide circulation of these tracts.

[196] BL Cotton MS Julius C. III, ff. 70, 191; C. H. Herford and P. Simpson eds., *The Works of Ben Jonson* (11 vols., Oxford, 1925–52), VIII, 207.

[197] Cotton MS Julius C. III, f. 28; E. Bourcier ed., *The Diary of Sir Simonds D'Ewes 1622–4* (Paris, 1974), 188.   [198] See BL Sloane MS 241, f. 20.   [199] Parry, 'Cotton's Counsels', 83.

his political purposes for what we would call scholarly integrity. The portraits of Simon de Montfort and Henry himself are one-sided and
wooden. *Henry III*, writes Daniel Woolf, 'is perhaps the most extreme
Jacobean example of the deliberate distortion and compression of historical fact for the sake of offering counsel'.[200] Cotton had important
general advice to give: the need for economy, for the reinvigoration of
the Privy Council, for the court to set an example of reform to the
country, for a monarch who would lead and govern 'in his own
person'.[201] Yet the genre in which he gave this advice was important to
him. Cotton expressed undisguised contempt for those who devised
'imaginary and fantastic forms of Commonwealths', as for those who
'flatter their own belief and ability that they can mould any state to these
general rules which in particular application will prove idle'.[202]
Historical example and parallel was for Cotton the best medium for conveying counsel. By corollary, the basis of the best political advice was
knowledge of precedent circumstances which might cast light on present
occasions.

In each of his political commissions therefore Cotton surveyed the
past, not primarily out of a legalistic attachment to precedents, but for
the best courses in similar circumstances. Tracts that read at first as mere
catalogues of precedents always contain advice – and sometimes warnings. In his 'Manner and Means how the Kings of England have from
time to time Supported and Repaired their Estates', Cotton lists a
number of past courses for raising money. But he warns against waste
and extravagant expenditure on favourites, strongly counsels reform and
cautions the king about expedients which, though lucrative, are impolitic.[203] Impositions, for example, he describes boldly as 'of late so
stretched as it is feared it will prove the overthrow of trade, neither do I
find this course at any other time'.[204] In a piece written for James I to
counter the arguments for war emanating from Prince Henry's circle,
Cotton staunchly backs the king's policy of neutrality and flatters his
standing, but issues another reminder of the need for the monarch not
to dissipate his estate: 'as well by reason of state as rules of best government the revenues and profits *quae ad sacrum patrimonum principis*

---

[200] Woolf, *Idea of History*, 160–2.
[201] Cotton, 'A Short View of the Long Life and Reign of Henry III', in *Cottoni Posthuma*, 1–27, 26.
The dating of this remains a problem. Re-reading it, I feel sure that as published, it applied to
1627, rather than 1614, when Cotton claimed he wrote it (cf. Camb. UL MS Gg.II.28).
[202] Cotton, 'Henry III', p. 3.
[203] Cotton, 'The Manner and Means how the Kings of England have from time to time Supported
and Repaired their Estates', *Cottoni Posthuma* (1672 edn), 168–9.   [204] Ibid., 188.

pertinent, which belong to the sacred patrimony of the crown, should remain firm and unbroken'.[205] In histories as well as masques and other literary panegyrics, criticism could be combined with compliment.[206]

Because Cotton always read the past for its direct applicability to the present moment, it is not surprising that his use and interpretation of the past altered with changed circumstances. Graham Parry confirms my sense that increasingly Cotton's writings 'emphasized the need for the full participation of Parliament in government', as experience again demonstrated the dangers of bad counsel.[207] In the 1625 speech he wrote or drafted, Cotton comes to quite a different view of his own Jacobean past and so of the most suitable precedents from which to learn. In his tract 'That the Sovereign's Person is required in Great Councils', Sir Robert collects the precedents which support the king's right to be involved in impeachment proceedings but concludes: 'He dares not say precedents are warrants to direct; the success . . . as the knowledge of them sometimes have made ill example by extension of regal power through ill counsels with ill success.'[208] The counsel to moderation owes more to contemporary circumstances than the precedents themselves.

Cotton's most widely distributed pamphlet, which he published under his own name in 1628, was his least historical piece. *The Danger Wherein the Kingdom Now Standeth and the Remedy* was written in January 1628, prob-ably in response to a request by the Privy Council.[209] Though it drew on medieval precedents – Cotton evoked the fates of Edward II and Richard II – the past that most shaped it was the recent past, of Cotton's own memory (or idealization), of Queen Elizabeth's reign and early James. And, more than any other work, it was focused on the present. Cotton catalogued his contemporaries' (and his own?) fears for the liberty of the subject threatened by loans, conscription and arbitrary arrest; the dangers of invasion from Spain; and concern for the safety of Protestantism. Most of all he pointed to the failure of counsel and dis-trust of the Duke of Buckingham. By way of remedy he counselled a return to more moderate courses and a parliament to win back hearts and purses.

---

[205] Cotton, *Wars with Foreign Princes Dangerous to Our Commonwealth* (1657), 57.

[206] See K. Sharpe, *Criticism and Compliment: the Politics of Literature in the England of Charles I* (Cambridge, 1987), pace M. Butler, 'Reform or Reverence? The Politics of the Caroline Masque', in J. R. Mulryne and M. Shewring eds., *Theatre and Government under the Early Stuarts* (Cambridge, 1993), 118–56.   [207] Parry, 'Cotton's Counsels', 90.

[208] *Cottoni Posthuma* (1651), 55.

[209] Sharpe, *Sir Robert Cotton*, 182–3; Cust, *Forced Loan*, 81–4; Cotton, *The Danger Wherein the Kingdom Now Standeth and the Remedy* (1628; STC 5863). See Love, *Scribal Publication*, 313.

It was just such counsel that drew James Howell to an edition of
Cotton's writings in 1651. A royalist who had written a political allegory
to support the king's cause on the eve of civil war, Howell spent much of
the 1640s in prison. During his confinement, he looked back on, and
may have written his familiar letters to reconstruct, a past in which sensible men had advocated moderate courses. Howell must have known
Cotton, as he knew Selden and Jonson. He cited the great historical
scholars – Camden, Raleigh, Selden (and Coke) – and, like Cotton, collected proverbs and axioms. In 1651, at a time of uncertainty for the
future of government, he turned, like so many, to the best of Elizabethan
practice, which Howell saw encapsulated in Cotton's life and writings.[210]
As he explained in his preface: 'what a great Zelot he was to his Countrey
. . . in all Parlements, where he served so often, his main endeavours were
to assert the public Liberty, and that *Prerogative* and Privilege might run
in their due Channels'.[211] A recent sketch of Howell's career goes a long
way to explain his edition of *Cottoni Posthuma* in 1651. Evidently, however,
the volume was more than a book for that moment. The whole collection was reissued in 1657, 1672 and 1679; individual pieces were separ-
ately republished in 1641, 1642, 1651, 1655, 1657, 1659, 1661, 1665, 1675,
1679, 1681, 1689 and beyond.[212] As Cotton reinterpreted the past with
changing circumstances, so generations re-read his writings and applied
them to new conditions: 'The usefulness of such works depended as
much on the response of the reader, on his ability to draw connections
with a current situation as it did on the wit of the author.'[213] There is a
whole history to be written of such readings. But do they echo the spirit
of Sir Robert Cotton? Howell had no doubt that they did. Cotton, he
felt sure, shared his belief that one studied and read to make 'useful
application of it' and that Cotton wrote in the same spirit that he read
– for use and application.[214]

As we begin to reconstruct the reading habits of the Renaissance, we
come to understand how typical such views were and how they operated
in general and in particular. Whether at the theatre, or reading the classics or the fables, contemporaries read to derive morals for their own

---

[210] On Howell, see D. Woolf, 'Conscience, Constancy and Ambition in the Career and Writings of
   James Howell', in J. Morrill, P. Slack and D. Woolf eds., *Public Duty and Private Conscience in
   Seventeenth-Century England* (Oxford, 1993), 244–78.
[211] Howell, *Cottoni Posthuma* (1651), sig. A3v.
[212] A sample provides some idea of the reapplication of Cotton's writings to other moments: his
   'Henry III' was published in 1641, 1651 and 1681, his 'Treatise Showing the Sovereign's Person
   is required in Great Councils' in 1641, and his 'Wars with Foreign Princes' (under other titles)
   in 1655, 1665 and 1675.   [213] Woolf, *Idea of History*, 168.
[214] Woolf, 'Conscience, Constancy', 242.

time, the commonplace book being often the site of the readers' medi-ations between old texts and modern circumstances.[215] Authors wrote in and for a culture in which readers not only applied a text, but searched between its lines and decoded meanings.[216] Histories were no exception; they may even have replaced the drama as a principal medium of con-temporary comment; they were seldom read for their 'contribution to scholarship', our own academic benchmark of worth. When that quin-tessential antiquary Simonds D'Ewes, who pored over charters and rolls, picked up Hayward's history of Henry IV, he was 'the rather drawn to read further because his reign came somewhat near our hard times'.[217] Amongst the ivory towers of Oxford, the Queen's College scholar Thomas Crosfield was no less alert to present concerns. In 1627 he noted: 'There is a little book published comprising several passages of state his-torically related as they were carried in the long reign of King Henry III, with some observations or applications to our state at this present which by reason of favourites and discontented peers resembles in many things that ancient government.'[218] Cotton's readers do not appear to have doubted that he wrote to impart counsel and to convey values – or that he had something important to say.

x

That sense of importance has not been shared by modern commenta-tors. Blair Worden did not think Cotton's ideas very impressive; Clive Holmes was harsher still about Sir Robert's 'rambling and platitudinous sentiments'.[219] As with Cotton's historical activities, such judgements rest on anachronistic criteria of importance – and once again perhaps on the issue of originality. As Blair Worden observed, much of what Cotton believed and counselled was part of the general currency of the age, even platitudinous. But the rearticulation of commonplace and tra-ditional values at a time when they appear to be in danger gives partic-ular force to the familiar, and reinvests old paradigms with powerful contemporary endorsement. As Richard Cust observes of Cotton's arguments in 1628: 'There was . . . nothing unusual in such views. What is interesting is the fact that they then were presented at all, that someone

---

[215] For one example see Annabel M. Patterson, *Fables of Power: Aesopian Writing and Political Theory* (Durham, N.C., and London, 1991).

[216] See Annabel M. Patterson, *Censorship and Interpretation* (Madison, Wis., 1984).

[217] Bourcier, *Diary of D'Ewes*, 138.

[218] Quoted in F. J. Levy, *Tudor Historical Thought* (San Marino, 1967), 270.

[219] Holmes, *Hist. Journ.*, 24 (1981), 1026.

felt that it was necessary to restate the principles which had normally been taken as read.'[220]

What were those principles and how did Cotton restate them? One, as I have argued, was balance and moderation in government. We have seen Cotton warn against the straining of the prerogative to excessive heights, but he had a greater horror of populism and disobedience. What was needed, he noted in passing in a treatise on Chancery, was to sustain a mean between the extremes of majesty and common law.[221] In his discussion of 'Other Descriptions . . . of the Parliament', his metaphors became as platitudinous as the ideas expressed. The relations of king, Lords and Commons were an imitation of the natural corpus of man, head, breast and body, 'and harmonical because so well turned a bass, mean and treble, there proceedeth an exquisite consert and delicious harmony'.[222] The point is that, at a time when experience was beginning to suggest their redundancy, Cotton not only restated these ideals *for* his age, he tried to demonstrate how they could be maintained in practice. The principles were not at fault, only the way in which they were applied. Before the Petition of Right rendered contentious the issue of imprisonment without due process, Cotton observed that before and after Magna Carta 'the kings of this realm . . . did exercise their kingly authority in that behalf which was so far from offending the subject for a long time'.[223] The question was not one of fundamental conflict between government and liberty. Subjects needed to obey, but a monarch 'should consider that nothing is more worth his apprehension than to see his subjects well satisfied of his actions'.[224] And nothing satisfied men more than a sense of the king's commitment to customary courses and values.

Such was also Cotton's solution to the mounting tensions within the church which have recently been the subject of much historiographical debate. Cotton had no time for popery; in 1624 he and D'Ewes discussed 'the danger and detestableness of popery since the Council of Trent'; and he advised James on how to check the influx of Jesuit priests.[225] But the antiquary was no fanatic. Not least because his maternal grandfather

---

[220] Cust, *Forced Loan*, 82; cf. Sharpe and Lake, *Culture and Politics*, introduction.
[221] BL Add. MS 36016, f. 38v.   [222] BL Egerton MS 2975, f. 32.
[223] Add. MS 36016, f. 37v; Sir Edward Coke had also accepted the royal power of imprisonment without cause: Sharpe, *Faction and Parliament* (1985 edn), xiii.
[224] Bodl. MS Tanner 103, f. 198.
[225] Bourcier, *Diary of D'Ewes*, 190; Cotton, 'Twenty Four Arguments Whether it be More Expedient to suppress Popish Practises . . . By the Strict Execution touching Jesuits . . .', in *Cottoni Posthuma*, 111–59.

and uncle had been recusants, Cotton appreciated (as did James I) that Catholics could be loyal Englishmen, as they had proved in 1588.[226] The solution to the Catholic challenge lay not in making martyrs but in reinvigorating the Church of England, and restoring the old and best times of Elizabeth: 'In those days there was an emulation between the clergy and the laity; and a strife arose whether of them should show themselves most affectionate to the gospel. Ministers haunted the houses of the worthiest men, where Jesuits now build their tabernacles, and poor country churches were frequented with the best of the shire. The word of God was precious, Prayer and Preaching went hand in hand together.'[227] Prayer and Preaching: the two words seem intended to conjoin what increasingly religious quarrels were putting asunder. Cotton made no direct comment on the quarrels between the Arminians and puritans.[228] When Sir John Eliot asked his assistance in 1629 to deal with the Arminian question, Cotton, to bring about 'a happy conclusion of your dispute of religion', advised firm adherence to the Elizabethan settlement, to 'the Catholic body of the church of England'.[229] Similarly the authors of the 'Topographical Description of England' praised an Elizabethan church whose doctrine was proved out of the Scriptures, Church Councils and the Fathers and rejected as factious the names of Lutheran and Calvinist.[230] 'How', Cotton asked in urging all to subscribe to one faith and church, 'can we draw others to our church, if we cannot agree where and how to lay on our foundation?'[231]

These traditional ideals for church and state informed Cotton's personal political ideology and morality – a belief above all in one's duty to serve the commonweal. When he described his own activities, scholarly and political, Sir Robert most often used the language of public duty and service. In the books he donated to Sir Thomas Bodley's library he inscribed his gift as 'for the public good';[232] his great library of manuscripts he collected, he claimed, 'out of my duty to the public'; his collections and learning, 'the labours of my life', he was 'most ready to offer to all public service'.[233] Men's self-descriptions are not always the best key

---

[226] *VCH, Hunts.*, I, 365: Sir Francis and Sir Henry Shirley. Cotton, 'Twenty Four Arguments', 146.

[227] Cotton, 'Twenty Four Arguments', 149–50.

[228] For a guide to the current state of historiography, see K. Fincham ed., *The Early Stuart Church, 1603–42* (Basingstoke, 1993).

[229] Sharpe, *Sir Robert Cotton*, 108–9, 181, 186; Port Eliot, MS X, f. 37.

[230] Sloane MS 241, f. 22ᵛ and ch. 2 passim.   [231] Cotton, 'Twenty Four Arguments', 144.

[232] Tite, '"Lost or Stolen or Strayed"', 263.

[233] Inner Temple Library, Petyt MS 537/18/50: Cotton to Speaker of House of Commons, 16 May 1614.

to their principles. But in Cotton's case his contemporaries spoke of his employment for the public good and his love of his country 'which yourself seek first to adorn'.[234] For his part his editor often heard Cotton say 'that he himself had the least share in himself but his country . . . had the greatest interest in him', and as a good Stoic, Howell commended a man 'in a perpetual pursuit after Vertu and knowledge'.[235]

Cotton saw his service performed in the very advice that historians have scorned as platitudinous. It was, we might say, *deliberately* not original advice. But neither was it the tired repetition and evocation of outmoded values that had no relevance to the needs of the day. Clive Holmes is right to observe that Cotton's conservative ideals of moderation, harmony and public service need to be discussed as part of the ideology of the 'country'. Yet Cotton regarded them no less as the best values for the court – and indeed served ministers whom he believed embodied them.[236] Sir Robert expressed some concern that the government might be becoming out of touch with the mood in the localities, but while the Huntingdonshire baronet was still called upon to give counsel in 1628, there was no need for him to conclude that those beliefs divided the country from the court, or parliament from the crown. Advice in the form of the politic history was advice for court *and* country.[237]

The politic history is a genre that belongs to the revival of interest in the classics, particularly Tacitus, and of commentaries on the classics in the late sixteenth century.[238] The influence of 'Taciteanism', more notoriously of Machiavellianism, produced an ambivalent response in early modern England.[239] On the one hand, the ideals of a Christian commonweal, of government as an ethical activity and of the need to subordinate private interest to the public good, remained the prevailing paradigm. On the other, experience showed all too clearly that *realpolitik*, intrigue and ambition characterized human and public behaviour, that Machiavelli and his disciples described accurately what men did, if not what they ought to do. Historians were particularly prone to reveal the ambivalence towards Machiavellian doctrines that characterized late

---

[234] BL Cotton MS Julius C. III, ff. 358–9.   [235] *Cottoni Posthuma*, sig. A3v.

[236] Holmes, *Hist. Journ.*, 24 (1981), p. 1027; on the need to reconfigure 'Court' and 'Country', see Sharpe and Lake, *Cululture and Politics*, 7–8.

[237] Cf. M. Smuts, 'Court-Centred Politics and the Uses of Roman Historians, c. 1590–1630', in Sharpe and Lake, *Culture and Politics*, 21–43.

[238] Ibid.; see also P. Burke, 'A Survey of the Popularity of Ancient Historians, 1450–1700', *History and Theory*, 5 (1966), 135–52.

[239] F. Raab, *The English Face of Machiavelli* (1964); Sharpe, *Politics and Ideas*, 25–8.

Elizabethan and Jacobean culture. As Daniel Woolf puts it well, 'Ralegh's ambivalence to the *realpolitik* of Tacitus and Machiavelli represents a conflict in early Stuart historiography between the duty to recommend effective worldly policy and the desire to advocate moral behaviour, a conflict which Ralegh (who was not alone) never resolved.'[240] Reviewers were sceptical about my claims for the influence of these ideas on Sir Robert Cotton. In some instances they were right to point out that such influence – of Giovanni Botero, for example – cannot be conclusively demonstrated. But there are notes on Guicciardini among Cotton's manuscripts, and *pace* Blair Worden, there is evidence that Cotton read Machiavelli who is cited in his treatise on the Jesuits.[241] Re-reading Cotton's maxims, I can hear him struggling with the conflict that Ralegh never resolved, even, more than Ralegh, endeavouring to resist acknowledging the force of Machiavellian observations. Yet whilst rejecting Machiavellian morality, Cotton adopted a central message of the Florentine: that success in public affairs depended upon acting in a manner appropriate to time and circumstance. For Sir Robert this meant no new amoral or radical courses. English history taught that the strongest regimes and best times were those in which the best examples and courses were followed and enacted. Accordingly, his advice to act on the moment was reiterated in the traditional language of statesmen behaving as skilful musicians, 'qui artem musices non mutant sed musices modum'.[242] Following the Taciteans, Cotton drew up axioms for the conduct of politics, but when it came to conveying advice he enfolded them in a history – a history not of classical times but of a medieval English king who had applied traditional remedies to the problems of his day.[243] Cotton's scholarship was always directed to 'useful application' in public life.[244] No less his public counsels, whatever they owed to new Italian influences, were presented as the lessons of English tradition and history.

XI

What then of Cotton's importance for and reputation in early Stuart English scholarship and politics? None has ever questioned the

---

[240] Woolf, *Idea of History*, 48.
[241] BL Cotton MS Titus B. I, ff. 6–53v; Cotton, 'Twenty Four Arguments', 123 (Machiavelli cited); Worden, 'Unmatched Antiquary'.
[242] *Cottoni Posthuma*, 131; 'Wisdom perfecteth her rules and ordinances by observation of time', Egerton MS 2975, f. 93.   [243] Sharpe, *Sir Robert Cotton*, 235–40.
[244] J. Howell, *Epistolae Ho-elianae*, ed. J. Jacobs (1890), 526.

centrality of his library and Colin Tite's researches are adding to our appreciation of just how important it was; Edmund Bolton's claims for its standing in Europe as well as England may soon appear description rather than hyperbole.[245] Similarly, few have doubted the role Cotton played in helping fellow scholars, not only with books, but with suggestions, contacts and notes. Again we are gaining a fuller picture of how widespread and sometimes how deep that assistance was, how far Cotton was a facilitator for a generation of scholars. He was asked to be an unpaid research assistant, an adviser on what to include in books, and sometimes a partial or co-author, often not acknowledged in the manner that our own standards would require.

That said, few modern commentators have had much to say for him as a scholar. To John Kenyon, he was a 'dilettante . . . in love with abstruse and curious learning which he assembled without the least discrimination'.[246] Fritz Levy dismissed him as 'an intellectual satellite of Camden'.[247] Though more favourable, the latest historian of early Stuart historical writing was forced to conclude that 'as neither historian nor antiquary . . . was Cotton himself especially outstanding'.[248] By the twentieth-century historian's criteria of scholarly judgement, such evaluations are not unreasonable. Lurking behind them, however, is an anachronistic disdain for a figure who, for all his resources, never made a major original contribution to scholarship and who (here one might have expected more sympathy) failed to finish books. Moreover, such judgements smack of the academic's continuing contempt for the scholar involved in the world of affairs, the figure who left the pure groves of academe for the corrupting influences of the public sphere. Even Colin Tite dismisses Cotton's political pieces as 'more ephemeral achievements'.[249] Cotton himself, however, would have demanded to be judged in the round – as a public figure *and* scholar – because the two spheres were not separate for him.

Unfortunately, as a politician, he has not enjoyed a much better press: Holmes thought him 'pompous'; Kenyon considered him 'entirely without political sense'. These read as strange verdicts on a man who was weekly called upon to advise MPs, ministers and monarchs, and whose advice was often taken – both at the time and later. The calling of the 1628 parliament, for instance, may have been due to his 'Danger

---

[245] BL Cotton MS Julius C. III, f. 29. Bolton said it made Paulus Jovius's library look like a charnel house.   [246] 'Antiquarian at Court', *Times Lit. Suppl.* (16 May 1980), 561.

[247] *Amer. Hist. Rev.*, 86 (1981), 127.   [248] Woolf, *Idea of History*, 159.

[249] Tite, *The Manuscript Library of Sir Robert Cotton*, 3.

and Remedy'; and there is much to suggest that during the 1630s Charles I carried out the programmes of reform at court and fiscal expedients outlined in Cotton's 'Henry the Third' and 'Manner and Means'. It was Cotton's 'cousin' Sir John Borough who, following the precedents outlined by the antiquary in 1610, drew Charles I's attention to knighthood fines, and other prerogative rights exploitable for fiscal gain.[250] But it was Charles I himself who appears to have directly taken up Cotton's advice: in his endeavour to reform the court, economize on the household, reinvigorate the Privy Council and, dispensing with favourites, 'dispose of affairs of most weight in his own person'.[251] Certainly, like Sir Robert, the king never doubted that 'Princes' Manners, though a mute law, have more of life and vigour than those of letters.'[252]

Cotton too was held in great esteem by those who, like him, stressed the utility of historical study, and the need for governors to be learned in its lessons. In the extraordinary collection of Sir William Drake's papers (in the Ogden bequest at University College London) that esteem is made abundantly clear.[253] Sir William Drake was the son of Sir Francis Drake of Esher and Joan Tottel, who inherited his considerable estate, Shardeloes in Buckinghamshire, from his maternal grandfather in 1626. Drake attended Christ Church, Oxford, and the Middle Temple, where he was bound with Sir Simonds D'Ewes.[254] He was a man of voracious appetite for learning, and especially for reading histories and antiquities, in manuscript and printed works, English and continental. In his quest for manuscripts on English law and parliament, Drake, like most of his contemporaries, was directed to the library of Sir Robert Cotton and, after 1631, to Sir Thomas Cotton.[255] He borrowed from Cotton as he did from D'Ewes, who may have introduced him to Sir Robert.[256] But Drake does more than add another name to the list of those borrowing from the Cottonian library. For Drake was, like Cotton,

---

[250] Cotton, 'Manner and Means'; BL Add. MS 34234, f. 169: extracts from Tower records by Borough (on whom see Harl. MS 6018, f. 149).

[251] Cotton, 'Henry III', 23–4, 25 (reform of waste), 26.   [252] Ibid., 25.

[253] For a guide to this collection, see S. Clark, 'Wisdom Literature of the Seventeenth Century: a Guide to the Contents of the "Bacon–Tottel" Commonplace Books', *Trans. Camb. Bib. Soc.*, 6 (1976), 291–305; 7 (1977), 46–73. Volumes 7, 8, 11, 23, 26, 29, 33–6, 38, 45, 48, 51–2 are in Drake's own hand. Recently the Huntington Library purchased another of Drake's notebooks, containing his political diary for the 1630s and Long Parliament (HM 55603). Harold Love also points to the very large number of Cotton's tracts in circulation, *Scribal Publication*, 87–9.

[254] M. Jansson, *Two Diaries of the Long Parliament* (Gloucester, 1984), xiii–xx; Phillips Sale Catalogue, 18 Mar. 1993; *VCH, Buckinghamshire*, III, 141, 145–8, 153.

[255] Huntington Lib. MS HM 55603, ff. 1 and *1 (Drake annotated his notebooks from each end; the Huntington Library has asterisked folios running from the back); University College London, Ogden MS 7/7, f.113ᵛ.   [256] Huntington Lib. MS HM 55603, f. 1.

a man of affairs. He sought and obtained the reversion of an office;[257] in 1640 he sat as MP for Amersham; and throughout the 1630s, whilst he was in England and travelling on the continent, he kept diaries and note-books – of public events, and of his reading.[258] Drake read and anno-tated the classical histories and humanist commentators on them: Xenophon and Plutarch, Tacitus and Cicero. But most of all, he read and constantly re-read the works of Lipsius, Cardanus, Bodin, and espe-cially Machiavelli, Guicciardini and – the man Drake saw as their English disciple – Francis Bacon. And there was a method to Drake's reading: he distilled from his studies a collection of maxims and rules for the conduct of his personal and public life, believing that 'when a man is deliberate and governed by order, rules and principles, no difficulty he meets with faints or abates his courage'.[259] Drake had little time for study as contemplation. To enable a man for action he thought nothing more important than the constant study and application of histories to the times: 'He that is well read in history seems to be of every country, to have lived in all ages and to have assisted at all councils.'[260]

Such a philosophy as well as a quest for manuscripts drew Sir William Drake to Sir Robert Cotton. Evidently, one of Drake's friends, 'Mr Pots' (Sir John Pots of Norfolk?), thought Cotton made such little use of his books, that – he told Sir William – he was like a man that had many weapons and never fought.[261] Drake clearly did not agree. His notes reveal that he read and annotated Cotton's writings more often than he borrowed from the antiquary's library. He laboured to obtain Cotton's account 'of the house of Austria practice', presumably the speech deliv-ered in the 1624 parliament.[262] He reminded himself to see 'Sir Robert Cotton's advice to help the King without aid of parliament'[263] and it evi-dently impressed him: 'read often' Cotton's project, he counselled himself, and 'let my fancy work upon the reading'.[264] Indeed Cotton became one of Drake's English models for his own development as a rhetorician and a writer. Significantly, after all his vast reading, he had decided to take Queen Elizabeth's and James I's chief minister, Lord

---

[257] Drake's negotiations for various offices are found in HM 55603. He purchased the reversion of a post in the Fine Office in the Court of Common Pleas; see G. E. Aylmer, *The King's Servants: the Civil Service of Charles I, 1625–1642* (London and New York, 1961), 97–8.

[258] Drake sat for Amersham in the Short and Long Parliaments. Jansson prints his parliamentary notebook from Ogden MS 7/51, but this now needs to be supplemented by his notes for his speech and other parliamentary proceedings in HM 55603.

[259] Ogden MS 7/8, f. 87.   [260] Ogden MSS 7/7 f. 90; 7/23, f. 23.

[261] HM 55603, f. *4.   [262] Ogden MS 7/7 f.132.   [263] Ibid. f. 100ᵛ.

[264] Ibid. ff. 161,169.

Salisbury, as his pattern, but noted: 'to supply his defect of writing many things read much Lord Bacon and Sir Robert Cotton's writings'.[265] The pairing of Bacon and Cotton was no mere whim of the occasion. Elsewhere, Drake instructed himself to 'read often Sir Francis Bacon's, Sir Robert Cotton's works'.[266]

It is not clear whether Drake knew Cotton personally, though it would seem quite likely. Certainly he noted that the Duke of Buckingham laboured to secure a match for Cotton's son, and, while he was overseas, he was informed of the search of Cotton's study following the discovery of the Dudley project (which Drake read).[267] Whether he knew him or not, however, Drake regarded Cotton as a man of affairs and valued his writings, as his collections, for their use, rather than their 'scholarship' in our sense of the word. He regarded Cotton's library as an 'arsenal' rather than repository for disinterested scholarly research.[268] He read Cotton, as he read Machiavelli, Guicciardini and Bacon, for his advice for the present, as much as his comments on the past. Sir William Drake's papers offer rich evidence of how a highly educated Englishman read his histories in the Renaissance, and how, at every point, historical learning was applied to present circumstances.[269] They remind us that, for all that subsequent generations of scholars have praised Cotton for assembling one of the greatest repositories for the academic study of the medieval past, Cotton's contemporaries perceived him, and valued him, differently: as a collector, writer and historian always engaged with his seventeenth-century present – with its political values, problems and disputes.

---

[265] Ibid. f. 148ᵛ.   [266] Ibid. f. 112ᵛ.   [267] Ibid. ff. 57ᵛ, 100ᵛ.   [268] HM 55603, f. *4.
[269] I am preparing two articles on 'The Mental World of Sir William Drake' and 'Sir William Drake and the Origins of the English Civil War'. (See now K. Sharpe, *Reading Revolutions: the Politics of Reading in Early Modern England* (forthcoming, New Haven and London, 2000).)

PART FIVE

Reviewings

CHAPTER TEN

Religion, rhetoric and revolution in seventeenth-century England

Religion, in recent years, has come as a salvation to historians of the English civil war. During the 1970s a group of historians on both sides of the Atlantic, often called revisionists, launched an assault on a view of seventeenth-century English history that had prevailed since 1688. Together these historians discredited the 'Whig' view that the story of English history, and especially of the Stuart century, was one of the triumph of parliaments over a series of monarchs' attempts to establish absolutism. Parliaments, they argued, were occasional assemblies ill-equipped to govern. MPs, more preoccupied with local than national matters, did not seek power, and their language was conservative rather than revolutionary; most shunned confrontation let alone bloody conflict.[1] Though well researched, powerfully argued, and often persuasive, these revisions left a major question unanswered: What did cause the English civil war? Stung by the witty retort of their critics – that they had succeeded in explaining why a civil war did *not* take place in seventeenth-century England[2] – the revisionists moved from their iconoclastic destruction of the old picture to endeavour to sketch a new. For none could deny that the civil war was the greatest fissure, and only violent revolution, in the English body politic, nor that it produced a vibrant political discourse of passion, ideological fervour and theoretical sophistication. One young scholar attempted to direct attention back to the language of liberty and property, law and contract, as the principal

---

[1] Among the best-known revisionist studies are C. S. R. Russell, 'Parliamentary History in Perspective, 1604–29', *History*, 61 (1976), 1–27; Russell, *Parliaments and English Politics 1621–1629* (Oxford, 1979); M. Kishlansky, 'The Emergence of Adversary Politics in the Long Parliament', *Journ. Mod. Hist.*, 49 (1977), 617–40; and K. Sharpe ed., *Faction and Parliament: Essays on Early Stuart History* (Oxford, 1978).

[2] See J. Morrill, *The Revolt of the Provinces* (1980), x; and Morrill, *The Nature of the English Revolution* (1993), 188.

rhetorics that scripted revolution, but he spoiled some suggestive possibilities with a crude, overschematized case.[3]

For the most part both revisionists and the next generation of disciples and critics shifted the focus to a different arena of contest: to religion and the church.

The old Whig thesis, of course, had also a religious dimension. For
most historians of the eighteenth, nineteenth and even twentieth centuries, the story of English history was as much that of the triumph of
protestantism over popery as of parliaments over absolutism. Some, discerning in protestantism the spiritual independence and individualism
that were the motors of secular political movements, described the
English civil war as a puritan revolution.[4] But in religious as in political
historiography, during the 1970s a group of revisionists upset the old
views and assumptions. The history of the early Stuart church, they
maintained, was not one of a struggle between Anglicans and puritans.
Not only were the very categories, they asserted, anachronistic or
blurred, the church as a whole was conjoined by the theological cement
of predestinarian Calvinism. Revolutionary puritans, the conclusion followed, were as mythical as revolutionary parliaments.[5]

Yet, once again, the importance of religious issues, of religious belief
and rhetoric, could not be denied. What then, the question remained,
fractured the ecclesiastical consensus to make theological and liturgical
preferences and differences vital determinants of political events and
allegiances in the years leading to civil war? The ecclesiastical revisionists found their villains not now among the ranks of puritans but in the
Arminians who, they argued, came to some prominence in the last years
of James I's reign, still more on the succession of his son. The
Arminians, the argument runs, rejected the predestinarian theology that
had become a consensus, advanced a more ceremonial form of worship
that smacked of popery, and enforced a rigid and novel conformity that
fundamentally altered and narrowed the Church of England.[6] Through

---

[3] See J. P. Sommerville, *Politics and Ideology in England 1603–1640* (1986); see also K. Sharpe, *Politics
and Ideas in Early Stuart England* (1989), 283–8.

[4] For example, S. R. Gardiner, *History of England from the Accession of James I to the Outbreak of the Civil
War* (10 vols., 1883–4), passim; cf. J. P. Kenyon, *The History Men: the Historical Profession in England
since the Renaissance* (1983), 222; see also C. Hill, *Puritanism and Revolution* (1958); and M. Walzer, *The
Revolution of the Saints* (Cambridge, Mass., 1965).

[5] See N. Tyacke, 'Puritanism, Arminianism, and Counter Revolution', in C. S. R. Russell ed., *The
Origins of the English Civil War* (1973), 199–234; cf. Tyacke, *Anti-Calvinists: the Rise of English
Arminianism c. 1590–1640* (Oxford, 1987); and P. Collinson, *The Religion of Protestants* (Oxford, 1982).
Tyacke's thesis became a textbook orthodoxy.

[6] As I have argued elsewhere, Tyacke and others are slippery with their definitions of
Arminianism.

their innovations – and the positions of power they obtained under Charles I to advance them – they drove former conformists into opposition and created the puritan revolutionaries who had hitherto found happy accommodation within the established church.[7] The English civil war was, they concluded, the reaction to an Arminian revolution.

To some political revisionists, wandering in the dark, these findings appeared as a blinding light of conversion on the road to Damascus. For the ecclesiastical historians had, like the political revisionists, emphasized the conservatism, even consensualism, of seventeenth-century Englishmen. But they had also found a magic key: an explanation of how a conservative culture could explode into radical conflict, thereby resolving the revisionists' dilemma. As a consequence, Nicholas Tyacke's thesis about the rise of English Arminianism became the mainstay of Conrad Russell's account of the origins of the English civil war.[8]

Others were not so easily persuaded. Ecclesiastical historians who took a longer view of the Church of England questioned the thesis of an Arminian revolution at all its key points. They refuted the claim that the Church of England was ever characterized by a commitment to double predestination, to reprobation as well as election; they denied that many labelled by Tyacke and others as Arminians were ever exponents of Arminius's views on free will; they exposed the falsity of simply reading theological positions from liturgical preferences (or vice versa); and they suggested, in the place of the clear dichotomies of Arminians versus Calvinists, a far more subtle spectrum of attitudes to theology and liturgy. The 'Arminian revolution', they concluded, was a myth.[9]

A contemporary *perception*, however, that much was amiss – in the church as well as the state – cannot be denied. Increasingly, some came to doubt the orthodoxy of King Charles, and by 1640 the fear of a popish conspiracy to subvert church and state was widespread.[10] Similarly, trust in the monarchy – to govern for the good of the commonweal, defend the realm and uphold the laws – was dangerously diminishing, to the point where normal political differences were less easily resoluble by traditional political means. The questions remain:

---

[7] See Collinson, *Religion of Protestants*.

[8] Russell, *Origins of the English Civil War*, introduction; and Russell, *The Causes of the English Civil War* (Oxford, 1990), chs. 3, 4 and passim.

[9] See P. White, 'The Rise of Arminianism Reconsidered', *Past and Present*, 101 (1983), 34–54; and White, 'Arminianism Reconsidered', *Past and Present*, 115 (1987), 201–29; S. Lambert, 'Richard Montagu, Arminianism, and Censorship', *Past and Present*, 124 (1989), 36–68; and the letters of Ian Green and myself in the *Times Lit. Supp.* (August, September 1987), 384, 899, 922, 955, 1017.

[10] C. Hibbard, *Charles I and the Popish Plot* (Chapel Hill, N.C., 1983); and A. Fletcher, *The Outbreak of the English Civil War* (1981).

How did those perceptions and fears arise? How was that trust eroded? And the question most neglected: How were the anxieties about the church and state connected in the consciousness of the seventeenth-century actors? While some historians have begun to suggest that the religious rhetoric cannot be separated from secular political rhetoric – that 'popery' articulated a range of anxieties[11] – for the most part the relationship of secular and religious issues and languages has not been reconfigured, or even explored.

We have been awaiting, then, a truly post-revisionist re-examination of the relationship of ideas to events in the early Stuart decades and a study of religion defined more broadly than the focus on questions of theology and debates between university-educated divines has allowed. We need, in other words, a study of the political culture of seventeenth-century England, conceived as that network of languages, customs, practices and rituals through and by which contemporaries discerned and constructed meaning and the values of their society.[12] Religion, studied as it should be in this broader cultural context, is then seen to incorporate the (sometimes contested) rituals of parish life – baptism, communion, funeral; the fabric of the church and lay–clerical relations; the place of things spiritual in the culture and customs of aristocratic elites and the populace – as well as issues of theology and liturgy. Overall, we need to understand how a complex contemporary political culture or ideological system, constructed of both secular and religious components, simultaneously embraced ideas of harmony and order and voices of discord and fragmentation; how circumstance could reshape and combine different traditional rhetorics and values into new perceptions and programmes; how the culture first functioned to contain conflict and then was ruptured and reconstituted by it. We await, in fine, a nuanced post-revisionist study of the cultural (a better term I think than 'intellectual') origins of the civil war, and of the rhetorics, religious and secular, that made and were remade by revolution.

II

In *The Early Stuart Church, 1603–1642* (Stanford, Calif., 1993), Kenneth Fincham and his contributors attempt to survey for students the current

---

[11] See the stimulating essay by Peter Lake, 'Anti-Popery: the Structure of a Prejudice', in R. Cust and A. Hughes eds., *Conflict in Early Stuart England* (1989), 72–106.
[12] This has been attempted in K. Sharpe and P. Lake eds., *Culture and Politics in Early Stuart England* (Houndmills and Stanford, 1994).

state of research on these questions and to take the debate forward. The old protagonists are here in the left and right corners. Tyacke attempts another answer to his critics with an essay on Archbishop William Laud.[13] Where, for Patrick Collinson, Laud was 'the greatest calamity ever visited on the Church of England',[14] Tyacke here argues that he 'deserves to rank among the greatest archbishops of Canterbury since the Reformation' (p. 51). But Tyacke still wishes to press the case he has never satisfactorily proved: that Laud was not merely perceived to be but actually was a doctrinal Arminian. He offers some new evidence, which deserves close consideration – even though the 1622 sermon commemorating James I's accession (printed by royal order) scarcely 'constitutes a declaration of Arminian sympathies' (p. 60).[15] Otherwise the essay is a disappointing rerun of Tyacke's old assertions about Laud (the proscription of Calvinist preaching and the 'Laudian' altar policy), all of which have been thrown into question by recent scholarship.[16] In the opposite corner the scholar who originally laid down the challenge crystallizes the argument of his book that there was no Arminian revolution in early Stuart England.[17] Peter White maintains that the Church of England was never committed to strict predestinarian theology, that from the beginning the Anglican settlement was characterized by moderation, and that James I and Charles I alike were committed to sustaining it.[18] In so far as the 1630s saw changes in the style of churchmanship, these owed more to the vigour and clericalism of the new regime than to any novel doctrinal or liturgical inclinations. Predestination, White concludes, should not be the device for categorizing early modern churchmen because it was not the 'crucial determinant' in a spectrum of beliefs nor the central issue for the church (p. 212).

There is little surprise, then, in the rounds of the principal protagonists in the Fincham volume, albeit it is valuable to have their views clearly restated. The interest of the book, however, lies most in its novel emphases and new contributions. The editor, in a useful introduction, now acknowledges the need to shift the argument from the narrow focus

---

[13] See Tyacke, *Anti-Calvinists* (paperback, edn, Oxford 1990) preface.

[14] Collinson, *Religion of Protestants*, 90.

[15] See J. Bliss and W. Scott eds., *The Works of William Laud* (7 vols., Oxford, 1847–60), I, 33–50.

[16] See Ian Green, '"For Children in Yeeres and Children in Understanding": the Emergence of the English Catechism under Elizabeth and the Early Stuarts', *Journal of Ecclesiastical History*, 37 (1986), 392–425; K. Sharpe, *The Personal Rule of Charles I* (New Haven and London, 1992), ch. 6; and J. Davies, *The Caroline Captivity of the Church* (Oxford, 1992), reviewed below.

[17] See P. White, *Predestination, Policy and Polemic: Conflict and Consensus in the English Church from the Reformation to the Civil War* (Cambridge, 1992).

[18] Cf. G. W. Bernard, 'The Church of England, c. 1529–1642', *History*, 75 (1990), 183–206.

on predestination to study issues of order, worship, clerical authority and attitudes to church history. Fincham also accepts some of the central criticisms made of the Tyacke case and of his own earlier arguments. The view that the 'sting of puritanism had largely been drawn by the accommodating climate of the Jacobean church' he rightly dismisses as 'over optimistic' (p. 7). The Jacobean church, he ventures, was not a stable and harmonious body; there were links between moderate and more radical puritans; Charles I 'inherited' rather than created suspicion of puritan conspiracy (p. 13). In so far as there was a different Caroline style, it was neither completely novel nor universally unpopular. Reactions differed widely, with Sunday sports, an emphasis on ritual, even an (alleged) ban on predestinarian teaching enjoying some appeal. 'So,' Fincham concludes, 'for all our talk of polarization under Archbishop Laud, it appears that Protestant fragmentation in the 1640s . . . was a direct consequence not of the 1630s but of the political crisis after 1642.'[19] It is a conclusion of course that leaves 'the precise contribution of religion to the coming of civil war . . . open to debate' (p. 21).

It is a conclusion, too, by which Fincham is so evidently discomfited that he often seems to contradict it himself. In his essay with Peter Lake on the ecclesiastical policies of James and Charles, for instance, he switches to the view that by the middle years of the first Stuart reign reluctant conformists were won over and the 'radicalism of puritanism had ostensibly been removed' (p. 28; cf. p. 7). Fincham seems uneasy about a James I whose ecclesiastical positions and policies still await satisfactory exegesis, for the James who patronized evangelical Calvinists also promoted Arminians, as the James who often failed to press strict conformity also harshly denounced puritans. Was James himself a predestinarian? Were his shifts of patronage and policy a response to political circumstance? Fincham sees the outbreak of the Thirty Years War and the puritan call to arms as the decisive moment in turning James against all puritans, moderate as well as radical. But James's commitment to confessional unity, his Hookerian vision of church and state, his inclination to ceremony and order, disposed him always to distrust those he denounced as a sect, fit only for the habitude of woods and caves, beyond civil society – a view not so different from his son's as most historians have maintained.[20] Where Charles did differ markedly from his father was, as Fincham nicely argues, in his insistence that disputes 'be

---

[19] Cf. Sharpe, *Personal Rule*, 933–5.
[20] See above, chs. 3 and 4, especially pp. 136–8, 165–7.

resolved not fudged' (p. 43). It was the resoluteness and vigour of execution rather than the policies themselves that gave a different tone to the Caroline regime in church and state. Most of all, the new king's more aggressive clericalism and obsessive concern with reverence and order were part of a broader change in political culture after 1625.

Other contributions to *The Early Stuart Church* helpfully move the focus to these broader issues and away from the narrow theological questions that exercised only a few. Anthony Milton usefully surveys the debates about the pre-Reformation church, the visibility and historic succession of the Church of England and its relation to Rome, albeit he draws too sharply the distinguishing line between Charles and James – who was quite willing to deny the pope was Antichrist, regard Rome as a true church, and to stress the continuity of the English church with the medieval church.[21] Judith Maltby rightly berates those who, attracted to the noise of the godly minority, have all but ignored the conformists, the 'Prayer Book Anglicans' as she calls them, of the church.[22] Far from sympathizing with puritans, she argues, those mainstays of the parish exhibited little interest in theological issues but were devoted to canonical worship, ceremony, baptismal rites, altars and (often) rails. Maltby is not at all clear on why she regards such views as being in opposition to Laudian reforms – perhaps not least because, along with other contributors, she tends to oversimplify Laud's programmes. She fails to read the petitions on church matters sent to parliament in the 1640s in the political contexts that shaped them. But her appeal to study those who objected to being labelled unregenerate from the pulpit and who identified with the Prayer Book and canons is a vital corrective and a timely pointer to new directions for research.

Andrew Foster, in a sensible examination of lay–clerical relations from the 1590s to 1640, persuasively argues that an assertive clergy, with a growing sense of their special status, may have done more than purely doctrinal disputes did to destabilize the church. Not least, though he attributes a role to Laudian sacramentalism, Foster is able to explain how a clericalism assertive from 1616 fuelled a reaction that culminated in attacks on churchmen of all doctrinal preferences in 1641.[23] Looking closely at the diocese of Peterborough, John Fielding, in the most

---

[21] Milton himself cites Laud's *Conference with Fisher*, conducted in 1622, as evidence of a changing attitude towards Rome during James's reign.

[22] For further exposition we eagerly await the publication of Christopher Haigh's research on the early Stuart church.

[23] It is worth remembering that the attack on the episcopacy in 1641 was not confined to Arminians or ceremonialists – a point not sufficiently pondered by Tyacke and Russell.

exciting and original essay in the volume, offers both a powerful critique of the historiographical consensus and some challenging suggestions for a new picture. The evidence from Peterborough, he is unequivocal, contradicts any idea of a Jacobean tranquillity, and it upsets some other neat categorizations as well. The Calvinist parson John Williams was a keen supporter of Sunday sports; Bishop Piers, seen as Laud's hench-man at Bath and Wells (1632–41), proceeded in Peterborough with tact and caution; vocal dissenters from the Laudian regime were openly preaching during the 1630s.[24] Most importantly, Fielding persuasively argues that far from driving the moderates into extremists' arms, 'the authority behind the policies of the 1630s caused moderate Calvinists . . . to draw away from their radical colleagues' (p. 111). Rejecting the thesis of a Calvinist consensus as 'simplistic' and the issue of predesti-nation as 'almost irrelevant', Fielding draws attention – crucially – to the issue of and concepts of order (pp. 111, 113). It was, he concludes, the issue of order that led a large conformist constituency to share the Arminians' fear of puritan populism and separated the staunchly Calvinist but royalist Lord Montagu from his puritan companions.[25] Fielding astutely reminds us that religious issues and, still more, theolog-ical questions should not be seen as distinct from broader political devel-opments.

It is no surprise that our best historian of seventeenth-century relig-ion is already leading the field to a broader conceptualization of the 'relig-ious' and its integration with political and cultural history. In his essay here Peter Lake urges us to see Laudianism less as a theology or even a novel programme and more as a 'distinctive style' (p. 163). At its heart, Lake argues, was an effort to redraw the boundaries between the sacred and the profane, a desire that shaped attitudes towards altars, the clergy, the Book of Sports, ceremonies, clerical and lay hierarchies, and the architecture of church and worship. Laudianism, as Lake defines it, held a coherent view of the church, Christian community and commonweal that has to be studied as an aspect of the Caroline style (and ideology) of government. There are some questionable claims here. To say that Laudianism placed external ceremonies 'at the very centre of . . . true religion' is to ignore Laud's own insistence that men should not place 'the principal part of . . . piety in them' (p. 167);[26] the statement that Laud

---

[24] Cf. Sharpe, *Personal Rule*, 648–9.
[25] On Montagu, see E. Cope, *The Life of a Public Man: Edward, First Baron Montagu of Boughton, 1562–1644*, American Philosophical Society, no. 142 (Philadelphia, 1981).
[26] *Works of Laud*, II, 312.

insisted on altars railed at the east end needs modifying in the light of new research, especially that of Julian Davies; passages about the 'levelling effects of Laudian clericalism' are more suggestive than persuasive (p. 178). But there are wonderful insights in Lake's exposition of the politics of church architecture, of a variegated community stretching from altar back to church porch, and their complementary relationship to secular architectures and social arrangements.[27] It is an essay like this that opens up the riches of a cultural, social and political, as well as theological, history of the church. And it is for its pointers to these new directions more than its summation of the old that *The Early Stuart Church* is most to be – dare I risk the pun – lauded.

One scholar is conspicuously absent from Fincham's seminar on the early Stuart church. For some years now, Julian Davies has been the awkward student who asked the leading question or questioned the leading interpretation.[28] Against the grain, Davies denied the importance of Arminianism and that Laud was an Arminian; argued that the archbishop's and others' positions on the altar controversy were oversimplified and misunderstood; and maintained that the Book of Sports was the more contentious and divisive issue in the Caroline church, albeit the differences did not run in or parallel to neat party lines. Most of all, against Tyacke and his disciples Davies insisted that theological preferences should not be read from attitudes to ceremony or vice versa. The reluctance to give him a fair hearing or to engage with his early formulations (several of Fincham's contributors refer to Davies while perpetrating the errors he has identified) has had a happy consequence. Davies has deepened his researches by work in over fifty record repositories throughout England and Wales and study of a vast range of administrative, court, visitational, diocesan and – usually much neglected – parish records.

In *The Caroline Captivity of the Church: Charles I and the Remoulding of Anglicanism* (Oxford, 1992), Davies explodes a bomb under almost every buttress of the Tyacke case. For one, he rejects the notion that the Book of Sports was an Arminian assault on puritan sabbatarianism. Laud himself was a strict observer of the sanctity of the Sabbath, as were Lancelot Andrewes and John Cosin. The archbishop never strictly enforced the reading of the Book, whereas the Calvinists Joseph Hall

---

[27] The religious history of the Stuart period has made too little use of visual evidence.

[28] His views have, as he hints, been less than welcome at some gatherings, such as the Tudor–Stuart seminar at the Institute of Historical Research, when defensive efforts were made by Russell and others to discredit Davies's early researches.

and John Davenant, as well as the Arminian Matthew Wren, did. Though Charles, like Queen Elizabeth or his father (on whose own book he had modelled the Book of Sports), was no sabbatarian, he had certainly not intended to contravene the statutes of 1625 and 1628 for Sunday observance;[29] indeed, in defining what was permissible and not permissible the Book could be and was used by the courts to strengthen such legislation. The Book of Sports, Davies concludes, was less about sabbatarianism than it was a test of conformity to authority: 'Dr Tyacke's "Arminian Sunday" is . . . misleading' (p. 203). Another incendiary is detonated under the altar. It has become an entrenched orthodoxy, wrongly repeated by many of Fincham's contributors, that Laud ordered tables to be placed at the east end, in a north–south position behind rails, at which communicants knelt to receive before what had become an altar of sacrifice. For Tyacke and others, this was the ceremony that expressed the sacramental theory of grace at the centre of Arminian theology. Davies shows, with formidable learning, that none of these assumptions stands. In the first place he reminds us that two Calvinists instigated the east-end altar at St Gregory's and that others, such as Bishop Davenant of Salisbury, enforced it. Laud for his part did not enforce an altarwise position nor receiving at the rails. Rather than clear Arminian or Calvinist positions, Davies shows in almost tedious detail, there was a wide variety of practice, reflecting different views on the placement of the altar at the east, its position (north–south), rails, and receiving communion at the rails. Those who still wish to insist on a Laudian altar policy now have a mass of evidence to answer.

Its foundations fractured at two points of historiographical support, the myth of Laudian Arminianism itself comes under Davies's assault. The Jacobean church, he concurs with White, was not an edifice cemented by a common Calvinist bond but a 'community with multifarious doctrinal views', in which it was quite 'possible to be reformed . . . without being Calvinist' (p. 89). Arminianism attained less importance in contemporary discussion than in present historiography. In so far as predestination was an issue, it was predestination to *reprobation* (not emphasized by Calvin, nor in the Thirty-nine Articles) that became controversial, and even here there was no simple bipolarization but a spectrum of positions. To reject reprobation, even to be anti-Calvinist, was not necessarily to espouse an Arminian theology of grace. As Davies, fol-

---

[29] 1 Car. 1 cap. 1, cap. 23; 3 Car. 1 cap. 2.

lowing Sears McGee and others, rightly puts it, Laud may have rejected reprobation, but pace Tyacke's efforts, 'the evidence . . . is certainly insufficient to indict him of Arminianism' (p. 95).[30] And if Laud's Arminianism must be doubted, he continues, so it must be also concluded, 'The Arminianization of the decade is a myth' (p. 122). For there was no campaign to restrict Calvinist preachers or catechisms; and no programme to publish Arminian tracts. Rather, Charles I's declarations and preface to the Thirty-nine Articles proscribed public controversy, leaving each to behave in private as he chose. Against Russell's tendentious assertions, Davies provides demonstration that the policy was enforced impartially.[31] To see, as many historians have, the decade of the 1630s 'through spectacles of Arminian versus Calvinist' is to see it through William Prynne's glasses – darkly (pp. 48, 122).

Such powerful critique of traditional historical explanation always leaves the critic with a problem. Whatever the historical reality, or the uncritical dependence of Tyacke, Russell and others on Laud's detractors, it remains the case that significant contemporaries did perceive Laud to be the spawn of a papist and an Arminian threat and did fear dangerous innovations in the Caroline church. Davies is not always ready to acknowledge these perceptions or, where he is, successful in explaining them. But his thesis is not mere negation. Though he rejects the chimera of an Arminian revolution, he identifies a Laudian and Caroline mode of churchmanship that effected important changes and aroused concerns. In one of the best analyses of Laud's beliefs, Davies shows him to have been most influenced by 'the patriotic reorientation and historical reinvestment of Anglicanism', which, in early Stuart England, placed greater emphasis on the visibility and Catholicity of the church (p. 54).[32] Laud stressed the historic continuity of the church, with bishops as the essential link and, like the Fathers, emphasized the holiness of places, objects and outward expressions. Though Laud was little interested in theological dispute and doctrinally tolerant, not all were able or willing to perceive that his emphasis on externals and his

---

[30] See S. McGee, 'William Laud and the Outward Face of Religion', in R. L. De Molen ed., *Leaders of the Reformation* (1984). Laud preached against Arminianism (see Davies, *Caroline Captivity*, 122; and Sharpe, *Personal Rule*, 286).

[31] See C. S. R. Russell, *The Fall of the British Monarchies, 1637–1642* (Oxford, 1991), 15, for an example of assertion as an alternative to argument.

[32] With the accession of James I, there was a change in the visual representation of the Greek Fathers. Gaultier's title page to the works of Chrysostom (1613) depicts the Fathers with halos. See M. Corbett and R. Lightbown, *The Comely Frontispiece: the Emblematic Title Page in England, 1550–1660* (1979), 41.

admiration for the pre-Reformed church were not popish. The arch-bishop's hounding of the Stranger churches – most of all his misjudged prosecution of Prynne, Burton and Bastwick – exacerbated the mis-understanding of his real goals and programmes. But what most cast him as the enemy of reformed Protestantism was not so much his own actions but his service to the king. To Davies, it was not Laud but the king who set the religious agenda of the reign, and a king who had his own brand of churchmanship – 'Carolinism' he calls it – distinct from and more damaging than the archbishop's. Davies's Carolinism was not a theology: doctrine for Charles was of little importance. What mattered most to the king was order – in the fabric of the church and modes of worship, among the clergy and laity. Charles linked the sacramental worship of God with the rituals of divine kingship to which he devoted such attention; the approach to the altar, as to the king, involved a hier-archy of chambers and stages of holiness.[33] And he feared in the volun-tarism of strict Calvinism a threat of disorder in state and church, which led him to read in every act of nonconformity a challenge to his rule. To Davies, Charles I's 'Caesaro-sacerdotalism' was more aesthetic and political than theological in its basis. Whatever its roots, however, in his arbitrary exercise of power as head of the church Charles, Davies con-cludes, violated the conscience, fundamentally altered the moderation of Elizabethan and Jacobean Anglicanism, and so fractured the Jacobean 'consensus': 'Religion became the major cause of the British civil war not because of the bugbear of Arminianism, but because Charles I was in conscious rebellion against lay and popular Protestantism' (p. 17).

It is a conclusion that comes as a – largely unpersuasive – surprise. For though Davies is at pains to reject the arguments of G. W. Bernard and others that Charles merely upheld an Anglican moderation in changed circumstances against a more active puritan radicalism, he – untypically – never argues the point.[34] Stricter conformity, an enhanced clericalism, a suspicion of puritan voluntarism and an inclination to ritual were spe-cific neither to the person of Charles I nor to his reign. Davies himself acknowledges that some of Charles's religious preferences were part of a changing climate and that others rested on a 'groundswell of support' in the localities; he never explains exactly how or why Charles came to be suspected of being popish.[35] Moreover, rather contradicting himself, he appears uneasy about the role of religion in the origins of the civil

[33] Cf. Gardiner, *History of England*, VII, 36; Sharpe, *Politics and Ideas*, 108–10; and Sharpe, *Personal Rule*, 28off.   [34] See Bernard, 'The Church of England'.
[35] I have argued elsewhere that the explanation lies as much with foreign as with domestic policy and circumstances.

war. 'But was religion', he asks, 'the same determinant of the divisions before 1641, during the regime, and after its collapse as it was in the split of 1641–42?' (p. 313). Because the answer must be a clear *no*, the precise role of religion remains in doubt. Again Davies is a better critic of existing views than author of a persuasive new thesis. For he is right to insist that religion has been too distinctly separated from other values and ideologies. Charles I attracted suspicion and opposition not least for his enhancement of the clergy and his commitment to re-endowing the church with lands – which in the eyes of the lay gentry threatened to overturn the victories of the Reformation (p. 291).[36] These royal policies were intimately bound up with Charles I's 'sacramental notions of personal authority', an ideology of kingship as well as churchmanship (p. 299). Charles, in short, could not easily make a distinction between nonconformity in the church and a challenge to his rule. Before we conclude with Davies that this was simple political miscalculation, we need to reconsider whether the 'subversive potential' of puritan voluntarism was contained in early Stuart England, or whether (as Charles feared) revolutionary puritanism was waiting for its moment (p. 10).[37]

III

It is both regrettable and remarkable that none of the historians at work reconfiguring the religious alignments and rhetorics of early Stuart England has paid serious attention to the literary texts of the age – the drama, the play of conscience, the devotional lyric – as obvious loci of shifting theological and liturgical sensibilities. And though they are leading historians in so many investigations of the political culture of the age, literary critics too have largely ignored religious texts, preferring to study the drama and poetry most obviously engaged with power, public life, theatricality and display.[38] One critic has even suggested that the anthropology underlying new historicism has limited its value as a methodology for explicating that interiority in which questions of faith are worked out. 'New Historicism,' Richard Strier has argued, 'unlike Renaissance English culture, . . . has a radically secular focus.'[39]

---

[36] See Sharpe, *Personal Rule*, 312–14.   [37] See Sharpe, *Politics and Ideas*, 28–31.
[38] Clear examples of the failure to consult religious texts are the works of Stephen Greenblatt, Jonathan Goldberg and Louis Montrose.
[39] R. Strier, '"Old" Historicism, "New" Historicism, and the Reformation' (paper delivered at 'Religion and Culture in the English Renaissance', conference held at UCLA and the Huntington, March 1993). Cf. Deborah Shuger, *Habits of Thought in the English Renaissance: Religion, Politics and the Dominant Culture* (Berkeley and Los Angeles, 1990).

Certainly in recent years the vast critical scholarship on Shakespeare has largely focused on the identification of new political (usually discordant and radical) voices, as opposed to the issues of church and state that pre-occupied his Elizabethan and Jacobean contemporaries.

In *Shakespeare and the Politics of Protestant England* (Lexington, Ky., 1992), Donna Hamilton sets out to restore Shakespeare's plays to contemporary discourse about church and state, to conjoin the religious and political issues that have been falsely separated, and to historicize a number of plays as precise comment on particular ecclesiological controversies. The preface promises a fruitful redirection. Religious questions of conformity and conscience were, as Hamilton reminds us, central to the (secular) debates about authority and obedience which informed Shakespeare's drama and to which that drama contributed. But our confidence that the promise will be fulfilled fades rapidly. In her introductory chapter, for all her sensitivity to the complexities of court faction and politics, Hamilton makes simplistic assumptions about the nature of patronage and its relation to ideological programmes, about the relationship of individual conscience to radical ideas of subjectivity, and about the fit of religious positions to ideas of law, prerogative and kingship – ideas here rather reductively polarized. Assertions that the High Commission was 'an institution without rival in its capacity for oppression' or that 'puritanism dominated mainstream English Christianity' inspire little confidence in historians (pp. 7, 9). Sadly, the particular readings of the plays command no more.

There can be no doubt that in some cases Hamilton is onto something. The argument that *Henry VIII* spoke not only to Jacobean disputes about royal finance and parliament but also to contests between Catholic and godly factions in 1612–13 – even the suggestion about some correspondences between Henry's divorce and that of the Jacobean Earl of Essex – is persuasive. Many other observations are provocatively stimulating: the valence of siting *The Comedy of Errors* in the Ephesus of Paul's epistle; the role of Imogen in *Cymbeline*; and most of all Shakespeare's replication and evocation of languages used in and freighted by contemporary religious polemic. But Hamilton's closer readings to press her argument about allegorical topicality not only dissatisfy; they are guilty of a tendentiousness bordering on contempt for the text. Few will be even half persuaded to see in *Twelfth Night* Malvolio 'constructed quite explictly along the lines of the hostile rhetoric of the conformists', or Toby as a representative of ecclesiastical persecution (p. 96). Few will follow Hamilton in decoding Adriana in *Errors* as the suspicious wife who equals the church, or the Dromios as the representatives of victimized puritans. Few will re-read *Measure*, as we are here urged to do, as a play about the ex officio oath and the question of conformity.

At times, Hamilton seems unsure about her own case. Though she wishes to characterize Shakespeare as 'ideologically similar' to the faction around the Earls of Leicester and Essex and Sir Philip Sidney (a group committed to the maintenance of liberties and promotion of godly programmes at home and abroad), the playwright often fails to conform to type (p. xi).[40] He excises anti-Catholic rhetoric from his sources; he appeals to a broad inclusive Catholic church rather than the invisible church of the elect; allegedly, he even recommends to James I that he 'validate all his subjects, even those who maintained a spiritual allegiance to Rome' (pp. 31, 61). To note that the plays often conclude with an injunction to 'cooperation and unity' is not to say anything novel but does raise questions about the precise meaning of those injunctions and their relation to the Leicester–Sidney position on church politics (p. 193).

If Hamilton fails as a close reader and critic, she is clearly extremely well read in the broader discourses about church–state relations and persuasive that in some way Shakespeare needs to be re-read in that discursive context. Such recontextualizations prompt suggestive reconsiderations of the religious valence of Shakespearean debates about conscience and duty, love and honour, sincerity and dissimulation. Whether they will point up precise historical allegories must remain in serious doubt.

Study of literary figures and texts tends more often to question or complicate historical categories than to confirm them. This should neither disappoint nor surprise the historian. For often the play or poem offered a space that contemporaries used to explore the tensions and contradictions – in themselves and in their age – and so presents the historian with valuable evidence of those uncertainties and efforts to resolve them.[41] For the history of the early Stuart church George Herbert presents a perfect example. Though the subject of revived critical interest, Herbert has remained unstudied and probably unread by ecclesiastical historians, perhaps because of his resistance to categorization. Herbert has been called an Arminian and a high churchman, a

---

[40] On the Sidney circle, see S. L. Adams, 'The Protestant Cause: Religious Alliance with the West European Calvinist Communities as a Political Issue in England, 1585–1630' (D.Phil. diss., Oxford University, 1973).

[41] The Jacobean drama and metaphysical poems are genres that obviously illustrate the way in which literary works complicate historical categories.

Calvinist and a puritan, and labelled conservative and radical. As Christopher Hodgkins argues in *Authority, Church, and Society in George Herbert* (Columbia, Mo., 1993), the debates about Herbert in the end centre on the 'meaning of "Anglicanism"' (introduction, p. 10). Hodgkins sensibly insists, as ecclesiastical historians have not, on the need to consider theology, liturgy and churchmanship discretely rather than as aspects of a uniform ideology of churchmanship. In matters of theology, he feels sure that Herbert should be counted as a Calvinist. Though in a 'discreet and wary' manner, Herbert was even prepared, when it was under assault, to defend the doctrine of double predestination (p. 21). But for most of the Elizabethan period, Herbert's Calvinism was easily reconcilable with conformity. And Herbert was a conformist. He was devoted to the liturgy and discipline and ceremonies of the church. He believed that all of the 1604 Canons should be enforced to sustain the 'orderly carriage' of worship; he even retained the title 'priest' for those who 'serve up God' in the communion (pp. 55, 107, 134). Herbert saw no disjuncture between Calvinist theology and a love of decency, nor according to Hodgkins did he need to in the Elizabethan and Jacobean church. What, Hodgkins argues, fissured Herbert as well as his church and society was the new conformity of the Laudians. Herbert, he maintains, remained a double predestinarian, rejected the Laudians' emphasis on the holiness of places and objects, and privileged inner experience. Most of all he remained committed to the community as well as uniformity of the Elizabethan church settlement – to Anglicanism – while the polarization of Laudians and puritans threatened its disintegration. 'As the gap widened between puritan "Nonconformists" and William Laud's "New Conformists," Herbert walked the increasingly lonely way of the Elizabethan "Old Conformists"' (p. 11).[42] His verse sought to effect a reintegration of self and society as well as church and state.

Hodgkins is subtle in showing how Herbert's Calvinism and high churchmanship combined, helpful in explaining how Herbert appealed alike to the puritans Edward Taylor and Richard Baxter and high Anglicans Henry Vaughan and Izaak Walton, and interesting on the relationship of the structural instabilities of his verse to the destabilizing of his (and others') values and world. He is most insightful and persuasive when he moves from Herbert's poetry to interpret his world. In less satisfactory passages, dubious historical generalizations are deployed as

[42] All types of conformity here listed require closer definition.

critical tools for interpreting the verse, vitiating both historical and critical exegesis. There are many examples. It is not true that Calvinist catechisms were outlawed during the 1630s.[43] It is quite inaccurate to claim that conformists in the Jacobean church 'generally admitted' that episcopal government was indifferent (pp. 43–4). It is absurd to suggest that neither James I nor the Arminians 'had much use for conscience' (p. 85).[44] Moreover, Hodgkins rehearses many of the false assumptions about Arminianism and Laudianism that Davies and others have discredited. And this leads Hodgkins to draw a stark contrast between Herbert and Laud that is not always persuasive, nor is it sustained by the verse. Hodgkins acknowledges that they had in common a commitment to being 'thorough', but there is more. The Herbert who stressed the importance of catechizing, the purity of the priestly role, decency and order, and the certainty of 'uniform doctrine and practice' for the 'Commonwealth's spiritual and temporal unity' was not separated by a gulf from William Laud (pp. 43–4). Indeed lines such as

> wine becomes a wing at last.
> For with it alone I flie to the skie,

seem close to a sacramentalism usually associated with Laudians.[45] Pace Hodgkins, Herbert's devotionalism appears more 'emotional . . . than narrowly logocentric' (pp. 163, 174). Though his poetical references to ecclesiastical externals are metaphorical, they are also aids to devotion. 'The Windows', to take an example, may stand as a metaphor for the preacher but the 'colours and light' that 'bring / A strong regard and aw' evoke the literal more than the metaphoric (p. 172). Hodgkins is right to argue that for Herbert such outward objects had to give way to true experience, but wrong to contrast him with a Laud who maintained exactly that.[46] So where to Herbert the 'fault or virtue lies not in the externals themselves, but in the ignorance or understanding the people bring to them', Laud rejected both superstition and contempt for externals.[47] Both men looked to an ideal (or idealized) unity in the past; both feared its disintegration. In Laud's diary no less than Herbert's poetry, the quest for public order is also a search for personal integrity, for an external unity that might conjoin the lonely soul to God as well as unite the subjects of the state in a Hookerian commonweal.

[43] See Green, 'Emergence of the English Catechism'.
[44] Cf. above, ch. 4; and Laud's diary (*Works of Laud*, III, passim).
[45] 'The Banquet', lines 42–3, in *The Works of George Herbert*, ed. F. E. Hutchinson (Oxford, 1964), 182.
[46] See, for example, *Works of Laud*, II, 312.
[47] See F. Hargrave, *A Complete Collection of State Trials* (11 vols., 1776–81), I, 492.

Herbert, the author of *The Countrey Parson*, was also very much a courtier. One brother, Henry, was the Master of the Revels; another, Edward, ambassador to France. Herbert then looked forward to a court career, progressing from an appointment as university orator at Cambridge to succeed Sir Francis Nethersole, who became Secretary of State. Evidently his ambitions and hopes, like those of so many others, were not fulfilled, and in 1630 Herbert pursued, as had Donne, what was likely to have been the consolation prize of ordination and a living. But Herbert was formed in and by a public political world of patronage and power, and his personal spirituality and religious verse were shaped by the language and experience of that world. In *Prayer and Power: George Herbert and Renaissance Courtship* (Chicago, 1991), Michael Schoenfeldt gives us a quite brilliant analysis of the conjunction (as well as disjuncture) between Renaissance worlds we anachronistically divide: material and spirit, public and private, amorous and political.

In a splendid discussion of the discourse of patronage, which no historian should miss, Schoenfeldt demonstrates how Herbert 'translates . . . lessons of civil behavior into the terms of . . . sacred conversation with God', how courtesy literature mingles with manuals of devotion (p. 61). God is conceived in terms of a great master or landlord whom the 'tenant' seeks in his 'manor' (p. 79). The poems of *The Temple* often depict God as a generous magnate, His Lord's Supper a feast to which one is invited by a feudal overlord. Like a monarch, God is conceived as a figure who can use the imposition of pain as an instrument of power. Writing in a discursive context in which Foxe's *Book of Martyrs* had linked physical pain with religious commitment, Herbert speaks in *The Temple* of a God who does 'rack' and 'stretch' him between heaven and hell (p. 125). Yet God is also a figure of love, and approach to Him as to a mistress was for Herbert scripted and regulated by the contemporary language and practice of courtship: 'Herbert . . . discovers that his longing for the favor and love of God occurs at the nervous intersection of political, sexual, and religious courtship' (p. 229).

The discourses of power permeate all areas of Herbert's devotional experience: they announce fear as well as love of authority, the sense of distance from and subordination to authority, the need to petition and praise authority, secular and divine. But Herbert is not merely the subject or object of authority; he is also the author of his own power, his own being in the face of authority, royal and divine. We have begun to learn how the ambiguities of Renaissance culture permitted the voice of criticism and dissent within the conventional vocabularies of praise and encomium.[48] In his analogies between heavenly and earthly power, Herbert finds space to 'record a sporadic but striking series of anti-hierarchical and anti-authoritarian sentiments': criticism of class, courtly pretension and exploitation (p. 91). And while applauding power, Herbert attempts to appropriate it – through speaking and writing. The poet who began his career as an orator retained a strong sense of the power of writing – not least in a Jacobean England where the monarch himself was a poet and pamphleteer:

> My God if writings may
> Convey a Lordship any way

Poetry was a mediation of social distance, a form of address to a patron, even the greatest lord of the land (quoted in *Prayer and Power*, p. 187).

The rhetorical strategies that could empower the subject in a hier-archical social and political world served simultaneously to enable a relationship with God. In an important sense, the language of patronage helped Herbert to resolve the ontological problem of serving an omnipotent being: 'Negotiation with absolute political power', Schoenfeldt puts it, 'provides a model for dealing with divinity' (p. 112). Fear and love mediate the relationship between humanity and divinity, and so close the awful distance of God's majesty to bring Him into the Christian's interior life. To interiorize God is to claim His power. And as in the secular realm, the claim to power is made through language: through petitioning God – praying – and through representing and praising Him. Herbert offers his God what he promises his patron: eternal praise in verse. The reciprocity always present in the patron–client relationship is inscribed on the Christian dialogue with God. 'Devotional utterance is never for Herbert simply the impotent outpouring of mortal desire into the vacuum of divine omnipotence. Rather it is prayer, a mode of deeply rhetorical speech, that intends to move its auditor to a particular course of action' (p. 155). In Herbert's lines the self is not just a suffering object of God's whim, gaze and omnipotence but is made into an agent, a director of God's will, even the voice of 'artful aggression' against Him (p. 157). The rhetoric of sacrifice and subjection – characteristic not only of the language of religious poetry but also of the stances required of poets within the patronage system – can also provide the occasion for display of the self and its abilities.[49] That 'self', Schoenfeldt concludes

---

[48] See, for example, David Norbrook, *Poetry and Politics in the English Renaissance* (1984); and K. Sharpe, *Criticism and Compliment: the Politics of Literature in the England of Charles I* (Cambridge, 1987).

[49] One thinks immediately of Jonson's and Donne's poems to patrons.

his argument, is most manifest in sexuality. And so rescuing Herbert's eroticism from the critics' cultural repressions, he shows how the discourse of sexual desire critiques the regulations of courtesy by which power sustained itself and how it opened to Herbert a mode of comprehending the Christ made flesh. In 'Love (III)', Herbert finds a God of and in love – 'My love, my sweetnesse' (p. 265).

It is impossible in a review to convey all the wonderful richness to be found in this study, which is no less than a cultural history of courtesy, politics, sexuality and devotion in Renaissance England. Always sensitive to the ideological complexities and ambiguities of this age, Schoenfeldt offers suggestive insights into the relationship of power to its own inversion, the role of writing in fashioning a public and private subjectivity, the multivalence of love as a sexual, religious and political discourse – most generally, the inherent rhetoricity of this culture and the pervasiveness of power (and the discourse of power) in the Renaissance imagination and spirit. When Schoenfeldt writes of Herbert's ability 'to fold into a single text a variety of discourses and situations', he pens a (too modest) review of his own quite exceptional achievement (p. 256).

Schoenfeldt's success stems, we should note, from an unusual and bold methodological eclecticism. In recent years, as the new historicists and cultural materialists have held sway, older critical theories and practices have been discredited. Too often this meant sacrificing the best of the 'old' scholarship, including formal analysis and close reading.[50] Here Schoenfeldt draws on Foucault, Bakhtin and Caroline Bynum, but he offers marvellous close readings of the language, structure and form of Herbert's lines. Moreover, a trained new historicist practitioner moving skilfully across texts, visual and verbal, which encoded the culture, Schoenfeldt also impresses more than most by his broad reading in the contemporary literature. Apart from its excessive delights in paradox and attachment to the word *ventriloquize*, this is too a refreshingly lucid work which should attract the wide readership it deserves. *Prayer and Power* is criticism and cultural history at its best.

IV

The language of manners, patronage and courtesy that so permeated Herbert's devotions was not the only secular language in early modern

---

[50] I ventured some such remarks at the conference 'Religion and Culture in the English Renaissance' (see n. 39) and am grateful to the panel participants for helpful discussion.

England. J. G. A. Pocock has brilliantly charted the histories of the discourses of custom, grace and law, virtue and commerce, from the sixteenth century to the eighteenth.[51] We still await studies that illuminate the operation of these vocabularies at specific moments, their relationship to other cultural texts and practices and to the course of politics and events.[52] Recently, the critics of revisionism, quite rightly taking Conrad Russell and others to task for ignoring ideology, have turned attention back to the voices and vocabularies of opposition: to the ideology of the 'country' and to the language of law and liberty.

Court, Country, and Culture (Rochester, N.Y., 1992), edited by Bonnelyn Y. Kunze and Dwight Brautigam, is a collection of essays in honour of Perez Zagorin that takes its title from Zagorin's pioneering study of 1970, *The Court and the Country*. Zagorin argued that in the concerted opposition movement called 'the country' were to be found the origins of the English civil war. Later research seriously damaged the thesis of court/country polarization, not least by demonstrating that few early Stuart Englishmen could easily be contained within one category or the other, that the civil war saw a split within both court and country rather than simply between them.[53] Yet for all the criticisms there could be no doubt that the terms *court* and *country* carried ideological freight and needed to be reconsidered as political language through which contemporaries articulated ideals and problems in their political culture.[54] Sadly, this volume falls short of taking up that opportunity. An essay by one of the editors, revisiting Zagorin's thesis, is ill-informed, misconceived and badly written. Brautigam writes of anti-absolutists believing it the purpose of the monarch to 'enhance the common good' when it is clear that everyone shared the belief (p. 59). Opposition to absolutist theories was not confined to MPs. While 'country' ideology clearly played a role in the downfall of Buckingham, Brautigam has no idea how to accommodate the fact that the favourite's impeachment was led by courtiers. A vague passage about 'conflict between early Stuarts and their subjects' would hardly be acceptable from an undergraduate. The absence of any reference to a seventeenth-century source is not the only reason why this essay fails to advance our understanding. Too many of the other contributors also have nothing new to say. Gordon Schochet's essay on the

[51] J. G. A. Pocock, *The Ancient Constitution and the Feudal Law* (1957; 2nd edn, Cambridge, 1987); *The Machiavellian Moment* (Princeton, N.J., 1975); and *Virtue, Commerce and History* (Cambridge, 1985).
[52] Cf. Sharpe and Lake, *Culture and Politics*, introduction; and see the splendid book by G. Burgess, *The Politics of the Ancient Constitution: an Introduction to English Political Thought 1603–1642* (Basingstoke and London, 1992). [53] See Sharpe, *Criticism and Compliment*, 6–11.
[54] See Cust and Hughes, *Conflict*, 19–21; Sharpe and Lake, *Culture and Politics*, 7–8.

English revolution in the history of political thought is a rather tired review of some secondary literature that fails to problematize the use of 'Ranter' and Fifth Monarchist writings and the like as evidence of political thinking in the lower orders. Linda Peck offers a summary of her *Patronage and Corruption in Early Stuart England* (1991), and here too seems uncertain what to make of some interesting material – especially that concerning the ambivalences audible in the languages of patronage.[55]

There are brighter moments. Paul Seaver's well-researched essay on gentle apprentices promises an interesting book. Peter Lake develops his study of Laudian conformity by an analysis of its scripturalism – a valuable reminder that the Bible was not the property only of the godly. Edward Hundert, in an essay outside our scope here, brilliantly re-reads Henry Fielding in order to explicate the interaction of theatre and ideas of identity. Two additional essays, widely differing in approach, offer the only valuable contributions here to our understanding of seventeenth-century secular ideology. Antonio D'Andrea in a fascinating vignette shows how the history of the word *aspire* opens windows onto a changing political culture. John Guy boldly assays a survey of the relationship between royal prerogative and the liberty of the subject from Magna Carta to the Bill of Rights. Though somewhat uneven, this is a stimulating piece, full of good sense, about the tensions revealed in theories of sovereignty through changing circumstances and 'continual negotiations' (p. 65). The meaning and rhetoric of 'imperium', law and liberties, he shows, were, for all the language of continuity, always in flux.

The history of liberty is the subject of a huge research project initiated by J. H. Hexter and lavishly funded by a number of foundations and corporations. At the very centre of the project is seventeenth-century England where was taken, according to Hexter and his panel, 'the decisive first step in the direction of modern freedom' (p. 1). *Parliament and Liberty from the Reign of Elizabeth to the English Civil War* (Stanford, Calif., 1991) has been launched as the flagship of the large freedom fleet in preparation. If so it would be better to abandon the enterprise here. For if new research is a major criterion, the sponsors appear to have obtained very poor results for their money. Hexter's introduction all too clearly sets a tone. Rambling and self-indulgent, it descends to the rehearsal of textbook clichés, untroubled by much recent scholarship. And defining freedom anachronistically in twentieth-century terms, it serves less to understand early modern Englishmen

[55] See K. Sharpe, review of this work, in *History*, 77 (1992), 504–5.

than to grade them for their degree of success in attaining it. His more substantial contribution on the Fortescue case and the Apology of 1604 provides some valuable detail but in no way sustains his assertion that its authors formulated a Lockean theory of property. David Sacks's endeavour to detect a labour theory of liberty will dumbfound anyone who has read the parliamentary debates – not least because it was a notion too radical even for some Leveller pamphleteers.[56] In a meandering, self-contradictory piece much in need of an editor, Sacks only finds his way when he leaves the flux of ideas to set his feet firmly in Bristol politics. There is an important story to tell about the developing idea of liberty as 'not only protection from external oppression but membership in a commonwealth governed through representation and consent', but Sacks does not tell it (p. 121).[57] Robert Zaller contributes to the theme only by taking the liberty to say almost nothing for twenty pages at others' – not least the reader's – expense.

Some essays, if they do not quite redeem the enterprise, certainly belong in better company. Thomas Cogswell takes a crucial issue: the relationship of war to changing ideas of liberty. Summarizing his book, he argues that the Commons never got the war they wanted and hence were reluctant to make sacrifices for it.[58] Whether the war they wanted – an early modern form of gunboat diplomacy – was viable is questionable, and Cogswell may not be ready enough to admit that (as parliamentary regimes discovered in the 1640s) all governments have to override the rights of subjects in wartime.[59] Indeed there is much to ponder in Cogswell's observation that war defined the issue sharply: 'The preservation of Continental religious and political liberties from the Habsburg behemoth was not worth sacrificing their own' (p. 249). Johann Sommerville usefully tracks the association of the liberty of the subject both with the privileges of parliaments and the idea of privilege, but by 1642 such associations were more problematic than he acknowledges. Charles Gray, in a rather discursive essay, shrewdly cautions against excessive 'paeans' for the Petition of Right as a charter of liberties and, always aware of politics, challengingly suggests that

---

[56] On this question, see C. B. Macpherson, *The Political Theory of Possessive Individualism: Hobbes to Locke* (Oxford, 1962); cf. K. V. Thomas, 'The Levellers and the Franchise', in G. E. Aylmer ed., *The Interregnum: the Quest for Settlement, 1646–1660* (Basingstoke and London, 1972), ch. 2.

[57] Cf. I. Berlin, 'Two Concepts of Liberty', in *Four Essays on Liberty* (Oxford, 1969).

[58] See T. Cogswell, *The Blessed Revolution: English Politics and the Coming of War, 1621–1624* (Cambridge, 1989).

[59] As D. Hirst puts it in another essay in the volume, 'Fighting any war demands stern measures'. See Hirst 'Freedom, Revolution and Beyond', *Parliament and Liberty*, 256.

seventeenth-century England was '*impeded* by an undue faith that the right way could be discovered in the law' (p. 193, emphasis added).

The contributions to *Parliament and Liberty* from Clive Holmes and Derek Hirst, though based on little new research, are the best in the volume. Holmes shows that as the crown, in desperate fiscal need, stressed the doctrine of necessity, which had warrant in Tudor precedent, so opponents emphasized the language of property. Both, he argues, drew from the ideology of the commonwealth, a multivalent language that, articulated from the centre, was increasingly appropriated by the middle sort in the localities to critique government action. As a consequence, ideas that had been 'integrated functionally in the old consensus' became 'theoretically disparate ideas' – an interesting way of looking at the fracturing of shared discourses and assumptions (p. 154).[60] Hirst, in a lively essay, studies how what had been 'vague consensus about liberty' became 'both defined and fragmented' (p. 253). During the revolutionary decades, *liberty* was claimed by many more and came to mean different things to all – not least the division of powers and freedom from standing armies. The history of freedom, Hirst observes – against the spirit of the enterprise – is 'by no means simply progressive' (p. 263). Those who had seen tyrannous parliamentary government in the 1640s had quite other attitudes to royal prerogative, privilege and liberty than their early Stuart predecessors; few had much regard for the Petition of Right. In the only essay here to attempt historical definition, Hirst well illustrates what Clarendon so acutely observed: 'though the name of liberty be pleasant to all kinds of people, yet all men do not understand the same thing by it' (p. 252).

v

There is as little about religion in *The Making of Modern Freedom* as about secular languages and ideologies in Fincham's and Davies's studies of the early Stuart church. These realms of discourse, however, were usually inseparable in early modern England. And during the 1640s and 1650s, from monarchical apologies to radical levelling, political pamphlets were written in the language of scripture, just as the Bible itself became the site of an overtly politically contested hermeneutics. With the dismantling of church and state, the shared languages of politics were not only cast into contest but shorn of meanings endowed by

---

[60] Cf. Sharpe and Lake, *Culture and Politics*, introduction.

custom and experience. During the Commonwealth and Protectorate, writers – of all political inclinations – had to reconstruct social meanings through discursive strategies that could link old notions and feelings to new circumstances. Despite a vast scholarly industry devoted to groups like the Levellers and Ranters, there has been little study of the strategies – rhetorical, generic, linguistic – through which various groups endeavoured to construct and sell their ideal republic, nor any investigation of the audiences and readings that shaped those strategies.

Elizabeth Skerpan, in *The Rhetoric of Politics in the English Revolution* (Columbia, Mo., 1992), investigates 'what happens to the discourse of a political community when the ideological assumptions forming that discourse are challenged' (p. 1). Arguing persuasively that politics, discourse and genre were inextricably connected and that audiences were alert to the politics of the form and genre as well as content of writing, she attempts a formalist rhetorical analysis of the political pamphlets from the eve of civil war to the Restoration. Skerpan begins with an account of a governmental failure that was, she suggests, as much due to rhetorical as political miscalculation. Archbishop William Laud, she argues, never understood the need to reach an audience outside his own circle of power; his speech in 1637 at the trial of Prynne, Burton and Bastwick, far from defending his cause, spoke only to the converted.[61] In contrast to Laud's forensic (and 'essentially private') oratory, the defendants, appropriating the language of martyrology from Foxe, linked their personal cause 'to a public and patriotic rhetoric which won over a large general audience' (pp. 58–9). After 1642, political fortunes depended not only on arms but also on the skill in winning the debate in the 'public sphere', the swelling body that participated in public life.[62] For some time, even after the outbreak of civil war, there were some shared assumptions about the body politic, and the polemicists who won conviction were those who skilfully appropriated those shared fundamentals for their partisan cause. The Royalists' appearing to put loyalty to Charles above that to the state left the field to the Parliamentarian pamphleteers who rhetorically best integrated their own interests with God, country and (even) king, discursively disenfranchising Charles I from the languages that validated monarchical rule.[63] The events of

---

[61] See S. R. Gardiner ed., *Documents Relating to the Proceedings against William Prynne in 1634 and 1637* (Camden Soc., 1877); *State Trials*, I, 486–95.

[62] See J. Habermas, *The Structural Transformation of the Public Sphere*, trans. Thomas Burger (Cambridge, Mass., 1989).

[63] See, for example, the Commons' defence of the militia ordinance, in S. R. Gardiner ed., *Constitutional Documents of the Puritan Revolution, 1625–1660* (Oxford, 1899), 256–75.

1648–9 swept away those common languages, along with the monarchy. Regicide presented a discursive, as well as constitutional and political, challenge and opportunity: 'to create a new political community out of language' (p. 85). Not only an opportunity but also a necessity: for if the new government were to survive it needed to invent a new language of legitimacy. This was difficult enough in the face of a public consciousness which had been formed through images and vocabularies of monarchy. What made it near impossible was the Royalists' (perhaps the king's) learning – at last but brilliantly – the tactics of rhetorical politics. Until recently the *Eikon Basilike*, though much read, has not been analysed as a text of artful form and verbal strategy.[64] Skerpan locates its extraordinary success in the choice of the epideictic genre, which permitted a flexible and eclectic combination of argumentative strategies. She shows how this genre enabled the speaker to unite, and unite with, the audience by evoking and identifying with the integrative values of community. Stealing the Parliamentarians' and even puritans' clothes, or rather scripts, the *Eikon*, denying partisanship, won the king and his son the prince a larger support than they had enjoyed since 1642. Though she never quite explains how, Skerpan is clear that the *Eikon* was the crowning (literally) Royalist achievement.

So successful was its rhetoric, the *Eikon* stimulated a radical suspicion (perhaps, as she does not say, always latent in puritanism) of rhetorical embellishment itself. The *Eikon Alethine*, for example, published in August six months after the 'King's book', warned against 'the allurements of effeminate Rhetorick'.[65] But by employing the old Parliamentarian language to ally the presbyterians to the Royalist cause, pamphlets like the *Eikon* put radical writers on the defensive – a defensiveness audible on every page of Milton's *Eikonoklastes*. Where the monarchists were able to adapt and take over an existing language of legitimacy, the republicans had the legacy of no indigenous discourse to represent a new order. Although, as Thomas Hobbes lamented, the histories of Greece and Rome presented models of republican rule,[66] their languages did not serve the Good Old Cause. 'No classical genre', Skerpan suggests in a stimulating aside worthy of more reflection, 'can truly be adapted to question the fundamental premises of a society' (p. 153). Though a large uncommitted public remained to be converted, the republicans never

---

[64] See T. Corns, *Uncloistered Virtue: English Political Literature, 1640–1660* (Oxford, 1992), reviewed below; and S. Zwicker, *Lines of Authority: Politics and English Literary Culture, 1649–89* (Ithaca, 1993), ch. 2.   [65] Skerpan does not comment on the gendering here.

[66] See B. Worden, 'Classical Republicanism and the English Revolution', in H. Lloyd Jones, V. Pearl and B. Worden eds., *History and Imagination* (1981), 182.

found the way to reach them. Republican politics were doomed by the failure of republican rhetoric.[67]

Rhetorically as well as politically, however, Restoration had to be fought for. After the unpopular innovations and divisions of the 1650s, the monarchists sought a language that would 'reassure readers of the continuity of the world as they remembered and idealized it' (p. 171), and they skilfully revived evocative organic languages of wholeness and harmony. While Prince Charles on the continent began to 'touch' to cure the king's evil, loyalist polemicists endeavoured to write away the previous years as a sickness that had infected the body politic. Drawing on the successful parliamentary tracts of 1642, they invested the monarchy with the ideals of moderation, harmony, liberty and the public good. Only Milton and Harrington among the radicals contested it to the last. But Milton himself seemed uncertain of his audience. By focusing on the rights of the individual, the radical pamphleteers had 'undermined the very conventions that advanced public discourse', leaving the republicans of 1659–60 to speak into a void (p. 208). Though Milton saw the need to find an integrative public voice, the radical cause floundered in an appeal only to the sects. The monarchists found the language that scripted the plot of Restoration and united the nation behind the king as spiritual and temporal head.

Historians will find much to dispute, even deplore, in Skerpan's book. As other literary practitioners of interdisciplinary studies, she is less well informed about important historical contexts than she should be. Excessively reliant on and uncritical of secondary literature, she asserts discredited positions as if they were unproblematic. The use of terms like 'rising middle class' or 'Parliamentarians' to describe any before 1642 is no longer acceptable, if it ever was. The view that most members of the Long Parliament were puritans is almost certainly nonsense. There are also uncomfortable contradictions in her case. On the one hand we are told that 'even before the king actually raised his standard, English public discourse had bifurcated'; on the other we are assured of the endurance of 'common forms of discourse' (pp. 36, 38, 39, 58, 65). Many vital questions remain unanswered and, in some cases, unasked. How did ideas of the 'state' independent of the king develop by 1642 in a shared monarchical culture? How was the legal language of parliament related to the godly rhetoric of the puritan opposition, and to what extent was their alliance inherently unstable? Why did the radicals, who

---

[67] And also more generally by the failure to find a republican representation or style, visual as well as verbal.

had so skilfully appealed to the public in 1637, narrow their address by
the adoption of the forensic genres that had led the government to
defeat? How conscious were readers in 1659 of the idealizing rhetoric of
nostalgia as a strategy to influence, rather than simply to describe,
events? Despite the importance of rhetoric in her approach, often a
passage frustrates by Skerpan's failure to analyse closely the form, style
and language of treatises or to relate their arguments to their genre,
form and tropes. Her decision to leap from the debates over the *Eikon* in
1649 to 1659 precludes study of some Leveller, Digger and most Ranter,
Quaker and other millenarian treatises, which gave voice to new languages, agendas and groups – those hitherto outside the 'public sphere':
the poor, women, the possessed. Consequently the political and discursive context of the debates of 1659–60 is not satisfactorily set, and the
appeal of a reaction to the sectarian fragmentation – of language itself
– is not fully comprehensible. Most of all Skerpan is not always sure
whether rhetorical failure was a consequence of political defeat or, as she
would incline most to suggest, political fortune was determined by skill
in oratory and rhetoric. Did, in other words, the republican experiment
fail because it was not defended well or was the ineffectuality of republican discourse a consequence of the failure of republican politics?
Milton's problem in 1659, for instance, was not primarily a lack of rhetorical art, but rather contempt for popular rule – his narrow political
base.

Such criticisms and shortcomings, however, should not distract us
from the importance and merits of this study. Although her measuring
tool is too mechanistic, Skerpan is the first to evaluate the pamphlets of
the Commonwealth and Protectorate as rhetorical performances, and
she helpfully points to the centrality of rhetorical strategy to political
outcome. During the civil war, even more than in Herbert's time, writing
offered the power not only of self-construction but also of forging a new
political order. Skerpan's observations on this score are often suggestive.
It is interesting to learn how the last section of the *Eikon*, the address to
the prince, moves from past to future; the discussion of self-contradictions within radical discourse adds an important chapter to the story, still
to be told, of the failure of a republican culture. There is a full argument
to be developed in the observation that 'through narration the writer can
literally tell the story of the society as he wishes it to exist, presenting it
as if it does exist' (p. 196). The suggestion that the increase in the number
of philosophical tracts expressed the pamphleteers' 'growing uncertainty' would repay further examination (p. 168). What Skerpan demon-

strates beyond doubt is that the politics of rhetoric (as well as the rhetoric of politics) across the whole seventeenth century is a crucially important area for the investigations of both historians and critics.

The potential of this subject and the range of possible approaches are well illustrated in a collection of essays exploring the prose of the 1640s and '50s from Marxist, feminist, ecological and post-structuralist perspectives. It is worthy of note that none of the contributors to *Pamphlet Wars: Prose in the English Revolution* (London, 1992) is an academic historian: the volume indeed stands as an example of both the fertile cultural histories currently being written by scholars in other disciplines, especially literature, and the less fertile consequences of ignorance and suspicion of 'periodizing'.[68] From a historian's point of view, the undoubted value of this book owes nothing to its editor. The thin, brief introduction by James Holstun missed an opportunity to set a critical and historical context for the particular essays; mere précis is not a substitute for situating. The judgements of both the history and historiography of the English revolution appear to be formed more by ideological passion than learning. Holstun is evidently unaware that far from being a slogan of 'a feminized public identity for radical males' bent on overturning Jacobean patriarchy, the phrase 'nursing fathers' was a scriptural term deployed by James I (as by Elizabeth) himself (p. 9). Such misgivings are only sadly confirmed by Holstun's own essay on Winstanley. Opening sentences about 'a more humane and egalitarian collective life' suggest the autobiography of the 1960s student more than historical analysis of the Diggers. Throughout the piece the border between history and politics – and between autobiography and analysis – is not policed (p. 159). Holstun is cavalier with the chronology of population growth and economic conditions, which were easing before the civil war, and emotional in his treatment of enclosure, the benefits of which were not merely the invention of Tory apologists. This is hardly surprising given his readiness to leap from seventeenth-century England to 'the genocidal origins of the American nation' or 'genocidal germ warfare' in Brazil (pp. 170, 198). While Holstun is right to point up that deference in early modern England was less a natural condition than 'a site for uneasy compromise', his essay abandons history for romance – for wishful thinking about a past and present led by agents of green politics, radical reform and revolution against capitalism (p. 173). Holstun endeavours to pre-empt such criticism by denouncing 'periodizing' as

---

[68] *Pamphlet Wars* is a hardback edition of *Prose Studies*, vol. XIV, no. 3, for which Holstun, the editor, has failed to provide an index.

the spurious stand of 'anti-socialist historians' (pp. 195, 200). What he needs to learn is that refining a sensitivity to the languages and values of a past period while struggling against the intrusions of one's own is what distinguishes all historical scholarship from crude ideologizing polemic.

Happily, other essays in *Pamphlet Wars* demonstrate that innovative approaches and even political commitments need not send scholarly standards into exile. Joan Hartman shows how the political fortunes of Charles I were greatly improved in 1641 by a change of style in the royal polemic – a change effected by the pen of Edward Hyde. So successful were Hyde's rescriptings perceived to be that parliament was compelled to contest them by denying royal authorship, as Milton was to do in response to the *Eikon Basilike*. I regretted the brevity of this discussion, which goes beyond Hyde's appropriation of parliamentary language for the king and opens the important subject of changing ideas of authorship – the notion of intellectual property and thus the relationship of the speaking or writing agent to the exercise of authority. Certainly the 1640s are a – perhaps *the* – crucial chapter in a history of language and power. John Wilkins expressed the widely held view that man could be improved by a reform of language; John Cleveland expected that once linguistic errors were corrected, authority would return to rightful rulers; Thomas Hobbes maintained that a common language, if need be imposed from above, was an essential condition of political stability. As Sharon Achinstein argues here, the frequent references to Babel expressed fears of political as well as linguistic anarchy: a fear of marginalized and heterodox voices making themselves articulate in the public sphere. Babel represented the contest in the 1640s for political legitimacy; the conservatives therefore pressed the case that 'only the King has the authority to validate language' (p. 41). The Charles I who himself appointed a standard grammar for use in schools may not have needed tutoring on this point.[69]

Those who control language order the world, as much in the seventeenth century as today. Byron Nelson may be right to discern in the writings of the Ranters a frustration at the inadequacy of language to render their experiences – in other words at their exclusion by and from the controlling discourses of church and state. And he makes a point, too often neglected, when he distinguishes between *meaning* and *use* of language.[70] Unfortunately his essay descends into a feeble

---

[69] *Cal. Stat. Pap. Dom., 1637*, 530.
[70] A distinction between language as content and as symbol – which Pocock and Skinner often fail to make.

attempt to rescue the Ranters from recent historiographical denials and becomes, like its subject, an emotive rant rather than persuasive discussion.[71] Few will be convinced by comparisons of the Ranters with Wittgenstein or by claims that their sardonic spirit contributed to Restoration drama.

The most original and best essays in *Pamphlet Wars* are explorations of female speech, writing and agency. Anne McEntee takes on a neglected subject in her essay on female petitioning during the 1640s and '50s. The very first action of these petitioners – speech – as she argues, laid down a political as well as linguistic claim: 'In demanding the right to define themselves politically, and hence publicly, the women called for a diminution of the male privilege of cultural inscription' (p. 93). Predictably, the patriarchal backlash, expressing a long-suppressed fear, attempted to brand the women as Amazons, associating their unorthodox politics with deviant sexual behaviour, or alternatively endeavoured to re-domesticate the female petitioners: 'The House gave an answer to your Husbands.'[72] Less predictably, perhaps, the women – initially – defined and confined themselves within the nomenclature and structure of patriarchal language and order, describing themselves as 'tradesmen's wives and widows' identified by the absent but significant other (p. 93). Evidently, however, they began to find in the Bible the validating models of autonomous female political action: the woman of Tekoa, Esther and – a figure freighted with the authority of Queen Elizabeth – Deborah. Significantly, as they found a voice and became more central in Leveller demonstration, the women, to raise money for the cause, sold their bodkins and wedding rings, the symbols of cultural femininity and the domestic sphere. By 1651 'we women' had replaced 'we wives' in the address of female petitioners (p. 109). Rachel Trubovitz, in a slighter piece, adds the suggestion that it was the spiritual equality preached by the sects that secured for women this new authority; more generally, that the civil war loosened gender categories.[73] Deep attachment to traditional sexual politics, however, remained – even the 1651 petitioners, if not ironic, stereotyped themselves as 'chattering like cranes' rather than speaking gravely like more majestic beasts (p. 145). But as in so many aspects of culture, the Restoration did not simply restore the gender status quo. For one, public female promiscuity, be it on stage, in verse or at court, acknowledged (albeit uncomfortably) a female sexuality, which

[71] See C. Davis, *Fear, Myth, and History* (Cambridge, 1986).
[72] *England's Moderate Messenger*, 23–30 April 1649, p. 3.
[73] Cf. K. V. Thomas, 'Women and the Civil War Sects', *Past and Present*, 4 (1958), 42–62.

in turn opened a cultural space for autonomous female identity and agency.[74]

In an innovative essay in *Pamphlet Wars*, Susan Wiseman traces the intercourse of sexual and political discourse during the Commonwealth and Protectorate and its legacy for the post-Restoration world. Filmer, she reminds us, supported monarchical authority by representing the state as the family. Not surprisingly, therefore, the link was made between subversive female politics and uncontrolled female sexuality – but more surprisingly, perhaps, between Henry Marten's republicanism and his loose sexual mores.[75] Despite the reactions, however, the fractures of civil war – in gender politics as in state politics – could not simply be repaired. Wiseman contributes nicely to the subject by analysis of Henry Neville's *Isle of Pines*, written in 1668. Not merely a scurrilous narrative, Neville's fictional patriarchal colony, she shows, is a political critique of paternal rule itself, in which patriarchy is inversely associated with disorder. It is in rich and suggestive feminist readings like these that we can discern a programme for exciting work on the politics of civil war and Restoration culture.

Skerpan and the contributors to *Pamphlet Wars* focus on the politics of prose. In *Uncloistered Virtue: English Political Literature 1640–60* (Oxford, 1992), Thomas N. Corns sets himself the ambitious task of historical and critical analysis of all political literature from 1640 to 1660 – pamphlets along with the poetic genres that 'are not to be appraised by the simpler procedures appropriate for prose polemic' (p. 99). In a fine work, impressive for its historical learning and critical acumen and sense, Corns aims to return to all texts – even those that do not as obviously as pamphlets announce their polemics – 'the political potency they once possessed' (p. 1). From the bold start, it becomes clear that here is a scholar never content uncritically to accept the established orthodoxy – even when it is not that of his own discipline. Corns begins in fact by debunking myths and undermining generalizations that have been read into the very literary texts that complicate and question them. On the eve of civil war and during the conflict itself, he argues, there was no simple stylistic contrast between Royalist and Parliamentarian: in appearance, manners – or prose. Stereotypes had to be constructed and the constructions of both pejorative and positive types, though related in only 'highly medi-

---

[74] This is nowhere more apparent than in the paintings and engravings depicting aristocratic women in late seventeenth-century England.
[75] 'Marten's sexual deviance stands for his political deviance' (*Pamphlet Wars*, 144).

ated fashion to reality', helped to form and sustain the parties and their programmes (p. 9).[76] Secondly, Corns sounds a healthy note of caution to historians who too enthusiastically take religion, with Sir Benjamin Rudyard, as the 'primum quaerite'. 'Religion', he sagely observes, 'covered a considerable range of issues, some relating to changes in the prevailing doctrinal concerns of the Church of England, some to matters of ceremony, some to individual acts of malpractice by clergymen, . . . some to the larger and more theoretical question of the power structure within the government of the Church' (p. 11). Still more he rejects the simplistic polarizing of writers on the doctrine of salvation, using Peter White's term *spectrum* to characterize a range of views that permitted intermediate positions as well as extremes. Corns, it is clear, is not going to confine his texts within the labels – Calvinist and Arminian, court and country, Royalist and Parliamentarian – that still in much writing substitute for fresh analysis. Rather, relocating a number of canonical and non-canonical texts in their immediate polemical contexts, he is able to gesture towards a more complex history as well as more nuanced criticism.

It is not surprising that Corns, author of the excellent study *The Development of Milton's Prose Style* (Oxford, 1982), erects a grand edifice around the foundation and keystones of chapters on Milton: the Milton of civil war, regicide and imminent Restoration. In 1641, when their author was preoccupied with ecclesiastical and doctrinal politics, Milton's *Of Reformation* and *Of Prelatical Episcopacy* were penned to write episcopacy into oblivion. Corns analyses the strategies of Milton's polemics: the incorporation of the reader, the ruthless tendentiousness with evidence, the forensic frame of reference, the intention to heighten difference so that reconciliation becomes impossible. Yet, as Corns also acknowledges, Milton eschewed rational engagement with others' arguments; his strategy 'cannot work on a sensibility that is not already puritan' (p. 18). And as puritanism itself fragmented during the 1640s, so the changing style of Milton's prose perforce marked the shifts in circumstance, the divisions within Protestantism between not only Milton and his enemies but Milton and erstwhile allies, even within Milton himself. *The Reason of Church Government*, as we know, was the first of his tracts to which Milton put his own name. As Corns explains, the gesture marks 'an uncertain transition from the voice that speaks collectively from

[76] This point needs careful consideration by all who cling to the simple court–country thesis.

within the Presbyterian tradition to the assertion of the centrality of individual perception and conscience' (p. 31).[77] Milton was writing a new radicalism on himself as well as himself on a new radical agenda. In the divorce tract, in *Tetrachordon* and in *Areopagitica*, Milton most obviously broke ranks with the presbyterian majority and claimed his own individual position. As the reactive attacks came, Milton rewrote the presentation of himself, moving from invocation of godly authority to that of education and property, changing stylistic practices to win different audiences. The regicide and creation of an independent republic gave Milton both a new employment and a new community. He justified the trial in *The Tenure of Kings and Magistrates*; he once again abandoned the individualistic 'I' for the pronoun that might help forge 'a new "we" of godly Englishmen' (p. 203). Soon his brilliant and eclectic rhetorical skills were called on to defend the godly commonwealth from a treatise that stole its own rhetoric and colours. Corns struggles, like Milton himself, to give force to *Eikonoklastes*; he questions the verdict that it was a failure on the curious and unpersuasive ground that it enjoyed potency later as a Williamite pamphlet. Here Corns's usually sensitive historicization lets him down, and we fail to comprehend how Milton's failure to find a stratagem for contesting the *Eikon Basilike*, his remaining the subject of a discourse defined by the king's book, undermined not only his but the whole Good Old Cause.[78] Ten years later he was faced with writing a hopeless last call to save that cause, *The Readie and Easie Way to Establish a Free Commonwealth*. Again Corns valiantly pleads for its rhetorical power – a 'guileful pamphlet, . . . resolutely and carefully targeted', exhibiting 'polemical control' (pp. 280–3). But in the end he is too good a critic not to acknowledge that the very images of restored monarchy it sought to discredit and erase dominate the page, as they do the politics of the moment. By the second edition, when the inevitability of Restoration loomed, Milton removed the name of the bookseller and printer, symbolically exiling himself from the public sphere.

At each point in Milton's extraordinary literary career, Corns analyses the politics of style as shaped by the polemical and historical context. He eschews idealizing. Milton subordinated grand principles to the dictates of polemical moments: 'To look for philosophical coherence in Milton's controversial prose is merely to mistake the decorum of its

[77] And perhaps to a broader shift towards a concept of individual conscience. See the brilliant essay by Keith Thomas, 'Cases of Conscience in Seventeenth-Century England', in Morrill, Slack and Woolf, *Public Duty and Private Conscience*, 29–56.
[78] See Zwicker's much more satisfying reading in *Lines of Authority*, ch. 2.

genre' (p. 56; cf. p. 53). We would like to know more than we learn here about Milton's personal synthesis of godliness and republican politics, individual conscience and his vision of commonwealth; regrettably, Milton's least successful prose pamphlets are those least successfully handled. Most of all the choice of genre – the election of the sonnet form, the abandonment of verse, the polemical freight of the poems – receives no satisfactory discussion. Yet overall, despite a somewhat flat tone, Corns's Milton chapters present a fascinating narrative of the history of civil war polemic and politics.

Another narrative is that centred on the writings of Levellers, Diggers and Ranters, which have preoccupied historians but received little critical analysis until recent years. As usual Corns has little time for romantic sentimentalism: the Levellers' spokesmen were not the lowly heroes fighting an elite; indeed they 'were not socially or culturally much distinct from Cromwell's circle' (p. 132). They endeavoured to find a broad community of support – largely through writing. But, not least on account of their literacy, they lacked mass support and remained 'an elite embarrassed by its elitism', and Corns shows how this fundamental contradiction sat at the heart of Leveller discourse as well as politics (p. 135). Lilburne in particular, he suggests, embodied this problem in his deployment of forms of speech and writing which, deflecting attention from the larger issues, were alien to radical purposes. The dilemma was more acute for other groups, like the Diggers, who lacked the literate and educated constituency of the Levellers. Digger pamphlets had to speak for the poor rather than to them, and so were often directed to the authorities as well as against them. Where the Ranters were concerned, Corns echoes other commentators in emphasizing the inadequacy of language itself for the politics of revelation.[79] But his analysis is refreshingly free of obfuscation and excessive special pleading.[80] 'The confusion of literal and metaphorical categories', he admits, 'are [*sic*] as tedious as they are perplexing' (p. 184). However, what contemporaries and historians have often perceived as madness may have been a strategic response to the paradox of persuading men to decentre rationality. Corns shows how not only Ranter prose but also the very physical structure of their books subverted the formalism that dimmed the inner light. Interestingly he points to the rhythms, sounds and associations of

---

[79] Cf. Byron Nelson, 'The Ranters and the Limits of Language', in *Pamphlet Wars*, 60–75.
[80] See too Nigel Smith, *Perfection Proclaimed: Language and Literature in English Radical Religion 1640–1660* (Oxford, 1989).

Coppe's language, which reject coherence for spiritual self-representa-
tion. Yet for all his dutifully serious attention, Corns remains doubtful
about the purpose of the Ranters' discourse, and even about their 'seri-
ousness' (p. 193). Perhaps too many pages have been wasted on endeavours to find meaning in the writings of the civil war's madmen.

Indeed, for all its sound sense on the radical prose of the 1640s and
'50s, *Uncloistered Virtue* makes its freshest and most original contribution
in its discussion of poetry, and in particular of the neglected verse of
Royalists during years of republican rule. Richard Lovelace's *Lucasta* and
Robert Herrick's *Hesperides* were both ready for publication in 1648 and
reflect the experience of a decade of political crisis, civil war and military defeat. Lovelace regrets the peace of Berwick and seeks a firm
response, 'one gallant thorough-made Resolve', that quality Machiavelli
called *virtu*, which might conquer fortune herself (p. 71).[81] Lovelace's civil
war poems, Corns points out, evoke worlds of chivalric romance but
they do so not out of nostalgic disengagement but to 'generate connections between Civil War royalism and the chivalric loyalism of the feudal
era', to bind a party to a cause (p. 74).[82] The eroticism of Lovelace's verse
functioned similarly: in the atmosphere of strict puritan morality, erotic
verse was ideological and combative. Yet beyond a challenge to puritan
values, the celebration of sensuous passion also expressed a devotion to
the king. As the poet puts it in the famous 'To Lucasta, Going to the
Warres': 'True, a new mistresse now I chase.'[83] *Lucasta*, Corns argues, in
all its modes, 'constructed a model for ideological survival' (p. 79). While
we might wonder at the response of a king who rejected sensuality for
the austeries of Platonic love and its political valence, we must welcome
Corns's preparedness to read this Cavalier verse as something more than
frothy escapism.[84] There is a vastly important subject in Caroline lyrics
that the politics of criticism has hidden.[85]

Herrick's *Hesperides*, as Corns argues, seems even more resistant to historicizing criticism. Articulating the experience of defeat in the late
1640s, the verse at times seems 'empty, poignant, impotent' (pp. 91, 93).
But Corns is persuasive in discerning ideological force in *Hesperides*, in its

---

[81] Corns does not comment on the political charge of the term *Thorough*, Wentworth's and Laud's
    slogan for their philosophy of government.
[82] Cf. J. S. A. Adamson, 'Chivalry and Political Culture in Caroline England', in Sharpe and Lake,
    Culture and Politics, 161–98.
[83] 'To Lucasta, Going to the Warres', in T. Clayton ed., *Cavalier Poets* (Oxford, 1978), 256.
[84] Cf. Sharpe, *Criticism and Compliment*, ch. 3 and passim.
[85] See K. Sharpe and S. Zwicker eds., *Politics of Discourse: the Literature and History of Seventeenth-Century
    England* (Berkeley, Los Angeles and London, 1987), introduction.

neoclassical simulations, its 'very literariness' and its notions of time. Rather than pastoral retreat, the parallels between the natural world and events in England present the promise of a new spring and a validation as 'natural' of a life-style not only controversial but also militarily defeated.[86] Herrick's celebrations of Christmas and traditional pastimes, Corns perceives, were counter-revolutionary – literally so when crowds defied the injunctions against Christmas. Moreover, *May poles, Hock-carts, Wassails, Wakes* represented not only popular festival but also images of agrarian hierarchies and communities on which the old order had been founded.[87] Defying the social dislocations of levelling and the sects, Herrick's poems 'proffer a vision of the contemporary social order as natural, inevitable and immutable' (p. 113) – the ultimate triumph of ideological polemic in any era. Sexuality again is presented as part of that condition, natural – even religious – and 'beyond the reach of puritan control' (p. 114). Corns notes the link in *Hesperides* between what appear, at first reading, the distinct secular and religious sections of the volume. The values of the Laudians – ritual, ceremonial – connect the two. And the emphasis on Christ as tragic actor (Corns fails to note that in 'The *Crosse* shall be thy Stage', *stage* can mean *scaffold*) evokes a Christic Charles ready to sacrifice for his people. *Hesperides*, like *Lucasta*, was not the despondent poetry of defeat. Corns lays down a persuasively bold statement to challenge a critical tradition that has neglected or slighted Royalist verse: 'If royalist generals could have organized their forces as well as royalist poets could marshall their wits the outcome of Edgehill and Marston Moor and Naseby might well have been different' (p. 128).

With the regicide and erection of the republic, however, Herrick's new spring seemed not to be dawning. How did former Royalists respond to the new orders of Commonwealth and Protectorate? In a brief and unsatisfying review of Marvell, especially disappointing on *Upon Appleton House*, Corns suggests that Marvell's 'early ideological wanderings' at last found stability, as did those of many, 'in the simplicities of a revived (Cromwellian) monarchism' (p. 244).[88] In the second edition of *Lucasta*, Corns discerns Lovelace's shift from eroticism to a coarseness that announced the abandoning of aristocratic, courtly aesthetics and

---

[86] There is an important subject in the ideological strategy of 'naturalizing' political authority and programmes in the Renaissance. See Terry Eagleton, *Ideology: an Introduction* (1991), ch. 2; and Peter Burke, *The Fabrication of Louis XIV* (New Haven and London, 1992), 128ff.

[87] Cf. D. Underdown, *Revel, Riot and Rebellion: Popular Politics and Culture in England 1603–1660* (Oxford, 1985).

[88] On *Appleton House*, see D. Hirst and S. Zwicker, 'High Summer at Nun Appleton, 1651: Andrew Marvell and Lord Fairfax's Occasions', *Hist. Journ.*, 36 (1993), 247–70.

politics – a change in sensibilities that demands fuller and broader treatment. The best discussion in the volume is devoted to the little-studied Abraham Cowley. In his earlier verse, sexuality and politics, 'the roles of lover and exiled servant', are said to 'interanimate each other' (p. 252). But Cowley returned to the England of Oliver Cromwell and, it may be thought, to accommodation with the regime. Far from it: Corns opens insights into a volume, Cowley's *Poems* of 1656, which he sees as inscribing a cultural royalism at a time when the Royalist cause was at its lowest ebb. Following Cowley's own injunction to readers to have their sharpest wits about them, Corns time and again brilliantly finds criticism in poetry others have simply read as pro-Cromwellian. Even Cowley, however, came to despair. His unfinished *Davideis*, which awaits (as do other Royalist romances) a full exegesis, may, it is suggested, announce an admission of defeat.

Uncloistered Virtue is a book that anyone interested in the riches of interdisciplinary study must greet with almost unqualified praise and enthusiasm. Corns is not only a subtle close reader, he is also usually extremely well informed historically. A master at situating a text in its polemical moment, he is able to offer suggestive political readings of poems that have resisted them. How much more richly complex the civil war appears in these readings than in the reductions of those historians who deny literature entry to their narrow arenas of evidence! Even when Corns, as he does in places, dissatisfies or frustrates, it is usually because he is beginning to raise new questions or to see from a new perspective. Moreover, he writes not only with a sound sense but also with a lucidity that happily contrasts with the vague slogans of some postmodern critics. *Uncloistered Virtue* is a work that will repay re-readings, as it makes one eager to read Lovelace and Cowley and others again. An author cannot desire more than that.

VI

The literature of the 1640s and '50s, like the paintings and engravings of those decades, testifies to the continuing force of royalism in the imagination and the culture of the Interregnum. Ironically, though republicanism and radicalism failed to find the images and voices that might have secured cultural and political domination, republican rhetoric and passion were not silenced by the Restoration. As Corns observes in a concluding chapter, the old court culture could not be re-established. Indeed, between the lines of Restoration panegyric and in the midst of

Restoration festival and celebration, we detect the acknowledgement and fear of other positions, oppositional elements that continued to stalk the imagination and threaten the regime well after Charles II was stably re-established on his throne. During the civil war decades of contest and division, a uniform culture had itself become contested and divided; after 1660, for all the rhetoric of harmony, those differences continued to mark the political and literary culture and increasingly came to define the course of politics itself.[89]

For the past few years, Richard Greaves has devoted himself to researching the activities of the radical underground in England, Scotland and Ireland, and among exiles on the continent, from the Restoration to the 1688 Revolution. *Secrets of the Kingdom: British Radicals from the Popish Plot to the Revolution of 1688–1689* (Stanford, Calif., 1992), the last volume of a trilogy, picks up the narrative with the Popish Plot and traces it to the influence of the radicals on William's invasion and the revolution settlement.[90] Greaves shows how the Popish Plot emerged in an atmosphere thick with suspicions and rumours of plotting that were fostered by the radical press. In 1679 the Whig pamphleteers laboured to support the Duke of Monmouth and to win popular support for Shaftesbury and Exclusion. Interestingly, civil war pamphlets refuting the historic origins of royal authority were reprinted and widely disseminated, undermining popular support for the monarchy; in 1682 a portrait in the Guildhall of James, Duke of York, was desecrated by one of the mob. In Scotland the Covenanters, never won to the Restoration settlement, maintained close links with Dutch republicans and Scottish exiles in Rotterdam and Utrecht.[91] Contacts were spread across the border: in 1680 2,000 Scots and English nonconformists met in Northumberland, re-exciting the fears of Anglo-Scots radical union that had undermined Charles I's government. The Scottish conventicle sermons were certainly radical calls to arms to defend the faith; and the meetings of the so-called United Societies in hills and woods for scripture reading and prayer reminded many of Covenanter organization.

Back in London, and polite society, the Whigs organized and orchestrated their campaign of exclusion in clubs and over dinners (the various

---

[89] See Zwicker, *Lines of Authority.*

[90] The other volumes in the trilogy are Greaves, *Deliver Us from Evil: the Radical Underground in Britain 1660–1663* (New York, 1986); and *Enemies under His Feet: Radicals and Nonconformists in Britain 1664–1667* (Stanford, Calif., 1990).

[91] Historians who have called for more attention to British history have largely ignored the important cultural differences between England and Scotland, where the mystification of kingship and authority was never as developed as in England.

meanings of the word 'party' may emerge from the political dinner),[92] but with no less menace. Wildman (former president of a republican club) proposed and Shaftesbury was prepared to entertain assassination of both the king and his brother. Plans to shoot them at the theatre, to attack them at Rye House in Hertfordshire, and to seize the Tower were drawn up by various radical factions. With their failure, tactics changed to the orchestration of risings in Scotland and England, with the hope of assistance from the Netherlands. Though the conspirators were foiled, such was the atmosphere of fear and suspicion that when Charles II died of natural causes, it was rumoured that he had been murdered. With the accession of James II, Monmouth committed himself to rebellion. His failure divided the radicals, who were already quarrelling over tactics and religion, but it also drove William of Nassau into an alliance with the English discontents, an alliance that was far from a foregone conclusion. Some of the radicals in exile returned to England with William; their earlier manifestos helped to shape the articles of the Declaration of Rights.

Greaves shows beyond doubt that far from being a bogey constructed by Tory apologists to justify authoritarianism and repression, the radicals were a very real threat: organized, with a theory of resistance, and prepared to pursue their ends by violence. He charts their activities, sects and factions in three countries, drawing on a very wide range of evidence in continental and English archives. This is a book of immense learning, full of useful information. Greaves is painstaking in evaluating evidence – of Russell's guilt, for instance, or about the controversy surrounding the cause of the Earl of Essex's death. In the end, however, it is a book that is often dull and disappointing. Too often Greaves seems to place a self-denying ordinance on analysis and argument. We need a much fuller discussion of the religious differences that fractured the radicals' ranks and of the role of religion in their programmes. Greaves suggests that they followed, even in 1688, Calvin rather than Locke but never explains why, nor entertains John Dunn's argument that Locke's own theory of resistance owed much to Calvinism.[93] We read fascinating snippets about the wearing of colours, the desecration of pictures, the dissemination of propaganda prints (especially from the Netherlands); but Greaves never brings them together into an analysis of the culture of radicalism and its relationship to official ideology and rep-

---

[92]   Cf. Sharpe and Zwicker, *Politics of Discourse*, 7.
[93]   See J. Dunn, *The Political Thought of John Locke: an Historical Account of the Argument of the Two Treatises of Government* (Cambridge, 1969).

resentation.[94] Nor does he develop any study of the languages of criticism, and so fails to understand how the linked charges of popery and promiscuity were intended (and served) to delegitimize the king and court.[95] The sexual politics and sexual rhetoric of both courtly and opposition culture call out for examination. Most of all, while he laboriously traces men and movements, Greaves says little about the radicals' ideas and never closely analyses the pamphlets, so that their precise contribution to political theory and polemic remains unclear. This last failing opens up a larger question: whether the word *radical*, or even *radicals*, is not too clumsy a catchall for a variety of beliefs and agendas. Certainly some definition of these terms over three decades and in different countries would have sharpened the discussion. All in all, *Secrets of the Kingdom* lays down the bare outline for a story. A historian of more inquisitive spirit needs to turn it into the best sort of thriller, where finally we know *why* as well as *what*.

Working from evidence entirely different from Greaves's, Nancy Maguire fully supports the thesis that the politics and political culture of Restoration England were dominated by the memory of regicide and fear of radicalism. 'An almost paranoid fear of the repetition of civil disorder', she writes in *Regicide and Restoration: English Tragicomedy 1660–1671* (Cambridge, 1992), 'agitated most Englishmen' (p. 49). Maguire's sources are the plays, principally the tragicomedies, performed at court and on the public stage between 1660 and 1671. These texts, almost entirely neglected by historians, she clearly shows to be rich documents of political values and political anxieties. Charles II himself not only attended plays frequently – probably twice a week – but also, like his father, occasionally commissioned them. Still more important, most of the playwrights were themselves politicians who had connections with the Stuarts: Thomas Shadwell, John Caryll, Henry Cary and Thomas Porter, for example, were the sons of Royalists and Caroline officeholders. These were men with personal political agendas and commitments; in *The Duke of Lerma*, to take a case, Sir Robert Howard, one of the instigators of Clarendon's impeachment, may even have 'devised his accusation' against the minister (p. 125). Most of all, they were all men dedicated to a propaganda campaign to rebuild the monarchy. In some cases personal interest rallied them to the cause. Those playwrights like Sir William Davenant who had made their accommodation with the

---

[94] Cf. Burke, *Fabrication of Louis XIV*, ch. 10.
[95] Cf. A. Bellany, '"Raylinge Rymes and Vaunting Verse": Libellous Politics in Early Stuart England', in Sharpe and Lake, *Culture and Politics*, 285–310.

Protectorate may have felt strongly in 1660 a need to prove their loyalty to the king.[96] In all cases, loyalists discerned the need to counter the republican threat and the vestiges of republican culture. One strategy, of course, was simply to return to old rhetorics of harmony and hierarchy and to revive the genres that had encoded them so as to, we might say, erase regicide and republic from the historical imagination and cultural history of England. But the fact and powerful memory of regicide rendered this problematic: 'Kingship', Maguire argues in a wonderfully suggestive sentence, 'could no longer be felt as an imaginative whole after the execution of Charles I' (p. 4).[97] Instead of erasure, therefore, the playwrights embraced the theme of regicide and endeavoured to use it as a form for both exorcising the past and underpinning a new present. As other aspects of Restoration culture, the plays exhibited a doubleness – a looking back and forward, an endeavour to restore an old and build a new world, a reminder to audiences of the tragic martyrdom of one king but the triumph of his cause and of another king. Such needs and circumstances presented playwrights with a technical – or generic – problem. Neither the masque, with its philosophical certainty of the force of the divine royal presence, nor the dramatic tragedy, overtaken by the most tragic of all scenes enacted on the scaffold at Whitehall, served the politics of the moment. The playwrights found their solution in the tragicomedy, which generically embraced and enabled the representation of menacing regicide transmuting into stable restored kingship. Maguire is at her most interesting in analysing the genre of tragicomedy as a window onto a broader cultural ambivalence:

> Within this uncertain and insecure culture the crashing polarities of regicide and restoration, idealism and pragmatism, past and present, security and instability, demanded a genre which allowed multiple perspectives, which tolerated a sense of change and flux . . . The simple vision of tragedy no longer worked and tragi-comedy, mirroring the double vision and ambiguity of the Restoration, inevitably contributed to the political method of the decade, as well as becoming its instinctive mood. (p. 42)[98]

Because there were no perfect indigenous dramatic models, the first experiments with the genre nervously stumbled, several plays in the early 1660s having alternative endings. Some playwrights, like Davenant, attempted adaptations of Shakespeare; still more copied Fletcher. Increasingly, however, it became obvious that the new world required a new politics and a new drama to represent, even to construct, it. For in

---

[96] Cf. A. H. Nethercot, *Sir William Davenant* (1938).

[97] Cf. Sharpe, *Politics and Ideas*, 67–71.

[98] See also S. Zwicker, *Politics and Language in Dryden's Poetry: the Arts of Disguise* (Princeton, 1984).

the 1660s it might still be that, in the words of *The Indian Queen*, 'Princes are sacred', but experience had confirmed the Hobbesian dictum acknowledged in the same play: 'power once lost, farewell their sanctity' (p. 69). As well as this national experience, and not least because of his personal experience, Charles II's own personality 'fostered the pragmatism of the new political theory' (p. 11). Though he touched for the king's evil and organized an elaborate mystical coronation ritual, the third Stuart was a very human king, whose practical daily life did not always sit comfortably with the magical image of monarchy. Here again the tragicomedy, with its capacity for divided idealizing main plot and satirical subplot, was able to express the 'culture's conflicting experience of kingship' (p. 138) – and, we might add, of power and politics themselves.

As she traces the history of the new genre from the anxious uncertainties of 1660 to the stabilities of the late 1660s, Maguire also tracks the gradual development of a new political culture. By 1668 Howard's *Lerma* and Davenant's *Tempest* announced a move away from panegyric to criticism of the king and court. Plays began to stage resourceful and loyal subjects rather than powerful kings. Mystical, divine-right monarchy, she suggests, gave way in dramatic representations to de facto kingship and pragmatism: as Leonidas says in *Marriage à la Mode*, 'You are a King, Sir; but you are no God' (p. 161). By 1670 younger playwrights like Dryden, less imbued with the experiences of civil war, developed a different vocabulary of praise, counsel and criticism. They both reflected and powerfully contributed to a more pragmatic representation of politics and a new, demystified politics of representation.

Regicide and Restoration fails to resolve several problems and misses many opportunities. Maguire completely misunderstands the early Stuart masque and is therefore unpersuasive both about abortive attempts to revive it and about its relationship to Restoration drama: the chapter on masque is the weakest. She is often in danger of idealizing and simplifying pre-civil war drama, as though arguing that the tensions she discerns after 1660 were completely absent before. She is too prone to simplify the narrative of the 1660s to one of divine right giving way to de facto kingship and pragmatism, when it is often an author's simultaneously embracing and acknowledging the contradiction that strikes us. Her occasional gestures towards semiotics and cultural theory, Lotman and Uspensky, add mainly platitude – and evidence that Maguire is herself uncomfortable with a theoretical turn.[99] Important questions posed by her argument and central to it are not answered.

[99] See Y. M. Lotman and B. A. Uspensky, 'On the Semiotic Mechanism of Culture', *New Literary History*, 9 (1978), 211–32.

Why was Fletcher chosen by those grappling to find a new dramatic genre? (He was not the only playwright to stage narrow escapes and sudden twists.) Where did the new form of drama come from? How influential was French theatre? The sexual politics of Restoration drama calls out for more than the scant attention it receives here. Maguire notes the references to *Tyrannick Love*, the focus on adultery, and the convention of joining good characters in marriage, but she never explores the relationship of these themes to the old drama of love and honour nor the valence of the discourse of love, sexuality and marriage in the politics, culture and society of Charles II's reign. While we are often persuaded by insightful general observations, the particular readings of plays never quite fulfil the promise. The cut-off date for her investigation seems arbitrary, and it robs us of the opportunity to study either the politics of generic adaptation, during the years of burgeoning party politics, or the revival of issues of divine right, loyalism and radicalism during the Exclusion Crisis.

Yet there is much of value in *Regicide and Restoration*, both in particular and in general. The importance of the new actresses and the enlarged female roles in the drama introduced audiences to novel representations of women and perhaps to the imagination of broader social activity for them, especially at a time when actresses became royal mistresses and countesses. Not only the connections between playwrights and politicians but also the integrations of drama and power emerge clearly here: 'True Monarchy's supported by our play' was more than an anonymous playwright's empty boast (p. 77). Lady Castlemaine's wearing the crown jewels in a production of *Horace* may even lead us to ponder the extent to which a monarchical culture demystified in practice depended for its image on its representations – on not only actors but also Charles himself 'playing the king'. Certainly, Maguire leads us to some very important reflections on the culture of Restoration England: the tendency towards 'compartmentalizing . . . and, above all, keeping emotions out of play' (p. 95); the fading magic of both power and theatre; the capacity to construct a myth, knowing it to be mythical – all are markers of a consciousness quite different from the Renaissance culture of pre-revolutionary England. In her observation of 'the continuous tension between concealment and display', Maguire points to a new political culture (brilliantly explicated by Steven Zwicker) and to fundamental changes in notions of public and private selves (p. 145). In reading from the plays the contemporary grasp of the necessity to limit and contain disagreement and division, she offers another perspective on the history of party and on the political institutionalization of difference. Most of all in *Regicide and Restoration,* Maguire opens the lid on a treasure chest of riches. After reading her who can doubt that the historians who confine themselves to letters, pamphlets and tracts, ignoring the plays that constructed as well as reflected a new political culture, will write an impoverished history of the Restoration?

VII

Some years ago when I first surveyed a group of books on literary culture and politics, the great promise for early modern history appeared to lie in interdisciplinary studies: in a historicizing of literary texts and a broadening of the range of evidence used by historians.[100] Yet for all the gestures to the interdisciplinary, that promise has not been fulfilled. Here, it is sad for a historian to have to admit, the fault lies almost entirely with academic historians. For, with a few exceptions, historians have not taken up the opportunity or challenge presented by new historicists and other critics. Nor have they broadened or enriched their jejune conception of political culture. Of the books here under review, therefore, it is those written by authors from disciplines other than history – notably, literary studies – that most excite and stimulate. If historians – rightly – bemoan the critics' failure to historicize closely, it behoves them to join with the best critical scholarship in a truly interdisciplinary programme to further explore and explicate the culture of early modern England.[101] To be successful any such programme must also bring in (or bring back) an art history not only concerned with formalist analysis but also engaged with questions of ideology, representation, dissemination and reception.[102] For language was in Renaissance England only one of the means by which symbols bequeathed and communicated meaning, and perhaps linguistic symbols cannot be fully understood isolated from those other genres and symbolic systems.

The subject of religion in seventeenth-century culture and politics calls out for just such an interdisciplinary approach. Historians are only

---

[100] See K. Sharpe, 'The Politics of Literature in Renaissance England', *History*, 71 (1986), 235–47.

[101] As we have seen in the books reviewed above, literary critics who rely on secondary historical works and historians who read literary texts mediated through criticism both ultimately fail in the interdisciplinary objective of historicizing texts. I am grateful to Steven Zwicker for discussion of this issue and for a critical reading of this essay.

[102] This agenda was brilliantly laid out by Sir Roy Strong in 1965 (Conference on British Art, Yale University, 21 April 1965; typescript of proceedings in Huntington Library). The issue remains almost as pressing today.

just beginning to explore religion as a visual, sensual and emotional experience – as opposed to a theological system or polemical sermon. Only further enquiry along such lines, using devotional lyric and religious representations, will explicate the changing roles of religion in the culture and help us to understand how religion contributed to the mystification of power; whether puritan iconophobia undermined the republican cause; whether and how religious discourse became a language of diminished potency in Restoration England, or whether, as Jonathan Clark would argue, it adapted to become a central discourse of an English *ancien régime*.[103]

A broader, more contextualized history of religion is also needed to elucidate the relationship of religious to other discourses – political and social, classical and pagan, amorous and sexual. How did the languages of pagan Greece and Rome and of scripture combine in the consciousness of the Anglican gentleman and godly republican? What fostered the slow emergence of the idea of conscience as an autonomous personal sphere? Did changing notions of the individual subject require the separation of religion from other languages and spaces? Were aesthetic revolutions the motor of changing religious sensibilities or driven by them?

Several of the books we have examined have focused attention on the issue of order – in religious and secular life. But no historian has attempted an exegesis of its usage or meanings in the seventeenth century, or of the response of a static concept to the fact of change. What did *order* mean to those who witnessed the execution of a king in 1649, or the erection of a new monarchy in 1660, or the deposition of a divinely anointed king in 1688? How did ideas of order, premised on ideals of harmony and organic community, adapt to accommodate and socially validate party division and contest, the pursuit of individual profit, even selfishness and duplicity? How did notions of moral and sexual order transmute from the sterilities of Platonic love to the debaucheries of Rochester, and what was the consequence for society and the state? To what extent was the necessity for and idea of order internalized in later Stuart England, forming the emergent individual as a self-policing agent? And what role did religion perform in constructing changing ideas of order?

Such questions return to the most fundamental question for any society: how do rulers and subjects discern and construct meaning and

---

[103] See J. C. D. Clark, *English Society 1688–1832: Ideology, Social Structure, and Political Practice during the Ancien Régime* (Cambridge, 1985).

a system of cohabitation and how do those constructions and systems adapt to changed circumstances? Indeed, it may be that with respect to the seventeenth century 'religion' is the shorthand we use to describe the meaning(s) and system(s) that English people constructed for themselves. If so, it becomes all the clearer that a fully satisfactory history of early modern religion awaits a broader and richer cultural history of that century of revolutions.

CHAPTER ELEVEN

Celebrating a cultural turn: political culture and cultural politics in early modern England

The historiography of seventeenth-century England has produced some of the finest, and most important, historical scholarship of any period or country. Be it political, religious or social history, works on the gentry controversy, the civil war, religion and magic, or the crisis of the aristocracy have deservedly been read by scholars of other periods and disciplines and have influenced the approaches to other centuries and subjects. Over the last twenty years the controversies over revisionism and the English civil war have reverberated into the historiography of other revolutions and have excited large discussions about the nature of historical evidence and narrative, and about the historian's own reading and positioning. Most recently the beginnings of a cultural turn in early modern studies – an openness to the theoretical and critical perspectives of other disciplines, principally literary studies – have led to a relaxing of the borders between political, social and cultural history, and to a reconstruction of political history itself.[1]

Professor David Underdown, an English scholar who migrated to America, has been at the pinnacle of early modern studies for over thirty-five years. Among his earliest publications were the classic instances of the impeccable monograph – *Pride's Purge* is perhaps still the best political analysis of a seventeenth-century moment.[2] In *Somerset in the Civil War*, Underdown made an early and important contribution to the new trend of local studies that tested generalizations about national politics and signalled the need to pay more attention to popular, as well as elite, politics and allegiance.[3] Over the next decade, whilst the clashes over revisionism sharpened, Underdown pursued a bold analysis of the relationships of popular culture and popular politics from 1603 to 1660.

---

[1] See Kevin Sharpe and Peter Lake eds., *Culture and Politics in Early Stuart England* (Houndmills and Stanford, 1994).

[2] David Underdown, *Pride's Purge: Politics in the Puritan Revolution* (Oxford, 1971).

[3] Underdown, *Somerset in the Civil War and Interregnum* (Newton Abbot, 1973).

Developing the agrarian historian's contrast between the economies of arable and pasture and woodland, Underdown extended the argument to press a correspondingly clear differentiation of local society, religion, customs, gender relations and politics that helped to shape the choice of sides in 1642.[4] Few reviewers found the ecological origins of the English civil war persuasive. But none doubted that *Revel, Riot and Rebellion* both demonstrated the relationship of village culture to ideas of order and deference, and pointed up the need for a history of politics that would transcend the traditional study of political institutions and their records to interrogate the broader political culture – of region and nation – inscribed in symbols, rituals and customs as well as quarter sessions records and subsidy rolls.[5] That broader sense of the political inspired Underdown's excellent local study of Dorchester, in which political conflicts, elite and popular, were convincingly related to cultural conflicts – from differences about the priorities of daily life to rival desires for change, aspirations for reform, and visions of the hereafter.[6] *Fire from Heaven* not only extends political analysis from the elite to the ordinary folk of early modern England, it embraces as the field of the political historian a terrain that had no place in *Pride's Purge*. It reconfigures political history itself.

It is interesting to recall that Underdown's work has plotted this trajectory while other political historians, both revisionist scholars and their critics, have remained, for the most part, preoccupied with high politics and devoted to the narrative told in meticulous detail.[7] Indeed there have been few Underdown students or disciples, and still fewer of them have followed their mentor into the history of popular culture, gender relations and popular politics. In 1995, a collection of essays was published in Underdown's honour, edited by Susan D. Amussen and Mark A. Kishlansky, entitled *Political Culture and Cultural Politics in Early Modern England*. This festschrift is unusual in not consisting largely of pieces by former students but in collecting essays by a group of 'colleagues' who claim to have been, in varying ways, influenced by Underdown's work.

---

[4] Underdown, *Revel, Riot and Rebellion: Popular Politics and Culture in England 1603–1660* (Oxford, 1985).

[5] See John S. Morrill, 'The Ecology of Allegiance in the English Civil War', *Journ. Brit. Studies*, 26 (1987), now reprinted in Morrill, *The Nature of the English Revolution: Essays* (1993), 224–41. Cf. Kevin Sharpe, *Politics and Ideas in Early Stuart England* (1989), 293–303.

[6] Underdown, *Fire from Heaven: Life in an English Town in the Seventeenth Century* (New Haven, Conn., 1992).

[7] This is as true for Richard Cust, *The Forced Loan and English Politics 1626–28* (Oxford, 1987), and Thomas Cogswell, *The Blessed Revolution: English Politics and the Coming of War* (Cambridge, 1989), as for Conrad Russell's *Parliaments and English Politics* (Oxford, 1979) or *The Fall of the British Monarchies* (Oxford, 1991).

Though an odd assembly, the range of contributors, senior and younger scholars, 'old revisionist' and 'anti-revisionist', signals another important move away from the old camps and categories that have begun to stifle early modern studies and towards a methodological eclecticism and openness to other disciplines that pays tribute to and transcends Underdown's own work. Not only a fitting celebration of David Underdown's career, *Political Culture*, together with other recent collections,[8] lays out a new agenda for the next generation of early modern scholars.

The most traditional of the essays addresses high politics very much in the spirit of Underdown's own brilliant analysis in *Pride's Purge*. John Morrill attempts a systematic re-examination of the career of John Pym in the Long Parliament and offers important correctives to the prevailing view based on J. H. Hexter's *King Pym*.[9] In a polite demolition of Hexter, exposing the thin (at times non-existent) evidential base of a number of his assertions, Morrill rejects the view that Pym was the craftsman behind the important parliamentary money ordinances of 1643 or the directives that established the regional associations for war administration. In an important few pages he scrutinizes the claims made for King Pym as the leading parliamentary orator, demonstrating that many printed speeches assigned to him were fabrications, that the corpus of his published speeches was small (eleven), and that Pym contributed little to some of the vital set-piece debates of the parliament, even those on religion and finance. As a consequence, King Pym is dethroned or emerges, in Morrill's words, in the 'more credible position as an extraordinarily determined and devoted team member'.[10] Rather than a lone leader, Pym was 'used by others' to run committees and maintain lines of communication between the houses – a man of business, as he might have been called by a historian of the Tudor parliaments.[11] This is an important essay that reminds us of the continuing importance of careful and detailed analysis of parliamentary politics, the refusal to take others' work on trust, and the scrutiny of manuscript as well as printed evidence, which characterizes the best revisionist scholarship. Yet (as some would say of revisionism in general), the essay is more effective in its critique of the old story than in rewriting Pym and

---

[8] See Sharpe and Lake, *Culture and Politics*, introduction and passim.

[9] J. H. Hexter, *The Reign of King Pym* (Cambridge, Mass., 1961).

[10] Susan D. Amussen and Mark A. Kishlansky eds., *Political Culture and Cultural Politics in Early Modern England* (Manchester and New York, 1995), 43.

[11] Cf. M. A. R. Graves, 'The Management of the Elizabethan House of Commons: The Council', in 'Men of Business', *Parliamentary History*, 2 (1983), 11–38.

raises a number of problems that it does not solve. Morrill is never really explicit about who were the others Pym served, nor who (if any) led a parliament (whose predecessor in the spring had appeared divided and directionless) so decisively towards radical challenge to the king. His acknowledgement that, while Pym was not a leader in the legislation programme, he was prominent in the cases against Laud and Strafford and 'most expert in identifying and articulating the great popish design'[12] suggests less that Pym's importance has been exaggerated and more that – not least through his tactical shifts? – the traditional priorities of bills against grievances gave way to high political manoeuvre. One would have liked more in this essay on Pym's relationship to other MPs, politicians and 'back-benchers', and, as well as a count of authentic speeches, some close analysis of Pym's rhetoric that so effectively sustained the paranoia about popery which, more than anything, inhibited political settlement. Furthermore, reconsideration of Pym's aspirations for court office and the consequences of the collapse of the Bedford plan (to bring opposition peers and MPs into the king's counsels) seems essential for an understanding of his (changing) tactics and standing in the Commons, not least his move from the summer of 1641 to 'a radical redefinition of parliament as a great Council of the realm'.[13] Finally, whatever the reality or extent of his dominance, the *perception* of Pym as leader of the Commons, his representation in letters, pamphlets, news books, royal propaganda, squib and cartoon, needs to be placed alongside the close re-reading of parliamentary speeches and journals. This is to ask too much of an essay, but it is a tribute to both Morrill's contribution and the perspectives offered by the festschrift as a whole that in these pages we have the beginnings of a new understanding of Pym, the politics of the Long Parliament and the politics of reputation and rhetoric that helped to form the public sphere.

Where Morrill debunks the historian's Pym, Peter Lake subjects the self-presentation of Bishop Joseph Hall to criticism. Hall's historical reputation, perhaps as he intended, has followed the title of his famous *Via Media*, published in 1626 and written at some point in the preceding year.[14] At the height of the controversy over Richard Montagu's *Appello Caesarem* and Arminianism, Hall's pamphlet announced an irenic middle course that might settle the issue and unite the parties in a Church of

---

[12] *Political Culture*, 44.

[13] *Political Culture*, 24; see Clayton Roberts, 'The Earl of Bedford and the Coming of the English Revolution', *Journ. Mod. Hist.*, 49 (1977), 600–16.

[14] Joseph Hall, *Via Media: the Way of Peace* in *The Works of the Rev. Joseph Hall* (12 vols., Oxford, 1837), X, 471–98; Lake dates the work to 1625/6, *Political Culture*, 70.

England that he located between the Roman and reformed churches. It is Lake's argument that it was a stance of moderation and irenicism that should not be taken at face value. For when carefully re-read, in the context of his other writings, Hall's *Via Media* revealed sympathies and commitments that were critical of the Arminians and close to the Calvinists. Hall's sermon of 1623, Lake argues, showed him to be resolutely opposed to the Spanish match and, whilst he echoed the irenic Jacobean rhetoric that could accept Rome as a true church, he simultaneously appealed to the antipopery that elided the differences between Protestants. Where Montagu was concerned to denounce Calvinists as puritans, beneath Hall's language of moderation Lake identifies a 'universalist Calvinism' that was intended subtly to tell against Montagu whilst claiming an impartial adjudication between him and his critics. Hall's book, Lake concludes, was 'a skillful deployment' rather than simple statement of moderation: it was 'both irenic and polemical'.[15]

As with his other essays warning historians not to take words at face value, or read from silence,[16] this is a clever and suggestive reading, persuasive in its reminder that in this political culture 'moderation', 'peace' and 'unity' were positions – and positions that any who sought to persuade (not least the king) needed to claim and appropriate. I am less persuaded by the attempt, even the method, of reading the *Via Media* from the context of Hall's other works, notably the sermon of 1623. Putting aside a sense that this sermon is a less 'direct' attack on the Spanish faction than is claimed,[17] the argument that Hall made his position more explicit over the next two years curiously underplays the declaration of war with Spain and the radically changed political circumstances that a skilful courtier (as well as bishop) had to negotiate. War against Spain necessarily sharpened antipapal rhetoric and emphasized the need for unity among Protestants. Hall's desire for settlement was clearly more than a rhetorical guise, but what kind of settlement did he seek? Lake refers to Hall's 'anti-Arminian asides' in the *Via Media* and argues that, for all the rhetoric, he reaffirmed a modified Calvinist position on justification and predestination against Montagu and the Arminians. As laid out here, however, Hall's position appears to offer genuine concessions to the critics of double-predestination. Hall 'asserted a general will of God that all men should be saved' and praised 'acute Arminius' along

---

[15] *Political Culture*, 75.

[16] See, for example, Peter Lake, 'The Collection of Ship Money in Cheshire during the 1630s: a Case Study of Relations between Central and Local Government', *Northern Hist.*, 17 (1981), 44–71.

[17] See Joseph Hall, 'The Best Bargain', preached 21 September 1623, in *Works*, V, 150–9.

with 'our learned and judicious Bishop Overall'.[18] Though Lake in one place refers to this as an 'invoking' of Overall's name, he elsewhere acknowledges that the influence of Overall on Hall was 'real enough'.[19] Moreover, the argument of rhetoric cuts both ways. As Lake acknowledges, where Featley and Carleton attacked Montagu as heterodox, 'Hall's response . . . was a good deal less confrontational and polarised in its language and argumentative procedures.'[20] Doubtless that response was strategic. But the point here is not only Lake's argument that language can veil other agendas; it is also the reverse: that contemporaries might have read the language, the appeal to Overall, rather than the hidden agenda. This was evidently true in Charles I's case. For, if Hall intended to persuade Charles to a Calvinist resolution of the controversy, he failed; the king silenced both sides, in a manner that followed Hall's *words*: 'There is no possible redress but in a severe edict of restraint to charm all tongues and pens upon the sharpest punishment from passing those moderate bounds.'[21] In other words, whatever Hall's *real* position – and I am not fully persuaded that it was as detached from his rhetoric as Lake would have it – it was the middle way he appealed to that had influence at the highest level of policy. Language, as we have come to see, can sometimes carry other freight than the load it is meant to deliver.

Another group of contributors pay tribute to Underdown's career by offering local studies that illuminate the broader political culture with varying degrees of success. Richard Cust uses the rich archival material in the Huntington Library meticulously to re-examine the rivalry in Leicestershire between the Greys and Hastings as a contest over values as well as for local supremacy. The ambiguous language of aristocratic humanism – language, he argues, of lineage and virtue, of harmony and competition, the multivalent meanings of honour and service – could be deployed differently and strategically to advance a case. Whilst the norms of gentry society were inscribed in common languages, the struggle between the families 'revolved around the two sides trying to gloss common themes in different ways' – and in different ways on different occasions. Though this is an essay of exemplary detail and interesting suggestions, in the end the local case does not easily sustain the broader argument, nor are the larger questions, about the discourse of honour,

---

[18] *Political Culture*, 69–70.   [19] Ibid., 76–7.   [20] Ibid., 76, 77.
[21] Ibid., 70; cf. James F. Larkin ed., *Stuart Royal Proclamations, Vol. II: Royal Proclamations of King Charles I, 1625–46* (Oxford, 1983), no. 43, 90–1; no. 105, 218–20.

for example, sufficiently contextualized. Was the language of honour and virtue a discourse that conjoined the old aristocracy and the gentry or one that still divided them? How far did the Jacobean peace reshape the ideas of honour and service? Were (different) religious beliefs and sympathies at odds with the shared values of chivalry and display? How far were contemporaries aware of the economic, social and political changes that had complicated ideals of public service and private interest? Was the appeal to traditional languages a polemical move, a belief in the continuing valence of, or a real desire for, older values in the process of transition?[22] It is to Cust's credit that a case study of a family rivalry can give rise to such questions. But it would take an engagement with discourse analysis of a broader spectrum of texts, a more open methodology – quite simply, a bolder approach to the subject – to begin to answer them.

Molly Mclain takes the local study into the still largely unmapped terrain of the Restoration county community.[23] Studying the riot in Wentwood Forest, Monmouthshire, she demonstrates how, quite unlike the forest riots of the 1630s led by the poor, dispossessed of common rights by entrepreneurial landlords, the Wentwood riot was orchestrated by some of the most powerful men in the country. And more than a mere protest against enclosure, she argues, the riot graphically announced the determination of the Monmouthshire gentry, who had grown in political independence during the civil wars, to check the attempts of the Marquis of Worcester to re-establish his dominance. As the marquis retaliated by removing local gentlemen from office, a fight began in the course of which the gentry proved willing, quite cynically, to exploit national fears and to slur Worcester with charges of tolerating Catholics and acting 'arbitrarily'. The report of the two MPs for Monmouthshire, Sir Trevor Williams and William Morgan, brought the dispute directly 'into the realm of party politics'.[24] With the support of the Whigs, the MPs used the mounting anxieties about a popish plot to promote a bill removing Worcester as Lord President of Wales. But, just as they drew on national fears to strengthen themselves in a local conflict, so the turn of the tide in Westminster left them weak and exposed in the Marches. The dissolution of the parliament in 1681 and the swell of loyalism saw Worcester safe as Lord President and promoted to a dukedom. The new

[22] For discussions of some of these questions, see J. S. A. Adamson, 'Chivalry and Political Culture in Caroline England', in Sharpe and Lake, *Culture and Politics*, 161–98.

[23] Though, see Andrew M. Coleby, *Central Government and the Localities: Hampshire 1649–1689* (Cambridge and New York, 1988).   [24] *Political Culture*, 124.

duke took his revenge on his enemies and Williams was imprisoned for inability to pay a fine for scandalous libel; the Lord Chancellor decided the Wentwood Forest case in Worcester's favour. The political struggle played for high stakes was lost by the county gentry.

Mclain's essay reveals how little we know about the late seventeenth-century localities and indicates how important such studies may be for a full understanding of national and party politics. There are rich suggestions here that might have been pointed up and further developed. We need to know *how* 'the development of the civil war years encouraged a sense of political independence among the . . . gentry' and in what ways the society and political culture of the county community had been transformed by 1660 – for all the pretence of a simple return to the status quo *ante bellum*.[25] Though an appeal, even a polemical appeal, to the centre was not a new strategy for the contestants in local disputes,[26] the presentation of that contest as a national issue, and in the language of party, marks an important shift in political culture to a politicization which, as Mark Kishlansky argued for electoral behaviour, transformed local into national values.[27] That Worcester, for all his ancestral power and office, also depended for his victory on an abrupt turn of the national mood, also raises questions about the position of the aristocracy in the new political order that have hardly begun to be addressed. If the next generation of scholars is to answer them, they will need to start from and then transcend the parameters of the enquiry Mclain initiates here.

Carl Esterbrook follows Mclain across the traditional divide of seventeenth-century historiography to examine the relationship between the cathedral and community in Wells before and after the civil war. He argues for a startling transformation in the relations of civic corporation and cathedral close. Before the civil war, the cathedral and its dean were major powers in the city: legally through the church courts and economically as a landlord and through control of major city thoroughfares. And such powers were demonstrated and reinforced in the elaborate pageants and displays (interestingly including pagan goddesses and miners in puritan garb) that Dean Haydon regularly staged on the city streets. For all the restoration of the church as well as

---

[25] *Political Culture*, 119.

[26] See W. T. MacCaffrey, 'Talbot and Stanhope: an Episode in Elizabethan Politics', *Bull. Inst. Hist. Research*, 33 (1960), 73–85.

[27] Mark Kishlansky, *Parliamentary Selection: Social and Political Choice in Early Modern England* (Cambridge, 1986); see also Victor L. Stater, *Noble Government: the Stuart Lord Lieutenancy and the Transformation of English Politics* (Athens, Ga., 1994).

monarchy in 1660, the cathedral and clerical establishment never regained such a hold; rather, Esterbrook argues persuasively, the civil war effected a shift to 'civic autonomy'. During the 1640s and '50s, the citizens of Wells had freely moved goods through gates the cathedral had previously closed to traffic, and had even opened formerly sacred spaces to commercial activity. Together with the evasion of rents and decline of ecclesiastical courts, such inroads punctured the mystique of clerical authority. After 1660 the mayor's court presided over even religious issues as the corporation saw a change to 'a significantly non-clerical political culture'.[28] Interestingly, the shift of power was marked by changes in ritual and display. At first the guild processions simply pointed up the identity with the city rather than close; 'eventually, however, the corporation came to appropriate ecclesiastical ritual itself for the expression of civic identity and authority' – even celebrating the cathedral's patronal feast day as a civic festival.[29] As Esterbrook puts it, Wells Cathedral had become the cathedral 'of Wells'.

Just as the essays by Cust and Mclain gesture to a society defeudalized by revolution (it is worth recalling that feudal dues and incidents were not restored in 1660), Esterbrook presents a case study in the desacralization of seventeenth-century England. As Jonathan Clark has warned us, such a story should not be told as a Whig narrative of progression to secularism and reason;[30] Esterbrook himself points to the popularity of organs and ceremonies in the 1660s and the revived interest in sacred music in the 1690s. Yet the shift to a more autonomous secular culture shown in miniature here mirrors our sense of change on the larger canvas. Still more interestingly, the appropriation of ecclesiastical ritual forms (just as a century earlier much Elizabethan ritual had appropriated Catholic forms) speaks of a continuing desire for power to be, if not sacralized, to some extent mystified rather than exposed in the utilitarian glare of Hobbesian atomism. Such an observation not only casts light on the ambiguities about the rationalization of authority in Augustan England, it cautions the historian that to privilege the rational discourse of politics over the rituals and symbols of state is to lose sight of contradictions and to depict in monochrome a political canvas of many, and clashing, hues.[31]

---

[28] *Political Culture*, 150. [29] Ibid., 151.
[30] J. C. D. Clark, *English Society 1688–1832* (Cambridge, 1985).
[31] We await a good study of rituals of state in late seventeenth-century England, but see G. Reedy, 'Mystical Politics: the Imagery of Charles II's Coronation', in P. Korshin ed., *Studies in Change and*

In the history of the nation as well as the locality, one of Underdown's most important contributions has been to broaden the arena of the political interrogated by historians and to extend the materials studied as evidence of the history of politics. It is very much in this spirit that Tom Cogswell castigates historians of early Stuart England for a concentration on elite texts and urges research on underground verse and ballads in which, he argues, a truly popular politics may be discerned. Following Harold Love and others, Cogswell reminds us that even in the first great age of print culture, many popular verses and songs still circulated in manuscript, beyond the controls of any censorship of the press.[32] Scandalous songs were passed from alehouse to alehouse, and along migration routes, and were copied into gentry commonplace books and often eventually printed. According to Cogswell, they constructed as well as reflected a new popular political awareness. And more than merely rehearsing political issues and debates, he maintains, this literature of mordant satire and ridicule of ministers and courtiers undermined any notion of a consensual political culture. Indeed, the 'polarisation which had been such a marked feature of the "underground" media facilitated the abrupt formation of two increasingly antithetical camps in the early 1640s'.[33] Popular literature, in other words, helped to forge the camps that contested the civil war.

Following the excellent work of Alastair Bellany and Adam Fox,[34] Cogswell's essay is far less 'cutting edge' than the strident claims he makes for it; but it is an important, if not unproblematic piece, nonetheless. For too long historians have disregarded literary sources from elite epics to popular song, although they offer unique insights into contemporary perceptions and anxieties. In the case of the lower orders, they form an important counter to the evidence of court depositions through the prism of which the history of popular consciousness is too often refracted. However, vulgar verse and song present the historian of politics with more problems than Cogswell confronts or even discusses. First,

Revolution (Menston, 1972), 19–42; John Ogilby, *The Entertainment of His Most Excellent Majestie Charles II in his passage through the city of London to his coronation* (1662), ed. R. Knowles (Binghamton, N.Y., 1988); L. Schwoerer, 'The Glorious Revolution in Spectacle', in S. Baxter ed., *England's Rise to Greatness, 1660–1763* (Berkeley, 1983), 109–49.

[32] Harold Love, *Scribal Publication in Seventeenth-Century England* (Oxford, 1993). This excellent book needs to be more widely read by all historians of early modern culture and politics.

[33] *Political Culture*, 292.

[34] See A. Bellany, '"Raylinge Rymes and Vaunting Verse": Libellous Politics in Early Stuart England', in Sharpe and Lake, *Culture and Politics*, 285–310; A. Fox, 'Ballads, Libels, and Popular Ridicule in Jacobean England', *Past and Present*, 145 (1994), 47–83.

it is by no means certain, as Cogswell appears to assume, that all verses express an autonomous popular voice. Squibs and libels could be penned by more elite scribes to undermine rivals and enemies, and in some cases the specificity of reference suggests that this was exactly what happened. We need to know much more about the authorship, production, distribution and communication of 'popular' verse before we conclude too confidently about popular political consciousness. The second difficulty, again one that Cogswell passes over too lightly, is that of reception. For Cogswell, 'the vital question centres on what contemporaries heard and read', but *how* they read, as we are beginning to learn, is of equal importance.[35] The diarist John Rous, for example, recorded a number of these rhymes 'for president of the time', though he declared that he hated them.[36] How did they help to form his political values? Were elite recorders and readers led to more critical perceptions of government by popular squibs or alarmed at the vulgar intrusion into the political arena? Did popular literature echo the debates and discussions of elite politics or express a class antagonism that ran across Cavalier and Roundhead divide? Did the relentless diet of sexual scandal fuel the stomach for opposition, or did it, as some would argue for the modern tabloid, induce a cynicism about *all* politics and politicians? For all his bold generalizations, Cogswell is very shaky on the move from underground verse to political action. He is unsure about whether 1640–1 marks a change, simultaneously criticizing those who see it as a crucial moment for the politics of ballad and describing it as a 'media revolution'.[37] He underplays the apparently popular ballads and verses that, in the 1640s as in the 1680s, pressed the royal case against disloyal and ambitious schemers. More generally, he fails to read alongside the libels and lampoons, the recurring preoccupation with order, stability and degree that characterized the moral politics of the crowd in early modern England.[38] In consequence, though Cogswell considers there to be 'no profound mystery about how contemporaries slipped so easily to violent confrontations in the early 1640s', most of his readers will still doubt the ease and seek a more sophisticated explanation for the move from sharp words to sharper swords, especially when so much of this literature itself appears concerned to halt violence.[39] Yet for all its

---

[35] *Political Culture*, 278.

[36] See Mary Anne E. Green ed., *The Diary of John Rous, Incumbent of Santon Downham, Suffolk, 1625–1642* (Camden Soc., 1st ser., 66, 1856); and Kevin Sharpe, *The Personal Rule of Charles I* (New Haven and London, 1992), 695–6.   [37] *Political Culture*, 288, 294.

[38] 'Loyalist' ballads in the 1640s and 1680s are no less common and no less worthy of study than opposition songs and squibs.   [39] *Political Culture*, 294.

problems, this is an important essay written with verve and vigour. If the precise relation remains vague, Cogswell convinces that there is an important connection between popular verse and politics and that a rich vein of literature awaits future research, not least on its language and rhetoricity, generic play and sexual politics.

Blair Worden's essay both complements Cogswell and points up some of the problems I have discussed. The career of the journalist Marchamont Nedham undoubtedly demonstrates the importance 'to Roundheads and Cavaliers alike, of the control of public opinion'. Whether through the verse libels discussed by Cogswell or the surge of polemical pamphlets after 1640, by the 1640s it was recognized that there was 'not so much as a young apprentice that keeps shop' or 'a labourer that holds the plough' who had not some acquaintance with the news brokers.[40] In the new market for news, none was more successful than Nedham. Yet Nedham's career graphically illustrates the problematics of the relationship between the author and his readers, or between news and politics. For Nedham began his career as a Parliamentarian pamphleteer, the voice of *Mercurius Britannicus*, transmogrified in 1647 into the Cavalier *Mercurius Pragmaticus*, and finally in 1650 became the leading propagandist of commonwealth under the banner of *Mercurius Politicus*. Unsurprisingly, scholars have tended to depict Nedham as a simple timeserver whose pen was up for auction and whose own views were neither discernible nor significant. Worden makes a more subtle case: 'Nedham may be important not only in spite of his mutability but because of it. He discovered, amid the polarisations of the puritan Revolution . . . that the very insincerities of journalism may protect a writer's independence of voice.'[41] And it is that independent authorial voice that Worden endeavours to trace through the vicissitudes of Nedham's career.[42] During the 1640s, he argues, Nedham's concern was to strip the monarchy of awe, to open a rational debate about politics. Though he could not be 'openly republican' in *Britannicus*, he went further than many MPs thought proper to press a pragmatic political theory based on 'interest' rather than traditional ties of allegiance or obligation. In 1647, however, hostile to the presbyterians who looked to make the settlement, Nedham

---

[40] *Political Culture*, 301, 307. On news brokers see Joad Raymond, *The Invention of the Newspaper: English Newsbooks, 1641–1649* (Oxford, 1996). I am grateful to Joad Raymond for allowing me to see this important book in advance of publication.   [41] *Political Culture*, 302.

[42] Cf. Worden, 'Milton and Marchamont Nedham', in D. Armitage, A. Himy and Q. Skinner eds., *Milton and Republicanism* (Cambridge, 1995), 156–80; and Worden, 'Marchamont Nedham and the Beginnings of English Republicanism', in D. Wootton ed., *Republicanism, Liberty and Commercial Society, 1649–1776* (Stanford, 1994), 45–81.

offered 'to write his Majesty back into his throne' and skilfully re-read classical and Renaissance histories to demonstrate the benefits of monarchy. Worden maintains, however, that Nedham was never an 'instinctive monarchist'; after the death of Charles I, he became a leading propagandist for commonwealth, pointing up Roman and continental models for a new republic. In co-operation with Marten and Chaloner, he found company in which he was 'able to bring his republicanism and his anti-Puritanism together' and so resolve the contradictions apparent in his career.[43]

In a characteristically elegant essay, Worden offers one of the best brief sketches of Marchamont Nedham that has been written. Importantly, he also shows how principles, rhetorics and positions could be appropriated, refashioned and polemically deployed for quite different ends in changing circumstances. Where he is less persuasive is in arguing for a consistency in Nedham's writings and thoughts. For all his antagonism to puritanism, Nedham's volte-face in 1647 appears all but inexplicable except in terms of a cynical bid for power or even survival. Moreover, though Worden rightly argues that Nedham questions the idea that political theory was a preserve of the elite, we are left with unresolved problems about his importance as a thinker. Worden acknowledges that his claims about interest were 'not consistently sustained', and that he resorted at times to more conventional arguments about virtue. His defence of the Commonwealth from Roman precedents finds (surprisingly) few echoes in the Thomason tracts; his influence appears almost non-existent in a Commonwealth that preferred to justify itself in the language of scripture and Providence.[44] And this raises more general questions about Nedham's journalism. If his skills as a polemicist were so highly valued, why was his own programme so spectacularly unsuccessful? For, despite his readership among apprentices and ploughmen, the populace neither supported regicide nor republic and popular opposition to the regime mounted after 1657. Perhaps, like Milton, Nedham misjudged his audience. Perhaps he only followed the directives of paymasters, republican and (again after 1660) royal, and was faced with making the best of a case. For all Worden's interesting exposition, something remains of the Nedham who was ready (as he said of Shaftesbury) to 'quit an unlucky side . . . at the noise of a new prevailing party'.[45]

The mass outpouring of political pamphlets – often of remarkable

[43] *Political Culture*, 324, 327.   [44] See above, ch. 7.   [45] *Political Culture*, 303.

sophistication – was only one of the ways in which civil war and revolution marked the literature as well as politics of early modern England.[46] In 1986, David Underdown's most influential student, Mark Kishlansky, began his study of *Parliamentary Selection* with a reading of *Coriolanus*, and then went on brilliantly to argue that the process of politicization across the seventeenth century transformed that political world and its texts so that a contested politics and culture became the norm of social experience.[47] Here, in a wonderful essay, Kishlansky addresses the editions of Aesop's fables as sites of that transformation and process of politicization. By a close reading of the fable of the frogs or 'the frogs desiring a king', as told in various editions and translations from the 1530s to 1680s, he traces the politicization of the acts of reading and interpreting, hence of the imagination itself.[48] The earlier editions, he finds, were more often used as an aid to teaching Latin than as political allegory. There was little commentary and the moral that followed the story was generalized and brief. Though some early seventeenth-century translations deployed language with obvious political freight ('subjection'), it was the civil war that transformed the writing and reading of Aesop's fables. In particular, John Ogilby's *Fables of Aesop Paraphrased* (1657) deployed full commentary on the fables to defend kingship and parody the Long Parliament. On the other side, Milton read the fable to deride 'the folly of those being free to seek a king'. It was Ogilby's lavish edition, however, that dominated the 1650s and 1660s. And later in the 1680s and early '90s, the editions by Barlow and L'Estrange continued to draw the lessons of the 'unsteadiness of the people', and the need for strong monarchy and passive obedience.[49] Aesop's fables had become a site of ideological contest, even of party politics. As Kishlansky concludes, 'The English Revolution politicised culture' and the Restoration 'could not unthink a political perspective'.[50]

As he hints along the way, this politicization of culture had broader reverberations. The shifting politics of gender appears, for instance, in one edition of the fable, in which it is a female frog which subverts the reign of King Log.[51] More interestingly, 'as the seventeenth century progressed, more "translators" became authors'; and Ogilby prefaced his

---

[46] See Steven Zwicker, *Lines of Authority: Politics and English Literary Culture* (Ithaca, 1993).

[47] Kishlansky, *Parliamentary Selection*, pp. 1–9.

[48] Cf. Annabel M. Patterson, 'Fables of Power: Aesopian Writing and Political History', in K. Sharpe and S. Zwicker eds., *Politics of Discourse* (Berkeley, Los Angeles and London, 1987), 271–96; and Patterson, *Fables of Power: Aesopian Writing and Political History* (Durham, N.C. and London, 1991). [49] *Political Culture*, 350, 354. [50] *Political Culture*, 375.

[51] The edition by Simon Sturtevant, *The Etymologist of Aesop's Fables* (1602; STC 23410).

edition with an engraving of himself rather than Aesop. Here Kishlansky might have further pondered the politics of this shift. For as Steven Zwicker and others have shown, the claim to authorship was inextricably linked with the political debates over property and authority.[52] More generally, the translator's self-proclamation as author marks an important moment in the emergence of ideas about authorial voice, individual interpretation and personal identity that were to transform political theory as well as literary production. And not only *production*. While Kishlansky's editions introduce us to a variety of authorial readings (in the commentaries and prefatory verses), the important issue of the readers' reception(s) remains unaddressed.

Yet there can be little doubt that, increasingly, the production of these texts responded to the market – to the demands and cultural habits of readers. Were then the readers of the early editions innocent of the politics of the fables, or was the politics of reading in the sixteenth century one of private hermeneutics, undirected by authorial exegesis? We know that the civil war transformed the reader as well as the writer into a more engaged participant in the text[53] – literally in the case of marginalia;[54] but did readers of Aesop come to choose editions, as they did their literary clubs, for their politics? Was the fable a barometer of changed cultural and political habits, or did it write a new political culture? Kishlansky does not pursue all of these questions. But by a clever, and long overdue, extension of 'the linguistic turn' into literary text, he opens a rich new agenda for research on how the early modern English constructed meanings for themselves and how they 'first became aware of the political dimensions of their lives'.[55]

In his most recent work, David Underdown has brought to the centre of social and political history the issues of gender roles and changes in gender relations in seventeenth-century England. It is appropriate then that four of the contributors to this festschrift take up the themes of gender, identity, love and politics. The boldest, and in some ways most exciting, claim is that made by Lisa Jardine in an essay on companionate marriage versus male friendship. 'The term "love"', she asserts, 'modulates during the period . . . from a formally acknowledged desig-

---

[52] Zwicker, *Lines of Authority*, ch. 2. Professor Joe Loewenstein is writing a study of the idea of literary property; I am grateful to him for allowing me to read some papers in advance of publication.   [53] See Sharon Achinstein, *Milton and the Revolutionary Reader* (Princeton, 1994).
[54] Steven Zwicker is currently writing on 'Habits of Reading in a Polemical Culture'. I am grateful to him, Bill Sherman and Heidi Brayman for discussions about marginalia and the politics of reading.   [55] *Political Culture*, 339.

nation of duty and affection towards the authority figure who governs one's life to a more self-centred, freely-willed directing of emotion.'[56] This modulation occurs not only in changing ideas of heterosexual love and marriage, but in new types of relationships amongst men – in both cases elected intimacy replaces traditional obligation, forging new political as well as personal relations. Jardine argues her case from a reading of Jacobean plays – *Lear* and, principally, Thomas Middleton's *The Changeling* – in which she discerns both the changes in relationships and residual textual traces of anxieties about them. Yet while we may be enticed by the thesis and fully persuaded that the drama may reveal 'gradual shifts in acceptable social practice which are not clearly articulated in other kinds of "documentary" historical evidence', the argument is not convincingly demonstrated here. For one, a reading of *The Changeling* can hardly bear the evidential weight of supporting such a large and important model of social change, and at times one feels the model is as much imposed on the text as argued from it. More generally, the description of the earlier relationships – of 'the steady, unchanging and dependable commitment of the feudal retainer' – appears a simplistic and idealized representation of earlier social relations.[57] If such is a seventeenth-century idealization, this only points up the need for the critic and historian to recognize that neither the drama nor any other documents offer clear windows onto the complexities of change, but rather ones tinted with not only anxieties but desires, myths and constructions of the past that may distort. There can be little doubt that Jardine is right to discuss links between changes in marriage and friendship on the one hand and larger social and political relations and issues (of will, election, desire and self, for example) on the other. But the nature and history of those links remain in this essay clouded and obscure.

Susan Amussen shifts the focus of early modern gender studies to investigate the 'cultural politics of manhood' in sixteenth- and seventeenth-century England. By examining courtesy books and other advice literature, Amussen proffers the firm conclusion that in early modern England, 'a man's sexual activities were not central to his manhood'.[58] Sexual conquest, she continues, played a limited role in ideas of masculine identity and men distanced themselves from rapes, sexual violence and even extra-marital sex. Gender roles, as evidenced by cross-dressing on (and off) the stage, were more fluid, and maleness

---

[56] *Political Culture*, 235.   [57] Ibid., 238.   [58] Ibid., 214.

was less defined by brute priapic power. Manhood was, in early modern
society, defined not by sexual criteria but by the attainment of independence, a status that not all ranks or generations of males could obtain.
To independence, the reformed model added respectability, confining
manliness to the propertied and monied, and, as it were, emasculating
as well as disenfranchising the lower orders. For all the originality of this
subject, Amussen's bizarre conclusions must startle anyone who has read
widely in early modern sources. Are not Tudor dynastic portraits testament to sexual prowess and fertility? Are not the plots of scores of
Jacobean and Caroline plays those of male power and sexual violence?
In popular ballads and bawdy verse is it not the men who cannot
perform sexually or handle their wives who are mocked and pilloried?
True, Christian advice manuals and courtesy literature stress different
ideals – of honour, gentle behaviour, grace – but Amussen here displays
little critical awareness that they were intended precisely as didactic antidotes to an often more brutal reality of unregulated sexual appetite, an
analogue in early modern England for anarchy. The polite codes of the
court only thinly veiled a world of sexual competition and conquest; in
the service of a household many young women were abused and
impregnated; among the lower orders even the threat of the whip did
little to reduce fornication and bastardy. If the magistracy stressed
family, responsibility and respectability as the ideal, that was less because
they were concerned with redefining masculinity than with preserving
order. And this brings us to the deep muddle in Amussen's essay over
matters of gender and class. For while she argues that masculinity was
not characterized by sexual violence, she acknowledges the apprentices'
riots against prostitutes and brothels. Whether Amussen is right to see
these riots as the resentment of young men who had not achieved full
manhood, or whether they expressed a morality of the urban middling
orders that awaits further elucidation must remain open to question.
One leaves this essay with a sense that an intelligent question about early
modern masculinity was spoiled in the pursuit by the naïve and simplistic adoption of modern theories about sex and power, gender identity
and instability, and class hegemony and control.

   Rachel Weil's essay centres on the story told (and published) by the
midwife Elizabeth Cellier as one of the many stories circulating at the
time of the popish plot (1678/9), in her case the counter allegation of a
presbyterian plot.[59] Weil's subject is the question, and contemporary

---

[59] For the context, see J. P. Kenyon, *The Popish Plot* (1972), ch. 6.

engagement with the problem, of what constituted credibility in the midst of the propaganda war between Whigs and Tories in 1679–80. Amid the confusion about what and whom to believe, she demonstrates, the genres of play and report – of fiction and fact, we might once have said – themselves were blurred as political testimony deployed dramatic strategies, and plot informers, in some cases reformed rogues, became central characters in the picaresque novel. As plot stories seemed endlessly reinterpretable and belief hinged not only on content but presentation, Weil argues, 'the popish plot . . . opened the way for a public discussion of credibility'.[60] It also, of course, opened the way for those normally outside the ranks of the credited to have a voice and a hearing as, amid the paranoia, the gossip of lowly paid informers – even women – was paid novel attention. Cellier published in *Malice Defeated* an account of a presbyterian plot to subvert the crown to which she proclaimed her loyalty. Constructing herself as a heroine of integrity, she related how other narrators had imprisoned her and tried to turn her against the Catholics, drawing on her job as midwife to claim the truth and justice of her account. By contrast, those who attacked her credibility gendered their assault by accusations of salacious sexual encounters and by dismissal of her stories as monstrous births. And the fact of her writing was used by her enemies as sustaining evidence of her impudence and unreliability. While the criteria of credibility were dissolving, polemicists still appealed to the authorities of the patron and the male to gauge and win belief.

Like Cellier's *Malice Defeated*, Weil's essay is by no means an easy read. Her argument is convoluted, and Cellier as the central subject moves in and out of focus. But some of these difficulties emerge from the sheer range of the suggestions Weil invites us to explore. After a civil war that had overturned oaths and sacrificed truth to propaganda, what now were the criteria of credibility?[61] When common folk had proved more loyal to monarchy than gentlemen, was reliability, as once had been thought, a quality only of the elite? And with the vulgar brought by the news pamphlets into the arena of politics, what devices (including the techniques of fiction) did authors need to deploy to carry conviction? What Weil's essay points to is no less than the need for a history of epistemology, of the cultural constructions and reconstructions of ideas of

---

[60] *Political Culture*, 193.
[61] For a different but complementary approach to this question see Barbara J. Shapiro, *Probability and Certainty in Seventeenth-Century England: a Study of the Relationships between Natural Science, Religion, History, Law, and Literature* (Princeton, 1983), not cited.

truth, belief and witness, a history that would also have to take on board the changing attitudes to authority and law, polemic and, in fine, politics itself. To see that Cellier sits on a point where many of these axes cross is also to recognize that gender too is part of all these narratives.

Perhaps the most succinctly argued of the essays concerned with gender is Ann Hughes's excellent and fresh discussion of Leveller literature. Hughes returns to the presentation and publication of Leveller petitions by women, which have recently received critical attention.[62] But unlike others, Hughes's main concern here is not the emergence of female political voices or agency. Rather, she reminds us, the 'public interventions by women were . . . carefully limited and controlled. The wives were supporting their husbands and defending their families, and it was made clear that theirs was not an independent voice.'[63] Women's petitioning, Hughes argues, was in fact part of a Leveller strategy to present themselves as respectable householders. Leveller language was dominated by the discourse of the household with its responsible male head and 'modest chaste and civil women', as the movement appropriated a validating political vocabulary to pursue its programme. Leveller women were presented as part of a unity, a movement, and Levellers were no less inclined than more conservative figures to slander sexually those women (not Levellers) who transgressed the codes of 'a friendly association of honest households'.[64] Where radical religious sects with women and naked preachers excited fears of a sexual, social revolution,[65] Leveller women were part of a Leveller claim to be the respectable face of change.

Hughes makes modest claims for her essay: 'I offer no neat conclusions . . . My aims have been . . . to demonstrate the advantage of examining the Levellers and gender together.'[66] But the modesty masks important and original insights and a brave independence of the feminist party line. In the course of her argument she has interesting things to say about John Lilburne's reading in Plutarch and Machiavelli and the Leveller faith in the political efficacy of text that would be worth exploring further.[67] Most of all, by moving from the traditional search for

---

[62] See A. M. McEntee, "'The [Un]Civill-Sisterhood of Oranges and Lemons": Female Petitioners and Demonstration, 1642–53' and R. Trubowitz, 'Female Preachers and Male Wives: Gender and Authority in Civil War England', both in J. Holstun ed., *Pamphlet Wars: Prose in the English Revolution* (London and Portland, Oreg., 1992), 92–111, 112–33.

[63] *Political Culture*, 170.   [64] Ibid., 181.

[65] See Christopher Hill, *The World Turned Upside Down: Radical Ideas during the English Revolution* (1972).

[66] *Political Culture*, 102.

[67] Commenting on the Levellers' close reading in 1647 of the parliamentary declarations of 1642–3, Hughes observes: 'It was as if textual analysis in itself could recall parliament to its original unity.'

emerging female activism, Hughes has other incisive observations about gender and politics. Parting company from Amussen, for example, she suggests that it was the impact of civil war and regicide that reformulated masculinity as chaste and ordered. And, as for the rise of sexual slander and pornography to ridicule opponents, Hughes argues that such literature 'may indicate the anxieties of men at their own divisions rather than that women have become more active'.[68] One would have liked to learn more from Hughes about how the revolution rendered notions of manhood 'generally problematic'; comparison of the gendered discourse of Levellers and other radical groups would have sharpened the discussion of Leveller language and strategy; there is no consideration here of the actual consequence of female petitioning, whatever the Levellers' intentions. Yet overall this is an essay that shows how rich the marriage of gender theory and close historical situating can be when performed by a scholar more interested in understanding the past than pursuing a contemporary agenda.

The essay that I turn to last, written by David Underdown's colleague at the Yale Center for Parliamentary History, takes up types of evidence and approach that Underdown has not himself pursued; but it further extends the claim of this volume to signal a cultural turn in early modern studies. Maija Jansson, in 'Remembering Marston Moor', begins with a proposal made by the Dutch to the new English commonwealth to place a pictorial tribute to victory in the civil war in the Banqueting House, where it would stand 'unto the people's view'.[69] The proponents cited the precedent of the tapestries commissioned by Lord Howard of Effingham to commemorate the Armada victory, tapestries which were reserved in 1650 from the royal collection for the use of the state. The proposal, however, came to naught and Jansson speculates interestingly on the reasons why. The proposal for a battle scene, she notes, would have been an entirely new artistic genre in England. England had avoided the Thirty Years War which had inspired engravers across Europe to record the clashes and horrors of warfare and so pushed secular art beyond the generic confines of portraiture. Perhaps also, the Commonwealth was too short of money, too preoccupied with other

---

[68] *Political Culture*, 175.

[69] That expression suggests access to the Banqueting House that was either always freer than we have assumed or newly so after 1649. Our assumptions about the audience for supposedly elite images need to be questioned at every point. I shall be exploring this subject in *Representations of Authority and Images of Power*.

matters, too indecisive and confused to give attention to a proposal for a painting. Perhaps a general lack of interest in the visual arts, in particular 'the absence of a peculiarly puritan secular visual aesthetic', condemned the project to oblivion. But *'perhaps'*, Jansson concludes, 'the Commonwealth erred in not embracing the proposal', in not representing or celebrating the providential victory over the enemies to liberty and property.[70]

This, I would venture, is a conclusion too measured. For if we turn from the empty space of commonwealth visual representation to the Royalists, we find a mass industry of paintings, copies, miniatures, engravings, frontispieces, medals, coins and cartoons pressing the divinity of kings and depicting republicans as the lecherous Machiavellian disciples of the devil. Many, drawing for their motifs on the *Eikon Basilike* (1649), kept the image of Charles I alive, as the representations of his son crowned by heaven sustained hopes of succession and restoration. There can be no doubt that the royalist dominance of the visual destabilized the Commonwealth, as Milton half discerned in his angry dismissal of an 'image doting rabble'. True, the Commonwealth pulled down images of Charles I in the Exchange, but pictures of kings in churches were exempted from iconoclasm and, more importantly, the Commonwealth failed to put anything in their place. The failure of a republican representation, I have argued elsewhere, may in the end be the reason for the failure of republican politics.[71]

More generally, Jansson's essay opens up the importance for the cultural turn of the study not only of the visual media but its more neglected ephemeral genres; the relatively inexpensive engravings that 'multiplied and dispersed' could be an effective weapon in the campaign to win support. Increasingly from the mid-seventeenth century, there was a market for engravings, and the dominance of the industry by Dutch émigrés undoubtedly gave a propaganda advantage to William in 1688.[72] As the public sphere was expanded, representation, putting a case, became the very essence of winning support, the principal art of politics and government. And part of effective representation was an address not only to present concerns but a control of the perceptions and memories of the past – especially of a civil war, the memories of which shaped the consciousness and politics of the English for the rest of the century, and perhaps until our own.

[70] *Political Culture*, 269–70 (emphasis mine).   [71] Above, ch. 7.
[72] There is still relatively little written on this subject. See Alexander Globe ed., *Peter Stent, London Printseller, c. 1642–1665* (Vancouver, 1985).

Art and memory, the construction of masculinity, the epistemology of credibility, the politics of Aesop's fables – it is not easy to think of another volume of essays on seventeenth-century England which embraces these subjects, still less a festschrift dedicated to a leading historian of politics. It is this that makes the volume so important and worthy of full consideration in a review essay, rather than brief note. Together with Sharpe and Lake's *Culture and Politics* and Gerald M. MacLean's *Culture and Society in the Stuart Restoration*[73] and other volumes in press or preparation, the essays in this collection signal a major shift in early modern studies, what I have called (with deliberate echo of an earlier move so brilliantly effected by Quentin Skinner and John Pocock) a 'cultural turn'. Here the debate about seventeenth-century England and the origins, nature and consequences of the English revolution transcends the sterile controversy over revisionism, and the notion of the political is extended from the narrow space of intrigue and manoeuvre at Westminster and Whitehall (or Edinburgh for that matter) into all the ways in which contemporaries endeavoured to construct values and represent themselves.[74]

Moreover, importantly, the volume is more than the sum of its parts. As I read and re-read the essays, I was often led to bring the perspective of one to the findings of another, and regretted that the authors had not entered into more of a dialogue with each other. I wished, for example, that John Morrill had taken up the issue of rhetoric and polemics for Pym that Lake explores in Hall, and that Lake had situated Hall's writings more closely in the shifting politics of religious controversy. I regretted both that Cust did not more broadly contextualize or theorize the linguistic shifts and ambiguities about honour, and that Jardine did not examine the changed nature of relationships in, say, the local household as well as on the stage. I would have liked Esterbrook to develop his discussion of the politics of display after civil war and for Jansson to explore the problematics of memory and visual culture into coins, seals, rituals and festivals. I wanted to urge Tom Cogswell to read Ann Hughes so that the important gender politics of the ballad and popular verse were not left unconsidered. Similarly, I wanted Kishlansky to consider the verses of Aphra Behn that prefaced one edition of Aesop alongside the engraving of Ogilby in another as important developments in the relationship of authorship to cultural and political authority. More generally, I

---

[73] Gerald M. MacLean, *Culture and Society in the Stuart Restoration: Literature, Drama, History* (Cambridge and New York, 1995).   [74] Cf. Sharpe and Lake, *Culture and Politics*, introduction.

wanted several essays to show more awareness of the consumption as well as production of texts – of questions of audience, reading, interpretation, response.

One might have looked to the introduction to take up such questions. Volumes of essays often depend upon a careful introduction that sets up the many questions they explore and draws together the conversation that has taken place between the book's covers. However, the introduction here disappointingly misses that opportunity. After a quite appropriate review of Underdown's career, it falls into a rather pedestrian summary of the essays and descends to banalities about 'historical and literary trends'. Too brief and too unambitious, it does not do justice to the quality of the pieces that follow, nor does it underline the new research agenda to which together they gesture. But by the end of this volume, few readers will fail to discern that *Political Culture and Cultural Politics* should ensure that the nouns of its title are no longer studied apart from the adjectives: that early modern studies and the history of politics more broadly have taken a revolutionary new cultural turn.

CHAPTER TWELVE

Representations and negotiations: texts, images and authority in early modern England

As our changing circumstances make some aspects of the past much more difficult to imagine or comprehend, so as if by way of compensation we are enabled to discern with new perspicacity other areas once shadowy or hidden. Modern society, at least in the West, has perhaps rendered feudal relations and ideas of chivalry and honour values far further removed from us than even from pre-war historians. On the other hand, the history of religious wars, once hard to teach to secular-minded students of the 1960s and '70s, became much more comprehensible with the rise of fundamentalism in the Middle East and America and with the escalation of terrorist violence. And who would doubt that our own experiences and anxieties have not only developed but virtually created the histories of family, gender and sexuality?

If our political history has been the least affected by historiographical change that may be because 'politics' has always been with us and, in essence, we often appear to believe, has little changed. For sure, revisionist historians have reinterpreted the history of seventeenth-century parliaments or nineteenth-century parties, but much of the political history written is still focused on dynasties and ministries, factions and parties, parliaments and elections, or popular movements and protests. Yet these are subjects and concepts that belong to us, or at least are most prominent in the modern age of politics, and even for that age they occlude important features of the exercise and experience of authority, the aesthetics and psychology of power.

In our own moment, the vocabulary of politics is, and for some time has been, a discourse of style, a lexicon of 'images', 'photo opportunities', 'sound bites' and 'spin doctors', a language of representations and 'rebrandings'. To the regret of some commentators this represents the decay of a democratic politics which was founded on the institutions of parliament and the hustings, on informed debate and issues of substance: it signals the vulgarization, the 'dumbing down' of politics. For other social critics the politics of style and representation is only another manifestation of a new postmodernity which has deconstructed orders, definitions and meanings, not only in society and state, but in epistemology and consciousness. Such contemporary analyses would themselves benefit from more historical perspective rather than loose talk about 'the end of history', but that is not my concern here. What I wish to take up is the importance of our contemporary experiences for the history of the pre-modern, in particular the politics of the English Renaissance state.

For as central to early modern as to contemporary politics were rhetoric, powerful oratory, the right image, the capacity to rebrand (after the Reformation or 1688, for example): that is the texts and arts of persuasion. Persuasion is at the heart of the exercise of all authority. The end of the Cold War and the collapse of the Eastern bloc have provided powerful testimony that even totalitarian regimes with mighty armies and secret police cannot survive without the co-operation of their people. Though the recent histories of Nazi Germany and Fascist Italy may make it discomforting, the exercise of authority always involves some complicity between rulers and subjects. In an early modern English state which, more even than its continental neighbours, lacked military power or a bureaucracy dependent on the monarch, government was from the top to the bottom a process shared between 'rulers' and 'ruled'. The humble constable or tithing man, often 'elected' by his parish, no less than the Lord Lieutenant, often self-selected by his status, were rulers as well as subjects, agents of a royal authority they constituted as well as represented. In such a system, the exercise of government was, even more than usual, a negotiation: an exchange between the needs and wishes of sovereigns, subordinates and subjects. A principal currency of that exchange, as historians have for long appreciated, was patronage: the offer or prospect of reward in return for service.[1] But while the mechanics of patronage have been thoroughly explored, too little has been written about the ideology, or social psychology, that underpinned it. For the 'system' of patronage expressed an ideology, an ideal of reciprocity, that much experience – and especially Machiavelli's political writings – exposed as a fiction. If, despite the brutal exposure of power by the Florentine, the ideology behind patronage survived for nearly two centuries, that was in part because the fiction was shared – by the ruled

---

[1] For one of the finest studies see J. H. Elliott, *The Revolt of the Catalans* (Cambridge, 1963). See too my 'Crown, Parliament and Locality: Government and Communication in Early Stuart England', in *Politics and Ideas in Early Stuart England* (1989), 75–100.

as well as the rulers. If we are to understand the exercise of authority, we must return such fictions to the narrative of political history.

For Marxist historians, ideologies and fictions of state were long regarded as devices through which a hegemonic government maintained social inequalities and the subordination of the proletariat: 'the ideal expression of the dominant material relationships', as Marx and Engels put it in *The German Ideology*.[2] More recently, critics on the left have complicated such a model by acknowledging, as does Foucault for instance, that while the organs of state education and discipline have formed subjects who have interiorized codes of order, authority also responds to the desires of subjects.[3] Other critics, deploying social psychology, have depicted the relationship of the subject with the state in terms of domestic discourse and 'family romance', with all the complexities of love and fear implicit in the relationship between children and parents – or sinners and God.[4] Again, contemporary events offer powerful demonstration of such arguments. For the life and death of Diana, Princess of Wales, articulated the desire of ordinary people to elevate, mystify and iconize figures of royal (as well as cultural – and this is important) authority, at the same time as criticisms of the Queen and Prince Charles for their remote hauteur expressed a simultaneous impulse to humanize monarchy and to deprive it of mystery and otherness – of its authority. Moreover, the funeral of the princess and the response of the royal family and government to it made overt the reciprocity of authority and the need for those in positions of power to respond to popular feelings in order to sustain their authority.

We should not and cannot draw simple parallels between modern British democracy and early modern England. Yet, I wish to argue, historical engagement both with the images and representations of authority, and the role of subjects in constructing as well consuming and experiencing those representations, is essential to our understanding of the sixteenth and seventeenth centuries.[5] For the image of the Virgin Queen and the cult of Charles the martyr were popular in a way that cannot be simply explained by elaborate propaganda machines (which anyway did not exist) or officially prescribed scripts. That they existed alongside other, less sacralized and more satirical images – even in the

---

[2] Cited in Raymond Williams, *Keywords: a Vocabulary of Culture and Society* (1976), 127.
[3] See M. Foucault, *The Order of Things* (1970); *Discipline and Punish* (1977).
[4] L. Hunt, *The Family Romance of the French Revolution* (Berkeley, 1992); cf. J. Fliegelman, *Prodigals and Pilgrims: American Revolution Against Patriarchal Authority* (Cambridge, 1982).
[5] I am currently researching a study of Representations of Authority and Images of Power in England, 1500–1700.

same mind – does not negate their importance, but does perhaps question the stark choices recent historiography has asked us to make between a consensus and conflict model of early modern political culture. Indeed study of the production and receptions of the texts and images of authority may help us to refigure the English Renaissance state and to reimagine, and re-enter the mind of, the early modern subject.[6]

Those who possessed, to quote Harold Love, 'a privileged understanding of the figurative nature of belief systems' and the 'master narratives of their culture' were the 'specialists in the use of figurative language', writers – and artists.[7] If much recent historiography on sixteenth- and seventeenth-century England has become atrophied and unable to explicate the rich complexities of political culture, it is not least because historians have ignored those specialists, writers and artists, and the ways in which texts and images performed.[8] Literary critics, however, have not only taken up these questions but have ventured, traditional historians might say dared, a new history of authority and government, based on readings of texts of power. Initially, writing within a broadly Marxist tradition, new historicist critics depicted a hegemonic political culture scripted successfully to underpin the divine authority of monarchs and to contain all dissent.[9] But more recently Stephen Greenblatt and others have written of a more complex circulation and exchange between authority and subjects.[10] And this revised model of 'negotiation' has been furthered by a cultural materialist criticism that has foregrounded the materiality and consumption of cultural texts, and more particularly by a reader-response criticism that emphasizes the role of readers in the determination of meaning.[11] What critics of English Renaissance texts now suggest is a dialogue about and for cultural authority – that is for authority itself.

This is nowhere more apparent than in studies of the theatre. In any age, the dialogic form of theatre permits and reveals the debates and differences about contemporary issues and social codes. In Elizabethan and early Stuart England, we now clearly see, playwrights, even a

[6] See my *Reading Revolutions: the Politics of Reading in Early Modern England* (New Haven and London, 2000).   [7] H. Love, *Scribal Publication in Seventeenth-Century England* (Oxford, 1993), 165.

[8] See above, ch. 1.

[9] For criticism of this emphasis on hegemony, see D. Shuger, *Habits of Thought in the English Renaissance: Religion, Politics and the Dominant Culture* (Berkeley and Los Angeles, 1990), esp. introduction.   [10] S. Greenblatt, *Shakespearean Negotiations* (Berkeley, 1988).

[11] See, for example, E. Freund, *The Return of the Reader: Reader-Response Criticism* (New York, 1987); S. Suleiman and I. Crossman eds., *The Reader in the Text: Essays on Audience and Reception* (Princeton, 1980).

'radical' Shakespeare, staged regicide and rebellion and exposed the dissimulations and intrigues that lay in the shadows of divine rule.[12] Various theatre historians and critics have endeavoured to 'explain' (the need for explanation being assumed) why heterodox views were tolerated and licensed, even by official court companies; and most have posited theories of licensed misrule in which criticism was accepted on the stage while it remained ambiguous and within bounds.[13] Such arguments, though suggestive, have never been fully persuasive when one considers both the size and experience of the playgoing public or scenes of popular insurrection and violence against kings, in history plays such as *Coriolanus* or *Edward II* for instance, which hardly seem oblique or coded. For too long perhaps the audience has been marginal to our explication of the politics of early modern drama.

The most recent research and writing on the Elizabethan theatre has played down the importance of court ties and aristocratic patronage to emphasize the place of theatre as a business in the burgeoning marketplace of early modern London.[14] In some respects theatre was in the fore of an emerging market economy. One of the few trades not regulated by a guild or fixed prices and wages, the business of playing was well placed to exploit the market of a rapidly expanding and wealthy capital city. Not only did the 'sharers', groups of writers, actors and managers, club together to finance the building of theatres to avoid the tax levied when the companies performed in inns. They also went in for expensive productions and lavish special effects in order to bring in the punters. As it is now studied, theatre was 'the Elizabethan equivalent of a multi million dollar business', rather like the Andrew Lloyd Webber productions of today.[15] In a manner not dissimilar to modern practice, the companies also conducted a form of market research, keeping a keen eye on the book trade as a barometer of changing fashion and taste. As today, parts were written with the resources of a company, and the talents and popularity of its leading actors, in mind. And, even more than today, the target audiences were genuinely popular: as well as the gentry and

---

[12] See, for example, J. Dollimore, *Radical Tragedy: Religion, Ideology and Power in the Drama of Shakespeare and His Contemporaries* (Brighton, 1983); J. Dollimore and A. Sinfield eds., *Political Shakespeare* (Manchester, 1985). Cf. J. Drakakis ed., *Alternative Shakespeares* (1985).

[13] The most important of these is A. Patterson, *Censorship and Interpretation: the Conditions of Writing and Reading in Early Modern England* (Madison, Wisc., 1984).

[14] J. H. Forse, *Art Imitates Business: Commercial and Political Influences in Elizabethan Theatre* (Bowling Green, Ohio, 1983); W. Ingram, *The Business of Playing: the Beginning of the Adult Professional Theater in Elizabethan London* (Ithaca, 1992); D. Bruster, *Drama and the Market in the Age of Shakespeare* (Cambridge, 1992); J. Haynes, *The Social Relations of Jonson's Theatre* (Cambridge, 1992).

[15] Forse, *Art Imitates Business*, 30.

craftsmen, the labourer and apprentice. At a penny, the same price as a drink or two in a tavern, a cheap stand at the playhouse was the 'best entertainment bargain' in early modern London.[16] And the audiences flocked in. Over 15,000 people a week attended performances of the Lord Admiral's and the Lord Chamberlain's companies, and it has been estimated that over 50 million visits to the theatre were made between the building of the Theatre in 1576 and the closing of the theatres in 1642.[17] As the crowds poured in, the actors and writers, especially if they had shares in the company, grew rich. The joiner James Burbage, one of the leading impresarios and entrepreneurs of the Elizabethan theatre, became wealthy enough to be a money-lender and owner of a livery stable who enjoyed the income of a modest gentleman with £368 a year.[18] And Shakespeare was able profitably to invest in property from the rich proceeds of his company shares and fees as an actor (perhaps in female roles), rather than his talents as a writer which added only small supplements to his income.[19] Theatre, it has been argued, was the prime 'new commodity and service' in a market economy that implicated all.[20]

In the most material sense, the court and courtiers became part of that business too. Not only did the entrepreneurial companies take their names from and enjoy some protection from royal or courtly patrons (the King's men, the Lord Chamberlain's men), the exchange between court and stage extended to the players' hiring costumes created for court interludes from the Office of the Revels; indeed the practice was so common that one, admittedly an aggrieved competitor, complained that the Yeomen of the Robes would hire 'her Highness's masks . . . to all sorts of persons that will hire the same'.[21] Though an earlier generation of theatre historians preferred not to dwell on it, the profit motive seems to have governed all. The players were the court's customers and also charged for their services. More important, not least thanks to the hired costumes, they fulfilled the desires of audiences: 'the glory of the Elizabethan stage may have been as much the product of the spirit of Elizabethan capitalism as it was the spirit of artistry'.[22]

But in no age is good theatre the mere reflection of social change; it helps to discern and even direct it. For Elizabethan and Jacobean England, it has been suggested, theatre succeeded so remarkably because it presented 'a new means of understanding the material foun-

---

[16] Ibid., 16.   [17] Bruster, *Drama and the Market*, 1.   [18] Forse, *Art Imitates Business*, 27.
[19] Forse points out that Shakespeare made c. £289 from acting in the year 1610–11, compared to £29 from writing: 'he was an actor who invested in property and wrote some plays on the side'. *Art Imitates Business*, 58–61. On the argument that Shakespeare performed female roles see ibid., ch. 3.   [20] Ibid., ch. 2 and p. 232.   [21] Ingram, *The Business of Playing*, 68–70.
[22] Forse, *Art Imitates Business*, 47.

dations of urban life'.[23] In an incisive book on *Drama and the Market in the Age of Shakespeare*, Douglas Bruster, beginning from the simultaneous construction of the first theatres and the Royal Exchange, studies the playhouse as a microcosm of a new material world of flux and inflation, a society in which commodity and consumption first seized the imaginations as well as emptied the purses of English men and women. Along with the synchronous erection of commercial and theatrical buildings, language and metaphor conjoined the worlds of play and business, commerce being described as a 'theatre' in which all, mingling promiscuously as in the playhouse, performed roles and transacted exchanges.[24] For actors were not merely in the forefront of a capitalistic exchange between service and payment, their service consisted in personation and representation. They made their living from commodifying themselves and constructing personae. And in these respects too the theatre appeared to stand for a theatrical notion of society, a world perceived as a comedy of manners in which the conception of the self was implicated in material concerns and transactions. The new genre of city comedy with its persistent themes of social flux, cuckoldry and commodification, represented and interrogated a new atomized universe in which traditional bonds and values, established degrees and notions of personal worth were being dissolved by money.[25]

Long, then, before economic and social theorists engaged with such changes, it was the theatre that began to construct a new 'social representation', and to participate in the creation and validation of new 'manners and fashions'.[26] The new dramatic realism, in short, helped to make social change itself real by staging what contemporaries had scarce begun to perceive. If theatre is 'part of society's ideological apparatus, of the means by which it understands and reproduces itself symbolically', Elizabethan and Jacobean theatre (and the early novels of Dekker, Deloney and others which owed much to theatre) valorized as well as symbolized profound changes in ideology as well as social relations.[27] It did not do so without ambiguity and anxiety. Tensions between new

[23] Bruster, *Drama and the Market*, xi.
[24] Bruster quotes John Hall: 'Man in business is but a theatrical person, and in a manner but personates himself', ibid., p. 7.
[25] Bruster explores in Elizabethan theatre the relationship, currently being discussed by critics of eighteenth-century England, between commodification and sex.
[26] Haynes, *Social Relations of Jonson's Theatre*, 5, 7–8. Haynes points out that former critics like L. C. Knights suppressed these aspects of early modern theatre not least as a consequence of their own 'feudal' sympathies and values.
[27] Ibid., 12. On Dekker and Deloney, see especially, D. Margolies, *Novel and Society in Elizabethan England* (1985); L. C. Stevenson, *Praise and Paradox: Merchants and Craftsmen in Elizabethan Popular Literature* (Cambridge, 1984).

commercial and older heroic values surface in several Shakespeare plays; writers such as Dekker and Deloney endeavoured to connect past and present by appropriating chivalric codes of honour and gentility for a new merchant and citizen class.[28] Most obviously, Ben Jonson denounced mere fashion and, nostalgic for older values of hospitality and community in personal and public life, satirized the social climbers and parasites who fashioned themselves and purchased their advancement. Yet as a recent brief but intelligent study argues, Jonson was fully involved, and implicated himself, in the world of commerce that he derides and mocks. His underworld characters who deploy their cunning for survival and advancement are not unsympathetic figures; and in *Bartholomew Fair* and *The Alchemist* the playwright almost acknowledges traditional order and festivity to be utopian visions.[29] As the induction on the stage to *Bartholomew Fair* makes clear, the dramatist was part of, not outside, a world of contract, commodity and barter, a society in which taste, that is cultural authority, would be determined by the biggest spenders.[30]

Patronized by courtiers and under the control of city magistrates, the theatre was also from its inception closely connected to government. And from the beginning it was an ambivalent relationship. From the time of the break from Rome, Henry VIII and Thomas Cromwell saw the potential value of theatre as a forum of propaganda and recruited John Bale and Richard Moryson to write antipapal, and later Protestant, plays.[31] Though after Cromwell's death Henry showed little interest in the stage, other government ministers continued to use theatre for direct political ends: in 1559 the Spanish ambassador even accused William Cecil of providing playwrights with material to mock Philip II of Spain.[32] The emergence of Elizabethan theatre, Professor Ingram has suggested, 'would not have happened in quite the way it did without the government exploitation of plays under the late Henry . . . and the early Edward'.[33] However, as some quickly appreciated, the religious and political dialogue opened by theatre might not easily be contained, and in the 1540s conservative councillors were shocked by the questions and criticisms of church and state (for example 'of a king how he should rule his realm') played out on the stage.[34] From the mid-century, therefore, there were moves to regulate the business of playing by licences and

---

[28] Stevenson, *Praise and Paradox*, passim.   [29] Haynes, *Social Relations of Jonson's Theatre*.
[30] Jonson, *Bartholomew Fair*, 'The Induction on the Stage'.
[31] Ingram, *The Business of Playing*, 78–9.   [32] Ibid., 84.   [33] Ibid., 90.   [34] Ibid., 80.

official patronage.[35] With the sharpening of factional rivalries and ideological differences, however, even aristocratic patronage of the theatre could not be equated with stability or royal control. The Dudleys had their own company performing in the provinces at the beginning of Elizabeth's reign; by the end it seems that Essex's enemies at court protected a seditious play targeted at the earl. James I's decision to confine patronage of the theatre to members of the royal family may have been a response to the immersion of theatre companies in factional rivalry, as well as a more general attempt at regulation.[36]

Efforts to control the stage, however, were never more than partially successful. And beyond the plays or interludes unofficially staged, or the impersonations of courtiers performed unobserved on the night, the failure to regulate was implicit in theatre itself – and in what made it potentially so useful to the state: the audience. The Privy Council clearly recognized the importance of plays in shaping public opinion. But public opinion also dictated, by means of the purse, what plays were staged or succeeded. As James Forse has shown, there was a close chronological relationship between the publication of popular books and the themes of plays which suggests the 'profit motive' as the principal determinant of the theatrical repertoire.[37] Any government attempt to use theatre as a vehicle for disseminating ideas was from the outset complicated and compromised by the reciprocity of the market.

Given that the market, like theatre itself, *was* society, reciprocity became more obviously a social and political condition. Audiences, after all, paid to watch kings and princes perform on the stage and to watch boys don the personae and – literally – the cloaks of majesty. It was no coincidence that Queen Elizabeth and King James began to speak of monarchs as figures on a stage: theatre was a way of conceiving and articulating social and political life as well as a site of their representation to the people. For the most part we can only imagine (though we should not shrink from indulging that) the contemporary experience of going to the theatre, in a London which also staged the rituals of divine monarchy, to see kings and queens personated by boys on the stage. But there were clearly some contemporaries who expressed concern about its effects. William Prynne, albeit often critical of theatre and authority, nevertheless feared that popular theatre undermined majesty: 'For if stage plays be meet ornaments for princes' palaces at times of greatest state and

---

[35] Ibid., ch. 3 passim.
[36] Ibid.; cf. 'Eddies of the Essex Episode', in Forse, *Art Imitates Business*, ch. 9.
[37] Forse, *Art Imitates Business*, 33, 41.

royal entertainment, great reason is there to suppress their daily acting
. . . for fear their assiduity, their commonness should make them despi-
cably base and altogether unmeet for such sublime occasions.'[38] If
Prynne foresaw the dymystification inherent in popular theatre, even
more remarkably a Buckinghamshire gentleman, Sir William Drake,
began to view majesty itself radically as a theatrical construct, sustained
by the desire of all to preserve the illusion:

> In a stage play all men acknowledge that he that plays the king's part may
> himself be the meanest, yet if a man should . . . call him by his own name while
> he stands in his majesty, one that acts his part with him may chance to break his
> head [for] marring the play. And so they said these matters be kings' games, as
> it were stage plays upon scaffolds, in which poor men are but the lookers on.[39]

If the theatre could never be fully brought under government control,
nor ultimately could the theatre of state be sustained without the will of
the subject. That was made dramatically evident when in 1649 Charles
I was executed on the scaffold outside the Banqueting House, the site of
the court entertainments of the Stuart monarchy.

If theatre epitomized the social changes and anxieties of the
Elizabethan and Jacobean age, and represented not only market
exchange but the element of reciprocity in political relations, the drama
offers historians rich evidence that hitherto few have investigated.
Recently, however, a group of American and English literary critics and
historians joined forces to attempt an innovative exploration of the relationship between theatre and politics in early modern London.[40]
Reading conventional historical sources, chronicles and pamphlets,
alongside play texts, they essayed an interdisciplinary study of spectacles
– on the stages of the theatre, the city and the nation. As with some
theatrical productions, the promise of the project far exceeds the performance. There are certainly valuable scenes. Among the contributions
paired essays on Stow's *Survey of London* nicely point up the tensions in
the text and city between a nostalgia for old charity, hospitality and communal celebration and the exaltation of acquisition, wealth and social
mobility. Similarly readings of *A Midsummer Night's Dream* incisively point
up the dependence of government on the 'manipulation of rhetoric'; the

---

[38] W. Prynne, *Histrio-mastix: the Player's Scourge; or Actor's Tragedy* (1633), 742–3.
[39] University College London, Ogden MSS, Bacon-Tottel collection 7/18 f. 153; on Drake, see my *Reading Revolutions*.
[40] D. Smith, R. Strier and D. Bevington eds., *The Theatrical City: Culture, Theatre and Politics in London, 1576–1649* (Cambridge, 1995) sets out promisingly to study the 'dramatic aspects of politics' as well as the politics of theatre, but the first is inadequately treated.

endeavour, represented in the wedding of Theseus, to appropriate for and focus on the ruler 'collective interests'; but ultimately the inability of the court to fix meaning in 'a complex place and time of ambivalences and multiple values', not least the ambivalence of the relationship between theatre and state.[41] Other essays raise, albeit they do not resolve, questions that historians have not often enough asked. Paul Seaver, for example, attempts to reconstruct the knowledge and perceptions that Londoners might have brought to a performance of Dekker's *Shoemaker's Holiday*. And Patrick Collinson, though almost certainly wrong in the case of puritans, appears unusually ready to recognize that the stage may have created as well as responded to language and social categories. But, for the most part, contributions to *The Theatrical City* represent a lost opportunity, in particulars and more generally. The essays on Marston's *The Fawn* fail satisfactorily to read the play in its moment of Jacobean succession, and one on Massinger descends to plot summary.[42]

The problem ironically appears to stem from what the method of pairing historians and critics seemed to promise. For often here, rather like a bad doubles pair at tennis, the 'partners' appear to have little mutual understanding or dialogue. As a consequence the historians' factual descriptions and language of 'reality' are too sharply contrasted with the critics' talk of representations and readings, belying that very integrity of art and authority that the volume set out to explore. It is not least because he is one of the few who theorizes the relationship of dramatic action to world that Martin Butler pens such an interesting study of Massinger's *New Way to Pay Old Debts* – one that emphasizes the involvement of the playwright in the contradictions he represents.[43]

Such perspectives were much needed in the lacklustre pieces on the Root and Branch petition and the Grand Remonstrance. The drama of pivotal parliamentary moments, especially in 1641 when the crowds clamouring outside the House of Commons brought a noisy audience (unwelcome to some) to the assembly, awaits exploration. Similarly historians have reprehensibly ignored the rhetoricity, the textuality of major speeches in and petitions to parliament.[44] Richard Strier makes a

---

[41] Ibid., 62, 66.
[42] Linda Peck and Lindley fail to historicize Marston and Massinger not least because they fail to consider the relation of the play to the world. (See L. L. Peck, 'John Marston's *The Fawn*' and K. Lindley, 'Philip Massinger's *A New Way to Pay Old Debts*', in Smith, Strier and Bevington, *Theatrical City*, 117–36, 183–92.
[43] M. Butler, 'The Outsider as Insider', in Smith, Strier and Bevington, *Theatrical City*, 193–208.
[44] See above, ch. 1, pp. 15–17.

start in identifying the deployment of sexual denigration and 'affective language' to demonize opponents and secure support, and in discerning the nervous discomfort manifested in the edgy syntax of the Remonstrance.[45] But, in the light of studies of the Elizabethan and Jacobean stage, we need to think much more about the House of Commons as a theatre, and about its relations to the London populace schooled from playgoing in dialogue about politics. We also need to think of MPs conscious of themselves as performing, and, like the actors and stage managers, performing a service for court *and* audience.

Certainly that is evident in the two most dramatic trials of the age, curiously not treated here: the state trial of first Thomas Wentworth, Earl of Strafford, then of the king himself.[46] Not only did the pamphlet literature from 1640 conspicuously draw on the language and dramatic techniques of the stage, the cast of characters, the timing of witnesses and evidence, the use of props, the self-conscious performing of the participants virtually rendered the trials magnificent spectacles with no charge for entry. Derek Hirst sensibly writes that 'the drama of justice was perhaps the most visible feature of the public life of London . . . in 1649'.[47] Metaphors of the stage dominated political discourse. As we begin to consider what that meant, we return to the ambivalences, the uncontrollability of the genre of drama, and the negotiations it required between performers and audience. For Charles I, having lost the control of the theatre of authority, at last at his trial learned to exploit that ambivalence to undermine the new regime. By masterly performance and powerful speech – in the courtroom and on the scaffold – he turned his trial into something of a triumph. And in a final text of artful theatricality he took up a powerful role that was to be replayed over decades: the part of martyr.[48]

II

When he wrote an attack on the *Eikon Basilike*, John Milton criticized the king's book as 'a piece of poetry'.[49] Though the charge was a curious

[45] R. Strier, 'From Diagnosis to Operation', in Smith, Strier and Bevington, *Theatrical City*, 233.

[46] On the theatricality of Strafford's trial and the pamphlet literature it engendered, see T. Kilburne and A. Milton, 'The Public Context of the Trial and Execution of Strafford', in J. Merritt, *The Political World of Thomas Wentworth, Earl of Strafford, 1621–1641* (Cambridge, 1996), 230–51.

[47] D. Hirst, 'The Drama of Justice', in Smith, Strier and Bevington, *Theatrical City*, 247.

[48] M. Grossman, 'The Dissemination of the King', in Smith, Strier and Bevington, *Theatrical City*, 261–2; cf. K. Sharpe, '"So Hard a Text"? Images of Charles I, 1616–1689' (forthcoming).

[49] J. Milton, *Eikonoklastes*, in M. H. Hughes ed., *Complete Prose Works of John Milton* (New Haven, 1962), III, 406.

and uncomfortable one, it betrays, as does every page of *Eikonoklastes*, the importance of poetry for politics. For long the political verse of the 1630s and '40s remained unstudied. In the past excluded by literary and political determinants from the canon, when 'Cavalier' verse became the subject of critical scrutiny it was read as the poetry of defeat and consolation, the verse of a disenchanted withdrawal from politics.[50] Only over the last decade have we seen a renewed critical approach to royalist verse and some appreciation of the complexity of its engagement with courtly values.[51] In James Loxley's *Royalism and Poetry in the English Civil Wars* we have one of the fullest and best studies for over twenty-five years.[52] As Loxley focuses attention not only on the better-known verse of Carew or Suckling but also on the panegyrical collections published by university poets to celebrate royal births, anniversaries and visits, old assumptions are dispelled and we are presented with valuable new perspectives on politics as well as poetry. Though it is a simple observation, the focus of university verse on the fecundity of the royal marriage both points up the centrality of dynastic security and complicates the dominance of Platonism in poetry that directly lauded sexual union and royal parturition.[53] More strikingly, against the critical consensus that characterizes royalist verse as elitist, Loxley argues that university volumes took up genres of celebration from outside the walls of academe and that royal panegyric made links with popular literature and festival, with 'the poetry of steeples and bells'. This 'assumption of equivalence between poetry and popular festivity' deserves to be taken more seriously in any consideration of attitudes to the king and court.[54] Indeed in a monograph that nicely complements the arguments, Timothy Raylor demonstrates how a body of wits who in the 1630s called themselves the Order of the Fancy were linked not only into court circles but were fully familiar with popular festivities, the playhouse and the alehouse, and wrote coarse street ballads. The members of the order, Raylor suggests, 'were exploring ways . . . of deploying classical literature in the taverns and on

---

[50] See K. Sharpe and S. Zwicker eds., *Politics of Discourse: the Literature and History of Seventeenth-Century England* (Berkeley, Los Angeles and London, 1987), introduction; E. Miner, *The Cavalier Mode from Jonson to Cotton* (Princeton, 1971).

[51] See C. Brown ed., *The Poems and Masques of Aurelian Townshend* (Reading, 1983); J. Kerrigan, 'Thomas Carew', *Proc. Brit. Acad.*, 74 (1988), 311–50; K. Sharpe, *Criticism and Compliment: the Politics of Literature in the England of Charles I* (Cambridge, 1987); T. Corns, 'The Poetry of the Caroline Court', *Proc. Brit. Acad.*, 97 (1998), 57–73; Corns ed., *The Cambridge Companion to English Poetry, Donne to Marvell* (Cambridge, 1993).

[52] J. Loxley, *Royalism and Poetry in the English Civil Wars: the Drawn Sword* (Basingstoke, 1997).

[53] See, for example, *Coronae Carolinae Quadratura . . .* (Oxford, 1636), where poets refer to royal births that 'do come so fast' and emphasize: 'we feel her pangs' (pp. iv, A1v, 132).

[54] Loxley, *Royalism and Poetry*, 32, 34.

the streets ... of mingling popular and elite culture'.[55] The object of this verse and traditional festival was the monarch.

Such assumptions were neither shared by all nor unproblematic. There are perhaps more discordant strains in the courtly verse of the 1630s than Loxley allows. But he is right to suggest that it was the outbreak of direct opposition in the Scots war that forced poets to struggle with the 'problems of representation' itself.[56] Not only did the last masque *Salmacida Spolia*, as Martin Butler showed, reveal tensions within royal counsels about peace and war, the representation of Charles as Philogenes and Henrietta Maria as an Amazon, and the celebration of the birth of Prince Henry on 8 July 1640 as 'ancient hero' and 'son of peace', continued and publicized those differences.[57] Such uncertainties characterized much courtly literature in 1640–1: the verse of Mennes and Smith, founders of the Fancy, 'teetered uneasily between serious reflection and comic relativism'.[58] Charles, we might say, ceased to be at the controlling centre of poetry as well as government.

Once the royal standard was raised, loyal poets faced a new opportunity and need to re-present the king. Not least, the king's entry into Lincoln, cheered by a throng that stretched four miles, suggested a politics very different to that of the London mob of 1640–1, and so revalidated the theme of popular celebration.[59] But now, the imminence of conflict and the 'invitation to take arms' voiced in loyal addresses constructed a new representation: one that had been a characteristic of Charles as prince but which had been overshadowed by the guardian of halcyon peace – the king as warrior. Loxley is excellent on the poetic strategies deployed to reconstitute the *cortegiano* of personal rule into the warrior knight of civil war. Yet, as he acknowledges, the transition posed difficulties and was effected at a price. For a king who led a party in civil war could no longer easily be heralded as the natural centre of all order. And a decentring of the monarch destabilized the verse which also derived its meaning from that order and centre. 'The contraction of royal authority into a merely partisan and partial phenomenon inevitably altered the nature of a poetics grounded upon that authority.'[60] Responding to the challenge, royalist poets did not just satirize their

[55] T. Raylor, *Cavaliers, Clubs and Literary Culture: Sir John Mennes, James Smith, and the Order of the Fancy* (Newark, Del., 1994), quotation, 101.   [56] Loxley, *Royalism and Poetry*, 64.

[57] Ibid., 64–5; M. Butler, 'Politics and the Masque: *Salmacida Spolia*', in T. Healy and J. Sawday eds., *Literature and the English Civil War* (Cambridge, 1990), 59–74.

[58] Raylor, *Cavaliers, Clubs and Literary Culture*, 166.

[59] *A True Relation of His Majesties Reception and Royal Entertainment at Lincoln* (1642).

[60] Loxley, *Royalism and Poetry*, 84.

puritan opponents; they endeavoured (they were not the last to do so) to claim epic status for contingent and partisan polemic; still more they depicted their enemies as a threat to all meaning and stable signification. They claimed, in Loxley's words, royal authority as the only means 'whereby poetry in particular and language in general may be secured against a collapse into . . . a Hobbesian state of nature'.[61] It was not a fanciful claim. Hobbes was to argue the need for some sovereign signifier, some ultimate determinant of meaning, and Milton did not doubt that to many the words of a king carried an authority second only to scripture.[62] That is why the publication of Charles I's letters seized at Naseby presented parliament with such a propaganda coup: the opportunity to expose and condemn the king by his own words. *The King's Cabinet Opened* (1645) used the imagery of theatre to suggest the literally dramatic unmasking of 'a dissembling king'.[63]

The royalist pamphleteers' response was to accuse publishers of the *King's Cabinet* of misreading and misrepresentation, and to stress the plainness and openness of the king's writing and mind.[64] Poets such as Martin Lluellyn followed the same defensive strategy. Others, notably Henry Vaughan and John Cleveland, took an opposite tack – depicting the letters as the mysterious scripts of a 'hieroglyphic king' beyond the ordinary readers' comprehension.[65] The contradictory portrayals of plainness and mystery owed much to the complex difficulties and needs, the 'tonal instabilities' of 1645.[66] But they also speak to the contradiction at the heart of all representation (on the stage and of the king): the need for both access and distance so as to realize the illusion. What the royalists understandably, necessarily, struggled to do during the 1640s was to remain in charge of representation. But parliamentarian pamphleteers did not only contest that representation and take control of it, in unmasking the king they came close to deconstructing the theatre state on which all authority depended.[67]

The resolution of these contradictions and the revalidation of the authority of theatre were effected by the king's death. As the Christ-like martyr, Charles could be plain and mysterious; the final reality of death authorized and confirmed the king's representation as *imago dei*. On the

---

[61] Ibid., 123.
[62] T. Hobbes, *Leviathan*, ed. R. Tuck (Cambridge, 1991), 39; Milton, *Eikonoklastes*, 339.
[63] Loxley, *Royalism and Poetry*, 130–2; *The King's Cabinet Opened* (1645, Thomason tract E293/28).
[64] See also Joad Raymond, 'Popular Representations of Charles I', in T. Corns ed., *The Royal Image: Representations of Charles I* (Cambridge, 1999), 47–73. [65] Loxley, *Royalism and Poetry*, 141–5.
[66] Raylor, *Cavaliers, Clubs and Literary Culture*, 186.
[67] I suggest in ch. 7 above that this move posed problems.

scaffold, in several senses, Charles was once again a fixed centre, the focus of all viewpoints as well as observers. And, accompanying that reclamation, the *Eikon Basilike* re-elevated the plain words of a Christic king to the status of holy writ. 'The king's book created a sacred author again capable of legitimising the royalist reading of words and actions.'[68]

Though the pamphlets as well as military exchanges of civil war presented new problems for royalist panegyrists, the 1640s neither marked a complete break with the poetry of the 1630s nor a retreat into disengaged escapism. Indeed the poet Mennes was given military charge of the counties of Anglesey, Carnarvonshire and Merioneth.[69] Books, including works like *Hesperides*, dedicated to Prince Charles sustained both royalist activism and royalist values and aesthetics. The royalist poets, we learn, 'forged the soldiery, arms and armour of a civil war fought with the pen'.[70] They continued to fight after 1649. In the nervous anxieties of Milton's *Eikonoklastes* we sense that at least one opponent feared they might win the polemical war.

Yet for all the force of the royal text, there had never been, and certainly could not be after 1642, absolute control over language, performance or meaning. Words and representations had always been interpreted differently. And during the 1640s and '50s, though the theatres were closed, the audiences of state grew with a burgeoning public sphere created by an outpouring of polemical pamphlets.[71] Not only did the fact of political division manifest differences of interpretation; pamphlets staged dramatic dialogues and invited the audience of readers to exercise their own judgement. The events and publications of the decade, Sharon Achinstein has interestingly argued, constituted a 'revolutionary reader' as a participant in political discourse and theatre, and so transmuted the subject into the citizen sharing in the business of government.[72]

There have been several, and recently some excellent, studies of the literature of the 1640s and '50s – especially of canonical authors such as Milton and Marvell.[73] What Steven Zwicker presents, in a brilliant new study of literary and political culture from 1649 to 1689, is an analysis of

[68] Loxley, *Royalism and Poetry*, 181–2.   [69] Raylor, *Cavaliers, Clubs and Literary Culture*, ch. 11.
[70] Loxley, *Royalism and Poetry*, 234.
[71] See J. Raymond, *The Invention of the Newspapers: English Newsbooks, 1641–1649* (Oxford, 1996); Dagmar Freist, *Governed by Opinion: Politics, Religion and the Dynamics of Communication in Stuart London, 1637–1645* (1997).   [72] S. Achinstein, *Milton and the Revolutionary Reader* (Princeton, 1994).
[73] See especially, T. Corns, *Uncloistered Virtue: English Political Literature, 1640–1660* (Oxford, 1992); N. Smith, *Literature and Revolution in England, 1640–1660* (1994); L. Potter, *Secret Rites and Secret Writing: Royalist Literature, 1641–1660* (Cambridge, 1989).

the production and performance of texts in the new conditions of overt partisanship and engaged public opinion.[74] Beginning with Milton's tortured efforts to deprive the royalists of the authority of aesthetic forms, to make poetry and theatre charges against the king, Zwicker traces the ways in which politics marked, and was reconstituted by, writing. One of his most original chapters reads Izaak Walton's *Compleat Angler*, that apparently most insistently apolitical of texts, as a royalist polemic. Interestingly, in the light of Loxley's and Raylor's studies of 1630s royalism, Zwicker points up the links made and claimed in Walton's work between learned and folk culture. Repudiating puritan sabbatarianism and dislocation of popular festivity, Walton reasserts 'an idealized Anglican community of manners and beliefs, of ancient, traditional and coherent relations among social classes and among members of an organic community'.[75] And in hymning the cycles and seasons, Walton makes nature itself critique the apocalyptic time of millenarian chronology and holds out the promise of a cyclical return to natural order – return to monarchy, and to its aesthetic forms. The naturalizing and normalizing of monarchy, the appropriation of pastoral and lyric forms for royalist politics, was a persistent theme of 1650s polemic which presented the defenders of republic with an aesthetic and political problem, which they never entirely solved. Where Milton, at least in 1649, hesitantly surrendered lyric to royalism, Marvell radically abandoned the genre to write a new aesthetic as well as politics for Cromwell as Lord Protector. In *The First Anniversary* of Cromwell's elevation, Marvell fashions the Protector as apocalyptic hero, a figure single-handedly creating new harmony and order, rejecting the corruptions of fallen nature and failed constitutions. Shrill, embattled and 'finally incoherent', Marvell's poem 'has meaning only within the social construct of an elect nation'.[76] Walton's, by contrast, 'is consoling and restorative'.[77] As we read the language of spring, rebirth and fertility that abounds in Restoration panegyric and popular verse, we cannot but conclude that, in a political as well as psychic sense, Walton's aesthetic was indeed restorative.

To see continuities from cavalier verse to Restoration panegyrics, however, is not to diminish the transformative force of civil war and Commonwealth on all genres of the aesthetic, as all political modes. Revolution made all aesthetic forms part of the contest for authority and allegiance. The puritans could not, and did not, surrender pastoral to

---

[74] S. Zwicker, *Lines of Authority: Politics and English Literary Culture, 1649–1689* (Ithaca, 1993), paperback edn, 1996.
[75] Ibid., 69; cf. D. Underdown, *Revel, Riot and Rebellion: Popular Politics and Culture in England 1603–1660* (Oxford, 1985).   [76] Zwicker, *Lines of Authority*, 88–9.   [77] Ibid., 89.

the royalists: on the other side, the king's party presented Charles II's escape from his enemies as a providential narrative of divine protection of Stuart kingship.[78] After 1660, for all the return of monarchical forms, no more than political contest did aesthetic contest demise. Indeed, despite the triumphalism, there was between the lines of Restoration panegyric an audible nervousness about how to re-present, even how to reconstitute kingship. In a study of Restoration drama, Nancy Klein Maguire showed the political and generic uncertainties that shaped in the end the mixed genre of tragicomedy.[79] While constitutionally the monarchy was no more mixed than before the war, in many respects it was an altered monarchy, with a king whose experiences had made him personally conscious of the reciprocity between ruler and people. Such contests, uncertainties and changes shaped aesthetics and politics, and the complex relations between them.

Charles II, from the beginning, appears to have endeavoured to conjoin the mystical and demystified, the elevated and popular elements that always existed in tension within royal representation. He touched for the king's evil yet sported with whores. As with Davidic parallels, there was a politics to pleasure after a decade of republic and puritanism. Royal panegyrists such as Dryden, Zwicker argues, tried to associate royal sexual profligacy with commercial abundance and empire. Charles's critics, on the other hand, contrasted royal debauchery with republican virtue, with, in Marvell's *Last Instructions*, a pastoral vision of the Dutch boldly appropriating the genre for criticism of the court. Rather than the fertile patriarch, Charles was represented by Marvell as a debauched whoremonger taking his selfish erotic pleasures from, and on, the English body politic. If Marvell audaciously reappropriated pastoral genres and patriarchal discourse to critique monarchy, Milton took them to reclaim epic for opposition. *Paradise Lost* also denies royalism a monopoly of sexual delight.[80] Indeed Milton's Eden of pastoral abundance and sexual bliss served to render corrupt, illegitimate and ungodly the monarch officially represented as Christ, father and provider.

Issues of sexuality, paternity and patriarchy continued to dominate Restoration politics, and, with the publication of Filmer's *Patriarcha* in

[78] See *Boscabel: or the History of His Majesties Most Miraculous Preservation After the Battle of Worcester* (1660); *The Royal Oak* (1660); A. M. Broadly, *The Royal Miracle* (1912); W. Matthews ed., *Charles II's Escape from Worcester: a Collection of Narratives Assembled by Samuel Pepys* (Berkeley, 1966). I shall pursue these texts in *Representations of Authority*.

[79] N. Maguire, *Regicide and Restoration: English Tragicomedy, 1660–1671* (Cambridge, 1992); above pp. 385–9.

[80] Zwicker, *Lines of Authority*, ch. 4; see too J. Turner, *One Flesh: Paradisal Marriage and Sexual Relations in the Age of Milton* (Oxford, 1987).

1680, debates about political legitimacy. Historians of politics and ideas have made us familiar with the politics of Exclusion and have resituated Locke's *Second Treatise* in the context of those debates and re-read the text as a response to Filmer.[81] What we learn from Zwicker is the need to extend these studies into aesthetic texts. For Dryden's *Absalom and Achitophel* attempted to cleanse patriarchalism of the damaging associations with tyranny and absolutism and to revalidate royal abundance. And he did so to reclaim a prelapsarian state of nature for the king, and – audaciously – to recast his Whig opponents as libertines. Secondly, having reclaimed legitimate abundance for the king, the laureate moved to denigrate the property that was central to Locke's notion of citizenship as personal greed and selfish interest. In *Absalom and Achitophel,* all the mantras of political debate are seized from the Whigs and refigured and reappropriated for the Stuarts. What it is important to note is Zwicker's point that Dryden's engagement with Locke was itself a matter of stylistics and aesthetics as well as politics. The *Second Treatise,* like the poem, was, too, a rhetorical performance, its measured tone a claim to a reason that was now culturally associated with authority and (as important) disassociated from zeal: to a reason that seemed to stand above party polemic. In Zwicker's words both Dryden and Locke 'aimed at and . . . achieved the elevation of poetry and philosophy' as they contended to define paternity, property, the state of nature and sovereign authority.[82] They did so because both appreciated the dependence of political legitimacy on aesthetic and cultural authority. We do not know enough to conclude what the success of the Whig coup in 1688 owed to a failure of royal representation in the reign of James II. But there can be little doubt that Toland's life and edition of Milton, as much as Burnet's *History*, endeavoured to sustain the Williamite regime, to validate political coup by aesthetic and cultural authorities.[83]

Though literary genres and tropes had carried political freight before, the civil war emphasized the complex interdependence of literary and political relations. What we see clearly in the 1640s and '50s is the contest for cultural validation. What is less apparent are how respective claims and appropriations were read, how and which texts persuaded. Interestingly the authors of civil war tracts appear – nervously – just as uncertain about the audience and effect of their writings. The explosion

---

[81] P. Laslett ed., *John Locke: Two Treatises of Government* (Cambridge, 1960); R. Ashcraft, *Revolutionary Politics and Locke's Two Treatises of Government* (Princeton, 1986); J. P. Sommerville ed., *Sir Robert Filmer, Patriarcha and Other Writings* (Cambridge, 1991).
[82] Zwicker, *Lines of Authority*, 162.   [83] Above, ch. 1, pp. 4–6.

of print created a new wider readership but also a remote and anonymous audience which, dedications suggest, authors were unsure how to address.[84] Moreover, both the civil war and popish plot involved claims and counterclaims, 'variety of opinions . . . everyone challenging truth to be of their party' and accusing others of lying.[85] The old theatre audiences which, as Jonson and others acknowledged, determined the fortunes of authors, now were invited to determine all truth and meaning, political as well as cultural worth. Somehow from these conditions emerged an appreciation that, like aesthetic taste, political preferences would, and could, also differ – that at last political fortunes would also be determined by a market of acceptance and support. Such a recognition in turn not only validated the politics of party, it also created a public sphere of news, squib and coffee house, a space in which the audience joined in all the action.[86]

Indeed by the end of the seventeenth century, to a larger extent, aesthetic tastes and political fortunes were determined by a measure of 'popularity'. The language of interest and commerce dominated social and political discourse, and the vocabulary of property, contract and exchange was central in political debate.[87] As we have seen, such was the language and condition of Elizabethan and Jacobean theatre and, as we review the place of the stage in seventeenth-century metropolitan and political life, it is tempting to speculate on the contribution of theatre to the new business of politics. A recent study of Mandeville encourages such considerations. For not only was Mandeville the infamous apologist for commerce and self-interest as the bonds of society, he also took the old idea of the *theatrum mundi* not for conventional ethical signification but as a description of the theatrical relations and self-fashioning of commercial society.[88]

The notion that 'character itself was in essence a social artefact, a construct of the demands of others' made all social life a set of persona-

---

[84] See my *Reading Revolutions*, ch. 1.

[85] J. Gauden, *The Love of Truth and Peace* (1640, E204/10), 27; R. Weil, "'If I did say so I lied": Elizabeth Cellier and the Construction of Credibility in the Popish Plot Crisis', in S. Amussen and M. Kishlansky eds., *Political Culture and Cultural Politics in Early Modern England* (Manchester, 1995), 189–212.   [86] See Sharpe and Zwicker, *Politics of Discourse*, introduction.

[87] See J. G. A. Pocock, *Virtue, Commerce and History* (Cambridge, 1985); J. P. Kenyon, *Revolution Principles* (Cambridge, 1977).

[88] E. Hundert, 'Performing the Passions in Commercial Society: Bernard Mandeville and the Theatricality of Eighteenth Century Thought', in K. Sharpe and S. Zwicker eds., *Refiguring Revolutions: Aesthetics and Politics from the English Revolution to the Romantic Revolution* (Berkeley, 1998), 141–72. See too Hundert, *The Enlightenment's 'Fable': Bernard Mandeville and the Discovery of Society* (Cambridge, 1984).

tions;[89] and, of course, it implied that politics too was a set of performances in response to demands rather than the enactment of moral truths. It is precisely this shift that was interrogated in a satirical pamphlet written in 1712 by Dr John Arbuthnot (a Harleian Tory and Physician Extraordinary to Queen Anne) – *The Art of Political Lying*.[90] Writing shortly after Mandeville had published *The Fable of the Bees*, Arbuthnot described modern society as a shared community of deceptions, a polity in which, since public opinion was powerful, all needed to lie to gain reputation and 'credit'. In a rather allusive but learned short book, Conal Condren analyses Arbuthnot's pamphlet as 'an index of the fragility of trust' in a world of party divisions, where the exchange of political gossip meant 'almost anything might seem a half truth'.[91] The world of Arbuthnot's satire is one in which the relation of language to externals is fluid and there is no sovereign signifier to anchor or determine meaning. Part political theory, part moral treatise, part satire and parody, *The Art of Political Lying* cannot easily be accommodated to modern disciplinary boundaries. It speaks for the relations of art and politics in the Augustan age. And in urging his readers to confront the slippery relations between truth and falsehood, representation and misrepresentation, Arbuthnot not only reapplied the ancient ambiguities of rhetoric to the first age of party, he began to describe the condition of modern politics.

III

The very title of Arbuthnot's satire, coupling 'art' and 'political lying', may appear almost natural to our generation born after the systematic propaganda of second world war and post-war cinema. And our contemporary expression 'photo opportunity' nicely conjoins image with a word and idea at the core of Machiavellian politics – a conjunction seemingly confirmed by Peter Mandelson's alleged admiration for *The Prince* and reputation as 'The Prince of Darkness'.[92] The modern parallels are both dangerous and suggestive. Dangerous because our understanding and use of the word propaganda implies a cynical manipulation and misrepresentation that were quite at odds with the

---

[89] Hundert, 'Performing the Passions', 170.
[90] C. Condren, *Satires, Lies and Politics: the Case of Dr Arbuthnot* (Houndmills, 1997).
[91] Ibid., 125.
[92] See B. Cathcart, *Were You Still up for Portillo?* (Harmondsworth, 1997), 15; D. Draper, *Blair's 100 Days* (1997), 19–22; *The Guardian*, 28 September 1996 (I owe this reference to the kindness of Joan Tumblety).

early modern meaning (dissemination of a faith) and Renaissance theories of representation. Suggestive because, despite those theories and political ideals, Machiavelli had advocated a politics of opportunity and interest, and had defended misrepresentation and dissimulation as acceptable means to the ends of advancement and power. For all that he was anathematized, Machiavelli's legacy was a persistent anxiety not only about political life but about too the potential of rhetoric for manipulation and of the arts of persuasion for misrepresentation. An age of confessional conflict only intensified those concerns.[93] Historians have studied intensively the impact of the anxieties induced by Machiavelli on the political thought and action of early modern Europe, but they have largely ignored the importance of his radical advocacy of feigning and personating as vital arts of politics for an understanding of the politics of art.

Indeed the politics of art, at least in early modern England, has itself been neglected by all but a handful of scholars. Perhaps not least in reaction to Marxist subordination of all cultural history to the structures of economy and class, twentieth-century art historians (like literary historians and 'new critics') retreated from an intellectual *history* of images to elevate art as timeless and universal. Much art history became and remains a study of form and technique, concentrated on the highest genres – painting and sculpture. The exception, indeed challenge, to this approach came principally from the Warburg Institute where Aby Warburg himself and his distinguished pupil, Ernst Gombrich, advocated and practised a contextualized and historicized intellectual and social history of art – in all its genres, woodcut and print as well as portrait. For early modern England the most important product of those influences has been the work of Sir Roy Strong who, from the late 1950s, transformed our understanding of the relations between art and power from the Reformation to the civil war.

As the welcome publication of his collected essays makes clear, Strong had an important historical argument to advance.[94] His early interest in Holbein and the reign of Henry VIII stemmed from his belief that Holbein represented the 'earliest deliberate propaganda campaign' in England. As Strong argued it, 'a small army of painters, sculptors and architects and craftsmen were employed throughout the 1530s to manifest in terms of paint, stone, wood, metal, glass and fabric the hard facts

---

[93] P. Zagorin, *Ways of Lying* (Cambridge, Mass., 1990).

[94] R. Strong, *The Tudor and Stuart Monarchy: Pageantry, Painting, Iconography*, I: *Tudor*; II: *Elizabethan*; III: *Jacobean and Caroline* (3 vols., Woodbridge, 1995).

of a political and religious revolution' – that is, the break from Rome.[95] On tapestries and movable furnishings, on illuminated manuscripts and in woodcut frontispieces to books, as well as on canvas, a 'visual campaign' was waged denouncing the pope and re-presenting the Tudor monarch as the new Constantine. Holbein, deploying the 'hallowed formulae of sacred art into tribute to a new and omnipotent monarchy', gave visual form to the claims to the Supreme Headship made in the Act in Restraint of Appeals.[96] Though the campaign was unsettled by the uncertainties that followed Henry's death, Strong argues that it was not abandoned. Antipapal propaganda was virulently conducted as Edward VI steered the country towards Protestantism, and, despite the iconophobia of the reformers, woodcuts and paintings continued to represent the king as protector of the word and the scourge of Antichrist (Figure 18).[97] After a minority and the Catholic reaction under Mary disrupted both court patronage and royal representation, Strong sees Elizabeth's reign as the continuation of the deployment of art for political power, and Hilliard as the true successor to Holbein.

The study of Elizabethan representations raises questions and problems which, as Strong writes today, 'never quite go away'.[98] For up to 1580 there were few portraits of the queen, and those constituted a series of different images rather than a programme. In famous paintings Elizabeth was depicted holding the sieve of chastity as Roman vestal virgin, as divine judge in a reworking of *The Judgement of Paris*, and as imperial heroine in the ermine portrait and 'Armada' portrait (Figure 19). Though we do not know who devised them, Strong has no doubt that such images were intended not only to underpin Elizabeth but also 'to sustain an island kingdom in the creation of an empire'.[99] Certainly there were official efforts made to control images of the queen. A draft proclamation of 1563 reveals early attempts at an approved image and in 1596 the Privy Council explicitly decreed that all offensive images of the queen should be destroyed.[100] Throughout her life Elizabeth was portrayed, in paintings that Strong describes as 'medieval', as a timeless icon, never ageing and ever youthful.[101]

Yet, the history of Elizabethan art is not, in the main, a story of official direction and control. As Strong points out, Hilliard was not on the royal payroll and, rather like the burgeoning acting companies, had to make

[95] Strong, *Tudor and Stuart Monarchy*, I, 6, 10.   [96] Ibid., 17, 52.

[97] See, Strong, *Tudor and Stuart Monarchy*, I, pp. 16–17, 88–92.

[98] Strong, *Tudor and Stuart Monarchy*, II, xii.   [99] Ibid., 15.

[100] C. Haigh, *Elizabeth I* (1988), 148.   [101] Ibid.; Strong, *Tudor and Stuart Monarchy*, II, 5.

Figure 18. Woodcut from Thomas Cranmer's *Catechism*, 1548, showing Edward VI with sword and Bible (by courtesy of Cambridge University Library)

Figure 19. The 'Armada' portrait of Elizabeth I, 1588 (courtesy of the Marquess of
Tavistock and the Trustees of the Bedford Estates)

his living by selling his services to others. As a consequence, 'a portrait
miniature was available . . . to anyone who could meet the bill' and the
genre of miniature evidently made that a bill affordable to a citizen's
wife.[102] At the same time as art sacralized and mystified Elizabethan
monarchy, the market both evidenced the desire for and distributed art
as a commodity. The 'democratization of the miniature' brought the
consuming urban elites to participate in the arts of representation.[103]

Indeed representations of Elizabeth I assumed, and were directed to,
a public which was perceived to be able to understand what they signified. One of Strong's greatest contributions has been to those dissemi-
nations of the royal image in public festival and procession. Elizabeth's
royal entry pageant for 1559 presented the queen as the true heir of York
and Tudor, the monarch who, embodying the virtues of wisdom, justice
and religion, would lead the realm from popish darkness to a flourishing

[102] Strong, *Tudor and Stuart Monarchy*, II, 217.
[103] Ibid., 217–23. Strong explains the politics by arguing 'each miniature was a personal vision of
his sovereign by the possessor' (p. 236).

Protestant nation. As we read the accounts of the pageant, we cannot doubt that it was a massive advertising campaign for a new reign and a new direction. But interestingly the impresarios were the Merchant Taylor Richard Hilles and Richard Grafton who had links back to the reformist circles around Thomas Cromwell. What the strong antipapal theme suggests, Strong posits, was that 'the religious zealots had framed a role for the queen'; and that, while she accepted that role, there was an element of counsel, even pressure, towards reform in the representation. If the queen was part audience and part spectacle, this was also true of others. Over a thousand people took part in the procession and the citizens, with their houses decorated and their balconies filled with cheering subjects, formed part of the show. Commentators from James I's reign on have questioned how much the multitude comprehended of these elaborate tableaux, and, as we shall see, scholarly scepticism about their impact has increased of late.[104] It is important, therefore, to be reminded of the efforts made to explain the message. As Strong explains, the texts of speeches, doubtless on the day drowned out by the noise of the crowds, were displayed for several days after the event; and the allegorical figures of Wisdom and Justice, if not easily recognizable from their costumes, had 'their names in plain and perfect writing set upon their breast easily to be read by all'.[105] Moreover, themes of royal representation were restaged in lord mayors' pageants which, as well as celebrating the livery companies and metropolitan pride, combined civic, popular and courtly concepts of the queen. Indeed at times of national crisis, as in 1585, the London mayoral pageant subordinated civic topoi to a homage to Elizabeth who again dominated the festival in 1590 after the Armada as the queen of bountiful peace.[106]

Elizabethan garter festivals extended the rituals of chivalry to the public at a time when Thomas Dekker and Thomas Deloney were helping to define virtues and values for merchants and craftsmen (Figure 20). As the reign progressed, 'the ceremonies became more of a public spectacle and the procession . . . was deliberately developed'.[107] Orders that knights who could not attend should enact the rituals wherever they were meant that even provincial audiences could participate, as they did

[104] Ben Jonson said of popular perception of spectacle, 'no doubt but their grounded judgements did gaze, said it was fine and were satisfied'. C. H. Herford and P. Simpson eds., *The Works of Ben Jonson* (11 vols., Oxford, 1925–52), VII, 91.

[105] J. M. Osborne ed., *The Queen Maiesties Passage through the City of London*, cited by Strong, *Tudor and Stuart Monarchy*, II, 44.   [106] See also D. Bergeron, *English Civic Pageantry, 1558–1642* (1971).

[107] Strong, *Tudor and Stuart Monarchy*, II, 63; cf. E. Ashmole, *The History of the Most Noble Order of the Garter* (1715).

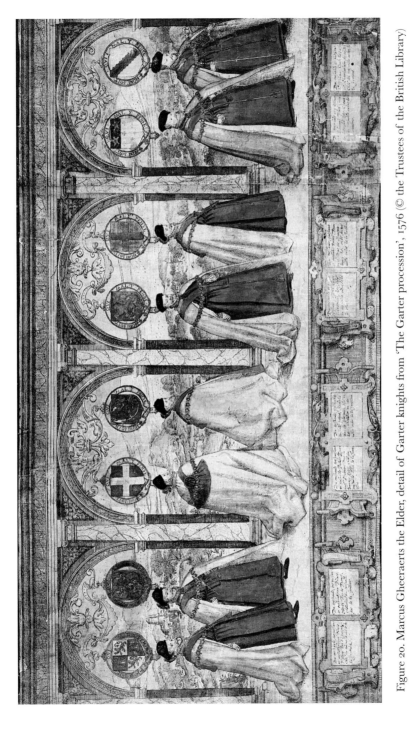

Figure 20. Marcus Gheeraerts the Elder, detail of Garter knights from 'The Garter procession', 1576 (© the Trustees of the British Library)

in 1577 on the great occasion of the firework display in Liverpool organized by the Earl of Derby in observation of the garter feast.

The reciprocity between presenter and audience, between queen and
subject, and the powerful role of the subject in these spectacles was most
manifest in the annual celebrations held to mark the queen's accession.
As Strong remarks, the festivities were 'both courtly and popular' – and
in consequence took directions that not all in authority condoned.[108]
The ringing of bells in 1590 led the mayor of Oxford to believe that a
dirge was being sounded for Queen Mary; and he had to be told that the
bells, long associated with popery, were being rung in honour of the
Protestant saint, the queen. The official services prescribing prayers for
a godly queen descended of Old Testament forebears spilled over into
less godly interludes, bonfires, firework displays and drunken revelry. But
'the complexities of eschatological and imperial theory are never far
away from the accession day themes' and the festivities literally played
out a Foxeian vision of British history, as if the woodcuts of cheap print
and popular piety had come to life on the streets.[109]

The reign of Elizabeth stands as a perfect illustration not simply of
the interconnectedness of art and power, but of the complex exchange
between authority and subjects in the production and dissemination of
a 'successful' image. Perhaps uniquely Elizabeth and her subjects found
a symbolic vocabulary, or vocabularies, that conjoined the mystical and
the popular: the representation of the queen as goddess and Good
Queen Bess. Though no representations were without ambiguities and
tensions, while the image of the queen by no means dispelled the harsh
realities of age, succession, factional strife and foreign threat, there can
be little doubt that the success of royal representation played no small
part in the stability of Elizabethan government and the historical reputation of the queen.

Any such conclusion suggests the need to consider whether, in the
case of the Stuarts, political problems and ultimately regicide owed
something to a corresponding failure of representation, a breaking of
the circle of reciprocity in matters cultural as well as constitutional.
Political historians have assumed such a connection. James I, they have
argued, paid no attention to his image. And under Charles, it is said, the
patronage of continental mannerist art distanced court taste from a

[108] Strong, *Tudor and Stuart Monarchy*, II, 123. See too D. Cressy, *Bonfires and Bells: National Memory and
the Protestant Calendar in Elizabethan and Stuart England* (1989), chs. 4, 8; R. Hutton, *The Rise and Fall
of Merry England: the Ritual Year 1400–1700* (Oxford, 1994), 146–51, 186–7.
[109] Strong, *Tudor and Stuart Monarchy*, II, 141.

national and popular aesthetic, and fostered suspicions of sympathies with popery that undermined trust in the king.[110] Given the hold this thesis has had, and still has, on the historiography, it is instructive to be reminded how long ago Roy Strong discredited it. For Inigo Jones, who epitomized the move to classicism, Strong shows, was obsessed with the British myth, the legend of the Trojan Brutus from whom the kings of Britain had supposedly descended. Jones interpreted and admired Stonehenge as evidence of ancient belief in one god; and he set out to educate taste so as to 'recreate once more the glories of ancient Britain'.[111] Jones, in other words, sought to advance in stone the British revival that James I advocated in speeches defending union and which historians such as Camden and Speed supported by study of British antiquities. 'It is important to grasp', Strong counsels, 'that [Jones's] architectural revolution was seen as Protestant and British and that any reading of it by way of Italianate crypto Catholicism is wholly wrong.'[112] And for all his architectural innovations, in organizing the accession day tilts that continued under James, Jones consciously replayed the refrains of Elizabethan chivalry and presented Prince Henry as a British hero. The Banqueting House ceiling followed the same project. The discovery in the manuscripts of Sir John Coke of plans for the ceiling suggest that it was Jones who drew up the programme for a visual narrative based on the Judgement of Solomon, and that it was James's vision of union (and his *Basilikon Doron*) that most influenced Jones's thinking.[113] Indeed far from Rubens introducing Catholic iconography to the royal rooms of state, Jones's ceiling symbolized the restoration under James of the ancient British church, in denial of papal supremacy. It was not the only echo of a Henrician (even Foxeian) assertion of British ecclesiastical purity and royal supremacy, for in one panel an open book bore the words 'in principo erat verbum'; and the word, as the frontispiece to the King's Bible had made clear, was a royal gift.

We cannot be sure, for all the unsupported assertions historians have repeated, how contemporaries viewed Jones's buildings or the Whitehall

---

[110] Such unargued assumptions underlie the widely read P. Zagorin, *The Court and the Country* (1969); P. Thomas, 'Two Cultures? Court and Country Under Charles I', in C. Russell ed., *The Origins of the English Civil War* (1973); R. Ashton, *The English Civil War, 1603–1649* (1978) and L. Stone, *The Causes of the English Revolution* (1972). I tried to refute these assumptions in *Criticism and Compliment*, ch. 1; see also J. Robertson, 'Caroline Culture: Bridging Court and Country?', *History*, 75 (1990), 388–416.   [111] Strong, *Tudor and Stuart Monarchy*, III, 105.   [112] Ibid.

[113] See G. Martin, 'The Banqueting House Ceiling: Two Newly Discovered Projects', *Apollo*, Feb. 1994, 29–34.

ceiling.[114] Strong suggests that it may have been commissions for Henrietta Maria that associated Inigo with Catholicism. Charles I himself not only saw the plans for the ceiling put into effect, he also showed interest in the British themes which found echoes throughout the court masques, and formed the subject of the king's reading in captivity.[115] Nor, for all the breathtaking innovations in technique effected by Van Dyck, were representations of Charles a complete break with the past. In what remains one of the best close readings of a painting, Van Dyck's *Charles I on Horseback* (Figure 21), Strong points out the continuities as well as shifts in representation of the king. While the equestrian portrait was a recent development in England and the portrayal of Charles as an emperor *à l'antique* novel, the canvas also presents the second Stuart as 'a saint presiding over his knights in prayer' and as 'a warrior leading his troops into battle'.[116] Images of the warrior Protestant knight may have contrasted with England's passivity, but the representation in itself blended new techniques and styles with traditional chivalric themes.

Imperator, knight, lover, hero and god . . . as Strong lists them, *Charles I on Horseback* is a painting of 'endless meanings'. What, perhaps, we need to appreciate is that, as well as being complementary, the various meanings could be read against each other – the warrior knight evoking very different associations and memories to the lover of a Catholic consort.[117] Milton certainly came to interpret paradisal landscape very differently to the representations in Van Dyck's canvases and Caroline masques, and to view the king's reign not as the fulfilment of, but obstacle to, a Foxeian providential narrative.[118] Undoubtedly widening political differences made the sustenance of a national royal image more difficult. But we should pause before we simply dismiss Caroline royal representation as political failure. For at least at court Van Dyck created on canvas a community of Councillors and peers united, for all their factional rivalries and religious differences, in a common style that naturalized aristocratic authority. Perhaps too in the tender and delicate portrayals of Charles with his wife and children, Van Dyck complemented the representation of the 'little god on earth' with that of a very

---

[114] James Robertson points out that in the Long Parliament, Sir Simonds D'Ewes had to ask who Jones was, 'Caroline Culture', 392.

[115] At Carisbrooke Charles read Villalpando's account of the reconstruction of the Temple of Solomon in *De Postrema Ezechielis Prophetae Visione* (1605), Strong, *Tudor and Stuart Monarchy*, III, 152.

[116] Ibid., 181.   [117] Cf. my 'The Royal Image: a Comment', in Corns, *The Royal Image*, 288–309.

[118] Some even read this contestation into *Comus*; see D. Norbrook, 'The Reformation of the Masque', in D. Lindley ed., *The Court Masque* (Manchester, 1984), 94–110.

Figure 21. Sir Anthony Van Dyck, 'Charles I on Horseback'
(by courtesy of the National Gallery, London)

human husband and father. Charles and Henrietta Maria were the 'first royal couple to be glorified as husband and wife', and in so presenting them Van Dyck appropriated for them the imagery and vocabulary of the domestic and emotional.[119] Years later it was the language of affect

---

[119] Strong, *Tudor and Stuart Monarchy*, III, 185.

and the image of the king as father that was to endow the *Eikon Basilike* with its rhetorical power and popular appeal.[120] For all that they did not save his life, the representations of Charles as divine ruler and tender father did much to save the crown.

As the stimulus of Strong's essays prompts us to attempt a narrative of representations, it also strikingly brings home how much about the period we do not know. Over thirty years ago Roy Strong mapped out at a conference the research questions that needed to be pursued in six-teenth- and seventeenth-century British art, and the need in tackling many of those questions for a history of art that would also be a literary and political history of the period.[121] Where his own pioneering work was concerned, against critics who corrected him and questioned his methods, he readily acknowledged the 'gaps and imperfections' that awaited address and hoped that another generation would address them. In particular areas his hope has been fulfilled. There is a rich lit-erature on the politics of festival and masques have recently attracted the serious attention they deserve. Tessa Watt and Margaret Aston have written excellent studies of the place of woodcuts and engravings in advancing the cause of religious reform.[122] As I write, the first ever exhi-bition of early modern British prints is open in London.[123] The work of Sir Oliver Millar, Francis Haskell, Arthur MacGregor and others, notably the organizers of the 1990 exhibition in Washington DC, have added much to our knowledge of Caroline art.[124] And yet even in the case of the greatest artist working in Britain, Van Dyck, we still lack a complete catalogue of portraits. More generally the field as a whole is 'still thinly populated', with artists such as Larkin, Walker, Lely and Kneller awaiting catalogues and critical study, and the representations of Mary, James I, Oliver Cromwell, Charles II, James II and William III urgently in need of scholarly research into paintings, engravings, sculp-ture, furniture, dress and jewels.

Such studies, when we have them, will need to take up questions and concerns that work in other disciplines has brought to the fore: questions

---

[120] E. Skerpan Wheeler, '*Eikon Basilike* and the Rhetoric of Self Representation', in Corns, *The Royal Image*, 122–40.

[121] R. Strong, 'Proceedings of a Conference on British Art in the Sixteenth and Seventeenth Centuries', 21 April 1965, typescript at Huntington Library.

[122] M. Aston, *The King's Bedpost: Reformation and Iconography in a Tudor Group Portrait* (Cambridge, 1993); T. Watt, *Cheap Print and Popular Piety, 1550–1640* (Cambridge, 1991).

[123] See A. Griffiths, *The Print in Stuart Britain, 1603–1689* (1998).

[124] O. Millar, *The Age of Charles I* (1972); *Van Dyck in England* (1982); *Sir Peter Lely* (1978). F. Haskell, 'Charles I's Collection of Pictures', in A. MacGregor ed., *The Late King's Goods* (London and Oxford, 1989); S. Barnes and A. J. Wheelock eds., *Van Dyck* (Washington, 1994).

of the changing materiality and meaning of images across the period. Uncertainties remain about the number and distribution of studio copies of works by Holbein and Van Dyck and so leave unanswered the question of the audience for these works in aristocratic and gentry houses. John Peacock's invaluable essay on the placement of paintings shows how much an understanding of the performance of images depends on further work on the politics of their arrangements.[125] We are only beginning to imagine what it meant to a Tudor magnate to 'own' a locket miniature of Queen Elizabeth or to a parliamentary general to buy a work formerly owned by Charles I; what it meant to a merchant to buy an engraving of the royal family or to a visitor to an alehouse to see a crude woodcut or cartoon. If, however, we are to understand the politics of representation, that is to say politics itself, we must return the image to all its histories – not just aesthetic history, but histories of production, distribution and reception. And, as with theatre, we must recognize and explore how changes in royal representation reflected as well as shaped changing perceptions of taste and authority. We must, that is, bring to the history of art not only the Warburgian engagement with ideology, but what contemporary artists never failed to consider: commerce, consumers and audience.

One of the first volumes in years to take up the chronological and thematic range of Strong's interests explores in a collection of essays aspects of art and patronage from Holbein to Kneller.[126] While too many pieces confine themselves unfruitfully to narrow concerns, the best contributions follow an interdisciplinary approach, to situate and read images in their histories. In a useful chapter, Susan Foister makes the simple but important point that it was demand for pictures that greatly increased – 'not just at court but also in the country' – and it was in part that demand that produced trained English painters by the end of the seventeenth century.[127] The focus and turning point was the reign of Charles I, the beginnings of connoisseurship – outside as well as within the circles of the court. An essay on Besner's funeral sculptures for Buckingham and Weston invites considerations, though they are not pursued here, of the fashioning of memory.[128] Very much in Strong's spirit, David Howarth

---

[125] J. Peacock, 'The Politics of Portraiture', in K. Sharpe and P. Lake eds., *Culture and Politics in Early Stuart England* (Houndmills and Stanford, 1994), 199–228.

[126] D. Howarth ed., *Art and Patronage in the Caroline Courts* (Cambridge, 1993).

[127] S. Foister, 'Foreigners at Court: Holbein, Van Dyck and the Painter-Stainers Company', in Howarth, *Art and Patronage*, 32–50, quotation, 42.

[128] R. Lightborn, 'Isaac Besner: Sculptor to Charles I and his Work for Court Patrons, *c.* 1624–1634', in Howarth, *Art and Patronage*, 132–67.

reads Jones's designs as 'texts of a carefully constructed system of social and political values'.[129] In an illuminating essay that should be read by all ecclesiastical historians, John Newman writes of church ornamentation as 'a team effort by parishioners' and suggests how Wren sought to reconcile 'warring prejudices' in religion as well as taste in his post-Restoration church architecture.[130] Perhaps significantly, one of the most interesting contributions is by a literary scholar. In an essay that combines close reading with an address to the social and ideological circumstances of its production and placement, Graham Parry studies the 'Great Picture' of Lady Anne Clifford (Figure 22) as a narrative of her triumph in securing her estates: as a 'self-documentation' and self-assertion in a patriarchal world.[131] The painting, only now receiving attention from feminist critics and historians of reading, demands interdisciplinary exegesis.[132] By conjoining a narrative of family and self with representations of books, musical instruments and portraits, the 'Great Picture' warns against any art history of early modern England that is not also social and intellectual history.

Encouragingly too there have been signs recently of a revival of historical, even Warburgian approaches to early modern England. In *Art and Magic in the Court of the Stuarts*, Vaughan Hart announces his purpose to explore art as symbol and cosmology. Indeed he begins from the purpose and role of the arts in the English Renaissance: their task 'whether architects, engineers or painters was to construct the royal image'; and, in particular, to capture and present the ruler's magical ability to perfect nature.[133] Refreshingly Hart takes seriously the politics as well as philosophy of Neoplatonism: a concern with the realization of perfect forms. As the Mercurian monarch was a work of art, so mastery of the liberal arts promised the perfection of man, nature and the polity. Masque, 'the supreme artistic celebration of Platonic order', was therefore viewed 'not as a theatre of illusion but as a glimpse of reality', that is of the highest forms.[134] Hart ties these Platonic conceits closely to British themes. Arguing the ubiquity of Trojan origins in Renaissance

[129] D. Howarth, 'The Politics of Inigo Jones', in *Art and Patronage*, 68–89; this piece nicely complements J. Newman, 'Inigo Jones and the Politics of Architecture', in Sharpe and Lake, *Culture and Politics*, 229–56.

[130] J. Newman, 'Laudian Literature and the Interpretation of Caroline Churches in London', in Howarth, *Art and Patraonge*, 164–88, quotations, 177, 186.

[131] G. Parry, 'The Great Picture of Lady Anne Clifford', in Howarth, *Art and Patronage*, 202–19.

[132] See B. Lewalski, *Writing Women in Jacobean England* (Cambridge, Mass., 1993), ch. 5; cf. M. E. Lamb, 'The Agency of the Split Subject: Lady Anne Clifford and the Uses of Reading', *Eng. Lit. Ren.*, 22 (1992), 347–68. [133] V. Hart, *Art and Magic in the Court of the Stuarts* (1994), quotation, 3. [134] Ibid., 17.

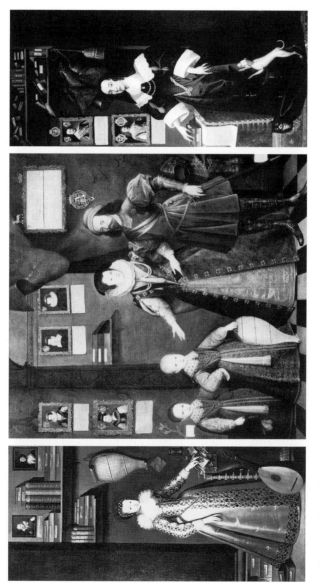

Figure 22. The 'Great Picture' of Lady Anne Clifford (1590–1676) (collection of Abbot Hall Art Gallery, Cumbria)

art, he suggests that both the first Stuarts sought to restore Albion
through a revival of antique arts and architecture. James I appeared with
his ancestor Brute on the Banqueting House ceiling, and masques for
Prince Henry and for James I and Charles I 'drew on renaissance Neo
platonism as a sign of the revival of British magical virtue'.[135] Inigo
Jones, as Strong suggested, was obsessed with British revivals, manifested
not only in masque but in his designs for the portico of St Paul's and
Temple Bar, monuments for a new Troy. 'Renaissance Neoplatonism
was thus used as a key expression and confirmation of the Stuart claim
to have restored a heroic British antiquity perhaps best entitled "Albion
and Jerusalem".'[136] The return of heroic British antiquity was not confined to the court. Lord mayors' shows for London staged Trojan
themes; heraldic literature and devices identified a golden age with
British chivalry; garden designs presented England as the original paradisal garden; and its monarch, assisted by the hydraulic magic of De
Caus and other designers, emerged as the restorer of ordered, harmonious nature. And as the magical properties of circles and triangles
shaped Jones's architectural schemes, so number mysticism lay behind
music and dance. By imitating the harmony of the spheres, it was
believed, the performers might draw down the favourable influences of
heaven and recreate, in the Banqueting House that united all the
Platonic arts, the perfections of the cosmos, with the king as the sun at
its centre. Similarly outside its walls, royal processions from Whitehall to
St Paul's were conceived as imitating the progress of the sun, with the
temple to a British sun king established half a century before Louis XIV
enjoyed the name.

Though at times the desire to detect British themes borders on the
overzealous, Hart persuasively demonstrates across all artistic genres a
'Platonism clothed in the national legends of a magical antiquity'.[137]
And while much more explanation was needed of how the themes of
Platonic harmony 'shifted from emphasising the monarch's duty to the
body politic to underlining his virtues as an absolute ruler', British
Platonism was clearly an important, and is a neglected, part of political
thinking.[138] The question that poses itself throughout is how these conceits and their politics were imagined and interpreted by others. British
themes clearly informed popular histories and literature, but did they in
popular texts construct James I and Charles I as magical kings? Rather
too late in his study, Hart acknowledges that these ideas of restorative

[135] Ibid., 34.   [136] Ibid., 58.   [137] Ibid., 190.   [138] Ibid., 189.

magic could be deployed for ideas of reform hostile to the established church and state; others, not least Milton, reinterpreted the place of Albion in an apocalyptic scheme with very different valence.[139] Yet there is clearly some relation between loss of faith in Platonic conceptions of the cosmos and changing perceptions of the monarchy; and Hart may be right in seeing both as changes in popular as well as learned thinking. The circular plans of Elizabethan theatres had attempted to evoke a marriage of heaven and earth. And in the frontispiece to the best-selling *Eikon Basilike*, Marshall redeployed several of the Platonic conceits to paint Charles as a mystical king and redeemer. Though the future lay in more 'earth bound' notions of authority, in 1649 the magic of monarchy may have for a time been strengthened by the theatre of regicide, as subjects dipped their kerchiefs in the royal blood.

Death was often the most powerful scene both on the stage and in the drama of politics, and an important new study argues for connections beyond contingency and mimesis.[140] Not only, Jennifer Woodward maintains, did the stage mirror the state funerals of the Tudor and Stuart royal dynasties, the funerals themselves constituted a 'theatre of death'. Like all successful performances, state funerals depended not only upon those who managed them, but upon a 'complicity between the actors, directors and audience' of the ceremonies. In an approach that would enrich understanding of all state festival, Woodward suggests that ritual was not concerned with unambiguous official messages; rather 'the power of ritual lies in its multivocality'.[141] 'Because symbols do not mean the same things to different people, and no one meaning is either explicitly included or excluded, all meanings, conscious and unconscious, can be embraced'; and through such ambiguities ritual can attain a cathartic impression of consensus.[142] It is from such a theorized perspective that Woodward examines early modern death and the funerals of Mary, Queen of Scots and Elizabeth I, James I, Prince Henry and Queen Anne.

In aristocratic and state funerals spatial organization, dress and insignia transferred all identities and meaning to symbols and images. Since the mourners at royal funerals did not witness the actual interment, the transfer of power to the heir was symbolically enacted in the offering ceremony and the funeral dinner, at which, by partaking of food, the

---

[139] See S. Achinstein, 'Milton and King Charles', in T. Corns, *The Royal Image*, 141–61.
[140] J. Woodward, *The Theatre of Death: the Ritual Management of Royal Funerals in Renaissance England* (Woodbridge, 1997).   [141] Ibid., 11.   [142] Ibid., 11.

guests 'accepted the heir's succession and acknowledged their obligation towards him'.[143] Doles for the poor extended these symbols of offer and acceptance. Though the Reformation brought changes, funerals retained many elements of medieval ritual, including bells, which may have evidenced a recognition of popular attachment to old ritual forms as well as to aspects of the old faith. For throughout the sixteenth century, state funerals appear to have involved a series of political calculations and negotiations between sovereigns and subjects. It may be, for example, that the splendour of the funeral for Sir Philip Sidney, the Protestant champion, was intended to distract attention from the issue of obsequies for Mary, Queen of Scots. If so, it failed for, possibly in response to pressure, a funeral was eventually held for Mary – albeit in Peterborough, far from the centre stage of politics. James I's decision to provide a lavish funeral and tomb effigy for Elizabeth was clearly intended to underpin his succession to his politic mother and to associate himself with the popularity of the queen (Figure 23). For Prince Henry's last rites, the inclusion of drums in the cortège of 2,000 may have served to veil the inglorious nature of his death from illness; at James's own funeral, the unusual presence of the prince and successor may have been intended to strengthen a new dynasty and to reinforce ideas of hereditary, divine-right kingship.

To be effective as propaganda, funerals needed to appeal to the public and that appeal, like any theatre, was founded on a complex of traditional tropes and immediate needs. There was no lack of interest in, or desire for, such spectacles. By 1612 it was said that the royal tombs at Westminster had become a tourist attraction with a guided tour available for a penny – interestingly the same cost as a play. Even during the 1630s the antiquary, John Weever, referred to the 'concourse of people [who] come daily to view the lively statues and stately monuments in Westminster abbey where in the sacred ashes of so many of the lord's annointed . . . are entombed'.[144] In response to such interest the funeral effigy of Prince Henry was left on public display, evidently insufficiently removed from the 'concourse' of visitors to prevent the theft of its robes in 1616. In James I's case, two effigies were commissioned – one for display and the other for the procession, 'with the intention of facilitating the overall performance'.[145] However, things did not always go right

---

[143] Ibid., 36; cf. M. Schoenfeldt, *Prayer and Power: George Herbert and Renaissance Courtship* (Chicago, 1991), ch. 5 and F. Heal, *Hospitality in Early Modern England* (Oxford, 1990).

[144] Woodward, *Theatre of Death*, 131, citing John Weever, *Ancient Funeral Monuments* (1631), 41.

[145] Woodward, *Theatre of Death*, 193–4.

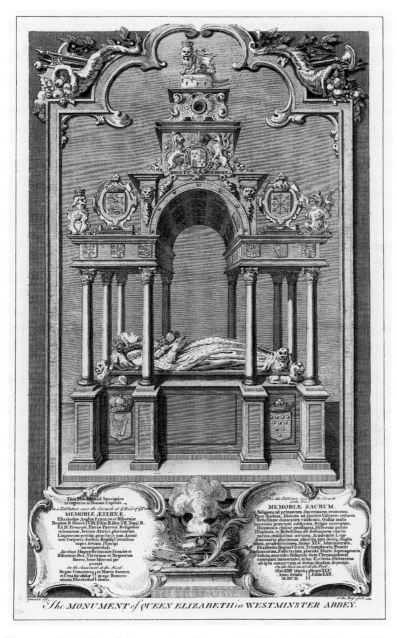

Figure 23. Maximilian Colt, engraving of the tomb of Elizabeth I in Henry VII's chapel, Westminster Abbey, finished 1606 (© Society of Antiquaries, London)

on the night, or rather day. At Anne's funeral, James forgot to invite the representatives of the City companies, and so, rather like the modern staged photograph, had to hold a second service. Even then, though it cost a great deal, Queen Anne's funeral procession did not impress, the newswriter Chamberlain describing it as a 'poor show'.[146] And the same disappointment was expressed a few years later at James's own funeral where a procession of well over 5,000, rather than symbolizing social order, became 'confused and disorderly' – the last before confusion and disorder overtook monarchy and commonwealth too.[147]

Though Woodward never quite manages to explain these individual failures, nor what most brought about the key changes in funeral ritual, we are left in no doubt as to their relation to changes in religion, culture and politics at large. As she hints in an all too brief discussion of funerals after 1625, the replacement of the effigy by the imperial crown in the funeral of Charles II relates to the shift to a more constitutional monarchy.[148] Closing with a modern parallel, *The Theatre of Death* notes the ten-foot portrait carried in the funeral procession of Kim Il Sung. Similarly overtly political in its symbolism, the tight control contrasted with the ambiguities and opportunities for subversion of Renaissance state funerals. Had her book appeared a little later, Woodward would not only have derived the benefit of a little more distance from her thesis, but would surely have closed with a different, more fitting parallel. For the funeral of Princess Diana did not only confirm the vitality of ritual and symbol and the power of representation and procession; simultaneously mystical and democratized, it starkly demonstrated the reciprocity in all state ritual, indeed on this occasion (perhaps as with Mary, Queen of Scots) even the superior force of popular will. In Diana's theatre of death, not for the first time, the audience determined how she would be played and remembered and, in so doing, they rewrote the script of regality too.

While monographs on Neoplatonic magic and the rituals of death further the research inspired by the Warburg Institute and advocated by Strong, David Howarth attempts the first overview of the relations between art and politics since Strong's *Art and Power*, itself the revision of a book first written twenty-five years ago.[149] Reminding readers that Carolines paid more attention to the sitter than the brush work or artist of a painting, Howarth urges less attention to 'originality' and aesthetic

---

[146] Chamberlain to Carleton, 14 May 1619, in N. M. McClure ed., *The Letters of John Chamberlain* (2 vols., Philadelphia, 1939), II, 237.   [147] Ibid., II, 616, 14 May 1625.

[148] Cromwell's funeral is also important, see *The Commonwealth Mercury*, 18–25 November 1658.

[149] D. Howarth, *Images of Rule: Art and Politics in the English Renaissance, 1485–1649* (Houndmills, 1997); Strong, *Splendour at Court: Renaissance Spectacle and Illusion* (1974).

qualities in art history. Noting too that neither Van Dyck nor Rubens appear in the index to Gardiner's magisterial history, he calls for a new political history that will be also cultural history.[150] To those ends his own survey takes in palaces and portraits, sculptures and artefacts, patronage and collecting and contemporary aesthetic and political ideas. As with all surveys, the coverage and conviction of the writing is uneven, especially where the core research has not yet been done. Edward VI and Mary Tudor receive inadequate discussion; and other than remarks about the king's lack of interest, the art of Jacobean England too little. Political historians will quibble at some statements and characterization of religious positions is at times unsure. Yet there are riches here both in particulars and in general. Howarth contributes a good and fresh chapter on tombs and memorial sculpture; the account of the Earl of Strafford's patronage of the arts and its politics is an original and important insight into a courtier's values and the Lord Lieutenant's representation of his devolved royal authority in Ireland. There are clear and helpful explications of individual portraits – the pelican portrait of Elizabeth, van Dyck's *Charles à la chasse* and Rubens's *Presentation of the Portrait*. Howarth helpfully summarizes work done on borrowings and influences when they aid understanding of what a canvas may have meant to contemporaries; and his own observations – that Elizabeth was always alone on canvas, that Peake's action painting of Prince Henry was a rare genre, that James I was the first monarch since Alfred to appear on a coin wreathed rather than crowned – stimulate further thinking about the politics of generic elections.

Valuably, *Images of Rule* directs students' attention to the performance of images. Elizabethan portraits, Howarth makes clear, depended for their effect on a reading of the emblems in jewels, clothes, furniture and other objects; the impact of portraits was conditioned by what hung next to them and how they were framed. Most of all, Howarth echoes what we have heard from theatre historians when he writes, 'propaganda depends as much on its capacity to penetrate a market as it does on any image it might carry'.[151] Writing in the 1990s Howarth is no longer afraid to discuss art in the language of commodity, advertisement and tourist attraction. Accordingly, collecting is compared to deal fixing and corporate investment, the print and its accessibility to a large market with cable televsion. Nor are the political implications of these conjunctions neglected. The expanding audience for art and images meant that

[150] Howarth, *Images of Rule*, 7. Rubens does in fact appear in Gardiner's index.
[151] Ibid., 116.

'an unlicensed print image might appear in a town hall anywhere', or that, as Thomas Fuller maintained, an engraved reproduction of Elizabeth's tomb was featured in 'most country churches'.[152] Fuller went on to note that, viewing such reproductions, 'each loyal subject created a mournful monument for her in his heart'. But widely disseminated images were available to be read and re-produced by subjects who were not always loyal. As the fine arts became commodified and politicized, images of rule too became possessed, interpreted and contested by subjects. In consequence, more than ever, 'the relation between sovereign and subject was one of reciprocity'.[153]

While Howarth was writing his social and political history of English Renaissance art, other scholars were challenging the very approach that studies images as propaganda for the early modern state. In 1995, in a lengthy article in the *Times Literary Supplement*, the popularizing historian Theodore K. Rabb asked: 'Who really understood the symbolism of Renaissance art?'[154] Rabb's question was an intelligent one, but there was little of intelligence or evidence in his attempt to answer it. Curiously Rabb maintained that the purchase by Ferdinand II of Tuscany of a picture of Oliver Cromwell 'seems to make a mockery of current emphasis on political purposes'. Paintings had often been used as a source of diplomatic information and as gifts (not least by Cromwell); and Ferdinand's desire to acquire a representation of the republican protector hardly seems apolitical. As for Rabb's assertion that political theorists paid little attention to art, the whole corpus of Platonic and Aristotelian ethical and political philosophy, on which early modern political thought was an extended commentary, rested on aesthetic theory. Machiavelli, I have suggested, subverted classical theories of representation no less than traditional political values; and Hobbes not only discussed representation and personation, his *Leviathan* was published with an engraved frontispiece which symbolized his argument and depicted its author.[155] Rabb concludes a weak piece with the statement that art was not politics but 'play', 'aesthetic enjoyment or ambition' (*sic*).

[152] Ibid., 166, 217. See too R. Titler, *Architecture and Power: the Town Hall and the English Urban Community, c. 1500–1640* (Oxford, 1991), ch. 6.
[153] Howarth, *Images of Rule*, 13; cf. the remarks in Sharpe and Zwicker, *Refiguring Revolutions*, introduction.
[154] T. K. Rabb, 'Play not Politics: Who Really Understood the Symbolism of Renaissance Art?', *Times Lit. Supp.*, 10 November 1995, 18–20.
[155] T. Hobbes, *Leviathan*, ed. R. Tuck (Cambridge, 1991), ch. 16, 111–15; for the frontispiece, see M. Corbett and R. Lightbown, *The Comely Frontispiece: the Emblematic Title Page in England, 1550–1660* (1979), 220–9.

The last phrase is a curious conjunction that undermines the argument, for ambition is not only a political activity but a term that contemporaries recognized, and feared, as a threat to social cohesion and commonweal.[156]

Nor were (or are) 'play' and 'aesthetic enjoyment' activities free of ideology.[157] In early modern England what constituted acceptable play or recreation became the subject of intense social debate and religious conflict;[158] and the very meaning of the aesthetic, as Sidney's *Apology for Poetry* and Davenant's preface to *Gondibert* and exchange with Hobbes testify, was not outside politics but deeply ideological and partisan territory.[159] Contemporaries of all beliefs recognized, some approvingly, some not, that art, visual rhetoric we might say, influenced and persuaded; and in the early modern state, influence and persuasion were the principal arts of politics. Where Rabb is right is to ask whether such attempts to influence worked: whether what the artist (or commissioner or patron of a work) intended was what was received. Rabb doubts it. How many, he asks, would have been able to interpret farming implements as the fruits of peace? 'Would anyone have recognised Pax from her caduceus?' In the first case, not only were farm tools a common symbol for anyone familiar with emblem literature, the quotidian symbol almost suggests a popular audience.[160] As for Pax, the answer is more difficult, but in early Stuart London entertainments, figures also bore a name – which informed the ignorant and schooled them in recognizing allegorical figures.[161] Allegory and symbol, after all, were not just an elite preoccupation; they were also a characteristic of popular literature and culture, of woodcuts as well as fables and tales.[162]

In a more serious essay and recantation, Sidney Anglo, one of the pioneering scholars of pageantry in Tudor England, writes that he is no

[156] The *OED* cites a seventeenth-century definition of ambition as 'ardent . . . or inordinate desire to rise . . .', cf. A. D'Andrea, 'Aspiring Minds: a Machiavellian Motif from Marlowe to Milton', in B. Kunze and D. Brautigam eds., *Court, Country and Culture* (Rochester, 1992), 211–22.

[157] For a fine recent discussion, see L. Marcus, *The Politics of Mirth: Jonson, Herrick, Milton, Marvell and the Defense of Old Holiday Pastimes* (Chicago, 1986).

[158] For the controversy over the book of sports see Marcus, *Politics of Mirth* and K. Parker, *The English Sabbath* (Cambridge, 1988). See too E. Duffy, 'The Godly and the Multitude in Stuart England', *The Seventeenth Century*, 1 (1986), 31–55.

[159] See W. Davenant, 'The Author's Preface to his . . . Friend, Mr Hobbes', in Davenant, *Gondibert: an Heroick Poem*, ed. D. F. Gladish (Oxford, 1971), and the discussion in Zwicker, *Lines of Authority*, 17–24.

[160] On the large numbers of emblem books in England see P. Daly, *The English Emblem and the Continental Tradition* (New York, 1988) and M. Bath, *Speaking Pictures: English Emblem Books and Renaissance Culture* (1994).   [161] Above, p. 440.

[162] Watt, *Cheap Print*; M. Spufford, *Small Books and Pleasant Histories* (1981).

longer convinced of the propaganda role of festivals and rituals. Though they were enjoyed as 'entertainment', they were, he now suggests, ineffective as 'a means of communication and influence'.[163] Here it might be helpful to suggest that the way the question is phrased does not help to find an answer. For Anglo assumes a top-down view of propaganda and influence, indeed of culture and politics. He questions, that is, how far official statements and elite ideas impacted on the populace. What we have begun to see, however, from work on Elizabethan theatre, Caroline poetry and early modern ritual, is that the polarized model of elite and popular culture and politics cannot be sustained. To suggest more of a common culture is not to argue that all interpreted its texts in the same way, or at the same level of 'sophistication'. But it is to view citizens as well as magnates participating in an allegorical and symbolic commonweal, as today we all participate in a commodity culture of sexual imagery.[164] Again the modern parallel may be enlightening. Advertisers endeavour to reach all potential customers, but even advertisements for the same corporation or product play out a number of messages which reflect different strategies in the boardroom, much as, Greg Walker reminds us, various elements at court competed to represent the royal image.[165] And, while they seek to reach us all, advertisements in different styles and genres, different places and times, target different – smaller and larger, more and less educated – audiences. We might benefit by thinking about early modern representations in the same terms. Lord Beaverbrook once remarked that he knew that half of his then large budget on advertising was wasted; but he did not know which half. Today sophisticated market research helps advertisers and promoters to gauge public reaction and to recast their messages. Neither early modern businesses nor government had such tools. Yet theatre historians show playhouse managers keeping a watchful eye on the popular book trade.[166] And early modern governments certainly kept a careful ear for the mood of the people.[167]

Representations and images of rule in early modern England were

---

[163] S. Anglo, *Spectacle, Pageantry and Early Tudor Policy* (2nd edn, 1997), preface; Anglo, *Images of Tudor Kingship* (1992).

[164] See P. Griffiths, A. Fox and S. Hindle eds., *The Experience of Authority in Early Modern England* (Houndmills, 1996), introduction.

[165] G. Walker, *Persuasive Fictions: Faction, Faith and Political Culture in the Reign of Henry VIII* (Aldershot, 1996), ch. 3. Walker shares some of Anglo's scepticism about an orchestrated and effective propaganda programme.   [166] Forse, *Art Imitates Business*, 33–42.

[167] A classic study, of course, is Geoffrey Elton's *Policy and Police: the Enforcement of the Reformation in the Age of Thomas Cromwell* (Cambridge, 1972).

not the illusory tricks performed by hegemonic authority to keep citizens subject. They were part of the theatre of politics in which the expectations and desires of the audience helped shape the show, the symbols and metaphors through which (as in all ages) men and women worked out the complex relationship between themselves and the artifice of government. To observe that at all times royalty has to stand before subjects 'at once dynastic and domestic, remote and accessible, magical and mundane' is not to say that there can be no history of the politics of royal representations.[168] Indeed as we view the change from the portraits of the goddess Elizabeth to the domesticated images of Queen Anne, we know that the story of these representations and negotiations remains the unwritten history of politics.[169]

---

[168] S. Schama, 'The Domestication of Majesty: Royal Family Portraiture, 1500–1800', in R. Rotberg and T. K. Rabb eds., *Art and History: Images and their Meaning* (Cambridge, 1988), 155–83, quotation, 183.

[169] T. Bowers, 'Queen Anne Makes Provision', in Sharpe and Zwicker, *Refiguring Revolutions*, 57–74; Bowers *The Politics of Motherhood: British Writing and Culture, 1680–1760* (Cambridge, 1996), pp. 35–89.

Index